OPTICAL SIGNAL PROCESSING

OPTICAL SIGNAL PROCESSING

Edited by Joseph L. Horner

Department of the Air Force
Rome Air Development Center (AFSC)
Hanscom AFB, Massachusetts

WITHDRAWN

ACADEMIC PRESS, INC.

Harcourt Brace Jovanovich, Publishers

San Diego New York Berkeley Boston
London Sydney Tokyo Toronto

ACADEMIC PRESS, INC.
1250 Sixth Avenue, San Diego, California 92101

United Kingdom Edition published by
ACADEMIC PRESS INC. (LONDON) LTD.
24–28 Oval Road, London NW1 7DX

Library of Congress Cataloging in Publication Data

Optical signal processing.

   Includes index.
   1. Image processing.   2. Optical data processing.
I. Horner, Joseph L. (Joseph LeFevre)
TA1632.O674   1987   621.36'7   87-903
ISBN 0–12–355760–7 (alk. paper)

PRINTED IN THE UNITED STATES OF AMERICA

87 88 89 90   9 8 7 6 5 4 3 2 1

Contents

I. White-Light Processors

1.1 Color Image Processing

Francis T. S. Yu

1.2 White-Light Fourier Transformations

G. Michael Morris and David A. Zweig

II. Pattern Recognition

2.1 Optical Feature Extraction

David Casasent

2.2 Unconventional Correlators

H. Bartelt

2.3 Optical Implementation of Associative Memory Based on Models of Neural Networks

Nabil H. Farhat and Demetri Psaltis

III. Temporal Signal Processing

3.1 Optical Architectures for Temporal Signal Processing

John N. Lee

3.2 Acoustooptic Synthetic Aperture Radar Processors

Demetri Psaltis and Michael Haney

3.3 Acoustooptic Signal Processors

Dennis R. Pape

IV. Nonlinear Optical Processors

4.1 Nonlinear Optical Waveguide Devices

H. A. Haus, and E. P. Ippen, and F. J. Leonberger

V. Transformations

5.1 Optical Transformations

Bahaa E. A. Saleh and Mark O. Freeman

List of Contributors

Numbers in parentheses indicate the pages on which the authors' contributions begin.

Harrison H. Barrett (335), Optical Science Center, University of Arizona, Tuscon, Arizona 85721

H. Bartelt (97), University of Erlangen, Physikalisches Institut, Erwin-Rommel-Strabe 1, 8520 Erlangen, Federal Republic of Germany

David Casasent (75, 389), Department of Electrical and Computer Engineering, Carnegie-Mellon University, Pittsburgh, Pennsylvania 15213

H. J. Caulfield (409), Center for Applied Optics, University of Alabama in Huntsville, Huntsville, Alabama 35899

J. N. Cederquist (525), Environmental Research Institute of Michigan, P.O. Box 8618, Ann Arbor, Michigan 48107

Roger L. Easton, Jr. (335), Center for Imaging Science, Rochester Institute of Technology, Rochester, New York 14623

Nabil H. Farhat (129), The Moore School of Electrical Engineering, University of Pennsylvania, 33rd & Walnut Streets, Philadelphia, Pennsylvania 19104

Arthur D. Fisher (477), Optical Sciences Division, Naval Research Laboratory, Washington, D.C. 20375

Mark O. Freeman (281), Department of Electrical and Computer Engineering, University of Wisconsin, Madison, Wisconsin 53706

Michael Haney (191), The BDM Corporation, McLean, Virginia 22102

H. A. Haus (245), Department of Electrical Engineering and Computer Science and Research Laboratory of Electronics, Massachusetts Institute of Technology, Cambridge, Massachusetts 02139

E. P. Ippen (245), Department of Electrical Engineering and Computer Science and Research Laboratory of Electronics, Massachusetts Institute of Technology, Cambridge, Massachusetts 02139

K. P. Jackson (431), IBM, Watson Research Center, P.O. Box 218, Yorktown Heights, New York 10598

B. V. K. Vijaya Kumar (389), Department of Electrical and Computer Engineering, Carnegie-Mellon University, Pittsburgh, Pennsylvania 15213

John N. Lee (165), Naval Research Laboratory, Washington, D.C. 20375-5000

F. J. Leonberger (245), United Technologies Research Center, Silver Lane, East Hartford, Connecticut 06108

G. Michael Morris (23), The Institute of Optics, University of Rochester, Rochester, New York 14627

Dennis R. Pape (217), Photonic Systems Incorporated, 1900 South Harbor City Boulevard, Melbourne, Florida 32901

Demetri Psaltis (129, 191), Department of Electrical Engineering, California Institute of Technology, Pasadena, California 91125

Bahaa E. A. Saleh (281), Department of Electrical and Computer Engineering, University of Wisconsin, Madison, Wisconsin 53706

H. J. Shaw (431), Edward L. Ginzton Laboratories, Stanford University, Stanford, California 94305

Cardinal Warde (477), Department of Electrical Engineering and Computer Science, Massachusetts Institute of Technology, Cambridge, Massachusetts 02139

Francis T. S. Yu (3), Department of Electrical Engineering, The Pennsylvania State University, University Park, Pennsylvania 16802

David A. Zweig (23), The Perkin-Elmer Corporation, Danbury, Connecticut 06810

Preface

It would be difficult to say just when the field of optical signal processing had its inception. Certainly the birth of the laser and the discovery of off-axis holography in the early 1960s got the field off to a running start. In the intervening years the field has seen several cycles of bloom and doom. Right now there seems to be a resurgence of interest and support for optical systems and devices as solutions to recurring technological problems.

There have always been two basic characteristics of our field. First, it is a hybrid technology, and second, it has been a practical field, proposing solutions, as opposed to developing even deeper and more encompassing theories. It is a hybrid in that it has utilized the tools, theories, and techniques from many diverse disciplines—physics, mathematics, engineering, and chemistry. This is also reflected in our academic training: some of us come from the physical sciences and some from the engineering sciences.

This book is in a sense a microcosm of all these facets. I have tried to get researchers from many different areas of optical signal processing to write synopses of their current work. It is also, by and large, a practical book, in which systems or algorithms that have been successfully tried and used are described. This book will be of special interest to workers and researchers in this field, students at a senior or graduate level, scientific administrators, and scientists and engineers in general.

I would like to thank the contributors and dedicate this book to them; most of the contributors are colleagues and friends whom I have known since the late 1960s, as we have matured (real meaning: grown old) together as the field has developed. I especially want to thank H. John Caulfield, Director of the Center for Applied Optics at the University of Alabama, Huntsville. Early on he encouraged and stimulated my interest in editing this book. I also thank my editors at Academic Press for their patience, help, and advice.

We all hope this book will be a useful addition to a growing field, which is still in the process of realizing its full and rightful potential.

I

White-Light Processors

1.1

Color Image Processing

FRANCIS T. S. YU

DEPARTMENT OF ELECTRICAL ENGINEERING
THE PENNSYLVANIA STATE UNIVERSITY
UNIVERSITY PARK, PENNSYLVANIA 16802

I. Introduction

Although coherent optical processors can perform a variety of complicated image processings, coherent processing systems are usually plagued with annoying coherent artifact noise. These difficulties have prompted us to look at optical processing from a new standpoint and to consider whether it is necessary for all optical processing operations to be carried out by coherent sources. We have found that many optical processings can be carried out using partially coherent light or white-light sources (Lohmann [1], Rhodes [2], Leith and Roth [3], Yu [4], Stoner [5], and Morris and George [6]). The basic advantages of white-light optical processing are (1) it can suppress the coherent artifact noise; (2) the white-light sources are usually inexpensive; (3) the processing environmental factors are more relaxed, for instance, heavy optical benches and dust free rooms are not required; (4) the white-light system is relatively easy and economical to operate; and (5) the white-light processor is particularly suitable for color image processing.

II. White-Light Optical Processing

An achromatic partially coherent processor that uses a white-light source [7] is shown in Fig. 1. The white-light optical processing system is similar to a coherent processing system except for the following: It uses an extended white-light source, a source-encoding mask, a signal-sampling grating, multispectral band filters, and achromatic transform lenses. For example, if we place an input object transparency $s(x, y)$ in contact with a sampling phase grating, the complex wave field, for every wavelength λ, at the Fourier plane P_2 would be (assuming a white-light point source)

$$E(p, q; \lambda) = \int\int s(x, y) \exp(ip_o x) \exp[-i(px + qy)] \, dx \, dy$$

$$= S(p - p_o, q) \qquad (1)$$

where the integral is over the spatial domain of the input plane P_1, (p, q) denotes the angular spatial frequency coordinate system, p_o is the angular spatial frequency of the sampling phase grating, and $S(p, q)$ is the Fourier spectrum of $s(x, y)$. If we write Eq. (1) in the form of a spatial coordinate system (α, β), we have

$$E(\alpha, \beta; \lambda) = S\left(\alpha - \frac{\lambda f}{2\pi} p_o, \beta\right) \qquad (2)$$

where $p = (2\pi/\lambda f)\alpha$, $q = (2\pi/\lambda f)\beta$, and f is the focal length of the achromatic transform lens. Thus we see that the Fourier spectra would disperse into rainbow color along the α-axis, and each Fourier spectrum for a given wavelength λ is centered at $\alpha = (\lambda f/2\pi)p_o$.

In complex spatial filtering, we assume that a set of narrow spectral band complex spatial filters is available. In practice, all the input objects are

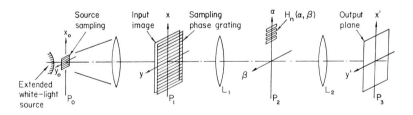

Fig. 1. White-light optical signal processor.

spatial frequency limited; the spatial bandwidth of each spectral band filter $H(p_n, q_n)$ is therefore

$$H(p_n, q_n) = \begin{cases} H(p_n, q_n), & \alpha_1 < \alpha < \alpha_2 \\ 0, & \text{otherwise} \end{cases} \tag{3}$$

where $p_n = (2\pi/\lambda_n f)\alpha$, $q_n = (2\pi/\lambda_n f)\beta$, λ_n is the main wavelength of the filter, $\alpha_1 = (\lambda_n f/2\pi)(p_o + \Delta p)$ and $\alpha_2 = (\lambda_n f/2\pi)(p_o - \Delta p)$ are the upper and lower spatial limits of $H(p_n, q_n)$, and Δp is the spatial bandwidth of the input image $s(x, y)$.

Since the limiting wavelengths of each $H(p_n, q_n)$ are

$$\lambda_l = \lambda_n \frac{p_o + \Delta p}{p_o - \Delta p} \quad \text{and} \quad \lambda_h = \lambda_n \frac{p_o - \Delta p}{p_o + \Delta p} \tag{4}$$

its spectral bandwidth can be approximated by

$$\Delta\lambda_n = \lambda_n \frac{4 p_o \Delta p}{p^2 - (\Delta p)^2} \simeq \frac{4 \Delta p}{p_o} \lambda_n \tag{5}$$

If we place this set of spectral band filters side by side and position them properly over the smeared Fourier spectra, the intensity distribution of the output light field can be shown to be

$$I(x, y) \simeq \sum_{n=1}^{N} \Delta\lambda_n |s(x, y; \lambda_n) * h(x, y; \lambda_n)|^2 \tag{6}$$

where $h(x, y; \lambda_n)$ is the spatial impulse response of $H(p_n, q_n)$ and $*$ denotes the convolution operation. Thus the proposed partially coherent processor is capable of processing the signal in complex wave fields. Since the output intensity is the sum of the mutually incoherent narrowband spectral irradiances, the annoying coherent artifact noise can be suppressed. It is also apparent that the white-light processor is capable of processing color images since the system uses all the visible wavelengths.

III. Source Encoding and Image Sampling

We now discuss a linear transform relationship between the spatial coherence (i.e., mutual intensity function) and the source encoding [8]. Since the spatial coherence depends on the image-processing operation, a more relaxed coherence requirement can be used for specific image-processing operations. Source encoding is to alleviate the stringent coherence requirement so that an extended source can be used. In other words, source encoding is capable of generating appropriate spatial coherence for a specific image-processing operation so that the available light power from the source can be more efficiently utilized.

A. SOURCE ENCODING

We begin with Young's experiment under an extended-source illumination [9], as shown in Fig. 2. First, we assume that a narrow slit is placed in the source plane P_o, behind an extended monochromatic source. To maintain a high degree of coherence between the slits Q_1 and Q_2 at plane P_2, the slit size should be very narrow. If the separation between Q_1 and Q_2 is large, then a narrower slit size S_1 is required. Thus the slit width should be

$$w \leqq \frac{\lambda R}{2h_o} \tag{7}$$

where R is the distance between planes P_o and P_1, and $2h_o$ is the separation between Q_1 and Q_2. Let us now consider two narrow slits S_1 and S_2 located in source plane P_o. We assume that the separation between S_1 and S_2 satisfies the following path-length relation:

$$r_1' - r_2' = (r_1 - r_2) + m\lambda \tag{8}$$

where the r_1' and r_2' are the distances from S_1 to Q_1 and S_2 to Q_2, respectively; m is an arbitrary integer; and λ is the wavelength of the extended source. Then the interference fringes due to each of the two source slits S_1 and S_2 should be in phase, and a brighter fringe pattern is seen at plane P_2. To increase the intensity of the fringes further, one would simply increase the number of slits in appropriate locations in plane P_o so that the separation between slits satisfies the fringe condition of Eq. (8). If the separation R is large, that is, if $R \gg d$ and $R \gg 2h_o$, then the spacing d would be

$$d = m\frac{\lambda R}{2h_o} \tag{9}$$

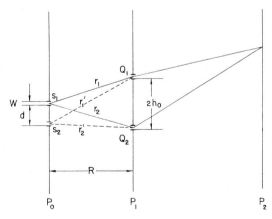

Fig. 2. Source encoding.

Thus, by properly encoding an extended source, it is possible to maintain a high degree of coherence between Q_1 and Q_2 and at the same time to increase the intensity of the fringes.

To encode an extended source, we would first search for a coherence function for a specific image-processing operation. With reference to the white-light optical processor shown in Fig. 1, the mutual intensity function at input plane P_1 can be written as [10]

$$J(\mathbf{x}_1, \mathbf{x}_1') = \int\int \gamma(\mathbf{x}_o) K(\mathbf{x}_o, \mathbf{x}_1) K^*(\mathbf{x}_o, \mathbf{x}_1') \, d\mathbf{x}_o \qquad (10)$$

where the integration is over the source plane P_o, $\mathbf{x}_o$, and $\mathbf{x}_1$ are the coordinate vectors of the source plane P_o and input plane P_1, respectively, $\gamma(\mathbf{x}_o)$ is the intensity distribution of the encoding mask, and $K(\mathbf{x}_o, \mathbf{x}_1)$ is the transmittance function between the source plane P_o and the input plane P_1, which can be written as

$$K(\mathbf{x}_o, \mathbf{x}_1) \approx \exp\left(i2\pi \frac{\mathbf{x}_o \mathbf{x}_1}{\lambda f}\right) \qquad (11)$$

Substituting $K(\mathbf{x}_o, \mathbf{x}_1)$ into Eq. (10), we have

$$J(\mathbf{x}_1 - \mathbf{x}_1') = \int\int \gamma(\mathbf{x}_o) \exp\left[i2\pi \frac{\mathbf{x}_o}{\lambda f}(\mathbf{x}_1 - \mathbf{x}_1')\right] d\mathbf{x}_o \qquad (12)$$

From this equation we see that the spatial coherence and source-encoding intensity form a Fourier transform pair, that is,

$$\gamma(x_0) = \mathrm{FT}[J(\mathbf{x}_1 - \mathbf{x}_1')] \qquad (13)$$

and

$$J(\mathbf{x}_1 - \mathbf{x}_1') = \mathrm{FT}^{-1}[\delta(\mathbf{x}_o)] \qquad (14)$$

where FT denotes the Fourier transformation operation. Equations (13) and (14) are the well-known Van Cittert–Zernike theorem [11, 12]. In other words, if a required coherence is provided, then a source-encoding transmittance can be obtained through the Fourier transformation. In practice, however, the source-encoding transmittance should be a positive real quantity that satisfies the physical realizability condition:

$$0 \leqq \gamma(\mathbf{x}_o) \leqq 1 \qquad (15)$$

B. Image Sampling

There is, however, a temporal coherence requirement for partially coherent processing. If we restrict the Fourier spectra, due to wavelength spread, within a small fraction of the fringe spacing d of a narrow spectral band filter $H_n(\alpha, \beta)$, then we have

$$\nu f \, \Delta\lambda_n \ll d \qquad (16)$$

where $1/d$ is the highest spatial frequency of the filter, ν is the spatial frequency limit of the input image transparency, f is the focal length of the achromatic transform lens, and $\Delta\lambda_n$ is the spectral bandwidth of $H_n(\alpha, \beta)$. The temporal coherence requirement of the spatial filter is, therefore,

$$\frac{\Delta\lambda_n}{\lambda_n} \ll \frac{2}{h_o\nu} \tag{17}$$

where λ_n is the central wavelength of the nth narrow spectral band filter, and $h_o = \lambda_n f/(2d)$ is the separation of the input image transparencies.

IV. Color Image Processing

As we have noted, the white-light optical signal processor is particularly suitable for color image processing. Since it would occupy an inexhaustible number of pages to describe all of these applications, we shall restrict ourselves to a few examples that may be interesting to the readers.

A. COLOR IMAGE DEBLURRING

One interesting application of white-light optical signal processing is the restoration of blurred color photographic images [13]. Since a linearly smeared image is a one-dimensional restoration problem, and the deblurring operation is a point-by-point filtering process, a fan-shaped deblurring filter can be used to compensate for the scale variation of smeared Fourier spectra due to wavelength.

We assume that a blurred image due to linear motion is

$$\hat{s}(x, y) = s(x, y) * \text{rect}\left(\frac{y}{W}\right) \tag{18}$$

where $\hat{s}(x, y)$ and $s(x, y)$ denote the blurred and unblurred images, respectively,

$$\text{rect}\left(\frac{y}{W}\right) \triangleq \begin{cases} 1, & |y| \leq \left|\frac{W}{2}\right| \\ 0, & \text{otherwise} \end{cases} \tag{19}$$

and W is the smeared length.

Let us insert this blurred image transparency into the input plane P_1 of a white-light optical processor as depicted in Fig. 1. The complex light distribution for every wavelength λ at the back focal length of the achromatic transform lens L_2 would be

$$E(\alpha, \beta; \lambda) = S\left[\alpha - \left(\frac{\lambda f}{2\pi}\right)p_o, \beta\right] \text{sinc}\left(\frac{\pi W}{\lambda f}\beta\right) \tag{20}$$

where p_o is the angular spatial frequency of the phase grating, and $S[\cdot]$ represents the Fourier spectrum of $\hat{s}(x, y)$, which is smeared into a rainbow of colors.

Let us assume that a fan-shaped broadband deblurring filter is provided, as described in the following equation:

$$H(\alpha, \beta; \lambda) = \delta\left(\alpha - \frac{\lambda f}{2\pi}p_o, \beta\right)\left\{\int\left[\text{rect}\left(\frac{y}{W}\right)\exp\left(-i\frac{2\pi}{\lambda f}\beta y\right)\right]dy\right\}^{-1}$$

$$= \delta\left(\alpha - \frac{\lambda f}{2\pi}p_o, \beta\right)\left[\text{sinc}\left(\frac{\pi W}{\lambda f}\beta\right)\right]^{-1} \qquad (21)$$

If we insert this deblurring filter in the spatial frequency plane, the complex light distribution, for every λ, at the output image plane would be

$$g(x, y; \lambda) = \text{FT}^{-1}\left[S\left(\alpha - \frac{\lambda f}{2\pi}p_o, \beta\right)H(\alpha, \beta; \lambda)\right]$$

$$= s(x, y)\exp(ip_o x) \qquad (22)$$

where FT^{-1} denotes the inverse Fourier transform. Thus the resultant output image intensity is

$$I(x, y) = \int_{\Delta\lambda}|g(x, y; \lambda)|^2\, d\lambda \cong \Delta\lambda\,|s(x, y)|^2 \qquad (23)$$

which is proportional to the entire spectral bandwidth $\Delta\lambda$ of the white-light source. Thus we see that the white-light optical processor is capable of deblurring color images.

Figure 3a shows a black-and-white photograph of a color image blurred due to linear motion. The body of the fighter plane is painted navy blue and white, the wings are mostly red, the tail is also navy blue and white,

Fig. 3. Color image deblurring. (a) Black-and-white color picture blurred by linear motion. (b) Black-and-white deblurred color image.

and the ground terrain is generally a bluish-green color. Figure 3b is a black-and-white picture of the deblurred color image obtained with the white-light processing technique; the letters and overall shape of the airplane are much clearer than in the blurred image. The river, the highways, and the forestry of the ground terrain are also far more distinguishable. We mention that the color reproduction of the deblurred image is rather faithful and that coherent artifact noise is virtually nonexistent.

B.   COLOR IMAGE SUBTRACTION

Another interesting application of white-light optical processing is color image subtraction [14]. Two color-image transparencies with a phase grating of spatial frequency p_o are inserted in the input plane of the white-light optical processor of Fig. 1. At the spatial frequency plane the complex light distribution for each wavelength λ of the light source may be described as

$$E(\alpha, \beta; \lambda) = S_1\left(\alpha - \frac{\lambda f}{2\pi}p_o, \beta\right)\exp\left(-i\frac{2\pi}{\lambda f}h_o\beta\right)$$
$$+ S_2\left(\alpha - \frac{\lambda f}{2\pi}p_o, \beta\right)\exp\left(i\frac{2\pi}{\lambda f}h_o\beta\right) \qquad (24)$$

where $S_1(\alpha, \beta)$ and $S_2(\alpha, \beta)$ are the Fourier spectra of the input color images $s_1(s, y)$ and $s_2(x, y)$, $2h_o$ is the main separation of the two color images s_1 and s_2, and p_o is the angular spatial frequency of the sampling phase grating. Again we see that the two input image spectra disperse into rainbow colors along the α axis of the spatial frequency plane.

For image subtraction, we should insert a sinusoidal grating in the spatial frequency plane. Since the scales of the Fourier spectra vary with respect to the wavelength of the light source, we must use a fan-shaped grating to compensate for the scale variation. Let us assume that the transmittance of the fan-shaped grating is

$$H(\alpha, \beta; \lambda) = \left[1 + \sin\left(\frac{2\pi}{\lambda f}h_o\beta\right)\right], \qquad \text{for all } \alpha \qquad (25)$$

Then the output image irradiance can be shown to be

$$I(x, y) \approx \Delta\lambda[|s_1(x, y - h_o)|^2 + |s_2(x, y + h_o)|^2 + \tfrac{1}{2}|s_1(x, y) - s_2(x, y)|^2$$
$$+ |s_1(x, y - 2h_o)|^2 + |s_2(x, y + 2h_o)|^2] \qquad (26)$$

where $\Delta\lambda$ is the spectral bandwidth of the white-light source. Thus the subtracted color image can be seen at the optical axis of the output plane. In practice it is difficult to obtain a true white-light point source; however, this shortcoming can be overcome with the source-encoding technique described in the previous section.

To ensure a physically realizable source-encoding function, we let a spatial coherence function with an appropriate point-pair coherence requirement be

$$J(|y - y'|) = \frac{\sin\left(\frac{N\pi}{h_o}|y - y'|\right)}{N \sin\left(\frac{\pi}{h_o}|y - y'|\right)} \, \text{sinc}\left(\frac{\pi W}{h_o d}|y - y'|\right) \tag{27}$$

where $N \gg 1$ is a positive integer, and $W \ll d$. Equation (27) represents a sequence of narrow pulses that occur at every $|y - y'| = nh_o$, where n is a positive integer, and its peak values are weighted by a broader sinc factor. Thus a high degree of spatial coherence can be achieved at every point-pair between the two input color-image transparencies. By applying the Van Cittert–Zernike theorem of Eq. (13), we find the corresponding source-encoding function to be

$$\gamma(|y|) = \sum_{n=1}^{N} \text{rect} \frac{|y - nd|}{W} \tag{28}$$

where W is the slit width, $d = (\lambda f / h_o)$ is the separation between the slits, f is the focal length of the achromatic collimated lens, and N is the total number of slits. Alternatively, Eq. (28) can be written in the form

$$\gamma(|y|) = \sum_{n=1}^{N} \text{rect} \frac{|y - n\lambda f / h_o|}{W} \tag{29}$$

from which we see that the source-encoding mask is essentially a fan-shaped grating. To obtain lines of rainbow color spectral light sources for the subtraction operation, we would use a linear extended white-light source with a dispersive phase grating, as illustrated in Fig. 4. In the white-light image subtraction operation, a broad spectral band sinusoidal grating such as

$$G = \frac{1}{2}\left(1 + \sin \frac{2\pi\alpha h_o}{\lambda f}\right) \tag{30}$$

should be used in the Fourier plane. Thus, with the prescribed broadband source-encoding mask of Eq. (29) and the fan-shaped sinusoidal grating of Eq. (30), as depicted in Fig. 4, the output image irradiance around the optical axis can be shown to be

$$I(x, y) = K \, |s_1(x, y) - s_2(x, y)|^2 \tag{31}$$

It is therefore apparent that a color subtracted image can readily be obtained with a white-light processor.

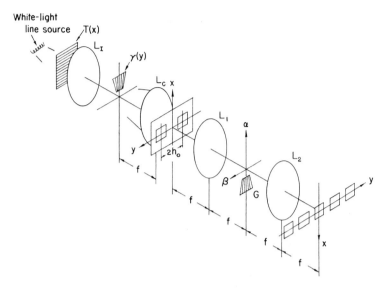

Fig. 4. White-light image subtraction system. $T(x)$ is a phase grating, γ a fan-shaped source-encoding mask, and G a fan-shaped sinusoidal grating.

We shall now provide a result of color image subtraction obtained by a white-light processing technique. Figure 5 is a set of black-and-white photographs of input color transparencies. Figure 5a shows a narrow, paved road photographed from the roof of a campus building. The road appears to be light gray under the hot summer sun, and the lawn is mostly green and yellowish. Figure 5b shows the same scene with a car passing by. The color of the car is orange-brown with various brightnesses. Figure 5c shows a black-and-white picture of the output subtracted color image obtained with the technique described. From this figure, we see that the shape of the car can be easily recognized. In reality, the shade of the car (i.e., subtracted image) varies from yellow-brown to orange-brown and the shadow of the car is generally yellow-green. Although the resolution of the subtracted image is still below the generally acceptable standard, this drawback could be easily overcome by using a finer design of the optical system.

C. COLOR IMAGE CORRELATION

Unlike human perception, conventional coherent optical image recognition systems cannot generally exploit the color or spectral content of the object under observation, which would enhance optical pattern recognition.

We now describe a white-light optical correlator that can exploit the spectral content of an object, that is, a correlator capable of recognizing

Fig. 5. Color image subtraction. (a), (b) Black-and-white pictures of input color objects. (c) Black-and-white picture of the output subtracted color image.

multi-colored objects of various shapes [15]. The need for color-pattern recognition is diverse and offers many applications. There are, however, two large categories in which color is extremely important: natural color variations and objects that are deliberately colored for identification, as, for example, in robotic vision.

We assume that a broadband matched filter is provided:

$$H(\alpha, \beta) = \sum_{\substack{n=-N \\ n \neq 0}}^{N} \left\{ K_1 |S(\alpha, \beta + f\nu_0\lambda_n)|^2 + K_2 |S(\alpha, \beta + f\nu_0\lambda_n)| \right.$$

$$\left. \cdot \cos\left[\frac{2\pi h}{\lambda_n f}\alpha + \phi(\alpha, \beta + f\nu_0\lambda_n)\right] \right\} \quad (32)$$

If this filter is inserted in the Fourier plane of a white-light processor, as depicted in Fig. 1, then the output complex light filter can be shown as

$$g(x, y; \lambda) = \sum_{n=1}^{N} C_1 s(x, y; \lambda) * s(x, y; \lambda_n) * s^*(-x, -y; \lambda_n)$$

$$+ \sum_{n=1}^{N} C_2 s(x, y; \lambda) * \left[s\left(x + \frac{h}{2}, y; \lambda_n\right) + s^*\left(-x + \frac{h}{2}, -y; \lambda_n\right) \right]$$

(33)

where $s(x, y; \lambda)$ is the color input object, $S(\alpha, \beta; \lambda)$ the corresponding Fourier spectrum, ν_0 is the sampling grating frequency, K_1, K_2, C_1, C_2, and h are arbitrary constants, $*$ denotes the convolution operation, the superscript $*$ represents the complex conjugate, and λ_n is the main wavelength of the nth order matched filter. The corresponding output irradiance is, therefore,

$$I(x, y) = \int_{\Delta\lambda_n} |g(x, y; \lambda)|^2 \, d\lambda$$

$$\simeq \sum_{n=1}^{N} \Delta\lambda_n \{ K_1 s(x, y; \lambda_n) * s(x, y; \lambda_n) \star s^*(x, y; \lambda_n)$$

$$+ K_2 [s(x, y; \lambda_n) * s(x + h, y; \lambda_n)$$

$$+ s(x, y; \lambda_n) \star s^*(x - h, y; \lambda_n)] \}$$

(34)

where $\star$ denotes the correlation operation. Thus we see that an autocorrelation of the input image is diffracted at $x = h$ at the output plane. Since we used a broad spectral band white-light source, the spectral content of the image can indeed be exploited.

Let us now provide a result of color object recognition obtained with this technique. Figure 6a shows a black-and-white photograph of a color aerial photograph with a (red) guided missile in flight. Figure 6b shows a visible (red) correlation spot obtained at the output plane of the correlator. Thus the white-light correlator has a feature for color pattern recognition that is based on both the spectral content and the shape of an input image.

Fig. 6. Color image correlation. (a) Black-and-white picture of an input color object. (b) Black-and-white picture of the output correlation spot.

D. Color Image Retrieval

Archival storage of color films has long been an unresolved problem for film industries around the world. The major reason is that the organic dyes used in the color films are usually unstable under prolonged storage and gradually fade. Although there are several techniques for preserving color images, all of them possess definite drawbacks. We have recently developed a white-light processing technique for color image retrieval [16], which would be the most efficient and effective technique.

A color transparency, the object to be encoded, is sequentially exposed with primary color illumination onto a black-and-white film. The encoding takes place by sampling spatially the primary color images of the color transparency with a specific sampling frequency and a prescribed direction onto a monochrome film. To avoid the moiré fringe pattern, the primary color images are sampled in orthogonal directions. Thus the intensity transmittance of the encoded films can be shown as

$$T(x, y) = K\{T_r(x, y)[1 + \text{sgn}(\cos \omega_r y)]$$
$$+ T_b(x, y)[1 + \text{sgn}(\cos \omega_b x)]$$
$$+ T_g(x, y)[1 + \text{sgn}(\cos \omega_g x)]\}^{-\gamma} \qquad (35)$$

where K is an appropriate proportionality constant; T_r, T_b, and T_g are the red, blue, and green color image exposures; ω_r, ω_b, and ω_g are the respective carrier spatial frequencies, (x, y) is the spatial coordinate system of the encoded film, and γ is the film gamma, and

$$\text{sgn}(\cos x) \triangleq \begin{cases} 1, & \cos(x) \geq 0 \\ -1, & \cos(x) \leq 0 \end{cases} \qquad (36)$$

To improve the diffraction efficiency of the encoded film, it is advisable to bleach it to convert it into a phase-type transparency. The amplitude transmittance of the bleached transparency can be written as

$$t(x, y) = \exp[i\phi(x, y)]$$

where

$$\phi(x, y) = M\{T_r(x, y)[1 + \text{sgn}(\cos \omega_r y)]$$
$$+ T_b(x, y)[1 + \text{sgn}(\cos \omega_b x)]$$
$$+ T_g(x, y)[1 + \text{sgn}(\cos \omega_g x)]\} \qquad (37)$$

and M is an appropriate proportionality constant.

If we place this bleached encoded film in the input plane of the white-light optical processor of Fig. 1, then the first-order complex light distribution, for every λ, at the spatial frequency plane P_2 can be shown to be

$$S(\alpha, \beta; \lambda) \simeq \hat{T}_r\left(\alpha, \beta \pm \frac{\lambda f}{2\pi}\omega_r\right) + \hat{T}_b\left(\alpha \pm \frac{\lambda f}{2\pi}\omega_b, \beta\right)$$

$$+ \hat{T}_g\left(\alpha \pm \frac{\lambda f}{2\pi}\omega_g, \beta\right) + \hat{T}_r\left(\alpha, \beta \pm \frac{\lambda f}{2\pi}\omega_r\right) * \hat{T}_b\left(\alpha \pm \frac{\lambda f}{2\pi}\omega_b, \beta\right)$$

$$+ \hat{T}_r\left(\alpha, \beta \pm \frac{\lambda f}{2\pi}\omega_r\right) * \hat{T}_g\left(\alpha \pm \frac{\lambda f}{2\pi}\omega_g, \beta\right)$$

$$+ \hat{T}_b\left(\alpha \pm \frac{\lambda f}{2\pi}\omega_b, \beta\right) * \hat{T}_g\left(\alpha \pm \frac{\lambda f}{2\pi}\omega_g, \beta\right) \tag{38}$$

where $\hat{T}_r$, $\hat{T}_b$, and $\hat{T}_g$ are the Fourier transform of T_r, T_b, and T_g, respectively, and the proportionality constants have been neglected for simplicity. We note that the last cross-product term would introduce a moiré fringe pattern, which can be easily masked out at the Fourier plane. It is therefore apparent that by proper color filtering of the smeared Fourier spectra, a true color image can be retrieved at the output image plane. Thus the output image irradiance would be

$$I(x, y) = T_r^2(x, y) + T_b^2(x, y) + T_g^2(x, y) \tag{39}$$

which is a superposition of three primary-encoded color images.

Let us now provide a result of the retrieved color image obtained with this technique, as shown in Fig. 7. We can see that the retrieved color is spectacularly faithful and has virtually no color crosstalk. The resolution and contrast are still below acceptance for widespread applications. However, these drawbacks can be overcome by using a more suitable film, for which a research program is currently under way.

E.   Pseudocolor Imaging

Most of the optical images obtained in various scientific applications are gray-level density images: for example, scanning electron micrographs, multispectral band aerial photographic images, x-ray transparencies, and infrared scanning images. However, humans can perceive details in color better than in gray levels; in other words, a color-coded image provides better visual discrimination.

We now describe a density pseudocolor encoding technique for monochrome images [17]. We assume that a gray-level transparency T_1 is available for pseudocoloring. By simple photographic contact printing processes, a negative and a product image transparency (T_2 and T_3, respectively) can be made. It is now clear that spatial encoding onto a monochrome film can

Fig. 7. Retrieved color image.

take place with the same procedure as described in color image retrieval. The intensity transmittance of the encoded film can be written as

$$T(x, y) = K\{T_1(x, y)[1 + \text{sgn}(\cos \omega_1 y)]$$
$$+ T_2(x, y)[1 + \text{sgn}(\cos \omega_2 x)]$$
$$+ T_3(x, y)[1 + \text{sgn}(\cos \omega_3 x)]\}^{-\gamma} \tag{40}$$

where K is an appropriate proportionality constant. To improve the diffraction efficiency of the encoded film, we again use a bleaching process so that the phase-encoded transparency becomes

$$t(x, y) = \exp[i\phi(x, y)] \tag{41}$$

where

$$\phi(x, y) = M\{T_1(x, y)[1 + \text{sgn}(\cos \omega_1 y)]$$
$$+ T_2(x, y)[1 + \text{sgn}(\cos \omega_2 x)]$$
$$+ T_3(x, y)[1 + \text{sgn}(\cos \omega_3 x)]\} \tag{42}$$

where M is an appropriate proportionality constant. If we insert this phase-encoded transparency at the input plane of the white-light processor of Fig. 1, the complex light distribution due to $t(x, y)$, for every λ, at the spatial frequency plane is

$$S(\alpha, \beta, \lambda) = \hat{T}_1\left(\alpha, \beta \pm \frac{\lambda f}{2\pi}\omega_1\right) + \hat{T}_2\left(\pm \frac{\lambda f}{2\pi}\omega_2, \beta\right)$$

$$+ \hat{T}_3\left(\alpha \pm \frac{\lambda f}{2\pi}\omega_3, \beta\right) + \hat{T}_1\left(\alpha, \beta \pm \frac{\lambda f}{2\pi}\omega_1\right) * \hat{T}_2\left(\alpha \pm \frac{\lambda f}{2\pi}\omega_2, \beta\right)$$

$$+ \hat{T}_1\left(\alpha, \beta \pm \frac{\lambda f}{2\pi}\omega_1\right) * \hat{T}_3\left(\alpha \pm \frac{\lambda f}{2\pi}\omega_3, \beta\right)$$

$$+ \hat{T}_2\left(\alpha \pm \frac{\lambda f}{2\pi}\omega_2, \beta\right) * \hat{T}_3\left(\alpha \pm \frac{\lambda f}{2\pi}\omega_3, \beta\right) \tag{43}$$

where $\hat{T}_1$, $\hat{T}_2$, and $\hat{T}_3$ are the smeared Fourier spectra of the positive, negative, and product images, respectively, and the proportionality constants have been neglected for simplicity. Again we see that the last cross product (i.e., the moiré fringe pattern) can be avoided by spatial filtering. Needless to say, by color filtering the first-order smeared Fourier spectra a moiré-free pseudocolor encoded image can be obtained at the output plane P_3. The corresponding pseudocolor image irradiance is therefore

$$I(x, y) = T_{1r}^2(x, y) + T_{2b}^2(x, y) + T_{3g}^2(x, y) \tag{44}$$

where T_{1r}^2, T_{2b}^2, and T_{3g}^2 are the red, blue, and green intensity distributions of the three spatially encoded images.

We shall now provide a set of color-coded x-ray images of a woman's pelvis, as shown in Fig. 8. The x-ray image was taken after a surgical procedure. A section of the bone between the sacroiliac joint and the spinal column has been removed. In Fig. 8a, the positive image is encoded in red, the negative image in blue, and the product image in green. By comparing

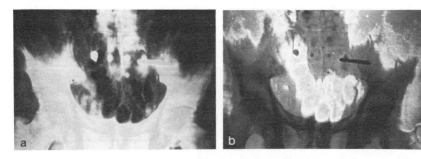

Fig. 8. (a) Black-and-white picture of a density pseudocolor encoded x-ray image. (b) Black-and-white picture of a reversed pseudocolor image of (a).

the pseudocolor-coded image with the original black-and-white x-ray picture, we see that the soft tissues can be better differentiated by the color-coded image, as demonstrated by the fact that the image contrast in the region containing the gastrointestinal tract is evidently superior in the color-coded image. Furthermore, Fig. 8b shows a reversal color-coded image of Fig. 8a. We see that the color mixture capability could be beneficial because an image in a different color combination may reveal subtle features that are otherwise undetected. For instance, the air pockets in the colon of the patient can be identified more easily in Fig. 8b than in Fig. 8a.

F. GENERATION OF SPEECH SPECTROGRAMS

The technique of generating a multicolor speech spectrogram with a white-light optical signal processor uses a cathode-ray tube (CRT) scanner to convert a temporal signal to a spatial signal onto a translating photographic film [18]. If this encoded film is moving over the input optical window of a white-light signal optical processor, as shown in Fig. 9, then a speech spectrogram can be generated at the output plane.

We stress that for converting a time signal to a spatial signal, the speed of the film motion must satisfy the inequality

$$v \geqq \frac{\nu}{R} \tag{45}$$

where R is the spatial resolution of the film, and ν is the highest frequency content of the time signal.

If the encoded signal format is loaded into a linear motion film transport at the input plane of the white-light optical processor of Fig. 9, a slanted

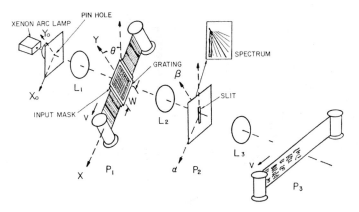

Fig. 9. White-light optical sound spectrograph.

set of rainbow-colored, smeared Fourier spectra in the spatial frequency plane can be obtained. We note that the effect of the phase grating at the input plane is to disperse the encoded signal spectra in a direction perpendicular to that of the recorded input format (i.e., the direction of the film motion), so that a set of nonoverlapping, slanted (or fan-shaped) rainbow-colored smear spectra can be displayed at the Fourier plane. It is now apparent that if a narrow, slanted slit is properly placed at the Fourier plane as illustrated in the figure, a frequency color-coded spectrogram can be recorded at the output plane with a moving color film. The color-coded spectrographic signal can also be picked up by a color TV camera for display, storage, transmission, and further processing by electronic or digital systems. We further note that by simply varying the width of the input optical window, one would expect to obtain the so-called wideband and narrowband spectrograms. In other words, if a broader optical window is used, then a high-spectral resolution that corresponds to a narrowband speech spectrogram can be obtained. However, by increasing the spectral resolution, we would expect to lose the spatial (i.e., time) resolution. Conversely, if the optical window is narrower, which corresponds to a wideband analysis, then a loss of spectral resolution is expected. Nonetheless, the loss of the spectral resolution would improve the time resolution of the spectrogram. This time–bandwidth relationship is in fact the consequence of the well-known Heisenberg uncertainty relation in quantum mechanics [19].

Let us now provide a multicolor speech spectrogram generated by a white-light processing technique. Figure 10 shows a black-and-white picture of a frequency color-coded speech spectrogram obtained with the proposed white-light technique. The frequency content is encoded from high

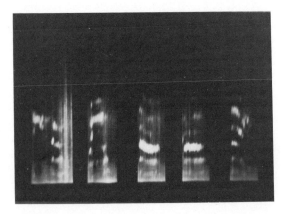

Fig. 10. Black-and-white picture of frequency color-coded speech spectrogram.

frequency (red), through intermediate frequency (green), to low frequency (blue). This color-encoded speech spectrogram represents a sequence of English words spoken by a male voice: "testing, one, two, three, four." On this color-encoded speech spectrogram, excellent characterization of format variation can easily be seen. Compared with its electronic and digital counterparts, the white-light signal-processing technique simplifies the processing procedure and is versatile to operate.

V. Concluding Remarks

We have mentioned some of the basic concepts and examples of white-light optical signal processing and have shown that the white-light processor is capable of processing the wave field in complex amplitude as a coherent processor. At the same time the processor is capable of suppressing artifact noise as an incoherent system. Since the white-light source emits all the visible wavelengths, the technique is particularly suitable for color image processing.

We also stress that optical methods offer the advantages of capacity, color, simplicity, and low cost. We can expect a gradual merging of the optical and flexible digital techniques. The continued development of optical–digital interfaces and various electrooptical devices will lead to a fruitful result: hybrid optical–digital signal processing techniques, utilizing the strengths of both processing operations. Furthermore, we believe that white-light signal processing is at the threshold of widespread application. We hope that this chapter may stimulate interested readers toward various imaginative signal processing applications with white light.

Acknowledgments

The support of the U.S. Air Force Office of Scientific Research and the Rome Air Development Center at Hanscom Air Force Base in the area of white-light optical processing is gratefully acknowledged.

References

1. A. W. Lohmann, *Appl. Opt.* **16**, 216 (1977).
2. W. T. Rhodes, *Appl. Opt.* **16**, 265 (1977).
3. E. Leith and J. Roth, *Appl. Opt.* **16**, 2565 (1977).
4. F. T. S. Yu, *Opt. Commun.* **27**, 23 (1978).
5. W. Stoner, *Appl. Opt.* **17**, 2454 (1978).
6. G. M. Morris and N. George, *Opt. Lett.* **5**, 202 (1980).
7. F. T. S. Yu, "White-Light Optical Signal Processing." Wiley (Interscience), New York, 1985.
8. F. T. S. Yu, *J. Opt.* **14**, 173 (1983).
9. S. T. Wu and F. T. S. Yu, *Appl. Opt.* **20**, 4082 (1981).
10. M. Born and E. Wolf, "Principles of Optics," 2nd Rev. Ed. Pergamon, New York, 1964.

11. P. H. Van Cittert, *Physica (Amsterdam)* **1**, 201 (1934).

12. F. Zernike, *Physica (Amsterdam)* **5**, 785 (1938).

13. T. H. Chao, S. L. Zhuang, S. Z. Mao, and F. T. S. Yu, *Appl. Opt.* **22**, 1439 (1983).

14. F. T. S. Yu and S. T. Wu, *J. Opt.* **13**, 183 (1982).

15. F. T. S. Yu and F. K. Hsu, *Appl. Opt.* **24**, 2135 (1985).

16. F. T. S. Yu, X. X. Chen, and S. L. Zhuang, *J. Opt.* **16**, 59 (1985).

17. F. T. S. Yu, K. Shung, and X. X. Chen, *IEEE Trans. Biomed. Eng.* **BME-32**, 199 (1985).

18. F. T. S. Yu, T. N. Lin, and K. B. Xu, *Appl. Opt.* **26**, 836 (1985).

19. F. T. S. Yu, "Optical Information Processing." Wiley (Interscience), New York, 1982.

1.2

White-Light Fourier Transformations

G. MICHAEL MORRIS

THE INSTITUTE OF OPTICS
UNIVERSITY OF ROCHESTER
ROCHESTER, NEW YORK 14627

DAVID A. ZWEIG

THE PERKIN-ELMER CORPORATION
DANBURY, CONNECTICUT 06810

I. Introduction

The usefulness of coherent optical correlators has been greatly restricted by the requirement for a smooth object format and by coherent artifact noise caused by small defects in the optical system, such as dust or scratches on a lens. To achieve a smooth object format, one must use either a transparency for the input object or some type of spatial light modulator. For a review of the status of spatial light-modulator development, see Chapter 7.2 by Warde and Fisher.

Several researchers have investigated the characteristics of noise in optical processing systems and its dependence on the spatial and temporal coherence of the illumination (Rogers, 1977, 1980; Chavel and Lowenthal, 1978a, b; Leith and Roth, 1979; Chavel, 1980; Leith et al., 1980; Thompson, 1983). Generally it is found that noise arising from optical-system imperfections (e.g., pupil-plane defects) is significantly reduced by using broad-spectrum and/or finite-sized sources; this is a primary motivation for investigating noncoherent optical processors.

Noncoherent optical processors can be divided into three categories depending on whether they use (1) quasimonochromatic, spatially incoherent illumination, (2) broadband, spatially coherent illumination, or (3) broadband, spatially incoherent illumination. Light that is quasi-monochromatic and spatially incoherent is easily generated by passing laser light through a rotating ground-glass plate or by spectral filtering a thermal source (e.g., a mercury arc lamp). Spatially incoherent processors operate as linear systems in intensity (see, e.g., Goodman, 1968), as opposed to coherent processors that are linear in complex amplitude. This class of processors is immune to optical-system noise, and object-phase noise is also suppressed. Hence rough objects or diffusely illuminated objects can be processed directly, thereby eliminating the need for an incoherent-to-coherent converter. Diffraction-based systems that use nonnegative spatial filters have been investigated by Lohmann (1968), Lowenthal and Werts (1968), Lohmann and Werlich (1971), Monahan et al. (1977), Potaturkin (1979), and Sherman et al. (1983). Also, various optoelectronic hybrid methods to achieve bipolar (complex) filtering operations, such as bandpass filtering and differentiation, using spatially incoherent illumination have been reported (Chavel and Lowenthal, 1976; Lohmann, 1977; Rhodes, 1977, 1980; Stoner, 1977, 1978; Lohmann and Rhodes, 1978; Furman and Casasent, 1979; Glaser, 1981; Angell, 1985; Leith and Angell, 1986; Mait, 1986). Detailed reviews of noncoherent optical processing schemes can be found in the works by Rogers (1977), Monahan et al. (1977), Rhodes and Sawchuk (1981), and Bartelt et al. (1982).

It is well known that an achromatic lens produces a Fourier transform pattern that is highly wavelength dependent. In fact, the size of the transform pattern varies linearly with the illumination wavelength. This wavelength dependence of the Fourier transform severely restricts the spectral bandwidth that can be used by a conventional Fourier processor, see Morris and George (1980a, b) and Yu (1985). In the second category of processors, the conventional Fourier processor is modified to use broadband, spatially coherent illumination. These processors function as a series of independent coherent processors, each operating at a different wavelength; this redundancy serves to reduce the effects of pupil-plane noise (Chavel, 1980).

Several system configurations based on wavelength-multiplexed filters have been devised (see, e.g., Yu, 1978; Yu and Chao, 1983; Goedgebuer and Gazeu, 1978; Ferriere et al., 1979; Case, 1979; Braunecker and Bryngdahl, 1982; Zerbino and Goedgebuer, 1985). In these configurations a separate spatial filter is made for each wavelength channel.

Another approach to increase the spectral bandwidth is to achromatize the optical Fourier transform operation (Katyl, 1972; Wynne, 1979; Morris and George, 1980c; Morris, 1981a, b; Collins, 1981; Upatnieks et al., 1982; Ferriere and Goedgebuer, 1982, 1983; Hopkins and Morris, 1983; Brophy, 1983; Leon and Leith, 1985; Zweig, 1985). The output of an achromatic Fourier transform system consists of an optical transform pattern whose size is independent of the illumination wavelength; this enables the processor to use the same frequency-plane filter that would be used in a monochrome coherent system. A major difference between the multiplexer and the achromatic transform approaches is that the multiplexer approaches operate over narrow bandwidth regions centered at specific wavelengths, whereas the achromatic transform methods operate over a broad continuous spectrum. It is noted that achromatic transform configurations also exhibit noise suppression capabilities since each wavelength performs as an independent coherent processing channel except at the object, transform, and image planes where all channels are identical.

The third category of noncoherent optical processors are the least restrictive; they operate with broadband, spatially incoherent light. Research on this category of noncoherent processors is motivated by the desire to realize an optical system that processes information using natural illumination, thereby eliminating the need for a spatial light modulator as well as the artifact noise associated with coherent processors. Almeida et al. (1979) have investigated an incoherent spatial filtering system in which white-light illumination is used to multiplex chromatically a continuum of inputs differing in their spatial Fourier spectral magnifications. Leith and Swanson (1980) developed an achromatic interferometer for white-light optical processing. Optical matched filtering in white-light illumination has been reported by George and Morris (1981, 1983). In these experiments an achromatic Fourier transform and a system to eliminate the lateral dispersion introduced by the frequency-plane filter were employed.

Optical systems have also been devised to realize cosinusoidal transforms in broadband incoherent light. An excellent treatment of geometrical-optics-based systems can be found in the book by Rogers (1977). Recently, George and Wang (1984) have developed an optical system to realize cosinusoidal transforms in spatially incoherent white light; their system is based on techniques of white-light interferometry (Brekinridge, 1978; Roddier et al., 1980).

In this chapter we concentrate on optical processors that use achromatic Fourier transform systems. As indicated, a number of lens systems have been designed to compensate for the chromatic size variation of the transform pattern. With the exception of the all-glass Fourier achromats of Wynne (1979) and Brophy (1983), the above systems use combinations of glass and holographic lenses to achieve the required wavelength dependence in the various lens groupings. However, the use of holographic lenses does introduce a complication: Holographic lenses suffer from a loss of diffraction efficiency at wavelengths other than that used in construction. This effect is due to a deviation from the Bragg condition and causes a background (or ghost) image in the output due to undiffracted light passing through the holographic lenses. To eliminate the undiffracted background image, Upatnieks *et al.* (1982) proposed an achromatic Fourier transform configuration that uses two off-axis holographic lenses with a grating between them; this off-axis geometry allows the undiffracted light to be blocked so that it does not interfere with the signal beam.

In Section II, we review briefly the basic principles of coherent and noncoherent optical processors. In this treatment the wavelength dependence of the system impulse response is included explicitly. In Section III, achromatic Fourier transform systems are analyzed using paraxial Fresnel diffraction theory. From the analysis a general solution for the required wavelength dependence of the various lens groupings is found; these solutions provide an excellent starting point for the first-order layout of the system. The optical design and optimization procedure for a diffraction-limited achromatic Fourier processor is described in Section IV.

II. Linear System Formalism

A. Coherence Theory for Linear Optical Systems

Consider a general linear system with an impulse response function given by $h(x, y; \xi, \eta; \nu)$, as shown in Fig. 1. For a given transverse component

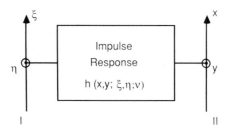

Fig. 1. Linear system with impulse response $h(x, y; \xi, \eta; \nu)$.

of the electric field, we associate a complex analytic signal $u(x, y; t)$ and define the spectral amplitude $U(x, y; \nu)$ to be the time-truncated Fourier transform of $u(x, y; t)$,

$$U(x, y; \nu) = \int_{-T}^{T} u(x, y; t) \exp(+i2\pi\nu t)\, dt \tag{1}$$

Using this definition one can express the spectral amplitude of the system output $U_{11}(x, y; \nu)$ in terms of the input spectral amplitude $U_1(x, y; \nu)$ as follows:

$$U_{11}(x, y; \nu) = \iint U_1(\xi, \eta; \nu) h(x, y; \xi, \eta; \nu)\, d\xi\, d\eta \tag{2}$$

In Eq. (2) the spatial coordinates in the input and output planes are denoted by (ξ, η) and (x, y), respectively, and ν denotes temporal frequency (i.e., $\nu = c/\lambda$, where λ is the wavelength and c the velocity of light).

When one considers the operation of an optical system with broadband illumination, by far the most convenient quantity to calculate is the cross-spectral density function $W(x_1, y_1; x_2, y_2; \nu)$ defined as

$$W(x_1, y_2; x_2, y_2; \nu) = \lim_{T \to \infty} \frac{\langle U(x_1, y_1; \nu) U^*(x_2, y_2; \nu) \rangle_s}{2T} \tag{3}$$

in which $\langle \cdots \rangle_s$ denotes an average over an ensemble of sources (see, e.g., Morris and George, 1980b; Wolf, 1982, 1986; Goodman, 1985). Note that the time-truncated field is used since, in general, the noiselike field $u(x, y; t)$ is not mean-square integrable. To simplify the notation in subsequent analysis, we shall suppress notation associated with the time truncation and simply write

$$W(x_1, y_1; x_2, y_2; \nu) = \langle U(x_1, y_1; \nu) U^*(x_2, y_2; \nu) \rangle \tag{4}$$

where $\langle \cdots \rangle$ is understood to represent time truncation and averaging in the sense of Eq. (3). The mutual coherence function $\Gamma(x_1, y_1; x_2, y_2; \tau)$ and the mutual intensity $J(x_1, y_1; x_2, y_2) = \Gamma(x_1, y_1; x_2, y_2; 0)$ are related to the cross-spectral density as follows:

$$\Gamma(x_1, y_1; x_2, y_2; \tau) = \int_0^\infty W(x_1, y_1; x_2, y_2; \nu) \exp(-i2\pi\nu\tau)\, d\nu \tag{5}$$

$$J(x_1, y_1; x_2, y_2) = \int_0^\infty W(x_1, y_1; x_2, y_2; \nu)\, d\nu \tag{6}$$

A quantity of primary interest in this chapter is the spectral intensity

$$I(x, y; \nu) \equiv W(x, y; x, y; \nu) = \langle |U(x, y; \nu)|^2 \rangle \tag{7}$$

which represents the optical power at a point (x, y) and frequency ν. Note that the total intensity is obtained by integrating the spectral intensity over all temporal frequencies as in Eq. (6).

If an input object $g(\xi, \eta; \nu)$ is inserted at plane I and illuminated by a field with spectral amplitude $U_{in}(\xi, \eta; \nu)$, then the spectral amplitude $U_1(\xi, \eta; \nu)$ leaving plane I is given approximately by

$$U_1(\xi, \eta; \nu) = U_{in}(\xi, \eta; \nu) g(\xi, \eta; \nu) \tag{8}$$

Using Eqs. (2), (7), and (8), one can write the spectral intensity $I_{11}(x, y; \nu)$ in the output plane II as

$$I_{11}(x, y; \nu) = \int\int\int\int g(\xi, \eta; \nu) g^*(\xi', \eta'; \nu) \langle U_{in}(\xi, \eta; \nu) U_{in}^*(\xi', \eta'; \nu) \rangle$$
$$\cdot h(x, y; \xi, \eta; \nu) h^*(x, y; \xi', \eta'; \nu) \, d\xi \, d\eta \, d\xi' \, d\eta' \tag{9}$$

Equation (9) is a general expression relating the spectral intensity in plane II to the cross-spectral density of the incident optical field.

It is useful to have the expression for $I_{11}(x, y; \nu)$ when the incident field is either spatially coherent or spatially incoherent. These limiting cases are best treated using a normalized form of the cross-spectral density function, that is, the magnitude of the complex degree of spectral coherence,

$$|\mu(\nu)| \equiv \frac{|\langle U(\xi, \eta; \nu) U^*(\xi', \eta'; \nu) \rangle|}{[\langle |U(\xi, \eta; \nu)|^2 \rangle \langle |U(\xi', \eta'; \nu)|^2 \rangle]^{1/2}} \tag{10}$$

in which $|\mu(\nu)|$ can assume values in the range $0 \leq |\mu(\nu)| \leq 1$.

1. Spatially Coherent Illumination

A field is said to be spatially coherent if $|\mu(\nu)| \equiv 1$; this can occur if and only if $U(\xi', \eta'; \nu) = k(\nu) U(\xi, \eta; \nu)$, where $k(\nu)$ is a deterministic function. It is convenient to express the spectral amplitude at points (ξ, η) and (ξ', η') in terms of the spectral amplitude at a reference point (ξ_0, η_0), that is,

$$U(\xi, \eta; \nu) = U_\nu(\xi, \eta) \frac{U(\xi_0, \eta_0; \nu)}{[I(\xi_0, \eta_0; \nu)]^{1/2}}$$

$$U(\xi', \eta'; \nu) = U_\nu(\xi', \eta') \frac{U(\xi_0, \eta_0; \nu)}{[I(\xi_0, \eta_0; \nu)]^{1/2}} \tag{11}$$

where the phasor amplitudes $U_\nu(\xi, \eta)$ and $U_\nu(\xi', \eta')$ are relative to the phasor amplitude at reference point (ξ_0, η_0). Using Eqs. (4) and (11) gives

$$W(\xi, \eta; \xi', \eta'; \nu) = U_\nu(\xi, \eta) U_\nu^*(\xi', \eta') \tag{12}$$

Substituting Eq. (12) into Eq. (9) gives the general expression for the spectral intensity when using spatially coherent illumination,

$$I_{11}(x, y; \nu) = \left| \iint g(\xi, \eta; \nu) U_\nu(\xi, \eta) h(x, y; \xi, \eta; \nu) \, d\xi \, d\eta \right|^2 \quad (13)$$

2. Spatially Incoherent Illumination

a. Delta-Function Correlation. For incoherent illumination in the idealized limit, $|\mu(\nu)| = 0$ for all points $(\xi, \eta) \neq (\xi', \eta')$. In this limit the cross-spectral density function of the incident field assumes the following form:

$$W(\xi, \eta; \xi', \eta'; \nu) = \kappa \langle |U_{in}(\xi, \eta; \nu)|^2 \rangle \delta(\xi - \xi', \eta - \eta') \quad (14)$$

where κ is a real constant.

Using Eqs. (9) and (14) gives the expression for the spectral intensity for spatially incoherent illumination,

$$I_{11}(x, y; \nu) = \kappa \iint |g(\xi, \eta; \nu)|^2 \langle |U_{in}(\xi, \eta; \nu)|^2 \rangle |h(x, y; \xi, \eta; \nu)|^2 \, d\xi \, d\eta \quad (15)$$

Note that with spatially incoherent illumination, the spectral intensity $I_{11}(x, y; \nu)$ depends on the intensity transmittance of the input object. Hence the output spectral intensity is not sensitive to variations of object phase.

b. Finite Coherence Area. A more realistic model for the cross-spectral density of the input illumination is obtained by assuming an input correlation interval that is consistent with illumination from a remote incoherent source. The Van Cittert–Zernike theorem serves as a guide to us in the choice of a realistic function for $W(\xi, \eta; \xi', \eta'; \nu)$.

Consider an input object that is illuminated by a source that has a cross-spectral density function in plane I given by

$$W_1(\xi, \eta; \xi', \eta'; \nu) = \langle |U_{in}(\xi, \eta; \nu)|^2 \rangle \mu(\Delta\xi, \Delta\eta; \nu) \quad (16)$$

The spectral intensity $\langle |U_{in}(\xi, \eta; \nu)|^2 \rangle$ of the incident illumination is assumed to be slowly varying, and the complex degree of spectral coherence $\mu(\Delta\xi, \Delta\eta; \nu)$ is taken by assertion to be

$$\mu(\Delta\xi, \Delta\eta; \nu) = \frac{[2J_1(\chi)]}{\chi} \quad (17)$$

in which J_1 is the Bessel function of order one and

$$\Delta\xi = \xi' - \xi$$
$$\Delta\eta = \eta' - \eta \quad (18)$$
$$\chi = \frac{\pi d}{\lambda z_0} (\Delta\xi^2 + \Delta\eta^2)^{1/2}$$

Equation (17) is appropriate for a primary circular source of diameter d that is located at a distance z_0 from plane I.

As a further simplification we associate with the complex degree of spectral coherence a correlation interval ε_0 such that $\mu(\Delta\xi, \Delta\eta; \nu)$ is significant when $(\Delta\xi^2 + \Delta\eta^2)^{1/2} \leq \varepsilon_0$ and is negligible outside of this region.

Making the change of variables $\xi' = \Delta\xi + \xi$ and $\eta' = \Delta\eta + \eta$ in Eq. (9) and using Eqs. (16)–(18) gives

$$I_{11}(x, y; \nu) = \int\int d\xi\, d\eta\, g(\xi, \eta; \nu) h(x, y; \xi, \eta; \nu) \langle |U_{in}(\xi, \eta; \nu)|^2 \rangle$$
$$\cdot \int\int d\Delta\xi\, d\Delta\eta\, g^*(\xi + \Delta\xi, \eta + \Delta\eta; \nu)$$
$$\cdot h^*(x, y; \xi + \Delta\xi, \eta + \Delta\eta; \nu) \mu(\Delta\xi, \Delta\eta; \nu) \qquad (19)$$

Finally, we assume that the input object is illuminated with light that is essentially incoherent, that is, the functions $g(\xi, \eta; \nu)$ and $h(x, y; \xi, \eta; \nu)$ are slowly varying within a coherence area $\pi\varepsilon_0^2$. With this assumption, Eq. (19) becomes

$$I_{11}(x, y; \nu) = \int\int d\xi\, d\eta\, |g(\xi, \eta; \nu)|^2 |h(x, y; \xi, \eta; \nu)|^2 \langle |U_{in}(\xi, \eta; \nu)|^2 \rangle$$
$$\cdot \int\int d\Delta\xi\, d\Delta\eta\, \mu(\Delta\xi, \Delta\eta; \nu) \qquad (20)$$

in which the $\Delta\xi$ and $\Delta\eta$ integrations extend over the range $0 \leq (\Delta\xi^2 + \Delta\eta^2)^{1/2} \leq \varepsilon_0$ and $\mu(\Delta\xi, \Delta\eta; \nu)$ is given in Eq. (17). The $\Delta\xi$ and $\Delta\eta$ integrations are performed by first changing variables to polar coordinates (r, θ), then applying Eq. (GR-6.511-7) of Gradshteyn and Ryzhik (1965) to the r integration. The resulting expression for the spectral intensity is

$$I_{11}(x, y; \nu) = \left[\frac{2}{\pi}\left(\frac{\lambda z_0}{d}\right)^2\right]\left\{1 - J_0\left(\frac{\pi d\varepsilon_0}{\lambda z_0}\right)\right\}$$
$$\cdot \int\int |g(\xi, \eta; \nu)|^2 |h(x, y; \xi, \eta; \nu)|^2 \langle |U_{in}(\xi, \eta; \nu)|^2 \rangle\, d\xi\, d\eta \qquad (21)$$

in which J_0 is the Bessel function of order zero.

Comparing Eqs. (15) and (21), one sees that the finite-coherence-area model gives the same expression as the δ-function description. However, κ, the real-valued constant in Eq. (15), is now explicitly given in terms of system parameters as follows:

$$\kappa = \left[\frac{2}{\pi}\left(\frac{\lambda z_0}{d}\right)^2\right]\left\{1 - J_0\left(\frac{\pi d\varepsilon_0}{\lambda z_0}\right)\right\} \qquad (22)$$

From Eq. (22) one sees that the precise value of κ depends on the definition of the coherence interval ε_0. For example, if one defines ε_0 to be the distance in which $\mu(\Delta\xi, \Delta\eta; \nu)$ drops from unity to zero, then $\kappa = 0.60\varepsilon_0^2$, where $\varepsilon_0 = 1.22\lambda z_0/d$. On the other hand, some authors (see, e.g., Born and Wolf, 1980) prefer to define the coherence interval as the distance that produces a departure of 12% from the ideal value of unity in $\mu(\Delta\xi, \Delta\eta; \nu)$. Using the latter definition, one obtains $\kappa = 1.46\varepsilon_0^2$, with $\varepsilon_0 = 0.32\lambda z_0/d$. These expressions are particularly useful in understanding the variation of output intensity as the correlation interval of the illumination is varied.

A numerical example may also serve to illustrate this important point about ε_0. In a typical setup it is not difficult to obtain an ε_0 of 15 μm using a white-light source and a modest degree of collimation. In this instance the output spectral intensity is in the ratio of $\varepsilon_0^2/(\lambda/2)^2$ brighter than for a fully incoherent source; this is ~2500 times brighter and shows that it is not desirable to make ε_0 needlessly small.

B. CONVENTIONAL OPTICAL FOURIER TRANSFORMS

1. F-to-F Transform Configuration

The canonical F-to-F transform arrangement is shown in Fig. 2a. An input object with amplitude transmittance $g(\xi, \eta; \nu)$ is placed in plane I

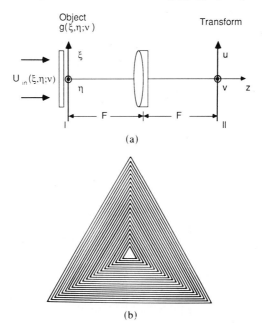

(a)

(b)

Fig. 2. (a) Canonical F-to-F optical Fourier transformation configuration; (b) input transparency consisting of a set of nested triangles; (c) optical Fourier transform of nested triangles obtained using spatially coherent white light (see color plate following p. 50).

and illuminated by an optical field with spectral amplitude $U_{in}(\xi, \eta; \nu)$. Plane II is the Fourier transform (or frequency) plane and is located in the rear focal plane of the lens. The lens transmission function is assumed to be of the form $t_L(x, y; \nu) = \exp[-i\pi(x^2 + y^2)/(\lambda F)]$.

The spectral amplitude in plane II is easily calculated (see, e.g., Goodman, 1968) and is given by

$$U_{II}(u, v; \nu) = \frac{-i}{\lambda F} \int\int g(\xi, \eta; \nu) U_{in}(\xi, \eta; \nu)$$

$$\cdot \exp[-i2\pi(f_\xi \xi + f_\eta \eta)] \, d\xi \, d\eta \tag{23}$$

in which $f_\xi = u/(\lambda F)$, $f_\eta = u/(\lambda F)$, and $\lambda = c/\nu$. Note that the conventional Fourier transform pattern scales linearly with the illumination wavelength (Fig. 2c). The expression for the impulse response function for the F-to-F transform configuration is obtained using Eq. (23) with $U_{in}(\xi, \eta; \nu) = 1$ and $g(\xi, \eta; \nu) = \delta(\xi - \xi', \eta - \eta')$:

$$h(u, v; \xi', \eta'; \nu) = \frac{-i}{\lambda F} \exp\left[\frac{-i2\pi}{\lambda F}(u\xi' + v\eta')\right] \tag{24}$$

With spatially coherent illumination, the spectral intensity in plane II is found using Eqs. (13) and (24):

$$I_{II}(u, v; \nu) = \frac{1}{(\lambda F)^2} \left| \int\int g(\xi, \eta; \nu) U_\nu(\xi, \eta) \right.$$

$$\left. \cdot \exp\left[\frac{-i2\pi}{\lambda F}(u\xi + v\eta)\right] d\xi \, d\eta \right|^2 \tag{25}$$

If the input object is illuminated with spatially incoherent illumination, the spectral intensity is found using Eqs. (15) and (24):

$$I_{II}(u, v; \nu) = \frac{\kappa}{(\lambda F)^2} \int\int |g(\xi, \eta; \nu)|^2 \langle |U_{in}(\xi, \eta; \nu)|^2 \rangle \, d\xi \, d\eta \tag{26}$$

From Eq. (26) it is seen that with spatially incoherent illumination all spatial-frequency information about the input object is lost in $I_{II}(x, y; \nu)$. $I_{II}(x, y; \nu)$ is simply a constant. To preserve the object–spatial-frequency information in plane II when using spatially incoherent illumination, one must modify the impulse response $h(u, v; \xi, \eta; \nu)$. George and Wang (1984) have demonstrated the implementation of a twin-imaging interferometer that produces a cosinusoidal impulse response. Their system can be used for diffraction pattern sampling in spatially incoherent white light.

2. Conventional Optical Fourier Processor

A conventional two-lens optical Fourier processor is shown in Fig. 3. An input object with amplitude transmittance $g(\xi, \eta; \nu)$ is placed in plane

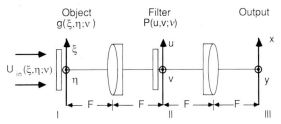

Fig. 3. Conventional two-lens optical Fourier processor: I, input plane; II, frequency plane; III, output (image) plane.

I. Plane II is the Fourier transform (or frequency) plane, which contains a pupil function $P(u, v; \nu)$. Plane III is the output (or image) plane of the processor. The F-to-F spacing between the various planes is chosen as a matter of convenience to simplify subsequent analysis. As above, each lens of the processor is assumed to have a transmission function of the form $t_L(x, y; \nu) = \exp[-i\pi(x^2 + y^2)/(\lambda F)]$.

The spectral amplitude $U_I(\xi, \eta; \nu)$ leaving plane I is given by

$$U_I(\xi, \eta; \nu) = U_{in}(\xi, \eta; \nu)g(\xi, \eta; \nu) \tag{27}$$

The spectral amplitude leaving plane II is written

$$U_{II}(u, v; \nu) = U'_{II}(u, v; \nu)P(u, v; \nu) \tag{28}$$

where

$$U'_{II}(u, v; \nu) = \frac{-i}{\lambda F} \iint U_I(\xi, \eta; \nu) \exp\left[\frac{-i2\pi}{\lambda F}(u\xi + v\eta)\right] d\xi \, d\eta \tag{29}$$

The spectral amplitude at plane III is obtained by taking the Fourier transform of $U_{II}(u, v; \nu)$:

$$U_{III}(x, y; \nu) = \frac{-i}{\lambda F} \iint U_{II}(u, v; \nu) \exp\left[\frac{-i2\pi}{\lambda F}(xu + yv)\right] du \, dv \tag{30}$$

Using Eqs. (27)–(30), one can write $U_{III}(x, y; \nu)$ as

$$U_{III}(x, y; \nu) = \iint U_I(\xi, \eta; \nu)h(x, y; \xi, \eta; \nu) \, d\xi \, d\eta \tag{31}$$

in which the coherent impulse response $h(x, y; \xi, \eta; \nu)$ is

$$h(x, y; \xi, \eta; \nu) = \frac{-1}{(\lambda F)^2} \iint P(u, v; \nu)$$

$$\cdot \exp\left[\frac{-i2\pi}{\lambda F}[u(x + \xi) + v(y + \eta)]\right] du \, dv \tag{32}$$

The spectral intensity in image plane III is easily calculated. When spatially coherent illumination is used, $I_{III}(x, y; \nu)$ is obtained using Eqs. (13) and (32). When spatially incoherent illumination is used, $I_{III}(x, y; \nu)$ is calculated using either Eq. (15) or (20) and Eq. (32).

Now consider the case in which $U_{in}(\xi, \eta; \nu) = 1$ and the pupil function $P(u, v; \nu) = P(u, v; \nu_0)$, where

$$P(u, v; \nu_0) = \frac{-i}{\lambda_0 F} \int\int p(\xi', \eta'; \nu_0) \exp\left[\frac{-i2\pi}{\lambda_0 F}(u\xi' + v\eta')\right] d\xi' d\eta' \qquad (33)$$

In Eq. (33), $p(\xi', \eta'; \nu_0)$ represents the amplitude transmission function of an object located in plane I, which is illuminated by spatially coherent light of frequency $\nu_0 = c/\lambda_0$. Using Eqs. (31)–(33), one can write the expression for the spectral amplitude in the image plane as

$$U_{III}(x, y; \nu) = \frac{+i\lambda_0}{\lambda^2 F} \int\int g(\xi, \eta; \nu) p\left[-\lambda_0 \frac{x+\xi}{\lambda} - \lambda_0 \frac{y+\eta}{\lambda}\right] d\xi \, d\eta \qquad (34)$$

With spatially coherent illumination, the spectral intensity in plane III is simply $I_{III}(x, y; \nu) = |U_{III}(x, y; \nu)|^2$. With spatially incoherent illumination, the spectral intensity is given by

$$I_{III}(x, y; \nu) = \left[\frac{\kappa\lambda_0}{\lambda^2 F}\right]^2$$

$$\cdot \int\int \left|g(\xi, \eta; \nu)^2 p\left[-\lambda_0 \frac{x+\xi}{\lambda} - \lambda_0 \frac{y+\eta}{\lambda}\right]\right|^2 d\xi \, d\eta \qquad (35)$$

From Eqs. (34) and (35) the output spectral intensity is seen to be the convolution of the object transmittance and a magnified impulse response function in which the magnification $M = \lambda/\lambda_0$. It is the wavelength dependence of the impulse response that limits the operation of the conventional Fourier processor to narrowband illumination. The origin of this dependence can be traced directly to the wavelength variation of the conventional Fourier transform system [see Eq. (23)]. By eliminating the wavelength variation in the Fourier transform subsystems, broadband (white-light) operation of the Fourier processor can be achieved over a continuum of wavelengths.

C.   Wavelength-Independent Fourier Transforms

From Eq. (23) and Fig. 2 it is seen that an achromatic lens produces an optical Fourier transform in which the transform size varies linearly with the illumination wavelength. The term *achromatic* indicates that the focal length of the lens is approximately independent of the illumination wavelength or, equivalently, that the size of an "image" is invariant to changes in wavelength. To realize an optical Fourier processor that operates with continuous broadband light, it is necessary to produce a Fourier transform whose scale does not change as the illumination wavelength is varied. The term *achromatic Fourier transform* or *Fourier achromat* will be used to describe a lens system that produces a Fourier transform whose scale is independent of illumination wavelength.

An ideal Fourier achromat produces a transform $G(f_\xi, f_\eta; \nu)$ for an input object $g(\xi, \eta; \nu)$ given by

$$G(f_\xi, f_\eta; \nu) = \frac{-i}{\lambda_0 F} \int\int g(\xi, \eta; \nu) \exp[-i2\pi(f_\xi \xi + f_\eta \eta)] \, d\xi \, d\eta \qquad (36)$$

in which ξ and η denote the spatial coordinates in the input plane, $u = f_\xi \lambda_0 F$ and $v = f_\eta \lambda_0 F$ are the coordinates in the transform plane, which are colinear with ξ and η, respectively. The product $\lambda_0 F$ is a constant. F can be thought of as the focal length of the transform system at the fixed wavelength λ_0. Since $\lambda_0 F$ is a constant, the size of the transform is independent of the illumination wavelength $\lambda = c/\nu$.

A block diagram for an idealized achromatic Fourier processor is shown in Fig. 4. It consists of an input plane I followed by a wavelength-independent Fourier transform, the frequency-plane II containing a filter with amplitude transmittance $P(u, v; \nu)$ followed by another achromatic Fourier transform, and the output (or image) plane III. For the linear system we can easily write the output spectral amplitude $U_{III}(x, y; \nu)$ in terms of the amplitude transmittance $g(\xi, \eta; \nu)$ as follows. The spectral amplitude incident on plane II, $U_{II,in}(u, v; \nu)$ is

$$U_{II,in}(u, v; \nu) = A_{12} \int\int U_{in}(\xi, \eta; \nu) g(\xi, \eta; \nu)$$

$$\cdot \exp\left[\frac{-i2\pi}{\lambda_0 F}(u\xi + v\eta)\right] d\xi \, d\eta \qquad (37)$$

in which A_{12} is a complex constant containing unessential propagation terms. A second application of Eq. (36) gives the output $U_{III}(x, y; \nu)$ in

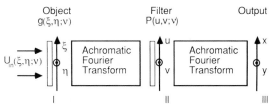

Fig. 4. Idealized achromatic (broadband) Fourier processor: I, input plane; II, frequency plane; III, output plane.

terms of the input $U_{II,in}(u, v; \nu)P(u, v; \nu)$ at plane II, as follows:

$$U_{III}(x, y; \nu) = A_{23} \iint U_{II,in}(u, v; \nu)P(u, v; \nu)$$

$$\cdot \exp\left[\frac{-i2\pi}{\lambda_0 F}(xu + yv)\right] du \, dv \qquad (38)$$

in which A_{23} is a complex constant. The choice for the filter $P(u, v; \nu)$ depends, of course, on the specific task that is to be performed.

Finally, taking $P(u, v; \nu) = P(u, v; \nu_0)$ as defined in Eq. (33) (i.e., the filter (pupil) function is independent of the illumination wavelength λ) and using Eqs. (37) and (38) yields the expression for the spectral amplitude in the output plane of an achromatic Fourier processor:

$$U_{III}(x, y; \nu) = A_{12}A_{13}U_{in}(\nu) \iint g(\xi, \eta; \nu)p[-(x+\xi), -(y+\eta); \nu_0] \, d\xi \, d\eta$$

$$(39)$$

in which we have taken $U_{in}(\xi, \eta; \nu) = U_{in}(\nu)$. Note that achromatic Fourier transformations provide a system impulse response that is independent of illumination wavelength provided that the filter function P is independent of wavelength. Of course, the object $g(\xi, \eta; \nu)$ may implicitly contain a wavelength dependence.

When processing with broadband, spatially coherent illumination, the spectral intensity at any wavelength is obtained by calculating $U_{III}U_{III}^*$, where U_{III} is given in Eq. (39). The total intensity is found by integrating the spectral intensity over the spectral bandwidth of the source.

When processing with broadband, spatially incoherent light, the system becomes linear in intensity as given in Eq. (15), and the appropriate impulse response is $|h(x, y; \xi, \eta; \nu)|^2 = |p(\xi, \eta; \nu_0)|^2$. In this case the spectral intensity $I_{III}(x, y; \nu)$ is given by

$$I_{III}(x, y; \nu) = \kappa|A_{12}A_{13}|^2|U_{in}(\nu)|^2$$

$$\cdot \iint |g(\xi, \eta; \nu)|^2|p[-(x+\xi), -(y+\eta); \nu_0]|^2 \, d\xi \, d\eta \qquad (40)$$

III. Achromatic Fourier Transform Systems

Several methods to produce an achromatic Fourier transform of an input object have been reported. Katyl (1972) used a geometrical optics method to predict the necessary lenses for an achromatic transformation. Morris (1981a) analyzed the process of achromatic Fourier transformation using diffraction theory. The diffraction theory approach leads to general conditions for the required lenses, and it facilitates consideration of subtle variations when partially coherent illumination is used. Other methods to realize achromatic transforms have also been reported. The required lens powers have been obtained using ray-matrix techniques (George and Morris, 1981), Y-N-U ray-tracing methods (Zweig, 1985), a chirp z transform method (Collins, 1981; Leon and Leith, 1985), and zone plate and achromat cascades (Ferriere and Goedgebuer, 1982, 1983).

A. DIFFRACTION ANALYSIS USING LENSES OF ARBITRARY DISPERSION

In this section the diffraction theory approach used by Morris (1981a) is described. Consider the lens arrangement shown in Fig. 5. The input object $g(\xi, \eta; \nu)$ is located in plane I. The focal length of the ith lens is denoted by $F_i(\lambda)$ $(i = 1, 2, 3)$. A, B, and C denote arbitrary, but fixed, spacings between the elements. The output plane of the system, plane II, is located directly behind the third lens $F_3(\lambda)$. The paraxial transmission function for a lens of focal length $F_i(\lambda)$ is assumed to be of the form

$$t_i(x_i, y_i; \nu) = \exp\left[\frac{-i\pi}{\lambda F_i(\lambda)}(x_i^2 + y_i^2)\right] \tag{41}$$

In Eq. (41), if $F_i(\lambda) > 0$, the lens is positive (or convergent); if $F_i(\lambda) < 0$, the lens is negative (or divergent).

A general expression for the spectral amplitude of the field in the output plane II is obtained as follows: Propagate the spectral amplitude leaving the object plane I a distance A; multiply by the transmission function of the first lens $t_1(x_1, y_1; \nu) = \exp\{-i\pi(x_1^2 + y_1^2)/[\lambda F_1(\lambda)]\}$; propagate this amplitude a distance B; multiply by the transmission function of the second lens $t_2(x_2, y_2; \nu) = \exp\{-i\pi(x_2^2 + y_2^2)/[\lambda F_2(\lambda)]\}$; propagate the spectral amplitude a distance C; and multiply by the transmission function of the

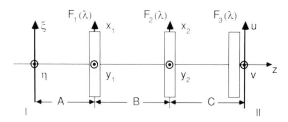

Fig. 5. General three-lens optical system. $F_i(\lambda)$ denotes the focal length of the ith lens $(i = 1, 2, 3)$. The input is located at plane I. Output plane II is located directly behind lens $F_3(\lambda)$.

third lens $t_3(u, v; \nu) = \exp\{-i\pi(u^2 + v^2)/[\lambda F_3(\lambda)]\}$. The details of the calculation are given in the paper by Morris (1981a). Here only the result is given. The spectral amplitude in plane II is found to be

$$U_{11}(u, v; \nu) = Q(\lambda) \exp\left[\frac{i\pi}{\lambda R(\lambda)}(u^2 + v^2)\right] \int\int d\xi\, d\eta\, g(\xi, \eta; \nu)$$

$$\cdot \exp\left[\frac{i\pi}{\lambda S(\lambda)}(\xi^2 + \eta^2)\right] \exp\left[\frac{-i2\pi}{\lambda T(\lambda)}(u\xi + v\eta)\right] \quad (42)$$

where

$$Q(\lambda) = \frac{-i}{\lambda ABCa_1(\lambda)\{a_2(\lambda) - [1/B^2 a_1(\lambda)]\}} \quad (43)$$

$$\frac{1}{R(\lambda)} = \frac{1}{C} - \frac{1}{F_3(\lambda)} - \frac{1}{C^2\{a_2(\lambda) - [1/B^2 a_1(\lambda)]\}} \quad (44)$$

$$\frac{1}{S(\lambda)} = \frac{1}{A} - \frac{1}{A^2 a_1(\lambda)} - \frac{1}{[ABa_1(\lambda)]^2\{a_2(\lambda) - [1/B^2 a_1(\lambda)]\}} \quad (45)$$

$$\frac{1}{T(\lambda)} = \frac{1}{ABCa_1(\lambda)\{a_2(\lambda) - [1/B^2 a_1(\lambda)]\}} \quad (46)$$

In Eqs. (43)-(46), $a_1(\lambda)$ and $a_2(\lambda)$ are simply shorthand notation for the expressions

$$a_1(\lambda) = \frac{1}{A} + \frac{1}{B} - \frac{1}{F_1(\lambda)} \quad (47)$$

$$a_2(\lambda) = \frac{1}{B} + \frac{1}{C} - \frac{1}{F_2(\lambda)} \quad (48)$$

Note that Eq. (42) is the general expression for $U_{11}(u, v; \nu)$ provided that $a_2(\lambda) - \{1/[B^2 a_1(\lambda)]\} \neq 0$ and $a_1(\lambda) \neq 0$.

B. CONDITIONS FOR ACHROMATIC TRANSFORMATION

1. General Solution

To find the lens arrangement(s) that will produce an ideal achromatic Fourier transform of an input object $g(\xi, \eta; \nu)$, we require the general field $U_{11}(u, v; \nu)$, in Eq. (42) to equal $G(f_\xi, f_\eta; \nu)$ in Eq. (36). This requirement is fulfilled provided that the terms in Eq. (42) satisfy the following constraints:

$$\frac{1}{R(\lambda)} = 0 \tag{49a}$$

$$\frac{1}{S(\lambda)} = 0 \tag{49b}$$

$$\frac{1}{T(\lambda)} = \frac{\lambda}{\lambda_0 F} \tag{49c}$$

in which the product $\lambda_0 F$ is an arbitrary constant, and λ is the illumination wavelength.

The constraints in Eq. (49) have simple physical interpretations. The constraint imposed by Eq. (49a) requires the phase curvature of the output spectral amplitude to be zero for all illumination wavelengths. The second constraint $1/S(\lambda) = 0$ is necessary to produce the Fourier transform of $g(\xi, \eta; \nu)$. In effect, it requires that the longitudinal (z-axis) dispersion of the transform system equal zero. The last condition, Eq. (49c), is needed to eliminate the variation of transform size with wavelength.

With these constraints, an exact solution for the wavelength dependence of each lens is found. Using Eqs. (46) and (49c), one can express $a_2(\lambda)$ in terms of $a_1(\lambda)$ as follows:

$$a_2(\lambda) = \left(\frac{F\lambda_0}{ABC\lambda} + \frac{1}{B^2} \right) \frac{1}{a_1(\lambda)} \tag{50}$$

Equations (45) and (50) are then substituted into Eq. (49b) to give

$$a_1(\lambda) = \frac{1}{A} + \frac{C\lambda}{BF\lambda_0} \tag{51}$$

The quantity $a_2(\lambda)$ is determined by substituting Eq. (51) into Eq. (50),

$$a_2(\lambda) = \frac{F\lambda_0}{BC\lambda} \tag{52}$$

The required power for the first lens, $1/F_1(\lambda)$, is obtained with Eqs. (47) and (51). The result is

$$\frac{1}{F_1(\lambda)} = \frac{1}{B} - \frac{C\lambda}{BF\lambda_0} \tag{53}$$

The power of the second lens, $1/F_2(\lambda)$, is found by equating Eqs. (48) and (52). One obtains

$$\frac{1}{F_2(\lambda)} = \frac{1}{B} + \frac{1}{C} - \frac{F\lambda_0}{BC\lambda} \tag{54}$$

The power of the third lens is obtained by substituting Eqs. (44), (51), and (52) into Eq. (49a) to give

$$\frac{1}{F_3(\lambda)} = \frac{1}{C} - \frac{B\lambda}{CF\lambda_0} - \frac{A\lambda^2}{(F\lambda_0)^2} \tag{55}$$

Using these expressions for the focal lengths, Eqs. (53)–(55), in Eqs. (42)–(48), one can verify that this three-lens system performs an ideal achromatic Fourier transformation. In the lens arrangement, the spacings A, B, and C, the constant $F\lambda_0$, and the illumination wavelength λ are independent variables. Once these parameters are specified, each lens of the system is completely determined.

In addition, it is noted that if one is interested only in the spectral intensity of the transform, the third lens $F_3(\lambda)$ is not required. The sole purpose of lens $F_3(\lambda)$ is to eliminate the chromatic variation of output-plane phase curvature.

a. Particular Solution. In the general solution Eqs. (53)–(55), there is a family of possible lens powers. The specific solutions depend on the values selected for the constants A, B, C, and $F\lambda_0$. In this section a particular solution that is easily interpreted in the context of Fourier optics is described. Consider the case in which the constants are as follows:

$$A = 0 \tag{56a}$$

$$B = C = F = 0.5 \text{ m} \tag{56b}$$

$$\lambda_0 = 514.5 \text{ nm} \tag{56c}$$

When one substitutes Eq. (56) into Eqs. (53)–(55), the required lens powers become

$$\frac{1}{F_1(\lambda)} = \frac{1}{F} - \frac{\lambda}{F\lambda_0} \tag{57}$$

$$\frac{1}{F_2(\lambda)} = \frac{2}{F} - \frac{\lambda_0}{F\lambda} \tag{58}$$

$$\frac{1}{F_3(\lambda)} = \frac{1}{F_1(\lambda)} \tag{59}$$

in which $F = 0.5$ m and $\lambda_0 = 514.5$ nm. Curves of the lens power versus wavelength for Eqs. (57) and (58) are shown in Figs. 6a and 6b, respectively.

The operational features of this transform arrangement can be seen by considering its longitudinal and lateral chromatic properties. To illustrate the longitudinal properties, consider a collimated beam of green light ($\lambda = 514.5$ nm) propagating along the z axis. From Eqs. (57) and (59) one

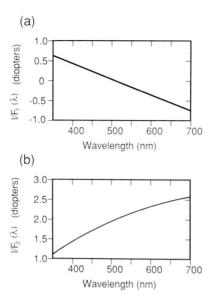

Fig. 6. Theoretical curves for lens power versus wavelength for (a) the first and third lenses [Eqs. (57) and (59)] and (b) the second lens [Eq. (58)]. With reference to Fig. 5, the distance between elements is $A = 0$, $B = C = 0.5$ m.

notes that the first and third lenses have no effect on the beam since the lens power is zero at this wavelength. The second lens, Eq. (58), has a power equal to 2 diopters and consequently focuses the beam at a distance of 0.5 m behind the second lens. Thus at $\lambda = 514.5$ nm it is seen that the system performs a canonical F-to-F Fourier transformation. At a red wavelength, the beam exiting the first lens is divergent. However, the second lens has more power in red light than in green. The power of the second lens $1/F_2(\lambda)$, has just the right power to bring the red beam into focus at the same distance as that of the green light, namely, 0.5 m. In a similar manner for a blue wavelength, the beam emerging from the first lens $F_1(\lambda)$ is convergent. The power of the second lens brings the blue beam to focus in the same plane as the red and green light. As noted previously, the function of the third lens $F_3(\lambda)$ is to eliminate the chromatic variation of the phase curvature in the transform field.

The lateral chromatic properties can be seen by comparing the system response for two different input fields. First, consider a collimated plane wave of arbitrary wavelength λ traveling at angle θ_0 with respect to the z axis. The tangential component of the spectral amplitude along the ξ-axis at plane I can be expressed by

$$U_I(\xi, \eta; \nu) = \exp[i(2\pi/\lambda)\xi \sin \theta_0] \tag{60}$$

Substituting $U_1(\xi, \eta; \nu)$, in Eq. (60), for $g(\xi, \eta; \nu)$, in Eq. (36), and evaluating the resulting integral gives the following expression for the spectral amplitude at plane II,

$$U_{II}(u, v; \nu) = -iF\lambda_0\, \delta(v)\, \delta\left[u - F\sin\theta_0\left(\frac{\lambda_0}{\lambda}\right)\right] \tag{61}$$

From Eq. (61) one notes that the lens system has a tremendous amount of lateral color, with the red wavelengths focusing closer to the optical axis than the blue wavelengths. Lateral color is defined as the difference in height of intercept of principal rays at the image plane (or in the present case, the transform plane) for two different colors, typically the C and F lines of hydrogen. For an achromatic Fourier transform system the lateral color in the output plane is given by

$$\text{lateral color} = F\lambda_0 \sin\theta_0\left(\frac{1}{\lambda_F} - \frac{1}{\lambda_C}\right)$$

Note that the lateral color of the system increases as the angle θ_0 increases.

Next consider as an input object a diffraction grating with transmission function

$$g(\xi, \eta; \nu_0) = \frac{1}{2}\left(1 + \cos\left[\frac{2\pi}{\lambda_0}\xi\sin\theta_0\right]\right) \tag{62}$$

Illuminating $g(\xi, \eta; \nu_0)$ with an axial plane wave of arbitrary wavelength, one finds the spectral amplitude in plane II, using Eq. (36), to be

$$U_{II}(u, v; \nu) = \frac{-iF\lambda_0}{2}\, \delta(v)\left[\delta(u) + \frac{1}{2}\delta(u - F\sin\theta_0)\right.$$

$$\left. + \frac{1}{2}\delta(u + F\sin\theta_0)\right] \tag{63}$$

From Eq. (63) it is seen that the transform pattern does not depend on the illumination wavelength λ. Hence the lateral color of the lens system exactly cancels the chromatic dispersion introduced by the input grating.

2.   Longitudinal and Lateral Chromatic Aberrations

In Section III.B.1 the conditions that produce an achromatic transform were discussed. Consistent with Eq. (49), an ideal achromatic Fourier transform system has no longitudinal dispersion, the phase curvature in the transform plane is zero, and the transform size is wavelength independent. Of course, in an actual lens system, using available glasses, one expects some degree of chromatic aberration. Consequently the performance of a given achromatic-transform design can be specified to first order by comparing its paraxial chromatic aberrations with the ideal case.

The longitudinal chromatic aberration L_{ch} of the transform system is defined as

$$L_{ch} = C - L(\lambda) \tag{64}$$

in which C is the distance between the lens of focal length $F_2(\lambda)$ and the transform plane in the ideal system, and $L(\lambda)$ is the actual distance between lens $F_2(\lambda)$ and the back focal plane of the system with illumination wavelength λ.

A general expression for the longitudinal dispersion of the system in Fig. 5 is found using Eqs. (42), (45), (47), and (48). The location of the focal plane, or equivalently the transform plane, is found by first substituting $L(\lambda)$ for C in Eq. (48) and then solving for the distance $L(\lambda)$, which eliminates the quadratic-phase term $\exp\{i\pi(\xi^2 + \eta^2)/[\lambda S(\lambda)]\}$ in Eq. (42).

Setting $1/S(\lambda) = 0$ in Eq. (45) and solving for $a_2(\lambda)$ gives

$$a_2(\lambda) = \frac{-A}{B^2[1 - Aa_1(\lambda)]} \tag{65}$$

Equation (47) is substituted into Eq. (65) giving

$$a_2(\lambda) = \frac{F_1(\lambda)}{B[F_1(\lambda) - B]} \tag{66}$$

Equating Eqs. (66) and (48) in which $L(\lambda)$ is substituted for C yields

$$\frac{1}{B} + \frac{1}{L(\lambda)} - \frac{1}{F_2(\lambda)} = \frac{F_1(\lambda)}{B[F_1(\lambda) - B]} \tag{67}$$

Equation (67) is solved for $L(\lambda)$ to give

$$L(\lambda) = \frac{1 - [B/F_1(\lambda)]}{[1/F_2(\lambda)] + [1/F_1(\lambda)]\{1 - [B/F_2(\lambda)]\}} \tag{68}$$

The expression for the longitudinal chromatic aberration is obtained by substituting Eq. (68) into Eq. (64).

The variation of transform size with wavelength is found as follows. The location of a particular object spatial frequency component f_ξ is given by the transform-plane coordinate

$$u(\lambda) = f_\xi \lambda T(\lambda) \tag{69}$$

or in normalized form,

$$\frac{u(\lambda)}{u(\lambda_0)} = \frac{\lambda T(\lambda)}{\lambda_0 T(\lambda_0)} \tag{70}$$

in which

$$T(\lambda) = ABCa_1(\lambda)\left[a_2(\lambda) - \frac{1}{B^2 a_1(\lambda)}\right] \tag{71}$$

is written from Eq. (46).

Substituting Eqs. (47) and (48) into Eq. (71) gives

$$T(\lambda) = \frac{[(A+B)F_1(\lambda) - AB][(B+C)F_2(\lambda) - BC]}{BF_1(\lambda)F_2(\lambda)} - \frac{AC}{B} \tag{72}$$

Equation (72) is rewritten to give $T(\lambda)$ in the following form:

$$T(\lambda) = A\left[1 - \frac{B}{F_1(\lambda)} - \frac{C}{F_1(\lambda)} - \frac{C}{F_2(\lambda)} + \frac{BC}{F_1(\lambda)F_2(\lambda)}\right]$$
$$+ BC\left[\frac{1}{B} + \frac{1}{C} - \frac{1}{F_2(\lambda)}\right] \tag{73}$$

Using Eq. (70) and Eq. (73) gives the expression for the chromatic variation of transform size. Note that, in general, the transform size depends on the object distance A (Fig. 6).

An example illustrating the use of Eqs. (70) and (73) may be helpful. Consider the transform size variation obtained with a single ideal achromatic lens of focal length F. For this case let $A = B = F/2$, $C = F$, $1/F_1(\lambda) = 0$, $1/F_2(\lambda) = 1/F$. Substituting these values into Eq. (73) gives $T(\lambda) = F$. Using this in Eq. (70) yields the well-known result $u(\lambda)/u(\lambda_0) = \lambda/\lambda_0$.

3.   Thin-Lens Layout

The wavelength variation for each of the required lenses is given in Eqs. (53)–(55). The approach to achieve the required lens powers is, however, at the discretion of the optical designer. As noted in Section I, most of the achromatic transform systems that have been reported use combinations of glass and holographic lenses to realize (or approximate) the required wavelength dependence on the different groupings. The exception is the all-glass Fourier achromat reported by Brophy (1983). The methods used to design an all-glass Fourier achromat are discussed in Section IV.

In this section, lenses that closely approximate the lens powers in Eqs. (57)–(59) are described. The analysis is based on thin-lens concepts in which the power of a thin lens is the sum of its component elements. It is found that each dispersive lens can be fabricated using a holographic zone lens in a cascade with a glass doublet. In Section III.3.b, curves of the longitudinal chromatic aberration, the chromatic variation of transform size, and the wavelength dependence of the phase curvature for the resulting system are compared with an ideal transform.

a. Dispersive Lens Design. The first lens of focal length $F_1(\lambda)$ [see Eq. (57) and Fig. 6a] can be obtained by cascading an achromatic lens of focal length F with a divergent holographic zone lens. The transmission function of the zone lens is given by

$$t_{H1}(x_1, y_1; \nu) = \exp\left[\frac{+i\pi}{\lambda_0 F}(x_1^2 + y_1^2)\right] \qquad (74)$$

In Eq. (74), λ_0 is a fixed number that can be thought of as the wavelength used in making the holographic element. Comparing Eqs. (41) and (74), one notes that $t_{H1}(x_1, y_1; \nu)$ behaves like a lens of focal length $F_{H1}(\lambda) = -F\lambda_0/\lambda$. Thus, adding the powers of the component elements, $1/F_{H1}(\lambda) + 1/F$, yields the desired lens power in Eq. (57).

The lens of focal length $F_2(\lambda)$ [see Eq. (58) and Fig. 6b] is more difficult to obtain than the first lens since the lens power is not linear in wavelength. The design approach for this lens is to cascade a convergent holographic zone lens with transmission function

$$t_{H2}(x_2, y_2; \nu) = \exp\left[\frac{-i\pi}{\lambda_0 \beta F}(x_2^2 + y_2^2)\right] \qquad (75)$$

and a glass lens of focal length $F_{L2}(\lambda)$. In Eq. (75), β is a fixed real number, and λ_0 denotes the wavelength used in recording the holographic lens. Again, the lens nature of $t_{H2}(x_2, y_2; \nu)$ is seen; by comparing Eqs. (41) and (75), one finds that $t_{H2}(x_2, y_2; \nu)$ is a lens of power

$$\frac{1}{F_{H2}(\lambda)} = \frac{\lambda}{\beta F \lambda_0} \qquad (76)$$

Subtracting Eq. (76) from Eq. (58) gives the required power of the glass element:

$$\frac{1}{F_{L2}(\lambda)} = \frac{1}{F}\left(2 - \frac{\lambda_0}{\lambda} - \frac{\lambda}{\beta \lambda_0}\right) \qquad (77)$$

The idea behind this lens combination is to use the holographic lens to produce the bulk of the dispersion and the glass element to provide the small corrections necessary to obtain the required power in Eq. (58). Hence the problem reduces to designing a lens with power $1/F_{L2}(\lambda)$ given in Eq. (77).

In Eq. (77) the parameter β has not yet been specified. With the proper choice of β it is seen below that the lens power $1/F_{L2}(\lambda)$ can be obtained to a good approximation with a glass doublet. The power of the thin doublet, denoted by $1/F_D(\lambda)$, is the sum of the powers of its component elements:

$$\frac{1}{F_D(\lambda)} = [n_A(\lambda) - 1]C_A + [n_B(\lambda) - 1]C_B \tag{78}$$

in which $n_A(\lambda)$ and $n_B(\lambda)$ denote the index refraction of glass A and glass B, respectively. C_A and C_B are constants associated with surface curvature. The optimum value for the constant β in Eqs. (76) and (77) is determined empirically by comparing the ideal lens power in Eq. (58) with the power obtained by summing $1/F_{H2}(\lambda)$ and $1/F_D(\lambda)$ in Eqs. (76) and (78). Using Schott glass BK7 and SF57 for glass A and glass B, respectively, one finds that the best fit to Eq. (58) is obtained with $\beta = 1.80$. Other constants are $F = 0.5$ m, $\lambda_0 = 514.5$ nm, $C_A = +16.421$ m^{-1}, and $C_B = -8.878$ m^{-1}.

In Fig. 7 the wavelength dependence of the lens combination consisting of a holographic zone lens and a glass doublet, $1/F_{H2}(\lambda) + 1/F_D(\lambda)$ in Eqs. (76) and (78), is compared with the required lens power in Eq. (58). The glass doublet is made with Schott glass BK7 and SF57. The constant β equals 1.80. It is seen that this combination provides a good fit to $1/F_2(\lambda)$ over the visible wavelength band.

b. Paraxial Chromatic Aberrations.   To first order, the performance of an achromatic transform system can be characterized by its paraxial chromatic aberrations. For a given transform design the various paraxial chromatic aberrations of the system are obtained by substituting the specific chromatic properties of each lens grouping $[F_1(\lambda), F_2(\lambda), F_3(\lambda)]$ into Eqs. (64), (68), (70), and (73).

Consider the transform system described in Sections III.B.3. From Eq. (57) the power of the first lens grouping—a lens achromat and a diverging

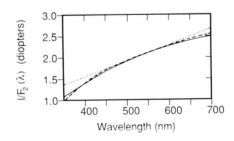

Fig. 7. Lens power versus wavelength for the ideal lens in Eq. (58) (solid line), a single holographic lens (dotted line), and a thin-lens cascade consisting of a holographic zone lens [Eq. (76)] and a glass doublet [Eq. (78)] (dashed line).

holographic zone lens—is given by

$$\frac{1}{F_1(\lambda)} = \frac{1}{F} - \frac{\lambda}{F\lambda_0} \tag{79}$$

in which $F = 0.5$ m and $\lambda_0 = 514.5$ nm. The second lens group consists of a convergent holographic zone lens of focal length $F_{H2}(\lambda)$ in cascade with a glass doublet of focal length $F_D(\lambda)$. The power of this combination is given by

$$\frac{1}{F_2(\lambda)} = \frac{1}{F_{H2}(\lambda)} + \frac{1}{F_D(\lambda)} \tag{80}$$

The lens powers $1/F_{H2}(\lambda)$ and $1/F_D(\lambda)$ are defined in Eqs. (76) and (78) with glass A = BK7, glass B = SF57, and $\beta = 1.80$. From Eq. (59) it is seen that the third lens grouping is identical to the first when the object distance A equals zero:

$$\frac{1}{F_3(\lambda)} = \frac{1}{F_1(\lambda)} \tag{81}$$

The chromatic aberrations of this arrangement are found by substituting Eqs. (79)–(81) into the general equations: longitudinal dispersion, Eqs. (64) and (68); transform size variation, Eqs. (70) and (73); and transform-plane phase curvature, Eq. (44).

The results, denoted by I, are plotted in Figs. 8–10. In Fig. 8 it is seen that the transform system is actually apochromatic since there are three wavelengths united at a common focus. In Fig. 9 one notes that the transform size has only a slight wavelength dependence. Over the visible spectrum (400–700 nm), the maximum deviation from the ideal value of unity is 0.018. Figure 10 shows that the paraxial phase curvature of the transform field has a maximum deviation of 0.0432 m^{-1} from the ideal value of zero. In both cases the maximum deviation occurs at $\lambda = 700$ nm.

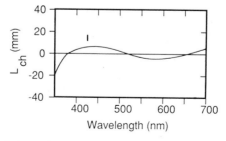

Fig. 8. Longitudinal chromatic aberration of system obtained using lens powers given in Eqs. (79)–(81).

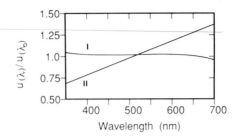

Fig. 9. Chromatic variation of transform size obtained using (I) the lens powers given in Eqs. (79)–(81) and (II) a single achromatic lens. $\lambda_0 = 514.5$ nm.

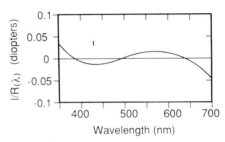

Fig. 10. Phase curvature of the optical field at plane II versus wavelength for the lens system defined by Eqs. (79)–(81).

c. In-Line and Off-Axis Geometries.   i. *In-Line Systems.*   In the Fourier achromat described in Section III.B.3, both diverging and converging holographic lenses are used. With Eqs. (79) and (80) as a starting point, an in-line Fourier achromat was designed and optimized using computer lens-design techniques (Hopkins and Morris, 1983). In the in-line Fourier achromat shown in Fig. 11, each holographic lens consists of an off-axis grating in contact with an off-axis holographic lens. With this arrangement, good efficiency is obtained over the entire aperture due to the volume diffraction effects of a thick hologram with a relatively high carrier frequency. However, at wavelengths off Bragg resonance, a portion of the beam is not diffracted by the holographic lens; this direct (or undiffracted) beam from each holographic lens is the major source of unwanted background radiation (or ghost images) in the transform plane. A diagram illustrating the source of the two ghost images is shown in Fig. 12.

Transform output of the system is shown in Fig. 13 (see color plate following p. 50) in which the object consisted of a set of nested triangles (see Fig. 2b). In this case the object was illuminated using spatially coherent white light. In Fig. 13a, the reddish inverted triangle is due to undiffracted

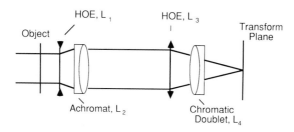

Fig. 11. Layout of in-line Fourier achromat (distances not to scale).

light arising from the diverging holographic lens. In effect the glass element in the first lens grouping produces a transform of this undiffracted light at the second lens grouping, which also transforms it, thereby producing an inverted red triangle. The second ghost image is due to light that is diffracted by the diverging holographic lens but passes directly through the converging holographic lens. In this case the glass doublet focuses the light beyond the transform plane, thereby producing a dispersed or wavelength-dependent image. These background terms can be minimized by placing a stop at the second lens group to block the inverted triangular image (Fig. 13b) or by using a bandpass filter (Fig. 13c).

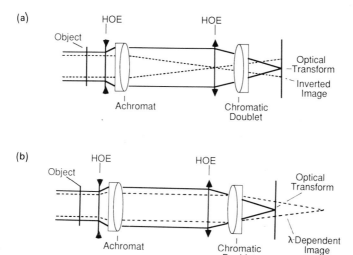

Fig. 12. In-line Fourier achromat showing the origin of unwanted background contributions. Solid lines indicate the ray paths under proper operation. Dashed lines show background contributions due to undiffracted light from (a) the first holographic lens and (b) the second holographic lens element.

The bandwidth of a holographic optical element depends on its thickness, carrier-frequency, and type (Stone and George, 1982, 1985; Sjolinder, 1984). However, a general understanding of the bandwidth that can be expected from a lens configuration consisting of several holograms can be obtained by considering holographic diffraction gratings of a representative spatial frequency.

The bandwidth of a grating (30° angle at 630 nm) is shown in Fig. 14 for a range of element thicknesses (Stone and George, 1985). For a 7.5-μm-thick emulsion, the theoretical prediction of bandwidth is 210 nm between the 90% points and 370 nm between the 70% points. While the precise bandwidth of a grouping of holograms needs to be evaluated for the particular configuration, in rough terms, if there are four separate zone-plates and gratings in a Fourier achromat, the bandwidth will be on the order of 200 nm to 70% points (approximately 0.9^4). This is an appreciable bandwidth.

ii. *Off-Axis Configurations.* An excellent solution to the background problem was provided by Upatnieks *et al.* (1982), who suggested the use

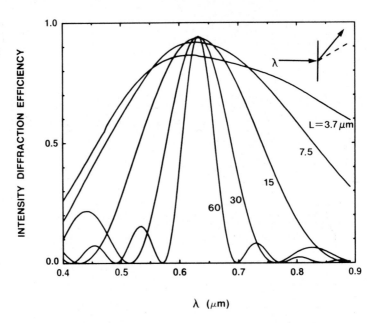

Fig. 14. First-order diffraction efficiency for a 30°-bias phase grating versus wavelength (with no angular detuning) for a range of element thicknesses. As the thickness decreases, the peak efficiency drops, and the sinc curve shape loses symmetry. [Reprinted with permission from Stone and George (1985)].

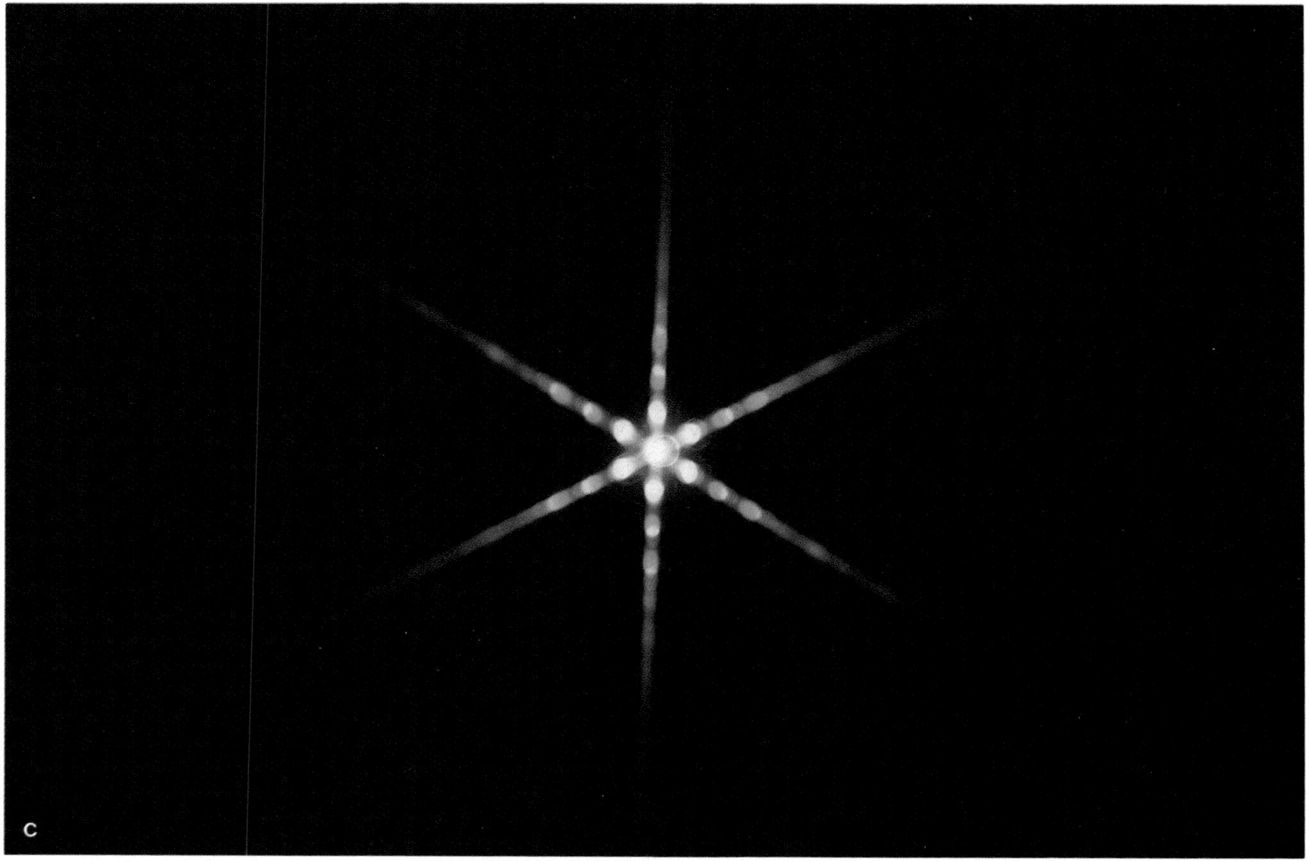

Fig. 2c

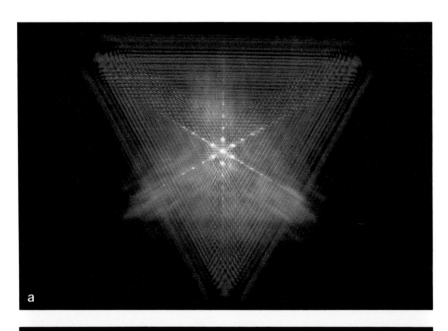

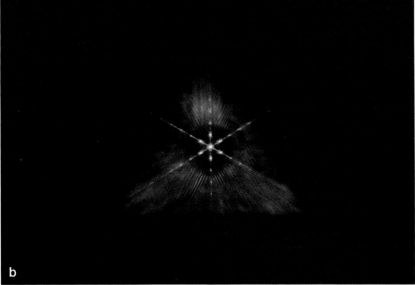

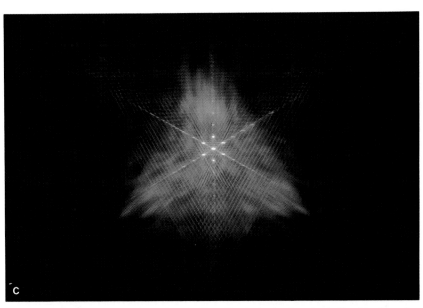

Fig. 13. Transform output for object in Fig. 2b obtained using the in-line Fourier achromat shown in Fig. 11 and spatially coherent white light: (a) optical transform with background contributions due to undiffracted light from the first HOE (inverted red triangle) and the second HOE (small λ-dependent triangle); (b) transform output obtained when a small on-axis stop is placed at the second HOE to block the background contribution from the first HOE; (c) transform output with spectral bandwidth limited to 200 nm (no stop at second HOE).

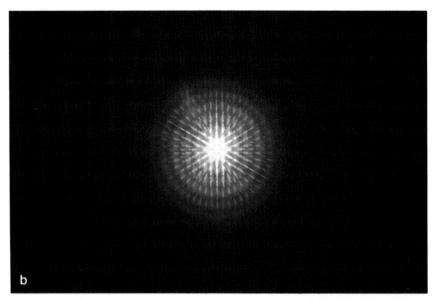

Fig. 16b

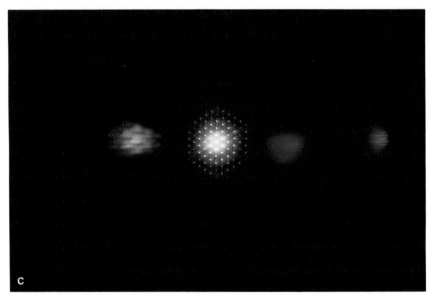

Fig. 16c

of an off-axis configuration in which off-axis holographic lenses L_1 and L_3, are used with a grating G positioned in between as shown in Fig. 15. This off-axis arrangement enables one to separate (or block) undiffracted and spurious orders. George and Morris (1983) implemented this off-axis geometry by modifying the system designed by Hopkins and Morris (1983), but with limited success. The addition of the off-axis arrangement produced substantial aberrations in the transform pattern. Subsequently, Zweig (1985) designed, computer optimized, and constructed a Fourier achromat for off-axis operation. Zweig's system produces diffraction-limited output over a 20-mm field at spatial frequencies up to 30 lines per millimeter using light of 200-nm bandwidth. Transform output for this Fourier achromat is shown in Fig. 16. In this case the off-axis angle $\theta_0 = 2°$ (Fig. 15) permits the achromatic transform to be separated from the various spurious orders. The design strategy for an off-axis Fourier achromat is discussed in detail in Section IV.

C. ACHROMATIC FOURIER PROCESSORS

In Section III.B, the lenses required to produce an achromatic transform with spatially coherent white light were specified. In this section the synthesis of an achromatic Fourier processor is considered. Since the three-lens system given by Eqs. (53)–(55) produces an achromatic transform that is accurate in both amplitude and phase, two achromatic transform systems can simply be cascaded as shown in Fig. 17a. From the diffraction-theory treatment, it is evident that the third and sixth lenses simply multiply the incident wavefront by a quadratic phase term to obtain a planar wavefront at planes II and III, respectively. In an optical processor in which one detects the intensity in the output, the phase correction at plane III is irrelevant, so L_6 is unnecessary. Figure 17b shows a reduced form of Fourier processor that is still capable of ideal performance: broadband Fourier transform at plane II and intensity only at plane III.

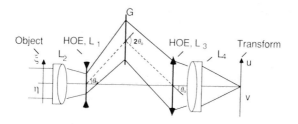

Fig. 15. Off-axis Fourier achromat (distances and angles not to scale).

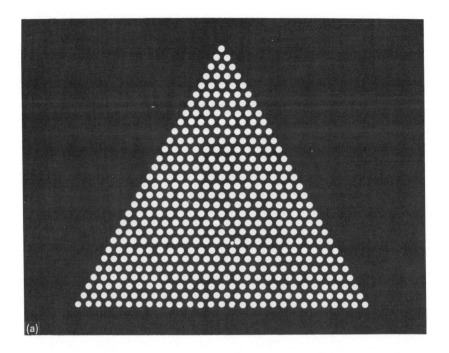

Fig. 16. (a) Input transparency consisting of a triangular array of dots with a spacing of 6 dots/mm; (b) optical transform obtained using a single achromatic lens with spatially coherent white light; (c) transform output obtained using off-axis Fourier achromat with spatially coherent white light. Note that the 2°-bias angle is sufficient to separate the undiffracted (left-hand side) and spurious orders (right-hand side) from the achromatized transform. [For (b) and (c) see color plate following p. 50.]

Morris (1981b) has shown that it is possible to eliminate lens L_3 as well or, more precisely, to combine the effects of lens L_3 into lenses placed between planes II and III. If this is done, the transform at plane II is no longer, strictly speaking, a Fourier transform since the spectral amplitude contains a wavelength-dependent phase term,

$$\Phi_3(u, v; \nu) = \exp\left[\frac{+i\pi}{\lambda F_3(\lambda)} (u^2 + v^2)\right] \tag{82}$$

in which $1/F_3(\lambda)$ is given in Eq. (55). However, the effects of $\Phi_3(u, v; \nu)$ can be included by modifying lenses L_4 and L_5, as shown in Fig. 17c.

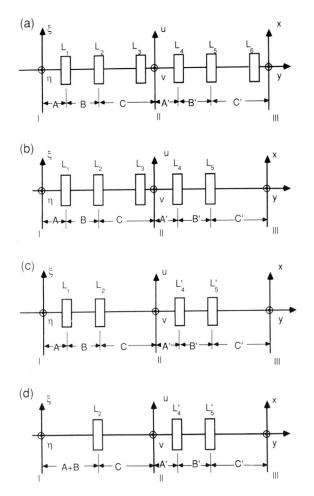

Fig. 17. General configurations for broadband optical processing and imaging: (a) lenses required for full implementation of lens powers given in Eqs. (53)–(55); (b) reduction for intensity-only output at plane III; (c) incorporation of the effects of lens L_3 into lenses between planes II and III; and (d) reduction for processing with broadband, spatially incoherent light only.

The required lenses L_4' and L_5' can be determined by applying the diffraction theory treatment described above between planes II and III as follows.

The spectral amplitude leaving plane II is taken to be

$$U_{\mathrm{II}}(u, v; \nu) = U_{\mathrm{II,in}}(u, v; \nu)P(u, v; \nu) \qquad (83)$$

where $P(u, v; \nu)$ represents a general frequency-plane filter and

$$U_{\text{II,in}}(u, v; \nu) = Q(\lambda) \exp\left[\frac{i\pi}{\lambda F_3(\lambda)}(u^2 + v^2)\right]$$
$$\cdot \int d\xi\, d\eta\, g(\xi, \eta; \nu) \exp\left[\frac{-i2\pi}{\lambda_0 F}(u\xi + v\eta)\right] \qquad (84)$$

where again $1/F_3(\lambda)$ is given in Eq. (55). Following the procedure described in Section III.A, the spectral amplitude in plane III is written in terms of $U_{\text{II}}(u, v; \nu)$:

$$U_{\text{III}}(x, y; \nu) = Q'(\lambda) \exp\left[\frac{-i\pi}{\lambda R'(\lambda)}(x^2 + y^2)\right] \int\int du\, dv\, U_{\text{II}}(u, v; \nu)$$
$$\cdot \exp\left[\frac{i\pi}{\lambda S'(\lambda)}(u^2 + v^2)\right] \exp\left[\frac{-i2\pi}{\lambda T'(\lambda)}(xu + yv)\right] \qquad (85)$$

where

$$Q'(\lambda) = \frac{-i}{\lambda A'B'C'a_4(\lambda)\{a_5(\lambda) - [1/B'^2 a_4(\lambda)]\}} \qquad (86)$$

$$\frac{1}{R'(\lambda)} = \frac{1}{C'} - \frac{1}{C'^2\{a_5(\lambda) - [1/B'^2 a_4(\lambda)]\}} \qquad (87)$$

$$\frac{1}{S'(\lambda)} = \frac{1}{A'} - \frac{1}{A'^2 a_4(\lambda)} - \frac{1}{[A'B'a_4(\lambda)]^2\{a_5(\lambda) - [1/B'^2 a_4(\lambda)]\}} \qquad (88)$$

$$\frac{1}{T'(\lambda)} = \frac{1}{A'B'C'a_4(\lambda)\{a_5(\lambda) - [1/B'^2 a_4(\lambda)]\}} \qquad (89)$$

$$a_4(\lambda) = \frac{1}{A'} + \frac{1}{B'} - \frac{1}{F_4'(\lambda)} \qquad (90)$$

$$a_5(\lambda) = \frac{1}{B'} + \frac{1}{C'} - \frac{1}{F_5'(\lambda)} \qquad (91)$$

in which $a_5(\lambda) - 1/[B'^2 a_4(\lambda)] \neq 0$ and $a_4(\lambda) \neq 0$. Using Eqs. (83)–(85) gives

$$U_{\text{III}}(x, y; \nu) = Q(\lambda)Q'(\lambda) \exp\left[\frac{i\pi}{\lambda R'(\lambda)}(x^2 + y^2)\right]$$
$$\cdot \int\int d\xi\, d\eta\, g(\xi, \eta; \nu) \int\int du\, dv\, P(u, v; \nu)$$
$$\cdot \exp\left\{\frac{i\pi}{\lambda}\left[\frac{1}{F_3(\lambda)} + \frac{1}{S'(\lambda)}\right](u^2 + v^2)\right\}$$
$$\cdot \exp\left\{\frac{-i2\pi}{\lambda}\left[\left(\frac{x}{T'(\lambda)} + \frac{\lambda\xi}{\lambda_0 F}\right)u + \left(\frac{y}{T'(\lambda)} + \frac{\lambda\eta}{\lambda_0 F}\right)v\right]\right\} \qquad (92)$$

If plane III is to be an image plane for plane I, then we require that the quadratic phase term in u and v integrations in Eq. (92) vanish for all wavelengths, that is,

$$\frac{1}{F_3(\lambda)} + \frac{1}{S'(\lambda)} = 0 \tag{93}$$

The image size can be made independent of wavelength by requiring

$$\frac{1}{T'(\lambda)} = \frac{\lambda}{\lambda_1 F'} \tag{94}$$

in which the product $\lambda_1 F'$ is an arbitrary, real constant.

Using Eqs. (93), (94), (55), and (88)–(91) gives the expressions for the optical power of lenses L'_4 and L'_5, respectively:

$$\frac{1}{F'_4(\lambda)} = \frac{1}{B'} + \frac{1/F_3(\lambda) - C'\lambda/(B'F'\lambda_1)}{1 + A'/F_3(\lambda)} \tag{95}$$

$$\frac{1}{F'_5(\lambda)} = \frac{1}{B'} + \frac{1}{C'} - \frac{F'\lambda_1}{B'C'\lambda}\left[1 + \frac{A'}{F_3(\lambda)}\right] \tag{96}$$

With reference to Fig. 17c, an expression for the spectral amplitude $U_{III}(u, v; \nu)$ that is produced by lenses given in Eqs. (53), (54), (95), and (96) can be written as

$$U_{III}(x, y; \nu) = \int\int d\xi\, d\eta\, g(\xi, \eta; \nu) h(x, y; \xi, \eta; \nu) \tag{97}$$

in which

$$h(x, y; \xi, \eta; \nu) = -\left[\frac{1}{(\lambda_0 F)(\lambda_1 F')}\right] \exp\left[\frac{i\pi}{\lambda R'(\lambda)}(x^2 + y^2)\right]$$

$$\cdot \int\int du\, dv\, P(u, v; \nu)$$

$$\cdot \exp\left\{-i2\pi\left[\left(\frac{x}{\lambda_1 F'} + \frac{\xi}{\lambda_0 F}\right)u + \left(\frac{y}{\lambda_1 F'} + \frac{\eta}{\lambda_0 F}\right)v\right]\right\} \tag{98}$$

Note that the achromatic Fourier processor illustrated in Fig. 17c can operate with either spatially coherent illumination [Eqs. (13) and (97)] or spatially incoherent illumination [Eqs. (15) and (97)].

Also note that if the system is to operate only with spatially incoherent white light, then the first lens L_1 can also be eliminated without compromising system performance (Fig. 17d). The lens powers for the processor shown in Fig. 17d are given by Eqs. (54), (95), and (96).

IV. Design of an Achromatic Fourier Processor

In practice, the utility of an achromatic Fourier transform depends on the ability to design and construct an achromatic Fourier transform (AFT) lens. The requirements on spectral bandwidth, transform resolution, aperture size, space-bandwidth product, spectral efficiency, and system dimensions must all be balanced to achieve the desired performance. For example, there is a direct tradeoff between spectral bandwidth and space-bandwidth product. Applications involving a narrow spectral range (e.g., diode laser optical correlators) can expect to achieve space–bandwidth products approaching those of conventional Fourier transform lenses. For broadband illumination (as found in stellar speckle interferometry), the maximum space–bandwidth product is limited by the constraints of the larger spectrum.

As has been shown, an achromatic Fourier-transform lens system is strongly dispersive. In most previous systems the required chromatic dispersion is achieved by the use of holographic lenses which have an effective Abbe V number of −3.45. It is also possible to generate the requisite amount of dispersion by using properly chosen glass combinations and large spaces between lens groups. Thus an all-glass lens system is also capable of producing an achromatic Fourier transform.

In this section we describe the design procedure for an achromatic Fourier transform lens of either the all-glass or holographic type. We also discuss the process of optimizing the design by using a computer design code such as CODEV.* In addition, an example of one such design is shown.

A. First-Order Layout

1. *Holographic and Glass Lens Systems*

In the previous section it was shown that an achromatic Fourier transform (in amplitude) can be produced by using two thin-lens groups L_1 and L_2 (Fig. 17c). The power of each lens group is given in Eqs. (53) and (54), respectively.

The first step is to convert these lens equations into a form that can be used in a lens design program. A thin lens has a power Φ given by the equation

$$\Phi = (n-1)(c_1 - c_2) = (n-1)c \tag{99}$$

where n is the index of refraction, c_1 and c_2 are the curvatures of the front and back surface of the lens, and c is the difference between the front and

---

*CODEV is a registered trademark of Optical Research Associates, Pasadena, California.

back curvatures. Since the index of refraction varies with wavelength, a single lens cannot be an achromat. A thin-lens doublet, however, can be achromatized if the total curvature of the first and second elements, c_a and c_b, respectively have the following values (see, e.g., Kingslake, 1978):

$$c_a = (c_{a1} - c_{a2}) = \frac{\Phi_{total}}{(V_a - V_b)\, \Delta n_a} \tag{100}$$

$$c_b = (c_{b1} - c_{b2}) = \frac{\Phi_{total}}{(V_b - V_a)\, \Delta n_b} \tag{101}$$

where Φ_{total} is the desired power of the achromatic doublet, V is the Abbe V number, and Δn is the index in F light (468.13 nm) minus the index in C light (656.27 nm). For first-order calculations, each holographic lens is represented as a conventional thin-lens with a large index of refraction that is proportional to wavelength (Sweatt, 1977). The concept of this model can be seen by considering a ficticious glass that has an index of refraction

$$n(\lambda) = (n_0 - 1)\frac{\lambda}{\lambda_0} + 1 \tag{102}$$

where n_0 is the index value at λ_0. A lens made with this glass would have a power described by substituting Eq. (102) into Eq. (99):

$$\Phi = c(n_0 - 1)\frac{\lambda}{\lambda_0} \tag{103}$$

The power of this element is proportional to wavelength, which is the first-order property of a holographic lens. This model becomes extremely accurate as the index n_0 increases (Sweatt, 1977, 1978). A holographic lens must be represented by very weak curvatures to compensate for the enormous index.

For the achromat in Φ_1, a number of glass pairs have been analyzed. Schott BK7 and SF8 glasses work well in the first achromatic doublet. For the achromat in Φ_2, various glass combinations have been tested with the lens design program CODEV to match the powers of each holographic optical element (HOE) glass doublet lens group to the theoretical power of Φ_2. Using the zoom option of CODEV, one can specify the target focal lengths at five different wavelengths. The best results are produced with either Schott BK7 and SF56 glasses or Schott SK16 and SF56 glasses.

2. All-Glass Fourier Achromat

The thin-lens equations that have been previously derived for a Fourier achromat require highly dispersive elements. Such dispersion is unavailable in common glass materials although it can be obtained in gradient-index lenses (Ryan-Howard and Moore, 1985). It is apparent that an all-glass Fourier achromat cannot be designed using the present thin-lens equations. The procedure to design on all-glass Fourier achromat have been described by Wynne (1979) and Brophy (1983). Brophy has shown that three highly dispersive lens groups can produce an achromatic Fourier transform. As was previously stated, a Fourier achromat must have a focal length inversely proportional to wavelength. This is to say that if a group of rays enters the lens parallel to the optical axis, the rays will impinge upon the transform plane at an angle

$$U = \frac{U_0 \lambda}{\lambda_0} \tag{104}$$

where U_0 is the ray angle at the reference wavelength λ_0. In addition, a ray incident at angle Q on an AFT lens crosses the transform plane at a height

$$Y = \frac{(QF)\lambda_0}{\lambda_1} = \frac{Y_0 \lambda_0}{\lambda} \tag{105}$$

where F is the focal length of the lens at the reference wavelength λ_0.

We choose a set of discrete wavelengths to represent the region of interest. If Eqs. (104) and (105) are satisfied at those wavelengths, then we assume to first order that they are satisfied everywhere in the spectrum. For simplicity, we consider three sample wavelengths. To satisfy two equations at three different wavelengths requires six free variables. A solution for two doublets contains six degrees of freedom: four lens powers and two air spaces. Unfortunately, the solution for two doublets gives rise to negative air spaces. A solution of three doublets is necessary to produce real powers and lens separations. Brophy (1984) has shown that the three-doublet solutions can be divided into two groups. Group 1 solutions consist of three positive-power doublets. Group 2 solutions consist of a negative-power doublet sandwiched between two positive-power doublets. The negative lens in the group 2 solutions causes off-axis rays to diverge from the optical axis as they head toward the third doublet. As a result of the diverging rays, the third doublet in the lens must have a large aperture to collect the light. This property makes group 2 lenses impractical to construct. The group 1 solutions overcome this problem by folding the off-axis rays back toward the optical axis. This makes group 1 solutions preferable for achromatic transform lenses that are needed to handle moderate to high spatial frequencies (>10 cycles/mm).

To generate a large amount of dispersion in each glass doublet, it is necessary to choose two glasses with as large a difference in V number as possible. Good success has been achieved by Brophy using Schott BK7 and SF56, which are at opposite ends of the glass chart.

Although the doublets are sufficient to satisfy the first-order design, they are incapable of correcting for the complex combination of wavelength-dependent aberrations that are found in achromatic transform systems. Three or more elements in each lens group are necessary for aberration correction.

3. Computer Optimization Strategy

Once a first-order design is found, it is necessary to consider a strategy for optimization. There are two distinctly different strategies for modeling a Fourier achromat.

To first order, a Fourier achromat can be treated as an imaging system with an off-axis object at infinity (Brophy, 1983). Under this assumption, the AFT lens produces an image with a "magnification" inversely proportional to wavelength:

$$\frac{Y(\lambda_1)}{Y(\lambda_2)} = \frac{\lambda_2}{\lambda_1} \tag{106}$$

where $Y(\lambda)$ is the height at which an off-axis ray crosses the transform plane. A second result of this assumption is that all on-axis rays come to focus on axis at the same plane:

$$Y_0(\lambda_1) = Y_0(\lambda_2) = Y_0(\lambda_3) = 0 \tag{107}$$

Equations (106) and (107) force the lens system to behave as a Fourier achromat. However, these equations do not control the aberrations of the lens. Aberration control must be addressed by other options in the merit function. A number of lens-design codes have a default merit function that may be adequate for some achromatic transform lenses.

The Fourier achromat lens is optimized separately at a number of different wavelengths using the zoom-lens option now commonly available with many optimization programs. Each wavelength is entered in a different zoom position. Thus the wavelengths are zoomed while the lens remains fixed. A merit function is constructed that couples the off-axis ray heights at different wavelengths $Y(\lambda)$ by the inverse of the wavelength ratio. Equivalently, one could require that the focal length at each wavelength be inversely proportional to the wavelength.

A second design strategy is to simulate the achromatic Fourier transform in the optimization process. The function of a Fourier achromat is to take the light diffracted from a grating like structure and form a wavelength-independent spatial frequency map. If a diffraction grating is placed in the input plane of an AFT lens and is illuminated with collimated white light, the diffracted light from a single order should come to the same place in the focal plane regardless of the wavelength [Eqs. (62) and (63)]. The grating frequency and the orientation can be varied by using the zoom-lens option. This method eliminates the need to define any special optimization values. The default merit function can be used to optimize for as many wavelengths as the designer chooses. By contrast, the previous method requires the optimization parameters to be changed for each change in wavelength.

After specification of the first-order layout, optimization is turned over to the optical design program. For the initial stages of optimization, it is best to work with thin lenses and to allow only the glass lens curvatures and lens-group separations to vary. Glass thickness is usually not important in the initial stages of a lens design. For a system using holographic lenses, it is best to hold the holographic lens powers constant in the initial stages of the design.

B. DESIGN EXAMPLE

To illustrate these techniques we discuss a step-by-step design of a holographic achromatic Fourier processor. In addition to the achromatic Fourier transform lens we have added the second half of the processor which converts the transform back into an image as in Fig. 17c.

1. Design of an Achromatic Fourier Transform Lens

The system under investigation is an achromatic Fourier processor capable of operating over the visible spectrum (400–700 nm) with spatially coherent illumination. The diameter of the entrance pupil is 20 mm, and the focal length is not specified at the outset. For initial lens separations we choose $B = C = 500$ mm and let the constant $\lambda_0 F = 0.25$ mm^2. The power of Φ_1 is found directly by substituting the values stated above into Eq. (53):

$$\Phi_1(\lambda) = 0.002 - 3.887\lambda \qquad (108)$$

For Φ_2, an achromat–holographic lens cascade is fit to Eq. (54) as described above to give

$$\Phi_2(\lambda) = 0.004 - (1.029 \times 10^{-6})\lambda \qquad (109)$$

For the achromatic lens element in Φ_1, the glasses used are Schott BK7 and SF8. The achromat in Φ_2 is constructed with BK7 and SF56. The first-order layout is optimized using CODEV. A 20-mm diameter diffraction grating is placed 5 mm in front of the first thin lens group. The grating has a spatial frequency of 15 lines per millimeter. The system is optimized at three wavelengths (650 nm, 550 nm, and 450 nm) for the 0 and ±1 diffracted orders. After eight optimization cycles, the rms spot size is reduced to

138 μm. The lens design program changes the first-order parameters, making $B = 637.46$ mm, $C = 208$ mm, and $F = 175.36$ mm with $\lambda_0 = 500$ nm. The resulting elements Φ_1 and Φ_2 agree closely with the theoretical powers corresponding to the new values of B, C, and F. This thin-lens system could be improved further by adding thickness to the lenses and by allowing the power of the HOEs to vary, but the relatively large value of the spot size at this point indicates that the performance of this design is limited. To allow for better aberration correction, Φ_2 is redesigned using two glass doublets to help correct for the aberrations produced by the holographic lenses. The wavelength-independent term of Φ_2 is divided in half. A BK7-SF56 doublet is constructed to produce half the necessary power, and an SK16-SF56 doublet produces the remainder. CODEV is used to fit this thin-lens group to the theoretical power of Φ_2. The redesigned system is optimized using the same method described previously. After seven optimization cycles, the rms spot size is 1.53 μm (the merit function does not account for diffraction). At this point the system can be reoptimized for gratings of larger spatial frequencies.

Once the thin-lens system is complete, a real-lens system can be formed by adding thickness to each element and a spacing between all elements. The elements of Φ_1 are given a thickness of 3 mm. Elements of Φ_2 are set to a thickness of 8 mm. Holographic lenses are required to be at least 30 mm from any other element (to allow for alignment in the laboratory). The minimum spacing between any two elements is constrained to be greater than 1 mm. The number of wavelengths used is increased from three (650, 550, and 450 nm) to five (650, 600, 550, 500, and 450 nm). Three ZOOM positions are used corresponding to gratings frequencies of 0, 20, and 30 lines/mm, respectively. The CODEV merit function is modified slightly using the aperture–weight option (WTA). The WTA option modifies the importance of rays in different parts of the aperture. A large WTA value causes the program to place greater emphasis on the central rays than on the perimeter rays. The default WTA value is 0.65. For this optimization cycle, WTA is set at 0.25 to improve the performance in the outer ring of the aperture.

In optimizing the system, CODEV tends to make the focal length very small, which causes problems in converting the transform back into an image. For this design, the focal length is constrained so that $F = 220$ mm. The ray plots for gratings with 0, 20, and 30 lines/mm are given in Fig. 18. These ray plots describe the focal spot size at each wavelength. The ray plot at each wavelength has a characteristic slope that increases as the objects spatial frequency increases. The slope of the line describes the amount of defocus present in the system. The lateral color is reasonably well corrected when no grating is present. In Fig. 18, one notes that the lateral color increases as the grating frequency increases. At 30 lines/mm,

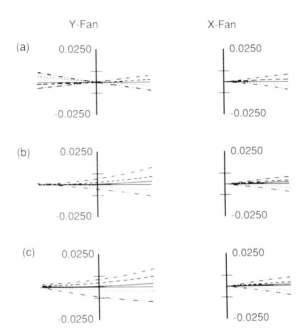

Fig. 18. Ray plots of an in-line Fourier achromat with a grating in the input plane. The grating frequency is (a) 0 lines/mm; (b) 20 lines/mm, and (c) 30 lines/mm. The tick marks along the vertical axes indicate the diffraction-limited spot (Airy disk) diameter.

the secondary spectrum is barely tolerable. Lateral color is the limiting factor in the design of a Fourier achromat.

2. *Design of an Achromatic Fourier Processor*

After the Fourier achromat has been optimized to an acceptable degree, the next step is to convert the transform to an image. For the back half of the processor, the theoretical power of each element is given by Eqs. (95) and (96). The same approach used to calculate the initial value for Φ_2 is followed. For the selected values of A', B', C', and $F'\lambda_1$ the powers of the resulting Φ_4' and Φ_5' are calculated at a number of different wavelengths. A best-fit hologram–glass lens combination is determined and CODEV is used to fit the lenses to the theoretical data. For the optimized thin-lens system, $B = 525.1$ mm and $C = 488.8$ mm. The focal length of the Fourier achromat $F = 434.4$ mm at $\lambda_0 = 550$ nm. For the back half of the processor various parameters are tried. The best results are obtained with $B' = C' = 500$ mm, $A = A' = 5$ mm. The magnification is set to one (i.e., $F\lambda_0 = -F'\lambda_1$).

The design strategy for the back half of the processor is different from that for the front half. In the previous sections, the Fourier achromat was assumed to take plane waves and produce point foci. For converting the transform into an image, the aperture plane of the Fourier achromat becomes the object plane of an imaging system. A point object is modeled as a point with an aperture between the object and the lens. The diameter of the aperture determines the maximum frequency content of the object.

For optimization the distance between the object and first lens is $A = 5$ mm. All parameters of the Fourier achromat are fixed. A 0.195-mm diameter aperture (corresponding to the ray angle of a 30 lines/mm grating illuminated with 650-nm light) is placed in the object plane. Three ZOOM positions are defined, corresponding to an object at a radius of 0, 5, and 9.5 mm, respectively. The image magnification is set to +1 (upright image). The glass curvatures and the lens group separations in the back half of the processor are allowed to vary. The object distance is kept constant. The layout is optimized at three wavelengths (650, 550, and 450 nm) for 12 consecutive cycles. The rms spot size is 185 μm. To improve the system further, the HOE powers and the distances between the glass lenses are allowed to vary. Another ten optimization cycles reduces the merit function (and the rms spot size) to 26.8 μm. At this point in the design, lens thicknesses are added and a final solution obtained.

3. Off-Axis Holographic Lenses

To eliminate undiffracted and spurious orders, an off-axis HOE configuration, introduced in Section III.B.3, is used. We use the term Λ-cascade to describe this configuration (Fig. 15). The use of off-axis holographic lenses does, however, create some problems. Holographic lenses suffer from aberrations caused by changes in field angle and construction–reconstruction wavelength shifts [Close (1975)]. These aberrations result when the reillumination wavefront does not exactly match one of the construction conjugates. The amount of aberration depends on the average grating frequency over the surface of the holographic element. An off-axis holographic lens is essentially a diffraction grating and a holographic zone lens cascaded together. The average spatial frequency of such a combined element is biased by the large frequency of the diffraction grating. Thus the aberrations in an off-axis HOE are significantly greater than those in either an on-axis holographic lens or a conventional glass lens.

It is clear that using off-axis holographic lenses adds a significant design problem. The off-axis geometry is necessary to eliminate the undiffracted component from the transform and image, but a large off-axis angle severely degrades the image quality. A compromise between these competing requirements is demonstrated by considering the Λ-cascade in Fig. 19. There are nine possible undiffracted components, depending on which elements

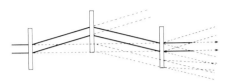

Fig. 19. Undiffracted and spurious components present in a Λ-cascade (dotted lines). Only one component (indicated with an arrow) continues in the same direction as the diffracted component (solid line).

diffract the light and which elements do not. One component passes undiffracted through all three elements and still ends up on the image plane. All other components are displaced from the usable part of the image plane. If each HOE in the Λ-cascade has a reasonably large diffraction efficiency ($>80\%$), then the dc component can be reduced to 1% or less of the total intensity. This displacement solution requires smaller off-axis angles than the method that involves blocking the light. In this way the undiffracted light can be separated without introducing large aberrations. It is found that the off-axis angle θ_0 needed for displacement of the undiffracted and spurious orders is approximately 2°. A Λ-cascade is inserted into the Fourier achromat design, and the resulting transform is examined. Analysis of the ray plots indicates there is little change in the performance of the lens due to the off-axis geometry. The back half of the system is added to the off-axis front half, and the image is inspected. It is found that the resulting image in plane III (Fig. 17c) is severely degraded. This is because the off-axis geometry introduces a position-dependent phase term in the transform plane that the back end of the processor is not designed to correct. Converting the HOE pair in the back half of the system into a 2° Λ-cascade only exacerbates the image degradation. The aberrations introduced by the off-axis HOE geometry are highly wavelength-dependent. Thus the use of additional glass elements such as cylindrical lenses or tilted spherical lenses does not correct the highly dispersive wavefront distortions introduced by the Λ-cascade. It is necessary to use computer-designed holograms that generate aspheric wavefronts to compensate for the off-axis aberrations. Since the achromatized transform is hardly affected by the off-axis geometry, it is decided that there is no need to use computer-designed holograms in the front half of the processor. The aspheric terms improve the transform quality, but they make the HOEs more difficult to construct and align. The correction can be contained in the off-axis lenses of the back half of the processor.

The off-axis system is optimized using CODEV. Holographic elements are represented as localized diffraction gratings using the CODEV HOE option. The location of each point source is entered into CODEV. The

TABLE I

DESIGN SPECIFICATIONS FOR AN ACHROMATIC FOURIER PROCESSOR

Element no.	Surface no.	Surface radius (mm)	Thickness (mm)	Aperture diameter (mm)	Material
Object		Infinite	5.0000		
1	1	(Stop)	0.0000	0.195	
2	2	290.340	3.0000	18.201	SF8
2	3	182.160	0.0000	18.192	
3	4	182.160	3.0000	18.192	BK7
3	5	Infinite	30.0000	18.216	
			321.1844	18.606	PHI 1
			321.1844	55.377	GRT
			44.3715	41.554	PHI 2
4	6	135.900	11.6000	41.203	BK7
4	7	−203.200	1.0000	40.214	
5	8	750.000	6.0000	39.598	SF56
5	9	57.420	6.8500	38.026	
6	10	55.720	8.0000	39.812	SK16
6	11	−153.700	1.6000	39.367	
7	12	−97.700	16.0000	38.999	SF56
7	13	−216.650	139.1147	38.330	
8	14	30.710	3.0000	6.571	BK7
8	15	44.000	0.0000	6.266	
9	16	44.000	3.0000	6.266	SF8
9	17	49.880	17.7230	5.944	
			91.3900	5.127	PHI 3
			91.3900	31.907	GRT
			41.6993	44.087	PHI 4
10	18	−127.000	11.6000	53.588	BK7
10	19	230.220	4.2000	58.617	
11	20	−3707.220	8.0000	60.011	SF56
11	21	−133.390	3.8000	61.588	
12	22	268.300	16.0000	63.929	SK16
12	23	−108.700	1.1000	64.486	
13	24	−139.630	8.8000	63.801	SF56
13	25	−332.230	1131.2471	64.297	
Image		Infinite		17.955	

Hologram Construction Parameters:

Construction wavelength:	488.0 nm
Diffraction order:	1
Substrate radii:	Infinity

PHI 1   Hologram formed by two point sources at $(X1, Y1, Z1)$, $(X2, Y2, Z2)$

$X1 = 0.000000E+00$	$Y1 = 0.000000E+00$	$Z1 = 0.663957E+03$	CONVERGING
$X2 = 0.000000E+00$	$Y2 = 0.818187E+02$	$Z2 = 0.234298E+04$	CONVERGING

Grating frequency at node of the substrate: 71.52 lines/mm

TABLE I (*Continued*)

GRATING (GRT)	Hologram formed by two point sources at $(X1, Y1, Z1)$, $(X2, Y2, Z2)$

$X1 = 0.000000E + 00$ $Y1 = -0.348995E + 08$ $Z1 = -0.999390E + 09$ DIVERGING
$X2 = 0.000000E + 00$ $Y2 = -0.348995E + 08$ $Z2 = 0.999390E + 09$ CONVERGING

Grating frequency at node of the substrate: 143.03 lines/mm

PHI 2	Hologram formed by two point sources at $(X1, Y1, Z1)$, $(X2, Y2, Z2)$

$X1 = 0.000000E + 00$ $Y1 = -0.594003E + 02$ $Z1 = 0.170100E + 04$ CONVERGING
$X2 = 0.000000E + 00$ $Y2 = 0.000000E + 00$ $Z2 = 0.661447E + 03$ CONVERGING

Grating frequency at node of the substrate: 71.52 lines/mm

PHI 3	Hologram formed by two point sources at $(X1, Y1, Z1)$, $(X2, Y2, Z2)$

$X1 = 0.000000E + 00$ $Y1 = 0.000000E + 00$ $Z1 = -0.853397E + 02$ DIVERGING
$X2 = 0.000000E + 00$ $Y2 = -0.323370E + 01$ $Z2 = -0.926007E + 02$ DIVERGING

Grating frequency at node of the substrate: 71.52 lines/mm

In addition to the point sources, a phase function is used to define the hologram. It is in the form of a sum of monomials in (X, Y), where the coordinates are on the surface of the substrate.

Power of X	Y	Coefficient
0	2	$-0.114100E - 04$

GRATING	Hologram formed by two point sources at $(X1, Y1, Z1)$, $(X2, Y2, Z2)$

$X1 = 0.000000E + 00$ $Y1 = -0.348995E + 08$ $Z1 = -0.999390E + 09$ DIVERGING
$X2 = 0.000000E + 00$ $Y2 = -0.348995E + 08$ $Z2 = 0.999390E + 09$ CONVERGING

Grating frequency at node of the substrate: 143.03 lines/mm

PHI 3	Hologram formed by two point sources at $(X1, Y1, Z1)$, $(X2, Y2, Z2)$

$X1 = 0.000000E + 00$ $Y1 = 0.961300E + 01$ $Z1 = -0.275276E + 03$ DIVERGING
$X2 = 0.000000E + 00$ $Y2 = 0.000000E + 00$ $Z2 = -0.234859E + 03$ DIVERGING

Grating frequency at node of the substrate: 71.52 lines/mm

In addition to the point sources, a phase function is used to define the hologram. It is in the form of a sum of monomials in (X, Y), where the coordinates are on the surface of the substrate.

Power of X	Y	Coefficient
0	2	$0.277556E - 05$
2	1	$0.223342E - 06$
0	3	$0.222432E - 06$

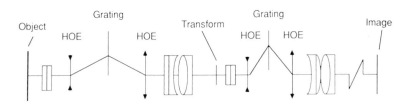

Fig. 20. Layout of an off-axis achromatic Fourier processor (not to scale). Detailed specifications of the system are given in Table I.

program then calculates the resulting grating frequency at different locations on the HOE surface. If there is any aspheric term, it is represented as a phase function in terms of the HOE surface coordinates.

The final achromatic Fourier processor design is listed in Table I. This off-axis processor is capable of transforming and imaging objects containing spatial frequencies of up to 30 lines/mm over a 20-mm object field and a spectral bandwidth of 200 nm (450–650 nm). At the transform plane, the system can produce a 14-μm focal spot anywhere across a 7.26 mm diameter. The f number of the processor at the mean wavelength $\lambda_0 = 500$ nm is $f/11$ at the transform plane and $f/26$ at the image plane.

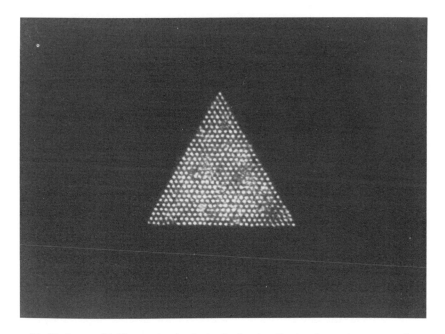

Fig. 21. Image of half-tone triangle obtained using the off-axis achromatic processor shown in Fig. 20.

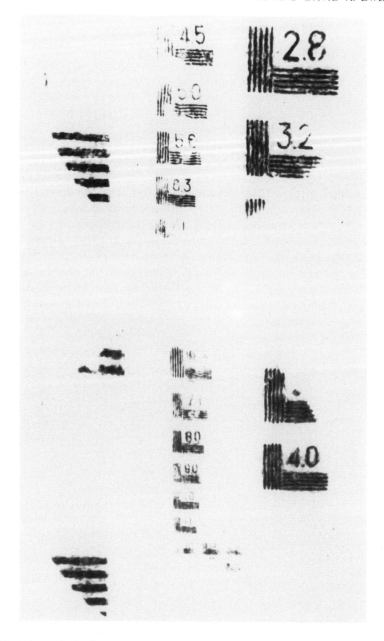

Fig. 22. Achromatic Fourier processor images of two sections of a USAF 1951 resolution target.

C. Experimental Results

The achromatic Fourier processor was constructed using the elements listed in Table I. A schematic layout is shown in Fig. 20. Holographic optics were formed in dichromated gelatin using the recipe prescribed by Leonard and Guenther (1979). The holographic lenses have an off-axis angle of 2°. Each holographic lens is actually a 30° off-axis grating cemented to a 28° off-axis holographic lens. The combined element has an effective 2° off-axis angle with high diffraction efficiency (>85%). Figure 16b shows the Fourier transform of a triangle made from circular half-tones using a conventional Fourier processor and broadband illumination produced by a Hg arc-lamp. The half-tone has a spatial frequency of 6 dots/mm. The chromatic smear in the transform is apparent. Figure 16c shows the transform of the same object using the achromatic Fourier processor. The chromatic smear is significantly reduced. The undiffracted component is visible to the right of the achromatized transform, displaced far enough so that it does not overlap any part of the transform. The undiffracted component is primarily blue due to the fact that HOE diffraction efficiencies decrease in the blue and red ends of the spectrum. The image of the half-tone triangle is shown in Fig. 21. The object is easily recognizable; however, there is some noise or scattered light, primarily due to imperfections in the holographic elements. Nevertheless, the image is well defined. The image resolution of the achromatic Fourier processor is analyzed with the use of a USAF 1951 bar target in Fig. 22. The processor is capable of resolving beyond group 10 (30 lines/mm) in the center and lower portions of the field.

V. Summary

Broadband optical Fourier processors are analyzed in the context of coherence theory. System operation with spatially coherent white light and spatially incoherent white light is considered. Fresnel diffraction theory is used to obtain first-order solutions for the lenses required to produce an achromatic Fourier transform of an input object [Fig. 4 and Eqs. (53)–(55)]. The achromatic Fourier transform system serves as the basic building block for broadband optical processors.

Experimental results are given for achromatic transform systems in which the required dispersive lenses are realized using combinations of holographic and glass elements. In-line and off-axis system configurations are analyzed. The design of in-line systems is simpler than off-axis arrangements, but undiffracted light from the holographic lenses contribute to background noise in the transform plane (Figs. 12 and 13). Off-axis geometries add a substantial design problem but offer greatly improved performance (Figs. 15 and 16).

General configurations for broadband optical processing and imaging are shown in Fig. 17. The design and operation of an achromatic Fourier processor, based on the first-order layout in Fig. 17c, is given in Section IV.

Acknowledgments

We wish to thank D. Faklis for his numerous and helpful comments, and we are grateful to Ms. D. Savage and Ms. R. Morris for their help with the preparation of the manuscript. Portions of the authors' research reported herein were sponsored by the New York State Center for Advanced Optical Technology and the U.S. Army Research Office.

References

Almeida, S. P., Case, S. K., and Dallas, W. J. (1979). *Appl. Opt.* **18**, 4025-4029.
Angell, D. K. (1985). *Appl. Opt.* **24**, 2903-2906.
Bartelt, H., Case, S. K., and Hauck, R. (1982). *In* "Applications of Optical Fourier Transforms" (H. Stark, ed.) pp. 499-536. Academic Press, New York.
Born, M., and Wolf, E. (1980). "Principles of Optics," 6th Ed., p. 511. Pergamon, Oxford.
Braunecker, B., and Bryngdahl, O. (1982). *Opt. Commun.* **40**, 332-336.
Brekinridge, J. (1978). *Opt. Eng.* **17**, 156-159.
Brophy, C. (1983). *Opt. Commun.* **47**, 364-368.
Brophy, C. (1984). Ph.D. Thesis, Univ. of Rochester, Rochester, New York.
Case, S. K. (1979). *Appl. Opt.* **18**, 1890-1894.
Chavel, P. (1980). *J. Opt. Soc. Am.* **70**, 935-943.
Chavel, P., and Lowenthal, S. (1976). *J. Opt. Soc. Am.* **66**, 14-23.
Chavel, P., and Lowenthal, S. (1978a). *J. Opt. Soc. Am.* **68**, 559-568.
Chavel, P., and Lowenthal, S. (1978b). *J. Opt. Soc. Am.* **68**, 721-732.
Close, D. H. (1975). *Opt. Eng.* **14**, 408-419.
Collins, G. D. (1981). *Appl. Opt.* **20**, 3109-3119.
Efron, U., ed. (1984). 'Spatial Light Modulators and Applications." *SPIE Semin. Proc.* **465**.
Ferriere, R., and Goedgebuer, J.-P. (1982). *Opt. Commun.* **42**, 223-225.
Ferriere, R., and Goedgebuer, J.-P. (1983). *Appl. Opt.* **22**, 1540-1545.
Ferriere, R., Goedgebuer, J.-P., and Vienot, J.-C. (1979). *Opt. Commun.* **31**, 285-289.
Furman, A., and Casasent, D. (1979). *Appl. Opt.* **18**, 660-665.
George, N., and Morris, G. M. (1981). *In* "Current Trends in Optics" (F. T. Arecchi and F. R. Aussenegg, eds.) pp. 80-94. Taylor & Francis, London.
George, N., and Morris, G. M. (1983). *SPIE Semin. Proc.* **388**, 12-22.
George, N., and Wang, S. (1984). *Appl. Opt.* **23**, 787-797.
Glaser, I. (1981). *Opt. Eng.* **20**, 568-573.
Goedgebuer, J.-P., and Gazeu, R. (1978). *Opt. Commun.* **27**, 53-56.
Goodman, J. W. (1968). "Introduction to Fourier Optics." McGraw-Hill, New York.
Goodman, J. W. (1985). "Statistical Optics." Wiley, New York.
Gradshteyn, I. S., and Ryzhik, I. M. (1965). "Table of Integrals, Series and Products." Academic Press, New York.
Hopkins, R. E., and Morris, G. M. (1983). *Kinam, Ser. C* **5**, 135-149.
Katyl, R. H. (1972). *Appl. Opt.* **11**, 1255-1260.
Kingslake, R. (1978). "Fundamentals of Lens Design," pp. 40-43. Academic Press, New York.
Leith, E. N., and Angell, D. K. (1986). *Appl. Opt.* **25**, 499-502.

Leith, E. N., and Roth, J. A. (1979). *Appl. Opt.* **18**, 2803-2811.

Leith, E. N., and Swanson, G. (1980). *Appl. Opt.* **19**, 638-644.

Leith, E. N., Roth, J. A., and Swanson, G. (1980). *SPIE Semin. Proc.* **232**, 2-8.

Leon, S., and Leith, E. N. (1985). *Appl. Opt.* **24**, 3638-3642.

Leonard, C. D., and Guenther, B. D. (1979). "A Cookbook for Dichromated Gelatin Holograms," Tech. Rep. RR-82-5. U.S. Army Missile Command, Redstone Arsenal, Alabama.

Lohmann, A. W. (1968). *Appl. Opt.* **7**, 561-563.

Lohmann, A. W. (1977). *Appl. Opt.* **16**, 261-263.

Lohmann, A. W., and Rhodes, W. T. (1978). *Appl. Opt.* **17**, 1141-1151.

Lohmann, A. W., and Werlich, H. W. (1971). *Appl. Opt.* **10**, 670-672.

Lowenthal, S., and Werts, A. (1968). *C.R. Hebd. Seances Acad. Sci., Ser. B* **266**, 542-545.

Mait, J. N. (1986). *J. Opt. Soc. Am., A* **3**, 437-445.

Monahan, M. A., Bromley, K., and Bocker, R. P. (1977). *Proc. IEEE* **65**, 121-129.

Morris, G. M. (1981a). *Appl. Opt.* **20**, 2017-2025.

Morris, G. M. (1981b). *Opt. Commun.* **39**, 143-147.

Morris, G. M., and George, N. (1980a). *Opt. Lett.* **5**, 202-204.

Morris, G. M., and George, N. (1980b). *Appl. Opt.* **19**, 3843-3850.

Morris, G. M., and George, N. (1980c). *Opt. Lett.* **5**, 446-448.

Potaturkin, O. I. (1979). *Appl. Opt.* **18**, 4203-4205.

Rhodes, W. T. (1977). *SPIE Semin. Proc.* **118**, 86-93.

Rhodes, W. T. (1980). *Opt. Eng.* **19**, 323-330.

Rhodes, W. T., and Sawchuk, A. A. (1981). *In* "Optical Information Processing: Fundamentals" (S. H. Lee, ed.), pp. 69-110. Springer-Verlag, Berlin and New York.

Roddier, F., Roddier, C., Martin, F., Baronne, A., and Brun, R. (1980). *J. Opt.* **11**, 149-152.

Rogers, G. L. (1977). "Noncoherent Optical Processing." Wiley, New York.

Rogers, G. L. (1980). *J. Opt. Soc. Am.* **70**, 1012-1014.

Ryan-Howard, D. P., and Moore, D. T. (1985). *Appl. Opt.* **24**, 4356-4366.

Sherman, R. C., Grieser, D., Gamble, F. T., Verber, C. M., and Dolash, T. (1983). *Appl. Opt.* **22**, 3579-3582.

Sjolinder, S. (1984). *Opt. Acta* **31**, 1001-1012.

Stone, T. W., and George, N. (1982). *Opt. Lett.* **7**, 445-447.

Stone, T. W., and George, N. (1985). *Appl. Opt.* **24**, 3797-3810.

Stoner, W. (1977). *Appl. Opt.* **16**, 1451-1453.

Stoner, W. (1978). *Appl. Opt.* **17**, 2454-2467.

Sweatt, W. C. (1977). *J. Opt. Soc. Am.* **67**, 803-808.

Sweatt, W. C. (1978). Ph.D. Thesis, Univ. of Arizona, Tucson.

Thompson, B. J. (1983). *SPIE Semin. Proc.* **388**, 3-9.

Upatnieks, J., Duthie, J. G., and Ashley, P. R. (1982). "Matched Filtering with Achromatic Optical Correlators," Tech. Rep. RR-82-5. U.S. Army Missile Command, Redstone Arsenal, Alabama.

Wolf, E. (1982). *J. Opt. Soc. Am.* **72**, 343-351.

Wolf, E. (1986). *J. Opt. Soc. Am., A* **7**, 76-85.

Wynne, C. G. (1979). *Opt. Commun.* **28**, 21-25.

Yu, F. T. S. (1978). *Opt. Commun.* **27**, 23-26.

Yu, F. T. S. (1985). "White-Light Optical Signal Processing." Wiley, New York.

Yu, F. T. S., and Chao, T. H. (1983). *Appl. Phys., B* **32**, 1-6.

Zerbino, L. M., and Goedgebuer, J. P. (1985). *Opt. Commun.* **55**, 248-252.

Zweig, D. A. (1985). M.S. Thesis, Univ. of Rochester, Rochester, New York.

II

Pattern Recognition

2.1

Optical Feature Extraction

DAVID CASASENT

DEPARTMENT OF ELECTRICAL AND COMPUTER ENGINEERING
CARNEGIE-MELLON UNIVERSITY
PITTSBURGH, PENNSYLVANIA 15213

I. Introduction

Workers in the field of optical data processing have recently devoted much attention to producing feature spaces in parallel, and the resulting architectures are quite attractive for pattern recognition. This approach to optical pattern recognition (OPR) is unique since optical feature extraction represents a fixed optical system, with no variable filters, that can compute the features of any input object. Most optical processing systems are specific to each application, and optical feature extractors different from them in their flexibility for use in various applications, which is provided by applying different discriminant functions to the output feature vectors produced by the system. These discriminant function operations are typically performed in digital post-processing (to achieve the necessary flexibility for diverse applications). Many approaches to OPR exist [1, 2]. Here we address only optical feature extraction. In optical correlators and most OPR systems, various filter functions are required for various objects and applications. This is not the case for optical feature extractors, which compute certain (usually geometrical) properties of an input object. These are subsequently operated upon to determine the class of the input object. Feature extractors also provide the ability to determine the object's location, orientation, and scale, whereas optical correlators usually provide only object location information. Optical correlators cannot provide general distortion invariance, although advanced techniques using synthetic discriminant functions and other methods promise such a capability. However, the processors can be applied only to a limited number of object classes, whereas feature extractors have potential use for a far larger number of classes and the ability to achieve distortion invariance. Thus optical feature extractors, besides extending the repertoire of operations achievable on an optical processor, have various other properties.

In Section II we provide a brief introduction to feature extraction and the linear algebra associated with processing the features produced. Section III considers the simplest of optical feature extractors, the optical Fourier transform (FT) and the use of operations that are more easily performed optically than by other methods—such as wedge ring detector (WRD) sampling—to obtain distortion invariance and to reduce the dimensionality of the feature space. Section IV addresses optical Hough transform feature space work, the lowest-level optical feature space that we shall consider. It also offers significant potential for the use of one-dimensional devices in processing two-dimensional image data. This also represents a feature space from which many other feature spaces can be obtained. In Section V space-variant optical feature spaces are considered. Here we introduce the concept of a high dimensionality feature space and the concept of performing the feature extraction and classification using optical techniques (rather than digital ones). Our chord distribution optical feature space discussed in Section VI includes a description of techniques to obtain object distortion parameter information from an optically generated feature space. In Section VII the most extensive optical feature space study is highlighted. The moment feature space processor described in this section includes a two-level classifier that minimizes the probability of error, extensive database test results, and various other properties of this feature space. Space limitations prevent extensive discussion of these various systems and their results, so references are provided to amplify the major issues associated with each of the optical feature space works discussed.

II. Optical Feature Extraction

Figure 1 shows a simplified feature extractor. An input object $f(x, y)$ is presented to the system and features of it are calculated and organized into the elements of a feature vector $\mathbf{x}$. (We shall denote vectors and matrices by boldfaced lower- and upper-case letters, respectively.) Specific features

Fig. 1. Block diagram of a simplified generic feature extraction processor.

can be extracted from this space (the feature-extraction operation), and the space can be transformed to a lower-dimensionality feature space v (e.g., a space with basis vectors, with independent features, or with better discrimination capability). The discrimination between various object classes is achieved by the vector inner product (VIP) operations between the feature vector (x or v) and up to N discriminant functions w_n. Analysis of these scalar output VIPs is included in the process of classification, which determines the best estimate of the class of the input object under investigation. The outputs from the full feature extraction processor are the class of the object, its orientation and other distortion parameters, and the confidence of these estimates. A training set of data (N images of the objects in each class) is presented to the algorithm, and these are used to select features, to determine all thresholds in the system, and to design the discriminant functions to be used. Test data are then employed to test the performance of the system.

Many techniques for feature selection exist, and many discriminant measures are possible. An attractive measure that one can easily relate to is the Fisher ratio [3]

$$ J = \frac{|\text{difference of the means of the projections of two classes}|^2}{\text{sum of the scatter for the projections of two classes}} \tag{1} $$

If the Fisher ratio is calculated for each feature (rather than for a projection of the feature vector) for the two classes of data, one can select the features to be those with the largest Fisher ratios (since these features provide the best class separation and the most descriptive representation of the training set data provided). If the features selected do not provide sufficient class separation, the feature vectors x_n for different classes can be made independent by transformation to a space $y = Ax$ with independent features. This transformation can be achieved if the rows of A are the eigenvectors of the covariance matrix Σ_x of the feature data $\{x\}$. This is a Karhunen–Loeve [KL] transform [3], which yields statistically independent features and does not increase the separation of the projections (unless only the dominant KL vectors are retained). The Gram–Schmidt (GS) technique [3] can be used to produce linear combinations of the original features that are independent of each other. Both feature extraction and transformation to a feature space with orthogonal basis functions also achieve dimensionality reduction of the feature space. This is usually intended to improve discrimination, but its primary objective is to simplify the required post-processing by performing dimensionality reduction. The KL eigenvector techniques are generally the most attractive because they allow optimum data compression.

One can compute the dominant eigenvector for one class of data and use this as the discriminant function $\mathbf{w}$. This is referred to as principal-component analysis (the eigenvalues define how much of the class information is present in a given principal component and, hence, the expected performance obtained by using this one principal component or eigenvector). One can retain the several most dominant eigenvectors and use these as the $\mathbf{w}_n$ discriminant vectors. This is referred to as KL data compression. The KL and eigenvector methods are appropriate only for intraclass (one-class) recognition since they mainly achieve dimensionality reduction rather than discrimination. One can use the dominant eigenvectors for each of the two classes of data. These vectors often achieve discrimination (especially if the two classes are sufficiently different), but there is no assurance that this will be the case. For interclass discrimination, other techniques are preferable. For example, one can calculate the discriminant vector $\mathbf{w}$ that maximizes the Fisher ratio in Eq. (1) and use this as the linear discriminant function (LDF) $\mathbf{w}$. The Fisher vector can also be extended to multiple classes of data by the use of several Fisher feature vectors. For a two-class problem, one can also form the correlation matrix for each class of data and diagonalize the sum of these correlation matrices. The transformation matrix that achieves this diagonalization can then be applied to the covariance matrix or correlation matrix of each class of data. It is known that this transformation yields a new space with the same eigenvectors for each class of data. However (and this is the important issue), the largest eigenvalues for one class are the smallest ones for the other class. Thus, by selecting the eigenvectors with eigenvalues that are most different from 0.5, we insure good interclass discrimination. These vectors $\mathbf{w}_n$ are referred to as Fukunaga–Koontz (FK) discriminant vectors. In our specific optical feature space case studies, we shall employ all of these discriminant function techniques. Other aspects of optical feature extraction will be detailed as appropriate for specific feature spaces.

III.   Fourier-Transform Feature Space and Unique Sampling

A spherical lens can form the two-dimensional FT of the two-dimensional input image data in parallel. This simple system (Fig. 2) is thus the preferable

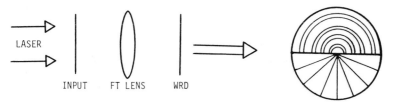

Fig. 2. Wedge–ring detector (WRD)-sampled optical Fourier transform feature space processor.

one to use and is the most attractive optical feature space to employ (in cases for which it is adequate). The FT space is well known for allowing significant data compression [4]. We choose to emphasize a specific compression method that uses a unique sampling and feature extraction of this FT feature space, is simple to implement in optics, and provides a feature space with approximate distortion invariance (a most desirable feature space property) and reduced dimensionality. The technique is to sample the FT plane with wedge- and ring-shaped detector elements (right-side of Fig. 2). Typically 32 wedge and 32 ring elements are used, and compression of the FT space to 64 wedge and ring features is thus achieved. The typical silicon wedge–ring detector is 25 mm in diameter. The magnitude FT is shift-invariant, the wedge output data are scale-invariant (this distribution shifts with rotations), and the ring outputs are rotation-invariant (this distribution shifts with scale changes). Extensive use of this feature space has been made [5–7]. The study in [7] offers examples of the performance of the various discriminant function methods noted in Section II for several two-class problems. This feature space has use in the classification of various scene regions [5] and for various commercial inspection applications [6]. The major advantages of this technique are its simplicity, dimensionality reduction, and the in-plane distortion invariance that it provides.

   More recent work has demonstrated the ability to fabricate such a detector using holographic optical elements (HOEs) and computer-generated holograms (CGHs) [8]. This was achieved and recently demonstrated by CGH synthesis of uniform gratings with different spatial frequencies and orientations in various wedge and ring regions of the FT plane. Figure 3a shows this CGH WRD, and Fig. 3b shows its output with uniform illumination. Figure 3b contains ten wedge outputs (the top two rows of the diffraction peaks) and ten ring outputs (the bottom two rows of diffraction peaks). The advantage of such a CGH WRD sampling unit with discrete detectors is the improved sensitivity and higher speed it provides (due to the use of separate photodetector outputs) and its reduced cost and size.

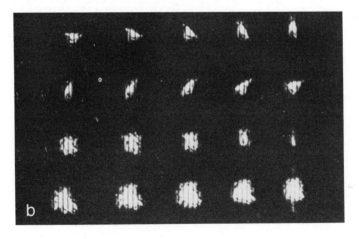

Fig. 3. (a) Computer generated hologram WRD and (b) output detector plane pattern for a ten-wedge and ten-ring detector system.

This FT WRD feature space is attractive for many applications. For inspection and object discrimination problems in which the two object classes to be separated are very similar, or in cases in which all image pixels are necessary, this feature space is not appropriate. This is the first feature extraction technique that one should consider and address for a given problem.

IV. Hough-Transform Feature Space

Most optical feature extractors produce global object features and are thus high-level processors. The optical Hough transform (HT) is an exception since its outputs are low-level image features, specifically the normal distance ρ and angle θ of all lines in the input image. This feature space can be optically produced in several ways [9, 10] including the use of CGHs [11]; it is best described by Fig. 4. This system shows the input image rotated by a Dove prism. For each rotated angle θ, the image is integrated in the one dimension along a line at an angle θ to yield an output $f_\theta(\rho)$, where ρ is one-dimensional spatial output variable and θ the angle of rotation of the input object. The full $f(\rho, \theta)$ output has peaks at ρ and θ descriptors for each line in the input image. In a more mathematical vein, this feature space can be described as the mapping of each input image pixel into a sinusoid. The accumulation of all such sinusoids exhibits the peaks noted above.

Besides the fact that these are low-level local features, this feature space is unique since it can also be used to produce FT WRD sampled outputs, moments, convex-hull descriptions, and other conventional image features [10] as well as allowing one to achieve two-dimensional correlations with one-dimensional correlations.

The WRD output pattern generation is now detailed. The algorithm employed follows. A one-dimensional slice at an angle θ of the two-dimensional FT of an image is the same as the one-dimensional FT of the projection or integration of the input image at an angle θ. Thus, if the successive $f_\theta(\rho)$ outputs at different angles θ are one-dimensional Fourier transformed (e.g., by an acoustooptic spectrum analyzer), proper detector processing can achieve WRD sampling of the two-dimensional FT space. To achieve this, half of the FT plane is sampled (in time, as θ varies) with one detector. These outputs yield the wedge detector-sampled WRD output

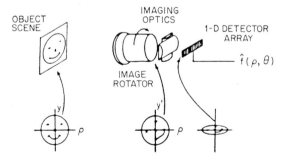

Fig. 4. Optical Hough-transform feature space processor. (From Gindi and Gmitro [10].)

data. The other half of the FT plane contains a linear time-integrating detector array. Its integrated outputs, after all θ input image values have been processed, are the ring outputs in a two-dimensional FT WRD plane. As detailed elsewhere [10], the first ten moments of the input object can also be obtained only from several $f_\theta(\rho)$ samples. Finally, the FT slice theorem can be extended to produce one-dimensional slices of the two-dimensional correlation of separate input images.

V. Space-Variant Feature Space and Optical Feature Extraction

In this feature space, we advance two new concepts: the use of a high-dimensionality feature space and the use of optical techniques for LDF feature extraction [12]. Conventional feature extractors emphasize dimensionality reduction and, hence, often suffer from noise (since an entire object is represented by only several numbers/features). Here we consider a high-dimensionality feature space, specifically a space-variant feature space. This space is produced by optical CGHs that implement a coordinate transformation (CT). The Mellin transform (MT) was one CT that was chosen. The MT of an input function $f(x, y)$ is obtained by the FT of the CT function $f(e^x, e^y)$. This MT feature space was chosen because its magnitude is scale-invariant [13]. A polar space was also chosen, that is, $f'(r, \theta)$, since the $f'(\theta)$ axis distribution is cyclically rotation-invariant. The combined feature space used involved the FT of a polar-log CT of the input data. The log CT in r is performed on the $f'(r, \theta)$ space and a magnitude FT of the result is performed giving $f(\omega_\xi, \omega_\theta)$. This resultant $f(\omega_\xi, \omega_\theta)$ feature space is shift-, scale-, and rotation-invariant and is thus most attractive.

Figure 5 shows the associated processor that produces this $f(\omega_\xi, \omega_\theta)$ feature space. We first form the magnitude FT of the input object at P1 by L_1 and ground glass at P_2. This centers the input object data at P_2 and still retains significant object information. The polar-log CT performed by a

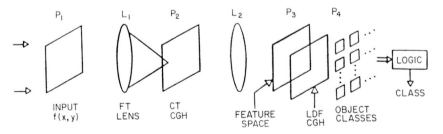

Fig. 5. Optical space-variant features space processor with parallel optical feature extraction included. (From Casasent and Lee [12].)

CGH at P_2 provides scale invariance (by the log CT operation in r) and rotation invariance (by the polar CT in θ). The location of the input object in this CT space shifts. To remove this shift, we form the magnitude FT of this $f'(r, \theta)$ pattern space by lens L_2 and thus produce our final $f(\omega_\xi, \omega_\theta)$ output feature space at P_3.

This feature space is of high-dimensionality (256×64 for a 64×64 object) and thus offers the potential for high noise performance (with increased LDF processing requirements). Prior work [13] with such feature spaces has employed correlators. In these systems the presence of an output peak indicated the presence of the input object, and the location of the output correlation peak indicated the scale and rotation of the object with respect to the reference. In the present system several LDFs are used at P_3 that encode different linear combinations of the $f(\omega_\xi, \omega_\theta)$ features; these LDFs are implemented as a CGH by gratings with various modulation levels placed at P_3. The angular orientation of these gratings determines the P_4 location in the final output plane to which data are deflected. The modulation level of each of these gratings determines the amount of each P_3 feature that is summed at the appropriate P_4 output detector location. We can space- and frequency-multiplex several optical CGH LDFs at P_3 and thus have each output plane detector correspond to the object class. In advanced versions of this processor we can use the various levels produced at the output P_4 plane detectors and thus significantly increase the number of classes that can be handled by this processor. Initial tests of the basic elements of this system have shown the ability to generate the required feature space in real-time on an SLM and the scale-, rotation-, and shift-invariant properties predicted for this feature space. Out-of-plane three-dimensional distortion invariance is achieved by the use of training sets of imagery from which the optimum features are selected and the optimum LDFs chosen. Initial simulations and laboratory tests of the CGH for such LDFs have shown the ability of these systems to achieve quite large three-dimensional distorted multiclass object recognition for a set of ten aircraft in different three-dimensional roll, pitch, and yaw distortions.

VI. Chord-Distribution Feature Space and Parameter Estimation

The chord-distribution feature space [14, 15] provides in-plane distortion invariance (i.e., in-plane scale, rotations, or translations of the input object) and the ability to achieve dimensionality reduction. Out-of-plane distortions refer to aspect angle variations of the input object. In our discussion of this feature space we include two new feature extraction issues: feature selection [15] and obtaining estimates of the object's distortion parameters from such a feature space [16]. To describe a chord distribution and its optical synthesis, we refer the reader to Fig. 6, which shows a general object shape. Between each pair of points on this object, a chord can be drawn. We show only a boundary object and one chord with its length r and angle θ, together with the projection values d_x and d_y for this chord. However, our technique accommodates objects with internal structure and is thus a most general and powerful extension of the chord concept. A chord exists between all pairs of object points $b(x, y)$ if both points have a pixel value of *one*. A chord thus exists between two points if

$$g(x, y, r, \theta) = b(x, y)b(x + r \cos \theta, y + r \sin \theta) = 1 \qquad (2)$$

The distribution of chord lengths and angles in polar coordinates is

$$h'(r, \theta) = \int_{-\Delta}^{+\Delta} \int_{-\Delta}^{+\Delta} g(x, y, r, \theta) \, dx \, dy$$

$$= \int_{-\Delta}^{+\Delta} \int_{-\Delta}^{+\Delta} b(x, y)b(x + r \cos \theta, y + r \sin \theta) \, dx \, dy \qquad (3)$$

where 2Δ is the one-dimensional extent of the object. In Cartesian coordinates, the chord distribution is

$$h(d_x, d_y) = \int_{-\Delta}^{+\Delta} \int_{-\Delta}^{+\Delta} b(x, y)b(x + d_x, y + d_y) \, dx \, dy \qquad (4)$$

To obtain the length distribution in r we form

$$h(r) = \int_{0}^{180} h(r, \theta) r \, d\theta \qquad (5)$$

and to obtain the angular distribution in θ we form

$$h(\theta) = \int_{0}^{R} h(r, \theta) \, dr \qquad (6)$$

We can obtain these $h(r)$ and $h(\theta)$ distributions by wedge and ring sampling the autocorrelation of the input image as shown in Fig. 7. We note that our

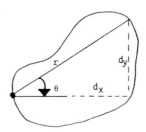

Fig. 6. General object showing a chord and its projections.

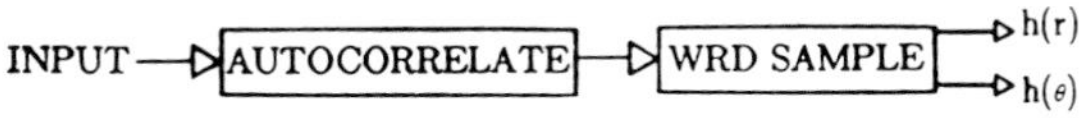

INPUT —▷ AUTOCORRELATE —▷ WRD SAMPLE ▷ h(r) ▷ h(θ)

Fig. 7. General optical-chord distribution feature space synthesis system.

chord-distribution synthesis technique also applies directly to gray-scale objects and objects with internal detail.

This feature space is easily achieved optically. The autocorrelation is shift-invariant, the $h(r)$ distribution is rotation-invariant, and the $h(\theta)$ distribution is scale-invariant. This feature space is thus in-plane distortion-invariant. We also note that the $h(r)$ and $h(\theta)$ distributions shift with input object scale and rotation, respectively. We now detail how one can achieve three-dimensional out-of-plane distortion invariance in this feature space. Similar techniques can be applied to other feature spaces. We detail this case to explain by example the basic technique. To achieve out-of-plane distortion invariance for two-class discrimination, we use M training images per class. For our case study, these are selected from 36 possible aspect views (in 10° increments) of two types of ships with all images obtained from a 90° depression angle. Figure 8 shows the broadside views of these two ships. The 64-dimensional covariance matrix for all views in both object classes was formed, and its eigenvectors and eigenvalues were computed.

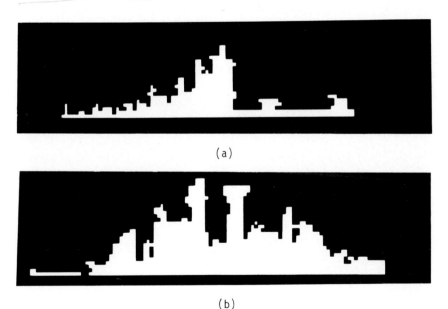

(a)

(b)

Fig. 8. Representative broadside ship images used in the chord feature space object classification and recognition experiments: (a) Moskva and (b) Albany.

In one test, the 12 dominant KL eigenvectors from this joint covariance matrix were used as the basis functions in which each input object was described as a vector of dimension 12. In subsequent tests, the three dominant eigenvectors were found to be adequate also. As a second discriminant function, the Fisher vector **w** was used. To compute **w**, the within-class scatter matrix S_W must be inverted. Its rank is $2M$, and its dimensionality is the number N of features. Thus inversion of S_W requires at least $N \leqq 2M$. If a WRD with 32 wedge and 32 ring elements is used, then $N = 64$; and thus we require $M = 32$ of the possible 36 images per class to be used for training (a larger value of M is required in practice since images with $10°$ aspect increments are not necessarily independent). Thus we reduced the number N of features used. To select the best features to use, we calculated J in Eq. (1) for each feature and selected the 12 features with the largest J values. We then found that we required only 12 training images per class. With these training images, we found that using the 12 KL chord LDF features gave perfect 100% recognition and classification of all 72 ship images. With 12 chord features (selected by the Fisher ciriteria), the Fisher LDF correctly classified 71 out of the 72 ship images for over 97% correct recognition.

We now address how estimates of the object distortion parameters (e.g., rotation and scale) can be obtained from such a feature space processor. Such properties are unique aspects of a feature space pattern-recognition system (not present in a correlator) and thus merit attention. Table I lists the effects of rotation θ_0, scale α, and translation on the chord distribution features $h(r)$ and $h(\theta)$. The effect of these distortions on the different chord distributions are noted in column 3 of the table, and the effect on the intensity (the measured quantity) of the associated features is noted in column 4. The invariant properties of the distributions are clearly seen, as are the methods by which α and θ_0 distortion estimates can be obtained.

TABLE I

PROPERTIES OF $h(r)$ AND $h(\theta)$ DISTRIBUTIONS

Parameter	Feature	Distribution property	Intensity effects
Rotation θ_0	$h(r)$	Invariant	None
	$h(\theta)$	Shifts $\propto \theta_0$	None
Scale	$h(r)$	Scales $r \to \alpha r$	α^{-5}
	$h(\theta)$	Invariant	α^{-5}
Translation	$h(r)$	Invariant	None
	$h(\theta)$	Invariant	None

Table II specifies the procedures to be used for the different distortion cases to determine the object class R and the distortion parameters α and θ_0 for each case. In this table we denote the stored chord distributions for reference object class R by $h_R(r, \theta)$. We note that only one $h_R(r)$ and one $h_R(\theta)$ distribution in one dimension is required for one scale/rotated/translated view per object class R.

We now show initial demonstration results of the use of this feature space for object class and distortion-parameter estimation for aircraft identification. Figure 9 shows our training set of data (one view with scale $\alpha_0 = 1$ and orientation $\theta_0 = 0°$ for each of three aircraft). Figure 10 shows three of the test images fed to the processor of Fig. 7 using the algorithm in Table II. These images are various scaled and rotated views of a B727. The objective is to determine the class and the α and θ_0 parameters of the input object. Consider the input in Fig. 10a. To obtain the class estimate we compare the input $h(r)$ distribution with the $h_R(r)$ distribution for all of the reference classes R. As seen in Fig. 11a, the B727 class is clearly the preferable (and correct) estimate. To estimate the rotation of the input object we compare $h(\theta)$ for the test input (with $\theta_0 = 11°$) with the B727 reference (with $\theta_0 = 0°$). The resultant shift in the two patterns (Fig. 11b) provides a $\theta_0 = 10.5°$ estimate that is limited only by the linear interpolation accuracy of the wedge ring detector considered. When Fig. 10b (a scaled

TABLE II

SCALE AND IN-PLANE ROTATION-INVARIANT
MULTICLASS CHORD PDF FEATURE PATTERN RECOGNITION

Case	Procedure	Remarks	Results
(A) Rotation θ_0 only	Compare $h(r)$ and $h_R(r)$ Compare $h_R(\theta + \theta_0)$ and $h(\theta)$	$h(r)$ is rotation invariant $h(\theta)$ shifts with θ_0	Class R estimate Confirms R estimate Provides θ_0 estimate
(B) Scale α only	Compare $h(\theta)/h_R(\theta)$ for each θ	Constant ratio provides R; ratio provides α estimate	Class R and scale α estimates
	Compare $h(r)/h_R(\alpha r)$	Confirms above estimate	Confirms R and α estimates
(C) Rotation θ_0 and scale α	Compare $h(\theta)/h_R(\theta + \theta_0)$ for all R and all shifts θ_0	Constant ratio provides R and θ_0; ratio gives α	Initial estimates of R, θ_0, α
	Compare $h(r)/h_R(\alpha r)$	Confirm above estimates	Confirm R and α estimates

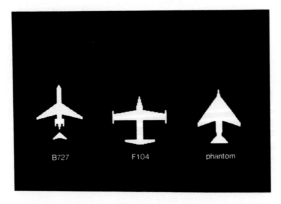

Fig. 9. Training-set data for aircraft tests: B727, F104, and phantom.

version of the B727) was the test input, the $h(\theta)$ distribution was used; and from the $h(\theta)/h_R(\theta)$ ratio for the reference B727, the scale estimate $\alpha = 1.36$ was obtained (in excellent agreement with the actual $\alpha = 1.33$ value). The variation of the $h(\theta)/h_R(\theta)$ ratio for the B727 reference was quite small (0.0146) and much less than for the other nearest reference object (the phantom, whose $h(\theta)/h_R(\theta)$ variance was 6.20).

VII.   Moment Feature Space and Unique Properties

The moments are an optically generated feature space on which significant research has been performed, and thus we detail these results more

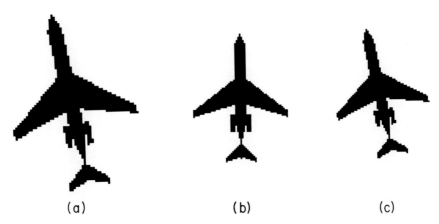

(a)   (b)   (c)

Fig. 10. Test-set data for aircraft evaluation: (a) $\alpha = 1$, $\theta_0 = 11°$; (b) $\alpha = 1.33 = 75\%$, $\theta_0 = 0°$; (c) $\alpha = 1.33$, $\theta_0 = 11°$.

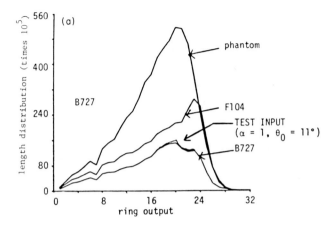

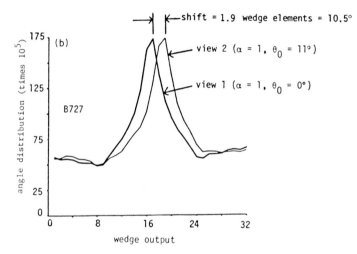

Fig. 11. Class estimation (a) and rotation estimation (b) for test input for the chord processor of Fig. 7a.

extensively than those for the other feature spaces, although the general remarks advanced in this section are appropriate for other optically generated feature spaces as well. The moments m_{pq} of an input object $f(x, y)$ are defined by

$$m_{pq} = \int\int f(x, y)x^p y^q \, dx \, dy \qquad (7)$$

The central moments (with translation and intensity invariance) are defined by

$$\mu_{pq} = \int\int f(x, y)(x - x_c)^p (y - y_c)^q \, dx \, dy \tag{8}$$

where

$$(x_c, y_c) = \left(\frac{m_{10}}{m_{00}}, \frac{m_{01}}{m_{00}} \right) \tag{9}$$

The moments

$$\eta_{pq} = \frac{m_{pq}}{m_{00}^{(p+q+2)/2}} \tag{10}$$

are scale-invariant. If they are calculated using μ_{pq}, they also become translation- and intensity-invariant. The moments are well-known geometrical descriptors of an input object. We can estimate object scale from m_{00}, object location (x_0, y_0) from m_{10} and m_{01}, object aspect from μ_{20}/μ_{02}, in-plane rotation from the eigenvector of the second-order moment matrix, and so on. The moments represent a feature space that is widely used in commercial computer vision modules.

This feature space can be optically computed in several ways. The simplest system to detail [17] is the one shown in Fig. 12. In this system the input image $f(x, y)$ is imaged onto a mask with transimittance $g(x, y)$. The output P_3 light distribution obtained (on-axis) is

$$u(0, 0) = \int\int f(x, y)g(x, y) \, dx \, dy \tag{11}$$

When the mask transmittance contains the various monomials $x^p y^q$, the P_3 distribution on-axis is the associated moment m_{pq}. If these monomials are spatially multiplexed on separate spatial frequency carriers, the P_3 distribution in two dimensions at appropriate detectors (whose locations are determined by the spatial frequency carriers on the mask) contains all moments generated in parallel. Practical considerations of noise usually restrict the

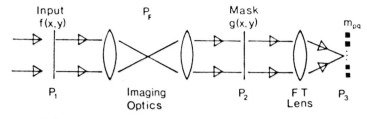

Fig. 12. Optical moment feature space generation system. (From Casasent et al. [17].)

use of moments to those below sixth-order (i.e., $p + q < 6$). These 21 moments can be generated in parallel on the optical system of Fig. 12. It is also possible to encode holographically the multiple monomials on a complex-valued mask using CGH techniques and to produce again all moments in parallel [18].

Excellent examples of the results of such systems are presented elsewhere [19, 20]. Here we shall discuss a total feature space system (Fig. 13) using a moment feature space. The general system consists on an optical processor to calculate the moment features $\hat{m}_{pq}$ of the input object to be classified, a first-level classifier that provides class and aspect estimates (which feed our reference database), and a second-level classifier that provides the final class estimates, the object-distortion parameter estimates, and the confidence of these estimates. We shall discuss this architecture, each element of the system, and its performance for a given case study. The database we consider (to allow quantified results) is a set of nine pipe parts with 36 images of each (128×128 pixels with a $50°$ depression angle) for a total of 324 images. We have grouped these nine pipe parts into four classes:

1. class 0 (hose tees),
2. class 1 (PVC tees),
3. class 2 (PVC elbows), and
4. class 3 (hose elbows).

The objective was to classify all 324 input objects into the correct one of four possible classes using the processor of Fig. 12 in the system architecture of Fig. 13.

Figure 13 uses a two-level classifier [19, 20]. The first-level classifier contains an aspect (A) estimator (the aspect is estimated as $\hat{A} = \hat{\mu}_{20} / \hat{\mu}_{02}$) and a tree classifier. The tree classifier uses μ_{pq} features and Fisher LDFs at each node of the tree to provide class estimates. We allow multiple paths

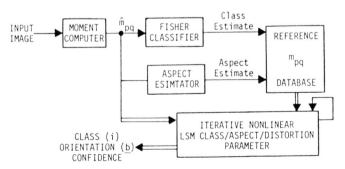

Fig. 13. Complete moment feature space processor architecture. (From Cheatham and Casasent [20].)

through the tree if decisions are close to a threshold. Several aspect estimates for each class are also allowed. The operations required in the first-level classifier are quite simple, requiring only a division and several VIPs. The purpose of the first-level is to reduce the number of class and aspect references for which the more computationally intensive second-level classifier must be applied.

The m_{pq} features have been shown to be jointly Gaussian random variables [19, 20] for in-plane distortions (because of digitization considerations). Thus the Bayesian minimum probability of error classifier is the least-squares solution. For a least-squares solution, the difference between the input measurement vector $\hat{\mathbf{m}}$ and the mean vector $\mathbf{m}_i$ for each class i is

$$g_i = [\hat{\mathbf{m}} - \mathbf{m}_i(\mathbf{b})]^T \Sigma^{-1} [\hat{\mathbf{m}} - \mathbf{m}_i(\mathbf{b})] \qquad (12)$$

If we can assume $\Sigma = \mathbf{I}$, the calculations in Eq. (12) are significantly simplified. As we shall show, use of $\Sigma = \mathbf{I}$ results in a loss of only 1% in the percentage of objects correctly classified. Since m_{pq} varies with in-plane distortions, we minimize g_i with respect to i and all distortion parameters (denoted by $\mathbf{b}$), hence $\mathbf{m}_i$ is a function of $\mathbf{b}$ in Eq. (12). We employ an iterative minimization solution for i and b in Eq. (12). This is more fully detailed elsewhere [19, 20].

The test results obtained for this application (and others) using this system were excellent. Without the aspect estimator, the second-level classifier algorithm had to be evaluated for 2.5 times more reference view classes i than when the aspect estimator was included. In both cases over 97% correct recognition was obtained. Thus the first-level classifier achieves its objective. We found that only six iterations were required in the iterative algorithm in the second-level classifier and that only 1% better performance (98.5%) was obtained if more exact Σ estimates (than $\Sigma = \mathbf{I}$) were used. In all cases, over 97% correct recognition was obtained with only nine reference aspect views out of 36 required for each of the object classes. In tests on real ship imagery [21], the accuracy of the position, scale, and rotation estimates produced by the system was found to be excellent (with perfect classification performance, with position estimate accuracies of 0.03–1.8 pixels, and with scale estimate accuracies of 0.2–2.3% for object scale changes as large as 50%).

A most attractive aspect of a moment feature space is the ease with which the computed moments can be corrected for various error sources [17]. The moments m_{pq} of $f(x, y)$ are related to the moments $\hat{m}_{pq}$ of the $f(x + x_0, y + y_0)$ shifted version of the object by

$$\hat{m}_{pq} = \sum_{i=0}^{p} \sum_{j=0}^{q} \binom{p}{i}\binom{q}{j}(-x_0)^i(-y_0)^j m_{p-i,q-j} \qquad (13)$$

We use Eq. (13) to convert the unipolar moments $\hat{m}_{pq}$ (calculated on our optical processor) to the bipolar m_{pq} required for pattern recognition. This simplifies the optical system since it can use output intensity values. The conversion from $\hat{m}_{pq}$ to m_{pq} involves a simple fixed matrix-vector multiplication of the computed moment feature vector. A more important fact is the relationship between the $\hat{m}_{pq}$ calculated with a nonlinearity described by t_{pq} present in monomial mask and the exact m_{pq} that would be computed using a perfect mask at P_2 of Fig. 12, that is,

$$\hat{m}_{PQ} = \sum_{p=0}^{P} \sum_{q=0}^{Q} t_{pq} m_{pq} \tag{14}$$

This result is most practical since optical processors cannot record perfect monomial masks. The exact $\mathbf{m_{pq}}$ vector can be obtained from the $\hat{\mathbf{m}}_{pq}$ vector computed on a non-exact optical processor by a simple matrix-vector multiplication. This is possible since the mask nonlinearities are fixed in space and time. The final optical system error sources we consider are lens aberrations, mispositioning of the components and blur, and degradation of the input image at P_1 (due to the real-time spatial light modulator used there). These error sources all affect the impulse response h of the system. The exact $\mathbf{m_{pq}}$ vector obtained with a perfect system is related to the calculated $\hat{m}_{pq}$ computed by

$$\hat{m}_{pq} = \sum_{i=0}^{p} \sum_{j=0}^{q} \binom{p}{i}\binom{q}{j} m_{pq} m_{p-i,q-j}^{h} \tag{15}$$

where m_{pq}^{h} are the moments of the impulse response $h(x, y)$. As before, the exact m_{pq} can be obtained from the measured $\hat{\mathbf{m}}_{pq}$ vector by a matrix–vector multiplication. This last correction can also be used to improve the resolution of the system and the input image.

For the various reasons discussed and from the extensive tests performed, this optically generated feature space has significant potential. In recent work [22], the calculation of the moments from sampled FT intensity coefficients has been demonstrated and studied. V. Kumar [23] has also proposed a method of calculating these moments from the Hartley transform of the images. This is most attractive since one feature space (the optical FT plane) can yield Fourier coefficients, WRD sampled features, as well as moments. A quite general optical pattern recognition system thus can result from a simple single feature space (the FT plane) that is easily calculated optically.

VIII. Summary and Conclusion

In these brief pages we have reviewed the concepts of feature extraction and classification and have noted the powerful properties of this pattern recognition technique. These included the ability of one optical processor to accommodate a variety of object recognition problems (without changes in any optical mask) and to provide object orientation information, and the possibility of accommodating a larger number of classes than is possible in other approaches. Such issues are vital for advanced artificial intelligence and robotics applications. The optical Fourier transform feature space (Section III) was described and shown to allow use of unique detectors (with wedge- and ring-shaped elements), thus producing a distortion-invariant feature space. The optical Hough-transform feature space (Section IV) is attractive since it is a low-level feature space and hence is one from which various other feature spaces can be produced on one optical processor with modest post-processing. The Mellin transform feature space (Section V) was described, and it was noted that it can be produced using computer-generator hologram techniques. Its high dimensionality and its in-plane distortion invariance make it attractive for advanced large-class recognition problems. The use of parallel optical feature extractors was discussed in conjunction with this feature space. The chord feature space (Section VI) is also easily computed optically and has in-plane distortion invariance. Our case study of this system provided details of feature extraction, training set selection, and discriminant function synthesis. We also included details and examples of the ability of this feature extractor to provide object orientation and distortion parameter estimates. Our moment feature space optical processor (Section VII) is also quite simple. It has the unique property of being correctable for most practical optical system errors. A full pattern-recognition system employing this feature space was detailed, and excellent class recognition and distortion parameter estimation performance was obtained. Space limited the number of optical feature spaces discussed. Other notable optical feature spaces that have been described include the Wigner distribution [24, 25] and analysis of the autocorrelation [26] pattern for an object.

Acknowledgments

The support of the CMU research included herein by the Air Force Office of Scientific Research (Grant AFOSR-84-0293) and the Internal Research and Development Funds of General Dynamics Pomona (Purchase Order No. 752647) is gratefully acknowledged.

References

1. D. Casasent, in "Handbook of Holography" (H. J. Caulfield, ed.), pp. 503–536. Academic Press, New York, 1979.
2. D. Casasent, SPIE Semin. Proc. 528, 64–82 (1985).
3. R. Duda and P. Hart, "Pattern Classification and Scene Analysis." Wiley, New York, 1973.
4. W. K. Pratt, "Digital Image Processing," Wiley, New York, 1978.

5. G. G. Lendaris and G. L. Stanley, *Proc. IEEE* **58**, 198–216 (1979).
6. H. L. Kasdan, *Opt. Eng.* **18**, 496–503 (1979).
7. D. Casasent and V. Sharma, *Opt. Eng.* **23**, 492–498 (1984).
8. D. Casasent, S. F. Xia, J. Z. Song, and A. J. Lee, *Appl. Opt.* **25**, 983–989 (1986).
9. G. Eichmann and B. Dong, *Appl. Opt.* **22**, 830–834 (1983).
10. G. Gindi and A. Gmitro, *Opt. Eng.* **23**, 499–506 (1984).
11. D. Casasent, *Opt. Eng.* **24**, 724–730 (1985).
12. D. Casasent and A. Lee, *Appl. Opt.* **25**, 3065–3070 (1986).
13. D. Casasent and D. Psaltis, *Progr. Opt.* **16**, 291–356 (1979).
14. D. Nichols, *Opt. Commun.* **48**, 242–246 (1983).
15. D. Casasent and W. T. Chang, *Appl. Opt.* **22**, 2087–2094 (1983).
16. D. Casasent and W. T. Chang, *SPIE Semin. Proc.* **579**, 2–10 (1985).
17. D. Casasent, R. L. Cheatham, and D. Fetterly, *Appl. Opt.* **21**, 3292–3298 (1982).
18. J. Blodgett, R. Athale, C. Giles, and H. Szui, *Opt. Lett.* **7**, 7–9 (1982).
19. D. Casasent and R. L. Cheatham, *Proc. ASME, Comput. Eng.* **1**, 1–6 (1984).
20. R. L. Cheatham and D. Casasent, *SPIE Semin. Proc.* **504**, 19–26 (1984).
21. D. Casasent and R. L. Cheatham, *OSA Top. Meet. Mach. Vision*, pp. ThD4-1–ThD4-4 (1985).
22. B. V. K. V. Kumar and C. A. Rahenkamp, *Appl. Opt.* **25**, 997–1007 (1986).
23. B. V. K. V. Kumar, *SPIE Semin. Proc.* **639**, 253–259 (1986).
24. B. V. K. V. Kumar and C. Carroll, *Proc. IOCC 10th*, pp. 130–136. IEEE Comput. Soc. Press, New York, 1983.
25. B. V. K. V. Kumar and C. Carroll, *Opt. Eng.* **23**, 732–737 (1984).
26. F. Merkle and T. Lorch, *Appl. Opt.* **23**, 1509–1516 (1986).

2.2

Unconventional Correlators

H. BARTELT

PHYSIKALISCHES INSTITUT DER UNIVERSITÄT
ERLANGEN-NÜRNBERG, D-8520 ERLANGEN,
FEDERAL REPUBLIC OF GERMANY

I. Introduction

When trying to convince someone of the importance of optical information processing, probably most optical scientists would stress the parallelism and the large processing capacity of optical systems. One of the most typical examples of this processing capacity is the optical implementation of the correlation and convolution operations, which are closely connected and have been implemented very successfully. The invention of the holographic matched filter for optical correlations by VanderLugt (1964) can be called a milestone in optical information processing. The correlation operation may be interpreted as a measure of similarity for two functions (e.g., two images). A similarity measure is the basis for any recognition process. The matched filter is therefore applicable to very general recognition operations: for instance, object detection in a noisy background or image enhancement and restoration (Considine and Gonsalves, 1978), and character recognition (Armitage and Lohmann, 1965) or pattern recognition (Casasent, 1979; Caulfield et al., 1980; Almeida and Indebetouw, 1982). Also, many other optical information processing operations can be interpreted as convolution or correlation. Therefore, even if these operations seem specific, they represent a general tool in optical information processing.

During the last few years many efforts have been made to improve optical correlation techniques to gain higher flexibility, less sensitivity to object modification, better signal discrimination, and the use of incoherent light or higher light efficiency. We shall describe some of these newer methods that go beyond the classical, holographic implementation of the matched filter. The discussion will be restricted to optical implementations of convolution or correlation for two-dimensional signals or, in simple words, to optical processing of images. The wide field of optical one-dimensional signal processing will be mentioned only briefly, and the applications of digitally computed correlations will be not covered; but many of the ideas and principles explained here for two-dimensional optical signal processing are similarly applicable in those related areas.

We start the following section with a short introduction into definitions and theorems of the correlation and convolution operations. Because of the great similarity of these operations, we shall discuss only correlation operations. But with slight modifications, the described systems can be adapted to perform convolution operations in a similar way. The correlation systems discussed here are grouped into two categories: First the classical, coherent filtering method is explained for introduction; then we proceed to more unconventional systems that use processing in Fourier space or in object space.

II. Definitions and Theorems

This section defines the notation used in this chapter and summarizes the most important theorems connected with convolution and correlation operations.

Correlation and convolution are integral operations that depend on two input functions $f_1(x, y)$ and $f_2(x, y)$ (see, e.g., Goodman 1968):

convolution $\quad f_1(x, y) * f_2(x, y) = \int\int f_1(x, y)f_2(x' - x, y' - y)\, dx\, dy$

$$(1)$$

correlation $\quad f_1(x, y) \star f_2(x, y) = \int\int f_1(x, y)f_2^*(x - x', y - y')\, dx\, dy$

(Integration boundaries are from $-\infty$ to $+\infty$ if not otherwise defined.)

The convolution operation will be denoted $(f_1 * f_2)$ and the correlation operation as $(f_1 \star f_2)$. If both input functions are identical $[f_1(x, y) = f_2(x, y)]$, the operations are often called autocorrelation (or autoconvolution). Otherwise, they are referred to as cross-correlation (or cross-convolution). Fourier transformation will be denoted FT.

Some useful theorems in Fourier mathematics are related to these operations:

Correlation theorem

$$FT[f_1(x, y) \star f_2(x, y)] = F_1(u, v) \cdot F_2^*(u, v) \tag{2}$$

where

$$F_1(u, v) = FT[f_1(x, y)]$$
$$F_2(u, v) = FT[f_2(x, y)]$$

Autocorrelation theorem

$$FT[f(x, y) \star f(x, y)] = |F(u, v)|^2 \tag{3}$$

where

$$F(u, v) = FT[f(x, y)]$$

Convolution theorem

$$FT[f_1(x, y) * f_2(x, y)] = F_1(u, v) \cdot F_2(u, v) \tag{4}$$

where

$$F_1(u, v) = FT[f_1(x, y)]$$
$$F_2(u, v) = FT[f_2(x, y)]$$

For recognition applications usually the correlation peak (at $x' = 0$, $y' = 0$) is measured. In this case the important fact is that the normalized, modulus square peak (peak intensity) is always higher for an autocorrelation then for a cross-correlation (Armitage and Lohmann, 1965):

$$\frac{\left|\iint f_2(x, y)f_2^*(x, y) \, dx \, dy\right|^2}{\iint |f_2(x, y)|^2 \, dx \, dy} \geqq \frac{\left|\iint f_1(x, y)f_2^*(x, y) \, dx \, dy\right|^2}{\iint |f_1(x, y)|^2 \, dx \, dy} \tag{5}$$

This inequality can be proven using the integral form of the Schwarz inequality. Therefore the measured intensity peak height in an optical correlation system can be directly used to recognize a specific input signal. The recognition process is, however, sensitive to changes in scale and/or rotation of one or both input functions. Additional transformations have been proposed to avoid this sometimes unwanted sensitivity (Casasent and Psaltis, 1976a, b, 1977; Szoplik and Arsenault, 1985; Leger and Lee, 1982). The correlation operation is shift-invariant (i.e., a shift of one of the input functions gives a shifted correlation function).

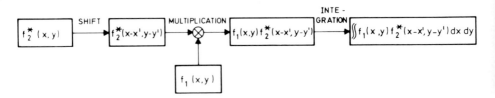

Fig. 1. Basic steps of a correlation operation in object space.

We now explain basic principles for practical implementation, concentrating for simplicity on the correlation operation. In general, implementation methods for the correlation operation can be classified into two categories: correlation by processing in object space and correlation by processing in Fourier space. These two groups can be further characterized by their different processing steps.

The object space version is obtained by the following steps (Fig. 1):

1. Variable shift by (x', y') of the function $f_2^*(x, y)$
2. Multiplication of $f_2^*(x - x', y - y')$ with $f_1(x, y)$
3. Spatial integration of the product

The main practical advantage of systems following this scheme lies in the fact that the necessary filter masks or transparencies are directly given by the input and reference functions. In many cases these functions are real or even positive, which makes the realization as optical masks simple.

Implementation by processing in Fourier space is based on the correlation theorem. The ability of lenses to perform Fourier transformations allows very compact optical correlation systems. The procedure consists now of the following steps (Fig. 2):

1. Fourier transformation of the function $f_1(x, y)$
2. Multiplication of $F_1(u, v)$ by the complex conjugate $F_2^*(u, v) = G(u, v)$ of the Fourier transform of $f_2(x, y)$

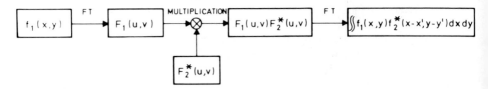

Fig. 2. Basic steps of a correlation operation in Fourier space.

3. Inverse Fourier transformation of the product $F_1(u, v) \cdot G(u, v)$. If instead of an inverse Fourier transformation the forward Fourier transformation is used, only the sign of the output coordinates changes.

These operations are well adapted to the properties of optical elements. Lenses are able to perform the Fourier transformations. The multiplication is realized by illuminating an optical spatial filter with a modulated wave. This setup will be explained in more detail in Section III.A.1. Sometimes a practical problem may occur in the production of the filter. The filter structure corresponds in general to a complex function. This fact makes it usually necessary to apply a hologram as a filter or to use additional multiplexing techniques. Therefore filter mask production can be rather complicated compared with the processing scheme in object space.

III.   Optical Correlation Systems

A.   FOURIER SPACE CORRELATORS

Because of its great importance the description of correlation systems starts with the Fourier space category. The classical optical correlator belongs to this group.

1.   The Classical Coherent Correlation System

The classical coherent optical correlator is based on the concept of the matched filter. Mathematically, matched filtering and correlation are equivalent operations. Matched filtering corresponds to a correlation operations in Fourier space. The filter $G(u, v) = F_2^*(u, v)$ is called the matched filter.

Historically, the matched-filter concept was taken from electrical engineering where it was applied to optimize recognition of a signal surrounded by noise. In optical signal processing it was also used for detection purposes, but usually with no noise assumed. Here the matched filter solves the problem of recognizing a specific object function, out of a given set, by generating a maximum output peak if the wanted object is presented to the system. This property of the matched filter can be shown using the Schwarz inequality as mentioned in Section II. One should note, however, that the matched filter is not the only filter with this property.

We shall now discuss this classical optical system as a basis for the more unconventional correlators. The typical optical spatial filtering setup is a $4f$ system, so called because its length is four times the focal length f of the lenses used (Fig. 3). In this system the first object function $f_1(x, y)$ is

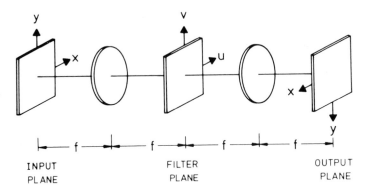

Fig. 3. Optical $4f$ system for spatial filtering.

placed as an optical mask in the front focal plane of the first lens (input plane) and illuminated by a monochromatic plane wave. Alternatively, an amplitude-modulated light wave can be used directly as input. In the back focal plane of the first lens, the Fourier transform $F_1(u, v)$ of $f_1(x, y)$ is obtained. The matched filter positioned in this plane is given by $G(u, v) = F_2^*(u, v)$. Hence the matched filter represents exactly the function required for a correlation by spatial filtering. Therefore, after another Fourier transformation by the second lens, the correlation function is produced in the output plane. Usually only the output intensity is measured, which is sufficient for recognition purposes.

The matched filter represents in general a complex function. An early practical solution to producing the matched filter from the known object function $f_2(x, y)$ was given by VanderLugt (1964). His idea can be described as recording a Fourier hologram of the function $f_2(x, y)$. To this end the Fourier transform $F_2(u, v)$ is superimposed with a plane wave $\exp(2\pi i u x_0)$ to give the following intensity interference pattern:

$$|H(u, v)|^2 = |F_2(u, v) + \exp(2\pi i u x_0)|^2$$

$$= |F_2(u, v)|^2 + 1 + F_2(u, v) \exp(-2\pi i u x_0)$$

$$+ F_2^*(u, v) \exp(2\pi i u x_0) \tag{6}$$

Such a hologram reconstructs, besides other terms, the original wavefront $F_2(u, v)$ [here multiplied with $\exp(-2\pi i u x_0)$] and also its complex conjugate $F_2^*(u, v)$ [here multiplied with $\exp(+2\pi i u x_0)$]; see Fig. 4a. If this hologram is used as a spatial filter, several different terms are obtained in the output plane. The input function is convolved with all terms of the hologram reconstruction. Fortunately the position of these terms is different due to the different modulations (Fig. 4b). One of the components (convolution with the twin image) represents exactly the correlation of $f_1(x, y)$ and $f_2(x, y)$.

It is not necessary to record such a Fourier hologram optically. The filter can be produced as a synthetic or computer-generated hologram, in which case the recording process is simulated by a computer. Because no optical setup or other physically existing object function is necessary to make the filter, this method gives much greater flexibility. Various computer-generated hologram types that are applicable for the correlation operation are described in Lee (1978) and Dallas (1980).

2. Modified Coherent Systems

Several modified versions of the basic set up in Fig. 4 are still applicable for correlation operations (Lohmann, 1975). As a first modification one can

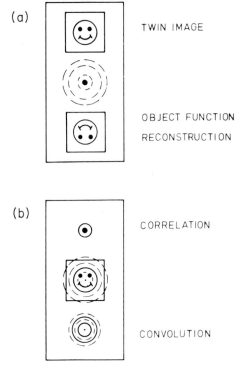

(a)
TWIN IMAGE

OBJECT FUNCTION
RECONSTRUCTION

(b)
CORRELATION

CONVOLUTION

Fig. 4. (a) Reconstruction terms from the Fourier transform of a Fourier hologram; (b) output terms from spatial filtering with a Fourier hologram.

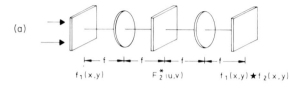

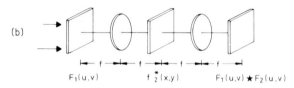

Fig. 5. Optical 4*f* setups for the correlation operation. (a) Correlation operation of $f_1(x, y)$ and $f_2(x, y)$; (b) correlation operation of $F_1(u, v)$ and $F_2(u, v)$.

exchange the position of object and filter function (Fig. 5). As a consequence, we obtain in the output plane a correlation of the Fourier transform $F_1(u, v)$ and $F_2(u, v)$. The intensity of the autocorrelation peak gives the same result in both cases:

$$\iint f(x, y)f^*(x, y)\, dx\, dy = \iint F(u, v)F^*(u, v)\, du\, dv$$

(Parseval's theorem)

$$(7)$$

In general, the overall shape of the correlation function for $F_1(u, v)$ and $F_2(u, v)$ is different from the correlation function of $f_1(x, y)$ and $f_2(x, y)$. In the case of a recognition process, one   of both operations may be preferable depending on the specific application in terms of the discrimination ability.

In a second modification the object function $f_1(x, y)$ may be shifted along the optical axis (Fig. 6). Then, in the back focal plane of the first lens, an additional quadratic phase factor $\exp(i\pi(u^2 / \lambda d + v^2 / \lambda d)$ occurs. This

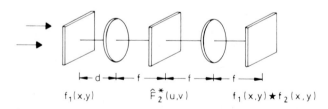

Fig. 6. Correlation operation with input function shifted along the optical axis.

effect can be compensated using a Fresnel matched filter where the complex conjugate of the Fresnel transform $\hat{F}_2^*(u, v)$ of $f_2(x, y)$ is used as optical filter mask:

$$\left| \mathrm{FT}\left[F_1(u, v) \exp\left(i\pi\left(\frac{u^2}{\lambda d} + \frac{v^2}{\lambda d} \right) \right) \hat{F}_2^*(u, v) \right] \right|^2 = |\mathrm{FT}[F_1(u, v)F_2^*(u, v)]|^2$$

$$= |f_1(x, y) \star f_2(x, y)|^2 \qquad (8)$$

where

$$\hat{F}_2(u, v) = \int\int F_2(u', v') \exp\left\{ \frac{i\pi}{\lambda d}[(u - u')^2 + (v - v')^2] \right\} du'\, dv'$$

In Section III.A.4 additional coherent correlators will be described, where the filter structure has been modified instead of the optical setup for improved signal detection.

3. *Spatially Incoherent Systems*

Until now, completely coherent illumination (e.g., from a laser light source) has been assumed. Under these conditions it is possible to perform correlation operations of truly complex input and reference functions. On the other hand, the use of incoherent light would present several practical advantages: Stability requirements are reduced, the signal to noise ratio is improved, and diffuse, reflecting, or self-luminous object functions (e.g., from a TV screen) are tolerable as input (Monahan *et al.*, 1977). The loss of the phase information channel means, however, that only positive (intensity) functions can be processed. In view of the practical advantages, this limitation may be preferable for many applications. The limitation to positive functions can be overcome to some extent by modulation techniques with bias, by multiplexing (e.g., using wavelength as an additional parameter), or by additional electronic post-processing (Lohmann, 1977; Görlitz and Lanzl, 1979; Bartelt, 1982).

We shall now describe the principle of a spatially incoherent correlator. The optical system is identical to the coherent system except for the illumination (Fig. 7). The light source should be spatially incoherent (i.e., extended but monochromatic). Such a light source is often experimentally realized by a laser beam that is modulated by a rotating ground glass in combination with a time integrating detector.

In general, the filtering effect or the performance of the transfer function $T(u, v)$ of a spatial filter, also called the pupil function $P(u, v)$, in an

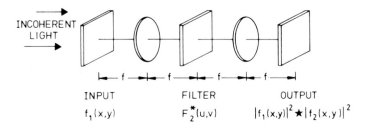

INCOHERENT
LIGHT

|← f →|← f →|← f →|← f →|

INPUT   FILTER   OUTPUT

$f_1(x,y)$ $F_2^*(u,v)$ $|f_1(x,y)|^2 \star |f_2(x,y)|^2$

Fig. 7. Optical incoherent correlation system.

incoherent system differs considerably from that in a coherent system and is described by the Duffieux formula:

$$T(u, v) = \frac{P(u, v) \star P(u, v)}{\iint |P(u, v)|^2 \, du \, dv} \qquad (9)$$

This description makes it difficult to derive a suitable pupil function directly for a specific transfer function. Fortunately, in the case of a matched filter, a simple solution is possible: The coherent matched filter is also one solution for the spatially incoherent system. The output intensity of the system shown in Fig. 7 is described by the correlation of the input intensity and the intensity of the Fourier transform of the filter function:

$$u(x', y') = \iint |f_1(x, y)|^2 |h(x - x', y - y')|^2 \, dx \, dy \qquad (10)$$

where $f_1(x, y)$ is the input function and $H(u, v) = \mathrm{FT}[h(x, y)]$ the filter function. For an intensity correlation of $f_1(x, y)^2$ and $f_2(x, y)^2$, any filter function $H(u, v)$ can be used, which, after a Fourier transformation, gives the amplitude of $f_2(x, y)$. One of many possible solutions is the conventional matched filter $H(u, v) = F_2^*(u, v)$. But the freedom to choose from a variety of filter functions allows even better solutions in most applications.

   Including a random phase $\phi_R(x, y)$ in the fabrication of the filters usually improves the light efficiency of the filter considerably (see also Section III.A.5):

$$H(u, v) = \mathrm{FT}[f_2(x, y) \exp(i\phi_R(x, y))] \qquad (11)$$

A shift of the filter function along the optical axis also results in an additional phase factor of $\exp[i\pi(x^2 + y^2)/\lambda d]$. This effect can therefore be used in a similar way to flatten the Fourier spectrum. Depending on the shift the Fourier transform of the filter also changes in scale:

$$\mathrm{FT}[F_2(u, v, z = 4f - d)] = \mathrm{const} \cdot \exp\left(i\pi \frac{x^2 + y^2}{\lambda d}\right) f_2\left(\frac{x}{\lambda d}, \frac{y}{\lambda d}\right) \qquad (12)$$

The quadratic phase factor is not harmful but usually increases the light efficiency. The scale change by shifting can be used for adapting the size of the filter response to the size of the object image.

A modification of the incoherent correlation would be a partially incoherent operation. This principle has been applied to make the correlation operation shift invariant [i.e., independent of the actual position of the input function (Armitage and Lohmann, 1965)]. This effect is especially useful if the position of the input function is unknown and if a fixed detector is used. The setup for this operation is shown in Fig. 8. The input object is illuminated by coherent light. In the Fourier plane a rotating ground glass is introduced to make the light spatially incoherent for the time-integrating detector. Since a shift of the input function is transformed into a linear phase factor, this information is destroyed when making the light spatially incoherent. This spatially incoherent light distribution is now used as input for the correlation processor. In this processor the intensity of the Fourier transform of the original input function is correlated with a reference intensity pattern $|F_2(u, v)|^2$:

$$R(u, v) = |F_1(u, v)|^2 \star |F_2(u, v)|^2 \tag{13}$$

The correlation peak in this system is always positioned on the optical axis. For character recognition applications it turns out that the wanted character function itself may be used as the reference filter mask. This is not the only possible filter, but it is a very practical one.

4. Temporally Incoherent Systems

The use of polychromatic (or temporally incoherent) light introduces some problems in Fourier type correlators. One of these problems is the wavelength dependence of conventional, optical Fourier transformers. The scale of the Fourier transformation changes inversely with the wavelength (Leith and Roth 1977, 1979; Morris and George, 1980; George and Morris, 1981; Warde et al., 1984; Leon and Leith, 1985). One can avoid this problem

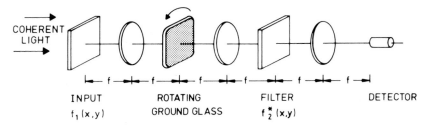

Fig. 8. Optical system for shift-invariant correlation.

by special achromatic Fourier transformers. For example, the lens systems can be corrected in such a way that the wavelength-dependent scale change is compensated (Morris, 1981).

But some methods have also been described in the literature that use the wavelength for multiplexed processing. In these cases the filter has to be wavelength dependent. This effect can be achieved, for example, with color filters or with thick holographic phase filters (Case, 1979). Later, more methods using wavelength multiplexing for object space correlations will be mentioned.

5. Filter Modifications

As mentioned, a common application of the correlation operation is the recognition process using a matched filter. But the matched filter is not the only filter structure that allows a recognition operation by transforming a specific input function into a peak pattern. We can take advantage of this fact in different ways by using modified filter functions. For interferometrically recorded matched filters on film, it is already almost impossible to avoid a nonlinear distortion. In practice this nonlinearity usually limits the dynamic range of the filter and often improves its performance (VanderLugt, 1969). For synthetic or computer-generated matched filters, it therefore makes sense to introduce this type of modification to improve the signal discrimination and to optimize the light efficiency. In this section we shall describe some modified filter types and discuss the practical advantages.

a. Additional Phase Functions.   One of the common problems in the application of a matched filter is its usually high dynamic range, which considerably reduces the light efficiency. We can influence this dynamic range of the matched filter without losing recognition ability. From Fourier holography, it is known that a random phase in an object function levels the amplitude of its Fourier spectrum. As a filter function for the recognition operation we can therefore use $F_R(u, v)$ with a random phase factor:

$$F_R(u, v) = FT[f_2(x, y) \exp i\phi_R(x, y)]$$

or   (14)

$$F_R(u, v) = F_2(u, v) * FT[\exp(i\phi_R(x, y))]$$

The additional random phase function causes no problems for an incoherent correlator where only intensities are effective. In the case of a coherent processor this modification of the filter requires an additional phase function $\exp(i\phi_R(x, y))$ at the input plane:

$$f_1(x, y) \to f_1(x, y) \exp(i\phi_R(x, y))$$ (15)

Now a correlation of $f_1 \exp(i\phi_R)$ and $f_2 \exp(i\phi_R)$ is computed, which is different from the correlation of f_1 and f_2 alone. But for certain recognition applications this is tolerable.

Another effect of this modification is that the recognition operation now becomes space-variant. A shift of the input function $f_1(x, y)$ [without a shift of the phase function $\exp(i\phi_R(x, y))$] gives a completely different correlation function and not just a shifted result. This limitation can be partly overcome by using a periodic phase function $\phi_p(x, y)$ instead of a random phase function (Lohmann and Thum, 1984). In this case a shift of $f_1(x, y)$ by a multiple of the period length p results in a shifted output function. This way one can increase the light efficiency of the filter and keep to some extent the advantages of space invariance.

b. Phase-Only Matched Filter. The optimum case with respect to light efficiency for a matched filter is realized by a phase-only filter structure (Horner and Gianino, 1984). One way to obtain such a filter is to omit the amplitude information of the matched filter:

$$F_2^{*\prime}(u, v) = \frac{F_2^*(u, v)}{|F_2^*(u, v)|} = \exp(i\psi(u, v)) \tag{16}$$

This loss of amplitude information in the filter has, in several practical applications, no negative effect for a recognition process. The importance of the Fourier phase information is already well known from image processing (Oppenheim and Lim, 1981). Kinoform elements, which are also phase-only Fourier filters, allow rather general image reconstructions (Lesem *et al.*, 1969). Therefore the good performance of the phase-only matched filter may be not surprising. Besides the improvement of the light efficiency, the output peak structure for the recognition process is also usually enhanced. Obviously the step from the matched filter to the phase-only matched filter can be described in spatial filtering theory as application of a $(1/|F_2(u, v)c|)$ filter. Since $|F_2(u, v)|$ usually has a strong peak structure (high amplitude for low spatial frequencies and low amplitude for high spatial frequencies), its inverse can be interpreted as a spatial high-pass filter. The result of the application of the phase-only matched filter is therefore, in general, a high-pass filtered conventional correlation function. In case of an autocorrelation the output peak is therefore strongly enhanced. Hence the signal-to-noise ratio or the discrimination ability of the filter is improved. On the other hand, this filter is also more sensitive to modifications of the input function such as rotation or scale change.

A computer simulation that illustrates the effect of the phase-only matched filter is shown in Fig. 9. Later, in Subsection f, we compare the relative merits of the performance of this phase-only matched filter with

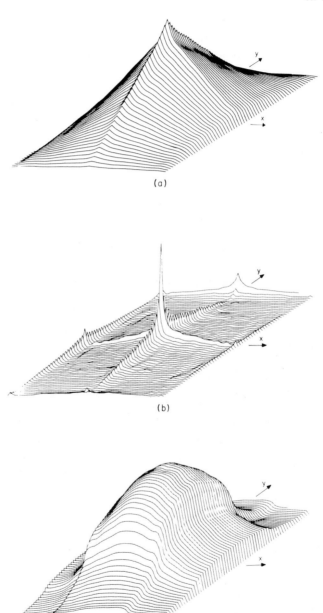

Fig. 9. Computer simulations (amplitude) with the test signal of Fig. 12a. (a) Correlation operation with matched filter; (b) correlation operation with phase-only matched filter; (c) correlation operation with amplitude-only matched filter.

other filter types. From the results of the phase-only matched filter, one may wonder how an amplitude-only filter performs. As expected, the investigation of this case shows that the recognition and discrimination ability becomes much worse (Fig. 9c).

c. Binary Phase-Only Matched Filter. With the good performance of the phase-only matched filter in mind one can go one step further in simplification. An additional restriction to binary phase-only structures would very much facilitate filter production. The technology of very large scale integration (VLSI) can also be used to make optical binary patterns with very high space–bandwidth products. There also exist spatial light modulators that can work in a binary phase-only mode.

For a discussion of its properties we describe a binary phase-only matched filter based on Eq. (16) as follows:

$$F_2^{*''}(u, v) = \begin{cases} +1, & \text{if } \psi \geq 0 \\ -1, & \text{if } \psi < 0 \end{cases} \tag{17}$$

An analysis of the binarization process shows that for the Fourier transform of the binary phase filter (compared with the Fourier transform of the phase-only matched filter) a noise term is added (Dallas, 1971a, b; Horner and Leger, 1985; Horner and Bartelt, 1985). The strongest part of the noise term can be described as a ghost image that is reversed in position $f_2'(-x, -y)$. Computer simulations have shown that, even with the additional noise level, a good correlation peak can be obtained. In the example of Fig. 10 the rms noise (as defined in the following subsection) has increased by a factor of four compared with the continuous phase filter.

We may also take advantage of the specific structure of the noise term to avoid its influence. To this end the reference object has to be placed properly in the object function area from which the filter function is completed. If the reference function is placed, for example, in the upper-left

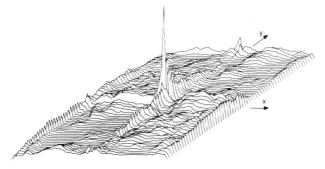

Fig. 10. Computer simulations (amplitude) with the test signal of Fig. 12a. Correlation operation with binary phase-only matched filter.

quadrant of the data field, the ghost image of the binary phase-only matched filter falls in the lower-right quadrant. With such a filter an input function $f_1(x, y)$ in an optical filtering setup is then convolved as well as correlated with $f_2(x, y)$. But both terms are spatially separated so that no significant overlapping occurs (Fig. 11b). Therefore binary phase-only matched filters can be made to perform like continuous phase-only matched filters.

A phase mismatch in the production of a binary phase-only matched filter is not very critical. To show the effect we assume a phase error of δ; then

$$F_2(u, v) = A_1(u, v)e^{i\delta} + A_2(u, v)\, e^{i\pi}\, e^{-i\delta} \tag{18}$$

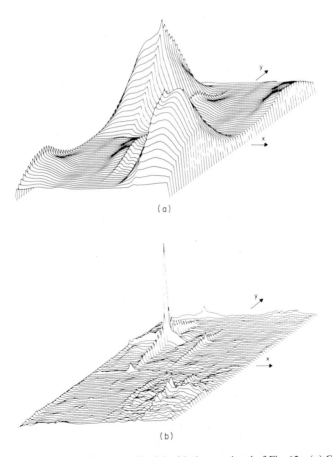

(a)

(b)

Fig. 11. Computer simulations (amplitude) with the test signal of Fig. 12a. (a) Correlation operation with a matched filter computed from a shifted reference function; (b) correlation operation with a binary phase-only matched filter computed from a shifted reference function.

The Fourier transform of this function can be described as

$$f_2'(x, y) = a_1(x, y)e^{i\delta} + a_2 e^{i\pi} e^{-i\delta}$$

$$= a_1(x, y) \sin(\delta) + e^{-i\delta}[a_1(x, y) + a_2(x, y)e^{i\pi}] \qquad (19)$$

In this result a noise term $a_1 \sin(\delta)$ is added, and a phase function $\exp(-i\delta)$ multiplies the result of the correct binary filter reconstruction. Only the additive noise term may become critical, but this term stays sufficiently small for small δ.

d. Two-Bit Correlation. Until now only a binarization of the matched filter has been discussed. Now we look into the consequences of an additional binarization of the input function. Since the input patterns of an optical correlator are usually real-valued images, we consider only an amplitude binarization. Such a binary data input would further simplify the correlation system and make possible an application of binary real-time light modulators. Now the input function will be represented by one amplitude bit per pixel and the matched filter by one phase bit per pixel. Therefore we shall call this operation a two-bit correlation.

Studies of the autocorrelation of amplitude binarized continuous signals were first published by Van Vleck and Middleton (1966). Under quite generous assumptions they derived the following rather simple and elegant result:

$$r_b(x) = \frac{2}{\pi} \sin^{-1} r_c(x) \qquad (20)$$

where $r_c(x)$ is the (one-dimensional) autocorrelation function of the continuous signal and $r_b(x)$ that of the binarized signal. Other studies found that, in special cases, binarizing the amplitude of the input object resulted in a better signal-to-noise ratio compared with the gray-scale correlation of the same signals (Kumar and Casasent, 1981).

To investigate the question of the performance of a two-bit correlation system we again show results of computer simulations. To this end a continuous test signal is binarized (Fig. 12):

$$f_1'(x, y) = \begin{cases} 0, & \text{if } f_1(x, y) \leq t \\ 1, & \text{if } f_1(x, y) > t \end{cases} \qquad (21)$$

The threshold t for binarization of the test signal was selected by first making a histogram of the pixel values and then picking the approximate median value. The spatial resolution of the input signal, including a dark frame is 128×128 pixels. Matched filters are computed from both the continuous and the binary test signal. For both types of input functions continuous filters, phase-only filters, and binary phase phase-only filters are derived and applied to the continuous and to the binarized input signals.

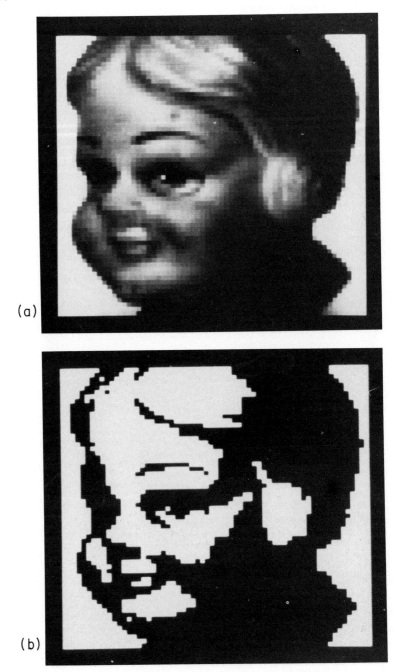

(a)

(b)

Fig. 12. Test signals. (a) Gray-level image; (b) binarized image.

TABLE I

COMPARISON OF DIFFERENT FILTERS FOR TWO-BIT CORRELATION

	Filter made from continuous amplitude			Filter made from binary amplitude		
	Matched filter	Phase-only filter	Binary phase-only filter	Matched filter	Phase-only filter	Binary phase-only filter
Continous amplitude input						
η_H	6.3%	3.3%	1.0%	3.1%	4.3%	0.9%
SNR	4:1	241:1	12:1	4:1	17:1	8:1
Peak intensity	1.0	125	36	1.3	63	16
Binary amplitude input						
η_H	1.5%	6.7%	2.5%	0.7%	19.0%	7.5%
SNR	4:1	34:1	21:1	7:1	62:1	36:1
Peak intensity	1.1	419	159	3.4	1191	471

The results of all these combinations are summarized in Table I, which shows light efficiency η_H, signal-to-noise ratio (SNR), and the peak correlation R_0^2 relative to the matched filter. These quantities will be explained in detail later. In the three-dimensional plots showing two typical cases (Figs. 13 and 14), the amplitude is plotted instead of the intensity to enable an easy, visual comparison of the noise performance. In these figures the peak

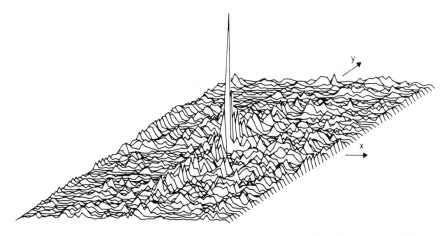

Fig. 13. Computer simulation (amplitude) of a correlation with binarized image and binary phase-only filter computed from gray-level image.

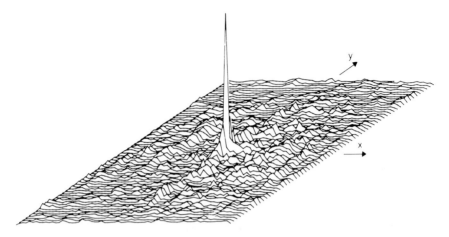

Fig. 14. Computer simulation (amplitude) of a correlation with binarized image and binary phase-only filter computed from binarized image.

heights are normalized and do not show the high increase (in many cases) in the absolute peak height of the phase-only filters.

In general the results prove that even the crude approximation of binarized filters and input signals can show good performance. One would expect the best results for the combinations of the input functions with the filters derived from the same functions. From the discussion in the preceding sections it is already known that phase-only filters usually yield better results. As can be seen from the table, the best results for the test pattern were obtained when the phase-only filter, made from the binarized test target, is correlated with the binarized test target. The poorest showing is the matched filter. Usually the binary amplitude input signal outperforms the operations of the continuous input signal. This effect may be explained by the increased portion of high spatial frequencies in the Fourier transform of the binary test pattern. In general the binarized combinations outperform the other corresponding combinations by a significant margin. Therefore binarized input and binary filters can serve as attractive alternatives to continuous correlations (Horner and Bartelt, 1985).

e. Tandem Component. VanderLugt-type matched filters are recorded as amplitude Fourier holograms. With such holograms it is not possible to achieve optimum light efficiency for general applications. The phase-only matched filter avoids light loss by absorption, but the correlation peak is still surrounded by side lobes. An almost perfect transformation of an input signal into a peak structure without light loss can be obtained with a computer-generated component consisting of two phase filters and a lens (tandem component, Bartelt, 1984, 1985). An intuitive way to explain the principle of the tandem component refers to the method of adding a diffuser function at the input plane, as explained in Subsection a. For the tandem component the diffuser function is specially computed for the wanted input signal. With this specially adapted phase filter, the Fourier spectrum of the input signal, including the phase mask, becomes flat in amplitude. The resulting matched filter is then automatically a phase-only structure.

A second approach to the principle of the tandem component starts from the idea of a wavefront transformation from the specific input pattern into a perfect peak function. Starting from the desired output peak, we can conclude that its Fourier transform must be a plane wave with constant phase and amplitude. The steps for arriving at this result can be seen from the setup in Fig. 15.

The amplitude in the filter plane should be made constant with help of a Kinoform-type phase element in the input plane (Lesem *et al.*, 1969):

$$f_1'(x, y) = f_1(x, y) \exp(i\phi(x, y)) \tag{22}$$

where f is the input signal, $\exp(i\phi)$ the first phase filter, and $|F_1'(u, v)| =$ const $= |FT[f_1'(x, y)]|$. No general analytic solution exists for finding $\phi(x, y)$ directly from the known data $f_1(x, y)$. In special cases a direct derivation is possible (Bartelt, 1984). In general, solutions can be approximated, for example, by applying the iterative techniques of Gerchberg and Saxton (1972) and Fienup (1981). The basic iterative method can be improved concerning convergency and final error of the approximation (Bartelt and Horner, 1985).

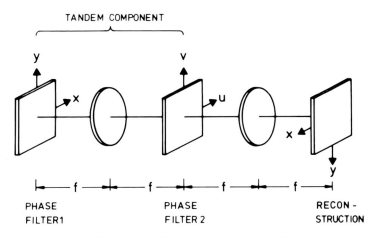

Fig. 15. Principle of the tandem component filter.

Assuming that we have found the desired phase function $\phi(x, y)$, then we can describe the Fourier transform of $f_1'(x, y)$ as

$$F_1'(u, v) = \exp(i\Phi(u, v)) \tag{23}$$

Therefore the matched filter in this case is given by

$$F_2^{*'}(u, v) = \exp(-i\Phi(u, v)) \tag{24}$$

With this matched filter the wavefront becomes constant in phase and amplitude. Its Fourier transform gives a perfect peak function. This result is obtained without losing light by absorption in the filter masks or by diffraction into higher orders.

A specific example for the performance of this type of correlation is shown in Fig. 16. For the experimental result the phase masks were simulated for simplicity by computer-generated amplitude holograms. This simplification reduces the actual light efficiency, but the system properties remain the same.

We should remember that the tandem component filter type is space-variant; so the input object has to be positioned properly. But with the method of using a periodic filter that was described in Subsection a, the disadvantages imposed by space variance can be limited. This method implies an additional constraint of periodicity for the first phase filter. Then the system again shows pseudo space invariance (i.e., an input function shifted by a multiple of the period length produces, except for a shift, the same correlation output). The additional constraint of periodicity for the first phase filter makes it more difficult to find a good approximation for the phase function $\phi(x, y)$. Therefore a higher noise level has to be tolerated. But computer simulation shows that the performance is tolerable for some applications (Fig. 17).

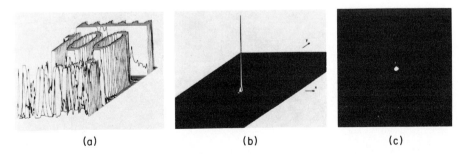

(a)   (b)   (c)

Fig. 16. Correlation-type operation with a tandem component filter. (a) Input test signal; (b) computer simulation of the output intensity; (c) experimental result with computer-generated amplitude holograms simulating the phase-only filters.

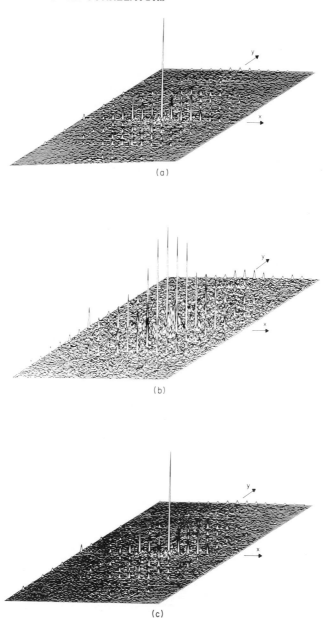

Fig. 17. Correlation-type operations with a periodic tandem component (computer simulation). (a) Intensity output for an input function with no shift; (b) intensity output for an input function shifted by half a period length; (c) intensity output for an input function shifted by a period length.

f. Comparison of the Performance of the Modified Filter Types. To be able to compare the performance of the filter types described in the preceding sections we now present the numerical results of computer simulations. It should be pointed out that these results depend on the specific patterns chosen as input. However, the data allow one to judge the relative merits of the filters. The object used in the computer simulations is the one shown in Fig. 12a. The object function has a resolution of 64×64 pixels surrounded by a dark frame, making a complete object field of 128×128 pixels. For the different filters, several parameters are derived that would be of importance for a recognition operation: peak height, light efficiency, and rms noise (Table II).

The peak height is the maximum intensity (modulus square) in the output plane.

For the light efficiency, a definition by Horner was applied (Horner, 1982; Caulfield, 1982):

$$\eta_H = \eta_M \frac{\iint_{A'} |f_1(x, y) \star f_2(x, y)|^2 \, dx \, dy}{\iint_A |f_1(x, y)|^2 \, dx \, dy} \tag{25}$$

where η_M is the proportionality constant, A' the area of the 50% peak response, and A the total area. This light efficiency η_H compares the energy in the output peak with the input light energy. The size of the 50% peak area is in all cases assumed to consist of 3×3 pixels. For simplicity we take $\eta_M = 1$.

For the rms noise measure, the energy of the correlation peak, $u_{i\,max}$, was compared with the energy outside the peak:

$$\text{SNR} = \frac{u_{i\,max}}{(\sum_{A-A'}^{i} |u_i|^2 / (N_A - N_{A'}))^{1/2}} \tag{26}$$

where $A - A'$ is the region outside the central 50% peak and $N_A - N_{A'}$ the

TABLE II

COMPARISON OF CORRELATION FILTER TYPES

Filter type	η_H (%)	SNR	Peak intensity
Matched filter	0.8	6:1	1
Phase-only filter	13.8	51:1	256
Binary phase-only filter	4.7	29:1	87
Tandem component	91.0	409:1	1853
Binary tandem component	58.8	153:1	1090

number of pixels in $A - A'$. This definition differs from the noise definition used for the derivation of the classical matched filter. Therefore, it is not surprising that in the results of Table II the modified filter types show much better performance than the original matched filter. On the other hand, one should keep in mind that with better performance, the filter operation usually becomes more sensitive to changes (scale or rotation changes and errors) in the input function. The results of Table II can be summarized in the following way: The tandem component filter gives the best results in every aspect, but with the limitation of space variance. The phase-only filter outperforms all filters with space-invariant properties. The binary phase-only filter still has advantages, according to this survey, over the amplitude-matched filter.

B. OBJECT SPACE CORRELATORS

The correlation systems based on Fourier optics are far more popular than the object-space correlators. But in the case of object-space correlators rather elegant solutions have been found. Compared with Fourier-space correlators the reference masks are usually relatively simple (e.g., real or even positive functions instead of complex filter functions). This is due to the fact that in an object-space correlator the reference function $f_2^*(x, y)$ is used directly as the filter. In case of positive functions this principle makes the filter production simple and does not show the light loss by diffraction present in holographic filters. Many object-space correlators are also applicable in incoherent light illumination; so self-luminous input facilities can be used (Monahan et al., 1977).

1. Scanning System

The scanning system for correlation shown in Fig. 18 directly implements the definition of the correlation integral [Eq. (2)] in an optical system. The

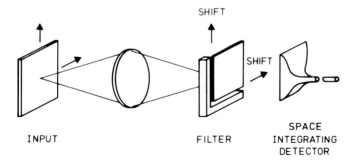

SHIFT

SHIFT

INPUT FILTER SPACE INTEGRATING DETECTOR

Fig. 18. Scanning system for a correlation operation.

input function is imaged into the plane of the reference pattern. The complete light irradiance passing through the reference pattern is measured with an integrating detector. By scanning in time (e.g., the reference pattern in two dimensions), one obtains sequentially the complete correlation data set:

$$\int\int f_1(x, y)f_2^*(x - x_0(t), y - y_0(t)) \, dx \, dy = f_1 \star f_2(x_0(t), y_0(t)) \qquad (27)$$

Using a two-dimensional lenslet array for optical replication of the input function, one can build a multichannel correlator (Glaser, 1982). In principle this multiplexing capacity can replace the need for the scanning operation. Alternatively the multichannel system can be used to perform several cross-correlations with various reference functions in parallel (Monahan *et al.*, 1977).

2. Shadow-Casting Method

The shadow-casting correlator takes direct advantage of the properties of spatially incoherent light (Marko and Platzer, 1981; Monahan *et al.*, 1977). It performs two-dimensional correlations without the need of any scanning procedure. The basic system is shown in Fig. 19.

The system requires diffusely scattering illumination with an intensity modulated by the input function. Such an input may be realized, for instance, by a ground glass in contact with an object transparency, an array of light emitting diodes, or a TV screen. The correlation process can be understood best from a geometrical optics point of view. The diffuse light source can be interpreted as emitting a superposition of parallel beams with different angles. The input function, illuminated with a specific parallel beam of angle α, produces a shadow image on the mask with the reference pattern. The shadow image is shifted depending on the angle α. The light representing the product of the shadow image and the reference pattern is then collected

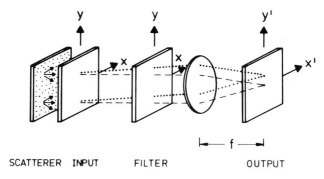

Fig. 19. Shadow-casting system for a correlation operation.

into a point at a specific position in the output plane. Since all possible angles are present in the light source, all correlation coefficients are calculated simultaneously by the system:

$$r(\alpha_x, \alpha_y) = \iint f_1'(x - d \sin \alpha_x, y - d \sin \alpha_y) f_2(x, y) \, dx \, dy \qquad (28)$$

where f_1' is the shadow image of f_1.

From this explanation the limitations of the method are obvious. Diffraction effects are not taken into account in this discussion of light rays. In general, diffraction limits the resolution of the correlation system. The number of resolvable pixels in the correlation function (the space–bandwidth product) depends directly on the mask separation and the mask size. Such systems have been proposed in several varying geometries (e.g., without lenses and with an additional scale change or a folded system for autocorrelation).

3.   *Wavelength Multiplexing*

A parameter that is applicable for multiplexing in temporally incoherent light is the wavelength. Proper use of this wavelength parameter avoids the need for mechanical shift in an object-space correlator. Since the wavelength is a one-dimensional parameter, such a system is able to perform only a one-dimensional correlation operation, but for two-dimensional signals. Two optical systems for this purpose will be described. In both cases a white-light source with a flat wavelength spectrum is assumed for simplicity.

In the first system (Fig. 20) the input function is illuminated by white light and is imaged through a dispersive element. For simplicity we assume that the wavelength-dependent shift of the dispersed image depends (besides a constant) linearly on the wavelength λ. The spectrally dispersed image is then used as illumination for the reference function. The correlation operation is completed by spatially collecting the light with a lens. The

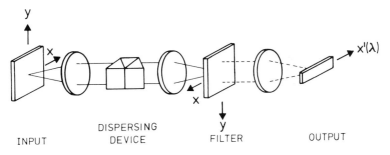

Fig. 20. Wavelength multiplexing correlator (Bartelt, 1979).

spectral intensity now contains the one-dimensional correlation data (positive functions f_1 and f_2 are assumed):

$$\iint f_1(x - c_0 - c_1\lambda,\, y)f_2(x, y)\, dx\, dy = [f_1 \star f_2](c_0 + c_1\lambda) \tag{29}$$

where c_0 and c_1 are constants of the dispersing device.

For display of the correlation function, the light can be dispersed again and measured by a wavelength-independent detector. An example is shown

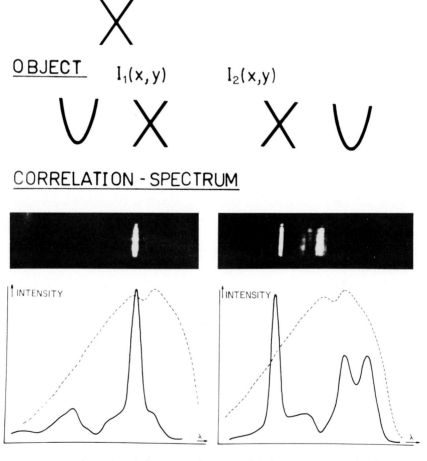

Fig. 21. Experimental result from a wavelength multiplexing correlator. Dashed line shows the actual spectral distribution of the used light source.

in Fig. 21. With the help of an additional one-dimensional mechanical scanning operation, the system can be extended to perform fully two-dimensional correlations (Bartelt, 1979).

Other elegant correlators in white light for one-dimensional correlations of two-dimensional signals were described by Lacourt (1978) and by Goedgebuer and Gazeu (1978). We shall discuss briefly the first system as an example. In this setup, two spectroscopes are directly combined (Fig. 22). The input function is again imaged through a dispersive device onto the reference function. The product of both is then imaged a second time through a spectroscope with different dispersive parameters. If one assumes a flat wavelength spectrum and a dispersion shift proportional to wavelength, the output measured with a wavelength-insensitive detector (e.g., a black-and-white film) is given by

$$r(x, y) = \int f_1(x - b_1 - c_1\lambda + c_2\lambda, y) f_2(x + b_2 + c_2\lambda, y) \, d\lambda \qquad (30)$$

where b_1 and b_2 are constants, and c_1 and c_2 are proportionality constants for the spectroscopes 1 and 2.

To show that this function indeed represents a correlation, we introduce a change of variables:

$$r\left(x\frac{c_1}{c_2}, y\right) = \frac{1}{c_2} \int f_1\left[z\left(1 - \frac{c_1}{c_2}\right) + x\frac{c_1}{c_2} - b_1, y\right] f_2(z + b_2, y) \, dz \qquad (31)$$

where $z = x + c_2\lambda$. If we ignore the constant shifts b_1 and b_2, we obtain a one-dimensional correlation between the function f_2 and the function f_1 scaled by a scaling factor $(1 - c_1/c_2)$. The correlation coordinate in the output plane is then (xc_1/c_2). The correlation operation also differs from the operation in the system of Fig. 21 in that a y-integration is not performed. The correlation is displayed separately for each horizontal line of the functions f_1 and f_2.

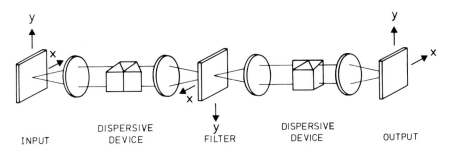

Fig. 22. Wavelength multiplexing correlator (Lacourt, 1978).

IV. Summary and Outlook

Due to the importance of the correlation operation in signal processing, a huge variety of systems has been proposed. Therefore it is impossible to cover all modifications in a single chapter, even with the restriction to optical correlation systems for two-dimensional signals. Optical systems are especially well suited to the group of two-dimensional signals because of their high multiplexing capacity and because of the inherent Fourier transformation capacity of optical lenses. However, as shown in the discussion of object-space correlators, not all optical correlation systems rely on the Fourier transformation property of lenses.

In addition to the optical systems for two-dimensional signals, a great class of optical correlators has been designed to process one-dimensional (and usually electronic) signals. Often the combination of an optical part with optoelectronic devices such as modulators, deflectors, and detectors makes such systems especially attractive (Bromley, 1974; Monahan *et al.*, 1977; Casasent, 1979; Leger and Lee, 1982; Upatnieks, 1983; Yu and Lu, 1984).

For the future these hybrid systems also have great potential for two-dimensional correlations. With the development of efficient electro-optical array devices (such as spatial light modulators and deflector arrays), a missing link between optics and electronics can be filled.

Finally, one can speculate even about the possibility of optical-digital correlators. Optical-digital computers, which are still in the research state, would find a wide field of applications in this direction.

References

Almeida, S. A., and Indebetouw, G. (1982). *In* "Applications of Optical Fourier Transforms" (H. Stark, ed.), p. 41. Academic Press, New York.
Armitage, J. D., and Lohmann, A. (1965). *Appl. Opt.* **4**, 461.
Bartelt, H. (1979). *Opt. Commun.* **29**, 37.
Bartelt, H. (1982). *Opt. Commun.* **42**, 87.
Bartelt, H. (1984). *Appl. Opt.* **23**, 1499.
Bartelt, H. O. (1985). *Appl. Opt.* **24**, 381.
Bartelt, H., and Horner, J. (1985). *Appl. Opt.* **24**, 2894.
Bromley, K. (1974). *Opt. Acta* **21**, 35.
Casasent, D. (1979). *Proc. IEEE* **67**, 813.
Casasent, D., and Psaltis, D. (1976a). *Appl. Opt.* **15**, 1798.
Casasent, D., and Psaltis, D. (1976b). *Opt. Commun.* **17**, 59.
Casasent, D., and Psaltis, D. (1977). *Proc. IEEE* **65**, 77.
Case, S. K. (1979). *Appl. Opt.* **18**, 1890.
Caulfield, H. J. (1982). *Appl. Opt.* **21**, 4391.
Caulfield, H. J., Hames, R., and Casasent, D. (1980). *Opt. Eng.* **19**, 152.
Considine, P. S., and Gonsalves, R. A. (1978). *In* "Topics in Applied Physics," Vol. 23: Optical Data Processing (D. Casasent, ed.). Springer-Verlag, Berlin and New York.

Dallas, W. J. (1971a). *Appl. Opt.* **10**, 673.

Dallas, W. J. (1971b). *Appl. Opt.* **10**, 674.

Dallas, W. J. (1980). *In* "Topics in Applied Physics," Vol. 41: The Computer in Optics Research (B. R. Frieden, ed.), p. 291. Springer, New York.

Fienup, J. R. (1981). "Transformations in Optical Signal Processing," SPIE Vol. 373, p. 147. SPIE, Bellingham, Washington.

George, N., and Morris, G. M. (1981). *In* "Current Trends in Optics" (F. T. Arecchi and F. R. Aussenegg, eds.). Taylor & Francis, London.

Gerchberg, R. W., and Saxton, W. O. (1972). *Optik* **35**, 237.

Glaser, I. (1982). *Appl. Opt.* **21**, 1271.

Goedgebuer, J.-P., and Gazeu, R. (1978). *Opt. Commun.* **27**, 53.

Görlitz, D., and Lanzl, F. (1979). *Opt. Commun.* **28**, 283.

Goodman, J. W. (1968). "Introduction to Fourier Optics." McGraw-Hill, New York.

Horner, J. L. (1982). *Appl. Opt.* **21**, 4511.

Horner, J. L., and Bartelt, H. (1985). *Appl. Opt.* **24**, 2889.

Horner, J. L., and Leger, J. R. (1985). *Appl. Opt.* **24**, 609.

Horner, J. L., and Gianino, P. D. (1984). *Appl. Opt.* **23**, 812.

Kumar, B. V. K. V., and Casasent, D. (1981). *Appl. Opt.* **20**, 1433.

Lacourt, A. (1978). *Opt. Commun.* **27**, 47.

Lee, W. H. (1978). *Prog. Opt.* **16**.

Leger, J. R., and Lee, S. H. (1982). *In* "Applications of Optical Fourier Transforms" (H. Stark, ed.), p. 131. Academic Press, New York.

Leith, E., and Roth, J. (1977). *Appl. Opt.* **16**, 2565.

Leith, E., and Roth, J. (1979). *Appl. Opt.* **18**, 2803.

Leon, S., and Leith, E. N. (1985). *Appl. Opt.* **24**, 3638.

Lesem, L. B., Hirsch, P. M., and Jordan, J. A. (1969). *IBM J. Res. Dev.* **13**, 150.

Lohmann, A. (1975). *Conf. Proc. IEEE Conf. Opt. Comput., Washington, D.C.* p. 153.

Lohmann, A. (1977). *Appl. Opt.* **16**, 261.

Lohmann, A., and Thum, A. C. (1984). *Appl. Opt.* **23**, 1503.

Marko, H., and Platzer, H. (1981). *NTZ Arch.* **3**, 231.

Monahan, M. A., Bromley, K., and Bocker, P. R. (1977). *Proc. IEEE* **65**, 121.

Morris, G. (1981). *Appl. Opt.* **20**, 2017.

Morris, G. M., and George, N. (1980). *Appl. Opt.* **19**, 3843.

Oppenheim, A. V., and Lim, L. S. (1981). *Proc. IEEE* **69**, 529.

Szoplik, T., and Arsenault, H. H. (1985). *Appl. Opt.* **24**, 3179.

Upatnieks, J. (1983). *Appl. Opt.* **22**, 2798.

VanderLugt, A. (1964). *IEEE Trans. Inf. Theory* **IT-10**, 748.

VanderLugt, A. (1969). Thesis, Chap. 5. Univ. of Reading, Reading, England.

Van Vleck, J. H., and Middleton, D. (1966). *Proc. IEEE* **54**, 2.

Warde, C., Caulfield, H. J., Yu, F. T. S., and Ludman, J. E. (1984). *Opt. Commun.* **49**, 241.

Yu, F. T. S., and Lu, X. J. (1984). *Appl. Opt.* **23**, 3109.

2.3

Optical Implementation of Associative Memory Based on Models of Neural Networks

NABIL H. FARHAT

THE MOORE SCHOOL OF ELECTRICAL ENGINEERING
UNIVERSITY OF PENNSYLVANIA
PHILADELPHIA, PENNSYLVANIA 19104

DEMETRI PSALTIS

DEPARTMENT OF ELECTRICAL ENGINEERING
CALIFORNIA INSTITUTE OF TECHNOLOGY
PASADENA, CALIFORNIA, 91125

I. Introduction

Steady progress in neuroscience and behavioral science during the last few decades is providing us with a level of understanding of the structural and functional properties of the brain that allows meaningful, albeit highly simplified, modeling of its neural networks. Several widely accepted observations can be made about the brain. It processes information in a collective manner with the aid of a network of a very large number of densely interconnected, relatively simple decision-making elements, the neurons. Each neuron makes a somewhat fuzzy decision on whether or not to change its state (firing or not firing) in the course of a computation depending on its weighted specific inputs from other neurons. It is estimated the brain has something of the order of 10^{10} to 10^{11} neurons, each making 10^3 to 10^4 connections to neighboring neurons. Information is stored by a process of electrochemical "learning" induced by representations of sensory data that modify the weights of the synapses (Hebb, 1949). The total number of synaptic interconnections where information is stored is extremely large, approaching 10^{14} or 10^{15}.

The number of connections in a neural network is in sharp contrast to the very sparse connectivity that exists in electronic circuits of computers. This structural difference is accompanied by a distinction among the types of problems that neural nets and conventional computers are particularly good at. For instance, we know that in arithmetic operations the brain is not nearly as efficient as a digital computer; but when it comes to performing tasks of recognition, classification, and association, it can outperform even the most powerful digital computer. This difference in capabilities stems directly from the collective nature of information processing in the brain as opposed to the predominately segmented and largely serial processing architectures of conventional digital computers. The difference between the way a neural net and a digital computer approach problems is evident in simple arithmetic problems. When we are asked what 3 times 8 equals, we do not need to calculate the result, we immediately give the answer 24 because in early age we memorized multiplication tables; we simply recognize the prompt and recall the associated answer.

One of the most impressive attributes of neural information processing is its fault tolerance, which ensures graceful degradation in performance. By the age of 50 many of us may have lost a nonnegligible number of brain cells (neurons), and yet no noticeable degradation in performance and capabilities is detected. We simply learn to do better with less. There is increasing evidence that neural interconnections are a dynamic nonceasing process which may also be a factor in checking deterioration. The robustness of information processing in the brain is not confined to tolerance to failure of components but also includes an ability to tolerate a degree of error and noise in the data presented and yet continue to perform the tasks of recognition, association, or classification that may be required. In other words the brain seems to be able to reconstruct signals from partial and noisy information, which gives it a superresolving capability by which a signal or entity can be reconstructed in its entirety from a partial version. As evidence of this, note the ease with which we recognize a face in a photograph when the photograph is partially mutilated or part of it is missing. Association and superresolution are important basic operations required in pattern recognition and in the solution of ill-posed problems encountered, for example, in vision and inverse scattering. We know, for example, that signal recovery from partial information is an ill-posed problem (Tikhonov and Arsenin, 1977). This problem appears to be handled readily by neural nets because of the nonlinear nature of their decision making, their massive interconnectivity, and the feedback employed (Poggio and Koch, 1985; Farhat and Miyahara, 1986). The problem of designing memories that can be used to supplement incomplete descriptions of members of an ensemble of patterns stored in a prescribed distributed fashion has been considered by many investigators (Gabor, 1969; Willshaw *et al.*, 1969; Longuet-Higgins *et al.*, 1970; Willsaw, 1971, 1972; Nakano, 1972; Anderson *et al.*, 1977; Little, 1977; Kohonen, 1972, 1978, 1984; Amari, 1977; Grossberg, 1982; Hopfield, 1982).

The parallelism and massive interconnectivity of neural nets happen to be also the main strengths of optical processing. Hence the interest in optical implementations of neural nets (Psaltis and Farhat, 1985; Farhat *et al.*, 1985). These studies and this review are aimed at drawing attention to the fit between optics and neural modeling with the hope that neural modeling can be combined with the capabilities of modern optics, including emergent optical technologies such as high-speed nonvolatile spatial light modulators (SLMs) (Tanguay and Warde, 1980; Ross *et al.*, 1983) and optically bistable devices (OBDs) (Miller *et al.*, 1981; Gibbs *et al.*, 1981). This may lead to optical architectures and processing systems that are attractive for associative memory, pattern recognition, and machine vision systems (Guest and Gaylord, 1980; Fisher *et al.*, 1985; Athale *et al.*, 1986; Yariv and Kwong, 1986; Soffer *et al.*, 1986; Cohen, 1986). In general, optics has distinct advantages and disadvantages vis-a-vis silicon-based processing systems (Lambe *et al.*, 1985; Graph, 1985). It is widely agreed that optics provides global communication ability and dense storage for memory. Semiconductors, on the other hand, are good for building gates with which combinatorial logic circuits, the mainstay of present day computers, are constructed. Optical computers whose structure and function are motivated by neural modeling can be advantageous compared with electronic implementations of the same architectures because the connectivity, which is the most distinctive characteristic of neural nets, also happens to be the advantage of optics.

In Section II of this chapter we discuss a linear systems approach to associative memory. In Sections III and IV, optoelectronic implementations of one and two dimensional neural nets are presented, and in Section V we discuss holographic associative memories. Finally, in Section V we make general observations on the features of the network approach to optical information processing and assess the future prospects of this field.

II. Linear Systems as Associative Memories

Optical information processing systems can perform very efficiently analog linear transformations on large input data sets, and as a consequence they have been applied to a variety of signal and image processing problems that require linear transformations. Associative memories is another application in which the ability of optical systems to perform linear transformations can prove useful. An associative memory can be implemented with a linear system by selecting the impulse response so that a desired output is produced for a set of specified inputs. If T is a matrix representing the impulse response of a system, then we require that

$$c^{(m)}\mathbf{v}^{(m)} = \mathbf{T}\mathbf{u}^{(m)} \tag{1}$$

for a set of vectors $\mathbf{u}^{(m)}$, $\mathbf{v}^{(m)}$ and constants $c^{(m)}$. the matrix $\mathbf{T}$ can be thought of as a memory that is addressed by the vectors $\mathbf{u}^{(m)}$ and produces the associated stored vectors $\mathbf{v}^{(m)}$. Here we are concerned with a specific class of autoassociative memory, which results when $\mathbf{u}^{(m)} = \mathbf{v}^{(m)}$ in Eq. (1). Autoassociative memories reproduce an input that exactly matches one of the stored vectors when the input is a partial or otherwise distorted version of one of the stored vectors that is sufficiently close to it. In this case Eq. (1) reduces to an eigenvalue equation, and the vectors are stored as eigenfunctions of the linear transformation $\mathbf{T}$. One way this can be accomplished is by constructing the matrix $\mathbf{T}$ as follows:

$$\mathbf{T} = \mathbf{VDV}^{-1} \tag{2}$$

where

$$\mathbf{D} = \begin{pmatrix} c^{(1)} & & & & & \\ & \cdots & & & 0 & \\ & & c^{(M)} & & & \\ & & & 0 & & \\ & 0 & & & \cdots & \\ & & & & & 0 \end{pmatrix}$$

$$\mathbf{V} = (\mathbf{v}^{(1)} \quad \cdots \quad \mathbf{v}^{(M)} \quad \mathbf{w}^{(M+1)} \quad \cdots \quad \mathbf{w}^{(N)})$$

N is the length of the vectors $\mathbf{v}$, and $M < N$ is the number of vectors stored in the $N \times N$ matrix $\mathbf{T}$. The vectors $\mathbf{w}$ are basis vectors in the subspace that is orthogonal to the space spanned by the vectors $\mathbf{u}$. Notice that in the diagonal matrix of eigenvalues $\mathbf{D}$ the eigenvalues are all zero for $m > M$. Thus the set of vectors $\mathbf{w}$ spans the null space of the linear transformation $\mathbf{T}$. If the matrix $\mathbf{T}$ as defined in Eq. (2) is multiplied by one of the stored vectors, the same vector is reproduced at the output scaled by the constant c. An arbitrary input vector $\mathbf{u}$ can be written as a linear combination of the eigenfunctions of the matrix $\mathbf{T}$:

$$\mathbf{u} = \sum_{m=1}^{M} d^{(m)}\mathbf{v}^{(m)} + \sum_{m=M+1}^{N} d^{(m)}\mathbf{w}^{(m)} \tag{3}$$

Let us consider the case in which all the eigenvalues are selected to be equal (i.e., $c^{(m)} = c$ for all m). Then the product of the vector **u** with the matrix **T** as defined in Eq. (3) can be written as follows:

$$\mathbf{Tu} = c \sum_{m=1}^{M} d^{(m)}\mathbf{v}^{(m)} \tag{4}$$

Thus the output is a linear combination of the stored vectors only. In general, if the correlation between **u** and a stored vector $\mathbf{v}^{(m)}$ is large, the corresponding coefficient $d^{(m)}$ is also large. Therefore the stronger contribution to the output comes from the stored datum with which it correlates best.

The role of the null space spanned by the vectors **w** is crucial in this scheme. If the null space were removed by making M equal to N, then any vector **u** would be simply replicated at the output scaled by the eigenvalue c. Clearly such a system does not perform useful computation. In general the fidelity with which the stored datum that best matches **u** is produced decreases monotonically with the ratio (M/N). This imposes the limit on the storage capacity of the memory. We discuss the issue of storage capacity in more detail later.

If the matrix **T** is formed by summing the outer products of the vectors **v** with **u** (or the outer products of each vector **v** with itself in the case of autoassociations), then Eq. (1) is satisfied approximately as long as M is sufficiently smaller than N. The outer product scheme has been used extensively because of its simplicity and bypassing of the need to invert a matrix even though it is not in principle as powerful as the true eigensystem approach. Moreover, the outer product scheme has been proposed as a model for the way information may be stored in neural networks; basically it is a linear approximation to Hebb's hypothesis about learning (Hebb, 1949), and thus much of the work on associative memories that has come from neural network modeling deals with the outer product scheme. For the case of autoassociative memory the matrix **T** formed as the sum of outer products is given by

$$\mathbf{T} = \sum_{m=1}^{M} \mathbf{v}^{(m)}\mathbf{v}^{(m)t} \tag{5}$$

where $\mathbf{v}^t$ is the transpose of **v**. The product of a vector **u** with **T** is also a linear combination of the stored vectors:

$$\mathbf{Tu} = \sum_{m=1}^{M} d^{(m)}\mathbf{v}^{(m)} \tag{6}$$

with $d^{(m)} = \mathbf{v}^{(m)t}\mathbf{u}$. In this case there is no guarantee that the output will be one of the stored vectors even if the input **u** is one of the stored vectors.

However, as before, the output is a linear combination of the stored vectors, and the vector that correlates best with the input is amplified the most.

In general it is desirable that an associative memory produce at its output the stored vector most closely associated with the input **u** (i.e., perform a closest-neighbor search). The linear models discussed produce a linear combination of all the memories with the correct stored vector emphasized. Therefore they do not produce the correct result but an approximation to it; the desired vector can be thought of as the signal term and the rest of the vectors as an additive interference that produces a noisy estimate of the stored datum. If the input and stored vectors are restricted to binary values, then it is possible to restore the output of the linear memory to the stored binary vector simply by thresholding. Consider Eq. (6) which represents the output of the linear system in the outer product scheme. We require that

$$\text{sgn}[\mathbf{Tu}] = \text{sgn}\left[\sum_{m=1}^{M} d^{(m)}\mathbf{v}^{(m)}\right] \tag{7}$$

where $\text{sgn}[x] = 1$ if $x > 0$ and -1 otherwise. If Eq. (7) is satisfied, then the addition of thresholding to the linear associative memory yields the precise binary stored vector that has the maximum correlation with the input vector **u**. If we knew the precise conditions under which the condition in Eq. (7) is satisfied then we would have a complete characterization of the performance of this type of memory. We do not yet have the complete answer to this question. We know that if the input vector **u** is one of the stored vectors $\mathbf{v}^{(m)}$, then condition (7) is satisfied if $M < N/4 \ln N$ (Venkatesh and Psaltis, 1985; McElice *et al.*, 1986). This gives an estimate of the storage capacity for the outer product scheme, defined as the maximum number of binary vectors that can be stored in the matrix **T** such that the output is equal to the input vector for all the stored vectors.

When **u** is not exactly equal to one of the stored binary vectors, then the output of the system is in general a binary-valued vector that is an approximation to the stored vector that correlates best with the input. We can use this estimate as the input to the memory and obtain a new estimate that is in general a better approximation to the stored vector. When this procedure is repeated a sufficient number of times, the correct stored vector is produced as an output. If the storage capacity is not exceeded, then once one of the correct outputs is produced it keeps reproducing itself (i.e., a stable point is reached). Hopfield (1982) has shown that, when the vector **T** is symmetric, the outer product formulation that guarantees stability is reached; Venkatesh and Psaltis (1985) have shown that this is also true in almost all cases for the eigenfunction scheme. The radius of attraction around a stored vector is defined as the maximum number of bits that an input vector can differ on the average from a stored vector and still produce, as a stable output, the correct association. The number of locations at which two binary vectors differ is the Hamming distance between them. Clearly this measure is equally important to the storage capacity. To our knowledge a strong theoretical result for the radius of attraction does not exist. In the eigenfunction scheme it is relatively easy to see, however, that there is a direct inverse relationship between the storage capacity and the radius of attraction. M in this case can be as high as N if the stored vectors are linearly independent. However, at this extreme all input vectors simply reproduce themselves at the output. Thus the radius of attraction is zero for all stored vectors. If $M = 1$, then any input vector converges to the stored word or its complement; thus the radius of attraction is the maximum N bits in this case. Of course the cases of interest lie in between. A single metric that can be used in evaluating the performance of these memories is the product of the radius of attraction plus one and the storage capacity. In computer simulations it has been found that this product can exceed N (its value at the two extreme cases discussed above), but we do not know where the optimum operating point is.

III. Optoelectronic Implementation of One-Dimensional Neural Nets

The outer-product method for storing binary vectors in an associative memory, discussed in the previous section, is now considered in more detail in terms of the components of the stored vectors. Given a set of M bipolar, binary $(1, -1)$ vectors $v_i^{(m)}$ for $i = 1, 2, 3, \ldots, N$, $m = 1, 2, 3, \ldots, M$, these are stored in a matrix $\mathbf{T}$ in accordance to the outer-product recipe,

$$T_{ij} = \sum_{m=1}^{M} v_i^{(m)} v_j^{(m)} \qquad i, j = 1, 2, 3, \ldots, N, \qquad T_{ii} = 0 \qquad (8)$$

If the memory is addressed by multiplying the matrix $\mathbf{T}$ with one of these vectors, say $\mathbf{v}^{(m0)}$, it yields the estimate

$$\hat{v}_i^{(m0)} = \sum_{j=1}^{N} T_{ij} v_j^{(m0)} = \sum_j^N \sum_m^M v_i^{(m)} v_j^{(m)} v_j^{(m0)} \qquad (9)$$

$$= (N-1) v_i^{(m0)} + \sum_{m \neq m0}^{M} a^{(m)} v_i^{(m)} \qquad (10)$$

where

$$a^{(m)} = \sum_{j=1}^{N} v_j^{(m)} v_j^{(m0)}$$

and $\hat{v}^{(m0)}$ consists of the sum of two terms: The first is the input vector amplified by $(N-1)$; the second is a linear combination of the remaining stored vectors and represents an unwanted cross talk term. The value of the coefficients $a^{(m)}$ is equal to $(N-1)^{1/2}$ on the average (the standard deviation of the sum of $N-1$ random bits), and since $(M-1)$ such coefficients are randomly added, the value of the second term is, on the average, equal to $[(M-1)(M-1)]^{1/2}$. If N is sufficiently larger than M, then with high probability the elements of the vector $\hat{\mathbf{v}}^{(m0)}$ will be positive if the corresponding elements of $\mathbf{v}^{(m0)}$ are equal to $+1$, and negative otherwise. Thresholding of $\hat{\mathbf{v}}^{(m0)}$ will therefore return $\mathbf{v}^{(m0)}$:

$$v_i^{(m0)} = \text{sgn}\left(\sum_{j=1}^{N} T_{ij} v_j^{(m0)} \right) \tag{11}$$

When the memory is addressed with a binary-valued vector that is not one of the stored words, then the vector–matrix multiplication and thresholding operation yield an output binary-valued vector that, in general, is an approximation of the stored word that is at the shortest Hamming distance from the input vector. As pointed out earlier, if this output vector is fed back and used as the input to the memory, the new output is generally a more accurate version of the stored word; and continued iteration converges to the correct vector.

The insertion and readout of memories using the outer-product scheme is depicted schematically in Fig. 1. Note that in Fig. 1b the estimate $\hat{\mathbf{v}}^{(m0)}$ can be viewed as the weighted projection of $\mathbf{T}$. Recognition of an input vector that corresponds to one of the state vectors of the memory or is close to it (in the Hamming sense) is manifested by a stable state of the system. In practice unipolar binary $(0, 1)$ vectors or words $\mathbf{b}$ of bit length N may be of interest. The above equations are then applicable with $(2b_i - 1)$ replacing v_i in Eq. (8) and b_i replacing v_i in Eq. (9). For such vectors the

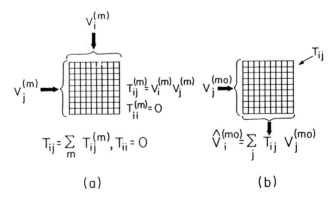

Fig. 1. Insertion (a) and readout (b) of memories.

SNR of the estimate $\hat{\mathbf{v}}^{(m0)}$ can be shown to be lower by a factor of the square root of two (Hopfield, 1982).

An example of the **T** matrix formed from four binary unipolar vectors, each being $N = 20$ bits long, is given in Fig. 2 along with the result of a numerical simulation of the process of initializing the memory matrix with a partial version of $b_i^{(4)}$ in which the first eight digits of $b_i^{(4)}$ are retained and the rest are set to zero. The Hamming distance between the initializing vector and $b_i^{(4)}$ is six bits, and it is nine or more bits for the other three stored vectors. It is seen that the partial input is recognized as $b_i^{(4)}$ in the third iteration, and the output remains stable as $b_i^{(4)}$ thereafter. This convergence to a stable state generally persists even when the **T** matrix is binarized or clipped by replacing negative elements by minus ones and positive elements by plus ones evidencing the robustness of the content addressable memory (CAMS). A binary synaptic matrix* has the practical advantage of being more readily implementable with fast programmable spatial light modulators (SLM) with storage capability such as the Litton LIGHTMOD (Ross *et al.*, 1983). Such a binary matrix, implemented photographically, is used in the optical implementation described below.

Several schemes for optical implementation of a CAM based on the outlined principle have been described. In one of the implementations (Psaltis and Farhat, 1985) an array of light-emitting diodes (LEDs) is used to represent the logic elements or neurons of the network. Their state (on or off) can represent unipolar binary vectors such as the state vectors $b_i^{(m)}$ that are stored in the memory matrix T_{ij}. Global interconnection of the elements is realized as shown in Fig. 3a through the addition of nonlinear feedback (thresholding, gain, and feedback) to a conventional optical vector–matrix multiplier (Goodman *et al.*, 1978) in which the array of LEDs represents the input vector, and an array of photodiodes (PD) is used to detect the output vector. The output is thresholded and fed back in parallel to drive the corresponding elements of the LED array. Multiplication of the input vector by the T_{ij} matrix is achieved by horizontal imaging and vertical smearing of the input vector that is displayed by the LEDs on the plane of the T_{ij} mask (by means of an anamorphic lens system omitted from Fig. 3a for simplicity). A second anamorphic lens system (also not shown) is used to collect the light emerging from each row of the T_{ij} mask on individual photosites of the PD array. A bipolar T_{ij} matrix is realized in incoherent light by dividing each row of the T_{ij} matrix into two subrows, one for positive and one for negative values, and bringing the light emerging from each subrow to focus on two adjacent photosites of the PD array that are electrically connected in opposition as depicted in Fig. 3b. In the system

---

*Strictly speaking such a matrix is ternary as it also contains zeros.

$b_i^{(1)}$	$b_i^{(2)}$	$b_i^{(3)}$	$b_i^{(4)}$
1	0	1	0
0	1	1	1
1	0	0	1
1	1	0	1
0	1	0	0
1	0	1	1
1	0	0	1
1	1	1	0
0	0	1	1
1	0	1	0
1	0	0	1
1	0	1	0
0	1	1	0
1	1	0	0
0	1	1	1
0	0	1	0
1	0	1	1
0	0	1	1
0	1	0	1
1	1	0	0

(a)

0	−2	0	−2	−2	2	0	2	0	4	0	4	0	0	−2	2	2	0	−4	0
−2	0	−2	0	0	0	−2	0	2	−2	−2	−2	2	−2	4	0	0	2	2	−2
0	−2	0	2	−2	2	4	−2	0	0	4	0	−4	0	−2	−2	2	0	0	0
−2	0	2	0	0	0	2	0	−2	−2	2	−2	−2	2	0	−4	0	−2	2	2
−2	0	−2	0	0	−4	−2	0	−2	−2	−2	−2	2	2	0	0	−4	−2	2	2
2	0	2	0	−4	0	2	0	2	2	2	2	−2	−2	0	0	4	2	−2	−2
0	−2	4	2	−2	2	0	−2	0	0	4	0	−4	0	−2	−2	2	0	0	0
2	0	−2	0	0	0	−2	0	−2	2	−2	2	2	2	0	0	0	−2	−2	2
0	2	0	−2	−2	2	0	−2	0	0	0	0	0	−4	2	2	2	4	0	−4
4	−2	0	−2	−2	2	0	2	0	0	0	4	0	0	−2	2	2	0	−4	0
0	−2	4	2	−2	2	4	−2	0	0	0	0	−4	0	−2	−2	2	0	0	0
4	−2	0	−2	−2	2	0	2	0	4	0	0	0	0	−2	2	2	0	−4	0
0	2	−4	−2	2	−2	−4	2	0	0	−4	0	0	0	2	2	−2	0	0	0
0	−2	0	2	2	−2	0	2	−4	0	0	0	0	0	−2	−2	−2	−4	0	4
−2	4	−2	0	0	0	−2	0	2	−2	−2	−2	2	−2	0	0	0	2	2	−2
2	0	−2	−4	0	0	−2	0	2	2	−2	2	2	−2	0	0	0	2	−2	−2
2	0	2	0	−4	4	2	0	2	2	2	2	−2	−2	0	0	0	2	−2	−2
0	2	0	−2	−2	2	0	−2	4	0	0	0	0	−4	2	2	2	0	0	−4
−4	2	0	2	2	−2	0	−2	0	−4	0	−4	0	0	2	−2	−2	0	0	0
0	−2	0	2	2	−2	0	2	−4	0	0	0	0	4	−2	−2	−2	−4	0	0

(b)

0	1	1	1	0	1	1	0	0	0	0	0	0	0	0	0	0	0	0	0	Partial input ($b_i^{(4)}$)	
−2	−4	6	4	−8	4	6	−4	2	−2	10	−2	−10	−2	0	−8	8	2	2	−2	1st Estimate	1st Iteration
0	0	1	1	0	1	1	0	1	0	1	0	0	0	0	0	1	1	1	0	1st Thresholding	
0	0	1	1	0	1	1	0	1	0	1	0	0	0	1	0	1	1	0	0	2nd Iteration	
0	1	1	1	0	1	1	0	1	0	1	0	0	0	1	0	1	1	1	0	3rd Iteration	Stable
0	1	1	1	0	1	1	0	1	0	1	0	0	0	1	0	1	1	1	0	4th Iteration	

(c)

Fig. 2. Numerical example of supplementing a partial input $N = 20$, $m = 4$. (a) Stored vectors, (b) interconnection or synaptic matrix, (c) results of initializing with a partial version of (b) showing convergence to a stable state on the third iteration.

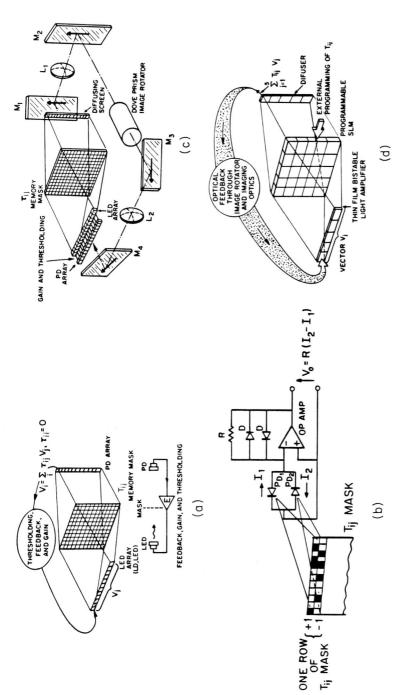

Fig. 3. Architectures for optical implementation of a content-addressable memory based on models of neural nets. (a) Matrix vector multiplier incorporating nonlinear electronic feedback, (b) optoelectronic scheme for realizing binary bipolar mask transmittance in incoherent light, (c) optical feedback scheme incorporating hybrid optical light amplifier array, (d) optical feedback with thin film bistable light amplifier and programmable connectivity matrix.

139

shown in Fig. 3a, feedback is achieved by electronic wiring. It is possible and preferable to dispose of electronic wiring altogether and replace it by optical feedback. This can be achieved by combining the PD and LED arrays in a single compact hybrid or monolithic structure that can also be made to contain all ICs for thresholding, amplification, and driving of LEDs. Optical feedback is particularly interesting when we consider that arrays of nonlinear optical light amplifiers with internal feedback (Porada, 1983), arrays of nonlinear optical switches (Gibbs *et al.*, 1981; Miller *et al.*, 1984) can be used to replace the PD/LED array. This can lead to simple CAM structures that may be interconnected to perform higher-order computations than the nearest-neighbor search performed by a single CAM.

A variation of the scheme presented in Fig. 3a was constructed to simulate optically a network of $N = 32$ neurons. The system, details of which are given below, was constructed with an array of 32 LEDs and two multichannel silicon PD arrays, each consisting of 32 elements. Twice as many PD elements as LEDs are needed to implement a bipolar memory mask transmittance in incoherent light in accordance to the scheme of Fig. 3b. A bipolar binary T_{ij} mask was prepared for $M = 3$ binary state vectors. The three vectors or words chosen, their Hamming distances from each other, and the resulting T_{ij} memory matrix are shown in Fig. 4. The mean Hamming distance between the three vectors is 16. A binary photographic transparency of 32×64 square pixels was computer-generated from the T_{ij} matrix by assigning the positive values in any given row of T_{ij} to transparent pixels in one subrow of the mask and the negative values to transparent pixels in the adjacent subrow. To insure that the image of the input LED array is uniformly smeared over the memory mask, it was found convenient to split the mask into two halves, as shown in Fig. 5, and to use the resulting submasks in two identical optical arms, as shown in Fig. 6. The size of the subrows of the memory submasks was made exactly equal to the element size of the PD arrays in the vertical direction, which were placed in register against the masks. Light emerging from each subrow of a memory submask was collected (spatially integrated) by one of the vertically oriented elements of the multichannel PD array. In this fashion the anamorphic optics required in the output part of Fig. 3a are disposed of, resulting in a simpler and more compact system. Further simplification can be achieved similarly by using an array of light-emitting line sources instead of the LEDs, which would dispose of the input optics and result in the compact associative memory chip concept depicted in Fig. 7. Considerable versatility can be added to such a chip by employing a computer-controlled dynamic nonvolatile SLM as a programmable synaptic mask as shown pictorially in Fig. 3d. Pictorial views of the input LED array and the two submask-PD array assemblies are shown in Figs. 8a and 8b, respectively. In Fig. 8b the left

Stored words:

```
Word 1 : 1 1 1 0 0 0 0 1 0 1 0 1 1 1 0 1 1 0 1 1 1 1 0 1 1 0 0 0 0 0 1 0
Word 2 : 0 1 1 0 0 0 0 0 0 0 1 0 0 1 0 1 0 1 0 0 1 1 1 1 0 1 0 1 1 0 1 0
Word 3 : 1 0 1 1 0 0 1 1 1 1 1 1 1 1 1 0 0 0 1 0 1 1 0 0 0 0 1 1 0 0 0 0
```

Hamming distance from word to word:

WORD	1	2	3
1	0	15	14
2	15	0	19
3	14	19	0

Clipped memory matrix:

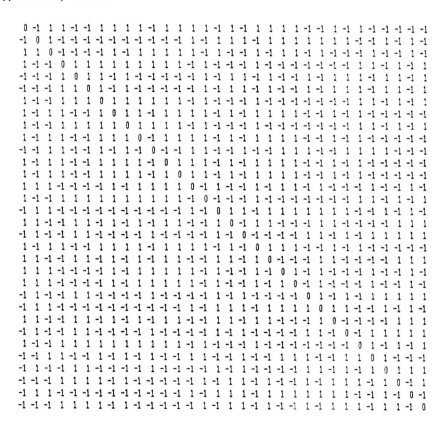

Fig. 4. Three stored words, their Hamming distances, and their clipped memory matrix.

Fig. 5. Two halves of binary memory mask.

memory submask-PD array assembly is shown with the submask removed to reveal the silicon PD array situated behind it. All electronic circuits (amplifiers, thresholding comparators, LED drivers, etc.) in the 32 parallel feedback channels are contained in the electronic amplification and thresholding box shown in Fig. 6a and in the boxes on which the LED array and the two submask-PD array assemblies are mounted (see Fig. 8). A pictorial view of a composing and display box is shown in Fig. 9. This contains an arrangement of 32 switches and a 32-element LED display panel whose elements are connected in parallel to the input LED array. The function of this box is to compose and display the binary input word or vector that appears on the input LED array of the system shown in Fig. 8a. Once an input vector is selected it appears displayed on the composing box and on the input LED box simultaneously. A single switch is then thrown to operate the system with the composed vector as the initializing vector. The final state of the system, the output, appears after a few iterations, displayed on the input LED array and the display box simultaneously. This procedure provides for convenient exercising of the system to study its response versus stimulus behavior. An input vector is composed, and its Hamming distance from each of the nominal state vectors stored in the memory is noted. The vector is then used to initialize the CAM, as described above, and the output vector representing the final state of the CAM, appearing almost immediately on the display box, is noted. The response time of the electronic feedback channels as determined by the 3-dB roll-off of the amplifiers was about 60 ms. Speed of operation was not an issue in this study, and thus low response time was chosen to facilitate hardware implementation.

The results of exercising and evaluating the performance of the system are tabulated in Table I. The first run of initializing vectors used in exercising the system were error-laden versions of the first word $b_i^{(1)}$. These were obtained from $b_i^{(1)}$ by successively altering (switching) the states of 1, 2, 3, ... up to N of its digits starting from the Nth digit. In doing so, the Hamming distance between the initializing vector and $b_i^{(1)}$ is increased linearly in unit steps as shown in the first column of Table I, whereas, on the average, the

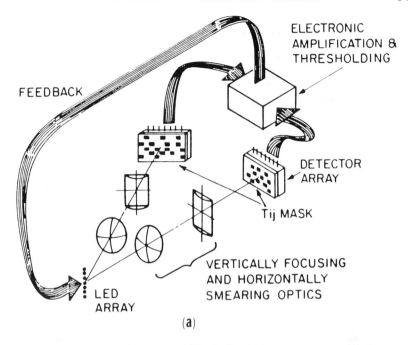

FEEDBACK

ELECTRONIC
AMPLIFICATION &
THRESHOLDING

DETECTOR
ARRAY

Tij MASK

VERTICALLY FOCUSING
AND HORIZONTALLY
SMEARING OPTICS

LED
ARRAY

(a)

(b)

Fig. 6. Arrangement for optical implementation of content addressable memory. (a) Optoelectronic circuit diagram, (b) pictorial view.

NONLINEAR FEEDBACK

THRESH.   AMP.

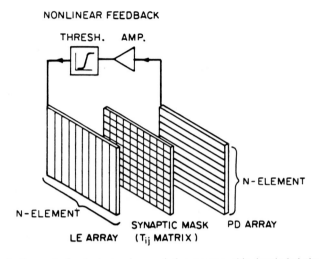

N-ELEMENT
PD ARRAY

N-ELEMENT
LE ARRAY

SYNAPTIC MASK
(T_{ij} MATRIX)

Fig. 7. Concept of optoelectronic associative-memory chip (exploded view).

Hamming distance between all these initializing vectors and the other two state vectors remained roughly the same, about $N/2 = 16$. The final states of the memory, that is, the steady-state vectors displayed at the output of the system (the composing and display box) when the memory is prompted by the initializing vectors are listed in column 2 of Table I. When the Hamming distance of the initializing vector from $b_i^{(1)}$ is less than 11, the input is always recognized correctly as $b_i^{(1)}$. The CAM is able therefore to recognize the input vector even when up to 11 of its digits (37.5%) are wrong. This performance is identical to the results obtained with a digital simulation, shown in parentheses in column 1 for comparison. When the Hamming distance is increased further to values lying between 12 and 22, the CAM is confused and identifies erroneously other state vectors, mostly $b_i^{(3)}$, as the input. In this range the Hamming distance of the initializing vectors from any of the stored vectors is roughly equal, making it more difficult for the CAM to decide. Note that the performance of the CAM and the resulting digital simulation in this range of Hamming distance are comparable except for the appearance of oscillations (designated by OSC) in the digital simulation when the outcome oscillated among several vectors that were not the nominal state vectors of the CAM. Beyond a Hamming distance of 22 both the optical system and the digital simulation identified the initializing vectors as the complement of $b_i^{(1)}$. This is expected because it can be shown using Eq. (1) that the T_{ij} matrix formed from a set of vectors is identical to that formed by the complementary set of the same

Fig. 8. (a) Pictorial views of input LED array and (b) memory submask/photodetector array assemblies.

vectors. The complementary vector can be viewed as a contrast-reversed version of the original vector.

Similar results of initializing the CAM with error-laden versions of $b_i^{(2)}$ and $b_i^{(3)}$ were also obtained. These are presented in columns 2 and 3 of Table I. Here again we see that when the Hamming distance of the initializing vector from $b_i^{(3)}$ ranged between 1 and 14, the CAM recognized the input correctly as $b_i^{(3)}$ as shown in column 3 of the table; and as such it did

Fig. 9. Word composer and final-state display box.

slightly better than the results of digital simulation. Oscillatory behavior is also observed here in the digital simulation when the range of Hamming distances between the initializing vector and all stored vectors approached the mean Hamming distance between the stored vectors. Beyond this range the memory recognizes the input as the complementary of $b_i^{(3)}$.

In studying the results presented in Table I, one can make several observations: The optically implemented CAM is working as accurately as the digital simulations and perhaps more accurately if we consider the absence of oscillations, which are believed to be suppressed in the system because of the smooth thresholding performed by the nonlinear transfer function of the electronic amplifiers compared with the sharp thresholding in digital computations. The smooth nonlinear transfer function and the finite time constant of the optical system provide a relaxation mechanism that substitutes for the role of the asynchronous switching that is required to provide convergence to a stable state (Hopfield, 1982). Generally the system is able to conduct successful nearest-neighbor searches when the inputs to the system are versions of the nominal state vectors containing up to about 30% error in their digits. It is worth noting that this performance is achieved in a system built from off-the-shelf electronic and optical components and with relatively little effort in optimizing and fine tuning the system for improved accuracy, thereby confirming the fact that accurate overall computation can be performed with relatively inaccurate individual components. It is also worth noting that despite accidental failure of two elements of the PD array, the net continued to perform as described in

TABLE I

Optical CAM Performance[a,b]

Hamming distance of initializing vector from $b_i^{(m)}$	Recognized vector ($m = 1$)	Recognized vector ($m = 2$)	Recognized vector ($m = 3$)
0	1 (1)	2 (2)	3 (3)
1	1 (1)	2 (2)	3 (3)
2	1 (1)	2 (2)	3 (3)
3	1 (1)	2 (2)	3 (3)
4	1 (1)	2 (2)	3 (3)
5	1 (1)	2 (2)	3 (3)
6	1 (1)	2 (2)	3 (3)
7	1 (1)	2 (2)	3 (3)
8	1 (1)	2 (2)	3 (3)
9	1 (1)	2 (2)	3 (3)
10	1 (1)	1 (1)	3 (3)
11	1 (1)	2 (2)	3 (3)
12	3 (3)	$\bar{3}, 2\,(\bar{3})$	3 (3)
13	3 (3)	$\bar{3}\,(\bar{3})$	$3\,(\bar{2})$
14	3 (3)	$1, \bar{3}\,(1)$	$3\,(\bar{2})$
15	1 (OSC)	1 (1)	$2, 3\,(\bar{2})$
16	3 (OSC)	1 (1)	$\bar{2}\,(\bar{2})$
17	3 (OSC)	1 (OSC)	$\bar{2}\,(\bar{2})$
18	3 (3)	$1\,(\bar{2})$	3 (OSC)
19	$3\,(\bar{2})$	$\bar{2}\,(\bar{2})$	$\bar{2}\,(\bar{2})$
20	$3\,(\bar{1})$	$\bar{2}\,(\bar{2})$	$\bar{2}\,(OSC)$
21	$1, 2\,(\bar{1})$	$\bar{2}\,(\bar{2})$	$\bar{3}\,(OSC)$
22	$3\,(\bar{1})$	$\bar{2}\,(\bar{2})$	$\bar{3}\,(OSC)$
23	$\bar{1}\,(\bar{1})$	$\bar{2}\,(\bar{2})$	$\bar{3}\,(OSC)$
24	$\bar{1}\,(\bar{1})$	$\bar{2}\,(\bar{2})$	$\bar{3}\,(\bar{3})$
25	$\bar{1}\,(\bar{1})$	$\bar{2}\,(\bar{2})$	$\bar{3}\,(\bar{3})$
26	$\bar{1}\,(\bar{1})$	$\bar{2}\,(\bar{2})$	$\bar{3}\,(\bar{3})$
27	$\bar{1}\,(\bar{1})$	$\bar{2}\,(\bar{2})$	$\bar{3}\,(\bar{3})$
28	$\bar{1}\,(\bar{1})$	$\bar{2}\,(\bar{2})$	$\bar{3}\,(\bar{3})$
29	$\bar{1}\,(\bar{1})$	$\bar{2}\,(\bar{2})$	$\bar{3}\,(\bar{3})$
30	$\bar{1}\,(\bar{1})$	$\bar{2}\,(\bar{2})$	$\bar{3}\,(\bar{3})$
31	$\bar{1}\,(\bar{1})$	$\bar{2}\,(\bar{2})$	$\bar{3}\,(\bar{3})$
32	$\bar{1}\,(\bar{1})$	$\bar{2}\,(\bar{2})$	$\bar{3}\,(\bar{3})$

[a] Values in parentheses are results of digital simulation.
[b] Values with overbars designate complementary vectors.

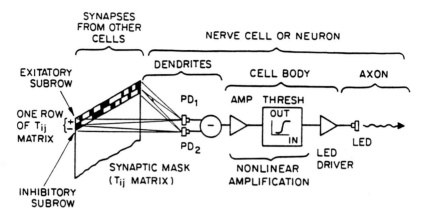

Fig. 10. Optoelectronic analog of a single nerve cell.

Table I (i.e., no noticeable change in performance was observed). In the above optoelectronic implementation, an artificial neuron can be divided into components that can be identified with their biological counterpart as shown in Fig. 10.

IV. Optoelectronic Implementation of Two-Dimensional Neural Nets

We now examine optoelectronic methods for storing and retrieving information arranged in two-dimensional format (e.g., images). Compatibility with two-dimensional data formats may be of practical interest in applications such as machine vision, and the potential exists for the optical implementation of networks containing larger numbers of neurons if they are arranged in two dimensions. The scheme that is described (Farhat and Psaltis, 1985) is a direct extension of the procedure for formation and readout of memories in the one-dimensional architecture discussed in the preceding section and summarized in Fig. 11. Given a set of two-dimensional bipolar binary patterns $v_{ij}^{(m)}$ with $i = 1, \ldots, N$, $j = 1, \ldots, N$, and $m = 1, \ldots, N$, these can be stored in an outer-product associative memory in the following manner: For each element of a pattern $v^{(m)}$ a new $N \times N$ matrix is formed by multiplying the value of this element with all the remaining elements of the matrix and setting the self-product equal to zero. The outcome is a new set of $N \times N$ binary bipolar matrices each having $N \times N$ elements. A formal description of this procedure is

$$T_{ijkl}^{(m)} = v_{ij}^{(m)} v_{kl}^{(m)} \tag{12}$$

which is a four-dimensional matrix. The overall memory matrix is formed

FORMATION OF T_{ij} MATRIX:

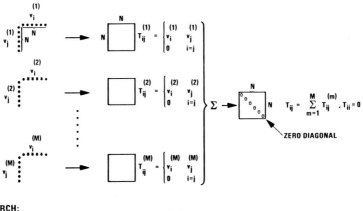

CAM SEARCH:

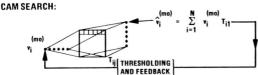

Fig. 11. Pictorial representation of formation and search of a two-dimensional connectivity matrix for a one-dimensional neural net.

by adding all matrices $T_{ijkl}^{(m)}$:

$$T_{ijkl} = \sum_{m=1}^{M} v_{ij}^{(m)} v_{kl}^{(m)} \tag{13}$$

A schematic representation of these procedures is given in Fig. 12.

Two-dimensional unipolar binary entities $b_{ij}^{(m)}$ are of practical interest. As in the one-dimensional case, these can be transformed into bipolar binary matrices by setting $v_{ij}^{(m)} = (2b_{ij}^{(m)} - 1)$ which are then used to form the T_{ijkl}. Also as in the one-dimensional case, the prompting entity can be unipolar binary $b_{ij}^{(m)}$, which would simplify optical implementations that use incoherent light.

Architectures for optical implementation of two-dimensional networks must contend with the task of realizing a fourth-rank memory matrix. Here a scheme is presented that is based on the partitioning of the four-dimensional matrix into an array of two-dimensional $N \times N$ submatrices.

Information is retrieved from this memory by forming, in a manner similar to Eq. (9), the product of an input $b_{kl}^{(m0)}$ with the four-dimensional matrix:

$$\hat{b}_{ij}^{(m0)} = \sum_{k,l}^{N} T_{ijkl} b_{kl}^{(m0)} \qquad i, j, k, l = 1, 2, \ldots, N \tag{14}$$

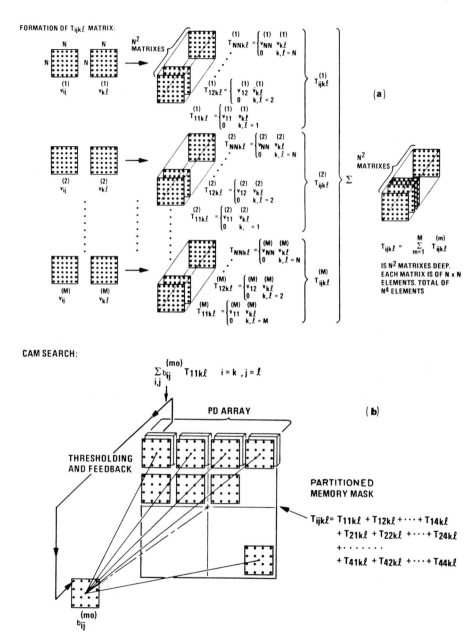

Fig. 12. (a) Formation of a four-dimensional connectivity matrix for a two-dimensional neural net and (b) memory search based on partitioning of the four-dimensional connectivity matrix.

This is followed by thresholding to obtain a new $N \times N$ matrix, which is used to replace $b_{kl}^{(m0)}$ in Eq. (14) for subsequent iterations. The procedure is repeated until the resulting matrix converges to the stored entity closest to the initiating matrix $b_{ij}^{(m_0)}$.

The operation in Eq. (14) can be interpreted as first partitioning of the four-dimensional T_{ijkl} matrix into a two-dimensional array of two-dimensional submatrices: $T_{11kl}, T_{12kl}, \ldots, T_{1Nkl}; \ldots, T_{21kl}, T_{22kl}, \ldots, T_{2Nkl};$ $\ldots, T_{N1kl}, T_{N2kl}, \ldots, T_{NNkl}$ as depicted schematically in Fig. 12b where the partitioned submatrices are arranged in a two-dimensional array. This first step is followed by multiplication of $b_{kl}^{(m_0)}$ by each of the partitioned submatrices, on an element-by-element basis and summing the products for each submatrix to obtain the first estimate $\hat{b}_{ij}^{(m_0)}$. A numerical simulation of a two-dimensional neural network of 5×5 neurons based on the above algorithm and partitioning of the T_{ijkl} memory matrix is presented in Figs. 13–15. Three two-dimensional unipolar binary entities $b_{ij}^{(m)}$, $m = 1, 2, 3$, are stored. These are shown in Fig. 13. The resulting T_{ijkl} matrix is given in Fig. 14 in partitioned form. The results of recall from partial versions (20%) of the three entities are presented in Fig. 15. These show that complete correct recall of each entity takes place after two iterations.

The summation operation called for in Eq. (14) is carried out in Fig. 12b by placing a spatially integrating photodetector behind each submatrix of the partitioned-memory mask which is assumed for the time being to be realized as pixel transmittance modulation in a hypothetical transparency capable of assuming negative transmittance values. The input entity $b_{ij}^{(m_0)}$, for example in Fig. 12b, is assumed to be displayed on a suitable LED array. The LED display of $b_{ij}^{(m_0)}$ is multiplied by the ideal transmittance of each partition submatrix by imaging the display on each of these with exact registration of pixels by means of a lenslet array as depicted in Fig. 16. The output of each photodetector, proportional to one of the components of Eq. 14, is thresholded, amplified, and fed back to drive an associated LED. The (i, j)th LED is paired with the (i, j)th photodetector. This completes the interconnection of the two-dimensional array of $N \times N$ neurons in the above architecture, where each neuron communicates its state to all other neurons through a prescribed four-dimensional connectivity matrix in which information about M, $N \times N$ matrices have been stored. The maximum number of two-dimensional entities that can be stored in this fashion is $M \approx N^2/(8 \ln N)$, which follows directly from the storage capacity formula for the one-dimensional neural-net case by replacing N by N^2.

The added complexity associated with having to realize a bipolar transmittance in the partitioned T_{ijkl} memory mask of Fig. 12b can be avoided by using unipolar transmittance. This can lead, however, to some degradation in performance. A systematic numerical simulation study (Lee and

NABIL H. FARHAT AND DEMETRI PSALTIS

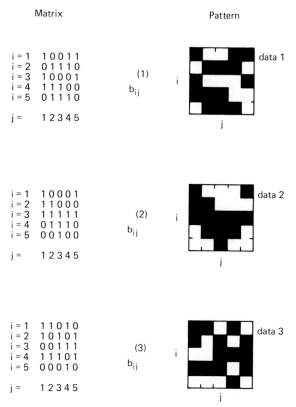

Fig. 13. Two-dimensional CAM simulation. Stored entities in matrix form (left) and in pictorial form (right).

Farhat, 1985) of a neural-net CAM in which statistical evaluation of the performance of the CAM for various types of memory masks (multivalued, clipped ternary, and clipped unipolar binary) and thresholding schemes (zero, threshold, adaptive threshold where the energy of the input vector is used as the threshold, adaptive thresholding and relaxation) was carried out. The results indicate that a unipolar binary memory mask can be used with virtually no sacrifice in CAM performance with the adaptive threshold and relaxation scheme. The scheme assumes an adaptive threshold proportional to the energy (light intensity) of the input entity displayed by the LED array at any time is used. The scheme of Fig. 12b can thus be realized by projecting an image of the input pattern directly onto an additional photodetection element. The detector output, being proportional to the total intensity of the input display, is used as a variable or adaptive threshold in a comparator against which the outputs of the PD elements positioned

	$k=1$	0	−1	−1	1	1	−1	0	1	1	−1	−1	1	0	−1	−1	1	1	−1	0	−1	1	−1	−1	−1	0
$i=1$	$k=2$	1	1	1	−1	−1	1	−1	1	−1	1	−1	−1	−1	1	1	−1	−1	1	1	1	−1	1	−1	1	−1
	$k=3$	1	−1	1	1	1	−1	−1	1	1	−1	−1	1	−1	−1	−1	−1	−1	−1	−1	1	1	1	−1	−1	1
	$k=4$	1	1	1	−1	−1	1	−1	−1	−1	1	−1	−1	−1	1	1	1	1	1	−1	1	−1	1	1	1	−1
	$k=5$	−1	−1	1	1	−1	1	−1	−1	1	1	1	1	−1	−1	1	−1	1	−1	1	−1	−1	1	1	−1	−1
	$k=1$	1	1	−1	−1	−1	1	−1	−1	−1	1	1	1	−1	1	−1	−1	−1	1	1	1	−1	1	1	1	−1
$i=2$	$k=2$	0	−1	−1	−1	1	−1	0	−1	1	−1	−1	−1	0	1	1	−1	1	1	0	−1	1	−1	1	−1	0
	$k=3$	−1	1	1	1	1	1	1	−1	−1	1	−1	−1	−1	−1	1	1	−1	−1	−1	−1	−1	−1	1	1	−1
	$k=4$	−1	1	1	1	1	−1	1	1	1	−1	1	1	1	−1	1	1	−1	−1	−1	−1	1	−1	−1	−1	1
	$k=5$	−1	−1	−1	−1	−1	−1	1	1	−1	−1	−1	1	−1	1	−1	1	1	1	1	1	1	−1	−1	1	1
	$k=1$	1	−1	−1	−1	1	−1	−1	1	−1	1	1	1	−1	−1	−1	1	1	−1	−1	−1	1	−1	−1	1	1
$i=3$	$k=2$	−1	1	−1	1	−1	1	1	−1	−1	−1	1	−1	−1	−1	1	1	−1	−1	−1	1	1	1	1	−1	−1
	$k=3$	0	1	−1	−1	1	1	0	1	1	−1	−1	1	0	1	1	−1	1	1	0	1	1	−1	1	1	0
	$k=4$	−1	1	1	1	−1	−1	−1	−1	1	−1	−1	1	1	1	1	−1	1	1	1	1	1	1	1	−1	−1
	$k=5$	−1	1	1	−1	−1	1	−1	1	−1	1	−1	−1	−1	−1	−1	−1	−1	−1	−1	−1	−1	−1	1	1	−1
	$k=1$	1	1	−1	1	−1	1	−1	−1	1	1	1	−1	−1	1	1	−1	−1	1	−1	1	−1	1	1	1	−1
$i=4$	$k=2$	−1	−1	1	1	1	1	1	1	−1	−1	1	1	1	−1	−1	1	1	−1	−1	−1	1	−1	1	−1	1
	$k=3$	−1	−1	−1	−1	1	1	−1	1	1	1	1	−1	1	1	1	1	1	1	1	−1	−1	−1	1	1	−1
	$k=4$	0	1	1	−1	1	1	0	1	−1	−1	1	1	0	−1	−1	−1	−1	−1	0	−1	1	−1	−1	−1	0
	$k=5$	−1	1	−1	1	−1	−1	−1	1	1	−1	−1	−1	1	1	−1	1	−1	1	−1	1	1	−1	−1	1	1
	$l=1$	−1	1	1	−1	−1	−1	−1	1	1	1	1	−1	−1	−1	1	1	1	−1	1	−1	−1	1	1	−1	−1
$i=5$	$k=2$	−1	−1	−1	1	1	−1	1	1	1	−1	−1	1	−1	1	−1	−1	−1	1	1	1	−1	−1	−1	1	1
	$k=3$	−1	1	−1	−1	−1	1	−1	−1	−1	−1	1	1	−1	−1	1	−1	−1	−1	−1	1	−1	1	−1	−1	−1
	$k=4$	−1	−1	−1	1	1	1	−1	−1	−1	−1	−1	1	1	1	−1	1	1	1	−1	1	−1	−1	−1	1	1
	$k=5$	0	1	−1	−1	1	1	0	1	1	1	−1	1	0	−1	−1	−1	1	−1	0	−1	1	1	−1	−1	0
	$i=$	1	2	3	4	5	1	2	3	4	5	1	2	3	4	5	1	2	3	4	5	1	2	3	4	5
	$j=$			1					2					3					4					5		

Fig. 14. Partitioned T_{ijkl} matrix of entities in Fig. 13.

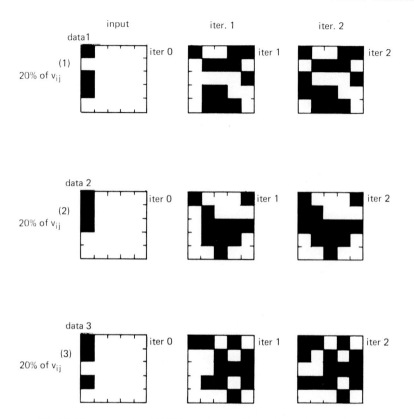

Fig. 15. Two-dimensional CAM simulation: Recognition of partial input.

behind the partitioned components of the T_{ijkl} memory mask are compared (subtracted). The comparator outputs are attenuated, and each is fed into a limiting amplifier with delayed feedback (relaxation). Each limiter–amplifier output is used to drive the LED that each photodetector is paired with. It is found (Lee and Farhat, 1985) that this scheme yields a performance equivalent to that of an ideal CAM with a multivalued connectivity matrix and zero thresholding. Note that although the initializing two-dimensional entities $b_{ij}^{(m_0)}$ are unipolar binary, the entity fed back after adaptive thresholding and limited amplification to drive the LED array are initially analog, resulting in multivalued iterates and intensity displays. However, after a sufficient number of iterations, the memory converges to the binary entities.

The ability to use unipolar binary memory matrices in the fashion described means that simple black-and-white photographic transparencies can be used as synaptic connectivity masks as suggested by the two schemes of Fig. 16. One scheme employs parallel optical feedback whereas the other

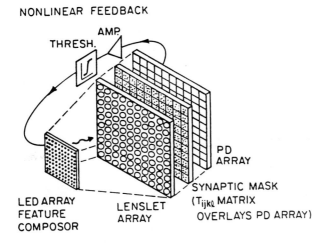

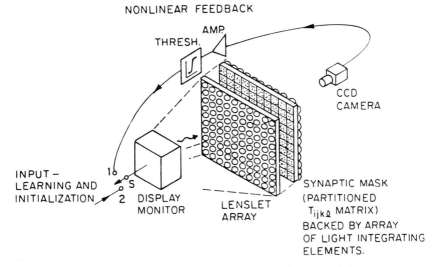

Fig. 16. Optoelectronic implementations of two-dimensional associative memory.

employs serial optoelectronic feedback. This latter scheme requires the use of a CCD television camera to enable time integration of the intensity distribution that is produced by the array of spatially integrating elements. These are diffusers situated behind each submask, and they randomly redistribute the light transmitted through each submask, thereby acting as integrating hemispheres. It is worth noting that this serial feedback scheme appears to be a novel means of achieving an arbitrary space-variant impulse

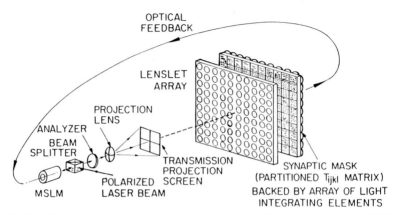

Fig. 17. Two-dimensional associative memory implemented with an electron-optic spatial light modulator.

response followed by a selected nonlinearity, which constitute two powerful operations in signal processing. A variation combining aspects of the above two schemes is shown in Fig. 17. In this arrangement, parallel nonlinear feedback is realized electron-optically with the aid of a microchannel spatial light modulator (MSLM) (Warde *et al.*, 1981; Warde and Thackara, 1982, also Chapter 7.2, this volume; Hara *et al.*, 1985, 1986). This device also provides an electronically controlled variable thresholding capability in which all parts of an output image relayed by the device falling below a given electronically adjustable intensity or brightness level are suppressed. The use of an MSLM in optical associative elements and computer architectures has also been described by Fisher, Giles and Lee (1985). An added advantage of a unipolar binary mask is the simplification in using a computer-driven nonvolatile spatial light modulator such as the Litton Magnetooptic SLM (Ross *et al.*, 1983) to realize a programmable CAM whose content can be altered, thus expanding its search capabilities using an electronic memory or a page-oriented holographic memory.

V. Holographic Associative Memories

Holography represents another link between optics and associative memories. It was recognized early (van Heerden, 1963; Gabor, 1969) that when a hologram of an object is recorded with a coded reference, the object is reconstructed when the hologram is illuminated with the same reference beam. Moreover, the reference beam can also be reconstructed by illuminating the hologram with the object beam. We can therefore think of the reference and object beams as being associated with each other. This is shown schematically in Fig. 18. The distinction in this case between an

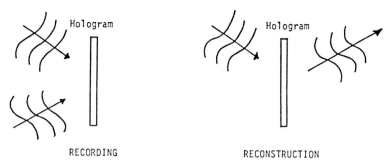

RECORDING   RECONSTRUCTION

Fig. 18. Holographic associative memory.

object and a reference becomes unimportant; we simply think of two patterns being associated with each other. Distorted partial versions of either pattern can also reconstruct the other, and if a portion of the recorded hologram is eliminated, the recorded pattern can be reconstructed with fidelity that degrades gradually as the portion of the hologram that is removed increases. These properties are reminiscent of the behavior exhibited by the outer-product associative memories discussed earlier. However, there is a crucial difference between holographic associative memories and the outer-product memories that limits our ability to store more than one pair of associated patterns on the same hologram.

To appraciate this distinction we consider a Fresnel hologram on which two separate pairs of associations are simultaneously recorded. Let f_1, f_2 and g_1, g_2 denote the two pairs and let the same symbols primed represent the Fresnel diffraction of the original patterns. The amplitude transmittance of the hologram can then be written as

$$T(x, y) = f_1'(x, y)f_2'^*(x, y) + g_1'(x, y)g_2'^*(x, y) + \text{bias terms} \qquad (15)$$

Now imagine this hologram being illuminated with a light beam that is modulated by the pattern $f_2(x, y)$, positioned with respect to the hologram in precisely the same manner as it was during recording. Then the light incident on the hologram is $f_2'(x, y)$, and the two terms of interest in the diffracted light are

$$f_1'(x, y)|f_2'(x, y)|^2 + g_1'(x, y)g_2'^*(x, y)f_2'(x, y) \qquad (16)$$

where $|f_2'(x, y)|^2$ is recognized as the intensity of the light diffracted from the object f_2. If the distance between f_2 and the hologram is sufficiently long, the intensity of the diffracted light will have very smooth variations. Consequently the first term of the reconstruction in Eq. (16) can be approximated by $f_1'(x, y)$. This diffracted light can be transformed with the aid of a lens to reproduce an image of f_1. If there is no special relationship between f_2 and g_2, the second term in Eq. (16) produces a highly convolved and unrecognizable image. In general the observed pattern due to this second term has a random, speckle like appearance, and its effect is to cause interference when we try to view the reconstruction of f_1. This behavior is also similar to that of the outer-product memory in that the "correct" association is obtained along with interfering cross terms. The difference is that the cross terms in the outer-product memory are suppressed by the square root of the space–bandwidth product of the input patterns. This does not happen in a hologram. In Eq. (16) the cross-product term is as strong as the first (signal) term. The only difference is that the reconstruction of the first term is recognizable as the pattern f_1 whereas the second term is noiselike. If we store two arbitrary images on the same hologram and reconstruct the hologram by illuminating it with one of the stored patterns, then on the average the signal-to-noise ratio of the reconstruction will be unity.

This limitation of holographic associative memories was perhaps recognized by Gabor who never mentioned the possibility of recording multiple associations on a single Fresnel hologram. It is, however, possible to record multiple associations using holography with one of two techniques: volume holography and multiplexing on planar holograms.

Sensitivity to the angle of illumination is a property that distinguishes volume from planar holograms. This property can be used to suppress the cross terms that appear in planar holograms; thus it is possible to store multiple associations in a volume hologram. Gaylord and coworkers at Georgia Tech (Guest and Gaylord, 1980) have explored associative memories using volume holography and have applied these memories to the optical calculation of look-up tables for performing binary multiplication. Here we shall discuss how multiplexed planar holograms can be used to synthesize associative memories that can store two-dimensional patterns and are functionally equivalent to the outer-product memories discussed in earlier sections.

The optical system shown in Fig. 19 was recently demonstrated experimentally (Paek and Psaltis, 1986) and is a modification of a system presented earlier (Psaltis and Farhat, 1985). As described in the previous section, the linear transformation that must be performed when we attempt to store two-dimensional patterns in an outer-product associative memory involves a four-dimensional kernel that cannot be directly implemented optically. Replacing the discrete one-dimensional vectors $v_i^{(m)}$ with continuous two-dimensional functions $f^{(m)}(x, y)$, we obtain the following four-dimensional function, which is analogous to the T_{ijkl} obtained in Eq. (13):

$$T(x, y, \hat{x}, \hat{y}) = \sum_m^M f^{(m)}(x, y) f^{(m)}(\hat{x}, \hat{y}) \tag{17}$$

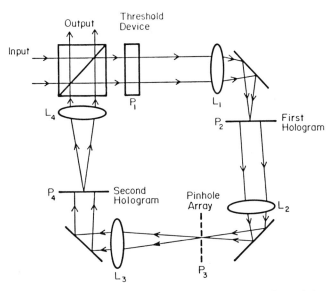

Fig. 19. Holographic implementation of a neural network model of associative memory.

We obtain an expression analogous to Eq. (10) for the output produced by the two-dimensional outer-product memory when it is addressed with an input image $f(x, y)$:

$$\hat{f}(\hat{x}, \hat{y}) = \iint T(x, y, \hat{x}, \hat{y})f(x, y) \, dx \, dy$$

$$= \sum_{m}^{M} \left(\iint f^{(m)}(x, y)f(x, y) \, dx \, dy \right) f^{(m)}(\hat{x}, \hat{y}) \qquad (18)$$

The two-dimensional integration over x and y in this equation is equivalent to a two-dimensional correlation between the images $f(x, y)$ and $f^{(m)}(x, y)$ evaluated at the origin of the correlation plane. This observation suggests that a coherent optical correlator (VanderLugt, 1964) can be used to implement each of these inner products. The overall system is shown in Fig. 19. An input image enters the system through the beamsplitter. A spatial light modulator is used in plane P_1 to detect the image incident on it and produce on its other side a thresholded version of the incident image. Lens L_1 produces at plane P_2 the Fourier transform of the light amplitude at P_1. A Fourier transform hologram is placed at P_2 that contains all the stored references. The hologram is constructed as shown in Fig. 20. The images that are to be stored in the memory are arranged side by side in a composite large transparency. A Fourier transform hologram of the composite is then

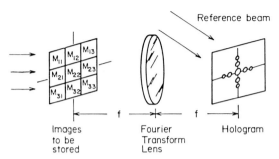

Fig. 20. Recording of the Fourier transform holograms used in the implementation of Fig. 19.

formed. Lens L_2 in Fig. 19 is also a Fourier transforming lens, which results in the light amplitude at plane P_3 being the correlation between the image at P_1 and the composite photograph. Due to the shift invariance of the optical correlator, the correlation patterns between the input and the individual images that make up the composite are formed spatially separated at plane P_3. Since we must keep only the inner products, not the full correlations (Psaltis *et al.*, 1986), an array of pinholes is placed at plane P_3 to sample each correlation pattern at its origin. Thus the amplitude of the light transmitted through each pinhole is approximately proportional to

$$\hat{f}^{(m)} = \int\int f^{(m)}(x - \hat{x}, y - \hat{y})f(x, y) \, dx \, dy \big|_{\hat{x}=0, \hat{y}=0}$$

$$= \int\int f^{(m)}(x, y)f(x, y) \, dx \, dy \qquad (19)$$

The light transmitted by each pinhole is collimated by lens L_3 and illuminates the second Fourier transform hologram placed at plane P_4. This second hologram is fabricated in the same way as the first and contains the same images. The final lens L_4 produces the Fourier transform of the light at plane P_4 back at plane P_1. Thus the optical system from P_4 to P_1 is also a correlator. If we approximate each pinhole by a delta function, then the light transmitted through each pinhole reconstructs the entire composite image stored in the hologram. The light transmitted though a pinhole on which the mth inner product is formed is located at plane P_3 at the position of the mth image in the composite photograph. As a result the reconstruction obtained at P_1 due to this pinhole is shifted such that the mth image appears centered around the optical axis. Therefore the light incident on plane P_1 is a superposition of all the stored images, each weighted by the appropriate inner product precisely as prescribed by Eq. (18). The spatial light modulator thresholds this light distribution, and the result becomes the input for the next iteration around the optical loop. When the system has reached stability, the result can be probed through the beam splitter as shown in Fig. 19.

VI. Conclusion

The implementation of optical associative memories described in this chapter establishes a link between neural network modeling and optics that we hope will prove useful in the implementation of optical information processing systems. A basic compatibility exists between what optics has to offer and what is required for the simulation of neural network models. As new models emerge and their sophistication increases, we can expect that optical implementations of these models will continue to show advantages over other approaches. Therefore neural networks and related models of computation may provide the appropriate algorithmic framework that will guide the development of optical information processing systems.

Acknowledgments

We acknowledge our colleagues Y. S. Abu-Mostafa, J. Hong, E. G. Paek, A. Prata, S. Venkatesh, and K. S. Lee with whom we have collaborated in several aspects of the work in this area.

This research is funded by DARPA as a joint project at Caltech and the University of Pennsylvania.

References

Amari, S. (1977). *Biol. Cybern.* **26**, 175–185.
Andersen, D. Z. (1986). *Opt. Lett.* **11**, 56–58.
Anderson, J. A., Silverstein, J. W., Ritz, S. A., and Jones, R. S. (1977). *Psychol. Rev.* **34**, 413–451.
Athale, R. A., Friedlander, C. B., and Kushner, B. G. (1986). *SPIE Semin. Proc.* **625**, 179.
Cohen, M. (1986). *SPIE Semin. Proc.* **625**, 215.
Condon, D. J., Reichenbach, M. C., Tarasevich, A., and Rhodes, W. T. (1985). *OSA Top. Meet. Opt. Comput., Incline Village, Nev.* Post-deadline pap., PD-2.
Farhat, N., and Miyahara, S. (1986). *Tech. Digest, Spring OSA Top. Meet. Signal Recovery Synth. II*, Hono, Hawaii, pp. 120–123.
Farhat, N., and Psaltis, D. (1985). *Tech. Digest, OSA Annu. Meet., Washington, D.C.* p. 58.
Farhat, N., Psaltis, D., Prata, A., and Paek, E. (1985). *Appl. Opt.* **24**, 1469–1475.
Fisher, A. D., Giles, C. L., and Lee, J. N. (1985). *Tech. Dig., OSA Top. Meet. Opt. Comput.* pp. WB4-1–WB4-4.
Gabor, D. (1969). *IBM J. Res. Dev.* **13**, 156–159.
Gibbs, H. M., McCall, S. L., and Venkatessan, T. N. C. (1981). *SPIE Semin. Proc.* **269**, 75–80.
Goodman, J., Dias, R. A., and Woody, L. M. (1978). *Opt. Lett.* **2**, 1.
Graph, H. P. (1985). *Workshop Neural Networks Comput., Santa Barbara, California.*
Grossberg, S. (1982). "Studies of Mind and Brain." Reidel, Dordrecht and Boston.
Guest, C., and Gaylord, T. (1980). *Appl. Opt.* **19**, 1201.
Hara, T., Sugiyama, M., and Suzuki, Y. (1985). *Adv. Electron. Electron. Devices* **64B**, 637–647.
Hara, T., Ooi, Y., Kato, T., and Suzuki, Y. (1986). *SPIE Semin. Proc.* **613**, 25.
Hebb, D. (1949). "Organization of Behavior." Wiley, New York.

Hecht-Nielsen, R. (1983). *SPIE Semin. Proc.* **360**, 180–189.
Hopfield, J. J. (1982). *Proc. Nat. Acad. Sci. USA* **79**, 2554–2558.
Kohonen, T. (1972). *IEEE Trans. Comput.* **C-21**, 353–359.
Kohonen, T. (1978). "Associative Memory." Springer-Verlag, Berlin and New York.
Kohonen, T. (1984). "Self-Organization and Associative Memory." Springer-Verlag, Berlin and New York.
Lambe, J., Thakoor, A. P., and Moopen, A. (1985). *JPL Rep.* **D 2825**.
Lee, K. S., and Farhat, N. (1985). *Tech. Dig. OSA Annu. Meet., Washington, D.C.* p. 48.
Little, W. A. (1974). *Math. Biosci.* **19**, 101–120.
Longuet-Higgins, H. C., Willshaw, D. J., and Buneman, O. P. (1970). *Q. Rev. Biophys.* **3**, 223–224.
McElice, R. J., Posner, E. C., Rodemich, E. R., and Venkatesh, S. (1986). Caltech Rep. Also, *IEEE Trans. Inf. Theory* (submitted).
Miller, D. A. B., Smith, D., and Colin, S. (1981). *IEEE J. Quant. Electron.* **QE-17**, 312–317.
Nakano, K. (1972). *IEEE Trans. Syst. Man Cybern.* **SMC-2**, 380–388.
Paek, E. G., and Psaltis, D. (1986). *Annu. Meet. Opt. Soc. Am., Seattle, Wash.* Abstr. I-MDD6.
Poggio, T., and Koch, C. (1985). *Proc. R. Soc. London, Ser. B* **226**, 303–323.
Porada, Z. (1983). *Thin Solid Films* **109**, 213–216.
Psaltis, D., and Farhat, N. (1985). *Opt. Lett.* **10**, 98–100.
Psaltis, D., Hong, J., and Venkatesh, S. D. (1986). *SPIE Semin. Proc.* **625**, 189.
Ross, W., Psaltis, D., and Anderson, R. (1983). *Opt. Eng.* **22**, 485–490.
Soffer, B., Dunning, G. J., Owechko, Y., and Marom, E. (1986). *Opt. Lett.* **11**, 118–120.
Tanguay, A. R., and Warde, C. (Eds.) (1983). Special issue on SLM's: Critical Issues, *Opt. Eng.* **22**, 663.
Tikhonov, A. N., and Arsenin, V. Y. (1977). "Solutions of Ill-Posed Problems." Winston, Washington, D.C.
VanderLugt, A. (1964). *IEEE Trans. Inf. Theory* **IT-10**, 139.
van Heerden, P. J. (1963). *Appl. Opt.* **2**, 387, 393.
Venkatesh, S., and Psaltis, D. (1985). *Workshop Neural Networks Comput., Santa Barbara, California.* Also, *IEEE Trans. Inf. Theory* (submitted), 1985.
Warde, C., and Thackara, J. I. (1982). *Opt. Lett.* **7**, 244–246.
Warde, C., Weiss, A. M., Fisher, A. D., and Thackara, J. I. (1981). *Appl. Opt.* **20**, 2066–2074.
Willshaw, D. J. (1971). Doctoral Dissertation, Edinburgh University, Scotland.
Willshaw, D. J. (1972). *Proc. R. Soc. London, Ser. B* **182**, 253–257.
Willshaw, D. J., Buneman, O. P., and Longuet-Higgins, H. C. (1969). *Nature (London)* **222**, 960–962.
Yariv, A., and Kwong, S. K. (1986). *Opt. Lett.* **11**, 183–186.

Temporal Signal Processing

3.1

Optical Architectures for Temporal Signal Processing

JOHN N. LEE

NAVAL RESEARCH LABORATORY

WASHINGTON, D.C. 20375-5000

I. Introduction

One-dimensional, serial data streams are predominantly the format encountered at the input of signal processors. This reflects the importance of time as a signal parameter and the high level of development of equipment and techniques for handling temporal data. Thus spatial data are often multiplexed into a time series, even when the data are intrinsically two-dimensional, for instance, in imagery where a temporal stream is formed by concatenating raster lines of a video display. The reasons for considering optical processing of such one-dimensional data include (i) very high bandwidth in the data channel, (ii) the existence of many channels of one-dimensional information, and (iii) a requirement to operate on a single channel repeatedly or over many variables simultaneously. Optics can be employed to implement particular operations at very high speed and/or many operations in parallel. On the most basic level, optics is capable of performing multiplication and addition of data samples, the former by mechanisms such as successive interactions with diffractive or transmissive-reflective media and the latter by mechanisms such as focusing light rays (space integration) or integrating photocharge (time integration). Multiplications and additions on arrays of data result in high-level mathematical operations. The most familiar of these larger operations is the Fourier transform integral, in which the multiplications and additions are incorporated in the basic structure of a single thin lens [1]. Another familiar example is the correlation integral. More generally it can be seen that optics has the capability for performing integral transforms. These examples involve signals in the continuous domain. Optics can, of course, also operate in discrete domains to perform operations such as the discrete Fourier transform (DFT), array beamforming [2], or more generally, matrix manipulations (e.g., matrix–vector multiplication). Many implementations have been considered and developed for these various operations. One finds, not surprisingly, that all approaches are not equally easy to implement nor are they equally suited to particular applications. A variety of architectural approaches to the basic mathematical operations are available, however, to accommodate various device limitations or differing application requirements. In the following section the basic operations are reviewed. Subsequent sections treat the various architectures for performing spectrum analysis, time-frequency analysis, and matrix manipulations needed in applications such as beamforming and associative processing.

II. Basic Operations

It is convenient to consider optics as capable of performing Fourier transforms, correlations, and matrix operations. This classification is somewhat artificial since there are clear connections between the classes, but it serves to emphasize potential applications.

A. FOURIER TRANSFORMATION

By placing a one-dimensional object having a complex transmission function

$$t(x_i) = a(x_i) \exp[-j2\pi b(x_i)] \tag{1}$$

a distance d in front of a lens of focal length f_l, as shown in Fig. 1, and illuminating with coherent light of wavelength λ, one obtains at one focal distance behind the lens the amplitude distribution [3]

$$U_f(x_f) = \frac{A \exp[(j\pi/\lambda f_l)(1 - d/f_l)x_f^2]}{j\lambda f_l} \int_L t(x_i) \exp\left[-j\frac{2\pi}{\lambda f_l}(x_i x_f)\right] dx \tag{2}$$

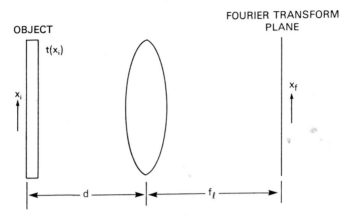

Fig. 1. Optical arrangement for Fourier transformation with a single lens.

where L is the spatial extent of $t(x_i)$, A is a constant, and the subscripts i and f arre used to denote the object and output spaces, respectively. When $f_l = d$, except for the finite limits on the integral, a Fourier transform of $t(x_i)$ results (to within a constant factor). The one-dimensional result given in Eq. (2) is obtained with a cylindrical lens. Use of a spherical lens results in a two-dimensional Fourier transform, but since the x and y variables in the exponential term in the integrand are separable, a spherical lens is usually used even for one-dimensional data. The optical arrangement of Fig. 1 is the most common for Fourier transformations. Alternative optical arrangements include (i) the use of two lenses separated by f_l with object and transform planes directly in front of the first lens and directly behind the second lens, respectively, and (ii) placement of the object between a single lens and its focal plane, which produces the proper Fourier transform amplitude but a curved phase front [3].

B. CORRELATION

The cross correlation of two signals $A(t)$ and $B(t)$,

$$R(\tau) = \int_T A(t)B(t-\tau)\, dt \qquad (3)$$

has a simple physical interpretation that is useful in optical implementation. A point-by-point multiplication is performed between overlapping portions of $A(t)$ and $B(t)$ at relative delay τ within a spatial aperture; optics is capable of performing this over large overlap intervals. (Spatial coordinates x_i are related to t by a constant factor such as the wave velocity in an acoustic-wave device.) There are two ways of implementing Eq. (3) at this point. In one approach the functions $A(t)$ and $B(t)$ are displayed over the spatial aperture with a particular value of $\tau = \tau_1$ as a relative time shift. The multiplied terms all along the aperture are summed (i.e., integrated) by focusing the light. The value for $R(\tau_1)$ is thus obtained. Shifting $B(t)$ relative to $A(t)$ a distance corresponding to an increment of τ to a new value τ_2 then leads to the calculation of $R(\tau_2)$, and so on. This procedure describes a space-integrating correlator. The shifting of $B(t)$ relative to $A(t)$ [i.e., generation of $B(t-\tau)$], is often performed with a traveling-wave device, such as an acoustooptic cell or an electronic shift register, and $R(\tau)$ is obtained as a time series from a photodetector. The space-integrating correlator requires that the functions not be longer than the aperture to ensure that the overlap region lies entirely within the aperture.

In the second approach to correlation one employs the multiplications that occur over a period of time at a particular point in a spatial aperture in which the two signals are traveling at the same velocity but in opposite directions. At any given point in the aperture the functions $A(t)$ and $B(t)$ are at a fixed τ for all times (e.g., $\tau = 0$ at the point where the functions first encounter each other). (Note: Broadcasting $A(t)$ over the aperture in which $B(t)$ is traveling has the same effect, although the total range of τ over the aperture is halved.) Hence, at a position corresponding to τ_1, one obtains $R(\tau_1)$ by integrating the products over the duration of the signals (e.g., by imaging onto a photodetector connected to a charge integrator). Other locations in the aperture x_i result in calculation of $R(\tau_i)$. This procedure describes a time-integrating correlator. In contrast to the space-integrating correlator there is no intrinsic limit on the length of the signals; hence very long signals can be employed and very high resolution obtained in the correlation function. On the other hand, the range of τ of the correlation function that can be displayed is limited by the spatial aperture, as will be discussed in more detail below.

An alternative description of this process can be related to the Fourier-transforming property of a lens. It can be shown that $R(\tau)$ can also be interpreted as multiplication in the Fourier transform domain [4], that is,

$$R(\tau) = \text{FT}[\text{FT}\{A(t)\} \cdot \text{FT}\{B^*(t)\}] \qquad (4)$$

where $\text{FT}\{A(t)\}$ and $\text{FT}\{B(t)\}$ are Fourier transforms of the respective functions, with FT denoting the Fourier transform operation. Implementation of the correlation integral is independent of which interpretation is used.

C. MATRIX ALGEBRA

Discrete data are generally formatted into vectors and matrices, and the basic operations on the data therefore involve scalar–vector, vector–matrix, and matrix–matrix manipulations. Also, matrix algebra is a paradigm for casting problems into a form amenable to parallel computation. The multiplications and additions required are performable with diffractive or transmissive optics. Of particular significance here is the ability of optics to broadcast light to, as well as combine light from, a number of data points, thereby allowing parallel computation (Fig. 2) for scalar–vector multiplication, vector–vector inner-product multiplication, vector–vector outer-product multiplication, and vector–matrix multiplication (optical components for shaping and directing the light beams have been omitted from the figure for clarity.) Matrix–matrix multiplications can be performed serially or in a single step. In the serial approach one can employ vector–matrix multiplication, in which a row of the first matrix (i.e., the vector) multiplies all the columns of the second matrix to produce one row of the resultant matrix at a time, or outer-product multiplication between corresponding columns of the first matrix and rows of the second, giving partial resultant matrices C_j as illustrated in Fig. 2c (with elements $c_{il} = a_{ij}b_{jl}$ formed for common index j); summing over all C_j gives the full matrix product. A single-step technique for matrix–matrix multiplication by performing many vector–matrix operations in parallel with the aid of holographic optical elements has also been proposed [5].

A significant aspect of optical matrix algebra processing is its potential applicability to any signal-processing problem expressible in a linear-algebraic formulation. In fact, the discrete version of the Fourier transform

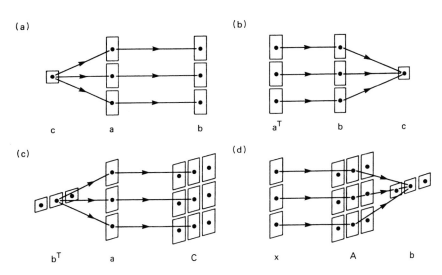

Fig. 2. Optical schemes for (a) multiplication of a scalar by a vector, (b) inner-product multiplication of two vectors, (c) outer-product multiplication of two vectors, and (d) multiplication of a vector by a matrix.

(DFT) and multichannel correlation are expressible as vector–matrix operations. The definition of the DFT,

$$G_k = \sum_{n=0}^{N-1} g_n \exp\left(-j\frac{2\pi nk}{N}\right) \tag{5}$$

is recognized as a product between the data vector $\{g_n\}$ and a matrix having as elements a_{nk}, the terms $\exp(-j\pi nk/N)$. A vector–matrix configuration can also easily be seen as a multichannel space-integrating correlator in which the vector is correlated against every column of the matrix.

Two important points need to be mentioned concerning the throughput possible with optically performed operations. One is that operations are usually carried out in the analog domain to maximize throughput. However, analog operation limits the number of possible grey levels to not much more than several hundred. This figure constitutes what may be considered the instantaneous dynamic range, or accuracy, of the processor, which is limited by factors such as spatial uniformity over an aperture. The full dynamic range can be much larger, processors having been built with dynamic ranges in excess of 60 dB [6], the range of signal amplitudes being limited by quantum noise or thermal noise at one end by signal accumulation capability at the other. Various encoding schemes have been investigated for obtaining high accuracy optical processors, but all entail some loss of throughput (see Chapter 6.1 by Casasent and Kumar and Chapter 6.2 by Caulfield).

A second limit on the throughput is due to the finite space-bandwidth (SBW) or number of resolvable spots in the aperture of any optical system. The SBW is ultimately determine by the limits imposed by optical diffraction. The angular spread of an optical beam due to a finite one-dimensional aperture of length L illuminated with light of wavelength λ is

$$\delta\theta \simeq \frac{\lambda}{L} \tag{6}$$

The maximum angular deflection of the light beam is directly proportional to the highest spatial frequency ν_{max} (i.e., $\theta_{max} \propto \lambda\nu_{max}$). Similarly, $\theta_{min} \propto \lambda\nu_{min}$. Since the spatial bandwidth B can be defined as $B = \nu_{max} - \nu_{min}$,

$$SBW = \frac{\theta_{max} - \theta_{min}}{\delta\theta} = LB \tag{7}$$

When one is using traveling-wave interactions, such as with acoustooptic devices, temporal apertures and bandwidths can be substituted in Eq. (7) to give a time-bandwidth product (TBW). For example, one-dimensional space-integrating optical correlators have been built with TBWs as high as 10,000 [6].

III. Spectrum Analysis of Continuous Functions

A lens-based Fourier transform as described above possesses intrinsic parallelism and speed, but this certainly does not mean such a transform technique applies equally well to all applications requiring spectral analysis. There are numerous, often conflicting, requirements in various applications, including (i) large numbers of points in the transform, (ii) high resolution in the transform, (iii) maximum speed in performing the transform or maximum input/ouput data rate, and (iv) maximum number of input channels. This section discusses architectures developed for meeting these requirements.

A. HIGH-SPEED TRANSFORMATION

Whereas the speed of the optical transform is ultimately limited by the transit time of the light from the object plane to the focal plane, actual speed is considerably slower; the input bandwidth is device-limited, or else the photodetection and readout of the transform is often the limiting factor. Input devices such as acoustooptic devices can be built with gigahertz bandwidths; hence the primary need has been to address bottlenecks at the outputs. Most available photodetector arrays integrate signals for some time interval (determining the ultimate output bandwidth for each channel), followed by a serial pixel-by-pixel readout of the array. The readout bandwidths available are often unable to accommodate the large transforms and the maximum input rates possible. A direct device-oriented approach is to increase the readout bandwidth using approaches such as a high-speed GaAs shift register line. An alternative device approach is to employ fully parallel readout of all pixels or serial–parallel readout involving small groups of pixels. However, device-oriented approaches often require specialized circuitry for implementation and subsequent post-processing. For example, large numbers of parallel channels may not be consistent with subsequent serial digital processing or rapid circuitry may be needed to reject channels that lack interesting information and to encode or multiplex remaining information-carrying channels.

An alternative that does not require new devices, but which involves a single high-speed photodetector channel, is the use of a correlation-based approach [7], often termed the chirp transform algorithm. This correlation approach is based on a reformulation of the Fourier transform integral

$$U(f) = \int_{-\infty}^{\infty} s(t) \exp(-j2\pi ft) \, dt$$

Substituting into the integral the identity

$$2ft = f^2 + t^2 - (t-f)^2$$

one obtains

$$U(f) = \exp(-j\pi f^2) \int_{-\infty}^{\infty} s(t) \exp(-j\pi t^2) \exp(j\pi(t-f)^2 \, dt \qquad (8)$$

Implementation of this equation can be done in three steps. In the integrand of Eq. (8) one can consider the input function $s(t)$ to be multiplied by the quadratic phase term $\exp(-j\pi t^2)$, known as a chirp or a linear FM, since there is a linear rate of frequency change. This is then followed by correlation with a second chirp, $\exp(j\pi(t-f)^2)$. Finally, the correlation result is post-multiplied by the third chirp, $\exp(-j\pi f^2)$, to obtain the proper phase function in the Fourier transform. The correlation operation is the most demanding portion of this algorithm and has therefore been the portion performed optically [6]. To obtain a temporal output in a single channel the correlation integral must be performed over a spatial domain (i.e., the variable t is a spatial one). In this case the size of the transform is determined by the time-bandwidth of the optical processing system. (In any case the number of transform points calculated is equal to the time-bandwidth.) It must also be noted that the chirp-multiplied signal must fill the aperture of the correlator before meaningful results are obtained (i.e., a single channel operates with at most a 50% duty fraction). Hence to obtain 100% time coverage two parallel channels must be employed in an alternating or "ping-pong" mode. A 1000-point space-integrating transform has been experimentally demonstrated at a bandwidth of 100 MHz and with about a 60-dB dynamic range [6].

The speed at which spectrum analysis must be performed is also driven by the need to obtain other signal parameters. In particular, measurement of the time of arrival (TOA) of a signal with high precision from spectral data requires that the transforms be performed in times consistent with the desired precision. However, TOA precision is inversely related to frequency resolution since the time aperture for the transform is directly related to TOA but inversely related to resolution.

B.   LARGE HIGH-RESOLUTION TRANSFORMS

The size of a one-dimensional Fourier transform performed using a lens as illustrated in Fig. 1 is limited by both the aperture and the bandwidth of the input device according to Eq. (7). Presently the limit for such a transform is about 2000 points. However, it is possible to obtain a very large one-dimensional transform by using two-dimensional optical processing techniques.

By breaking a long one-dimensional signal into N horizontal lines, each $1/N$ the length of the entire signal, and displaying the lines in a two-dimensional raster format, one above the other as in a video display, one can produce a two-dimensional "folded spectrum" of the signal [8]. The input raster lines are Fourier transformed with a two-dimensional spherical lens as shown in Fig. 1. If the input raster lines are of length a, then the Fourier transform of these lines results in a coarse spectrum consisting of spots separated by distances $\lambda f_l/a$ (i.e., diffraction-limited), where f_l is the focal length of the lens. The vertical spacing b of the input raster lines produces results like those with a diffraction grating; the vertical Fourier-transform pattern repeats at intervals of $\lambda f_l/b$. The bandwith of each coarse resolution cell is spread over one such vertical interval. Thus the output can be described by almost-vertical lines (orthogonal to the input raster), where the individual lines cover a small spectral bandwidth determined by the width of one coarse resolution cell or, equivalently, the length of the input raster line. The resolution in each output line is inversely related to the total length of the input signal.

The folded-spectrum technique described above employs space integration (i.e., the raster lines must display the entire one-dimensional signal). Hence a two-dimensional raster display technique with storage capability must be used. Data have been displayed using film written with a scanning light beam and with various video displays, including cathode ray tubes with long-image persistence times and liquid crystal display devices. However, it is not always desirable or possible to employ space-integrating techniques (e.g., due to device limitations). Time-integrating techniques can also be employed, especially when extremely high resolution is desired. The approach most suited to time-integration is use of the chirp transform algorithm.

The chirp transform algorithm expressed by Eq. (8) can also be implemented with integration over the time domain. By using a time-integrating correlator, described in Section II, one can employ a very long-duration chirp to obtain very large TBW or high resolution. Use of only one traveling-wave cell, however, limits the range of the output display as discussed earlier. A natural approach, therefore, is to extend the chirp transform to two dimensions, using one dimension to perform coarse frequency analysis with a fast chirp (short duration) and using fine frequency analysis with a slow chirp along the other dimension to fill in the frequencies between adjacent coarse-frequency bins. This may be implemented with the two-dimensional correlation function

$$R(\tau_x, \tau_y) = \int_T f_1(t)f_2(t - \tau_x)f_3(t - \tau_y) \, dt \tag{9}$$

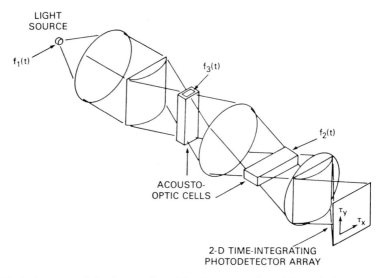

Fig. 3. Acoustooptic implementation of the time-integrating triple-product processor.

where $f_1 = S(t)c_1(t)c_2(t)$, with $S(t)$ the function to be analyzed, $f_2 = c_1(t) = \exp(jat^2/2)$, and $f_3 = c_2(t) = \exp(jbt^2/2)$. The slow chirp ($c_1$) has a period equal to the integration period T and determines the fine frequency resolution. The fast chirp is made to repeat many times during the integration period. It can be shown that a chirp transform performed with a chirp that repeats during the integration period produces a comb-filtered or discrete version of the spectrum, with comb-element width determined by the chirp bandwidth, and the number of comb elements equal to the number of times the chirp has been repeated [9]. Hence the output obtained from a two-dimensional time-integrating detector array is the same output raster as for the space-integrating case described above. A particular implementation of the two-dimensional chirp transform using orthogonal acoustooptic cells is shown in Fig. 3; this processor is actually a much more general one known as the time-integrating triple-product processor.

IV. Time–Frequency Analysis

It is well known that one-dimensional signals can be analyzed in a two-dimensional space to obtain more complete information about the signal (e.g., to allow signal identification or target characterization in radar or sonar). The most familiar of such two-dimensional mappings involves the generation of various time–frequency representations for the one-dimensional signals, which combine spectral analysis with temporal analysis. It is natural to look at optical-processing techniques, which possess inherent two-dimensional parallel processing capabilities, as a means of obtaining the desired two-dimensional representations. Consider first the familiar cross-ambiguity function (CAF), which gives the cross-correlation between the two signals along one axis, while along the orthogonal axis the correlation is seen as a function of the relative doppler frequency shift between the two signals. The CAF is defined mathematically as

$$A(\mu, \tau) = \int s_1(t) s_2^*(t - \tau) \exp(-j\pi\mu t) \, dt \tag{10}$$

where $s_1(t)$ and $s_2(t)$ are the two signals, μ the Doppler frequency, and τ the correlation shift variable. One way that Eq. (10) can be implemented is by time integration, using the triple-product processor of Fig. 3 and using the following as inputs to the processor: $f_1(t) = r_1(t) \exp(-jt^2/2)$, $f_2(t) = r_2(t)$, and $f_3(t) = \exp(+jt^2/2)$, where $r_1(t)$ and $r_2(t)$ are the real parts of $s_1(t)$ and $s_2(t)$, respectively. With the correct diffraction orders, Eq. (9) which describes the processor, becomes

$$R(\tau_x, \tau_y) = \exp\left(\frac{+j\tau_y^2}{2}\right) \int_T s_1(t) s_2^*(t - \tau_x) \exp(-j\tau_y t) \, dt \tag{11}$$

Comparison of Eqs. (10) and (11) shows that with phase weighting by the factor $\exp(-j\tau_y^2/2)$, one obtains the CAF where $\tau = \tau_x$ and $\mu = \tau_y/2\pi$.

It is also possible to generate $A(\mu, \tau)$ with a space-integrating technique that is also very illustrative. Simple modifications in the basic optical configuration used in the space-integrating technique also produce a variety of other time-frequency representations [10]. The basic optical configuration that has been developed for the generation of two-dimensional representations is briefly reviewed and is shown schematically in Fig. 4. A light source

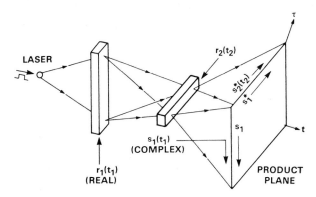

Fig. 4. Optical configuration to produce the complex product plane $s_1 s_2^*$ from real signals r_1 and r_2.

such as a laser diode is followed by two one-dimensional modulators oriented orthogonally to produce a two-dimensional product plane consisting of all possible cross products between the components of signals $s_1(t)$ and $s_2^*(t)$ displayed in the apertures of the one-dimensional modulators. The laser is pulsed if traveling-wave light modulators are employed as shown in Fig. 4. (Not shown in Fig. 4 are the optics required to collimate, expand, and shape the laser beam and the optics to produce images of the one-dimensional modulators in a common plane.) We also note, but shall not discuss, the capability to generate complex functions, such as $s_2^*(t)$ from real input $r_2(t)$, using light modulators. The configuration of the optics following the product plane determines the particular two-dimensional representation produced.

1. Cross-Ambiguity Functions (CAF)

This function, described by Eq. (10), can be produced by a spherical lens–cylindrical lens combination that images along one diagonal direction of the product plane and Fourier transforms along the other diagonal direction (Fig. 5). The imaging operation is along a direction that picks out those products corresponding to the kernel of a correlation integral; hence the imaged diagonal direction corresponds to the correlation time axis (τ). The Fourier transform implements the remainder of the ambiguity function integral; hence the direction of this diagonal corresponds to the Doppler axis (μ). By choosing a spherical lens of focal length f_l and placing it a distance f_l from the product plane $s_1 s_2^*$, a Fourier transform plane is produced a distance f_l beyond the lens. Addition of a cylindrical lens of focal length f_l produces imaging along the power direction of the cylinder at the same location as the Fourier transform plane (since the focal length of the spherical–cylindrical lens combination is $f_l/2$).

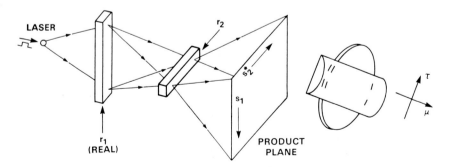

Fig. 5. Optical configuration to produce the cross-ambiguity functions.

2. Cross-Wigner Function

A spherical–cylindrical lens combination identical to that for the CAF is used, except that the linear axis of the cylinder is oriented along the other diagonal of the product plane, as shown in Fig. 6, to implement the cross-Wigner integral $W(t, \nu_0)$, defined as

$$W(t, \nu_0) = \int s_1(\tau)s_2^*(t-\tau)\exp(-j2\pi\nu_0\tau)\,d\tau \tag{12}$$

As a result of the reorientation of the cylinder the convolution of the signals is represented along one axis (t) whereas the mean frequency of the signals is represented along the other axis (ν_0).

3. Instantaneous Power Spectrum (IPS)

For a single signal $s_1(t)$, the IPS function

$$I(t, \nu) = s_1(t)\tilde{s}_1^*(\nu)\exp(-j2\pi\nu t) \tag{13}$$

where $\tilde{s}_1(\nu)$ is the Fourier transform of $s_1(t)$, produces the frequency spectrum of the signal as a function of time. Here the inputs to the one-dimensional modulators are identical, giving a product plane denoted by $s_1(t)s_1^*(t)$. Again the same spherical–cylindrical lens combination is used as for the CAF and the Wigner function, except that the cylinder is oriented parallel to one of the axes of the product plane (Fig. 7). The $s_1(t)$ is displayed along the t axis, whereas the frequency spectrum is displayed along the ν axis.

4. Mean-Frequency Selective Correlation (MFC) and Doppler-Frequency Selective Convolution (DFC)

For the special case of AM, monofrequency-carrier, signals, two new time-frequency distributions can be defined. These correspond to mean-frequency selective correlation (MFC) and Doppler-frequency selective

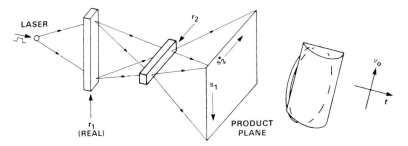

Fig. 6. Optical configuration to produce the cross-Wigner function.

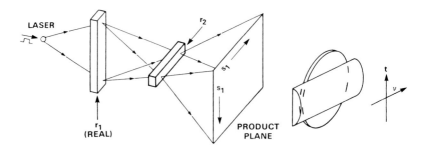

Fig. 7. Optical configuration to produce the instantaneous power spectrum.

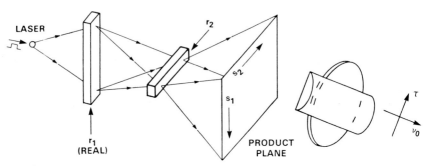

Fig. 8. Optical configuration to produce the mean-frequency selective correlation between two AM monofrequency signals.

convolution (DFC) [Eqs. (14) and (15)] and are convenient to implement on the same processors as for the CAF and the Wigner function, respectively (see Figs. 8 and 9):

$$\text{MFC:} \quad M(\nu_0, \tau) = \int_{-\infty}^{\infty} s_1(t)s_2(t-\tau)\exp(-j2\pi\nu_0 t)\, dt \qquad (14)$$

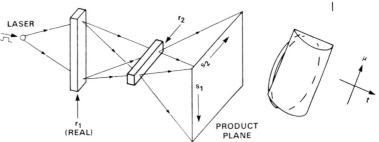

Fig. 9. Optical configuration to produce the Doppler-frequency selective convolution between two AM monofrequency signals.

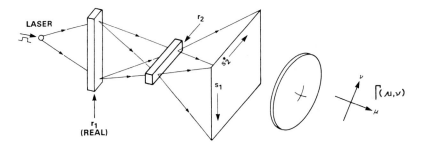

Fig. 10. Optical configuration to produce the cyclostationary function.

$$\text{DFC:} \qquad N(t_0, \mu) = \int_{-\infty}^{\infty} s_1(\tau) s_2(t - \tau) \exp(-j2\pi\mu\tau) \, d\tau, \qquad (15)$$

where $s_1(t)$ and $s_2(t)$ are complex representations of the real AM signals. Note the absence of conjugation in the integrals of Eqs. (14) and (15). By using $s_1(t) = a_1(t) \exp(j2\pi\nu_1 t)$ and $s_2(t) = a_2(t) \exp(j2\pi\nu_2 t)$ and applying the principle of stationary phase, we see that the main contribution of $M(\nu_0, \tau)$ occurs at $\nu_0 = \nu_1 + \nu_2$, whereas that to $N(t_0, \mu)$ occurs at $\mu = \nu_2 - \nu_1$. $M(\nu_0, \tau)$ at $\nu_0 = \nu_1 + \nu_2$ gives cross correlation between $a_1(t)$ and $a_2(t)$, and $N(t_0, \mu)$ at $\mu = \nu_2 - \nu_1$ gives cross convolution between $a_1(t)$ and $a_2(t)$. Thus it can be seen that MFC and DFC combine the properties of the ambiguity function and the Wigner distribution in an interesting fashion. In particular the auto-MFC provides a unique description of a multicomponent signal by displaying the autocorrelation functions of the various components while simultaneously giving information about their carrier frequencies.

5. Cyclostationary Function

This function, denoted $\Gamma(\mu, \nu)$ in Fig. 10, is produced by using only the spherical lens in the processors described above in a Fourier transform configuration. $\Gamma(\mu, \nu)$ can be recognized as the Fourier transform of the CAF along the τ axis. This function is useful for analysis of signals that have an underlying repetitiveness [11].

V. Discrete Operations

Discreteness often occurs in signal processing for a number of reasons. Data often can be sampled only at regular time intervals rather than continuously. A sensor array produces a corresponding number of data channels that need to be combined to obtained some processing gain over a single sensor channel; at any instant of time these channels constitute discrete data inputs to a processor. The important class of linear shift-invariant transforms (or filters) of data sequences has been the most common one considered for optics for implementation of spectrum analysis, correlation, frequency filtering, and so on. The general approach is to "tap" at points along the data sequence, multiply (e.g., by weighting factors or other data), and sum. Hence the next section discusses the implementation of the discrete Fourier transform as a general example of techniques for transformation of discrete data. Transformations of discrete data streams in applications such as beamforming and associative processing are then discussed.

A. DISCRETE FOURIER TRANSFORM ARCHITECTURES

In Section II it was shown how the discrete Fourier transform (DFT) could be performed as a vector–matrix multiplication. To avoid the requirement for a two-dimensional light modulator for the matrix, the DFT can be recast in a form resembling a discrete correlation. Writing the DFT of a sample set $\{g_n\}$ as

$$G_k = \sum_{n=0}^{N-1} g_n \exp\left(\frac{-j2\pi nk}{N}\right) \qquad (16)$$

one makes the substitution of the identity

$$nk = \frac{(k+n)^2 - (k-n)^2}{4} \qquad (17)$$

to obtain [12]

$$G_k = \sum_{n=0}^{N-1} g_n \exp\left(\frac{-j\pi(k+n)^2}{2N}\right) \exp\left(\frac{j\pi(k-n)^2}{2N}\right) \qquad (18)$$

The two exponential terms in Eq. (18) can be generated using a single complex chirp (not necessarily discrete) and propagation in opposite directions in a spatial aperture. By spatially arraying the N samples $\{g_n\}$ in the aperture at regular intervals, one can perform the required multiplications and additions. This corresponds to the space-integrating architecture, and as in a space-integrating correlator, a temporal output results. It is easily shown that if a real chirp is used in the implementation, the output contains the real and imaginary parts of the DFT in quadrature [13]. In a time-integrating architecture a data sample is uniformly spread over the aperture, and one steps through the data sequence in unison with the flow of chirps through the aperture [14]. The DFT results appear as a spatial pattern on a one-dimensional detector array, the positioning of the display being dependent on the relative time shift between the data sequence and the chirp signals.

The DFT of a large set of N samples can be obtained in entirety by a two-step process. If N can be factored as $N = N_1 N_2$, one can substitute the quantities $n = n_1 N_2 + n_2$ and $k = k_1 + k_2 N_1$ into the DFT equation to obtain [12]

$$G_{k_1 + k_2 N_1} = \sum_{n_2=0}^{N_2-1} \exp\left(\frac{-j2\pi k_2 n_2}{N_2}\right) \exp\left(\frac{-j2\pi k_1 n_2}{N_2 N_1}\right)$$

$$\times \sum_{n_1=0}^{N_1-1} \left[g_{n_1 N_2 + n_2} \exp\left(-\frac{j2\pi k_1 n_1}{N_1}\right) \right] \qquad (19)$$

A long one-dimensional transform can therefore be achieved by first performing a DFT of size N_1 and then multiplying by the phase factor

$$\exp\left(\frac{-j2\pi k_1 n_2}{N_2 N_1}\right)$$

and finally performing a second DFT of size N_2.

B. BEAMFORMING

The temporal outputs of an array of sensors may be combined to obtain enhanced detection of a signal source that produces a coherent wavefront at some angle α to the array, as illustrated in Fig. 11. The angular location of the source is obtained, and there is a signal-to-noise gain due to rejection

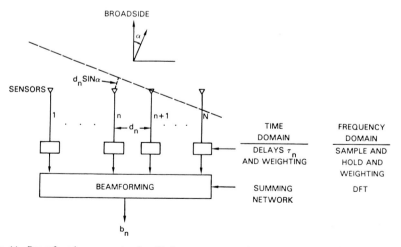

Fig. 11. Beamforming geometry for N-element array to detect plane-wave signal at angle α.

of localized interference not in the "beam" and to the small angle of acceptance by the beam for distributed background noise. Since one is dealing with a number of separate sensor channels, the beamforming operation is necessarily discrete in nature; additionally the data from each channel may be sampled rather than continuous. Beams may be formed using either time-domain or frequency-domain algorithms. The time-domain methods involve time-delaying, shading, and summing of the sensor outputs. With appropriate time delays, it can be easily seen that sensor signals x_n resulting from the same source add coherently to give an output

$$b(t) = \sum_{n=1}^{N} a_n x_n(t - \tau_n) \tag{20}$$

where τ_n is the delay applied to the nth sensor in an array of size N, and a_n is a constant weighting coefficient. The time delays are related to the angular location of the source from the boresight direction ($\alpha = 0$ in Fig. 11); between adjacent sensors the relative change in delay is

$$\tau_{n+1} - \tau_n = \frac{d_n \sin \alpha}{v}$$

(Fig. 11), where d_n is the spacing between the nth and $(n+1)$th sensor in the array, and v the signal velocity. For an equally spaced array all delays are a multiple of a basic τ. To obtain a second beam in a different-look direction, a different set of τ_n must be applied.

In frequency-domain methods a signal at frequency f_0 and angle α produces a differential phase term between adjacent sensors of

$$\exp\left[j2\pi f_0\left(\frac{d_n \sin \alpha}{v}\right)\right]$$

For an N-element array with equal sensor spacings d, the phase-shift term at the nth sensor relative to the first sensor is

$$\exp\left[j2\pi f_0\left(\frac{d \sin \alpha}{v}\right)n\right]$$

If the sensor signals x_n are sampled at some instant of time and summed, one obtains (with wavelength $\lambda = f_0/v$)

$$b = \sum_{n=0}^{N-1} x_n \exp\left[j\pi\left(\frac{d \sin \alpha}{\lambda}\right)n\right]$$

To obtain signal gain, each term must be multiplied by a phase factor. For reasons soon to be apparent the phase factor is chosen as

$$\exp\left(-j\frac{2\pi}{N}nk\right)$$

The new summation is

$$b_k = \sum_{n=0}^{N-1} x_n \exp\left[-j2\pi\left(\frac{d\sin\alpha}{\lambda}\right)n\right]\exp\left(j\frac{2\pi}{N}nk\right) \tag{21}$$

which is maximized when the exponential factors in every term cancel, that is, when

$$k = \frac{Nd\sin\alpha}{\lambda}$$

The quantity k is thus a phase corresponding to a beam at angle α. The choice of phase factor can be seen to result in a spatial DFT operation on the signal samples.

It is interesting to compare the time-domain and the frequency-domain approaches. In the time-domain case a single set of delays products a single beam. In the frequency-domain case a set of phase factors results in a sample in each of N possible beams. In a DFT the number of output points (or beams) must be equal to the number of input points (or sensors); hence, for an N-element array, frequency-domain beamforming produces N simultaneous beams, updated at the rate DFTs are performed. In time-domain beamforming the number of beams that can be formed is determined by the minimum temporal resolution possible. Finally, one can consider the two beamforming methods to be optimum for different signal types. In the time-domain case the optimum occurs for short-duration, impulselike signals since only one set of delays τ_n produces signal gain. In the frequency-domain case beamforming is done narrowband, in contrast to time-domain in a nondispersive wave medium in which there is no intrinsic restriction on bandwidth. An impulselike signal must therefore first be filtered into a number of frequency bands to be processed separately in the frequency-domain case. On the other hand, a long-duration cw tone would be handled with a single DFT in the frequency-domain case, whereas the time-domain approach would result in an ambiguity in τ_n every period, whereby a shift in τ_n of one wave period also produces gain. (In practice the spacings of the sensors is chosen on the assumption that one knows the highest signal frequency expected, that is, $d \leq \lambda_{\min}/2$; so the ambiguity in τ_n, or aliasing, does not arise.)

Optics can be used to improve the throughput of beamforming systems. In the time-domain case the need is to implement many beams simultaneously. In the frequency-domain case the need is to form a large number of simultaneous beams for many frequencies (often referred to as $\omega-k$ beamforming); the frequency analysis of a broadband signal prior to narrowband beamforming may be done either with another DFT (for discrete data) or with some Fourier transform device (for continuous data). One can perform the frequency analysis over many sensor channels in parallel; the outputs of the channels at a particular frequency can then be fed in parallel to a space-integrating DFT architecture for beamforming [13].

Broadband time-domain beamforming is not easily related to a standard optical architecture as with the frequency domain case. However, both space-integrating and time-integrating concepts can be employed. An example of each will be discussed.

A space-integrating, time-domain beamformer (illustrated in Fig. 12) employs a pulsed light source, collimating optics for producing a uniform two-dimensional optical beam, a multitransducer acoustooptic Bragg cell with one transducer per sensor, an imaging system, a computer-generated holographic mask (to be described later), a spherical lens used in a Fourier transforming configuration, and a parallel readout detector array for producing output beams.

We shall assume that the sensor output is sampled and hence the acoustooptic transducers are driven by discrete pulses of data. The time window of the acoustooptic cell must be long enough to accommodate the longest required delay between any two elements of the sensor array. The bandwidth of the cell must be high enough to resolve the individual samples, and the time-bandwidth product of the cell is determined by the total number of time samples needed from each sensor to form all the beams.

The operation is illustrated in Fig. 12 with an example of a four-element array. Suppose that beam b_1 is formed by the expression

$$b_1(t) = s_1(t - \tau_{11}) + s_2(t - \tau_{21}) + s_3(t - \tau_{31}) + s_3(t - \tau_{41}) \tag{22}$$

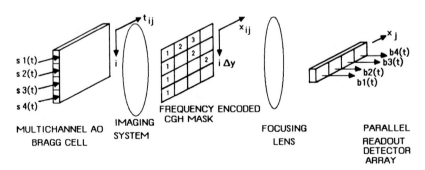

Fig. 12. Acoustooptic, space-integrating implementation of time-domain beamforming.

to associate one-dimensional arrays consisting of discrete data (either binary or analog) arrayed as n-element vectors. The matrix-algebra description of some of the basic concepts of associative processing are first described. How optics can be applied to implement associative storage and recall is then discussed.

A general information pattern can be expressed as a series of n discrete values written as a vector, the components of which might represent, for example, the amplitudes of a descriptor set such as spectral components. Using a matrix-algebra formulation, one can write associative recall of the vector $\mathbf{v}^k$ by the vector $\mathbf{u}^k$ as the vector-matrix product

$$\mathbf{v}^k = \mathbf{M}\mathbf{u}^k \tag{23}$$

where $\mathbf{M}$ is the association matrix to be determined, and the superscript k denotes that $\mathbf{u}^k$ and $\mathbf{v}^k$ are a specific associated pair of vectors. With m associated vector pairs one can construct matrices of size $n \times m$ denoted U and V, where the columns consist of the individual vectors. Equation (23) then becomes a full matrix equation

$$V = MU \tag{24}$$

and one may determine $\mathbf{M}$ from

$$M = VU^{-1} \tag{25}$$

However, the existence of the inverse U^{-1} requires that $n = m$ and that the vectors $\mathbf{u}^k$ be linearly independent. Before discussing how the more general case can be handled, we present a special case solution for $\mathbf{M}$ where U has linearly independent, orthonormal vectors, since it forms the starting point for one approach to the general solution.

When the vectors $\mathbf{u}^k$ are orthonormal to each other, we may form the outer product between the vectors $\mathbf{u}^k$ and $\mathbf{v}^k$ as illustrated in Fig. 2c. The matrix $\mathbf{M}$ is obtained as the sum of all the outer products of associated vector pairs.

$$\mathbf{M} = \mathbf{V}\mathbf{U}^T = \sum_{i=1}^{m} \mathbf{v}^i(\mathbf{u}^i)^T \tag{26}$$

Here T denotes the transpose operator, which in this case converts a column vector to a row vector. It is easy to see that for orthonormal $\mathbf{u}^i$ vectors, $\mathbf{M}$ as given in Eq. (26) gives the proper result when operating on any of the vectors $\mathbf{u}^k$:

$$\mathbf{M}\mathbf{u}^k = \sum_{i=1}^{m} (\mathbf{v}^i\mathbf{u}^{iT})\mathbf{u}^k = \sum_{i=1}^{m} \mathbf{v}^i(\mathbf{u}^{iT} \cdot \mathbf{u}^k) = \mathbf{v}^k$$

The recall operation can be implemented on a vector–matrix multiplier such as that discussed in Section II and illustrated in Fig. 2. $\mathbf{M}$ can be precomputed, knowing the entire set of associated vector pairs. If the input vector $\mathbf{u}^k$ is incomplete, one can threshold the resultant output vector and feed it back into the system as a new input vector; it has been shown that if the missing portions of $\mathbf{u}^k$ do not constitute too large a fraction of $\mathbf{u}^k$, this procedure eventually converges to the exact output desired, namely, $\mathbf{v}^k$ [15, 16, 18]. An optical implementation of a similar type of associative memory is discussed in [18] in which a somewhat different approach to the construction of the association matrix was used, an approach based on energy-type considerations.

When $\mathbf{U}^{-1}$ does not exist (e.g., $n \neq m$), one has the situation of solving a linear set of simultaneous equations with an unequal number of variables and constraints. When there are more variables than constraints, there are an infinite number of solutions for $\mathbf{M}$, one of which is $\mathbf{VU}^+$, where $\mathbf{U}^+$ denotes the pseudoinverse [19]. When there are more constraints than variables, there is often no solution; but $\mathbf{U}^+$ is the optimum solution in a least-squares sense. As an example, if $\mathbf{UU}^T$ has an inverse, then

$$\mathbf{U}^+ = \mathbf{U}^T(\mathbf{UU}^T)^{-1}$$

$\mathbf{M} = \mathbf{VU}^+$ has the property of giving the least-squares minimization of the quantity

$$\sum_{i=1}^{m} (\mathbf{v}^i - \mathbf{Mu}^i)^2$$

An optical implementation of an adaptive scheme has been described that allows one to obtain the pseudoinverse solution in an iterative manner [20]. This approach considers the association matrix $\mathbf{M}$ to be dynamic rather than static, characterized by the differential equation of storage,

$$\frac{d\mathbf{M}}{dt} = g'(\mathbf{v}^k - \mathbf{v})\mathbf{u}^{kT} \tag{27}$$

where $\mathbf{v}$ is the output at any given instant, $\mathbf{v}^k$ the desired output for associated input $\mathbf{u}^k$, and g' an adjustable gain factor. Implementation follows a difference-equation version of Eq. (27),

$$\mathbf{M}_{n+1} = \mathbf{M}_n + g\mathbf{v}^k\mathbf{u}^{kT} - g\mathbf{vu}^{kT} \tag{28}$$

where each associated vector pair is held constant for a time interval Δt, and $g = g' \Delta t$. The algorithm described by Eq. (28) has been investigated previously in adaptive systems [21], and proof that the system converges to the solution

$$M = VU^+$$

is given in [15].

Note that the implementation of Eq. (28) involves the computation of outer-product matrices such as $v^k u^{kT}$. In other words the exact solution for the orthonormal case described by Eq. (26) is the starting point for iteratively obtaining the exact solution for the general case via Eq. (28). The vector-matrix products, Eq. (23), initially do not produce output vectors v equal to v^k; a correction to the association matrix M is produced by subtracting the outer product of the input and v from the outer product of the input and v^k. The basic concept of adaptively updating M not only provides a means of obtaining the correct solutions in the general case, but also can potentially provide additional capabilities such as "accumulative learning" in which multiple presentations of a particular stimulus pair (u^k, v^k) strengthens the association, and the absence of a recurrence of a particular stimulus results in a "forgetting" behavior, which helps prevent saturation or "overflow" of the association matrix. This latter behavior could be especially important in high-speed analog implementations, such as with optics, and in situations in which the number of associations over a long period of time is large (e.g., due to changing signal environment), but the number required at any one time is relatively small.

VI. Summary

A large variety of optical techniques has been developed for processing of temporal data streams. One can view these techniques hierarchically. On the simplest level, optics performs multiplications and additions at high speed and/or in parallel. Higher-level building-block operations including Fourier transforms, correlations and matrix-algebra operations can then be implemented. Many specific signal-processing operations for broad classes of applications can be implemented using these building blocks. Among these are the analysis of waveforms to extract both temporal and frequency information, sensor-array beamforming for signal gain and target localization, and implementation of various transformations, both continuous and discrete, at high speed and/or over large data arrays. Discussion of specific hardware implementations of the various operations has been kept to a minimum because obtaining optimum optical implementations is often tied closely to the details of specific applications. Finally, at the highest level, optics can be considered a candidate technique for implementation of computationally-complete schemes such as associative processing that require not only modest dynamic range and accuracy but also massive interconnection and transformation of large arrays of data to obtain an alternate, more robust, means for signal detection and identification than the ones presently in widespread usage.

Acknowledgments

The author would like to thank Dr. A. D. Fisher and Dr. R. D. Griffin for many helpful discussions.

References

1. E. Abbe, *Arch. Mickrosk. Anat.* **9**, 413 (1873); A. Porter, *Philos. Mag.* **6**, 154 (1906).
2. R. L. Pritchard, *J. Acoust. Soc. Am.* **25**, 879 (1953).
3. J. W. Goodman, "Introduction to Fourier Optics," Chap. 5. McGraw-Hill, New York, 1968.
4. R. Bracewell, "The Fourier Transform and Its Applications." McGraw-Hill, New York, 1965.
5. P. N. Tamura and J. C. Wyant, *SPIE Semin. Proc.* **83**, 97 (1976).
6. N. J. Berg, J. N. Lee, M. W. Casseday, and B. J. Udelson, *Appl. Opt.* **18**, 2767 (1979).
7. L. Mertz, "Transformations in Optics," Wiley, New York, 1965.
8. C. E. Thomas, *Appl. Opt.* **5**, 1782 (1966).
9. T. M. Turpin, *SPIE Semin. Proc.* **154**, 196 (1978).
10. R. A. Athale, J. N. Lee, E. L. Robinson, and H. H. Szu, *Opt. Lett.* **8**, 166 (1983).
11. W. A. Gardner and L. E. Franks, *IEEE Trans. Inf. Theory* **IT-21**, 4 (1975).
12. J. M. Speiser and H. J. Whitehouse, Rep. NUC TN 1355R. Nav. Ocean Syst. Cent., San Diego, California, May 1974.
13. M. W. Casseday, N. J. Berg, and I. J. Abramovit, *in* "Acousto-Optic Signal Processing: Theory and Implementation" (N. J. Berg and J. N. Lee, eds.), p. 165. Dekker, New York, 1983.
14. J. N. Lee, S. C. Lin, and A. B. Tveten, *Appl. Phys. Lett.* **41**, 131 (1982).
15. T. Kohonen, "Self-Organization and Associative Memory." Springer-Verlag, Berlin and New York, 1984.
16. G. E. Hinton and J. A. Anderson, "Parallel Models of Associative Memory." Erlbaum, Hillsdale, New Jersey, 1981.
17. S. Grossberg, "Studies of Mind and Brain." Reidel, Boston, Massachusetts, 1982.
18. D. Psaltis and N. Farhat, *Dig. Congr. ICO, 13th, ICO-13, Sapporo, Jpn.* p. 24 (1984).
19. G. Strang, "Linear Algebra and Its Applications." Academic Press, New York, 1980.
20. A. D. Fisher, *Tech. Dig. OSA '85 Conf. Opt. Comput.* p. TuCl-1 (1985).
21. B. Widrow, *in* "Self-Organizing Systems" (M. C. Yavits, G. T. Jacobi, and G. D. Goldstein, eds.). p. 435. Spartan Books, Washington, D.C., 1962.

3.2

Acoustooptic Synthetic Aperture Radar Processors

DEMETRI PSALTIS

DEPARTMENT OF ELECTRICAL ENGINEERING
CALIFORNIA INSTITUTE OF TECHNOLOGY
PASADENA, CALIFORNIA 91125

MICHAEL HANEY

THE BDM CORPORATION
MCLEAN, VIRGINIA 22102

I. Introduction

Synthetic aperture radar (SAR) [1, 2] is a powerful imaging technique that has been used increasingly for over thirty years. The principal advantage of SAR is its ability to form fine resolution images at relatively long radar wavelengths with small antennas. The signals that are collected in a SAR system, however, are not already focused as is the case in real aperture imaging systems, and extensive processing is required to form the SAR image from the received radar signal. Optical signal processing (OSP) techniques have been applied to the collection and processing of SAR data since the introduction of the technique [3]. Coherent optical signal processors now routinely form radar images from data collected by spacecraft or aircraft. In fact, OSP technology is so well matched to the SAR data processing requirements that optical processors still account for a major portion of the SAR images produced, despite the tremendous advances made in digital signal processing technology over the last thirty years.

Optical signal processing techniques apply well to the SAR problem because the coherent detection of radar echoes received from the object field in SAR is analogous to the interferometric detection of the Fresnel diffraction pattern of an object that is illuminated with coherent light. Therefore the synthesis of the image of a single scatterer in SAR is equivalent to the optical reconstruction of a Fresnel hologram of a single point. This analogy has been exploited to build optical SAR processors in which the radar signals are recorded on photographic film and the radar images are produced by optically focusing the collection of zone plates that are recorded on the film. In recent years there has been increasing use of digital computers in SAR processing because of the higher accuracy and flexibility that these systems provide, coupled with the dramatic increase in the speed of electronic computers. Initially, optics was used for SAR processing because the speed limitation of electronic computers at that time was prohibitive. Processing speed alone is no longer a limitation of electronic implementations since it has now become feasible to build real-time digital SAR processors. New advances in the use of optics in SAR will most likely be in applications such as space-borne radars where the smaller power requirements and size of a real-time optical SAR processor will be advantageous.

Recent advances in light sources, modulators, and detectors have made possible the implementation of real-time optical signal processors that are relatively compact and have low power requirements. Laser diodes are now available as light sources that are small, efficient, have sufficient coherence, and can be modulated directly at very high bandwidths. Charge-coupled device (CCD) detector arrays are available to provide high-resolution output in optical signal processors. One-dimensional spatial light modulators, such as acoustooptic devices (AODs) and also less advanced two-dimensional devices with large space–bandwidth products, can be used as high bandwidth electronic-to-optical transducers. In this chapter we describe how these modern optoelectronic technologies can be used to implement a versatile, compact, and power-efficient real-time optical SAR processor [4–7].

II. Synthetic Aperture Radar

A. GEOMETRY

The side-looking SAR geometry is depicted in Fig. 1. The antenna is carried by a moving platform such as an aircraft or satellite. Typically the

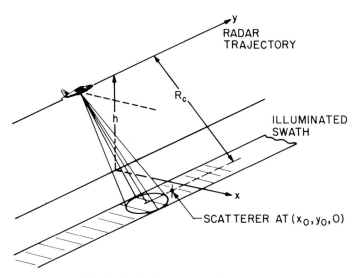

Fig. 1. Synthetic aperture radar geometry.

transmitting and receiving antennas are both located on the same vehicle, and usually one antenna is used for both transmission and reception. A periodic pulse train is transmitted as the platform moves with respect to the ground being mapped, and the sequence of radar echoes from the target scene is received by the radar at locations along the path of the airplane. The received signals are stored until all of the returns are collected. The sequence of radar returns are then processed to generate an image. The axes of the two-dimensional coordinate system in which the radar image is formed are usually referred to as range x and azimuth y. Range is in the direction perpendicular to the direction of the flight of the vehicle, and the azimuth direction is parallel to the flight.

Resolution in the range dimension is achieved by coding the transmitted pulses with a broadband signal and performing pulse compression on each return. Measurements of the time of arrival of the compressed pulses determines the range of individual points on the target scene. The range resolution achievable is $c/2B$, where c is the speed of light and B the bandwidth of the chirp code.

Fine resolution in the azimuth dimension is accomplished with a form of pulse compression as well. The data collection geometry imposes a relatively slow phase modulation on the sequence of radar returns due to the Doppler shifts associated with the nonzero radial velocity component between the moving radar and the target. This phase modulation does not vary measurably within any single pulse but is significant over a long sequence of pulses. The phase history expected for each point scatterer in the target field is known for a given trajectory, and hence the synchronously demodulated radar returns can be correlated against a known phase function to achieve azimuth pulse compression. The azimuth resolution achievable is v/B_a, where v is the velocity of the radar and B_a the Doppler bandwidth (i.e., the bandwidth that the radar echo would have due to the Doppler effect if the transmitted signal were a single-frequency sinusoid).

As the radar travels past each point scatterer, the return signal is upshifted in frequency as the scatterer is approached, has a zero Doppler shift at the point where the point scatterer is directly to the side of the radar, and has a negative shift as the radar moves away. Thus the longer a target stays illuminated in the azimuth direction the wider the induced Doppler bandwidth. In the side-looking geometry the length of the illuminated area (*footprint* of the antenna) is equal to the distance the radar traverses while collecting data from each point target. This distance is called the synthetic aperture of the radar, and it has the interesting and important property that the azimuth resolution obtainable with the SAR system is equivalent to the resolution that can be obtained with an antenna whose real aperture is equal to the synthetic aperture. This limit is realized if the number of pulses that are used by the SAR processor in forming the image is equal to the number of pulses that are transmitted during the time required to travel a distance equal to the beam's footprint on the ground. For side-looking SAR the footprint W is approximately equal to the product of the range to the scatterer R and the divergence angle of the antenna λ/d, where λ is the radar wavelength and d the width of the radar antenna. This minimum achievable azimuth resolution is then given by

$$\delta y = \frac{R\lambda}{2W} = \frac{d}{2} \tag{1}$$

where the factor of 2 is due to the two-way propagation path between each element of the synthesized array and the target. Thus we have the interesting result that the minimum azimuth resolution achievable is equal to one half the size of the antenna and is independent of the range to the target and the velocity of the radar.

B. SIGNALS

In this section we define the transmitted and received signals in a SAR system and establish the notation to be used throughout the chapter. We consider a radar that is carried on a platform moving with a constant velocity on a trajectory that is parallel to the ground at an altitude h. A strip on the ground parallel to the flight path is illuminated as depicted in Fig. 1.

A sequence of N radar pulses is transmitted during the time that the radar illuminates each point scatterer, and the echoes are received back at the radar. We assume that each transmitted pulse is linear frequency modulated (LFM). The total integration time is NT, where $1/T$ is the pulse repetition frequency (PRF) of the radar. The synthetic aperture is thus equal to vNT. The transmitted waveform is a periodic pulse train given by

$$s(t) = \sum_{n=0}^{N} \text{rect}\left[\frac{t - nT}{\tau}\right] \exp[j\pi b(t - nT)^2] \exp(j\omega t) \qquad (2)$$

where τ is the duration of each transmitted pulse, b the chirp rate of the LFM waveform, and ω the carrier frequency of the radar.

The formation of a focused image from the radar signal is a linear operation and as such is completely characterized by its impulse response. We consider, therefore, the formation of the image of a single point scatterer located at ground coordinates (x_0, y_0). The distance $R(t)$ between the antenna and the single point scatterer varies with time and it is equal to

$$R(t) = [\hat{x}_0^2 + (y_0 - v_r t)^2]^{1/2}$$
$$\simeq \hat{x}_0 + \frac{(y_0 - v_r t)^2}{2\hat{x}_0} \qquad (3)$$

where v_r is the felocity of the radar and $\hat{x}_0$ the distance between the radar antenna and the point target at the instant the target is directly to the side of the radar. The approximate expression for $R(t)$ is valid when the range $\hat{x}_0$ is much longer than the synthetic aperture of the system. The quantity $\hat{x}_0$ is equal to $(x_0^2 + h^2)^{1/2}$ (i.e., it is directly derived from the range coordinate x_0 on the ground but is not equal to it). This does not pose any difficulty other than when the final image is formed, its range coordinate must be rescaled accordingly. For the sake of clarity we shall deal in susequent analysis with only the range coordinate x_0.

The backscattered signal $r(t)$ that is received by the radar is proportional to $s[t - 2R(t)/c]$, where c is the speed of light. Using Eq. (2) and the approximate form of Eq. (3), we can write an approximate expression for the recieved signal $r(t)$:

$$r(t) \simeq \sum_{n=0}^{N} \text{rect}\left[\frac{t - 2x_0/c - nT}{\tau}\right] \exp\left[j\pi b\left(t - \frac{2x_0}{c} - nT\right)^2\right]$$
$$\times \exp\left[-j\omega \frac{(y_0 - v_r nT)^2}{x_0 c}\right] \exp\left(\frac{-2j\omega x_0}{c}\right) \exp(j\omega t) \qquad (4)$$

In this equation $R(t)$ is approximated further by x_0 in the first two terms that represent the LFM waveform, and the time-varying portion of the range delay was included in the term that involves the large radio-frequency ω

only. Moreover, it was assumed that the temporal variation of the range is negligible within the duration τ of a single chirp signal, which allows us to use the approximation $t \simeq nT$. These approximations are the basis of SAR imaging since they allow the range position x_0 of each point target to be determined by measuring the round-trip delay of the transmitted LFM signal using pulse compression techniques, whereas the term that contains the time-varying range delay in Eq. (4) provides an estimate of the azimuth position. This term is phase modulated quadratically as a function of the sampled time variable nT. An estimate of the azimuth position y_0 is obtained by measuring when the midpoint of this slow azimuth frequency modulation occurs. The signal $r(t)$ is, of course, a one-dimensional function of time; however, it is convenient to think of it as a two-dimensional function of "fast" and "slow" time variables. The fast time is $t_1 = t - nT$ and is proportional to the real time t except that the origin is reset to zero each time a pulse is transmitted. The slow time is the discrete variable $t_2 = nT$. We have used t_2 in the slow-varying azimuth phase function in Eq. (4) in place of the continuous variable t. Finally, we make the assumption that the received signal is heterodyned to baseband and therefore omit the term $\exp(j\omega t)$ from Eq. (4). With these definitions and approximations, and neglecting the inconsequential constant-phase term in Eq. (4), we can write a relatively simple final form for the received signal in the new two-dimensional coordinate system:

$$f(t_1, t_2) = \text{rect}\left[\frac{t_1 - 2x_0/c}{\tau}\right] \exp\left[jb_1\left(t - \frac{2x_0}{c}\right)^2\right]$$

$$\times \text{rect}\left[\frac{t_2 - y_0/v_r - NT/2}{NT}\right] \exp\left[j\frac{b_2}{x_0}\left(t_2 - \frac{y_0}{v_r}\right)^2\right] \tag{5}$$

C.   SIGNAL PROCESSING REQUIREMENTS

The signal in Eq. (5) is recognizable as a two-dimensional zone plate. The SAR processor must accept this signal and produce a focused point. The required operation for accomplishing this is the following two-dimensional linear operation:

$$g(x, y) = \sum_{t_2} \int f(t_1, t_2) h(t_1 - \alpha x, t_2 - \beta y, x_0) \, dt_1 \tag{6}$$

where

$$h(t_1, t_2, x_0) = \text{rect}\left[\frac{t_1}{\tau}\right] \exp[-jb_1 t_1^2]$$

$$\times \text{rect}\left[\frac{t_2 - NT/2}{NT}\right] \exp\left[-j\frac{b_2}{x_0} t_2^2\right] \tag{7}$$

and α and β are suitable constants. The operation described by Eqs. (6) and (7) is nearly shift invariant, with the exception that the kernel is scaled in the azimuth coordinate t_2 by the range x_0. This effect is referred to as range–azimuth coupling. In addition, the kernel is separable in the two variables of integration. These two facts simplify the digital or optical implementation of a SAR processor. For instance, in a digital implementation the processing time is shortened dramatically through the use of the fast-Fourier transform algorithm. As we shall see in the next section, the optical implementations are also facilitated greatly by this special form of the SAR kernel. Nevertheless, the SAR imaging operation remains computationally intensive, principally because the images are very large. For real-time operation we may require that the SAR image be formed in one second (approximately the time required to collect the data). In most cases the required processing rate is achievable with special-purpose digital electronic processors, and it is also well within the capabilities of analog optical processors. Therefore processing speed, which for years was a determining factor in choosing optics as the processing method, is no longer a primary issue when optical and electronic techniques are compared for SAR. Other requirements such dynamic range, flexibility, size, weight, and power consumption are more relevant for comparison. Generally, digital techniques provide higher dynamic range and probably more flexibility to adjust for varying parameters of the radar, whereas optics offers advantages in terms of lower power consumption and smaller size.

III. Acoustooptic Processor

A. ARCHITECTURAL CONSIDERATIONS

The transformation that needs to be performed in a SAR signal processor [Eq. (7)] can be implemented optically with relative ease since it is basically a Fresnel integral. Also, the fact that SAR is a two-dimensional signal-processing problem allows the inherent two-dimensional parallelism of optics to be used effectively. In the classical implementation of the an optical SAR processor, the recieved signals are recorded in two-dimensional format on photographic film, and then the image is brought into focus in both dimensions by Fresnel diffraction aided by anamorphic lenses that correct for range–azimuth coupling. To adapt this architecture so that it operates in real time, we need to replace the photographic film. One possibility is to retain the same basic architecture and replace the film with a real-time two-dimensional spatial light modulator [8]. This approach is limited by the lack of available spatial light modulators that are suitable for use in practical applications.

The alternative considered in this chapter is the use of an acoustooptic device (AOD) as the input transducer. The motivation for using AODs comes from the fact that they are well developed, at least by comparison with other spatial light modulators, and as a result it is possible to implement acoustooptic signal processors that are suitable for practical use. AODs are one-dimensional spatial light modulators, and therefore it is not possible to incorporate them directly into the classical SAR processor. The optical system architecture must be modified to accommodate a one-dimensional input device. We shall use a combination of time- and space-integrating processing, a method that we have applied to the processing of several two-dimensional problems [9]. With this approach the two-dimensional space in which two-dimensional input signals are represented and processed is constructed with one spatial dimension and time. In general this implies processing the two-dimensional signal one line at a time using spatial integration. This is followed by a temporal integration of the spatially processed lines of data on a two-dimensional detector array, which completes the two-dimensional signal-processing operation. It is possible to use AODs as input transducers in these architectures since only one spatial dimension is used at any one time.

SAR is a two-dimensional signal-processing problem that is particularly well suited for an acoustooptic implementation for several reasons. The first reason is the nature of the input signal itself. It is convenient to think of the input signal as a two-dimensional function [Eq. (5)], however, it is a one-dimensional signal of time. Therefore it can be directly applied to the AOD without raster recording, which is required in the classical architecture. Moreover, the two-dimensional kernel that must be implemented in this case [Eq. (7)] is also cooperative because it is separable in the two input variables t_1 and t_2. This allows the spatial and temporal processing to be done in a simple cascade configuration, the output of the space-integrating processor becoming the input to the time-integrating system. The format in which the focused SAR image is produced by the time- and space-integrating architecture is ideally suited for the side-looking geometry depicted in Fig. 1. In this case a long strip on the ground is being imaged. If the processing is done in real time, then the SAR processor produces one line of the focused image each time a radar pulse is transmitted, resulting in a continuous flow of information in and out of the processor. If a two-dimensional spatial light modulator is used as the input transducer, then framing is unavoidably introduced; a set of radar returns (lines) are raster recorded until the aperture of the two-dimensional input device is full, and a focused image of the corresponding patch on the ground is formed. The image of the next patch is formed subsequently. In a time- and space-integrating architecture it is possible to form the output image one line at a time. As a result the SAR image is produced in a continuous scrolling fashion, a mode of operation that is often preferable.

These generally desirable features of the acoustooptic SAR architectures are accompanied by an increase in the complexity of the resulting system and a reduction in the dynamic range at the output. The increased complexity comes primarily in the form of electronic circuitry that is necessary for driving the various electrooptic components in the temporally integrating portion of the system. Most of these signals, however, are already available as part of the radar that is used to collect the data. Therefore, in applications such as spaceborne SARs were the radar and the processor are located near each other the increase in hardware complexity is minimal. The limited dynamic range is a consequence of the use of time-integrating processing. The optical detector is used to accumulate photogenerated charge that is proportional to light intensity, a real and positive quantity. Bipolar signals are represented by adding a bias at the detector plane, and the dynamic range with which the focused SAR image is displayed is substantially smaller than the detector dynamic range.

B. RANGE FOCUSING

We now turn our attention to the implementation of Eq. (6) using an acoustooptic processor. We begin by rearranging Eq. (6):

$$g(x, y) = \sum_{t_2=-NT/2}^{NT/2} \exp\left[j\frac{b_2}{x_0}(t_2 - \beta y)^2 \right]$$
$$\times \int_{-\tau/2}^{+\tau/2} f(t_1, t_2) \exp[jb_1(t_1 - \alpha x)^2] \, dt_1 \qquad (8)$$

The form of this equation suggests that it is possible to implement the required two-dimensional integral by first carrying out the integral over t_1 for each value of t_2 and all x. The acoustooptic processor used to perform this operation is shown in Fig. 2. The received radar signal $r(t)$ is applied to the piezoelectric transducer of the AOD. The generated acoustic wave is proportional to $r(t - \hat{x}/v_a)$, where $\hat{x}$ is the spatial coordinate along the direction of propagation of the acoustic wave in the plane of the AOD. At time instances $t = mT$, the light source of the system is pulsed for a short interval. The duration of each light pulse is made shorter than the bandwidth of the signal $r(t)$ so that the traveling signal in the AOD is periodically sampled in time. Let us make the reasonable assumption that the acoustic delay T_a across the full aperture of the AOD is long enough to contain only one radar return at one time. This implies that $\tau < T_a < T$. Then the temporally sampled spatial representation of $r(t)$ in the AOD is strictly equivalent to its representation as a two-dimensional signal $f(t_1, t_2)$ with

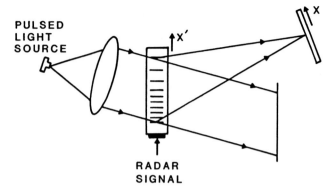

Fig. 2. Space-integrating acoustooptic range focusing technique.

$t_1 = \hat{x}/v_a$. The integration over the range variable t_1 can therefore be accomplished by integration over the spatial variable $\hat{x}$.

The acoustic signal that is seen by each light pulse is a grating whose spatial frequency changes linearly with distance. Such a grating acts as a one-dimensional Fresnel lens, and it diffracts the incident plane wave into a diverging and/or a converging cylindrical wave. For the arrangement shown in Fig. 2 a thick acoustooptic medium is assumed, which results in only one diffracted order, and the illumination geometry results in a converging cylindrical wave. The propagation of light for a distance z through free space is described by a Fresnel integral that is identical in form to the integral over t_1 in Eq. (8). Therefore the t_1 integration is performed by allowing the diffracted light to propagate until it comes to a focus. This happens at a distance

$$z = \frac{\pi v_a^2}{\lambda b_1}$$

away from the plane of the AOD. The position of the focused spot in the transverse direction is determined by the position of the chirp signal within the aperture of the AOD at the instant the light was pulsed. This is, in turn, determined by the range of the point target; a distant target produces a chirp closer to the piezoelectric transducer since it induces a longer delay on the transmitted pulse. The light distribution at the plane in which the diffracted light comes to focus represents the SAR image focused in the range dimension only. Imaging along the second (azimuth) direction is accomplished by temporally integrating the response from multiple radar pulses on a two-dimensional detector array, as discussed in the next section.

C. AZIMUTH FOCUSING

Under the previously stated assumptions the slight variations in range that occur as the radar flies by a point target do not affect the delay of the reflected linear FM signal, but they introduce a phase shift on the carrier frequency ω. These phase delays decrease quadratically in t_2 as the radar approaches a point target in the geometry of Fig. 1 and then increase quadratically after the radar has overflown the target and moves away from it. The integration over t_2 is a pulse compression operation that focuses the radar signal at the azimuth position at which the phase of the return signal stopped decreasing and started increasing.

In the acoustooptic range-focusing architecture discussed in the previous section, the information necessary for focusing in the azimuth direction is preserved in the phase of the range-focused image. Note that the light amplitude at the output plane in Fig. 2 represents the range-focused image; it is a complex quantity with a magnitude that remains constant from pulse to pulse but a phase that changes quadratically. Azimuth focusing is performed by temporally integrating the range-focused image on a detector array. Since detectors respond to light intensity, we must detect the range-focused image interferometrically to preserve the phase.

The interferometric detection scheme that we use is shown in Fig. 3. It uses a reference beam that is introduced through the same AOD that is used for the signal. This is accomplished by electronically adding a reference sinusoid to the signal $r(t)$ before it is applied to the AOD. The reference signal induces an acoustooptic grating with constant spatial frequency, which results in a diffracted plane wave in addition to the converging signal waves. At the plane where range focusing takes place the reference beam remains collimated and provides a reference for all possible range positions.

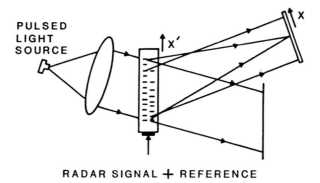

Fig. 3. Interferometric technique used to detect the azimuth phase history.

The frequency of the reference sinusoid must be coherent with the center frequency and the PRF of the radar, and hence the PRF of the light source. This is necessary to ensure that the interference between the reference and signal beams is observed when the light is integrated over multiple pulses.

This interferometric scheme was experimentally demonstrated with the set up of Fig. 3. A sinusoid was electronically added to a periodic chirp waveform and applied to the AOD. The light source used was a laser diode that was pulsed in synchronism with the PRF at which the chirp waveforms were generated. The diffracted light was then detected on a linear-detector array at the plane where range focusing occurred. Figure 4a shows the range-focused signal obtained without reference. Figure 4b shows the output when only the reference signal was applied. In Fig. 4c both the signal and reference were applied, and the relative phase was chosen so that constructive interference took place. Finally, Fig. 4d was obtained by adjusting the relative phase between the two signals so that destructive inteference occurred. Clearly the phase of the chirp waveform has been mapped to variations in the intensity that is detected.

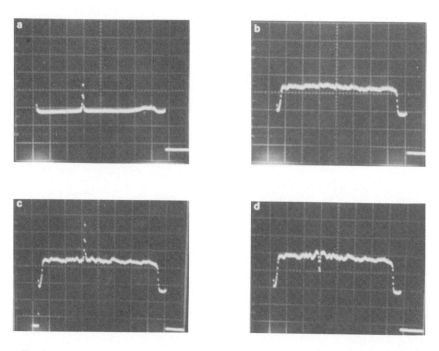

Fig. 4. CCD outputs showing range-dimension signals: (a) range-focused signal without reference, (b) output with only reference signal applied, (c) both signal and reference applied, and (d) same as (c) but with relative phase adjusted for destructive interference.

In reference to Eq. (8), the signal detected at the output of the inter-ferometer of Fig. 3 is the result of the integration in the variable t_1, with the range variable x being the spatial coordinate at the output plane. The second output variable y is obtained by expanding the light in the direction perpendicular to x. The full two-dimensional system is shown in Fig. 5, in which the laser diode is first collimated by a spherical lens and then focused to a horizontal line by a cylindrical lens to illuminate the AOD. The light diffracted by the AOD is recollimated in the vertical direction by a second cylindrical lens. As a result the range-focused image is smeared vertically at the output plane where a two-dimensional CCD detector array is placed. A mask is positioned immediately in front of the CCD. An example of the azimuth reference function used in the experiments is shown in Fig. 6 with range being in the horizontal direction. The intensity transmittance of the mask, $t_1(x, y)$, is a linear FM signal whose chirp rate varies with range to account for range–azimuth coupling:

$$t_1(x, y) = \frac{1}{2} + \frac{1}{2} \cos \frac{b_2(\beta y)^2}{x} \tag{9}$$

This function is the real part of the complex azimuth kernel in Eq. (8) with a bias added. This mask leads to the formation of the real part of the SAR image, and a second mask that is in quadrature with the first is required to obtain the full complex SAR image. This is one of several techniques possible to represent the complex signals that are encountered in the acoustooptic SAR processor. We shall proceed with the description of the processor without the details of the complex representation and discuss the various complex representation schemes in the next section.

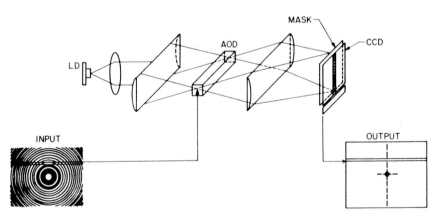

Fig. 5. Real-time acoustooptic SAR processor.

Fig. 6. Example of azimuth reference mask.

Let $I_{inc}(x, t_2)$ represent the light intensity incident at the output plane of the system in Fig. 5. The light incident on the CCD detector is the product $I(x, y, t_2) = I_{inc}(x, t_2)t_1(x, y)$. An integral part of CCD detector arrays is a mechanism for transporting photogenerated charge along one of the dimensions of the two-dimensional array. This charge-transported mechanism is normally used for reading out an image after it has been detected. In the acoustooptic SAR architecture the charge is continuously transferred during exposure. The motion of the photogenerated charge relative to the stationary reference mask performs the azimuth correlation when the light is temporally integrated on the CCD. The charge pattern that accumulates on the CCD after N light pulses have been integrated is given by

$$I_{CCD}(x, y) = \sum_{t_2=-NT/2}^{NT/2} I(x, y + v_c t_2, t_2)$$

$$= \sum_{t_2=-NT/2}^{NT/2} I_{inc}(x, t_2)t_1(x, y + v_c t_2) \qquad (10)$$

where $v_c = \delta y / T$ and δy is the pixel separation on the CCD. The quantity v_c can be thought of as the velocity with which charge propagates on the CCD. Equation (10) shows that the correlation between the function describing the variation of the incident light intensity with the slow time variable t_2 and the transmittance of the reference mask forms at each range position

x. Recalling that the fluctuations of the output light intensity were inter-ferometrically produced by the azimuth phase history and that the mask contains the azimuth reference, we conclude that the signal that accumulates on the CCD contains a term that is the SAR image focused in azimuth. A detailed analysis that includes all the bias components that arise from the interferometric detection, and the bias of the masks shows that $I_{CCD}(x, y)$ is equal to the real part of $g(x, y)$ in Eq. (8) plus a constant bias [4].

The experimental setup that was used to demonstrate the operation of the system is shown in Fig. 7. The laser diode is at the far left. In the implementation shown, the mask is imaged onto the CCD rather than being placed against it. Experiments were performed by generating simulated point target signals using a surface acoustic-wave device to generate chirp waveforms periodically. A constant-phase delay was applied to each chirp, and the delay was increased quadratically to simulate the azimuth phase history of a point target in the side-looking geometry. A photograph of such a simulated radar signal heterodyned to baseband and raster scanned for display on a CRT is shown in Fig. 8. The parameters of the simulated waveform were as follows: PRF = 0.5 kHz, chirp bandwidth = 20 MHz, chirp duration = 6 μs, center frequency = 60 MHz. The reference sinusoid that was added to the signal prior to its application to the AOD has a frequency equal to 60 MHz also. The clock that controlled the PRF of the chirp

Fig. 7. Experimental setup of Fig. 5.

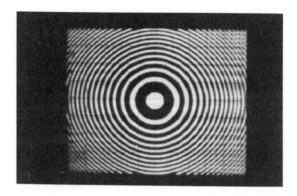

Fig. 8. Raster recording of simulated unfocused radar signal.

waveforms was used to trigger the laser diode pulser and the charge transfer on the CCD. An isometric display of the image that resulted in real time at the output of the CCD when the simulated radar signal for a single point target was applied at the input is shown in Fig. 9. The ridge that is clearly evident in Fig. 9 is one of the bias terms that results when the range-focused image is interferometrically detected. The range dimension is perpendicular, and azimuth is parallel to the ridge. Also evident on top of the ridge is a

Fig. 9. Isometric display of real-time processor output.

sharply focused point which is the image of the simulated point target focused in both dimensions. The plateau on which the bias ridge and the signal are riding is formed by the approximately uniform reference beam that was introduced to detect the range-focused image interferometrically. This bias term can be removed relatively easily since it is not signal dependent. However, the ridge is an unwanted signal-dependent bias that must be separated from the signal term to produce a clean SAR image. In the following section we discuss several possible bias subtraction schemes and the consequences of the bias on the dynamic range of the system.

D. BIAS REMOVAL AND DYNAMIC RANGE

The most direct method for separating the signal from the bias at the output is by the use of two separate CCDs. This arrangement is shown in Fig. 10. The light is split into two paths before it arrives at the output plane and it is detected by two identical CCDs at the range focus plane in both arms. The reference signal is added to the AOD as before and is also detected at the output along with the range-focused image. The azimuth reference mask is included only in one of the two arms, and azimuth focusing takes place in this arm only. In the second arm the interferometrically generated temporal variations temporally integrate to zero, and as a result only the bias components, including the signal-dependent bias, are detected. When the video signals from the two CCDs are electronically subtracted, the biases cancel, and only the desired signal remains. In practice the difference between the fixed-pattern noise of the devices is stored and also subtracted. The resulting bias-free signal is the real part of the complex

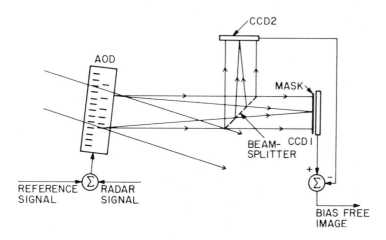

Fig. 10. Bias removal scheme.

SAR image which is displayed after first producing its magnitude squared. The full complex image and hence the magnitude squared of the complex image can be produced if we are willing to use three CCDs to represent the cosine and sine components of the azimuth reference mask and a third for calculating the bias.

The use of multiple CCDs has the advantage that complex images can be represented with space–bandwidth products that are comparable to the number of pixels on the CCD. If, however, it is important that only one CCD be used, bias removal can be accomplished in a number of ways. For instance, the real and imaginary parts of the azimuth reference can be spatially multiplexed on the same device. Alternatively the SAR image can be formed on a spatial carrier whose amplitude and phase are modulated by the complex SAR image. The bias terms are formed at baseband and can be removed by post-detection electronic filtering. The details of the carrier encoding methods are rather involved [10], but the principle is simple; both the input radar signal and the reference signals are placed on carriers, and the resulting correlations form on a carrier as well. The carrier can be introduced in either the range or the azimuth direction. We chose to demonstrate experimentally the bias subtraction method using a carrier in the azimuth direction and filtering the output video electronically in the slow time variable t_2, using a digital buffer that was capable of holding 12 video lines at any one time. The results of this experiment are isometrically displayed in Fig. 11. Clearly the bias terms have been removed, and a sharp image of the simulated point target has been formed.

The dynamic range with which the final SAR image is produced is determined by a number of factors, the most critical being the CCD dynamic range and the portion of the CCD dynamic range that is taken up by the bias components. It is important to realize, however, that this is an interferometric system; the output electrical signal that represents the SAR image is proportional to the light amplitude. Therefore 100 distinguishable signal levels at the detector output correspond to a factor of 10,000 in intensity (between the highest and lowest distinguishable scatters) in the displayed SAR image. In the classic SAR architecture, on the other hand, in which light intensity is detected, 100 levels in the light amplitude of the focused SAR image will require an optical detector capable of producing 10,000 levels. This advantage of coherent detection in terms of dynamic range is counterbalanced in part by the need to allocate a large portion of the CCD dynamic range to the bias terms. The portion of the detector dynamic range that can be used for representing the SAR image depends on the characteristics of the image itself. Images of simple point targets can be generated with nearly half the dynamic range of the CCD. The dynamic range drops as $1/M^{1/2}$, where M is the average number of equivalent point scatterers

Fig. 11. Isometric display of image of simulated point scatterer with bias components removed.

that are in the same range position within a distance equal to the synthetic aperture in the azimuth direction.

IV. Programmable Architecture

A. INTERFEROMETRICALLY GENERATED REFERENCE FUNCTION

In some applications the parameters of the radar–target geometry, such as the velocity and altitude of the aircraft and the direction in which the antenna is pointed, may change dynamically. The real-time SAR imager must have the ability to adapt rapidly to such changes to produce a well-focused image continuously. To accomplish this with the system of Fig. 5 the mask could be replaced by a real-time two-dimensional spatial light modulator on which the proper reference function is written. This is perhaps possible but is not necessary. Examination of the required two-dimensional reference function reveals that it is approximated well by a one-dimensional baseband LFM signal in the azimuth direction, with a scale that varies linearly in the range direction to account for the range–azimuth coupling. This approximation is valid because we assume that the overall range to the target is large when compared with the width of the strip that is being imaged. This suggests that a one-dimensional spatial light modulator can be used to enter the reference function in the processor in conjunction with an appropriate anamorphic lens arrangement to provide the scaling in the orthogonal direction. This approach can be implemented with a second AOD. Figure 12 is a schematic diagram of a specific implementation of this idea, and it is also descriptive of the experimental setup we used to demonstrate this technique. An electronic chirp signal is applied to an AOD along with a sinusoidal reference signal. After the acoustic signals have propagated to the center of the AOD, the laser diode is pulsed to freeze the moving diffraction grating in the same manner as the radar signal is sampled in the AOD of the SAR processor described previously. An anamorphic lens arrangement is used to spread the diffracted light uniformly in the x direction at the detector plane. The undiffracted light (not shown in Fig. 12) is blocked and not used. In the y direction the diffracted light from the sinusoidal reference signal in the AOD is a plane wave that is transformed into a cylindrical wave at the detector plane. The light diffracted by the chirp signal is a cylindrical wave that is transformed into a cylindrical wave of different curvature at the detector plane. The waves from the chirp and reference signals have different radii of curvature, and therefore, under the paraxial approximation, the resulting interference pattern on the detector will be a LFM signal in the y direction. The scaling that is required in the x direction to account for range–azimuth coupling is accomplished by tilting a cylindrical lens about the y axis. An azimuth filter that was generated as described above is shown in Fig. 13. Figure 13a shows the result without a tilted cylindrical lens. Figure 13b shows the effect of tilting the cylinder, which simulates the range–azimuth coupling as described above.

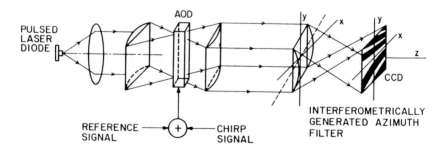

Fig. 12. Optical setup for the interferometric generation of the SAR azimuth filter.

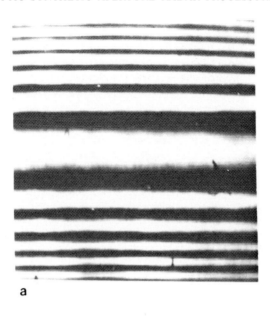

a

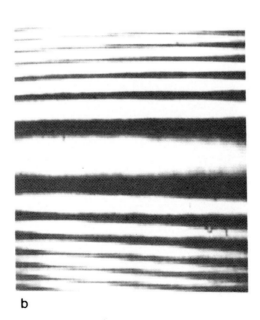

b

Fig. 13. Interferometrically generated reference functions: (a) without range/azimuth coupling and (b) with range/azimuth coupling.

An architecture using the interferometically generated filter has the flexibility to adapt to changes in the radar–target geometry by changing the characteristics of the electronically generated chirp. The parameters that may be changed include the starting frequency, the starting time, and the chirp rate of the azimuth reference signal. In the following section we describe one such architecture.

B. Crossed Bragg Cell Architecture

A programmable real-time SAR processing architecture is synthesized by integrating the interferometric technique for SAR azimuth filtering with the range-processing technique of Fig. 2. One possibility is to construct an additive interferometric architecture in which the AOD containing the radar waveform is placed in one arm of a Mach–Zehnder interferometer; the AOD containing the azimuth reference is oriented orthogonally to the first AOD and is placed in the second arm of the interferometer. An alternate and generally preferable solution is a multiplicative interferometric architecture in which the radar and azimuth subsystems are cascaded. In this implementation the intefering beams pass through the same optics, and thus the stability of this system is drastically enhanced compared with the two-arm interferometer. The cascaded system is shown in Fig. 14. The top view shows the path of the light beams in the range dimension. The light

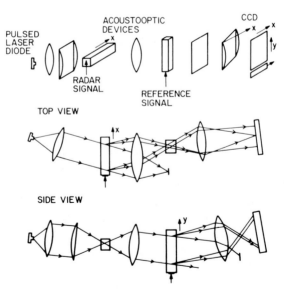

Fig. 14. Optical architecture for SAR imaging with the azimuth reference introduced through a second acoustooptic cell.

diffracted by the induced Fresnel-zone plate focuses on the CCD to perform the range compression. As in the original architecture this wave interferes with a beam that is collimated in the x direction that is due to the diffraction from the sinusoidal reference signal. Both beams pass through the second AOD containing the azimuth filter signal and a second sinusoidal reference. The sum of the signals corresponding to the azimuth kernel and a constant sinusoidal reference is periodically applied to the second AOD at the PRF of the radar signal. The light diffracted by the second AOD consists of a converging (or diverging) beam in the y direction and a collimated beam (shown in the side view) that passes through the tilted cylindrical lens. These two beams interfere at the detector plane to produce the azimuth filter. As in the original processor the radar signal is range focused at the detector plane, and its phase is detected by interferometric detection. The light that is diffracted due to the signal from the first AOD in this architecture, however, is rediffracted by the azimuth signal in the second AOD. This beam contains the product of the range-focused signal times the appropriate azimuth reference. At the same time the reference signal from the first AOD is rediffracted by the reference signal in the second AOD and provides a reference signal at the output plane. The two doubly diffracted beams interfere at the detector plane to produce an intensity that contains a term proportional to the correct range-focused signal and the azimuth filter, precisely as in the architecture with the fixed mask. Temporal integration on a scrolling CCD detector produces the final focused SAR image as before. An interesting feature of this architecture is that azimuth focusing can also be performed without shifting the charge in the CCD. Instead, the azimuth kernel in the AOD can be progressively shifted in y as a function of the slow time variable t_2. This is accomplished by generating the azimuth kernel at a slightly higher PRF than the PRFs of the radar and the laser diode. As a result the acoustic signals in the second AOD seen by two consecutive laser pulses are shifted versions of one another. This effect is entirely analogous to shifting the photogenerated charge in the CCD and can therefore be used to perform azimuth focusing.

The architecture shown in Fig. 14 was experimentally demonstrated except that in the experiment the two AODs were cascaded in reverse order. It was found that by placing the azimuth filter ahead of the range compression section, unwanted barrel distortion arising from the tilted cylindrical lens is avoided. An azimuth time–bandwidth product of 80 was selected for the simulated target. This allows a direct comparison to be made with experiments with the nonprogrammable architecture in which the same time–bandwidth product was used. An oscilloscope trace of the total signal applied to the reference AOD is shown in Fig. 15. This signal consists of the sum of a 60-MHz sinusoid and a LFM of equal amplitude, centered at

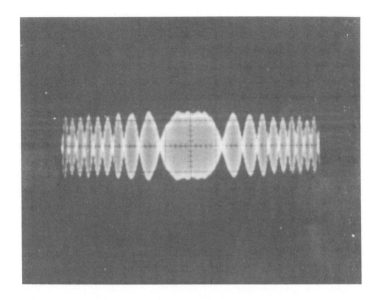

Fig. 15. Azimuth filter signal, 0.5 μs/division.

60 MHz, with a chirp rate of about 4×10^{12} Hz/s. The beating of the two signals in the scope trace reveals the chirped nature of the azimuth filter signal. The optical magnification along the y direction was adjusted so that the resultant interferometric azimuth filter had a space–bandwidth product equal to 80 over the aperture of the CCD. Simulated impulse response signals were generated as before. Figure 16 shows isometrically displayed images of a simulated point scatterer focused with the programmable architecture. A comparison of Figs. 16 and 9 shows that the operation of the multiplicative architecture is nearly identical to that of the nonprogrammable processor.

V. Conclusions

The relatively simple optical architecture of the acoustooptic SAR processor makes its miniaturization or even integration onto a single waveguiding substrate possible. The power requirement of such a system is only several watts, which compares favorably with current electronic implementations. These two features are the principal advantages of the system, whereas its principal disadvantage relative to an electronic implementation is less accuracy and dynamic range. There are several additional issues such as cost, programmability, and resolution that are important, but the optical and electronic real-time implementations are roughly equivalent in these

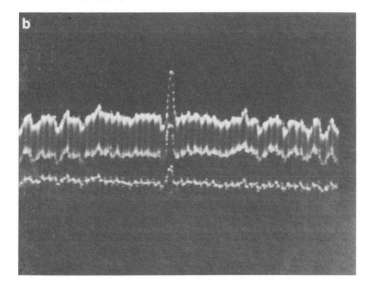

Fig. 16. Isometrically displayed images of simulated point scatterers without bias removal, viewed from two different aspects.

terms. Dynamic range versus power consumption and size are likely to be the deciding factors in selecting an implementation for a particular application. The feasibility of implementing a real-time acoustooptic SAR processor has been demonstrated. The next step ought to be the identification of applications in which the advantageous features of the optical implementations are needed the most and the development of processors that are designed specifically for such applications.

Acknowledgments

The authors thank Kelvin Wagner and Tom Bicknell for their help in several aspects of this work and for many discussions on the subject. This work was supported by the Air Force Office of Scientific Research, NASA through the Jet Propulsion Laboratory, and General Dynamics.

References

1. L. Cutrona, W. Vivian, E. Leith, and G. Hall, *IRE Trans. Mil. Electron.* **MIL-5**, 127 (1961).
2. L. Cutrona, *in* "Radar Handbook" (M. I. Skolnik, ed.), Chap. 23. McGraw-Hill, New York, 1970.
3. L. Cutrona *et al.*, *Proc. IEEE* **54**, 1026 (1966).
4. D. Psaltis and K. Wagner, *Opt. Eng.* **21**, 822 (1982).
5. D. Psaltis, M. Haney, and K. Wagner, *Proc. NASA Opt. Inf. Process. Conf.* p. 199 (1983).
6. M. Haney, K. Wagner, and D. Psaltis, *SPIE Semin. Proc.* **495** (1984).
7. M. Haney and D. Psaltis, *SPIE Semin. Proc.* **545** (1985).
8. D. Psaltis, A. Tanguay, and T. Bicknell, *Proc. NASA Opt. Inf. Process. Conf.* p. 47 (1981).
9. D. Psaltis, *Proc. IEEE* **72**, 962 (1984).
10. M. Haney, Ph.D. Thesis, California Inst. Technol., Pasadena, 1986.

3.3

Acoustooptic Signal Processors

DENNIS R. PAPE

PHOTONIC SYSTEMS INCORPORATED
MELBOURNE, FLORIDA 32901

I. Introduction

Optical technology, using the ability of spatially extended light to carry simultaneous information, provides a powerful means for processing information. The key component in an optical processor is the device capable of spatially encoding the light beam with information: a spatial light modulator. The high performance of the acoustooptic Bragg cell, a device capable of transforming a signal from a time-varying form to a spatial-varying form, is responsible for the extensive development of optical signal processing. This section discusses the properties of the bulk acoustooptic Bragg cell and its use in several signal processing operations including spectrum analysis and correlation. Additionally, the performance of several processors incorporating this technology is described.

II. Acoustooptic Processor Components

A. Acoustooptic Bragg Cell

1. *Principle of Bragg Interaction*

The acoustooptic effect is the diffraction of light by ultrasonic waves [1]. An acoustooptic device consists of a piezoelectric transducer bonded to a transparent medium capable of supporting sound propagation. An electrical signal input to the transducer is converted into an ultrasonic wave that carries both the amplitude and the phase of the electrical signal. The traveling ultrasonic wave manifests itself as a density wave, which through the photoelastic effect results in an index of refraction variation in the acoustooptic material. This index variation, or grating, carries the amplitude and phase information of the ultrasonic wave (and thus of the original electrical input). The amplitude and phase of the resulting light diffracted by the grating is thus proportional to that of the original electrical input.

The input electrical signal $s(t)$ is typically placed on a radio-frequency (rf) carrier of some center frequency ω_c. If, for an acoustooptic device of length L, the transducer is located at position $x = -L/2$ and the acoustic velocity is v, then the diffracted light amplitude at position x and time t immediately behind the acoustooptic device can be represented by the following function (we use here and elsewhere in this chapter the notation suggested by Vander Lugt [2]):

$$A(x, t) = a(x)s\left(t - \frac{T}{2} - \frac{x}{v}\right) \exp\left[\pm i\omega_c\left(t - \frac{T}{2} - \frac{x}{v}\right)\right] \quad (1)$$

where $a(x)$ indicates the variation in amplitude due to nonuniform illumination, acoustic attenuation and so on, and T is the time aperture of the device, as shown in Fig. 1. The sign in the exponential indicates the sign of the diffracted order.

In principle, all orders are diffracted from the acoustooptic device. When all orders are present, the device is said to be operating in the Raman–Nath regime. Since all orders carry the same information, however, it is advantageous to suppress the upper orders and maximize the optical energy in just the first order. This is called Bragg diffraction, and acoustooptic devices operating in this regime are called Bragg cells. Suppression of the upper orders is accomplished by making the length of the transducer (in the direction of optical propagation) large relative to the acoustic wavelength.

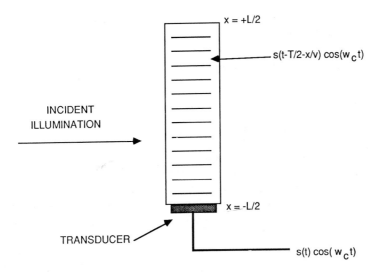

Fig. 1. Acoustooptic Bragg cell.

In this way the acoustic waves more nearly approximate plane waves, and the optical Bragg diffraction is analogous to x-ray Bragg diffraction from crystalline lattice planes.

The deflection or Bragg angle of the diffracted optical beam can be obtained by considering the acoustooptic interaction in momentum space [3]. Conservation of momentum in the acoustooptic interaction requires that the momentum vector of the diffracted optical beam $\mathbf{K}_d$ be equal to the vector sum of the momentum vectors of the incident optical beam $\mathbf{K}_i$ and the acoustic beam $\mathbf{K}_a$ (directed normal to the transducer):

$$\mathbf{K}_d = \mathbf{K}_i + \mathbf{K}_a \tag{2}$$

Since $K = 2\pi/\lambda$, and the incident optical wavelength is typically 400–800 nm whereas the acoustic wavelength is typically 1000–10,000 nm, the magnitude of $\mathbf{K}_d$ is approximately that of $\mathbf{K}_i$. This is shown graphically in Fig. 2, where $\mathbf{K}_d$ and $\mathbf{K}_i$ are drawn with constant magnitude in momentum space. Bragg matching is a consequence of momentum conservation, where the magnitude of the acoustic momentum vector $|\mathbf{K}_a|$ is given by

$$|\mathbf{K}_a| = 2|\mathbf{K}| \sin \theta_B \tag{3}$$

where $|\mathbf{K}| = |\mathbf{K}_d| \approx |\mathbf{K}_i|$ and the angle between the incident optical beam and the acoustic beam is the Bragg angle:

$$\theta_B = \lambda/2n\Lambda \tag{4}$$

where n is the index of refraction of the acoustooptic medium, λ the optical wavelength, and Λ the acoustic wavelength.

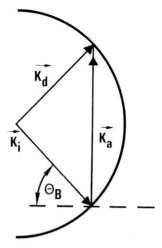

Fig. 2. Momentum space representation of isotropic Bragg interaction. (Vector quantities are denoted by arrows above symbols in figures and by boldface type in text.)

From Eq. (1) it is seen that the diffracted optical beam is shifted in frequency from that of the incident optical beam by an amount equal to the frequency of the acoustic beam. This shift may either increase (upshift) or decrease (downshift) the diffracted light frequency, depending on whether the optical illumination is against (upshift) or with (downshift) the direction of acoustic propagation.

2. Efficiency and Bandwidth

The efficiency of the acoustooptic interaction can be determined by solving the optical wave equation for propagation through an acoustooptic media. Expansion of the optical field in a Fourier series leads (in the Bragg regime) to a set of two coupled-mode first-order differential equations. The solution of these equations is the intensity in the diffracted and undiffracted optical beams relative to the incident optical beam [4]. The ideal efficiency of light diffraction into the first order is

$$\eta = \sin^2\left(\frac{\pi^2}{2\lambda^2} M_2 \frac{L}{HP_a}\right)^{1/2} \tag{5}$$

where H is the transducer height, M_2 the acoustooptic figure of merit (a material-dependent quantity that is proportional to the photoelastic constant), and P_a the acoustic power. At low acoustic power the efficiency is linearly proportional to the square root of the power and thus linearly proportional to the amplitude of the input electrical signal. The diffraction efficiency is reduced from the ideal value given in Eq. (5) by acoustic attenuation and acoustic diffraction. Good acoustooptic materials have high figures of merit, low acoustic attenuation and diffraction, and are obtainable with high optical quality. The most commonly used acoustooptic materials are listed in Table I. Here the value b characterizes the acoustic diffraction of the material in the plane perpendicular to optical propagation direction. For values greater (less) than 0, the material has less (greater) diffraction than an isotropic material.

Several techniques have been employed in recent years to increase Bragg cell efficiency and bandwidth. As seen from Eq. (4), the Bragg angle varies proportionally to the change in acoustic frequency. Thus to get exact Bragg matching over a wide bandwidth one must continually change the illumination angle of the Bragg cell. We want, of course, to use the Bragg cell with the incident optical beam orientation fixed. To achieve efficient acoustooptic interaction at a fixed Bragg angle, we must provide a wide angular spectrum of acoustic wave vectors. With a spectrum of wave vectors over an angular spread $\partial \theta_a$, as shown in Fig. 2, Bragg matching occurs over a band of momentum wave vectors:

$$\Delta K = 2|\mathbf{K}| \, \partial \theta_a \sin \theta_B \qquad (6)$$

The acoustic beam radiating from a transducer behaves similarly to light passing through a window in an opaque screen; in both cases the emanating waves diffract in accordance with the Huygens–Fresnel formulation, and it can easily be shown that the angular spread of the beam diffraction is inversely proportional to the length of the aperture, or in our case, the

TABLE I

ACOUSTOOPTIC MATERIALS

Material	Acoustic mode and axis[a]	Figure of merit (M_2) ($\times 10^{-18}$ s^3/g)	Velocity ($\times 10^3$ m/s)	Attenuation (dB/μs GHz^2)	Index of refraction	$b^{[b]}$
GaP	L [110]	44.6	6.32	3.80	3.31	−0.03
	S [110]	24.1	4.13	1.96	3.31	0.487
LiNbO$_3$	L [100]	7.00	6.57	1.0	2.2	−0.55
	S [100] 35°	14.0	3.6	1.0	2.2	−0.6
PbMoO$_4$	L [001]	36.3	3.63	6.3	2.39	−0.168
TeO$_2$	L [001]	34.5	4.2	6.3	2.26	0.2
	S [110]	793.0	0.62	17.9	2.26	−26.4

[a] L, longitudinal; S, shear.
[b] In the plane perpendicular to optical propagation.

length L of the transducer:

$$\partial \theta_a = \frac{\Lambda}{L} \tag{7}$$

However, the diffraction efficiency of an acoustooptic device is proportional to the transducer length, as shown in Eq. (5). Thus, in trying to gain bandwidth, diffraction efficiency is lost. In practice it is found that to achieve bandwidths of even 500 MHz with this conventional Bragg interaction, one is limited to diffraction efficiencies less than 10%. To achieve a useful device at the 1 GHz or higher bandwidth necessitates a different Bragg interaction technique.

One way to maintain a large value of L and hence high diffraction efficiency and yet still achieve Bragg matching over a wide bandwidth is to segment the transducer into separate elements. By driving the transducer array with a signal shifted 180° between elements, one can steer the acoustic beam vector away from the normal to the transducer array [5]. This is shown in Fig. 3, where now, instead of the acoustic vector $\mathbf{K}_a$ being fixed normal to the transducer, its direction varies with frequency. This is shown in Fig. 3 for two frequencies corresponding to $\mathbf{K}_{a1}$ and $\mathbf{K}_{a2}$. This technique allows the Bragg condition to be maintained over a wide bandwidth with a narrow angular spectrum of acoustic wavevectors. Hence the interaction length L can be kept at a large value for high diffraction efficiency. For a fractional bandwidth of $\frac{2}{3}$, the gain in efficiency of a phased array transducer over a single transducer element is approximately 3.

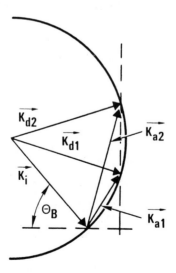

Fig. 3. Momentum space representation of phased-array Bragg interaction.

Another way to maintain a large value of L and simultaneously achieve wideband Bragg matching is through the use of the Bragg interaction in an anisotropic media [6]. In particular, tangential phase matching can be employed so that the acoustic wavevector direction is chosen to lie tangential to the diffracted light index ellipsoid, as shown in Fig. 4. Thus a wide range of K_a values can be made to satisfy the Bragg matching condition. Bandwidths in excess of 1 GHz are available using this technique.

The above discussion concerns methods used to obtain wide bandwidth Bragg cells. These cells find applications in wideband spectrum analysis, particularly channelized receivers, where large instantaneous bandwidth coverage is desirable. Another type of Bragg cell has smaller bandwidth but a large time–bandwidth product. These cells find applications in narrowband spectrum analysis in which fine frequency resolution is desired and in correlation processors in which a long time-history of the signal is necessary for processing. The slow shear acoustic mode in TeO_2 is used for this application. It has an unusually low acoustic velocity, as shown in Table I. Time–bandwidth products in excess of several thousand are available with these cells.

3. Dynamic Range

The dynamic range of a Bragg cell is the ratio of the intensity of the maximum diffracted light to the intensity of spurious diffracted light. The spurious response results from optical noise due to scatter from the cell and unwanted light diffraction when multiple frequencies are present simultaneously in the cell. Optical noise can be minimized during Bragg cell fabrication by using high optical quality acoustooptic material, by maintaining high-quality optical windows, and by using an antireflection coating on the windows. In this way optical noise can be kept less than 60 dB below the maximum diffracted light signal.

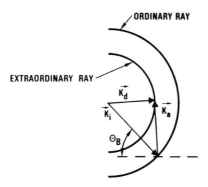

Fig. 4. Momentum space representation of anisotropic tangentially phased Bragg interaction.

Spurious response from simultaneous multiple frequencies in the cell, intermodulation products, are characterized using two input frequencies f_1 and f_2. When the two frequencies are restricted to an octave band, the dominant in-band intermodulation terms are the two-tone third-order products $2f_2 - f_1$ and $2f_1 - f_2$. Intermodulation products arise from two different phenomena. First, light diffracted from one acoustic grating may be rediffracted by other acoustic gratings [7]. The magnitude of this two-tone third-order product (at $2f_1 - f_2$) is given by

$$I = \frac{I_1^2 I_2}{36} \qquad (8)$$

where I_1 and I_2 are the diffraction efficiencies of the two input frequencies. A Bragg cell dynamic range of 50 dB thus requires the power in each of the two input frequency signals to result in less than 2% diffraction efficiency for each signal. The second source of intermodulation products is the nonlinear response of the acoustic material. Harmonics of each of the input acoustic waves interact with the fundamental frequency acoustic waves and with themselves to produce acoustic intermodulation products [8]. These products grow as the waves propagate, and thus the effect is dependent on the illumination aperture of the Bragg cell. The effect is also strongly dependent on signal power density, frequency, and the nonlinearity of the acoustooptic material. Wide bandwidth, high center-frequency cells, and long aperture cells are thus particularly sensitive to these effects.

4. *Multichannel Cells*

Two-dimensional optical signal processing can be accomplished with multichannel Bragg cells. These cells are constructed and function in the same manner as the single-channel devices except that instead of a single electrode a multielement electrode is used. These devices have not found wide application in optical signal processing because adjacent channel cross talk from acoustic diffraction limits their time–bandwidth product to less than 100. Recently, work has been reported in extending the time–bandwidth product of these cells using the self-collimating shear mode in GaP, which has a *b* value of 0.487 [9].

A list of acoustooptic Bragg cells for optical signal processing applications is given in Table II.

B. Light Sources and Photodetectors

Historically, gas lasers have been used as light sources for coherent optical processing systems. Some imaging systems, not requiring a coherent source, have used LEDs as well as other incoherent sources. The demand for small, rugged, low power, optical processors has led to the recent use

TABLE II

COMMERCIALLY AVAILABLE ACOUSTOOPTIC BRAGG CELLS FOR OPTICAL SIGNAL PROCESSING

Type	Center frequency (GHz)	Bandwidth (MHz)	Time aperture (μs)	Diffraction efficiency (%/W)	Source[b]
Wideband					
LiNbO$_3$ (L)	1.0	500	2.0	2.5	CTI
GaP (L)	1.0	500	0.5	50	CTI
GaP (L)	1.0	500	0.3	18 (815 nm)	H
LiNbO$_3$ (L)	2.0	1000	1.0	1.0	CTI
GaP (L)	2.0	1000	0.15	30	CTI
LiNbO$_3$ [S-35°]	2.3	1000	0.4	32	CTI
LiNbO$_3$ [S-35°]	2.5	1000	0.3	16 (815 nm)	H
Large time–bandwidth product					
TeO$_2$ (SS)	0.045	24	50	45	H
	0.050	30	40–80	250[c]	CTI
	0.075	50	40–80	150[c]	CTI
	0.090	50	40	40	H
Multichannel					
TeO$_2$ (L)					
64 channels	0.4	200	1.0	100	H
32 channels	0.4	200	5.0	60	CTI

[a] Measured at 6328 nm unless otherwise noted.
[b] CTI, Crystal Technology Inc.; H, Harris Corp.
[c] Measured with 1.7 μs aperture illuminated.

of injection laser diodes. These devices usually require external cooling for stability. They also have highly diverging and elliptical diffraction patterns which require beam shaping and collimating optics prior to the Bragg cell. The varied commercial applications for these devices have resulted in extensive improvements in performance in recent years.

Photodetectors form an important part of an optical signal processor [10]. One- and sometimes two-dimensional arrays are required for most applications. Both serial and parrallel readout, one-dimensional, silicon photodetector arrays are available with approximately 35 dB of dynamic range. The serial readout arrays contain up to 4096 pixels, and the parallel readout arrays contain about 500 pixels. Work is in progress to extend the dynamic range of the parallel arrays as well as to integrate transimpedance amplifiers on the array substrate for optical signal processing applications [11]. Additional improvements are required in photodetector array performance, however, to satisfy the unique requirements of optical signal processing systems.

III. Power Spectrum Analyzers

Perhaps the most widely used acoustooptic signal processor is the power spectrum analyzer [12]. An rf signal input to a Bragg cell can be transformed using a spherical lens such that the light distribution in the back focal plane of the lens represents the Fourier transform of the signal. Discrete photodetectors in this plane measure the light intensity at a particular spatial location corresponding to a particular frequency in the input rf signal. Such a processor is also called a channelized receiver (Fig. 5), since it is essentially an array of narrowband rf filters. This inherently parallel processor has many advantages over its single-channel electronic counterparts in modern signal analysis in which many signals with different frequency, amplitude, and pulse duration must be sorted simultaneously.

A. Principle of Fourier Transformation

A coherent optical processing system is shown in Fig. 6 [13]. A plane wave of monochromatic light illuminates a spatial light modulator in plane P_1. The spatially modulated plane wave $U(x, y)$ passes through the spherical lens in plane P_2 of focal length F. Exiting the lens is the spatially modulated wave $U'(x, y)$ given by

$$U'(x, y) = U(x, y) \exp\left[-iK\left(\frac{x^2 + y^2}{2F}\right)\right] \tag{9}$$

where K is the wave number of the plane wave. The wave propagates,

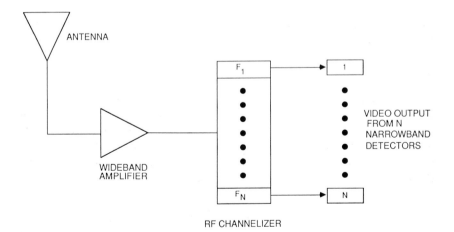

Fig. 5. Channelized receiver.

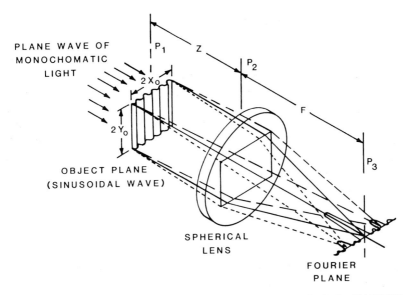

PLANE WAVE OF
MONOCHOMATIC
LIGHT

P_1 z

P_2

$2X_0$

F

$2Y_0$

OBJECT PLANE
(SINUSOIDAL WAVE)

P_3

SPHERICAL
LENS

FOURIER
PLANE

Fig. 6. Coherent optical processing system. (From Vander Lugt [13]. © 1974 IEEE.)

undergoing Fraunhaufer diffraction, to plane P_3, where it is of the form:

$$U(x_2, y_2) = \exp\left[-iK\left(\frac{x_2^2 + y_2^2}{2F}\right)\right]$$

$$\cdot \int\int_{-\infty}^{+\infty} U(x, y) \exp\left[-iK\left(\frac{xx_2 + yy_2}{F}\right)\right] dx\, dy \qquad (10)$$

Identifying the radian spatial frequencies $p = x_2 K / F$ and $q = y_2 K / F$, one recognizes $U(x_2, y_2)$ as the Fourier transform of $U(x, y)$.

B. PROCESSOR IMPLEMENTATION

The acoustooptic power spectrum analyzer is shown in Fig. 7. The acoustooptic cell is illuminated at the Bragg angle with coherent light focused in the z direction to approximately 80% of the height of the transducer and collimated in the x direction. With signal $f(t)$ as input to the Bragg cell, the amplitude $A(x, t)$ of the light leaving the cell is [from Eq. (1)]:

$$A(x, t) = a(x)f\left(t - \frac{T}{2} - \frac{x}{v}\right) \exp\left[-i\omega_c\left(t - \frac{T}{2} - \frac{x}{v}\right)\right] \qquad (11)$$

The light is then Fourier transformed in the back focal plane of the Fourier

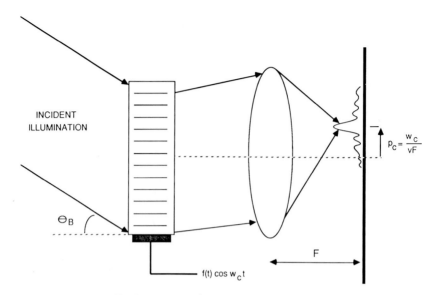

Fig. 7. Acoustooptic power spectrum analyzer.

transform lens. The light distribution in the focal plane is, Fourier transforming Eq. (11),

$$A(p, t) = \exp\left[i\omega_c\left(t - \frac{T}{2}\right)\right] \int_{-\infty}^{+\infty} f(x) \exp[-i(\omega - \omega_c)x]\, dx \qquad (12)$$

The transform is centered at a position p_c corresponding to the frequency ω_i of the input rf signal.

A photodetector array in the focal plane then converts the spatially resolved optical information back to the electrical domain for further processing.

C. CURRENT SYSTEMS

Kellman *et al.* [14, 15] describe a 500-MHz bandwidth acoustooptic channelized receiver with 1000 channels spaced at 500-kHz intervals. The minimum integration period was 0.25 ms, and the detector dynamic range was 33 dB. The post-processor had an A/D converter with 10 bits accuracy at a sample rate of 4 MHz.

More recently, the availability of high-performance injection laser diodes coupled with the relatively small size of acoustooptic Bragg cells and photodetector arrays makes possible the miniaturization of optical processing systems. A 50-channel miniature channelized receiver with a 500-MHz

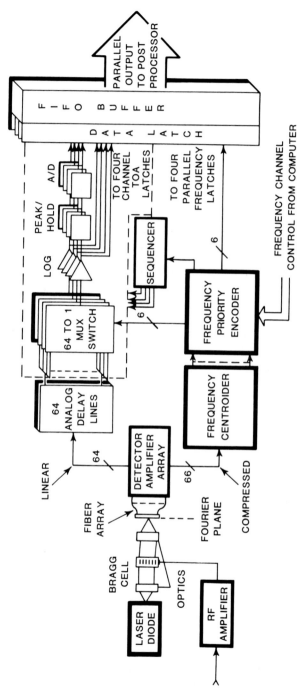

Fig. 8. High-performance acoustooptic Bragg cell spectrum analyzer. (From Yarborough [17].)

bandwidth is described by Coppock and Croce [16]. A linear fiber-optic array was used to channelize the output to discrete photodetectors. The single-tone dynamic range was measured to be 42 dB, and the two-tone third-order intermodulation product limited dynamic range was 35 dB. An electronic post-processor performed thresholding and centroiding, although no performance data are provided.

A very high-performance acoustooptic Bragg cell spectrum analyzer has been recently described by Yarborough [17] and is shown in Fig. 8. It uses the birefringent LiNbO$_3$ cell listed in Table II with a 1.25-GHz bandwidth. A 64-element linear fiber-optic array channels the output light from the Fourier plane to a detector amplifier array in nominal 20-MHz channels. Two video amplifier arrays are implemented. The upper branch provides a linear amplification to the post-processing electronics dedicated to measuring pulse amplitude and time of arrival. The lower branch provides compressed video output from frequency measurement.

Post-processing consists, first, of centroiding the output to determine the frequency bin of the signal. The system can measure up to four simultaneous pulses. A frequency priority encoder, detecting activity in a particular channel, directs a 64:1 multiplexer switch in the upper branch to select the channel for time-of-arrival and amplitude analysis. At the end of the analysis, the time-of-arrival word (24 bits), the amplitude word (6 bits), and the frequency word (6 bits) are all simultaneously available in output data latches. A summary of the performance of this processor is given in Table III.

TABLE III

PERFORMANCE OF ACOUSTOOPTIC CHANNELIZED RECEIVER

Instantaneous frequency coverage	1.25 GHz
Channelization	64
Channel bandwidth (nominal)	20 MHz
Dynamic range (instantaneous)	>30 dB
Sensitivity (estimated 10 dB SNR)	−80 dBm
Simultaneous signals	To 4
Pulse density capability	To 500,000 pps
Output format	36-bit parallel word
Pulse amplitude	6 bits
Time of arrival	24 bits
Frequency	6 bits
Output rate	Determined by input pulse rate
Time-of-arrival accuracy	±50 ns

Source: Yarborough [17].

IV. Interferometric Spectrum Analyzer

The dynamic range of the acoustooptic power spectrum analyzer is fundamentally limited by the square-law detection process of the photodetector. An architecture that detects light amplitude rather than intensity can, in principle, provide a system dynamic range (expressed in dB) twice that available from a power spectrum analyzer. An architecture providing this detection technique interferes a reference light signal with that produced by the power spectrum analyzer. One of the three resulting signals is proportional to the magnitude of the original signal input to the spectrum analyzer. This architecture, the interferometric spectrum analyzer [18, 19], not only provides inherent dynamic range improvement over that available from the power spectrum analyzer, but also provides other advantages such as improved crosstalk suppression and immunity to scattered light.

A. INTERFEROMETRIC PRINCIPLE

The basic interferometric spectrum analyzer architecture is shown in Fig. 9. The lower branch is the same as the power spectrum analyzer shown in Fig. 7. The upper branch is different from the lower branch in two aspects. First, the upper Bragg cell is driven by a reference signal. Second, a wedge is placed in the upper branch to offset the frequency components of the reference beam in the detector plane with respect to the corresponding frequency components of the input signal beam. The optical beams from the two branches are combined and transformed in the same manner as the power spectrum analyzer.

We denote the amplitude of the beam exiting the lower Bragg cell as $S_1(p, t)$ and the beam exiting the upper Bragg cell as $S_2(p, t)$. The form of

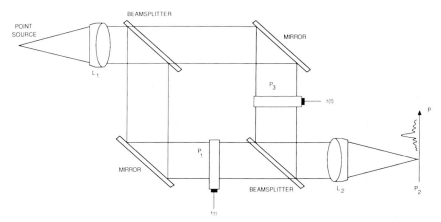

Fig. 9. Interferometric spectrum analyzer architecture. (From Vander Lugt [18].)

S is given in Eq. (1). The light intensity $I(p, t)$ at the photodetector plane P_2 is the square of the sums of the two signals from the two branches:

$$I(p, t) = |S_1(p, t) + S_2(p, t)|^2$$
$$= |S_1(p, t)|^2 + |S_2(p, t)|^2$$
$$+ 2|S_1(p, t)| |S_2(p, t)| \cos[2\pi\omega_0 t + \phi(p)] \qquad (13)$$

where ω_0 is the fixed frequency offset between the two signals introduced by the wedge described above, and $\phi(p)$ is the phase difference between the two signals. The first two terms are bias terms containing frequency components centered at baseband. The third term is the one of interest; it is proportional to the magnitude of the input signal offset to frequency ω_0. This term can be separated from the first two terms using a bandpass filter on each photodetector element.

B. PROCESSOR IMPLEMENTATION

The first demonstration of the improved dynamic range capability of the interferometric spectrum analyzer was reported by Shah et al. [20]. A Mach–Zehnder interferometer was configured using two 300-MHz bandwidth PbMoO$_4$ cells, each centered at 500 MHz. The illuminating source was a 5-mW HeNe laser. The photodetector plane consisted of a fiber-optic array connected to discrete silicon PIN photodiodes. The reference Bragg signal consisted of a linear chirp with a repetition rate of 1.2 MHz. A pseudo-noise sequence was also used as a reference with no significant difference observed. A discussion of other possible reference waveforms is given in [21]. The fixed-frequency offset of the interferometer, the "beat" frequency, was adjusted to be 5.4 MHz by tilting the beam combiner. The maximum signal level input to the Bragg cell corresponded to 1% diffraction efficiency to keep two-tone third-order intermodulation products sufficiently small to provide a minimum multitone dynamic range of 50 dB. The single tone CW dynamic range was measured to be 58 dB, at least 40% higher than that available from a corresponding power spectrum analyzer. The dynamic range for 5-μs pulses was observed to be 54 dB, decreasing to 20 dB for 60-ns pulses, with 100% probability of intercept. Details of improved performance from an interferometric spectrum analyzer are given in [22].

C. CURRENT SYSTEMS

The highest performance interferometric spectrum analyzer reported to date uses the almost common path architecture shown in Fig. 10 [23]. The entire system fits in a package $2 \times 4 \times 8$ in. Here two cube beamsplitters generate the interferometric paths. The reference and signal Bragg cells are

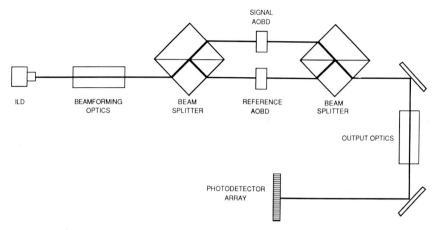

Fig. 10. Common-path architecture interferometric spectrum analyzer. ILD, injection laser diode; AOBD, acoustooptic Bragg deflector. (From Koontz [23].)

combined into a single unit using a two-channel 200-MHz bandwidth cell operating at a center frequency of 500 MHz. A linear fiber-optic array channelizes light in 1.6-MHz channels to discrete photodetectors connected to preamplifiers, bandpass filters, and signal conditioning electronics. The crosstalk from a signal 20 MHz away was <60 dBc. The system exhibited a single tone CW dynamic range of 60 dB and a two-tone third-order intermodulation limited dynamic range of 54 dB. Pulses of 650 ns are detected with 100% probability of intercept; 10-ns pulses are resolvable with reduced dynamic range.

V. Correlators

Correlation is one of the most important signal processing functions. In radar signal processing, target range and velocity can be determined by correlating the received with the transmitted signal. In communications signal processing, correlation is used to identify and decode signals. Acoustooptic Bragg cell processing provides an elegant approach to correlation using the delay line characteristics of the cell and the multiplicative nature of an optical system [24, 25].

A. PRINCIPLE OF CORRELATION

The correlation of two continuous functions $f(\tau)$ and $g(\tau)$ is defined by the relation

$$R(\tau) = \int_{-\infty}^{\infty} f(t)g(t - \tau)\, dt \tag{14}$$

To form the correlation one slides $g(\tau)$ by $f(\tau)$ and integrates the product from $-\infty$ to ∞ for each value of the displacement τ. If $f(\tau)$ and $g(\tau)$ are the same function, $R(\tau)$ is the autocorrelation; if different, $R(\tau)$ is the crosscorrelation. The richness of optical processing yields two architectures for implementing Eq. (14): space-integrating and time-integrating.

B.   PROCESSOR IMPLEMENTATION

1.   *Space-Integrating Processor*

A schematic of the space-integrating correlator is shown in Fig. 11. Two Bragg cells are mutually imaged with a lens producing the transform of the product onto a single photodetector. Here the received signal slides past the reference signal with the integration performed over space and the output from the photodetector displayed in time. The second Bragg cell, containing the reference signal, could be a fixed mask if real-time updating of the reference was not necessary.

The light exiting the first cell can be written, using Eq. (1), as

$$S_1(t, x) = C_1 f\left(t - \frac{x}{v}\right) \exp\left[-i\omega_c\left(t - \frac{x}{v}\right)\right] \qquad (15)$$

Similarly, the second cell produces the following result (where the input

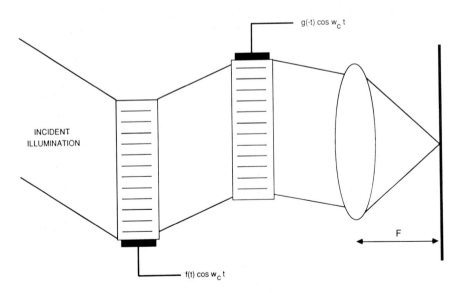

Fig. 11. Space-integrating correlator.

signal g is time reversed):

$$S_2(t, x) = C_2 g\left(-\frac{x}{v} - t\right) \exp\left[-i\omega_c\left(\frac{x}{v} - t\right)\right] \qquad (16)$$

The spherical lens forms the transform of the product of S_1 and S_2 in its back focal plane:

$$F(p, t) = C_1 C_2 \int_{-L/2}^{L/2} f\left(t - \frac{x}{v}\right) g\left(-\frac{x}{v} - t\right) \exp(-ipx) \, dx \qquad (17)$$

Using the change of variables $L = vt$ and $u = t - x/v$, Eq. (17), evaluated on-axis at $p = 0$, becomes

$$F(0, t) = C_1 C_2 v \int_{t-T}^{t} f(u) g(u - 2t) \, du \qquad (18)$$

where $F(0, t)$, of the same form as Eq. (10), represents the correlation of S_1 and S_2.

Several characteristics are to be noted of this system. To obtain the correlation the reference signal must be time-reversed and counter-propagated relative to the received signal. The output is time compressed by a factor of 2.

2. Time-Integrating Processor

A schematic of a time-integrating correlator is shown in Fig. 12 [26, 27]. Here the received signal modulates a point source illuminating the reference

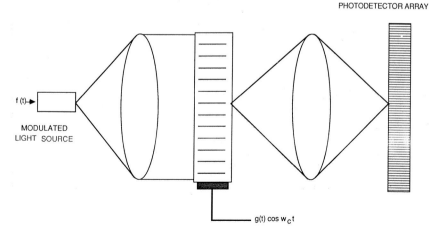

Fig. 12. Time-integrating correlator.

signal Bragg cell. The cell is imaged on a photodetector array with the integration performed in time and the correlation displayed as a function of distance across the array. The output at a point τ in the photodetector plane is

$$R(\tau) = \int_0^T f(t)g(t-\tau)\,dt \tag{19}$$

where $\tau = x/v$. Here the integration is not limited by the time duration of the signal in the cell; hence gain (integration × bandwidth) can be large. Also it is not necessary to time-reverse the reference signal. However, only a short time delay, the aperture time of the Bragg cell, can exist between S_1 and S_2.

C. CURRENT SYSTEMS

One of the many communication applications of a signal correlator is the acquisition of a noise-corrupted pulse code. A time-integrating optical correlator was designed to detect the presence and relative delay of a digital signal buried in both synchronous and random noise [28]. The Bragg cell had a 1-μs aperture and 200 MHz of bandwidth. The photodetector array had 1024 elements with variable integration time from 2 ms to several minutes. The light source could be modulated at rates up to 100 Mb/s. The system was tested using a pseudo-random sequence as the reference input to the light source and a signal to the Bragg cell composed of the reference corrupted by either clock or random noise. The system showed a correlation gain in excess of 50 dB with a resolution of 3 ns.

D. TWO-DIMENSIONAL CORRELATION

The full potential of optical signal processing is exploited with two-dimensional architectures. A powerful two-dimensional time-integrating optical processor is shown in Fig. 13 [29]. The light source, modulated by signal S_1, illuminates the first Bragg cell containing signal S_2. The diffracted output from the first cell passes through the second Bragg cell, orthogonal to the first and containing signal S_3, and is imaged at the detector plane. The result is the function

$$R(\tau_1, \tau_2) = \int_T S_1(t)S_2(t-\tau_1)S_3(t-\tau_2) \tag{20}$$

where $\tau_1 = y/v$ and $\tau_2 = x/v$. This triple-product processor can perform a number of operations.

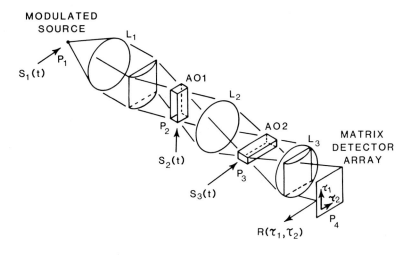

$$R(\tau_1, \tau_2) = S_1(t)\ S_2(t-\tau_1)\ S_3(t-\tau_2)\ dt$$

$$\tau_1 = y/v$$

$$\tau_2 = x/v$$

Fig. 13. Two-dimensional time-integrating optical processor. (From Kellman [29].)

One such operation is calculation of the ambiguity function:

$$A(\tau, \omega) = \int u(t)u^*(t - \tau)\exp(-i\omega t)\ dt \tag{21}$$

which, in radar processing, represents the correlation between the transmitted signal $u(t)\exp(-i\omega_c t)$ and the time-delayed (τ), Doppler shifted, received signal $u(t-\tau)\exp[-i\omega_c(1-\psi_d)t]$. Here ψ_d describes the signal's Doppler frequency shift and is twice the ratio of the target velocity to the speed of light. The transmitted signal is input to the modulator, the received signal input to the first Bragg cell, and a distributed local oscillator $\exp(-i\omega t)$ is input to the second Bragg cell. Thus, in the two-dimensional detector plane, the horizontal dimension represents the time delay and the vertical direction the Doppler frequency of the received signal.

A second signal processing function performed by the triple-product architecture is two-dimensional Fourier analysis [30]. By transforming in two-dimensions, one can obtain finer frequency resolution than that available with a one-dimensional processor. Here two chirps are used to produce a two-dimensional array of oscillators. One chirp, input to the vertical Bragg cell, has a repetition period equal to the detector array integration period. The other chirp, input to the horizontal Bragg cell, repeats many times over the detector integration period. Thus coarse frequency is represented in the horizontal direction on the array and fine frequency in the vertical direction. The signal to be analyzed is input to the point modulator. The result is the transform of the input located at spatial coordinates representing the frequency of the input.

E. ADAPTIVE FILTERING

Antenna side-lobe weighting and signal-noise cancellation are examples of signal processing problems that require filtering without *a priori* knowledge of the received signal. Adaptive techniques have been applied to both these problems using digital transversal filters [31, 32]. The fact that an acoustooptic Bragg cell is a natural delay line that can be tapped optically has led to several adaptive acoustooptic filter systems. Time-integrating architectures implemented in both the time [33, 34] and frequency [35] domains and space-integrating architectures also implemented in both the time [36] and frequency [37] domain have been reported. Because of its high performance, the space-integrating frequency-domain processor is described here.

Figure 14 shows the transversal filter arrangement of an adaptive filter, called a correlation cancellation loop. The weights C_i of the system are the correlation between the n-tapped input signal $s(t-\tau)$, where $\tau = nD$ and the residual signal $z(t)$:

$$C(\tau) = G \int_{t-T_1}^{t} z(u)s(u-\tau)\, du \qquad (22)$$

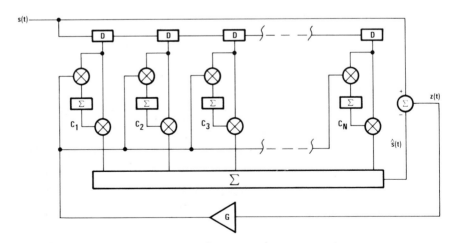

Fig. 14. Correlation cancellation loop. (From Vander Lugt [37].)

where G is the feedback loop gain. The estimate of the received signal is the convolution of the weights with their respective tapped signals:

$$\hat{S}(t) = \int_0^T C(\tau)s(t-\tau)\,d\tau \tag{23}$$

Substituting Eq. (22) into Eq. (23) and going to the frequency domain yields

$$\hat{S}(t) = G \int_{-\infty}^{\infty} Z_T(\omega, t)S_T(\omega, t)2\,e^{i\omega t}\,d\omega \tag{24}$$

where Z_T and S_T are the Fourier transforms of s and z, respectively. Since

$$Z_T(\omega) = S_T(\omega) - \hat{S}_T(\omega) \tag{25}$$

we find, using Eq. (24), that indeed a filter with transfer function

$$H(\omega) = \frac{Z_T(\omega)}{S_T(\omega)} = \frac{1}{|1 + GS_T(\omega)|^2} \tag{26}$$

is implemented so that a strong signal with energy at a particular frequency is suppressed.

This algorithm was implemented using the crossed Bragg cell [38] and Mach–Zehnder interferometric configuration shown in Fig. 15 [39]. Here the signals $s(t)$ and $z(t)$ are input to mutually imaged orthogonal Bragg cells. A lens integrates the result forming the tap weights in the plane of the third Bragg cell. This light output from this cell, input with signal $s(t)$,

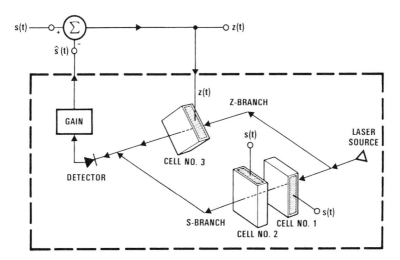

Fig. 15. Crossed Bragg cell Mach–Zehnder interferometric configuration. (From Beaudet *et al.* [39].)

is transformed to produce the signal estimate $\hat{s}(t)$; $\hat{s}(t)$ is subtracted electronically from $s(t)$ to form the error signal $z(t)$.

The stability of the feedback loop was found to be of paramount importance in achieving high-performance nulling. With minimization of the feedback loop delay, 32-dB notch depths were observed. Almost common-path architectures should lead to further gains in system performance [40].

VI. Summary

Acoustooptic signal processing is the most developed of the optical processing technologies due to the high performance of the acoustooptic Bragg cell. However, continued improvement in the performance of light sources and, more important, in photodetector arrays are necessary to realize the power of optical signal processing. Spectrum analysis and correlation are two of the signal processing functions in which Bragg cell technology is particularly effective in providing high performance in both radar and communication applications. Particularly powerful architectures are possible using the two-dimensional nature of optical technology. Finally, several small, rugged systems have been described showing the feasibility of using the technology in real-world applications.

Acknowledgments

The author wishes to acknowledge many stimulating discussions with Dr. Anthony (Bud) Vander Lugt, whose framework for the understanding of this subject has contributed to the discussion presented here.

References

1. A. Korpel, *Proc. IEEE* **69**, 48–53 (1981).
2. A. Vander Lugt, unpublished manuscript Harris Corp., Melbourne, Florida, 1985.
3. I. C. Chang, *IEEE Trans. Sonics Ultrason.* **SU-23**, 2–22 (1976).
4. W. R. Klein and B. D. Cook, *IEEE Trans. Sonics Ultrason.* **SU-14**, 123–134 (1967).
5. D. A. Pinnow, *IEEE Trans. Sonics Ultrason.* **SU-18**, 209–214 (1971).
6. R. W. Dixon, *IEEE J. Quantum Electron.* **QE-3**, 85–93 (1967).
7. D. L. Hecht, *IEEE Trans. Sonics Ultrason.* **SU-24**, 7–18 (1977).
8. G. Elston, *IEEE Ultrason. Symp. Proc., San Francisco, California* **1**, 391–397 (1985).
9. W. R. Beaudet, M. L. Popek, and D. R. Pape, *SPIE Semin. Proc.* **639**, 28–33 (1986).
10. G. M. Borsuk, *Proc. IEEE* **69**, 100–118 (1981).
11. E. J. Boling and J. W. Dzimianski, *SPIE Semin. Proc.* **477**, 174–177 (1984).
12. T. Turpin, *Proc. IEEE* **69**, 79–92 (1981).
13. A. Vander Lugt, *Proc. IEEE* **62**, 1300–1319 (1974).
14. P. Kellman, H. Shaver, and J. W. Murray, *Proc. IEEE* **69**, 93–100 (1981).
15. P. Kellman and T. Bader, *Opt. Eng.* **23**, 002–006 (1984).
16. R. A. Coppock and R. F. Croce, *SPIE Semin. Proc.* **477**, 138–143 (1984).
17. J. Yarborough, *J. Electron. Def.* **8**, 101–196 (1985).
18. A. Vander Lugt, *Appl. Opt.* **20**, 2770–2779 (1981).

19. M. L. Shah, E. H. Young, A. Vander Lugt, and M. Hamilton, *Proc. IEEE Ultrason. Symp.* pp. 743–746 (1981).
20. M. L. Shah, J. R. Teague, R. V. Belfatto, D. W. Thompson, and E. H. Young, *Proc. IEEE Ultrason. Symp.* pp. 740–742 (1981).
21. A. Vander Lugt and A. M. Bardos, *Appl. Opt.* **23**, 4269–4279 (1984).
22. L. M. Ralston and A. M. Bardos, "Wideband, Interferometric Spectrum Analyzer Improvement." Rep. No. AFWAL-TR-84-1029 Air Force Wright Aeronautical Laboratories/AADO, Wright Patterson AFB, Ohio, 1984.
23. M. Koontz, *SPIE Semin. Proc.* **639**, 126–130 (1986).
24. R. A. Sprague, *Opt. Eng.* **16**, 467–474 (1977).
25. W. T. Rhodes, *Proc. IEEE* **69**, 65–79 (1981).
26. R. A. Sprague and C. L. Koliopoulous, *Appl. Opt.* **15**, 89–92 (1976).
27. T. M. Turpin, *SPIE Semin. Proc.* **154**, 196–203 (1978).
28. F. B. Rotz, *SPIE Semin. Proc.* **202**, 163–169 (1979).
29. P. Kellman, *SPIE Semin. Proc.* **185**, 130–139 (1979).
30. T. Turpin, *SPIE Semin. Proc.* **373**, 117–124 (1981).
31. B. Widrow, P. E. Mantey, L. J. Griffiths, and B. B. Goode, *Proc. IEEE* **55**, 2143–2159 (1967).
32. B. Widrow, J. Glover, Jr., J. McCool, J. Kaunitz, C. Williams, R. Hearn, J. Zeidler, E. Dong, Jr., and R. Goodlin, *Proc. IEEE* **63**, 1692–1716 (1975).
33. J. R. Rhodes and D. E. Brown, *SPIE Semin. Proc.* **341**, 140–147 (1982).
34. W. A. Penn, D. R. Morgan, A. Aridgides, and M. L. Noble, "Acousto-Optic Adaptive Processor (AOAP)." F30602-81-c-0264, Rome Air Development Center, Griffiss AFB, New York, 1983.
35. J. L. Newman, Masters thesis AFIT/GE/EE/83D-51. Air Force Inst. Technol., Wright-Patterson AFB, Ohio, 1983.
36. D. Psaltis and J. Hong, *Appl. Opt.* **23**, 3475–3481 (1984).
37. A. Vander Lugt, *Appl. Opt.* **21**, 4005–4011 (1982).
38. A. Vander Lugt, *Appl. Opt.* **23**, 2275–2281 (1984).
39. W. R. Beaudet, A. M. Bardos, and A. Vander Lugt, *SPIE Semin. Proc.* **639**, 175–181 (1986).
40. J. D. Cohen, *Appl. Opt.* **24**, 4247–4259 (1985).

IV

Nonlinear Optical Processors

4.1

Nonlinear Optical Waveguide Devices

H. A. HAUS AND E. P. IPPEN

DEPARTMENT OF ELECTRICAL ENGINEERING AND COMPUTER
SCIENCE AND RESEARCH LABORATORY OF ELECTRONICS
MASSACHUSETTS INSTITUTE OF TECHNOLOGY
CAMBRIDGE, MASSACHUSETTS 02139

F. J. LEONBERGER

UNITED TECHNOLOGIES RESEARCH CENTER
HARTFORD, CONNECTICUT 06108

I. Introduction

Most nonlinear optical waveguide devices operate by controlling the reactive component of the susceptibility $Re(\chi)$, rather than the resistive component $Im(\chi)$. There is a good reason for this, at least at this stage of nonlinear-optical-materials development. Any nonlinear loss component has associated with it a linear loss component that produces unavoidable absorption. More seriously, the loss is difficult to control precisely, so it varies due to material growth and device fabrication. Reactive components

245

do not have loss, so in principle the wave need not experience attenuation. Further, fabrication errors in the construction of reactive waveguide devices can be usually compensated by bias adjustments.

All-optical modulators with which we shall be concerned in this chapter use the third-order nonlinear susceptibility $\chi^{(3)}$ through which an optical intensity controls changes in refractive index. Because $\chi^{(3)}$ is usually small, it is also necessary to choose a device geometry that increases the net effect of this control. To date this has been achieved either by resonance in an optical etalon [1] or by extended interaction length in an optical waveguide [2, 3]. Here we shall concern ourselves only with the latter method, which has the advantage that the price one pays for increasing the sensitivity is only a "pipeline" delay and not a slowing of the response time.

In a nonlinear guided-wave device the control intensity affects the signal wave by changing its propagation constant (phase velocity). To characterize this phase-velocity modulation one must first determine the propagation constant of an optical waveguide from the spatial index distribution. This is done in Section II, in which the well-known scalar wave equation is derived. However, contrary to the usual procedure we interpret the solution of the scalar wave equation as the transverse component of the vector potential rather than of the electric field. We show that the correct field patterns and dispersion relations for the modes of a fiber are obtained in this way. We develop the formula for the change of the propagation constant caused by a change of the dielectric tensor such as would be produced by an electric bias field or an optical intensity. This perturbation leads to a phase modulation of an optical signal passing through the waveguide.

There are two main methods for transforming a phase modulation into an amplitude modulation. One is by means of a waveguide coupler and the other by means of an interferometer. Both have been demonstrated in all-optical modulator arrangements. Such structures have the potential of very high-rate modulation. The interferometer is described in Section V, and its potential use as an all-optical XOR gate is brought out. Modifications of the structure can operate as any of the basic logic gates. The waveguide coupler is described in Section VI. Nonlinear materials that are candidates for device fabrication are discussed in Section VII.

II. Scalar Wave Equation for Mode Analysis

The scalar wave equation provides an intuitively helpful way to estimate the propagation constants of dielectric waveguides or optical fibers. Of course the equation is approximate because electromagnetic fields are vector fields. Yet one may obtain results that are usually of sufficient accuracy for many applications, in particular when the approach is refined as shown in this section.

It is customary when dealing with the scalar wave approximation for dielectric waveguide modes in a medium μ_0, $\varepsilon(x, y)$,

$$\nabla^2\psi + \omega^2\mu_0\varepsilon\psi = 0$$

to identify the electric field $\mathbf{E}$ with $\hat{\mathbf{x}}\psi$ or $\hat{\mathbf{y}}\psi$. This is not the optimum approach. In this brief review of the analysis of modes in dielectric waveguides and optical fibers we shall show that a better identification of ψ is with the vector potential. We shall show that errors in the field profiles are reduced thereby and that the use of the expressions thus obtained in a perturbational expression can lead to appropriate corrections for the propagation constant.

Consider a dielectric waveguide. The dielectric is uniform along the z-axis but varies in the $x - y$ cross section, having maximum dielectric constant at (and around) the origin $y = x = 0$. The dielectric may be dispersive. In this case one must analyze the system under sinusoidal excitation at a particular frequency. Maxwell's equations are

$$\nabla \times \mathbf{E} = -j\omega\mu_0\mathbf{H} \tag{1}$$

$$\nabla \times \mathbf{H} = j\omega\mathbf{D} \tag{2}$$

$$\nabla \cdot \mathbf{D} = 0 \tag{3}$$

$$\nabla \cdot \mu_0\mathbf{H} = 0 \tag{4}$$

with

$$\mathbf{D} = \varepsilon\mathbf{E} \tag{5}$$

if the dielectric is isotropic, as we shall assume in this section. Further, it has been assumed that no free charge density is present.

One can "solve" one of the four Maxwell's equations, Eq. (4), by setting

$$\mu_0\mathbf{H} = \nabla \times \mathbf{A} \tag{6}$$

Introducing this expression into Eq. (1) one finds

$$\nabla \times (\mathbf{E} + j\omega\mathbf{A}) = 0 \tag{7}$$

Therefore $\mathbf{E} + j\omega\mathbf{A}$ must be the gradient of a scalar potential Φ:

$$\mathbf{E} = -j\omega\mathbf{A} - \nabla\Phi \tag{8}$$

where Φ is as yet undetermined. Introduction of Eq. (8) in Eq. (2) with Eq. (5) gives

$$\nabla \times (\nabla \times \mathbf{A}) = \omega^2\mu_0\varepsilon\mathbf{A} - j\omega\mu_0\varepsilon\,\nabla\Phi$$

Using the identity for curl $\mathbf{A}$, one obtains

$$\nabla^2\mathbf{A} = -\omega^2\mu_0\varepsilon\mathbf{A} + \nabla[\nabla \cdot \mathbf{A} + j\omega\mu_0\varepsilon\Phi] - j\omega\mu_0\Phi\,\nabla\varepsilon \tag{9}$$

It is customary to choose the Lorentz gauge

$$\nabla \cdot \mathbf{A} + j\omega\mu_0\varepsilon\Phi = 0 \tag{10}$$

so that a simple wave equation results for $\mathbf{A}$ when the medium is uniform. In a nonuniform medium there is still coupling between $\mathbf{A}$ and Φ.

Thus far we have used Eqs. (4), (1), and (2). The last of the four Maxwell's equations, Eq. (3), gives

$$\nabla^2\Phi + \omega^2\mu_0\varepsilon\Phi + \frac{\nabla\varepsilon}{\varepsilon} \cdot (j\omega\mathbf{A} + \nabla\Phi) = 0 \tag{11}$$

Here again coupling occurs between Φ and $j\omega\mathbf{A}$.

Let us rewrite Eq. (9) with the use of the Lorentz gauge Eq. (10). Then we obtain

$$\nabla^2\mathbf{A} + \omega^2\mu_0\varepsilon\mathbf{A} = (\nabla \cdot \mathbf{A})\frac{\nabla\varepsilon}{\varepsilon} \tag{12}$$

In a nonuniform medium, ignoring the term containing $\nabla\varepsilon$, one also obtains the source-free wave equation. The procedure is then to make this approximation and to test, from the solutions obtained, the validity of the approximation. Some consequences of the approximations are immediately apparent. The source-free wave equation

$$\nabla^2\mathbf{A} + \omega^2\mu_0\varepsilon\mathbf{A} = 0 \tag{13}$$

permits solutions of the form

$$\mathbf{A} = \hat{\mathbf{x}}\psi(x, y)\exp(-j\beta z) \tag{14}$$

or

$$\mathbf{A} = \hat{\mathbf{y}}\psi(x, y)\exp(-j\beta z) \tag{15}$$

in media uniform along the z-direction, and the scalar function ψ obeys the scalar wave equation

$$\nabla_T^2\psi + (\omega^2\mu_0\varepsilon - \beta^2)\psi = 0 \tag{16}$$

where

$$\nabla_T \equiv \hat{\mathbf{x}}\frac{\partial}{\partial x} + \hat{\mathbf{y}}\frac{\partial}{\partial y}$$

Thus linearly polarized vector potentials are exact solutions of the approximate equations. Of course, the E- and H-fields obtained from these vector potentials are not linearly polarized, that is, the fields have true vector character (they are not equal to scalar functions multiplied by $\hat{\mathbf{x}}$ or $\hat{\mathbf{y}}$).

We find from Eqs. (8) and (10)

$$E = -j\omega A - j\frac{\nabla(\nabla \cdot A)}{\omega\mu_0\varepsilon} \tag{17}$$

Substitution of Eq. (14) into Eq. (17) gives

$$E = -j\omega\left[\hat{x}\left(\psi + \frac{1}{\omega^2\mu_0\varepsilon}\frac{\partial^2\psi}{\partial x^2}\right) + \hat{y}\frac{1}{\omega^2\mu_0\varepsilon}\frac{\partial^2\psi}{\partial x\,\partial y} - j\frac{\beta\hat{z}}{\omega^2\mu_0\varepsilon}\frac{\partial\psi}{\partial x}\right] \tag{18}$$

The magnetic field is

$$\mu_0 H = \nabla \times A = [-\hat{x}\times\nabla_T + j\hat{y}\beta]\psi\exp(-j\beta z) \tag{19}$$

for the $\hat{x}$-polarized vector potential. The $\hat{y}$-polarized potential gives rise to analogous expressions. Note that both the **E**- and **H**-fields have longitudinal components.

The scalar wave equation reduces the determination of the propagation constants and the mode eigenfunctions to the solution of the Schrödinger equation in a 2-dimensional potential "well" proportional to $-\omega^2\mu_0\varepsilon(x, y)$. It is clear that the negative curvature of ψ reaches its peak where ε is largest. It is also clear that the eigenmode spectrum for guided modes, which has an ε profile that approaches a constant as $|x| \to \infty$, is finite (Fig. 1). Only modes with $\beta^2 < \omega^2\mu\varepsilon_{min}$ decay exponentially outside the guiding region ($\varepsilon > \varepsilon_{min}$). There is only a finite number of such modes. A single-mode fiber

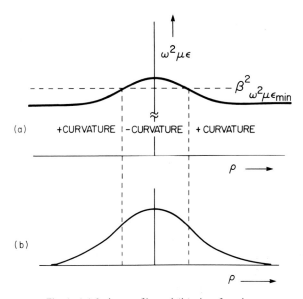

Fig. 1. (a) Index profile and (b) eigenfunction.

has a profile such that only one bound solution is found for ψ. Of course "single mode" is a misnomer, because there are always two modes present, of orthogonal polarizations and equal propagation constants, if the dielectric-constant distribution has circular cylindrical symmetry.

In an elliptical or a rectangular waveguide the two polarizations have different propagation constants. The splitting of the degeneracy can be evaluated perturbatively from Eq. (12). Suppose A_0 is the solution of Eq. (13) at frequency ω, possessing propagation constant β_0. Further suppose that A is the solution of Eq. (12) with propagation constant β. Multiply the complex conjugate of Eq. (13) scalarly by A, the solution of Eq. (12), multiply Eq. (12) scalarly by A_0^*, subtract, and integrate over the cross section. The result is

$$\int (A_0^* \cdot \nabla_T^2 A - A \cdot \nabla_T^2 A^*) \, da - (\beta^2 - \beta_0^2) \int A_0^* \cdot A \, da$$
$$= \int (\nabla \cdot A) A_0^* \cdot \frac{\nabla_T \varepsilon}{\varepsilon} \, da \qquad (20)$$

The first integral vanishes because of the boundary conditions at infinity. Solving for $\beta^2 - \beta_0^2 \approx 2\beta_0 \delta\beta$ one obtains

$$\beta_0 \, \delta\beta = - \frac{\int (\nabla_T \cdot A_0) A_0^* \cdot (\nabla_T \varepsilon / \varepsilon) \, da}{2 \int |A_0|^2 \, da} \qquad (21)$$

where we have replaced A by A_0 to first order in the perturbation. In a waveguide of abrupt index change $\nabla_T \varepsilon / \varepsilon$ is an impulse function of magnitude $(n_i^2 - n^2)/n^2$ where n_i is the internal index and n the external one. Thus, for polarization in the x-direction

$$\beta_0 \delta\beta \approx \frac{\oint (\partial\psi/\partial x)\hat{n} \cdot \hat{x}\psi^* \, ds}{2 \int |\psi|^2 \, da} \left(\frac{n_i^2 - n^2}{n^2} \right) \qquad (22)$$

where the integral in the numerator is a contour integral around the contour of index discontinuity, $\hat{n}$ is the normal to the contour, and the integral in the denominator is over the guide cross section.

EXAMPLE: CHANNEL WAVEGUIDE

For the analysis of the TE mode in a slab guide, Kogelnik and Ramaswamy [4] have used the normalized variables (as referred to the symmetric slab)

$$V \equiv \frac{\omega}{c} \frac{d}{2} (n_i^2 - n^2)^{1/2} \qquad (23)$$

and

$$b \equiv \frac{\beta^2 - (\omega^2/c^2)n^2}{(\omega^2/c^2)(n_i^2 - n^2)} \qquad (24)$$

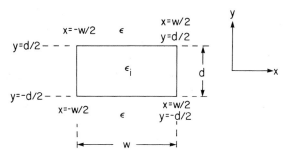

Fig. 2. The channel waveguide.

For the TE mode of the slab waveguide a universal plot can be made of V versus b. If one considers rectangular channel waveguides (Fig. 2), a new parameter enters, namely, the aspect ratio R. The scalar wave equation permits a set of universal plots for the channel waveguide (Fig. 3) with R as a parameter. To appreciate this fact consider the wave equation (16) in the case of a rectangular channel waveguide with index n_i of width w, height d, surrounded by the index n. With the definitions Eqs. (23) and (24), one can write

$$\frac{d^2 \, \nabla_T^2 \psi}{4V^2} + (1-b)\psi = 0$$

for $|x| < w$ and $|y| < d$ and

$$\frac{d^2 \, \nabla_T^2 \psi}{4V^2} - b\psi = 0$$

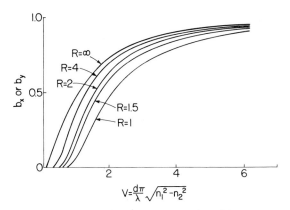

Fig. 3. Graph of b versus V for channel waveguide with R as a parameter.

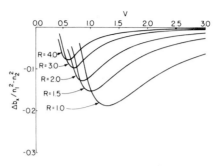

Fig. 4. Birefringence correction for x-polarization.

For either $|x| > w$ or $|y| > d$. These equations involve the normalized derivatives

$$\frac{d}{V}\frac{\partial}{\partial x}$$

and

$$\frac{1}{V}w\frac{\partial}{\partial y} \equiv \frac{R}{V}d\frac{\partial}{\partial y}$$

where $R \equiv w/d$, and also involve the normalized parameters b and V. Hence a universal graph of b versus V with R as a parameter is sufficient to characterize the dispersion of channel waveguides excluding material birefringence (Fig. 3).

The splitting of the degeneracy leading to the modal birefringence is proportional to the parameter $(n_i^2 - n^2)/n^2$. This parameter can be factored out of a simple perturbation formula for the change of propagation constant.

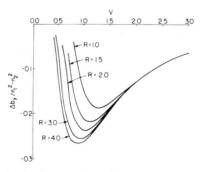

Fig. 5. Birefringence correction for y-polarization.

Introducing the normalization, Eq. (23), one can write for Eq. (22),

$$\delta b = \frac{\oint (d/V)(\partial\psi/\partial x)\hat{\mathbf{n}} \cdot \hat{\mathbf{x}}\psi^*(V/d)\,ds}{\int |\psi|^2 V^2 (da/d^2)} \frac{(n_i^2 - n^2)}{4n^2}$$

The integrals are normalized and hence "universal." The normalized change of the propagation constant is proportional to $(n_i^2 - n^2)/4n$. Thus universal plots entail one dispersion diagram for the scalar wave equation solution, of b versus V, with R as parameter (Fig. 3), and two for the birefringence corrections entailing the same parameters for the two polarizations [5] (Figs. 4 and 5).

III. Perturbational Formula for Change of Dielectric Tensor

Nonlinear interaction of optical modes or beams can take many forms. If the mode patterns are allowed to change, a large variety of phenomena can occur [6]. Generally, however, mode control is desirable so that the patterns of the input and output modes are unchanged in the interaction. In such cases the interaction is confined to a perturbation of a mode in a single-mode waveguide (or fiber). Because the optical nonlinearities are weak, the change of phase within a wavelength is always very small (less than one part in one thousand) so that perturbational methods can be employed to evaluate the change of phase or propagation constant. In this section we develop the expressions for such a change of propagation constant as produced by a change in the dielectric constant. Because the nonlinear susceptibilities are tensors, we shall consider the wave equation in an anisotropic medium under the assumption that the medium is an isotropic (scalar) medium in the absence of a perturbation. If this assumption is not warranted, perturbation methods analogous to those developed here for the nonlinear interactions can be employed to evaluate the modes and propagation constants of the linear problem unless the birefringence is very pronounced. We shall not be concerned here with these situations.

Maxwell's equations for a tensor dielectric medium are Eqs. (1)-(4) with Eq. (5) replaced by

$$\mathbf{D} = \boldsymbol{\varepsilon} \cdot \mathbf{E} \tag{25}$$

where $\boldsymbol{\varepsilon}$ is the dielectric tensor. Split $\boldsymbol{\varepsilon}$ into the isotropic "unperturbed" value $\mathbf{1}\varepsilon$ and the tensor perturbation $\delta\boldsymbol{\varepsilon}$. With this separation one can write for Eq. (9), reevaluated for this case,

$$\nabla^2 \mathbf{A} = -\omega^2 \mu_0 \varepsilon \mathbf{A} - \omega^2 \mu_0 \, \delta\boldsymbol{\varepsilon} \cdot \mathbf{A} + \nabla[\nabla \cdot \mathbf{A} + j\omega\mu_0\varepsilon\Phi]$$
$$- j\omega\mu_0 \Phi \, \nabla\varepsilon + j\omega\mu_0 \, \delta\boldsymbol{\varepsilon} \cdot \nabla\Phi \tag{26}$$

We again choose the gauge

$$\nabla \cdot \mathbf{A} + j\omega\mu_0\varepsilon\Phi = 0 \tag{27}$$

and obtain

$$\nabla^2 \mathbf{A} + \omega^2 \mu_0 \varepsilon \mathbf{A} = -\omega^2 \mu_0 \, \delta \boldsymbol{\varepsilon} \cdot \mathbf{A} + j\omega\mu_0 \, \delta \boldsymbol{\varepsilon} \cdot \nabla \Phi - j\omega\mu_0 \Phi \, \nabla \varepsilon \qquad (28)$$

This equation can also be solved by perturbation techniques, where the terms on the right-hand side are the cause of the change of β. The last term causes polarization birefringence, as was explained and analyzed. The medium perturbation $\delta \varepsilon$ contributes two terms, the first of which is much larger than the second. Indeed, $\omega\mu_0 \, \nabla \Phi$ is of the order of the gradient of the divergence of $\mathbf{A}$, which is small compared with $\omega^2 \mu_0 \varepsilon \mathbf{A}$. Thus the most important perturbation is due to $-\omega^2 \mu_0 \, \delta \boldsymbol{\varepsilon} \cdot \mathbf{A}$. Retaining only this perturbation, one has

$$\nabla^2 \mathbf{A} + \omega^2 \mu_0 \varepsilon \mathbf{A} = -\omega^2 \mu_0 \, \delta \boldsymbol{\varepsilon} \cdot \mathbf{A} \qquad (29)$$

As below, denote the solution of Eq. (13) for a given frequency ω by $\mathbf{A}_0$ and its propagation constant by β_0. The solution of Eq. (29) is $\mathbf{A}$ with propagation constant β. Multiply scalarly Eq. (29) by $\mathbf{A}_0^*$, and the complex conjugate of Eq. (13) by $\mathbf{A}$; subtract the result, and integrate over the guide cross section. The result is

$$\beta^2 - \beta_0^2 \simeq 2 \, \delta\beta \, \beta_0 = \frac{\int \omega^2 \mu_0 \mathbf{A}_0^* \cdot \delta \boldsymbol{\varepsilon} \cdot \mathbf{A} \, da}{\int \mathbf{A}_0^* \cdot \mathbf{A} \, da} \qquad (30)$$

This is the desired perturbation formula. The vector potential $\mathbf{A}$ may be replaced by $\mathbf{A}_0$ to the same degree of approximation. Further, for $\mathbf{A}$ in Eq. (30) can be substituted the transverse E-field. This ignores the contribution of the longitudinal E-field, which has been neglected when the term $\delta \boldsymbol{\varepsilon} \cdot \nabla \Phi$ has been dropped from Eq. (28).

In all optical modulators described in the next two sections, the dielectric changes are caused by the third-order susceptibility tensor $\chi^{(3)}$ due to an optical "control" field. If the frequency of the control field is ω_c and that of the signal field is ω_s, then the dielectric tensor change caused by the control field is

$$\delta\varepsilon_{ij} = \varepsilon_0 \chi_{ijkl}^{(3)}(\omega_s; \omega_s, \omega_c, -\omega_c) E_k(\omega_c) E_l^*(\omega_c) \qquad (31)$$

In the literature it is common to employ the definition of a nonlinear index n_2. The index change experienced by a wave is written

$$\Delta n = n_2 I_c \qquad (32)$$

where I_c is the intensity of the control field. If the signal field is linearly polarized along $\hat{\mathbf{x}}$ and the control field along $\hat{\mathbf{y}}$, then

$$2n \, \Delta n = 2nn_2 I_c = \frac{\delta\varepsilon_{xx}}{\varepsilon_0} = \chi_{xxyy}^{(3)}(\omega_s; \omega_s, \omega_c, -\omega_c)|E_y(\omega_c)|^2 \qquad (33)$$

Additional effects are produced at the signal frequency by the control field. These are the so-called coherence effects discussed in the next section.

IV. Coherent Coupling between Modes in a Nonlinear Optical Waveguide

When calculating changes of the dielectric tensor [Eq. (31)] and its modulating effect, one must keep in mind that perturbations are induced not simply by the control and signal beam intensities independently but also by the electric field interference between them. Such interference terms are known to produce coherent artifacts in nonlinear specoscopic measurements [7]. They are present whenever coherent (or partially coherent) optical fields are coupled by nonlinearities, even if there is no absolute phase coherence between control and signal fields and even if the fields have different carrier frequencies.

For simplicity of description, consider the case of control and signal beams traveling in the same waveguide mode, and assume that each is described by a single electric field component aligned along a single crystal axis. This polarization need not be the same for both control and signal waves, and they may have different phase velocities and frequencies. Thus we can write

$$\mathbf{E}(\omega_c, t) = \hat{\mathbf{x}} E_c(t)\, e^{j(\omega_c t - \beta_c z)} \tag{34}$$

and

$$\mathbf{E}(\omega_s, t) = \hat{\mathbf{y}} E_s(t)\, e^{j(\omega_s t - \beta_s z)} \tag{35}$$

where $E_c(t)$ and $E_s(t)$ describe the slowly varying envelope and phase variations of the control and signal beams respectively.

Now, as discussed in Section III [see Eq. (31)], the control beam intensity produces a change in the signal beam propagation constant through the dielectric tensor component

$$\delta\varepsilon_{yy} = \varepsilon_0 \chi^{(3)}_{yyxx}(\omega_s;\, \omega_s, -\omega_c, \omega_c) E_c^*(t) E_c(t) \tag{36}$$

The signal beam, however, is also affected by an additional term that causes scattering of the control beam into the signal beam,

$$\delta\varepsilon_{yx} = \varepsilon_0 \chi^{(3)}_{yxxy}(\omega_s;\, \omega_c, -\omega_c, \omega_s) E_c^*(t) E_s(t)\, e^{j(\omega_s - \omega_c)t - j(\beta_s - \beta_c)z} \tag{37}$$

which has the appropriate frequency, spatial periodicity, and tensor subscript to induce coupling between control and signal. If $E_c(t)$ and $E_s(t)$ have the same polarization (i.e., $x = y$), this term is the result of amplitude interference between the two, and the nonlinear coefficients in Eqs. (36) and (37) become equivalent. If $E_c(t)$ and $E_s(t)$ are orthogonal, an off-diagonal tensor element is produced by the periodically rotating sum polarization. The off-diagonal term then also couples the two orthogonal polarizations. Although the contribution described by Eq. (37) is conveniently described as a "scattering" term, there need be no power exchanged between control and signal. If $\chi^{(3)}$ is purely real, the scattering process occurs in quadrature, and only phase changes are produced. (If the effective $\chi^{(3)}$ has an imaginary component, then power transfer, and even gain for one of the beams, can also occur [8].)

When we multiply Eq. (36) by $E_s(t)$ and Eq. (37) by $E_c(t)$, we see that each term produces a nonlinear polarization proportional to $|E_c(t)|^2 E_s(t)$. Thus the relative magnitude of the coherent coupling contribution does not, to first order, depend upon the relative intensities of control and signal waves. But it does generally depend upon crystal symmetry and varies from material to material. It also depends critically upon the nonlinear response times of the medium, which can differ for the anisotropic and isotropic components, and on the coherence of the optical signals.

Let us define $A_{yyxx}(t)$ and $B_{yxxy}(t)$ as the impulse responses of $\chi^{(3)}_{yyxx}(\omega_s; \omega_s, -\omega_c, \omega_c)$ and $\chi^{(3)}_{yxxy}(\omega_s; \omega_c, -\omega_c, \omega_s)$, respectively. Then the total nonlinear polarization created at ω_s by the sum of the two fields is given (at say $z = 0$) by

$$
P^{(3)}(\omega_s) \propto E_s(t)\, e^{j\omega_s t} \int_{-\infty}^{t} A(t - t') |E_c(t')|^2 \, dt'
$$

$$
+ E_c(t)\, e^{j\omega_c t} \int_{-\infty}^{t} B(t - t') E_c^*(t') E_s(t')\, e^{j(\omega_s - \omega_c)t'}\, dt' \qquad (38)
$$

The first term in Eq. (38) results from the response of the medium to the control intensity. The second term is the contribution from the coherent interference of the control and signal fields. It is more complicated. It depends first on the electric field correlation between $E_c(t)$ and $E_s(t)$. If they have a relative phase that varies rapidly compared with the response of $B(t)$ (i.e., if either field is sufficiently incoherent), the integral vanishes. The same is obviously true if $B(t)$ cannot respond to the frequency difference $(\omega_s - \omega_c)$. If $B(t)$ is essentially instantaneous in its response, the full effect of coherent coupling obtains.

Consider now the special case when $\omega_s = \omega_c$. If both $E_c(t)$ and $E_s(t)$ are transform limited, their interference depends upon their relative input phases. Optical phase stabilization of the individual fields then might be necessary to avoid excessive amplitude noise in the nonlinear device. Fortunately, by introducing large enough differences in propagation constants to provide fringe averaging over the interaction distance, one can eliminate this absolute phase problem. So, using either birefringent propagation differences or different frequencies is desirable if coherent coupling effects are present.

Finally, some words about $A_{yyxx}(t)$ and $B_{yxxy}(t)$: If $E_c(t)$ and $E_s(t)$ have the same polarization, then trivially, $B_{xxxx}(t) = A_{xxxx}(t)$; and the magnitude of the coherent coupling depends only on the speed of the medium relative to the coherence time between $E_c(t)$ and $E_s(t)$. If $E_c(t)$ and $E_s(t)$ are orthogonally polarized, $A_{yyxx}(t)$ and $B_{yxxy}(t)$ can have different properties. $A_{yyxx}(t)$ may have an anisotropic component as well as an isotropic component depending upon the ratio A_{yyxx}/A_{xxxx}. As a function of time the degree of this anisotropy may even change (by molecular reorientation, for example). On the other hand, $B_{yxxy}(t)$ is purely anisotropic. Thus the coherent coupling term may be strongly diminished by a reorientation that is more rapid than the overall isotropic response (as is the case with the creation of excitons and free carriers in a semiconductor [9]).

In conclusion, the net effect of coherent nonlinear coupling is to increase the observed nonlinearity in all-optical devices by as much as a factor of two. Calculation of the exact magnitude requires knowledge of material nonlinearities, response times, and pulse coherence times, all of which can possibly be designed to maximize the overall effect. With this in mind one can simply use an "effective" nonlinearity in further theoretical analysis of different device geometries.

We are now ready to consider the operation of all optical nonlinear waveguide devices constructed of waveguide interferometers and waveguide couplers.

V. All-Optical Interferometer

The Mach–Zehnder waveguide interferometer can perform as a switch [10], multiplexer, or demultiplexer with index modulation by an applied electric field. Such applications can provide fast [20 gigabit (Gb)] modulation and switching if the switching is regular (the applied signal is narrow-band). Such applications take advantage of the large optical bandwidth inherent in optical waveguides but use driving electrodes that are either narrowband or low-pass, up to a cutoff frequency determined by the (skin-effect) losses of the electrode structure. The optical bandwidth of the waveguide is much greater than 20 GHz (a precise definition of available bandwidth depends on the application and the details of the structure). Modulation of optical signals by optical signals could achieve, in principle, rates much higher than 20 Gb. This was the reasoning that led to the construction of the all-optical waveguide modulator that could function as an XOR gate [2]. The schematic is shown in Fig. 6. A continuous stream of pulses is fed into a Mach-Zehnder waveguide interferometer that has, in addition, two optical waveguide inputs of different polarization from that of the central input. With a fixed applied voltage on the electrode, so that a relative phase shift of 180° is achieved, no output appears in the output guide. If a pulse is entered into one of the control guides, the 180° shift can be compensated, and the pulse emerges.

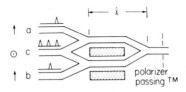

Fig. 6. Schematic of Mach–Zehnder interferometer as all-optical XOR gate.

With different biases and different uses of input and output ports, all basic logic gates can be realized (see Fig. 7). The speed of the gate is determined by the speed of the optical nonlinearity, and the required optical power can be reduced by increasing the length of the interferometer at a cost of delay of the response but not of the rate of the pulse throughput.

We describe first the all-optical interferometer modulation, its fabrication, and the experimental results. Because the all-optical logic gate, in any realization, is much larger in size than the electronic counterpart, one can expect uses of the all-optical gate in special applications and not as a component of an all-purpose processor. Section V.B shows the potential use of a version of the interferometer in a quantum nondemolition (QND) photon number measurement that operates at the limit of quantum detection theory. In Section V.C we show that the same apparatus could be used to tap a communication channel without net extraction of power. A fiber realization of such an interferometer could detect power levels characteristic of a semiconductor laser with a detection bandwidth of 1 MHz.

A.   EXPERIMENTS ON THE ALL-OPTICAL INTERFEROMETER

An all-optical waveguide interferometer was fabricated in X-cut, Y-propagating LiNbO$_3$ [2]. Lithium niobate was chosen because it was the only material with which interferometers had been built successfully at that time. The value of $\chi^{(3)}$ of LiNbO$_3$ was not known but was estimated by Miller's rule; the estimated control power was of the order of 1.5 kW peak

FUNCTION	INPUTS	PHASE SHIFT	COMMENTS
inverter	A	0	pulse stream in C
$\overline{\text{XOR}}$	A,B	0	pulse stream in C
AND	A,C	π	no pulse stream
XOR	A,B	π	pulse stream in C

Fig. 7. Gate operation as function of phase bias and choice of input ports.

in an interaction length of 2 cm. One could not hope to achieve such a high input power; thus it was decided from the outset to demonstrate the operation as a waveguide modulator.

Square pulses were assumed in the description of the operation of the gate. In reality the pulses from a mode-locked laser are not square, and therefore a phase shift of π cannot be obtained uniformly across the controlled pulse. In an X-cut, Y-propagating waveguide configuration, the natural birefringence of $LiNbO_3$ imparts different group velocities to the TE and TM mode. The controlled pulses "slide through" the control pulses in the interaction region, thus simulating a longer duration of the control pulses and giving a more uniform phase shift as seen by the controlled pulses. In $Ti:LiNbO_3$ waveguides the index discontinuity is small (weak guidance), and therefore the group velocities of the modes have essentially the unguided bulk value. Therefore $v_c = v_{TM} = c/n_0$ and $v_{a,b} = v_{TE} = c/n_e$ where, for $\lambda = 0.84 \, \mu m$, $n_e = 2.17$ and $n_0 = 2.25$ are the extraordinary and ordinary indices, respectively. For an interaction length $L = 2$ cm, the relative slip is about 5 ps. If the interaction length were much longer than 2 cm, the pulses would no longer be synchronized and would fail to interact.

Figure 8 shows the predicted pulse shape at the output and compares it with the input Gaussian pulse. The peak power of the control pulse was chosen to maximize the output energy. The distortion of the pulse shape due to the nonuniform phase shift over the duration of the pulse is kept very small. For $LiNbO_3$, in which the pulses travel at the velocities given, about 94% of the energy is transmitted. In an isotropic material the two pulses would travel at the same velocity and about 80% would be transmitted. The zeros obtained with this structure are real nulls and are not dependent on the pulse shape but only on the quality of the interferometer.

Figure 9 is a microphotograph of portions of the 3 cm long interferometer chip. Waveguides were formed by Ti indiffusion and were single mode at

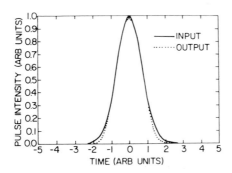

Fig. 8. Predicted output pulse shape and comparison with Gaussian input pulse.

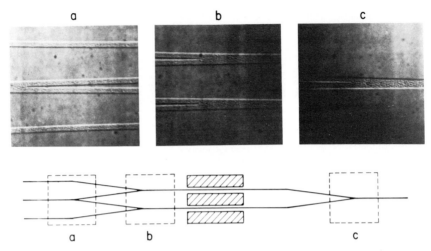

Fig. 9. Micrograph of portions of interferometer.

0.85 μm. Preliminary experiments were performed with a synchronously pumped rhodamine 6G laser and were found to produce intolerably high levels of optical damage in our Ti indiffused waveguides. To avoid this well-known damage effect [12] a laser was developed for operation at longer wavelengths. Using oxazine 750 [13] dissolved in propylene carbonate and ethylene glycol and synchronously pumped with a mode-locked Kr$^+$ laser, 5 ps pulses were obtained, tunable over the range of 720–900 nm. At the longest wavelengths, where optical damage was less, peak powers from the dye laser were also reduced. A compromise between maximizing the nonlinear gating signal and minimizing waveguide damage was found at 840 nm. At this point the peak power of the approximately transform-limited 5-ps pulses was about 200 W.

The experimental setup is shown in Fig. 10. The train of pulses from the dye laser goes through an acoustooptic modulator that reduces the average power by a factor of about 300 to reduce the optical damage. The same laser provides both the control and controlled pulses through beam splitters and polarizers.

A translation stage provides a variable delay between the pulses in each channel. The control pulse is modulated at a low frequency. The output is detected and amplified in a lock-in amplifier. The signal is then processed by a multichannel averaging system that is incremented by the variable delay. The output is recorded on a plotter or photographed directly from the screen of the multichannel averager.

To enhance the sensitivity a dc voltage was applied so that the interferometer was biased halfway between the points of maximum and minimum

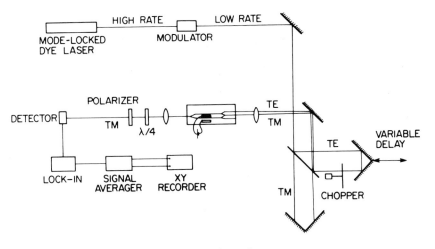

Fig. 10. Experimental setup.

transmission, which correspond to a phase of $(\pi/2) \pm n\pi$. Two traces were taken (Fig. 11) and stored in the multichannel averager. In one case the control pulse increases the throughput of the controlled pulses and in the other case decreases it.

From the experiment it was possible to estimate the value of n_2 (proportional to the matrix element $\chi^{(3)}_{xxzz}$),

$$n_2 \simeq 3 \times 10^{-9} \left(\frac{MW}{cm^2}\right)^{-1} \tag{39}$$

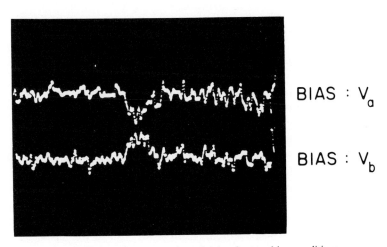

Fig. 11. Modulation as function of delay for two bias conditions.

The experiment indicates that the observed index nonlinearity is essentially instantaneous. The measured response is described by calculations that take into account the pulse shape and the velocity difference between control and controlled pulses. For the relatively short interaction lengths, material and waveguide dispersion could be ignored.

B. INTERFEROMETER QUANTUM NONDEMOLITION MEASUREMENT

Optical waveguides and optical fibers can be made to propagate one single mode. They are ideal mode selectors. The quantum mechanical description of a system is always based on an expansion in terms of the modes of the system. If the process under study excites many modes, the statistical scatter of measurements upon the system is generally enhanced. To cite a specific example, consider the "classic" example of a quantum measurement of the position of a particle by illumination through a microscope. The photons whose diffraction pattern reveals the position of the particle perturbs the momentum Δp_x due to the measurement so that

$$\Delta x \, \Delta p \geq \tfrac{1}{2}\hbar \tag{40}$$

In the microscope measurement it is not possible to establish a measurement accuracy with the equality sign in Eq. (40) because the control of the optical modes is not adequate.

With single mode fibers it is possible to carry out such measurements in principle, with the uncertainty relation for the photon field analogous to Eq. (40) obeyed with the equality sign, at least in principle. We shall now describe an idealized measurement performed by the nonlinear interferometer.

A quantum nondemolition (QND) measurement is the measurement of an observable of a quantum state that yields a value of the observable, which is found unchanged upon repetition of the measurement on the state. Thus the observable of the state is not demolished by the measurement [14].

Every quantum mechanical observable has a complementary variable. Measurement of the observable affects the complementary variable. A precise measurement of the observable with zero uncertainty leads to an infinite mean-square deviation of the complementary variable.

We shall show how the nonlinear interferometer can be used to perform a QND measurement of the photon number [15]. The schematic of the interferometer adapted to the QND measurement is shown in Fig. 12. The probe at frequency ω_p enters through the interferometer Y; the signal at frequency ω_s enters and leaves through the two couplers. Because the probe and signal frequencies are different, the coupler can be designed to be synchronous at the signal frequency but asynchronous (and "inoperative") at the probe frequency. A nonlinear medium extends over a length l.

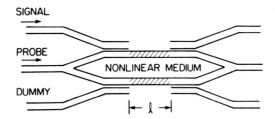

Fig. 12. Interferometer adapted to QND measurement.

Symmetry is preserved through dummy couplers and the same nonlinear medium placed symmetrically in the other arm.

Suppose that the polarization (mode) of the signal is in direction i and that of the probe in direction j. The signal propagating through the nonlinear medium with the coefficient $\chi^{(3)}_{iijj}$ produces a change of index Δn as seen by the probe that is evaluated from Eq. (33)*:

$$\Delta n = \frac{1}{2n(\omega_p)} \chi^{(3)}_{jjii} E^{(s)}_i E^{(s)*}_i \tag{41}$$

This change of index over a length l causes a phase shift of the probe wave Φ_p that is given by

$$\Phi_p = -\frac{\omega_p}{c} \Delta n \, l = -\frac{\omega_p l}{2cn(\omega_p)} \chi^{(3)}_{jjii} E^{(s)}_i E^{(s)*}_i \tag{42}$$

To express $|E^{(s)}_i|^2$ in photon number we use a volume of normalization V that is made up of the waveguide cross section and the length of the wavepacket. Then the signal photon number N_s is given by

$$\hbar\omega_s N_s = \frac{\varepsilon}{2} |E^{(s)}_i|^2 V \tag{43}$$

Thus Eq. (42) gives a relation between the signal photon number and the phase shift of the probe,

$$\Phi_p = -\frac{\hbar\omega_p\omega_s}{\varepsilon V c n(\omega_p)} l \chi^{(3)}_{jjii}(\omega_p; \omega_p, -\omega_s, \omega_s) N_s \equiv -FN_s \tag{44}$$

where

$$F \equiv \frac{\hbar\omega_p\omega_s l}{\varepsilon V c n(\omega_p)} \chi^{(3)}_{jjii}(\omega_p; \omega_p, -\omega_s, \omega_s) \tag{45}$$

*If coherence effects are taken into account, as explained in Section IV, $\chi^{(3)}_{jjii}$ contributes as well to Δn (i.e., a summation must be carried out over all permutations of the subscripts). The analysis carries through unchanged except that the $\chi^{(3)}_{jjii}$ has to be replaced by the sum over permutations. Further, the selfphase-modulation of the probe can cause additional noise. In principle, this noise can be avoided by use of a resonant Kerr effect [15].

The uncertainty in the measurement of the signal photon number is predicated on the accuracy of determination of Φ_p. The phase of the probe signal is subject to the uncertainty relation

$$\overline{\Delta\Phi_p^2} \geq \frac{1}{4\,\overline{\Delta N_p^2}} \tag{46}$$

and thus N_s cannot be determined within a range better than

$$\overline{\Delta N_s^2}\big|_{\text{meas}} = \frac{1}{F^2}\,\overline{\Delta\Phi_p^2} = \frac{1}{F^2}\,\frac{1}{4\,\overline{\Delta N_p^2}} \tag{47}$$

where we assume that the equality sign holds in Eq. (46). The measurement of N_s by a probe causes unpredictable phase changes of the signal, because the field fluctuations of the probe induce phase shifts of the signal by a formula analogous to Eq. (44),

$$\Phi_s = -\frac{\hbar\omega_p\omega_s l}{\varepsilon V c n(\omega_s)}\chi_{iijj}^{(3)}(\omega_s;\,\omega_s,\,-\omega_p,\,\omega_p)\,N_p = -G N_p \tag{48}$$

where

$$G \equiv \frac{\hbar\omega_p\omega_s L}{\varepsilon V c n(\omega_s)}\chi_{iijj}^{(3)}(\omega_s;\,\omega_s,\,-\omega_p,\,\omega_p) \tag{49}$$

Thus the phase fluctuations induced by the measurement are

$$\overline{\Delta\Phi_s^2}\big|_{\text{meas}} = G^2\,\overline{\Delta N_p^2} \tag{50}$$

Substitution of $\overline{\Delta N_p^2}$ from Eq. (47) is

$$\overline{\Delta N_s^2}\big|_{\text{meas}}\,\overline{\Delta\Phi_s^2}\big|_{\text{meas}} = \frac{1}{4}\frac{G^2}{F^2} = \frac{1}{4} \tag{51}$$

since from Kleinmann's symmetry relation [16] $G = F$. Thus we have found that the product of the uncertainty in the determination of the photon number and the mean-square phase fluctuation induced by the measurement obey the uncertainty relation of number and phase with an equality sign.

C. PROBING OF A CHANNEL WITH PCM

The QND measurement by the interferometer described in the preceding two sections has one most interesting property: It measures the photon number without changing it (i.e., with no absorption of photons). Thus a measurement of this kind could be performed on a stream of pulses along a fiber without extracting photons from the fiber. One can imagine a local area network that can be "tapped" with taps of zero insertion loss. The delay of 1 μs of the interferometer does not limit the bandwidth of detection but only causes a delay in the detected signal. Thus high-rate pulse streams could be probed by such taps. The action upon the information obtained from the tapping would have to be delayed by 1 μs. Shapiro has proposed similar taps, except that in his scheme the use of squeezed states was essential [17].

VI. Nonlinear Waveguide Coupler

A logic gate based on the waveguide coupler was proposed by Jensen [18]. He gave no experimental results. The difficulty with the waveguide coupler is that it is excited asymmetrically. The photorefractive effect in LiNbO$_3$ can rapidly destroy the symmetry of the structure and prevent proper operation. Nonlinear interactions in a waveguide coupler built in GaAs were demonstrated by Li Kam Wa et al. [3], using a quantum well (QW) structure. The carrier relaxation in such structures is of the order of 20 ns, and thus operation at rates faster than of the order of 50 Mb cannot be expected from such a device, and no data on the speed of the device were presented. However, one can speed up the relaxation rate by proton bombardment to 150 ps [19]; thus considerably higher bit rates could be expected at a corresponding increase of the power requirements and higher absorption. These are not high to begin with. The saturation intensity of a QW with 20-ns relaxation time is of the order of 500 W/cm^2. Semiconductor laser intensities are of the order of 500 kW/cm^2.

We start with a brief discussion of coupled waveguides and then consider the nonlinear interaction in these waveguides. The experimental results, although limited at this time, are presented.

A. COUPLED WAVEGUIDES

The evaluation of the propagation constant from the scalar wave equation outlined in Section II is not limited to a single waveguide. If two identical waveguides are in proximity, the dielectric profile leads to a solution of the wave equation in a symmetric double well. Such wells give two eigenvalues for ω, the lower values belonging to the symmetric solution e_s and the higher eigenvalue to the antisymmetric solution e_a. The dispersion diagram is as shown in Fig. 13. If one launches a field profile $e_s + e_a$ at $z = 0$, it turns into $e_s - e_a$ at a distance $\Delta\beta_z = \pi$. Power launched in guide (1) has been transferred to guide (2). This is the operating principle of symmetric waveguide couplers.

If the index is a function of intensity in the waveguide, then the coupler is nonlinear. When the power launched in guide (1) is so large that the index is changed to such an extent that well (1) lies lower than well (2),

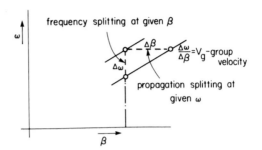

Fig. 13. Dispersion diagram of coupled guides.

the mode pattern changes. The transfer is incomplete or does not occur at all. These effects are understood most easily through the coupled mode formalism. We develop here the necessary background. For further details the reader is referred to the literature [20, 21].

Consider the spatial dependence of the amplitude a_1 of the mode with the field pattern $\mathbf{e}_1$ in guide (1) in the absence of guide (2). Its propagation constant is β_1, and thus

$$\frac{da_1}{dz} = -j\beta_1 a_1 \tag{52}$$

A similar equation holds for guide (2) with the field pattern $\mathbf{e}_2$:

$$\frac{da_2}{dz} = -j\beta_2 a_2 \tag{53}$$

Through proper normalization the power in the guides can be set equal to the square of the mode amplitude $|a_1|^2$ and $|a_2|^2$. When the two guides are put near each other, two changes occur. First, the fields of the guides overlap, and the power cannot be computed as the sum of the squares of the amplitudes of the individual modes. The power must be written

$$\text{power} = \sum_{i,j=1,2} \mathbf{P}_{ij} a_i^* a_j \tag{54}$$

where the matrix $\mathbf{P}_{ij}$ is nondiagonal because of the presence of crosspower terms but is Hermitian because the power is real. Second, the mode amplitudes couple, and excitation in one guide gets transferred to the other guide and vice versa. The coupling equations read

$$\mathbf{P}_{ij} \frac{d}{dz} a_j = -j\mathbf{H}_{ij} a_j \tag{55}$$

where

$$\mathbf{H}_{ij} = \begin{bmatrix} \beta_1 & \kappa_{12} \\ \kappa_{21} & \beta_2 \end{bmatrix}$$

Since power is conserved, the equation is obeyed:

$$\frac{d}{dz}(\mathbf{P}_{ij}a_i^* a_j) = 0 \tag{56}$$

When Eq. (55) is used in Eq. (56), one finds that power is conserved for arbitrary excitation amplitudes a_1 and a_2 if and only if

$$\kappa_{12} = \kappa_{21}^* \tag{57}$$

$\mathbf{H}_{ij}$ is a Hermitian matrix. Usually the crosspower is neglected, $P_{12} = P_{21} = 0$, and $P_{11} = P_{22} = 1$. Then Eq. (55) can be written

$$\frac{da_1}{dz} = -j\beta_1 a_1 + j\kappa_{12} a_2 \tag{58}$$

$$\frac{da_2}{dz} = -j\beta_2 a_2 + j\kappa_{21} a_1 \tag{59}$$

The solutions of Eqs. (58) and (59) for $\beta_1 - \beta_2$ can be used to confirm the operation of the symmetric guide coupler as described. If $\beta_1 \neq \beta_2$, one can choose a detuning $\beta_1 - \beta_2$ such that no power is transferred from guide (1) to guide (2). This can be seen from the solutions of the coupled equations that yield the propagation constant

$$\beta_{\pm} = \frac{\beta_1 + \beta_2}{2} \pm \sqrt{\left(\frac{\beta_1 - \beta_2}{2}\right)^2 + |\kappa_{12}|^2} \equiv \frac{\beta_1 + \beta_2}{2} \pm \beta_0 \tag{60}$$

and thus can be solved by the Ansatz

$$a_1 = \left[A_+ \exp(-j\beta_0 z) + A_- \exp(j\beta_0 z) \right] \exp\left(-j\frac{\beta_1 + \beta_2}{2} z\right) \tag{61}$$

$$a_2 = -\left[\left(\frac{\beta_+ - \beta_1}{\kappa_{12}}\right) A_+ \exp(-j\beta_0 z) \right.$$

$$\left. - \left(\frac{\beta_- - \beta_1}{\kappa_{12}}\right) A_- \exp(j\beta_0 z) \right] \exp\left(-j\frac{\beta_1 + \beta_2}{2} z\right) \tag{62}$$

With the boundary condition $a_1 = a(0)$ and $a_2 = 0$ at $z = 0$, one finds

$$a_1(z) = a_1(0)\left[\cos \beta_0 z + j\left(\frac{\beta_2 - \beta_1}{2\beta_0}\right) \sin \beta_0 z \right] \exp\left(-j\frac{\beta_1 + \beta_2}{2} z\right) \tag{63}$$

$$a_2(z) = a_1(0)\frac{j\kappa_{21}}{\beta_0} \sin \beta_0 z \exp\left(-j\frac{\beta_1 + \beta_2}{2} z\right) \tag{64}$$

Thus with $\beta_0 z = \pi$ one finds that $a_2(z)$ is unexcited, and no transfer occurs. We see from the definition of β_0, Eq. (60) that a detuning at fixed coupling (κ_{12}) may increase $\beta_0 z$ from $\pi/2$ at synchronism to π through an adjustment of $(\beta_1 - \beta_2)$.

In a nonlinear system the difference of the propagation constants, $\beta_1 - \beta_2$, is affected by the intensity of the signal in the guides, that is, β_1 and β_2 change proportionally to $|a_1|^2$ and $|a_2|^2$ whereas the coupling can be considered unaffected. We shall consider a symmetric structure. Suppose that the index changes due to the intensity in the guide so that

$$\beta_1 = \beta + b|a_1|^2 \tag{65}$$

and

$$\beta_2 = \beta + b|a_2|^2 \tag{66}$$

where b is proportional to the third-order nonlinearity coefficient. Introducing Eq. (65) and Eq. (66) into Eqs. (58) and (59) and setting $\kappa_{12} = \kappa_{21} = \kappa$, one obtains

$$\frac{da_1}{dz} = -j\beta a_1 + j\kappa a_2 - jb|a_1|^2 \tag{67}$$

$$\frac{da_2}{dz} = -j\beta a_2 + j\kappa a_1 - jb|a_2|^2 \tag{68}$$

These equations have closed form solutions [18]. To demonstrate this set

$$a_1 = A_1 e^{-j\phi_1} \tag{69}$$

$$a_2 = A_2 e^{-j\phi_2} \tag{70}$$

and introduce this Ansatz in Eqs. (65) and (66). One obtains four real equations for the real parameters A_1, A_2, ϕ_1, and ϕ_2. One can prove by manipulation of the derivatives that the power P_0,

$$P_0 \equiv |A_1|^2 + |A_2|^2$$

is independent of z, which is an obvious consequence of the fact that the structure is lossless. The nonlinearity affects only the phase of the waves. Not so obvious is the fact that the quantity

$$\Gamma \equiv 4A_1 A_2 \cos(\phi_1 - \phi_2) + \frac{2b}{\kappa} A_1^2 A_2^2 \tag{71}$$

also obeys $d\Gamma/dz = 0$ (i.e., is an invariant). Using this fact, one can derive an equation for $|A_1|^2 \equiv P_1$, the power in guide (1) [18].

$$\left(\frac{dP_1}{dz}\right)^2 = \kappa(4\kappa + \Gamma b)P_1(P_0 - P_1) - \tfrac{1}{4}\Gamma^2 \kappa^2 - b^2 P_1^2(P_0 - P_1)^2 \tag{72}$$

This equation integrates as an elliptic integral. Figure 14 (taken from reference [18]) shows the power P_1 as a function of distance for different input power P_1 into guide (1) with guide (2) unexcited, where $P_c \equiv 4\kappa/b$ and $Z = \kappa z$. Figure 15 shows the output in guide (1) for increasing power in guide (1) for a coupler of fixed length.

Li Kam Wa *et al.* [3] constructed a two-guide coupler incorporating a quantum well driven by a semiconductor laser. The experiment was done in strain-induced coupled waveguides above a substrate containing a multiple quantum well (MQW) structure comprising 25 wells each of 100 Å thickness. The waveguides were formed at the edge of 0.5 μm thick Au layers deposited on the top of the sample. The coupling length for complete power transfer was 1.7 mm. Jensen's theory gives for the critical power at which a coupler

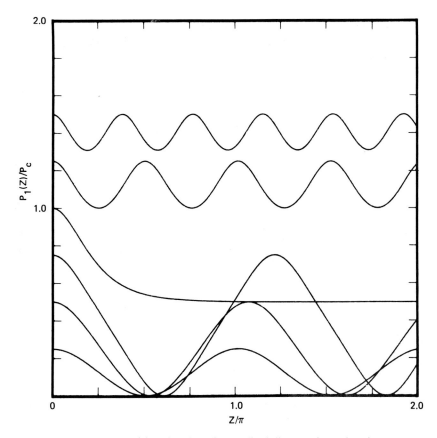

Fig. 14. Power in guide (1) as function of normalized distance, for various input powers. (From Jensen [18], © 1982 IEEE.)

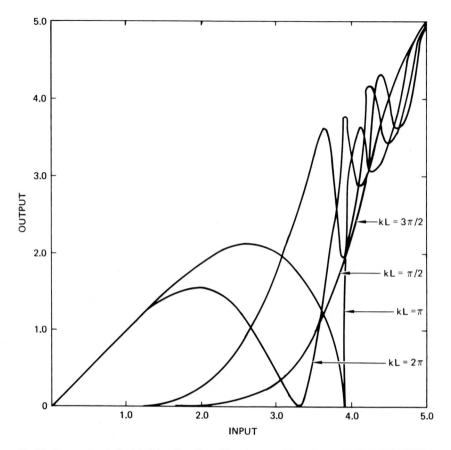

Fig. 15. Power at end of guide (1) as function of input power. (From Jensen [18], © 1982 IEEE.)

of critical length achieves equal division of power (Fig. 15)

$$P_c = \frac{A\lambda_0}{n_2 L_c} \tag{73}$$

where $L_c = \pi/2|\kappa|$ is the critical length (1.7 mm), A the guide cross section (10 μm^2), $n_2 = 10^{-7}$ cm$^2/W$ and $\lambda_0 = 0.85$ μm, the wavelength of the source. The value of n_2 was arrived at from the fact that the peak of the exciton absorption at the temperature of the sample (180 K) was estimated at 0.82 μm and the operating wavelength of the semiconductor laser diode was detuned from it at a wavelength of 0.85 μm. One finds

$$P_c = 500 \text{ μW} \tag{74}$$

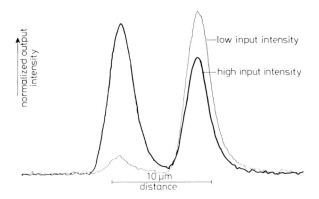

Fig. 16. Experimental results of Li Kim Wa *et al.* [3].

The laser diode produced of the order of 1 mW peak power with a pulsewidth of 20 ns and a 1-kHz repetition rate. The experimental output intensity with one guide excited in a sample of 1.7 mm length is shown in Fig. 16. One can see a definite change of the power transfer. At low intensity the second guide is very weakly excited. At the highest intensity the split approaches a 50/50 ratio.

VII. Nonlinear Waveguide Materials, Devices, and Design Considerations

For nonlinear optical waveguide devices to become practical, judicious choices among available materials and technologies must be made to determine the best development directions. In this section some of the design tradeoffs are discussed, and the status of various nonlinear waveguide technologies reviewed.

A. NONLINEAR MATERIALS

For many of these applications it is desirable to have a very fast nonlinearity. However, a rule of thumb is that for most materials a nonlinear figure of merit $n_2/\alpha\tau$ is constant within a factor of 10. Here α is the absorption coefficient and τ the response time (turn off) of the nonlinearity. This suggests that high speed and the necessary low absorption imply a relatively weak n_2. This is indeed the case for $LiNbO_3$. For other materials, such as some quantum-well structures, high n_2 is achieved in wavelength bands where, by Kramers–Kronig, there also exists high absorption. This can limit transmission lengths, a detriment in many-mm-long waveguide structures. (For such long structures it is desirable to have $\alpha \lesssim 1\ cm^{-1}$ to keep total insertion loss to tolerable levels.) Absorption also tends to produce heating, so that relatively slow thermal (relative to electronic) nonlinearities become significant and can limit response speed and high-speed switch extinction ratios. These generic arguments have led to a search for improved materials. Some of the most promising materials in which waveguides have been demonstrated include semiconductor-doped glasses, GaAs/GaAlAs quantum wells, and organic films. These are discussed below.

Semiconductor-doped glasses are a class of materials that contain microcrystallites (100–1000 Å diameter) of a semiconductor in a borosilicate glass host. Conventional color glass cut-off filters that contain varying amounts of CdS_xSe_{1-x} are one example of such materials. A plot of the measured spectral dependence of n_2 and induced absorption for one glass is shown in Fig. 17 [22]. Here 5-ns low-duty-cycle pulses were used. The change of sign of the index at the band edge is what one expects if the nonlinearity is due to band-filling effects. Response times of 30 ps have been reported, but an underlying slow (~ 10 ns) process, probably thermal in nature, was also observed [23]. If the glass also contains Na, it is possible to use ion-exchange technology [24] (e.g., Ag–Na exchange) to form optical waveguides. In this technique regions of Ag dopant have higher index of refraction. Work to date has demonstrated slab and channel guides [25], but nonlinear measurements have not yet been reported.

Work on optical waveguides with GaAs/GaAlAs quantum-well material is also in its early stages. A fair amount of data exist on the spectral dependence of n_2, and values near the band edge as large as $n_2 \sim 2 \times 10^{-4}$ cm^2/W (considerably enhanced over bulk material) have been reported [26]. Much of this work has been motivated by interest in bistable

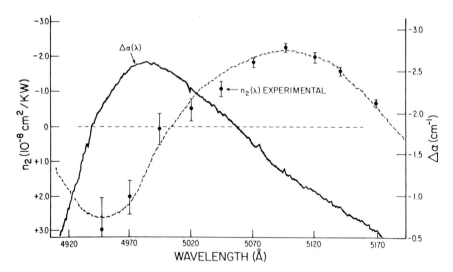

Fig. 17. Nonlinear refractive index of Cd $S_{0.9}Se_{0.1}$. (From Olbright and Peyghambarian [22].)

thin-film etalon devices. These results, as well as enhanced electroabsorption QW-waveguide modulation experiments, suggest that multiple quantum-well structures, operated at wavelengths of ≤ 300 Å from the gap, may be too lossy to be practical for waveguide use. The peak value of n_2 quoted above corresponds to band edge absorption of $\sim 10^4$ cm^{-1}, and the work of Wa *et al.* on nonlinear couplers had $\alpha \sim 15$ cm^{-1} at a wavelength of $\lambda = 0.85$ where $n_2 \sim 10^{-7}$ cm^2/W. This suggests that operation in specialized structures such as quantum-well pockets in passive guides, or one- or two-well structures, or operation far from the band edge may be required for nonlinear guided wave devices.

There has been a fair amount of work on organic materials grown specifically for high nonlinearity. Most of the reports of high nonlinearity have been on bulk crystals, which for a variety of reasons (including much surface scattering) have not yet been used to form waveguides. An advantage of working with organic materials is the large variety of host materials and dopant molecules available to synthesize crystals. Encouraging results have recently been obtained [27] for polydiacetylene (PTS) platelets (1 μm thick) which have been grown with good optical quality. To date only four-wave mixing experiments, in which the beams were incident perpendicular to the surface, have been reported for this material. Values of $\chi^{(3)}$ ranging from 9×10^{-10} esu at 6575 Å (near the band edge) to 5×10^{-10} esu at 7000 Å have been reported (Fig. 18). These are the largest values for fast, high-optical-quality material yet reported. Response speed was measured to be <6 ps. The absorption for these platelets was relatively high ($\sim 10^3$ cm^{-1} at 6625 Å) and $\sim 2 \times 10^2$ cm^{-1} at 7015 Å. This suggests that one must work further from the band edge for waveguide applications. For example, at $\lambda = 1.3$ μm the absorption should be adequately low, and measurements of near-IR $\chi^{(3)}$ suggest that reasonable nonlinearity could be attainable [28]. Recently, slab waveguides were reported [29], made by a solvent-assisted indiffusion of nonlinear molecules into an inert matrix. A variety of molecules was evaluated, including DAN ($n_2 \sim 5 \times 10^{-7}$ cm^2/W, $\tau \sim 2$ ms) and ONA ($n_2 \sim 10^{-13}$ cm^2/W, $\tau < 5$ ns). Further advances can be expected in this technology.

B. ULTRASHORT-PULSE SOURCES

Practical design and eventual application of nonlinear optical waveguides devices depend, finally, upon the characteristics of the optical sources and signals with which they are to be used. Material properties, device structures, and system requirements all must be compatible with practical laser systems. Speed and efficiency will be determined by the available optical pulse durations, energies, wavelengths, and coherence properties. Application will depend upon the size, reliability, and energy consumption of the sources.

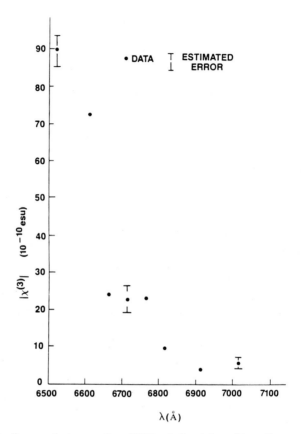

Fig. 18. Nonlinear optical properties of PTS polydiacetylene. (From Carter *et al.* [27].)

At present most investigations of nonlinear material properties and device performance rely upon the use of laboratory systems based on dye, Nd:YAG, or color-center lasers. These lasers provide great research flexibility with picosecond and femtosecond pulses, pulse energies ranging from nanojoules to microjoules, and broad wavelength coverage. But practical application of nonlinear optical waveguide devices depends upon their eventual compatibility with semiconductor diode lasers. Thus a few words on short-pulse diode lasers are in order.

An attractive feature of diode lasers is their ability to be modulated at high speed by direct current modulation. Because of their small size and high gain, resonator lifetimes are on the order of picoseconds, and transient excitation can result in optical pulses of 20–50 ps in duration. Demonstrated methods for producing such pulses include the use of rf modulation on top of a dc bias [30], step-recovery diodes and comb generators [31], and ultrafast electrical excitation with an Auston switch [32]. A disadvantage of these methods is that the rapid current modulation tends to result in frequency modulated, non-bandwidth-limited pulses [33]. To a certain extent this chirping can be controlled by laser design (i.e., DFB or cleaved-cavity structures) or compensated by group velocity dispersion. Whether these remedies are sufficient depends upon the application.

An alternative approach that also can result in shorter pulses is mode-locking in an external resonator. With an external resonator it is not necessary for the diode to generate a completely new optical pulse with each excitation pulse. Pulse shaping and control are facilitated by repetitive passes of the pulse through the diode and other elements of the resonator. A fraction of the pulse energy is transmitted through one of the mirrors to produce an output train with period corresponding to the resonator round-trip time. This mode-locked operation can be achieved either by active modulation of the diode in synchronism with the round-trip frequency [34] or by the passive method [35] of introducing a saturable absorber. Ho [36] has recently reviewed the literature on the subject. Among the best research results to date are 5-ps pulses at a repetition rate of 20 GHz for an actively mode-locked system [37] and subpicosecond pulses at rates of several GHz for passive systems [38, 39].

The average output powers of mode-locked lasers correspond to those of continuous wave (cw) devices: 1–10 mW. So typical pulse energies are in the range of 0.5–10 pJ depending upon repetition rate. Peak powers vary inversely with pulse duration and, fortunately, can be considerably higher than the damage-limit peak powers inferred from long pulse or cw operation.

C. Design Considerations and Summary

To see how material parameters and laser powers affect the design of devices, consider again the equation for nonlinear modulation of optical phase in a waveguide of length L:

$$\Phi = \frac{2\pi}{\lambda} \Delta n \, L \qquad (75)$$

where Φ is the induced phase change. In terms of the material figure-of-merit given above, this becomes

$$\Phi = \frac{2\pi}{\lambda} \left\{ \frac{n_2}{\alpha\tau} \right\} \cdot \{I\tau\} \cdot \{\alpha L\} \qquad (76)$$

Thus the effectiveness of the modulator at a particular wavelength is determined by the product of three terms. The first is the material figure-of-merit. The second, if we assume that the optical pulse duration is optimized to fit the material response time (or vice versa), is only the pulse energy. It is simply determined by the average power obtainable from the diode laser.

The third term in Eq. (74), αL, is a measure of the insertion loss of the modulator. How much is permitted is a function of system design, but obviously it cannot be made arbitrarily large. A reasonable assumption is $\alpha L = 1$. Therefore the real tradeoff here is between thermal dissipation (which affects Φ by changing temperature) and pipeline delay (which is proportional to L). Important examples at opposite ends of this trade-off are semiconductor waveguide devices (which have relatively large absorption losses associated with high nonlinearity) and optical fibers (which have such low losses that they become very attractive if long interaction lengths are permissible).

In summary, eventual practicality of all-optical waveguide modulators depends upon future advances in both nonlinear materials and semiconductor diode lasers, and progress can be expected on both fronts. We have found that use of a figure of merit, $n_2/\alpha\tau$, is helpful in comparing materials. But materials with the same figure of merit may require different device structures (i.e., different interaction lengths) for optimal use. The development of high power diode lasers and laser arrays can be expected to increase interest in nonlinear optical signal processing.

Acknowledgments

The work done at MIT was supported in part by the Joint Services Electronics Program under Contract DAAL03-86-K-0002. Sections V.B and V.C are based on work by Dr. Y. Yamamoto of Nippon Telegraph and Telephone (NTT) and on joint work done while one of the authors (HAH) spent two months at the NTT Laboratory in January and February 1985.

References

1. A. Migus, A. Antonetti, D. Hulin, A. Mysyrowicz, H. M. Gibbs, N. Peyghambarian, and J. I. Jewells, *Appl. Phys. Lett.* **46**, 70 (1985).
2. A. Lattes, H. A. Haus, F. J. Leonberger, and E. P. Ippen, *IEEE J. Quantum Electron.* **QE-19**, 1718 (1983).
3. P. Li Kam Wa, J. E. Stitch, N. J. Mason, J. S. Roberts, and P. N. Robson, *Electron. Lett.* **21**, 26 (1985).
4. H. Kogelnik and V. Ramaswamy, *Appl. Opt.* **8**, 1857 (1974).
5. H. A. Haus and W. P. Huang, *IEEE J. Lightwave Tech.* (to be published).
6. C. T. Seaton, J. D. Valera, R. L. Shoemaker, G. I. Stegeman, J. Chilwell, and S. D. Smith, *IEEE J. Quantum Electron.* **QE-21**, 774 (1985).
7. E. P. Ippen and C. V. Shank, in "Ultrashort Light Pulses" (S. L. Shapiro, ed.). Springer-Verlag, Berlin and New York, 1977.
8. J. Feinberg, D. Heiman, A. R. Tanguay, Jr., and R. W. Hellwarth, *J. Appl. Phys.* **51**, 1297 (1980).
9. B. S. Wherrett, A. L. Smirl, and T. F. Boggess, *IEEE J. Quantum Electron.* **QE-19**, 680 (1983); J. L. Oudar, D. Hulin, A. Migus, and F. Alexandre, *Phys. Rev. Lett.* **55**, 2075 (1985).

10. L. A. Molter-Orr, H. A. Haus, and F. J. Leonberger, *IEEE J. Quantum Electron.* **QE-19**, 1877 (1983).
11. H. Haga, M. Izutsu, and T. Sueta, *IOOC '83 Conf., Tokyo*, Pap. 30B2-3 (1983); also T. Sueta and M. Izutsu, *J. Opt. Commun.* **3**, 52 (1982).
12. A. M. Glass, *Opt. Eng.* **17**, 470 (1978).
13. G. D. Aumiller, *Opt. Commun.* **14**, 115 (1982).
14. V. B. Braginsky, Y. I. Vorontsov, and K. S. Thorne, *Science* **209**, 547 (1980).
15. N. Imoto, H. A. Haus, and Y. Yamamoto, *Phys. Rev. A* **32**, 2287 (1985).
16. D. A. Kleinmann, *Phys. Rev.* **126**, 1977 (1962).
17. J. H. Shapiro, *Opt. Lett.* **5**, 351 (1980).
18. S. M. Jensen, *IEEE J. Quantum Electron.* **QE-18**, 1580 (1982).
19. Y. Silberberg, P. W. Smith, D. A. B. Miller, B. Tell, A. C. Gossard, and W. Wiegmann, *Appl. Phys. Lett.* **46**, 701 (1985).
20. H. A. Haus, "Waves and Fields in Optoelectronics." Prentice-Hall, Englewood Cliffs, New Jersey, 1984.
21. A. Hardy and W. Streifer, *IEEE/OSA J. Lightwave Tech.* **LT-3**, 1135 (1985).
22. G. R. Olbright and N. Peyghambarian, *Appl. Phys. Lett.* **48**, 1184 (1976).
23. S. S. Yao, C. Karaguleff, A. Gabriel, R. Fortenberg, C. T. Seaton, and G. Stegeman, *Appl. Phys. Lett.* **46**, 801 (1985).
24. See, e.g., T. Findakly, *Opt. Eng.* **24**, 244 (1985).
25. C. M. Ironside, J. F. Duffy, R. H. Hutchins, W. C. Bangai, C. I. Seaton, and G. I. Stegeman, *Proc. Int. Conf. Integr. Opt. Opt. Fiber Commun., 5th, Venice* p. 237 (1985).
26. D. S. Chemla, D. A. B. Miller, P. W. Smith, A. C. Gossard, and W. Wiegman, *IEEE J. Quantum Electron.* **QE-20**, 265 (1984).
27. G. M. Carter, M. K. Thakur, Y. J. Chen, and J. V. Hryniewicz, *Appl. Phys. Lett.* **47**, 457 (1985).
28. J. P. Hermann and P. W. Smith, *Dig. Tech. Pap. Int. Quantum Electron. Conf., 11th, Boston, Mass.* Pap. T6, p. 656. IEEE, New York, 1980.
29. M. J. Goodwin, R. Glenn, and I. Bennion, *Electron. Lett.* **22**, 789 (1986).
30. H. Ito, H. Yokoyama, S. Murata, and H. Inaba, *IEEE J. Quantum Electron.* **QE-17**, 663 (1979).
31. C. Lin, P. L. Liu, T. C. Damen, D. J. Eilenberger, and R. L. Hartman, *Electron. Lett.* **16**, 600 (1980).
32. E. O. Gobel, G. Veith, J. Kuhl, H.-U. Habermeier, K. Lubke, and A. Perger, *Appl. Phys. Lett.* **42**, 25, 1983; J. M. Wiesenfeld, R. S. Tucker, P. M. Downey, and J. E. Bowers, *Electron. Lett.* **22**, 396 (1986).
33. C. Lin, T.-P. Lee, and C. A. Burrus, *Appl. Phys. Lett.* **42**, 141 (1983).
34. P.-T. Ho, L. A. Glasser, E. P. Ippen, and H. A. Haus, *Appl. Phys. Lett.* **33**, 241 (1978).
35. E. P. Ippen, D. J. Eilenberger, and R. W. Dixon, *Appl. Phys. Lett.* **37**, 267 (1980).
36. P.-T. Ho, in "Picosecond Optoelectronic Devices" (C. H. Lee, ed.). Academic Press, Orlando, Florida, 1984.
37. G. Eisenstein, R. S. Tucker, S. K. Korotky, U. Koren, J. J. Veselka, L. W. Stutz, R. M. Jopson, and K. L. Hall, *Electron. Lett.* **21**, 173 (1985).
38. J. P. Van der Ziel, W. T. Tsang, R. A. Logan, R. M. Mikulyak, and W. M. Augustyniak, *Appl. Phys. Lett.* **39**, 525 (1981).
39. Y. Silberberg, P. W. Smith, D. J. Eilenberger, D. A. B. Miller, A. C. Gossard, and W. Wiegmann, *Opt. Lett.* **9**, 507 (1984).

V
Transformations

5.1

Optical Transformations

BAHAA E. A. SALEH AND MARK O. FREEMAN
DEPARTMENT OF ELECTRICAL AND COMPUTER ENGINEERING
UNIVERSITY OF WISCONSIN
MADISON, WISCONSIN 53706

I. Introduction

Numerous advances have been made in the use of optics to perform transformations on analog signals since the publication of the classic paper of Cutrona, Leith, Palermo, and Porcello in 1960 [1]. In that paper the basic architectures for computing two-dimensional (2-D) Fourier transforms as well as 2-D linear shift-invariant filtering operations were laid out. In the following decades the new discipline of optical data processing attracted considerable interest, which resulted in the extension of the class of transformations achievable with optical processors. In 1977 Goodman [2] reviews the state of the art, which then encompassed linear shift-variant operations, coordinate transformations, and a number of special nonlinear filtering operations. Since then, progress in hardware (spatial light modulators, optical detectors, and holographic systems) has been paralleled by the introduction of new architectures and applications to an even wider class of transformations [3–8]. This chapter reviews some of those advances with an emphasis on geometric, shift-variant, nonlinear, and transdimensional transformations. Emphasis is also placed on the interrelations between the various transformations.

The classes of transformations and their interrelations are defined in Section I.A. Section I.B. introduces the basic principles of optical implementation of these transformations.

A.   Definition and Classification of Transformations

Consider the general transformation

$$\mathbf{g(u)} = T\{\mathbf{f(x)}\} \tag{1}$$

applied on an input function (signal or image) $\mathbf{f(x)}$ to produce a transformed output function $\mathbf{g(u)}$, as illustrated in Fig. 1. The variables $\mathbf{x}$ and $\mathbf{u}$ and the functions $\mathbf{f}$ and $\mathbf{g}$ belong to sets $\mathcal{F}$, $\mathcal{G}$, $\mathcal{X}$, and $\mathcal{U}$ which define their nature, $\mathbf{x} \in \mathcal{X}$, $\mathbf{u} \in \mathcal{U}$, $\mathbf{f} \in \mathcal{F}$, and $\mathbf{g} \in \mathcal{G}$. We shall denote the components of $\mathbf{x}$ and $\mathbf{u}$ by $\mathbf{x} = (x, y, z, \ldots)$ and $\mathbf{u} = (u, v, w, \ldots)$.

Transformations can be classified according to the nature of the variables $\mathbf{x}$ and $\mathbf{u}$, the functions $\mathbf{f}$ and $\mathbf{g}$ or the mapping T itself, as follows.

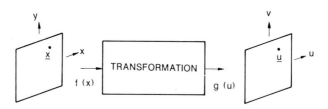

Fig. 1. Transformation of a function $f(\mathbf{x})$ into a function $g(\mathbf{x})$.

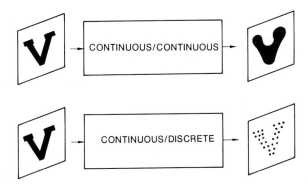

Fig. 2. Continuous/continuous and continuous/discrete transformations.

1. Classifications Based on Input and Output Fields

A transformation is classified as continuous–continuous, continuous–discrete, discrete–continuous, or discrete–discrete, depending on whether the independent variables **x** and **u** are continuous or discrete (Fig. 2). For example, a transformation that computes the Fourier series coefficients $g(u)$, $u = 0, \pm 1, \pm 2, \ldots$ of a function $f(x)$ would be classified as a continuous–discrete transformation. Components of **x** (or **u**) need not be of the same nature (continuous–discrete); for example, in the transformation that obtains the circular harmonics $g(r, p)$ from a 2-D function $f(r, \theta)$, the variable $\mathbf{u} = (r, p)$ has a discrete component $p = 0, \pm 1, \pm 2, \ldots$, representing the order of the harmonic, and a continuous component, namely, the polar coordinate r.

A transformation is classified on the basis of the dimensionality of the variables **x** and **u**, say N and M. We shall call the transformation an N-dimensional to M-dimensional (N-D/M-D) transformation. When $N \neq M$, the transformation is called transdimensional. An example is a 2-D to 1-D transformation obtained when a 2-D image $f(x, y)$ is scanned to generate a video signal $g(u)$ (Fig. 3).

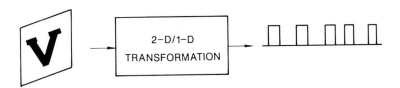

Fig. 3. Two-dimensional to 1-D transdimensional transformation.

2. Classifications Based on Input and Output Functions

The functions f and g may be complex-valued, real-valued, or binary-valued functions. They may be scalar or vector functions. In the case where f and/or g are vectors, the transformation can be modeled as a multiport system, having more than one input or output (Fig. 4). For example, the transformations of multiplication and cross-correlation have two input functions transformed into one output function. Likewise, transformations on color images operate on three input functions to generate three output functions.

3. Classifications Based on Mapping

a. Linear Transformations. A transformation is said to be linear if the transformation of a superposition of two inputs is the superposition of their transformations, that is,

$$T\{af_1(\mathbf{x}) + bf_2(\mathbf{x})\} = aT\{f_1(\mathbf{x})\} + bT\{f_2(\mathbf{x})\}$$

where a and b are constants. When this property is not satisfied, the transformation is said to be nonlinear.

A linear transformation is completely characterized by its impulse response function $h(\mathbf{u}, \mathbf{x}') = T\{\delta(\mathbf{x} - \mathbf{x}')\}$. This is the response to an input impulse at $\mathbf{x}'$. The input and output are related by the integral

$$g(\mathbf{u}) = \int h(\mathbf{u}, \mathbf{x}) f(\mathbf{x}) \, d\mathbf{x} \tag{2}$$

Throughout this chapter, when limits of integrals are not denoted, they cover the entire domain of the variables of integration.

b. Shift-Invariant Transformations. A transformation (for which $N = M$) is said to be shift-invariant if it is invariant to shifts of the input function

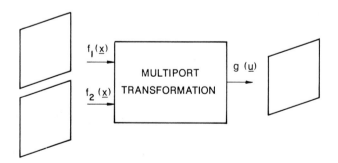

Fig. 4. Transformation of two functions $f_1(\mathbf{x})$ and $f_2(\mathbf{x})$ into one function $g(\mathbf{u})$.

$f(\mathbf{x})$, that is, $T\{f(\mathbf{x})\} = g(\mathbf{u})$ implies that $T\{f(\mathbf{x} - \mathbf{x}_0)\} = g(\mathbf{u} - \mathbf{x}_0)$ for all $\mathbf{x}_0$. A transformation that does not satisfy this property is said to be shift-variant.

The impulse response function of a linear shift-invariant system $h(\mathbf{u}, \mathbf{x}) = h(\mathbf{u} - \mathbf{x})$ is a function of only the difference $\mathbf{u} - \mathbf{x}$. The input and output are related by the convolution

$$g(\mathbf{x}) = f(\mathbf{u}) * h(\mathbf{u}) \equiv \int h(\mathbf{u} - \mathbf{x}) f(\mathbf{x})\, d\mathbf{x} \tag{3}$$

c. Point Transformations. Point (or zero-spread) transformations are transformations for which the value of the input $f(\mathbf{x})$ at any particular point $\mathbf{x}$ of the input field influences the value of the output function $g(\mathbf{u})$ at one and only one point $\mathbf{u}$ of the output field. In general, the output function at a point $\mathbf{u}$ may be affected by values at one or many points of the input field (Fig. 5).

A point-to-point (or one-to-one) transformation is a special case of a point transformation in which the value at a point in the output field is determined by the value of only one corresponding point in the input field (Fig. 5). If the correspondence $\mathbf{u} = \mathbf{x}$ is assumed, then

$$g(\mathbf{x}) = \psi[f(\mathbf{x}), \mathbf{x}] \tag{4}$$

where ψ is some function of f and $\mathbf{x}$. If a point transformation is shift-invariant, then that function is independent of $\mathbf{x}$,

$$g(\mathbf{x}) = \psi[f(\mathbf{x})] \tag{5}$$

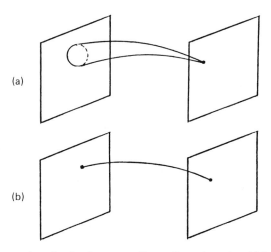

(a)

(b)

Fig. 5. Two examples of point (zero-spread) transformations, in which each point $\mathbf{x}$ of input contributes to only one point $\mathbf{u}$ of output. (a) General case and (b) a point-to-point transformation.

that is, the law for transforming f into g is independent of location $\mathbf{x}$. An example is the nonlinear transformation $g(\mathbf{x}) = \log[f(\mathbf{x})]$. The transformation may or may not be invertible. For example, the transformation $g(\mathbf{x}) = f^2(\mathbf{x})$ is not invertible (assuming f and g are real functions).

The concept of point transformations can also be generalized to multipoint transformations. A point in the input may contribute to two points in the output. An example is the transformation

$$g(\mathbf{x}) = f(\mathbf{x}) + f(-\mathbf{x})$$

which transforms an image into two superimposed copies, one straight and one inverted.

d. Geometric Transformations. Geometric, or coordinate, transformations are linear (in general, shift-variant) transformations obtained by changing the coordinate system using a mapping

$$\mathbf{u} = \boldsymbol{\psi}(\mathbf{x}) \tag{6}$$

that is,

$$f(\mathbf{x}) = g[\boldsymbol{\psi}(\mathbf{x})] \tag{7}$$

The mapping $\mathbf{u} = \boldsymbol{\psi}(\mathbf{x})$ itself may be linear or nonlinear.

When the mapping $\mathbf{u} = \boldsymbol{\psi}(\mathbf{x})$ is a one-to-one invertible mapping, $\mathbf{x} = \boldsymbol{\psi}^{-1}(\mathbf{u})$, and

$$g(\mathbf{u}) = f[\boldsymbol{\psi}^{-1}(\mathbf{u})] \tag{8}$$

The system then has an impulse response function

$$h(\mathbf{u}, \mathbf{x}) = \delta[\mathbf{x} - \boldsymbol{\psi}^{-1}(\mathbf{u})] \tag{9}$$

An example is the cartesian-to-polar transformation

$$\mathbf{u} = (r, \theta) = \left((x^2 + y^2)^{1/2}, \tan^{-1} \frac{y}{x} \right), \qquad \mathbf{x} = (x, y) = (r \cos \theta, r \sin \theta)$$

Of some interest also are noninvertible mappings $\mathbf{u} = \psi(\mathbf{x})$, for which many points $\mathbf{x}$ correspond to one point $\mathbf{u}$. In this case, one definition of the relation between $f(\mathbf{x})$ and $g(\mathbf{u})$ is

$$g(\mathbf{u}) = \int_{\Omega(\mathbf{u})} f(\mathbf{x}) \, d\mathbf{x} \tag{10}$$

where $\Omega(\mathbf{u})$ is the region in the $\mathbf{x}$-plane for which $\boldsymbol{\psi}(\mathbf{x}) = \mathbf{u}$. In the literature of sensory systems this region is called the receptive field. A comparison between Eqs. (10) and (2) reveals that this geometric transformation can be regarded as a special case of a linear system.

An example is the transformation

$$g(u) = \int f(u, y) \, dy \tag{11}$$

This 2-D/1-D transformation (which represents projection) can be regarded as a geometric transformation that transforms lines in the input plane into points on the output line. It can alternatively be regarded as a member of the class of linear shift-variant systems described by an impulse response function $h(u, \mathbf{x}) = \delta(u - x)$ (note that $\mathbf{x} = (x, y)$).

One might wonder whether an arbitrary linear transformation, such as Eq. (2), can be regarded as a geometric transformation. This is not so. First, geometric transformations cannot describe transformations that have spread (i.e., that are not point transformations). Second, an arbitrary linear zero-spread transformation not only maps one or many points in the input plane into a point in the output plane (as a geometric transformation does), but it also assigns varying weights (measures) to those points and adds them to determine the value of the output at that point.

e. Bilinear Transformations. A bilinear transformation is a transformation of a vector input signal $\mathbf{f}(\mathbf{x}) = \{f_1(\mathbf{x}), f_2(\mathbf{x})\}$ into one output signal $g(\mathbf{u})$, such that $g(\mathbf{u})$ is linearly related to each of the components $f_1(\mathbf{x})$ and $f_2(\mathbf{x})$,

$$g(\mathbf{u}) = \int\int f_1^*(x_1) f_2(x_2) h(\mathbf{u}; x_1, x_2) \, dx_1 \, dx_2 \tag{12}$$

where h is the transformation kernel. Three important examples of this transformation are the product

$$g(\mathbf{x}) = f_1^*(\mathbf{x}) f_2(\mathbf{x})$$

the cross-correlation

$$g(\mathbf{u}) = \int f_1^*(\mathbf{x}) f_2(\mathbf{x} + \mathbf{u}) \, d\mathbf{x}$$

and the convolution

$$g(\mathbf{u}) = \int f_1(\mathbf{x}) f_2(\mathbf{u} - \mathbf{x}) \, d\mathbf{x}$$

In the degenerate case, for which $f_1(\mathbf{x}) = f_2(\mathbf{x}) = f(\mathbf{x})$, we have the quadratic transformation

$$g(\mathbf{u}) = \int\int f^*(\mathbf{x}_1) f(\mathbf{x}_2) h(\mathbf{u}; \mathbf{x}_1, \mathbf{x}_2) \, d\mathbf{x}_1 \, d\mathbf{x}_2 \tag{13}$$

where now $f(\mathbf{x})$ is a scalar. Under some conditions of analyticity, a nonlinear relation between $f(\mathbf{x})$ and $g(\mathbf{x})$ that involves spread can be written in the form of a series expansion (similar to a Taylor's series expansion) known as the Volterra series expansion [9]. The first term is independent of f; the second is a linear operation on f, as in Eq. (2); the third is a quadratic operation on f, as in Eq. (13); the fourth is a transformation that involves triple products of the function $f(\mathbf{x})$ at triplets of points; and so on.

The above transformations and their optical implementations are discussed in detail in the following sections. Sections II–V discuss linear transformations of different kinds: Section II, geometric transformations; Section III, transdimensional transformations; and Section IV, different shift-variant transformations. Nonlinear transformations are the subject of Section V. We first give a brief review of the basic principles of optical implementation.

B. Principles of Optical Implementation

The first step in implementing a transformation $g(\mathbf{u}) = T\{f(\mathbf{x})\}$ is to represent the functions $f(\mathbf{x})$ and $g(\mathbf{u})$ with optical quantities. The usual quantities are optical fields (which represent complex-valued functions) and optical intensities (which are limited to real nonnegative functions) [10]. Other optical variables include amplitude or intensity transmittance or reflectance of masks, holograms, spatial light modulators, and other optical media. The two polarization components may also be used. The next step is to implement the transformation T using optical elements. A variety of optical elements exist including lenses, mirrors, prisms, apertures, masks, holograms, optical wave guides (e.g., optical fibers), optical modulators (e.g., acoustooptic, electrooptic, and liquid crystals), and, of course, propagation in free space (the least expensive optical element).

Such optical elements perform two important functions: *multiplication* (e.g., a mask multiplies an incident optical field by its transmittance) and *routing* (e.g., prisms, lenses, and holograms redirect light rays between points of two parallel planes). Light has the inherent property of *addition* or superposition (allowing us to add two optical fields). It is the combination of these three primary operations—multiplication, routing, and addition—that allows us to design architectures for the optical implementation of numerous transformations. Theoretically, all *linear* transformations can be implemented by use of these primary operations. Geometric transformations are implemented by use of the routing properties of some optical elements. Nonlinear operations are more difficult to implement. Some nonlinear operations (e.g., autocorrelations and bilinear transformations) utilize the quadratic relation between optical field and optical intensity. Others require highly nonlinear optical devices (e.g., thresholding devices for realizing logic operations).

Optical processors are inherently 2-D: They transform a 2-D signal into another 2-D signal. Transdimensional transformations can be used to convert the dimensions of the signal to be transformed (1-D, 3-D, or 4-D) to 2-D. This ability to change the dimensionality of the problem is the basis of some architectures of optical processing as will be seen in the remainder of this chapter. Another architectural principle is that of decomposing a desired transformation as a serial (cascade) or parallel combination of other operations whose optical realization is established. This principle will also be amply demonstrated.

II. Geometric Transformations

Geometric or coordinate transformations substantially expand the range of operations performable by optical systems by introducing controlled shift-variance. They have been used to correct for aberrations in imaging systems and TV systems [11–13], for redistributing illumination to produce custom-designed wave fronts [14–17], and in the areas of shift-variant data processing and pattern recognition [13, 18–29].

As mentioned in Section I.A, a geometric transformation maps each point $\mathbf{x}$ in the input field to a point $\mathbf{u} = \boldsymbol{\psi}(\mathbf{x})$ in the output field. We shall also denote this mapping in terms of its components $\mathbf{u} = (u, v)$, $\mathbf{x} = (x, y)$ in the form

$$u = \psi_1(x, y)$$
$$v = \psi_2(x, y) \tag{14}$$

Figure 6 shows some commonly encountered coordinate transformations. Figures 6a–6d are the results of, say, changing camera or viewing positions, whereas Fig. 6e shows two types of distortion common in less expensive lenses and displays. Figures 6f–6h show how appropriate transformations can result in invariances useful in pattern recognition; Fig. 6f, logarithmic transformation results in scale invariance; Fig. 6g, polar transformation results in rotational invariance; and Fig. 6h, combination of logarithmic and polar transformations gives invariance to both scale and rotation.

A. PRINCIPLE OF OPTICAL IMPLEMENTATION

Some geometric transformations are implemented by use of simple optical elements such as mirrors, prisms, and lenses. Fun-house mirrors and cheap "wavy" windows provide examples of interesting familiar geometric transformations. They also provide the key to producing desired transformations.

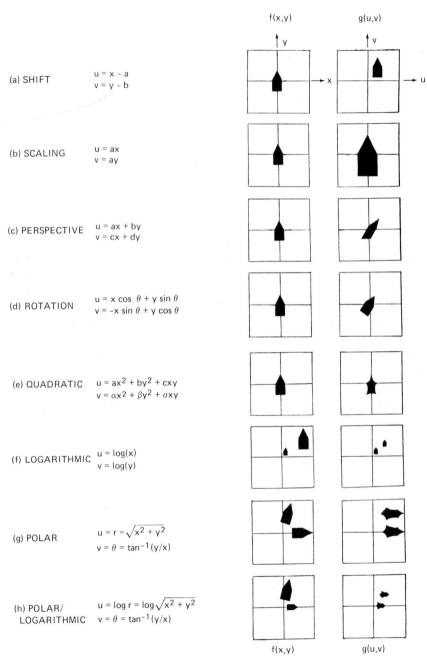

(a) SHIFT	$u = x - a$ $v = y - b$	
(b) SCALING	$u = ax$ $v = ay$	
(c) PERSPECTIVE	$u = ax + by$ $v = cx + dy$	
(d) ROTATION	$u = x \cos\theta + y \sin\theta$ $v = -x \sin\theta + y \cos\theta$	
(e) QUADRATIC	$u = ax^2 + by^2 + cxy$ $v = \alpha x^2 + \beta y^2 + \sigma xy$	
(f) LOGARITHMIC	$u = \log(x)$ $v = \log(y)$	
(g) POLAR	$u = r = \sqrt{x^2 + y^2}$ $v = \theta = \tan^{-1}(y/x)$	
(h) POLAR/ LOGARITHMIC	$u = \log r = \log\sqrt{x^2 + y^2}$ $v = \theta = \tan^{-1}(y/x)$	

Fig. 6. Examples of coordinate transformations.

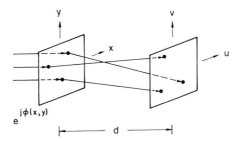

Fig. 7. Light at each point in the xy plane is steered to a new location in the uv plane by means of an optical phase element.

We need a methodology for synthesizing an optical element that performs an arbitrary geometric transformation.

The idea is based on the fact that local phase variation in a transmissive (or reflective) optical element (phase grating) introduces a tilt into the path of the transmitted optical ray (local plane wave). Therefore, by placing an element with the proper local phase variation next to the object to be transformed, one can redirect light from each point to a new point in some plane further down the optical axis. This is depicted in Fig. 7.

We now determine the relation between the desired coordinate transformation and the necessary local phase variation that must be introduced. We consider the element to be made of many small phase gratings, as shown in Fig. 8, illuminated by a uniform plane wave. To simplify the problem, we work with the x-dimension only. Let the element located at position x have frequency $q(x)$. It bends the incoming ray by an angle (assuming the paraxial approximation)

$$\theta(x) = \frac{q(x)}{k_0} \tag{15}$$

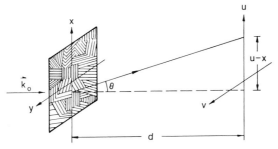

Fig. 8. The steering phase element consists of many small phase gratings. A ray is shown redirected through the angle θ from its original position $(x, 0)$ to its new position $(u, 0)$.

where $k_0 = 2\pi/\lambda$ is the wavenumber of the input light. We desire to direct this ray to a position $u = \psi(x)$ in a plane a distance d away. Therefore we should have

$$\theta(x) = \frac{u - x}{d} \tag{16}$$

or

$$\frac{q(x)}{k_0} = \frac{\psi(x) - x}{d} \tag{17}$$

Now, in the limit in which the grating elements have infinitesimal areas, we have a continuous grating, say, of amplitude transmittance $\exp[j\phi(x)]$. The local (or instantaneous) frequency associated with this varying phase is given by

$$q(x) = \frac{d\phi}{dx} \tag{18}$$

(This is analogous to the instantaneous frequency of an FM signal). It follows from Eqs. (15), (17), and (18) that

$$\phi(x) = \frac{k_0}{d}\left[\int \psi(x)\, dx - \frac{x^2}{2}\right] \tag{19}$$

Equation (19) is the desired relation between the phase of the optical element $\phi(x)$ and the geometric transformation $\psi(x)$.

It is apparent that, regardless of the particular coordinate transformation, the phase element must always contain a term of the type $-k_0 x^2/2d$ (i.e., a built-in lens of focal length d). A simple example is the case in which we are interested in steering all points in the input plane to the point $u = 0$ in the output plane ($\psi(x) = 0$). The optical element then has a phase $\phi(x) = -k_0 x^2/2d$ (i.e., just a lens).

The lens imbedded in the optical element can be removed and replaced with a glass lens. The combination of an optical element of phase

$$\phi(x) = \frac{k_0}{f}\int \psi(x)\, dx, \qquad \frac{d\phi}{dx} = \frac{k_0}{f}\psi(x) \tag{20}$$

and a lens of focal length f, performs the same geometric transformation $u = \psi(x)$. This is actually advantageous since, as we shall soon see, the phase element is usually a computer-generated hologram that contains a certain amount of quantization noise. Implementing the lens part of the phase function by use of a glass lens avoids the quantization noise for the lens term.

Equation (20) can be generalized to the 2-D case in which

$$\phi = \phi(x, y)$$

$$\frac{\partial \phi}{\partial x} = \frac{k_0}{f} \psi_1(x, y) \tag{21}$$

$$\frac{\partial \phi}{\partial y} = \frac{k_0}{f} \psi_2(x, y)$$

where $u = \psi_1(x, y)$ and $v = \psi_2(x, y)$ define the transformation $\mathbf{u} = \psi(\mathbf{x})$.

Bryngdahl [30, 31] was the first to introduce methods of performing arbitrary geometric transformations in optics. He derived the form of the phase element using the method of stationary phase as follows. For the setup shown in Fig. 9, the output $g(\mathbf{u})$ is given by the Fourier transform

$$g(\mathbf{u}) = \int f(\mathbf{x}) \exp[j\phi(\mathbf{x})] \exp\left[-j\left(\frac{k_0}{f}\right)(\mathbf{u} \cdot \mathbf{x})\right] d\mathbf{x} \tag{22}$$

which can be rewritten as

$$g(\mathbf{u}) = \int f(\mathbf{x}) \exp[jk_0 s(\mathbf{x})] \, d\mathbf{x}$$

$$s(\mathbf{x}) = \frac{\phi(\mathbf{x})}{k_0} - \frac{\mathbf{u} \cdot \mathbf{x}}{f} \tag{23}$$

The stationary phase method [32] of determining the above integral is strictly true only in the limit of infinitely large k_0 but remains an excellent approximation for any reasonably large value of k_0 (small wavelength λ). It states that the only significant contributions to the integral occur at the points where the gradient of s vanishes,

$$\mathbf{\nabla} s = 0 \qquad \left(\text{or } \frac{\partial s}{\partial x} = \frac{\partial s}{\partial y} = 0\right) \tag{24}$$

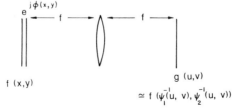

Fig. 9. Typical setup for performing a geometric transformation incorporating a physical lens in addition to the phase element.

at ts where

$$\frac{\partial \phi}{\partial x} = \frac{k_0}{f} u, \qquad \frac{\partial \phi}{\partial y} = \frac{k_0}{f} v \qquad (25)$$

from which Eq. (21) follows.

That the method of stationary phase yields the same result as geometrical optics is not a surprise since both geometrical optics and the method of stationary phase rely on the assumption of infinitely small wavelength. The output function, then, is given by

$$g(\mathbf{u}) = \frac{2\pi f(\mathbf{x}_0) \exp[jk_0 s(\mathbf{x}_0) + \pi/2]}{k_0 (s_{xx} s_{yy} - s_{xy}^2)^{1/2}} \qquad (26)$$

where $\mathbf{x}_0 = \boldsymbol{\psi}^{-1}(\mathbf{u})$ and s_{xx}, s_{yy}, and s_{xy} are partial derivatives of s with respect to x and s_{xy} are partial derivatives of s with respect to x and y evaluated at $\mathbf{x} = \mathbf{x}_0$. Note that some weighting distortion as well as a rather complicated phase term is introduced. However, for most cases the weighting distortion is a slowly varying function of $\mathbf{u}$ and can be treated as nearly constant, implying that the magnitude of $g(\mathbf{u})$ is essentially the desired one, that is,

$$|g(\mathbf{u})| \approx |f(\boldsymbol{\psi}^{-1}(\mathbf{u}))| \qquad (27)$$

The reader should be aware that both the ray-tracing derivation leading to Eq. (15) and the stationary phase derivation leading to Eq. (23) have ignored the spatial frequency content of the input itself. If the input $f(\mathbf{x})$ has substantial high-frequency content, then it too steers the input light, thus altering the desired geometric transformation.

Equation (21) is a recipe for determining the phase $\phi(x, y)$ of the optical element that realizes a geometric transformation $u = \psi_1(x, y)$, $v = \psi_2(x, y)$. One might wonder if any arbitrary geometric transformation can be synthesized using this technique. If $\phi(x, y)$ is to perform a continuous mapping, the first partial derivatives of ϕ (i.e., ψ_1 and ψ_2) must be continuous. Cederquist and Tai [33] pointed out that a further condition is

$$\frac{\partial \psi_1}{\partial y} = \frac{\partial \psi_2}{\partial x} \qquad (28)$$

or equivalently,

$$\frac{\partial^2 \phi}{\partial x \, \partial y} = \frac{\partial^2 \phi}{\partial y \, \partial x} \qquad (29)$$

In other words, the order of differentation is immaterial. This means that $\phi(x, y)$ must have continuous partial derivatives up through second order. It turns out that a large class of transformations related to conformal mappings satisfies Eq. (28). If

$$f(z) = u(x, y) + jv(x, y); \qquad z = x + jy$$

is analytic, meaning that it defines a conformal mapping, then the reflected transformation defined by

$$f(z^*) = u(x, -y) + jv(x, -y); \qquad z^* = x - jy$$

satisfies Eq. (28). Therefore conformal mappings must be implemented in reflected coordinates. For further discussion of this matter, the interested reader is referred to [33].

B. OPTICAL IMPLEMENTATIONS

Up to this point, the implementation of the required phase element has not been mentioned. Except for a few special cases, standard optical components with the desired phase variation are not available, and producing a custom optical element, say, by making a piece of glass whose thickness (or index of refraction) varies as $\phi(x, y)$, is usually impractical although it has been done [11, 12]. If light with the proper phase variation can somehow be made available, then recording an optically produced hologram is the best option. Most often, however, the only alternative is to use some form of computer-generated hologram (CGH). Many different methods for encoding a complex function onto a computer-generated mask have been devised. The space-bandwidth product achievable in all cases is limited by the display or plotting device used to produce the CGH. References [34] and [35] both provide good overviews of current CGH technology. References [36–39] are historically important in that they introduce four CGH techniques that remain some of the more commonly used today.

Both the Lohmann and Paris detour phase CGH [36] and Lee's computer-generated binary interferogram [38] have the advantage of being binary holograms (i.e., containing only two levels of amplitude transmittance). This makes them relatively easy to print on a wide variety of plotting devices and robust with respect to degradations incurred in photoreduction and development processes. Lee's delayed sampling CGH [37] was designed as a gray-level hologram but can also be produced in binary form. All three of these holograms are reconstructed in the first diffraction order, with much of the useful input light energy being wasted in spurious images produced in other diffraction orders (theoretical maximum diffraction efficiency is only about 10% for a binary amplitude hologram and about 40% for a binary phase hologram [40]). The kinoform [39], a pure phase hologram, is much harder to produce than those just cited. It is usually produced by coding the desired phase function as gray levels and then using a photo-graphic bleaching process on the final reduced hologram to turn gray-level variations into phase variations. It does, however, have the advantage of on-axis reconstruction with near 100% diffraction efficiency.

In Bryngdahl's initial work on optical geometric transformations [30, 31], he demonstrated a variety of transformations. An example of them is shown in Fig. 10. He has used both Lohmann and Paris' detour phase and Lee's

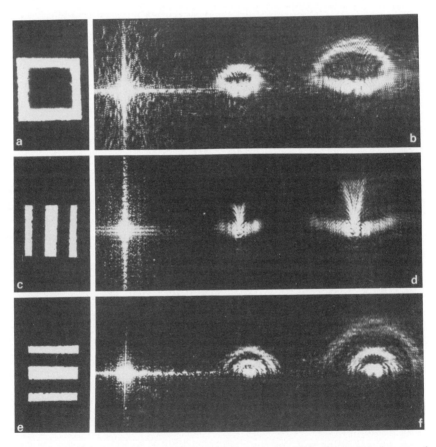

Fig. 10. Example of a conformal-type mapping. A region of the input plane is mapped into the interior of a circle according to the mapping $f(z^*) = p \exp(-z^*/q)$. The inputs are on the left with their corresponding outputs shown beside them on their right. The transformation appears in different scales in the first and second diffraction orders. (From Bryngdahl [31].)

binary interferogram methods for coding the CGHs. Another idea he raised was the possibility of breaking the phase function into the product of two phase functions, that is, having

$$\phi(x, y) = \phi_1(x, y)\phi_2(x, y) \tag{30}$$

If the functions ϕ_1 and ϕ_2 are printed on separate CGHs oriented at 90° to each other, then the results from all three transformations $\phi_1(x, y)$, $\phi_2(x, y)$, and $\phi(x, y)$ are available at the output of the system as shown in Fig. 11.

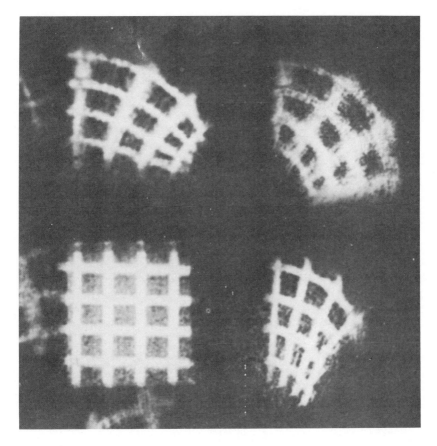

Fig. 11. By use of two CGHs oriented at 90° to each other, three geometric transformations are made available in one step. The input is shown on the lower left with transformations corresponding to ϕ_1 and ϕ_2 appearing beside and above it. The transformation corresponding to the product $\phi_1\phi_2$ appears in the upper right. (From Bryngdahl [30].)

C. CASE STUDIES

Casasent and Psaltis [20] and Yatagai *et al.* [18] have used the method described previously and the setup of Fig. 9 to implement the transformation

$$u = \psi_1(x, y) = \ln(x)$$
$$v = \psi_2(x, y) = \ln(y) \tag{31}$$

as a step in performing the optical Mellin transform (the Mellin transform will be further discussed in Section IV). Solving Eq. (21) with the above functional forms for ψ_1 and ψ_2 gives the following phase distribution.

$$\phi(x, y) = \frac{k_0}{f} [x \ln x - x + y \ln y - y] \tag{32}$$

Both implementations used Lee's binary interferogram [38] for coding the CGHs.

As pointed out in the discussion related to Fig. 6, a transformation of the form

$$u = \psi_1(x, y) = \ln r$$
$$v = \psi_2(x, y) = \theta \tag{33}$$

where $r = (x^2 + y^2)^{1/2}$ and $\theta = \tan^{-1}(y/x)$ are polar coordinates, results in invariance to changes in scale and rotation. This is a conformal mapping; so as pointed out earlier in Section II.B), the reflected version, (x, y) into $(\ln r, -\theta)$, must be implemented. Saito *et al.* [19] used this transformation with a W. H. Lee binary interferogram CGH [28] to build a scale- and rotation-invariant optical correlator. Cederquist and Tai [33] used the same transformation (scaled by a constant) as an intermediate step in an angle demultiplexing scheme for fiber-optics communications. Their CGH was implemented as a direct analog to a standard optical interferometric hologram as in [41]; namely, the amplitude transmittance was coded as a sampled version of

$$t(x, y) = a + b \cos[\phi(x, y) + \alpha x + \beta y] \tag{34}$$

where a and b are constants chosen to insure that the transmittance is nonnegative, and α and β are spatial carrier frequencies. The necessary phase function was found to be

$$\phi(x, y) = \frac{k_0}{f} \left[x \ln(x^2 + y^2)^{-1/2} - y \tan^{-1} \frac{y}{x} - x \right] \tag{35}$$

Their system is shown in Fig. 12, where hologram H_1 performs the $(x, y) \rightarrow$ $(\ln r, -\theta)$ transformation.

D. GEOMETRIC TRANSFORMATIONS NOT SATISFYING CONTINUOUS-PHASE ELEMENT CONDITION

An interesting transformation that does not satisfy the condition in Eq. (28) for realization by use of an optical element of continuous phase, is the mapping from rings of different radii to points to a line. This transformation, which was considered by Cederquist and Tai [33] for fiber-optics applications, has the form

$$u = \psi_1(x, y) = [x^2 + y^2]^{-1/2}$$
$$v = \psi_2(x, y) = 0$$
(36)

Obviously this does not ssatisfy the constraints of Eq. (28). Therefore a single-step transformation using a continuous-phase CGH is not possible. Cederquist and Tai considered two possible alternatives. They refer to the first as a discrete-phase CGH. The input coordinate plane is divided into a number of discrete regions. Light from each region is then mapped to a region in the output plane, using an independent coordinate mapping. The total CGH is then a composite of many discrete CGHs. A space–bandwidth constraint limits the number of regions that can be mapped [26, 33]. Say that the input plane is divided into $N \times N$ regions, and one wants to map each of these into any of $N \times N$ regions in the output plane (a worst case). Each of the discrete CGHs must then have a space–bandwidth product of $N \times N$, giving a necessary space–bandwidth product of $N^2 \times N^2$ for the

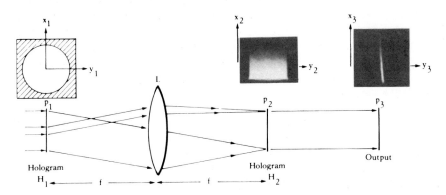

Fig. 12. Two-hologram system for mapping rings in plane P_1 into points in plane P_3. Hologram # 1 performs an $(x, y) \rightarrow (\ln r, -\theta)$ transformation, and Hologram # 2 projects onto the r-axis. (From Cederquist and Tai [33].)

total CGH. With available printing devices limited to perhaps $10,000 \times 10,000$ spots (optimistic), this limits the number of regions to only 100×100. Of course, in many cases this may be sufficient. For this particular case the input region was divided into 30 concentric rings. The total light in each ring was mapped to 30 different points along a line in the output plane.

The second alternative considered was to break the coordinate transformation into two consecutive steps, each implementable using a continuous-phase element. First, the $(\ln r, -\theta)$ mapping was performed as described above; second, an integration in θ was performed by a lens or a conventional optically generated hologram. The second step is a form of projection (as will be discussed in Section II.B). The total system is shown in Fig. 12. Cederquist and Tai concluded that for general coordinate transformations, continuous-phase CGHs in single or multiple steps offer the best solution. Discrete-phase CGHs are applicable where a large space–bandwidth product is not called for.

E. Multifacet Holographic Optical Elements

Multifacet holographic optical elements are a new type of hologram based on a hybrid fabrication technique [14–17]. They have applications to the general geometric (coordinate) transformation problem. As seen in earlier sections, for most coordinate transformations the flexibility of computer-generated holograms is required to produce the complicated phase variations called for. Unfortunately, this flexibility is accompanied by relatively poor diffraction efficiency and a space–bandwidth product limited by available display and plotting devices. Volume phase materials such as dichromated gelatin are capable of high (nearly 100%) diffraction efficiency and very fine resolution, but they must be recorded interferometrically and thus lack flexibility. It is natural then that techniques are being invented to combine the complementary advantages of the two types of holograms.

One technique is to make a CGH master and use its reconstructed output as the object wave for recording a volume hologram. This has been accomplished [42, 43], and high diffraction efficiency has been achieved. However, this method does not overcome the space–bandwidth limitation of the original CGH master.

The multifacet technique makes use of both the high diffraction efficiency and the large space–bandwidth products available in volume holographic materials. The design principle is conceptually simple. Although producing the complicated phase variations required for arbitrary coordinate transformations is usually impossible with conventional optical elements, the phase variation in any particular local region can often be approximated closely by a simple wavefront such as a plane, cylindrical, or spherical wave. The idea, then, is to divide the hologram into many simple subholograms and record each sequentially under computer control. The recording setup is shown in Fig. 13. A flexible aperture is placed lightly against the film to define an individual facet. With the reference beam fixed, the film is translated, and the object beam is changed according to the desired local transformation.

The reader, no doubt, sees the similarity between this and the discrete-phase CGH described earlier. Notice that the space–bandwidth constraint described in connection with the discrete-phase CGH no longer applies. With the interferometric construction, the required space–bandwidth product in each subhologram is no longer a problem to achieve. However, there is a new space–bandwidth constraint that is related to how small the individual facets can be made [17]. As the facets become smaller, the effect of diffraction from the defining aperture becomes more predominant. Assuming that the output plane is in the Fraunhofer region of an individual facet, Bartelt and Case [17] estimate the limiting size of the aperture as being when the spot size in the output plane corresponding to a single facet is the same size as the facet itself. This gives

$$W_{min} = (2\lambda d)^{1/2} \tag{37}$$

as the limiting size of the aperture, where W is the width of the aperture and d the distance to the output plane. Assuming that the light cannot be redirected through an angle greater than $\Delta\alpha$, the space–bandwidth product is limited to

$$N = \frac{d \tan(\Delta\alpha/2)}{W_{min}} \tag{38}$$

Figure 14 shows the results of using a multifacet hologram to perform a transformation from cartesian to polar coordinates. In (a) is the circular

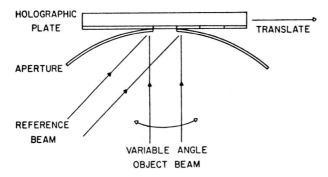

Fig. 13. Recording geometry for a multifacet hologram.

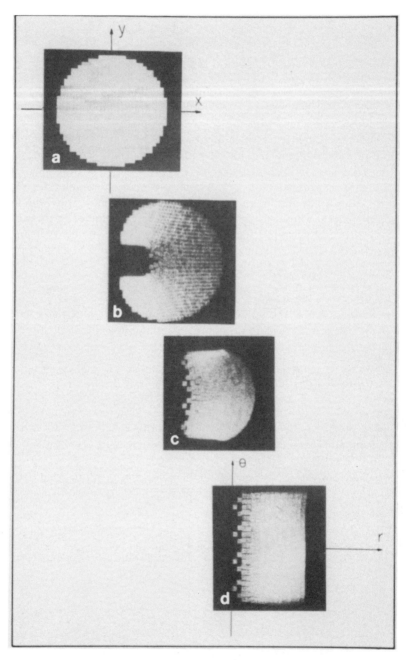

Fig. 14. Multifacet hologram performs an $(x, y) \rightarrow (r, \theta)$ coordinate transformation. The hologram plane is shown in (a). Two intermediate stages of the evolution of the light distribution (b) and (c) are shown, arriving at the desired transformation in (d). (From Bartelt and Case [17].)

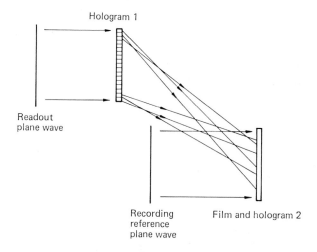

Fig. 15. Two-hologram system to perform a collimated geometric transformation. The recording geometry for the second hologram is shown. The redistributed light from Hologram #1 is used as the object beam for recording the second hologram.

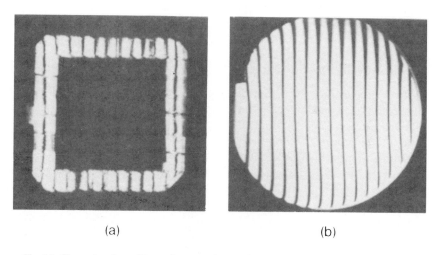

(a)   (b)

Fig. 16. Example of a collimated geometric transformation. Light has been redistributed from an input Gaussian beam into a square annulus. Interferograms showing the resultant wave front are presented: (a) the collimated output wave front and (b) a plane wave for comparison. (From Case, Haugen, and Lokberg [15].)

distribution of light at the plane of the hologram. Successive photographs, (b) and (c), show how the light pattern evolves on its way to the output plane in (d). Each facet was recorded with a plane wave object beam.

As with transformations performed using CGHs, the phase at the transformed plane is not controlled. Figure 15 shows a two-hologram system to collimate the transformed light distribution. Hologram #1 is a multifacet hologram that performs the geometric transformation. A second hologram is recorded using the transformed beam as the object wave. When the same setup is used with the recording reference plane wave turned off and the film replaced by the developed hologram, the emerging light is all in phase. The output of such a system is shown in Fig. 16 for the case in which the geometric transformation involved maps a Gaussian input beam into a uniform square light distribution [15].

III. Transdimensional Transformations

When the dimensions N and M of the variables $\mathbf{x}$ and $\mathbf{y}$ of the input $f(\mathbf{x})$ and output $g(\mathbf{u})$ of a transformation are not equal, the transformation is said to be transdimensional. We first examine transdimensional geometric transformations, then we consider other cases: projection and inner product which are cases of down-conversion $(M < N)$, and fan-out and outer-product transformations, which are cases of up-conversions $(M > N)$. Another interesting example of up-conversion is the computation of the local spectra of signals (e.g., the complex spectrogram or the Wigner distribution function). This is relegated to Section V (nonlinear transformations).

A. Geometric Transformations

Transdimensional transformations are often used to change the dimension of a signal to equal that of an available processor, a transmission channel, or a storage medium. For example, 2-D images are transformed by a TV camera into 1-D video signals, which are appropriate for transmission and broadcasting. A TV monitor transforms the received 1-D video signal back into a 2-D image, which is appropriate for viewing. The opposite process is also of interest. A 1-D signal can be transformed into a 2-D signal that is then processed by an optical processor and subsequently retransformed into a 1-D signal. This is one of the areas in which optical processing has played an expanding role in recent years [44–52]. Likewise, 3-D signals (e.g., time-varying images) are transformed into 2-D signals (as a sequence of images), recorded (e.g., on a movie film strip), and transformed back into a 3-D signal for playback [53]. Such transformations are usually geometric in nature as illustrated by the following cases.

1. *Two-Dimensional to One-Dimensional* (2-D/1-D)
   Transformation

A transformation of a 2-D image $f(x, y)$ into a 1-D signal $g(u)$ can be realized by a geometric transformation $u = \psi(x, y)$, where the points (x, y) lie on a sampling path in the x-y plane, for example, a set of parallel lines as shown in Fig. 17. This transformation is a form of sampling of $f(x, y)$. The transformation can be implemented using techniques of optical or electronic scanning. Alternatively, it can be realized using a holographic optical element as discussed in Section II.C. Note that because of the discreteness of the sampling lines the appropriate phase of the hologram would not be continuous.

2. *One-Dimensional to Two-Dimensional* (1-D/2-D)
   Transformation

A transformation of a 1-D signal $f(x)$ into a 2-D image $g(u, v)$ is implemented by assigning the value $f(x)$ to points on a line in the u-v plane defined parametrically by $u = \psi_1(x)$, $v = \psi_2(x)$. Thus $g(u, v)$ becomes an image containing a line singularity. Choice of the line is arbitrary. Examples of suggested lines are shown in Fig. 18.

A choice of the particular transformation depends on the purpose. For example, if the purpose of the transformation is to compute the Fourier transform of $f(x)$ by use of a 2-D optical processor, then the falling raster transformation in Fig. 18b is appropriate, because then the 2-D Fourier transform of $g(u, v) = T\{f(x)\}$ is simply related to the 1-D Fourier transform $F(u)$ of $f(x)$, as illustrated in Fig. 19 [52]. Other operations on $f(x)$ (e.g., correlation [51] and Fresnel transform) call for other 2-D mappings of $f(x)$ as explained in detail in [52]. These 1-D/2-D point transformations can be implemented using scanning or holographic techniques.

B. PROJECTION OR FAN-IN TRANSFORMATIONS

A projection

$$g(v) = \int f(x, v) \, dx \qquad (39)$$

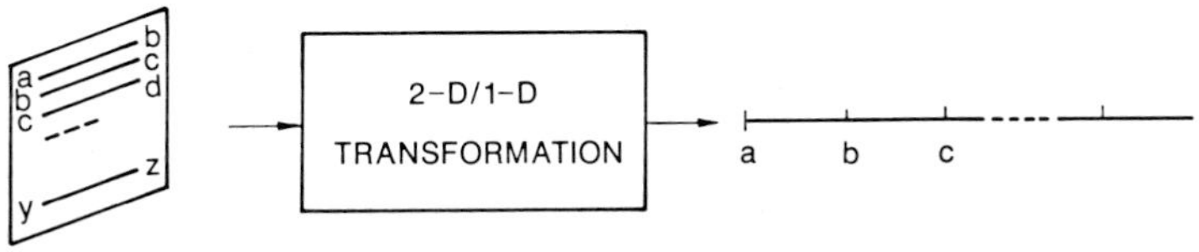

Fig. 17. Transformation of a 2-D function into a 1-D function by raster scanning.

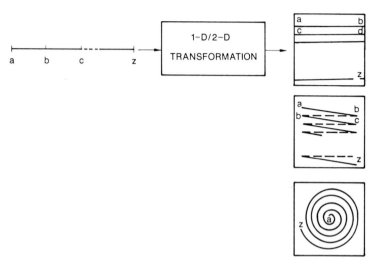

Fig. 18. Transformation of a 1-D function into a 2-D function containing a line singularity.

of a 2-D signal $f(x, y)$ on the y-axis is an important simple example of a noninvertible 2-D/1-D transformation. The simplest optical implementation utilizes the integrating property of a cylindrical lens. In fact, it is necessary to integrate along the x-direction and image along the y-direction as illustrated in Fig. 20.

A sophisticated explanation of this simple system introduces an important architectural principle. A new 2-D/2-D transformation defines a new

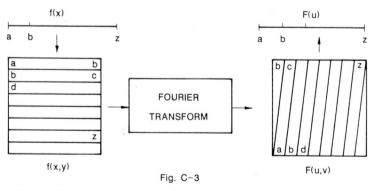

Fig. 19. One-dimensional function $f(x)$ in Fig. 18 is transformed into a 2-D function $g(x, y)$ by use of lines representing segments of $f(x)$. Its Fourier transform $G(u, v)$ contains line segments from which the Fourier transform $F(u)$ of $f(x)$ can be reconstructed. Windowing effects are ignored.

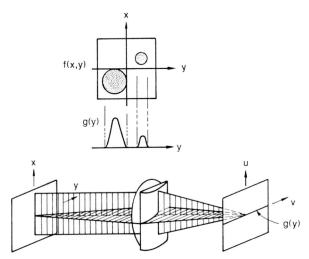

Fig. 20. Projection of a function $f(x, y)$ on the y-axis to obtain a function $g(y)$. The optical system images in the y-direction and integrates in the x-direction.

auxiliary 2-D signal,

$$\Gamma(u, v) = \int\int \delta(v - y) \exp(-jux) f(x, y) \, dx \, dy \qquad (40)$$

It is obvious that our desired signal $g(v)$ is related to the auxiliary signal by the geometric transformation of sampling along the v-axis,

$$g(v) = \Gamma(0, v) \qquad (41)$$

Now the transformation between the 2-D signals $f(x, y)$ and $\Gamma(u, v)$ is an astigmatic linear transformation that involves perfect imaging in the y-direction but Fourier transformation in the x-direction. Such a system can be easily implemented by use of a coherent optical processor as illustrated in Fig. 20.

Projections along different directions can be used to determine the Fourier transform of a 2-D function using 1-D Fourier transform processors (e.g., surface acoustic wave filters using a chirp-transform algorithm). According to the projection-slice theorem, the resultant 1-D transforms are slices of the 2-D Fourier transform along the corresponding directions. Such Radon-transform approaches are examined elsewhere in this book.

A projection transformation can also be regarded as a form of geometric transformation in which vertical lines in the input plane are mapped (in the sense of Eq. (10)) into points on the output line. In that sense it can be implemented using a hologram as described in Section II.D. The hologram, which can be recorded interferometrically by superimposing a uniform plane wave with a wave front produced by a line source, would then play the role of the astigmatic imaging and integration of Fig. 20.

C. INNER PRODUCT

An inner product of two inputs $f_1(\mathbf{x})$ and $f_2(\mathbf{x})$ is a scalar defined by

$$g = \int f_1^*(\mathbf{x}) f_2(\mathbf{x}) \, d\mathbf{x}$$

This N-dimensional to zero-dimensional transformation can be implemented optically by the simple scheme of Fig. 21, which is applicable to the $N = 2$ case. Other architectures for implementing the $N = 1$ inner product using acoustooptic cells are discussed in [54, 55].

D. FAN-OUT TRANSFORMATIONS

The simplest fan-out transformation is the 1-D/2-D transform

$$g(x, y) = f(x) \tag{42}$$

which fans out values of a function $f(x)$ along the y-direction. This can be regarded as a backprojection. It involves the spread of each point on the input line to a vertical line in the output plane. A simple optical implementation is depicted in Fig. 22.

Discrete fan-outs, in which one point in the input plane is mapped into a number of points in the output plane can be realized by use of diffraction gratings or specially designed holograms [56].

E. OUTER-PRODUCT TRANSFORMATION

The outer product

$$g(x, y) = f_1(x) f_2(y) \tag{43}$$

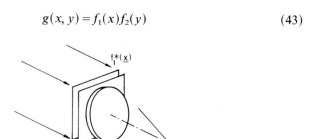

Fig. 21. Inner product of two functions implemented by a process of multiplication followed by integration.

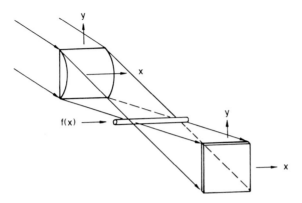

Fig. 22. Fan out of a function $f(x)$ as a function $\phi(x, y) = f(x)$.

is a simple example of a 1-D/2-D up-conversion of two 1-D input functions into one 2-D output signal. The idea behind implementation is to augment each signal by fanning it out into the other dimension,

$$F_1(x, y) = f_1(x)$$
$$F_2(x, y) = f_2(y)$$

and then form the product

$$g(x, y) = F_1(x, y) F_2(x, y)$$

An optical implementation is depicted in Fig. 23. Other approaches to outer-product computations based on serial and systolic processing have been reported [56].

IV. Linear Shift-Variant Transformations

Linear shift-invariant operations via the optical Fourier transform are usually considered the most natural type of operation for optical

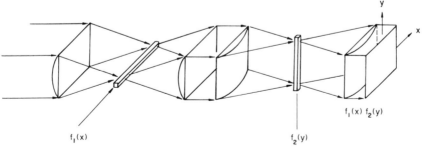

Fig. 23. Outer product $\phi(x, y) = f_1(x) f_2(y)$. The 1-D functions $f_1(x)$ and $f_2(y)$ are entered through acoustooptic cells.

implementation. This is ironic in a sense because the Fourier transform itself is a shift-variant transformation. While shift-invariant processing is adequate for many problems, there remain many tasks in the fields of image processing, pattern recognition, optical computing, and signal processing that require shift-variant operations. In Section II the implementation of one general class of shift-variant transformations, namely, geometric transformations, was discussed. The present section is intended to review some of the more promising ways in which arbitrary shift-variant operations can be performed optically.

We begin with a brief discussion of the simplest shift-variant transformation that coherent optics can perform, the Fourier transform, followed by a brief discussion of shift-invariant transformations; both subjects have been discussed extensively in the literature. We then present various methods of optical implementation of shift-variant transformations.

A. Fourier Transform

The Fourier transform is defined by

$$g(\mathbf{u}) = \int \exp(-j\mathbf{u} \cdot \mathbf{x}) f(\mathbf{x}) \, d\mathbf{x} \tag{44}$$

where $\mathbf{u}$ and $\mathbf{x}$ have the same dimension $N = M$. It is therefore a linear shift-variant transformation for which the impulse response function is

$$h(\mathbf{u}, \mathbf{x}) = \exp(-j\mathbf{u} \cdot \mathbf{x}) \tag{45}$$

For a given $\mathbf{x}$ this is a harmonic function of $\mathbf{u} = (u, v, \ldots)$ of angular frequency $\mathbf{x} = (x, y, \ldots)$. When $N = 2$ the function $\exp(-j\mathbf{u} \cdot \mathbf{x})$ represents the amplitude of a uniform plane wave at points in a plane (the $\mathbf{u}$-plane). Thus the response to an impulse, a point at position $\mathbf{x}$ in the input plane, is a cross section of a plane wave in the output plane. Therefore, to construct a Fourier transform operation optically, all we need is to make every point $\mathbf{x}$ in the input plane generate a plane wave of appropriate direction so that its cross section in the output plane is harmonic of angular frequency $\mathbf{x}$. Such a task is easily accomplished with coherent light by use of a lens in the well-known configuration of Fig. 24 [10].

One can also look at the Fourier transform operation from another perspective. The function $f(\mathbf{x})$ in the input plane can be analyzed as a sum of harmonic functions of different angular frequencies $\mathbf{q}$ and amplitudes $g(\mathbf{q})$ (where $g(\mathbf{q})$ is the Fourier transform of $f(\mathbf{x})$). The optical system of Fig. 24 routes the amplitude of the harmonic function of frequency $\mathbf{q}$ in the input plane to a point in the output plane of position $\mathbf{u} = (\mathbf{q}/k_0)f$.

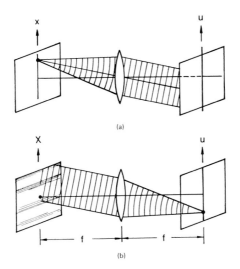

Fig. 24. (a) Fourier transformation as a system whose impulse response function is a cross section of a uniform plane wave. (b) Fourier transformation as a system that routes a harmonic function in the input plane to a point in the output plane.

B. SHIFT-INVARIANT TRANSFORMATIONS

Shift-invariant transformations can be cast in the convolution form

$$g(\mathbf{x}) = f(\mathbf{x}) * h(\mathbf{x})$$

Their implementation is based on the property that the Fourier transform of $g(\mathbf{x})$ is the product of the Fourier transforms of $f(\mathbf{x})$ and $h(\mathbf{x})$. This well-known spatial filtering method has in past years generated numerous applications [10].

C. ARBITRARY SHIFT-VARIANT TRANSFORMATIONS USING KNOWN TRANSFORMATIONS OF HIGHER DIMENSION

An arbitrary N-D shift-variant transformation ($N = M$),

$$g(\mathbf{u}) = \int h(\mathbf{u}, \mathbf{x}) f(\mathbf{x}) \, d\mathbf{x} \tag{46}$$

can be associated with a $2N$-D/N-D transformation that involves the operation of projection. This is accomplished by definining the auxiliary $2N$-D functions

$$\phi(\mathbf{x}, \mathbf{y}) = f(\mathbf{y}) \tag{47}$$

and

$$\Gamma(\mathbf{x}, \mathbf{y}) = h(\mathbf{x}, \mathbf{y})\phi(\mathbf{x}, \mathbf{y}) \tag{48}$$

and observing that

$$g(\mathbf{u}) = \int \Gamma(\mathbf{u}, \mathbf{y}) \, d\mathbf{y} \tag{49}$$

Implementation of this technique in the $N = 2$ case is obviously difficult because of the need for 4-D processing. In optics, the four dimensions are hard to come by. There are two transverse dimensions; perhaps use can be made of the third longitudinal direction and maybe time or wavelength for the fourth dimension. No universal solution has yet been discovered. Some techniques resulting in dimensionality reduction or involving spatial or temporal multiplexing are discussed in following sections. However, when the function to be transformed is only 1-D, the required 2-D kernel can be implemented using the two transverse spatial dimensions available in optical systems. This makes optical implementation reasonably straightforward.

Optical implementation for $N = 1$ follows three steps, described in Eqs. (46)–(49):

1. A fan-out transformation changing $f(x)$ into $\phi(x, y)$ is implemented using a cylindrical lens.
2. The product $\Gamma(x, y) = h(x, y)\phi(x, y)$ is implemented.
3. The projection of $\Gamma(x, y)$ is computed using the techniques discussed in Section III.B (e.g., by a 2-D operation of perfect imaging in the x-direction and Fourier transform in the y-direction followed by sampling).

This system (Fig. 25) was suggested in 1965 by Cutrona [57] and more recently by Goodman *et al.* [24]. It requires two cylindrical lenses in addition to the noncritical illumination lens L_1. Goodman and colleagues [24, 26, 58]

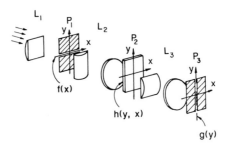

Fig. 25. One possible optical arrangement to perform an arbitrary 1-D linear shift-variant transformation.

have suggested two other architectures requiring only one cylindrical lens in one and none in the other. They point out that this is advantageous since high-quality cylindrical lenses are not readily available. Elimination of cylindrical lenses comes at the expense of a more complicated mask with complex amplitude transmittances, thus necessitating the use of holograms.

D. GEOMETRIC TRANSFORMATION PROCESSING

As seen in the previous section, geometric transformations are one class of shift-variant transformations that can often be implemented optically using the methods discussed in Section II. Many times (but not always) a general shift-variant transformation can be separated into sequential steps of geometric transformation combined with some operation for which optics excels, such as a shift-invariant transformation or a Fourier transform. This is depicted in Fig. 26 which shows a preprocessing and a postprocessing geometric transformation. One of the two is sometimes sufficient.

The basic concept is intuitively appealing. Consider turning a shift-variant operation into a shift-invariant operation using a geometric transformation. The input data are spatially rearranged, via a geometric transformation, to compensate for the spatial variation of the shift-variant operation. Thus only an operation that is invariant to spatial location remains. Finally, a second geometric transformation rearranges the filtered data to the form desired for output.

This technique of achieving shift-variant operations is known as coordinate transformation processing. It was first developed by Sawchuk [27–29] for use in digital restoration of blurred images and by Robbins and Huang [13], who applied it to digital removal of the effects of aberrations in an imaging system. Its most common use in optical systems has been as a

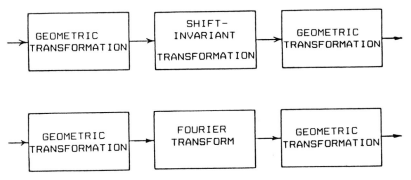

Fig. 26. Linear shift-variant transformations can be implemented using more easily realizable operations with the aid of coordinate transformations.

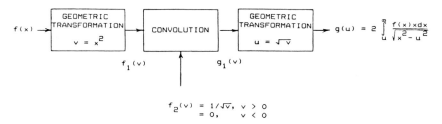

$$f_2(v) = 1/\sqrt{v}, \quad v > 0$$
$$\quad\quad = 0, \quad\quad v < 0$$

Fig. 27. Abel transform is realized using a combination of a shift-invariant operation and two coordinate transformations.

method for achieving shift-variant correlators in optical pattern recognition. As was shown in Fig. 6, a logarithmic transformation results in scale invariance and a polar transformation results in rotational invariance. Casasent and Psaltis have proposed general ways to combine these and other geometric transformations to obtain optical correlators that are invariant to changes in position, scale, and rotation [20–23]. Full optical implementation of this type of optical correlator has been performed by Yatagai *et al.* [18] and by Saito *et al.* [19].

The difficulty with this technique is that there is no general rule for finding the pre- and postprocessing geometric transformations for a given class of processors (e.g., shift-invariant) that would make the overall system realize a given shift-variant transformation. In the following we show some important examples.

Figures 27 and 28 illustrate the method for two simple 1-D examples [26]. The Abel transform is the projection of a circularly symmetric 2-D function onto one dimension. In Fig. 27 the necessary input and output geometric transformations as well as the intermediate shift-invariant kernel, which together result in an Abel transform, are shown.

The Mellin transform, it turns out, is closely related to the Fourier transform. By application of the input geometric transformation

$$x' = -\ln x \qquad\qquad (50)$$

Fig. 28. Mellin transform is realized using a combination of a Fourier transform and a coordinate transformation.

the Mellin transform becomes a Fourier transform in the new coordinate system, as shown in Fig. 28 [20]. The logarithmic transformation, as discussed earlier, indicates that the Mellin transform is invariant to changes in scale.

Coordinate transformation processing places a limit on the allowed space–bandwidth product of the input in two ways. First, as noted in Section II, to make the purely optical methods of geometric transformation work, the input $f(\mathbf{x})$ can contain only spatial frequencies that are much lower than those of the phase element used to perform the coordinate mapping. In some cases this dictates that nonoptical methods must be used to produce the geometric transformation. One possibility is transforming the coordinate system via nonuniform scanning of the input and then introducing the transformed input into the optical system using some sort of spatial light modulator [20].

Second, the nature of the geometric transformation itself often tends to increase the space–bandwidth product of the transformed input relative to the untransformed input. This results as a consequence of multiplying two finite space–bandwidth product functions, in this case the input and the phase grating. The space–bandwidth product of the input must be limited so that after the geometric transformation, the space–bandwidth product of the optical processing system is not exceeded. Casasent and Psaltis have shown that for the Mellin transform the increase in space–bandwidth product can be as great as five times the input space–bandwidth product [21].

E. MULTIPLEXING TECHNIQUES

Techniques have been devised by Walkup, Marks, and their co-workers whereby a shift-variant transformation can be separated into a number of discrete operations [25, 59–62]. These include approximating the shift-variant kernel by a piecewise isoplanatic function (i.e., piecewise shift-invariant), expanding the input function on an orthonormal basis, and a technique based on shift-variant sampling theory. Since all the techniques result in similar optical implementations, we center this discussion around a sampling approach.

It is common in discrete systems to perform shift-invariant operations on continuous signals by sampling them at the appropriate Nyquist rate. Marks *et al.* [62] have derived a generalized sampling theorem that gives the analogous rate necessary for dealing with shift-variant operations. Briefly, for the 1-D case, if the input has a bandwidth of W_1 and the shift-variant kernel has a variational bandwidth of W_v, then if the input is sampled at points spaced by $1/2W$, where

$$W = W_1 + W_v \qquad (51)$$

a shift-variant transformation takes the form

$$g(u) = \int h(u - x; x) f(x) \, dx$$

$$= \sum_n f(x_n) h(u - x_n; x_n) * \text{sinc}(2Wu) \tag{52}$$

where $x_n = n/2W$, and the shift-variant kernel has been reexpressed in the revealing form $h(u - x; x)$ (i.e., a shift-invariant form for each separate point x). In Eq. (52) the integral has been broken into a weighted sum of 1-D impulses responses (trivially shift-invariant) followed by a low-pass filter. Further, if we assume that the input $f(x)$ has a finite space–bandwidth product, then the summation is over only a finite number of terms.

One basic scheme for implementing the 2-D version of Eq. (52) uses a multiplexed volume hologram as shown in Fig. 29. The input is sampled by the sampling mask. After being Fourier transformed by a lens, each sampled input point corresponds to a plane wave traveling in a different direction at the hologram plane. On the volume hologram are recorded the Fourier transforms of the various impulse responses of the summation in Eq. (52). They are recorded using different reference beam angles in such a way that they are accessed only by the plane wave corresponding to the point in the input for which they were sampled. The Bragg extinction condition is counted on to eliminate crosstalk by the various plane waves.

Although the system of Fig. 29 is useful to illustrate the basic concept behind the holographic multiplexing technique, it has some serious drawbacks. It is known [63] that the Bragg condition is satisfied by a cone of angles rather than by just a single angle when the range of angles is not restricted to a plane. Therefore one could expect significant corsstalk if the sampling rates are high. Encoding the reference beams with white-noise-like phases obtained using diffusers has been suggested as a way to get around the crosstalk problem [63]. On playback, each input sample would be

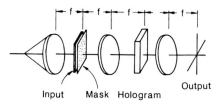

Fig. 29. Optical arrangement for implementing 2-D linear space-variant transformations by sampling the input with a mask and multiplexing the respective impulse responses on a volume hologram.

addressed using the same diffuser with which its impulse response had been recorded. The recording and playback steps are shown in Fig. 30. Zero cross-correlation between different diffuser phases is then the mechanism for eliminating crosstalk.

As an alternative to the spatial multiplexing techniques described above, Marks [59] has proposed a number of processors based on temporally multiplexing the impulse response terms of Eq. (52). Rather than all impulse responses being recorded on one hologram, each impulse response is separately introduced into a shift-invariant processing system, and each input sample is processed sequentially in time. The summation is achieved by using the sequential outputs as object beams to expose a single hologram. Thus the crosstalk is eliminated at the expense of time.

These do not exhaust the methods that have been proposed for performing shift-variant transformations. The purpose here has been simply to introduce some of the principles and problems.

F. MIXED CONTINUOUS AND DISCRETE SHIFT-VARIANT TRANSFORMATIONS

Another interesting class of shift-variant operations is that for which the input and/or output fields contain a mixture of continuous and discrete coordinates. An important example of this class is the expansion of a function in a basis.

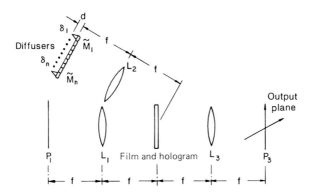

Fig. 30. Eliminating crosstalk between the various impulse response terms in a spatially multiplexed hologram by use of phase-coded reference beams. The hologram is recorded using lens L_1, by sequentially introducing the desired impulse response terms into plane P_1 and using a different diffuser for each exposure. On playback, lens L_3 is used. The input is placed in contact with the point source array illuminating the diffusers, and the output appears in plane P_3.

1. *Expansion of a Function in a Basis*

When a function $f(\mathbf{x})$ is expanded in a basis $\{h(x, p)\}$, the coefficients of expansion are given by the projections

$$g(\mathbf{p}) = \int f(\mathbf{x})h(\mathbf{x}, \mathbf{p}) \, d\mathbf{x} \tag{53}$$

The function $f(x)$ is then transformed into a set of coefficients $\mathbf{q}(\mathbf{p})$ where $\mathbf{p} = (p, q, \ldots)$ is a vector of integers. An example is the basis $h(x, p) = \exp(-j2\pi px/T)$, which generates the Fourier series expansion of a periodic 1-dimensional function. Another is the basis $h(x, y, p, q) = x^p y^q$, used to generate the moments of a 2-D function (see Chapter 2.1 by Casasent). Such expansions are applied to images for the purpose of pattern recognition; here $f(\mathbf{x})$ represents an image, $g(\mathbf{p})$ represents its features, and $h(\mathbf{x}, \mathbf{p})$ is a basis chosen to optimally classify the image.

The principle of optical implementation is based on the observation that each coefficient is obtained by taking the inner product of the input function with the corresponding basis function. Realization of that operation has been discussed in Section III.C. The complete shift-variant transformation entails forming all the inner products in parallel using some method of multiplexing. Two methods of performing the inner product can be used: evaluating the Fourier transform of the product $f(\mathbf{x})h(\mathbf{x}, \mathbf{p})$ at zero frequency and evaluating the cross-correlation function between $f(\mathbf{x})$ and $h(\mathbf{x}, \mathbf{p})$ at zero delay. Multiplexing schemes for both approaches are presented below.

When the Fourier transform method is used, the functions $\{h(\mathbf{x}, \mathbf{p})\}$ are frequency multplexed by forming the function

$$t(\mathbf{x}) = \sum_p h(\mathbf{x}, \mathbf{p}) \cos(\boldsymbol{\omega}_0 \cdot \mathbf{x} + \mathbf{p} \, \Delta\omega \cdot \mathbf{x}) \tag{54}$$

that is, each function is mounted on a different sinusoidal carrier. The product $t(\mathbf{x})f(\mathbf{x})$ is formed and Fourier transformed. Sampling at frequency $\mathbf{p} \, \Delta\omega$ gives the coefficient $g(\mathbf{p})$ (see Chapter 2.1 by Casasent).

Space multiplexing is used with the correlation method. A function

$$r(\mathbf{x}) = \sum_p h(\mathbf{x} - \mathbf{p} \, \Delta x, \mathbf{p}) \tag{55}$$

is generated by placing the different functions of the basis at different locations. The input $f(\mathbf{x})$ is cross-correlated with $r(\mathbf{x})$; the desired coefficients $g(p)$ are found by sampling the cross-correlation function at the locations $\mathbf{p} \, \Delta x$. Cross-correlation can be implemented by making a mask of the inverse Fourier transform of $\mathbf{r}(\mathbf{x})$ and placing it in the Fourier plane of a filtering system. Lee *et al.* [64–66] suggested multiplying each of the basis functions $h(\mathbf{x}, \mathbf{p})$ with a random phase function prior to encoding the mask. The input function is also multiplied by the same random phase function before performing the cross-correlation. The concept is the same as that used to eliminate crosstalk, as discussed previously in relation to performing space-variant transformations by a sampling method. The complete setup is shown in Fig. 31. This approach helps reduce the dynamic range required to print the mask. Further, if the phase noise is uncorrelated, the cross-correlation function would be negligible except at sampling points, thus allowing the packing of more coefficients in a given area.

2. Expansions in a Subspace

A more complicated situation arises when a function of two variables, say $f(x, y)$, is to be expanded in an orthogonal basis in the subspace of one variable, say y. The appropriate transformation has the form

$$g(x, p) = \int h(y, p)f(x, y) \, dy \tag{56}$$

The transformation applies to a continuous input function $f(x, y)$ and generates a mixed continuous and discrete output function $g(x, p)$.

For each p, this transformation resembles a 1-D shift-variant transformation, of the type in Eq. (2), with $h(y, p)$ playing the role of the input and $f(x, y)$ playing the role of the kernel. In general, the optical implementation would proceed as described in Section IV.C, namely, fan out $h(y, p)$ and multiply the result by $f(x, y)$ to obtain an auxiliary function $\Gamma(x, y, p)$, which is projected on x using a combination of imaging and Fourier transform, followed by sampling to obtain $g(x, p)$. The process could be repeated for each value of p or, depending on the form of $h(y, p)$, could lend itself to multiplexing in the kernel or output planes.

An important example of the transformation given in Eq. (56), which also serves to introduce an alternate optical implementation, is the decomposition of a 2-D function into its circular harmonics. Circular harmonics are

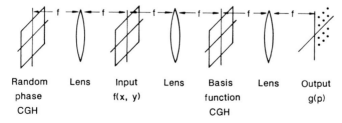

Random phase CGH   Lens   Input f(x, y)   Lens   Basis function CGH   Lens   Output g(p)

Fig. 31. Optical processor for expanding on a basis. The inner products are formed using cross-correlation with a random phase term included to eliminate correlation at points other than the desired sampling locations.

used, for example, in pattern recognition to generate features possessing rotational invariance [67–69]. Further, if one precedes the circular harmonic decomposition by a 2-D Fourier transform, a Hankel transform results [70].

Let the input function be presented in polar coordinates. The circular harmonic expansion is then

$$f(r, \theta) = \sum_p g(r, p) \exp(jp\theta) \tag{57}$$

where $g(r, p)$ is the radial dependence of the pth circular harmonic. The specific form of Eq. (56) becomes

$$g(r, p) = \frac{1}{2\pi} \int_0^{2\pi} f(r, \theta) \exp(-jp\theta) \, d\theta \tag{58}$$

which is immediately recognizable as the 1-D Fourier series of the function $f(r, \theta)$ in the variable θ. This leads to the simple optical implementation shown in Fig. 32. The input is presented in polar coordinates by means of an optical or electronic coordinate transformation. A combination of cylindrical and spherical lens images in r and Fourier transforms in θ. The output is then sampled along lines corresponding to integer values of the θ frequency variable.

One could envision many other examples of mixed continuous and discrete shift-variant transformations. The parallel processing power of optical systems should be exploited when possible to perform the complete transformation as a single optical operation with outputs corresponding to the discrete index multiplexed in the output space.

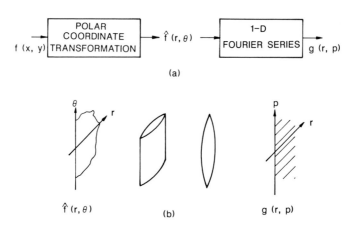

Fig. 32. (a) Circular harmonic decomposition consists of a polar coordinate transformation followed by a 1-D Fourier series. (b) Optical setup for performing the 1-D Fourier series.

V. Nonlinear Transformations

Nonlinear transformations can be classified into zero-spread transformations (point nonlinearities) and nonlinear transformations with spread. This section discusses the optical implementation of both classes. Other reviews of this topic include [71, 72].

A. ZERO-SPREAD NONLINEAR TRANSFORMATIONS

Numerous zero-spread nonlinear transformations have been implemented optically. New useful nonlinear transformations can also be realized by combining zero-spread nonlinear transformations with linear transformations involving spread.

Zero-spread nonlinear transformations can be further classified into shift-invariant and shift-variant classes. Among shift-invariant point nonlinearities, the following transformations (Fig. 33) have been used in optical data processing.

1. Quadratic Transformation

The quadratic transformation $g = |f|^2$ is basic to optical processing since it relates the detected optical intensity to the optical field. This transformation is basic to the functioning of many processors.

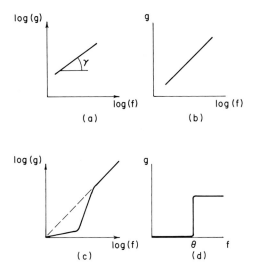

Fig. 33. Examples of point nonlinearity: (a) photographic film (b) logarithmic nonlinearity, (c) saturable absorber, and (d) thresholding.

2. Film Nonlinearity

The transformation $g \propto f^{-\gamma}$ represents the relation between the transmittance of a photographic emulsion and its exposure in the linear region (where γ is the contrast index). Film nonlinearity poses a problem when implementing linear coherent (or incoherent) optical transformations. An appropriate value of γ must be selected to render the overall process linear [10]. However, a large γ is sometimes called for when high-intensity values are to be emphasized, that is, when detecting peaks of the output of a matched filter.

3. Logarithmic Transformation

The transformation $g = \log(f)$ is important in homomorphic filtering [73]. Operations such as the inverse Fourier transform of the logarithmically transformed Fourier transform proved to be valuable in the processing of speech and images [74, 75].

4. Saturation Transformation

The transformation $g = f[1 - a/(b+f)]$, shown in Fig. 33, describes light transmission through some organic dyes operating as saturable absorbers [76] (f and g are optical intensities, and a and b are constants). Photochromic materials exhibit similar behavior [77]. When plotted on a logarithmic scale, this transformation exhibits three distinct approximately linear regions. The intermediate region can be approximated by $g = f^{\gamma}$, where γ is usually a large contrast index.

Such nonlinear elements, which can be used in real time, are useful not only in implementing a nonlinear modification to the gray level of an image, but also in performing mixing operations needed to multiply two images (e.g., the quadratic transformation $g = f^2$ operating on the sum $f_1 + f_2$ contains the product term $f_1 f_2$). Applications of this type have been implemented by Lee [72]. The main difficulty with such elements is the requirement of high-intensity light sources.

5. Thresholding (or Hardlimiter) Transformation

This is the transformation $g = \frac{1}{2} + \frac{1}{2} \operatorname{sgn}(f - \theta)$, where $\operatorname{sgn}(f) = 1$ or -1 for $f > 0$ or $f < 0$, respectively, and θ is the threshold of the hardlimiter. It is an idealization of the nonlinearity $g = f^{\gamma}$, when γ is very large. It is important in operations such as gray-level slicing and logic operations on binary signals.

6. Feedback

Feedback can also be used to introduce nonlinearity. If a transparency whose transmittance is the signal f is illuminated uniformly and the transmitted light fed back to the input, then the transmitted light g would be related to f by the transformation $g = f/(1 - f)$.

We now turn to shift-variant zero-spread nonlinear transformations. Here the nonlinear relation between f and g varies with location. Examples follow.

a. Frequency Modulation. This transformation [78–80] maps a signal $f(\mathbf{x})$ into a frequency-modulated version,

$$g = \cos[\omega_x(f)x + \omega_y(f)y]$$

where the frequencies $\omega_x(f)$ and $\omega_y(f)$ are functions of f. The process is illustrated in Fig. 34. An example is theta modulation [79], for which

$$\omega_k = \omega_0 \cos(af), \qquad \omega_y = \omega_0 \sin(af)$$

where ω_0 and a are constants. Here the signal f is coded into a grating whose local frequency is $\omega_0/2\pi$ and whose orientation angle $(\theta = af)$ is proportional to the gray level of the local input f. The process can be implemented by use of liquid-crystal spatial light modulators operating in the variable-grating mode [80, 81].

When this encoded signal is Fourier transformed, the Fourier components that correspond to different gray levels are separated. One such component may be selected; an inverse Fourier transform identifies locations of the selected gray level. The result is a level slicing operation [81]. If, instead, the different Fourier components are modified selectively by use of a mask, and an inverse Fourier transform is realized, the operation is equivalent to modification of the gray level by a relation governed by the mask function. Details are described in [81].

b. Halftone Encoding. Halftone encoding is a form of pulse-width or pulse-area modulation in which an input real-valued signal f is transformed into a binary-valued signal g [82–84]. One recipe is

$$g(\mathbf{x}) = \frac{1}{2} + \frac{1}{2} \operatorname{sgn}[f(\mathbf{x}) + f_s(\mathbf{x}) - \theta]$$

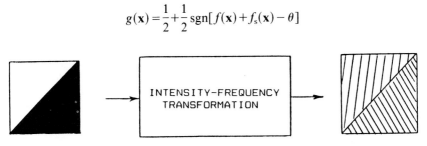

INTENSITY–FREQUENCY
TRANSFORMATION

Fig. 34. Intensity-to-frequency transformation.

where $f_s(\mathbf{x})$ is a periodic function of dots or lines and θ a constant threshold. The resultant signal g is composed of dots or lines whose local width W is some function of the local input signal $W = \psi(f)$. The process is best illustrated in the 1-D case using triangular-shaped pulses, as in Fig. 35.

This transformation can be combined with a linear shift-invariant filter to obtain an interesting overall nonlinear transformation. For example, using a filter that passes only frequencies in the vicinity of one of the Fourier components of the periodic function $f_s(\mathbf{x})$ gives a resultant output that is proportional to $\sin^2[\alpha W]$, where α is a constant. The overall system is equivalent to a point nonlinearity $g = \sin^2[\alpha\psi(f)]$. This is an interesting nonmonotonic nonlinearity [2].

B. BILINEAR AND QUADRATIC TRANSFORMATIONS

The bilinear transformation is defined in Eq. (12). Under conditions of shift-invariance, it becomes

$$g(\mathbf{u}) = \int\int f_1^*(\mathbf{x}_1)f_2(\mathbf{x}_2)h(\mathbf{u}-\mathbf{x}_1,\mathbf{u}-\mathbf{x}_2)\,d\mathbf{x}_1\,d\mathbf{x}_2 \tag{59}$$

In the degenerate case the two input signals are the same: $f_1(\mathbf{x}) = f_2(\mathbf{x})$.

Because of the quadratic nature between optical intensity and optical field, the bilinear transformation arises naturally in numerous optical systems. This includes coherent optical systems (using an intensity detector), partially coherent systems, and coherent imaging systems with random time-varying pupil functions (using an averaging detector). Other examples can be found in references [85–87].

The most direct method of implementing a bilinear transformation of an N-D signal is to replace it with a $2N$-D linear transformation, thus trading dimensionality for order of nonlinearity [88–90]. We construct the auxiliary signals

$$\phi(\mathbf{x}_1,\mathbf{x}_2) = f_1^*(\mathbf{x}_1)f_2(\mathbf{x}_2) \tag{60}$$

$$\Gamma(\mathbf{u}_1,\mathbf{u}_2) = \int\int \phi(\mathbf{x}_1,\mathbf{x}_2)h(\mathbf{u}_1-\mathbf{x}_1,\mathbf{u}_2-\mathbf{x}_2)\,d\mathbf{x}_1\,d\mathbf{x}_2 \tag{61}$$

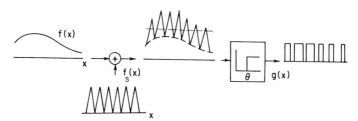

Fig. 35. Intensity-to-pulse width transformation.

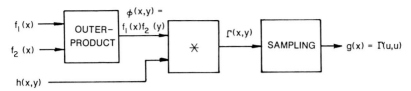

Fig. 36. Bilinear transformation.

We can easily see that our output signal $g(\mathbf{u})$ can be obtained from the auxiliary signal $\Gamma(\mathbf{u}_1, \mathbf{u}_2)$ by sampling along diagonal points,

$$g(\mathbf{u}) = \Gamma(\mathbf{u}, \mathbf{u}) \tag{62}$$

Therefore the processing is performed in three steps. The auxiliary function $\phi(\mathbf{x}_1, \mathbf{x}_2)$ is formed by an outer product of $f_1(\mathbf{x}_1)$ with $f_2(\mathbf{x}_2)$. The linear transformation (61) is realized using, for example, a coherent optical processor, and the output is sampled by placing a detector at diagonal points. The scheme is illustrated in Fig. 36, and the optical setup for the 1-D case ($N = 1$) is shown in Fig. 37.

When $N = 2$, a 2-D/1-D transdimensional transformation can be used to obtain a 1-D representation, conduct the bilinear transformation, and then convert back to a 2-D signal. The system then becomes the following sequence of transformations: 2-D/1-D sampling → 1-D/2-D outer product → 2-D linear transformation → 2-D/1-D diagonal sampling → 1-D/2-D scanning.

Another method of realizing a bilinear transformation is to decompose it as a combination of linear transformations and elementary operations of multiplication or squaring. This is possible if the kernel $h(\mathbf{x}_1, \mathbf{x}_2)$ is expandable in the form

$$h(\mathbf{x}_1, \mathbf{x}_2) = \sum_n \lambda_n \phi_n^*(\mathbf{x}_1) \phi_n(\mathbf{x}_2) \tag{63}$$

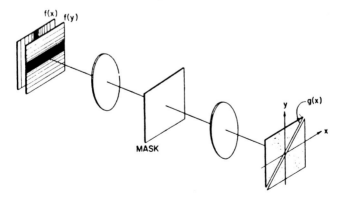

Fig. 37. Implementation of bilinear transformation of 1-D functions.

The bilinear transformation then becomes

$$g(\mathbf{u}) = \sum_n \lambda_n [f_1^*(\mathbf{u}) * \phi_n^*(\mathbf{u})][f_2[(\mathbf{u}) * \phi_n(\mathbf{u})] \tag{64}$$

and in the degenerate (quadratic) case

$$g(\mathbf{u}) = \sum \lambda_n |f(\mathbf{u}) * \phi_n(\mathbf{u})|^2 \tag{65}$$

Therefore the bilinear operation embodies operations of convolutions, multiplications (or absolute-value squaring), and summations, as illustrated in Fig. 38.

Implementation can be done using a serial system that computes the convolutions (using a coherent optical processor) and the multiplications (using, for example, a light valve), or squaring (using a detector), and accumulates the results to perform the summation. A scheme that uses a parallel system in which the convolutions and multiplications of the different terms are computed simultaneously has been developed for the degenerate case [91, 92].

C. DOUBLE-DOMAIN REPRESENTATIONS OF SIGNALS (LOCAL SPECTRA)

Another important example of nonlinear transformations of second order is the Wigner distribution function (WDF) [93, 94]. The WDF and other local spectral distributions are also examples of trans-dimensional distributions (up-conversions), for which a signal is represented in the combined

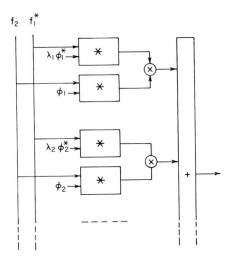

Fig. 38. Parallel implementation of bilinear transformation using convolutions, multiplications, and summations.

space and frequency (or reciprocal) domains as a function of both position and frequency.

An indication of the local spectral characteristics of a signal $f(\mathbf{x})$ at a location $\mathbf{x}$ can be obtained by computing its Fourier transform as seen through a window centered around the location $\mathbf{x}$. The result is a function $g(\mathbf{u}, \mathbf{x})$ known as the space–frequency representation of the signal, where $\mathbf{u}$ represents frequency.

Two important definitions are used: the complex spectrogram (CS) [95],

$$g(\mathbf{u}, \mathbf{w}) = \int f(\mathbf{x})\, W^*(\mathbf{x} - \mathbf{w})\, \exp(-j\mathbf{u} \cdot \mathbf{x})\, d\mathbf{x} \tag{66}$$

and the Wigner distribution function (WDF),

$$g(\mathbf{u}, \mathbf{w}) = \int f(\mathbf{w} + \tfrac{1}{2}\mathbf{x}) f^*(\mathbf{w} - \tfrac{1}{2}\mathbf{x})\, \exp(-j\mathbf{u} \cdot \mathbf{x})\, d\mathbf{x} \tag{67}$$

The variables $\mathbf{u}$ and $\mathbf{w}$ represent frequency and position, respectively. The function $W(\mathbf{x})$ is a window function. It is evident that the WDF is a self-windowed CS. The WDF is related to the ambiguity function (which is used extensively in radar theory) [96–98] by a $2N$-D Fourier transform operation. Other properties of the CS and WDF can be found in numerous references [93].

If f is N-dimensional, then g is $2N$-dimensional. The transformation is an up-conversion transdimensional transformation. The CS is a linear transformation, whereas the WDF is nonlinear (quadratic). Both involve spread. Several optical implementations have been suggested [97–105]. One architecture is not unlike that used previously to implement projection, shift-variant transformations, and bilinear transformations. An auxiliary function of the higher dimension $2N$ is defined:

$$\phi(\mathbf{x}, \mathbf{y}) = f(\mathbf{x})\, W^*(\mathbf{x} - \mathbf{y}) \qquad \text{(CS case)} \tag{68}$$

$$\phi(\mathbf{x}, \mathbf{y}) = f\left(\mathbf{y} + \frac{1}{2}\mathbf{x}\right) f^*\left(\mathbf{y} - \frac{1}{2}\mathbf{x}\right) \qquad \text{(WDF case)} \tag{69}$$

The transformation can now be written in the form

$$g(\mathbf{u}, \mathbf{w}) = \int\!\!\int h(\mathbf{u}, \mathbf{w}; \mathbf{x}, \mathbf{y})\, \phi(\mathbf{x}, \mathbf{y})\, d\mathbf{x}\, d\mathbf{y}$$

$$h(\mathbf{u}, \mathbf{w}; \mathbf{x}, \mathbf{y}) = \exp(-j\mathbf{u} \cdot \mathbf{x})\, \delta(\mathbf{w} - \mathbf{y}) \tag{70}$$

It is readily apparent that (70) is a $2N$-D/$2N$-D linear transformation with an impulse response function $h(\mathbf{u}, \mathbf{w}; \mathbf{x}, \mathbf{y})$ that represents an astigmatic system performing perfect imaging in the $\mathbf{y}$-direction and Fourier transform in the $\mathbf{x}$-direction.

When $N = 1$, the implementation uses a 2-D astigmatic coherent optical system such as that in projection. The auxiliary function $\phi(x, y)$ can be entered by use of two acoustooptic cells carrying the two 1-D functions $f(x)$ and $W(x)$ and by optical rotations and multiplication to implement the product of (68) or (69).

Optical implementation of the local spectrum of an image $(N = 2)$ is obviously more difficult because the output is 4-D. Systems in which 2-D slices of that output are obtained sequentially and in parallel have been developed [102–105].

Another approach is based on the Radon transform method [105]. The 2-D Fourier transform in (70) is implemented by a series of 1-D line-integral projections. One-dimensional Fourier transforms are performed by use of efficient 1-D processors. The resultant output gives 1-D slices through the 4-D WDF or CS.

D. Logic Operations on Binary Images

The transformation of a binary-valued input image $f(\mathbf{x})$ into a binary valued output image $g(\mathbf{u})$ is an operation of considerable interest in pattern recognition. If the transformation is a point-to-point transformation, then only one operation is meaningful: the NOT operation (to NOT or not to NOT at each position $\mathbf{x}$). However, if the transformation involves spread, then the value $g(\mathbf{u})$ at a point $\mathbf{u}$ is a logic operation L on the values of $f(x)$ at a neighborhood, $\mathbf{x} \in \Omega(\mathbf{u})$,

$$g(\mathbf{u}) = L\{f(\mathbf{x}), \mathbf{x} \in \Omega(\mathbf{u})\} \tag{71}$$

Examples are the transformations of contraction and expansion [106, 107]. the contraction operation is defined by the following rule: Set $g(\mathbf{u})$ to *zero* if $f(\mathbf{x})$ is not *one* at all $\mathbf{x} \in \Omega(\mathbf{u})$. The region $\Omega(\mathbf{u})$ is usually a region surrounding but not including *u*. The expansion operation is the complementary: Set $g(\mathbf{u})$ to *one* if $f(\mathbf{x})$ is not *zero* everywhere in $\Omega(\mathbf{u})$. Such operations are useful in linking together segments of broken lines and in removing noise and defects near edges in binary images.

Optical implementation of logic operations of the type in Eq. (71) is based on the fact that it can always be decomposed as a combination of a linear transformation with spread,

$$g_0(\mathbf{u}) = \int_{\Omega(\mathbf{u})} h(\mathbf{u}, \mathbf{x}) f(\mathbf{x}) \, d\mathbf{x} \tag{72}$$

Followed by a zero-spread point nonlinearity,

$$g(\mathbf{u}) = \psi[g_0(\mathbf{u})] \tag{73}$$

which is in general nonmonotonic and discontinuous. For example, to realize the expansion operation,

$$h(\mathbf{u}, \mathbf{x}) = 1, \qquad \mathbf{x} \in \Omega(\mathbf{u})$$

$$= 0, \text{ elsewhere}$$

and $\psi(.)$ is a simple thresholding operation. The two operations can be implemented using previously discussed techniques [107].

The class of transformations for which Ψ is a single threshold is called linearly-separable. Linearly-separable Boolean operations are implemented by threshold logic. Threshold logic applied to binary input variables $x_1, x_2, \ldots$ generates a binary output variable according to the rule

$$Y = 1, \quad \text{if } \sum_{j=1}^{n} a_j x_j > \theta$$

$$Y = 0, \quad \text{otherwise,}$$

(74)

where a_j are real-valued weights. Applied to our continuous imaging problem, this is equivalent to

$$g(\mathbf{u}) = 1, \quad \text{if } \int h(\mathbf{u} - \mathbf{x}) \, d\mathbf{x} > \theta,$$

$$g(\mathbf{u}) = 0, \quad \text{otherwise,}$$

(75)

that is a cascade of convolution followed by a simple threshold—two operations amenable to efficient optical implementation.

To appreciate the nature of linearly-separable logic operations, examine the operation $Y = L\{x_1, x_2, \ldots, x_n\}$ in a geometrical framework. The 2^n possible input combinations or vectors of the Boolean function can be mapped onto the vertices of a cube in an n-dimensional Euclidean space. Each vertex corresponds to a possible input vector and has a value of 1 or 0 depending on the function that is being implemented. The problem in finding a single threshold is that of computing an optimal set of weights or coefficients $\{a_n\}$ that satisfy Eq. (74). This set of coefficients defines an n-dimensional hyper-plane such that all the logic 1 vertices lie on one side of the plane and all the logic 0 vertices lie on the other side. Not all Boolean functions are linearly-separable and hence not all functions can be implemented with a single threshold gate. The possible threshold gates for Boolean functions of up to 8 variables have been tabulated along with their weights [109]. The weights may be positive or negative. Methods exist for recording negative weights holographically or even with incoherent optical systems [110]; a negative threshold can be eliminated by inverting the inequality of (75).

Recent work in the study of nonlinear filtering of images has produced a class of operations known as stack filters. The median filter is the best known of these filters [111]. It has been shown [112] that stack filters can be constructed from positive Boolean functions. Positive Boolean functions are those that do not contain complemented variables. The linearly-separable Boolean functions with positive weights are a subset of this class. This does not imply that all linearly-separable functions are positive since there exist linearly-separable functions (those with negative weights) that are not positive Boolean functions. There also exist positive functions that are not linearly-separable. Both of these classes are subsets of unate Boolean functions, which have the property that their expressions do not contain variables and their complements.

The binary median filter is an interesting subclass of stack filters which is also linearly-separable. This is because the filters output is just the majority of the input 1's and 0's and the majority gate is one of the basic gates in threshold logic. This formed the basis of the optical implementation of the general median filter reported recently [113]. The possibilities of using this class to construct optical nonlinear filters are apparent.

VI. Conclusions

We have aimed at providing a general classification of the various transformations of interest in computing, signal and image processing, and optics. Dimensionality, linearity, spread, and shift invariance were the main bases for the classification. The interrelations between the categories were delineated, highlighting the important notion that many transformations can be decomposed as serial or parallel combinations of more elementary ones. Optical implementations have used this concept to great advantage.

Some of the elementary transformations that are directly realizable by use of optical techniques are multiplication, addition, routing (geometric transformation), Fourier transform, 1-D/2-D fan out, 2-D/1-D fan in (projection), and some point nonlinearities. Through more than two decades of activities in this area, the above "primary" transformations have been combined in forms that are simple and complex, straightforward and tricky, to achieve a hierarchy of other transformations, that is still growing.

One very interesting newcomer to this hierarchy is stochastic transformations [108]. Here the input signal is deterministic, and the output is random (with statistical averages determined by the input). It is a general form of a random number generator. Implementation is based on the random nature of photons.

Acknowledgment

This work has been supported in part by the National Science Foundation.

References

1. L. J. Cutrona, E. N. Leith, C. J. Palermo, and L. J. Porcello, *IRE Trans. Inf. Theory* **IT-6**, 386–400 (1960).
2. J. W. Goodman, *Proc. IEEE* **65**, 29–38 (1977).
3. S. H. Lee, ed., "*Optical Information Processing Fundamentals.*" Springer-Verlag, Berlin and New York, 1981.
4. H. Stark, "*Applications of Optical Fourier Transform.*" Academic Press, New York, 1982.
5. F. T. S. Yu, "*Optical Information Processing.*" Wiley, New York, 1983.
6. W. T. Rhodes, J. R. Fienup, and B. E. A. Saleh, eds., "*Transformations in Optical Signal Processing,*" SPIE Vol. 373 (1984).
7. *Proc. IEEE* **72**, July (1984).
8. *Opt. Eng.* **25**, Jan. (1986).
9. M. Schetzen, "The Volterra and Weiner Theories of Nonlinear Systems." Wiley, New York, 1980.
10. J. W. Goodman, "Introduction to Fourier Optics." McGraw-Hiill, New York, 1968.
11. A. W. Lohmann and N. Streibl, *Appl. Opt.* **22**, 780 (1983).
12. G. Hausler and N. Streibl, *Opt. Commun.* **42**, 381 (1982).
13. G. M. Robbins and T. S. Huang, *Proc. IEEE* **60**, 862 (1972).
14. S. K. Case and V. Gerbig, *Opt. Commun.* **36**, 94 (1981).
15. S. K. Case, P. R. Haugen, and O. J. Lokberg, *Appl. Opt.* **20**, 2670 (1981).
16. S. K. Case and P. R. Haugen, *Opt. Eng.* **21**, 352 (1982).
17. H. Bartelt and S. K. Case, *Opt. Eng.* **22**, 497 (1983).
18. T. Yatagai, K. Choji, and H. Saito, *Opt. Commun.* **38**, 162 (1981).
19. Y. Saito, S. Komatsu, and H. Ohzu, *Opt. Commun.* **47**, 8 (1983).
20. D. Casasent and D. Psaltis, *Proc. IEEE* **65**, 77 (1977).
21. D. Casasent and D. Psaltis, *Appl. Opt.* **16**, 1472 (1977).
22. D. Casasent and M. Kraus, *Appl. Opt.* **17**, 1559 (1978).
23. D. Casasent and D. Psaltis, *Appl. Opt.* **17**, 655 (1978).
24. J. W. Goodman, P. Kellman, and E. W. Hansen, *Appl. Opt.* **16**, 733 (1977).
25. J. F. Walkup, *Opt. Eng.* **19**, 339 (1980).
26. J. W. Goodman, *in* "Optical Information Processing Fundamentals" (S. H. Lee, ed.), pp. 235–260. Springer-Verlag, Berlin and New York, 1981.
27. A. A. Sawchuk, *Proc. IEEE* **60**, 854 (1972).
28. A. A. Sawchuk, *J. Opt. Soc. Am.* **63**, 1052 (1973).
29. A. A. Sawchuk, *J. Opt. Soc. Am.* **64**, 138 (1974).
30. O. Bryngdahl, *J. Opt. Soc. Am.* **64**, 1092 (1974).
31. O. Bryngdahl, *Opt. Commuun.* **10**, 164 (1974).
32. M. Born and E. Wolf, "Principles of Optics," p. 753. Pergamon, New York, 1965.
33. J. N. Cederquist and A. M. Tai, *Appl. Opt.* **23**, 3099 (1984).
34. W. J. Dallas, *in* "The Computer in Optical Research" (B. R. Frieden, ed.), pp. 291–366. Springer-Verlag, Berlin and New York, 1980.
35. W. H. Lee, *in* "Progress in Optics" (E. Wolf, ed.), Vol. XVI, pp. 119–232. North-Holland Publ., Amsterdam, 1978.
36. A. W. Lohmann aand D. P. Paris, *Appl. Opt.* **6**, 1739 (1967).
37. W. H. Lee, *Appl. Opt.* **9**, 639 (1970).
38. W. H. Lee, *Appl. Opt.* **13**, 1677 (1974).
39. L. B. Lesem, P. M. Hirsch, and J. A. Jordan, Jr., *IBM J. Res. Dev.* **13**, 150 (1969).
40. B. R. Brown and A. W. Lohmann, *IBM J. Res. Dev.* **13**, 160 (1969).
41. J. J. Burch, *Proc. IEEE* **55**, 599 (1967).
42. S. K. Case and W. J. Dallas, *Appl. Opt.* **17**, 2537 (1978).

43. H. Bartelt and S. K. Case, *Appl. Opt.* **21**, 2886 (1982).
44. C. S. Weaver, S. D. Ramsey, J. W. Goodman, and A. M. Rosie, *Appl. Opt.* **9**, 1672–1682 (1970).
45. W. T. Rhodes and J. M. Florence, *J. Opt. Soc. Am.* **65**, 1178 (1975).
46. W. T. Rhodes, *SPIE Semin. Proc.* **128**, 322 (1977).
47. D. Casasent and R. Kessler, *Opt. Eng.* **16**, 402–405 (1977).
48. H. Bartelt and A. W. Lohman, *Opt. Commun.* **42**, 87–91 (1982).
49. W. T. Rhodes, *in* "Transformations in Optical Signal Processing" (W. T. Rhodes, J. R. Fienup, and B. E. A. Saleh, eds.), SPIE Vol. 373, pp. 11–20 (1984).
50. T. M. Turpin, *in* "Transformations in Optical Signal Processing" (W. T. Rhodes, J. R. Fienup, and B. E. A. Saleh, eds.), SPIE Vol. 373, pp. 117–124 (1984).
51. W. W. Stoner, W. J. Miceli, and F. A. Horrigan, *in* Transformations in Optical Signal Processing" (W. T. Rhodes, J. R. Fienup, and B. E. A. Saleh, eds.), SPIE Vol. 373, pp. 21–30 (1984).
52. H. O. Bartelt and A. W. Lohman, *in* "Transformations in Optical Signal Processing" (W. T. Rhodes, J. R. Fienup, and B. E. A. Saleh, eds.), SPIE Vol. 373, pp. 3–10 (1984).
53. J. Hofer-Alfeis and R. Bamler, *in* "Transformations in Optical Signal Processing" (W. T. Rhodes, J. R. Fienup, and B. E. A. Saleh, eds.), SPIE Vol. 373, pp. 77–88 (1984).
54. W. T. Rhodes and P. S. Guilfoyle, *Proc. IEEE* **72**, 820–830 (1984).
55. D. Casasent, *Proc. IEEE* **72**, 831–849 (1984).
56. J. W. Goodman, *Opt. Acta* **32**, 1489–1496 (1985).
57. L. J. Cutrona, *in* "Optical and Electro-optical Information Processing" (J. T. Tippett, D. A. Berkowitz, L. C. Clapp, C. J. Koester, and A. Vanderburgh, eds.), Chap. 6. MIT Press, Cambridge, Massachusetts, 1965.
58. P. Kellman and J. W. Goodman, *Appl. Opt.* **16**, 2609 (1977).
59. R. J. Marks, II, *Appl. Opt.* **18**, 3670 (1979).
60. R. J. Marks, II and T. F. Krile, *Appl. Opt.* **15**, 2241 (1976).
61. R. Kasturi, T. F. Krile, and J. F. Walkup, *Appl. Opt.* **20**, 881 (1981).
62. R. J. Marks, II, J. F. Walkup, and M. O. Hagler, *J. Opt. Soc. Am.* **66**, 918 (1976).
63. T. F. Krile, R. J. Marks, II, J. F. Walkup, and M. O. Hagler, *Appl. Opt.* **16**, 3131 (1977).
64. J. R. Leger and S. H. Lee, *J. Opt. Soc. Am.* **72**, 556 (1982).
65. Z. H. Gu, J. R. Leger, and S. H. Lee, *J. Opt. Soc. Am.* **72**, 787 (1982).
66. Z. H. Gu and S. H. Lee, *Opt. Eng.* **23**, 727 (1984).
67. H. H. Arsenault, Y. N. Hsu, K. Chalasinska-Macukow, and Y. Yang, *SPIE Semin. Proc.* **359**, 266 (1982).
68. Y. Yang, Y. N. Hsu, and H. H. Arsenault, *Opt. Acta* **29**, 627 (1982).
69. T. Szoplik and H. H. Arsenault, *Appl. Opt.* **24**, 3179 (1985).
70. B. Davis, "Integral Transforms and their Applications" pp. 237–240. Springer-Verlag, Berlin and New York, 1978.
71. A. A. Sawchuk and T. C. Strand, *in* "Applications of Optical Fourier Transform" (H. Stark, ed.), Chap. 9. Academic Press, New York, 1982.
72. S. H. Lee, *in* "Optical Information Processing Fundamentals" (S. H. Lee, ed.), p. 261. Springer-Verlag, Berlin and New York, 1981.
73. A. V. Oppenheim and R. W. Schafer, "Digital Signal Processing." Prentice-Hall, Englewood Cliffs, New Jersey, 1975.
74. H. Kato and J. W. Goodman, *Opt. Commun.* **8**, 378–381 (1973).
75. W. K. Pratt, "Digital Image Processing." Wiley, New York, 1978.
76. K. T. Stalker and S. H. Lee, *J. Opt. Soc. Am.* **64**, 545 (1974).
77. J. R. Meyer-Arendt and N. J. Wilder, *J. Opt. Soc. Am.* **59**, 1516 (1969).
78. B. Morgenstern and A. W. Lohman, *Optik* **20**, 450 (1963).
79. J. D. Armitage and A. W. Lohman, *Appl. Opt.* **4**, 399–403 (1965).

80. B. H. Soffer, D. Boswell, A. M. Lackner, A. R. Tanguay, Jr., T. C. Strand, and A. A. Sawchuck, *SPIE Semin. Proc.* **218**, 81 (1980).
81. A. A. Sawchuk and T. C. Strand, *in* "Transformations in Optical Signal Processing" (W. T. Rhodes, J. R. Fienup, and B. E. A. Saleh, eds.), SPIE Vol. 373, pp. 69-74 (1984).
82. T. C. Strand, *Opt. Commun.* **15**, 60-65 (1975).
83. S. R. Dashiell and A. A. Sawchuck, *Opt. Commun.* **15**, 66-70 (1975).
84. H. Kato and J. W. Goodman, *Appl. Opt.* **14**, 1818-1824 (1975).
85. R. K. Raney, *J. Opt. Soc. Am.* **57**, 1180-1189 (1967).
86. B. E. A. Saleh, *Opt. Acta* **26**, 777-799 (1979).
87. B. E. A. Saleh, *in* "Transformations in Optical Signal Processing" (W. T. Rhodes, J. R. Fienup, and B. E. A. Saleh, eds.), SPIE Vol. 373, pp. 125-134 (1984).
88. B. E. A. Saleh, *Appl. Opt.* **17**, 3408-3411 (1978).
89. E. W. Kamen, *J. Nonlin. Anal. Theor. Methods Appl.* **3**, 467-481 (1979).
90. N. S. Subotic and B. E. A. Saleh, *Opt. Commun.* **52**, 259-264 (1984).
91. B. E. A. Saleh and N. Subotic, *Opt. Commun.* **43**, 111-113 (1982).
92. N. S. Subotic, H. K. Liu, and B. E. A. Saleh, *Opt. Acta* **32**, 91-105 (1985).
93. T. A. C. M. Claasen and W. F. G. Mechlenbrauker, *Philips J. Res.* **35**, 217-250 (1980).
94. M. J. Bastiaans, *Opt. Commun.* **25**, 26-30 (1978).
95. L. R. Rabiner and R. W. Schafer, "Digital Processing of Speech Signals." Prentice-Hall, Englewood Cliffs, New Jersey, 1978.
96. A. Papoulis, *J. Opt. Soc. Am.* **64**, 779-788 (1974).
97. R. J. Marks, II, J. F. Walkup, and T. F. Krile, *Appl. Opt.* **16**, 746 (1977).
98. R. J. Marks, II and M. W. Hall, *Appl. Opt.* **18**, 2539-2540 (1979).
99. M. J. Bastiaans, *Appl. Opt.* **19**, 192 (1980).
100. K. H. Brenner, H. O. Bartlet, and A. W. Lohman, *Opt. Commun.* **42**, 32 (1982).
101. J. Z. Jiao, B. Wang, and H. Liu, *Appl. Opt.* **23**, 1249 (1984).
102. R. Bamler and H. Glunder, *Proc. Int. Conf. Opt. Comput., Cambridge, Mass.*, 1983, pp. 117-121.
103. N. Subotic and B. E. A. Saleh, *Opt. Lett.* **9**, 471-473 (1984).
104. M. Conner and Y. Li, *Appl. Opt.* **24**, 3825-3829 (1985).
105. R. L. Easton, Jr., A. J. Ticknor, and H. H. Barrett, *Opt. Eng.* **23**, 738-744 (1984).
106. P. Margos and R. Schafer, *IEEE Int. Conf. Acoust. Speech Signal Proc.* **2** (1984).
107. S. H. Lee, *Opt. Eng.* **25**, 69-75 (1986).
108. G. M. Morris, *J. Opt. Soc. Am.* **1**, 1292 (1984).
109. S. Muroga, "Threshold Logic and its Applications." Wiley, New York, 1971.
110. F. T. S. Yu, "Optical Information Processing," Ch. 8. Wiley, New York, 1983.
111. J. P. Fitch, E. J. Coyle, and N. C. Gallagher, *IEEE Trans. Acoust., Speech, Signal Process.* **ASSP-32**, 1183-1185 (1984).
112. P. D. Wendt, E. J. Coyle, and N. C. Gallagher, *IEEE Trans. Acoust., Speech, Signal Process.* **ASSP-43**, 898-911 (1986).
113. E. Ochoa, J. P. Allebach, and D. W. Sweeney, *Annu. Meet. Opt. Am., Seattle*, 1986, p. 7.

5.2

Tomographic Transformations in Optical Signal Processing

ROGER L. EASTON, JR.* AND
HARRISON H. BARRETT

OPTICAL SCIENCES CENTER
UNIVERSITY OF ARIZONA
TUCSON, ARIZONA 85721

I. Introduction and Definitions

The traditional motivation for processing signals by optical means is due primarily to two factors. The first is the ability of coherent optical systems using spherical elements to perform the Fourier transform, and the second is the inherent capability of optical systems to operate on two-dimensional (2-D) data planes. For 2-D signals (e.g., images), optical processing is of obvious utility; but even if the signals to be processed are one-dimensional (1-D), optical techniques can allow parallel processing of several channels. The increased system throughput thus obtained may make optical processing attractive relative to more precise (but as yet slower) digital electronic technologies.

The main thrust of research in optical signal processing has been directed at applying either or both of the capabilities of rapid Fourier transformation and parallelism. However, there are problems restricting the utility of optical

*Present address: Center for Imaging Science, Rochester Institute of Technology, Rochester, New York 14623.

335

processing that are well known to those working in the field and that diminish its attractiveness relative to digital electronic processing. Primary among these are the limitations of available 2-D input/output devices (spatial light modulators and detector arrays) and (for coherent systems) speckle noise. These limitations are responsible for restricting the use of optical processing to a few applications in which the limitations are not significant (e.g., off-line synthetic aperture radar processing). In marked contrast to the situation for 2-D hardware, signal-processor technology for temporal (1-D) signals is quite advanced in capability and flexibility, and hence it may be profitable to apply that 1-D technology to 2-D operations, if possible. In effect, this would allow a tradeoff between rapid parallel processing and precise serial processing in a hybrid system. Several algorithms are available to derive 1-D signals from a 2-D input and reconstruct the 2-D processed signal. A familiar example of such an operation is the television raster, which creates a 1-D temporal signal from 2-D imagery by scanning and rederives the 2-D image by stacking segments of the temporal signal (Rhodes, 1981b). The raster transduction was used in optical signal processing by Thomas (1966) to generate a 2-D array from a long 1-D temporal signal to use as input to a 2-D optical processor. Several other dimensional transduction operations were considered by Bartelt and Lohmann (1981). One that is becoming more familiar can be called a tomographic transformation, in which a 1-D data set is derived from a 2-D signal by integration along sets of parallel lines. The relation between these two sets of data has some nice mathematical properties that make the transformation potentially very useful in both analog and digital signal processing.

A. History and Development

The mathematical basis for the tomographic transformation was derived in 1917 by Johann Radon, an Austrian mathematician. Radon (1917) proved that the complete set of 1-D projections of continuous 2-D or 3-D functions with compact support contain all of the information in the original function. The projections are derived by integration of the 2-D function over sets of parallel lines or by integration of the 3-D function over parallel planes. The derivation of the 1-D projections from the function is the forward Radon transform. Radon also derived expressions for reconstruction of the function from its projections—the inverse Radon transform. Generalization of the theory has made it applicable to functions of higher dimensionality (John, 1955). Another development was made by Cormack (1963, 1964), who formulated the mathematical expansion of projections into circular harmonics (i.e., a discrete angular Fourier series representation of the projection data).

Radon was primarily interested in using projections to find solutions of Poisson's differential equation in electrostatics, but his work has been applied to a myriad of scientific disciplines since the 1950s, including crystallography, radio astronomy, geophysics, nuclear magnetic resonance, radiative scattering, and diagnostic radiology. This explosion of interest is evident by the number of publications on the subject, especially in the last 15 years or so. For a good discussion of applications and an extensive bibliography see Deans (1983). No doubt the application of the Radon transform most familiar to the lay public is in diagnostic radiology. The new fields of x-ray computed tomography (CT), emission computed tomography (ECT), and magnetic resonance imaging (MRI), which enable imaging of cross-sectional slices of the body of a patient from sets of projection data, have received much attention in the press. Indeed, the medical application of Radon's theory is the source of its now familiar name, tomography, which is derived from the Greek word for slice. Each of these new medical wonders owes its existence to Johann Radon and the subsequent researchers who generalized and applied the mathematical theory.

In the applications listed above, Radon's mathematical theory is used to solve an inverse problem in which the source function is mathematically reconstructed from the projection data. Of course, the complete infinite set of projections is never collected, making it impossible to reconstruct the source function uniquely; only some "best" estimate can be found. We shall not overly concern ourselves here with such niceties as they are somewhat removed from the purpose at hand and have been considered at length elsewhere (Rowland, 1979; Barrett and Swindell, 1981). Rather, we wish to investigate the use of the Radon transform as a dimensional transducer in signal processing. The discrete nature of the data set will still be of some concern to us, mainly due to nonuniform sampling of Cartesian space by the transformation, but our main purpose is the identification of signal processing operations that are possible and profitable to perform by tomographic transformation. For some of these the processed 1-D data alone may be sufficient for the task at hand; but often it will be desirable to reconstruct the processed 2-D signal from the processed projections, and so some consideration will be given to optical methods of generating the inverse Radon transform.

B. BASIC THEORY

In the literature there are several extensive mathematical developments of the theory of the Radon transform (see, e.g., Helgason, 1980; Deans, 1983; Barrett, 1984). Consequently, we shall keep our discussion brief and emphasize applicability rather than completeness or mathematical rigor. Also, we shall generally restrict our treatment to the 2-D problem with occasional remarks about application to 3-D when warranted.

1. *Forward Radon Transform, Projections*

Given a 2-D function $f(\mathbf{r}) = f(x, y)$ (we shall denote vectors by boldface characters), a single projection along an azimuth angle ϕ can be derived by integration along all lines at azimuth $\phi + \pi/2$ (Fig. 1). The 1-D function thus generated has as independent variable the perpendicular distance of the integration line from the origin. This distance is the magnitude of the vector $\mathbf{p}$, where $\mathbf{p} = (p, \phi)$ in polar coordinates. It is also useful to define a unit vector $\hat{\mathbf{n}} = \mathbf{p}/|\mathbf{p}| = (1, \phi) = [\cos \phi, \sin \phi]$. (Note that square brackets denote Cartesian coordinates, and parentheses denote polar coordinates.) Naturally, for each set of integration lines at different angles relative to the

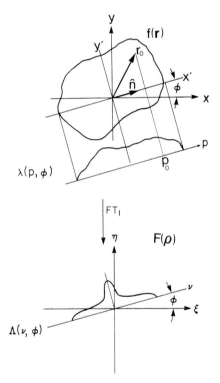

Fig. 1. Geometry of the projection operation and the central-slice theorem. The azimuth angle ϕ is defined by the unit vector $\hat{\mathbf{n}}$, and $[x', y']$ define the rotated coordinate system. The value of the function at $\mathbf{r}_0$ is projected to $p_0 = \mathbf{r}_0 \cdot \hat{\mathbf{n}}$. The 1-D Fourier transform of the projection $\lambda_\phi(p)$ yields a central slice through the 2-D Fourier transform $F(\boldsymbol{\rho})|_{\boldsymbol{\rho} = \hat{\mathbf{n}}\nu}$.

x-axis, a different projection is derived. A common notation for a projection is $\lambda(p, \phi)$, implying that λ is a 2-D function. But since all operations on the projection act on the spatial coordinate p alone, we can consider the projection to be a 1-D function parametrized by the azimuth angle ϕ. Depending on one's mathematical preference, $\lambda(p, \phi)$ can be defined in a number of equivalent ways. For example, we can consider a projection to be obtained by integration over lines parallel to the y'-axis in a system of coordinates $[x', y']$ rotated at angle ϕ relative to the original $[x, y]$ axes. However, there are distinct advantages obtained by defining a projection as a 2-D integral transform. The kernel of this transform is a 1-D Dirac delta function that selects the projection azimuth ϕ as defined by the polar unit $\hat{n} = (1, \phi)$. We want to determine the value of the projection coordinate p that is influenced by a point in the 2-D function located at $\mathbf{r} = (|\mathbf{r}|, \theta) = [r \cos \theta, r \sin \theta]$. As is apparent from Fig. 1, $\mathbf{r}$ must be located on the line normal to $\hat{n}$ at a perpendicular distance from the origin defined by

$$p = r \cos(\theta - \phi) = (r \cos \theta \cos \phi + r \sin \theta \sin \phi) = \mathbf{r} \cdot \hat{n} \tag{1}$$

Hence multiplying $f(\mathbf{r})$ by $\delta(p - \mathbf{r} \cdot \hat{n})$ collapses the area integral to a set of line integrals for the azimuth defined by $\hat{n}$, giving

$$\lambda(p, \phi) = \iint_{\infty} d^2 r f(\mathbf{r}) \, \delta(p - \mathbf{r} \cdot \hat{n}) \tag{2}$$

where the subscript ∞ denotes integration over the entire space spanned by the variables of integration. The transformation has mapped the Cartesian coordinates $[x, y]$ to a new system (p, ϕ), which is called Radon space. We have a choice about the limits on the new coordinates. If we consider p to be bipolar $(-\infty \leq p \leq \infty)$, then $\lambda(p, \phi) = \lambda(-p, \phi + \pi)$. We can therefore limit ϕ to the region $(0 \leq \phi \leq \pi)$. If we require p to be positive, then ϕ runs over 2π radians. The former choice is usually preferred since it simplifies the mathematical development. A plot of the Radon transform in (p, ϕ) space (Fig. 2) is termed a sinogram since a point in Cartesian space maps to a sinusoid in Radon space. From Eq. (2) it is easy to see that the Radon transform is linear and space variant. It is often convenient to express the projection operation in operator notation, for instance, $R_2[f(\mathbf{r})] = \lambda(p, \phi)$, where the subscript 2 denotes that the function being transformed is two-dimensional.

The projection operation described by Eq. (2) can be easily extended to functions of higher dimensionality (Barrett, 1984). For example, a 1-D projection of a 3-D function can be obtained by integration over parallel 2-D planes. Hence the 1-D Dirac delta function in Eq. (2) now reduces the volume integral to a planar integral. The transform collapses the 3-D

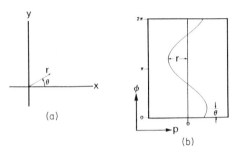

Fig. 2. Mapping of a single object point at $\mathbf{r} = (r, \theta)$ to sinogram space. (a) Cartesian space and (b) Radon space. The locus of all line integrals passing through the point $\mathbf{r}$ is a sinusoid of amplitude r and phase θ.

function $f(x, y, z)$ to a set of 1-D projections (e.g., $\lambda(p, \phi, \theta)$) parametrized by the two angles defining the unit normal to the planes of integration.

2. Central-Slice Theorem

Now that the forward Radon transform has been defined, we need to investigate its properties that may be useful for signal processing. Foremost of these is the central-slice theorem, which relates the Fourier transform of a 2-D function to the 1-D Fourier transforms of its projections. The theorem arises because the kernel of the Radon transform is a Dirac delta function of the scalar product of the conjugate variables $\mathbf{r}$ and p, as the kernel of the Fourier transform is a function of the scalar product of conjugate variables $\mathbf{r}$ and $\boldsymbol{\rho}$. As is customary, we define the Fourier transform of a 2-D function $f(\mathbf{r})$ as

$$\mathrm{FT}_2[f(\mathbf{r})] \equiv F(\boldsymbol{\rho}) = \iint_\infty d^2 r f(\mathbf{r}) \, e^{-2\pi i \boldsymbol{\rho} \cdot \mathbf{r}} \tag{3}$$

where FT_2 is the 2-D Fourier transform operator from coordinate $\mathbf{r} = [x, y]$ to spatial frequency $\boldsymbol{\rho} = [\xi, \eta]$. In this notation, functions denoted by a lower-case character are the coordinate-space representation (e.g., $f(\mathbf{r})$), and the corresponding frequency-space representation is signified by the upper-case character (e.g., $F(\boldsymbol{\rho})$). If we perform the 1-D Fourier transform of the projection defined by Eq. (2), we obtain

$$\mathrm{FT}_1[\lambda(p, \phi)] \equiv \Lambda(\nu, \phi) = \int_{-\infty}^{\infty} dp \, \lambda(p, \phi) \, e^{-2\pi i p \nu} \tag{4}$$

Substitution of Eq. (2) into Eq. (4) yields

$$\Lambda(\nu, \phi) = \int_{-\infty}^{\infty} dp \left[\iint_\infty d^2 r f(\mathbf{r}) \, \delta(p - \mathbf{r} \cdot \hat{\mathbf{n}}) \right] e^{-2\pi i p \nu} \tag{5}$$

Exchanging the order of integration, we obtain

$$\Lambda(\nu, \phi) = \int\int_\infty d^2r f(\mathbf{r}) \int_{-\infty}^\infty dp \, \delta(p - \mathbf{r} \cdot \hat{\mathbf{n}}) \, e^{-2\pi i p\nu}$$

$$= \int\int_\infty d^2r f(\mathbf{r}) \, e^{-2\pi i \hat{\mathbf{n}}\nu \cdot \mathbf{r}} \qquad (6)$$

Comparing Eq. (6) with Eq. (3), we can identify the relation between $\Lambda(\nu, \phi)$ and $F(\mathbf{\rho})$:

$$\Lambda(\nu, \phi) = F(\mathbf{\rho})|_{\mathbf{\rho}=\hat{\mathbf{n}}\nu} = F(\hat{\mathbf{n}}\nu) \qquad (7)$$

So the 1-D Fourier transform of a Radon projection at azimuth angle ϕ relative to the x-axis yields one line through the origin of the 2-D Fourier transform of the function $f(\mathbf{r})$. This line (central slice) in Fourier space is oriented at the same azimuth angle ϕ but relative to the ξ-axis (Fig. 1). The central-slice theorem can be represented in operator notation by

$$FT_2 = FT_1 R_2 \qquad (8)$$

It is important to note that the 2-D frequency-space representation generated via the Radon–Fourier transform has a sampling density in Cartesian space that falls off as ν^{-1} (Fig. 3). This sampling nonuniformity

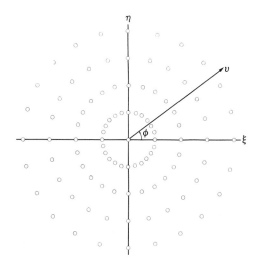

Fig. 3. Sampling nonuniformity of the Radon–Fourier transform in Cartesian frequency space obtained via the central-slice theorem. The 2-D input $f(\mathbf{r})$ is uniformly sampled in both radius p and azimuth ϕ. After performing the 1-D Fourier transforms and displaying in the radial format required by the central-slice theorem [Eq. (7)], it is apparent that the sampling density decreases as ν^{-1}.

must be compensated whenever a Cartesian-space representation is derived from a Radon-space representation (e.g., for display of the 2-D Fourier transform) or (as will be shown) when reconstructing the 2-D source function by the inverse Radon transform. Also note that the duality of coordinate- and Fourier-space representations ensures that a dual to the central-slice theorem exists. That is, the inverse Fourier transform of a projection in Fourier space is a central-slice of the coordinate space representation of the 2-D function.

A theorem similar in nature to central slice relates parallel projections weighted by a phase factor to parallel, rather than meridional, lines of the 2-D Fourier transform (Farhat *et al.*, 1983). If a weighted projection is defined as

$$q(x, \eta_0) = \int_{-\infty}^{\infty} dy\, f(x, y)\, e^{2\pi i \eta_0 y} \tag{9}$$

the 1-D Fourier transform of the weighted slice is found to be

$$\int_{-\infty}^{\infty} dx\, q(x, \eta_0)\, e^{2\pi i \xi x} = \int_{-\infty}^{\infty} dx \int_{-\infty}^{\infty} dy\, f(x, y)\, e^{2\pi i (\xi x + \eta_0 y)}$$

$$= Q(\xi, \eta_0) \tag{10}$$

Systems for optically generating and processing weighted projections have been proposed (Gmitro *et al.*, 1983) but are substantially more complicated than comparable systems for central slices.

3. *Filter Theorem*

Another very useful attribute of the Radon transform can be derived easily via the central-slice theorem. Consider the convolution of two 2-D functions $f(\mathbf{r})$ and $g(\mathbf{r})$. Using operator notation, we can take the 2-D Fourier transform of the convolution:

$$FT_2[f(\mathbf{r}) ** g(\mathbf{r})] = FT_2[f(\mathbf{r})] \times FT_2[g(\mathbf{r})] \tag{11}$$

where the number of asterisks denotes the dimensionality of the convolution. Equation (11) can be rewritten using the operator notation for the central-slice theorem [Eq. (8)], giving

$$FT_2[f ** g] = FT_1 R_2[f ** g]$$

$$= FT_1 R_2[f] \times FT_1 R_2[g]$$

$$= FT_1[\lambda_f(p, \phi)] \times FT_1[\lambda_g(p, \phi)] = \Lambda_f(\nu, \phi) \times \Lambda_g(\nu, \phi) \tag{12}$$

where the subscripts f and g are used to denote which function is being projected at the common azimuth angle ϕ. Applying the inverse 1-D Fourier transform operator to Eq. (12) yields

$$\mathrm{FT}_1^{-1}\,\mathrm{FT}_1\,R_2[f ** g] = R_2[f ** g] = \lambda_{f**g}$$
$$= \mathrm{FT}_1^{-1}[\Lambda_f \times \Lambda_g] = \mathrm{FT}_1^{-1}[\Lambda_f] * \mathrm{FT}_1^{-1}[\Lambda_g]$$
$$= \lambda_f * \lambda_g \tag{13}$$

where the common coordinate variables have been suppressed. In words, this shows that the projection of a 2-D convolution of two functions is the 1-D convolution of the projections of the functions. From this conclusion it is just a short conceptual hop to the realization that the same relationship holds for 2-D correlations. Thus we now have the mathematical capability of deriving the projection of a 2-D filtering or correlation operation simply by performing 1-D filtering or correlation of the projections of the original functions. This is a very powerful result and holds much promise for application to optical processing.

4. Inverse Radon Transform

Since most of the research into the Radon transform has been directed at the solution of inverse problems, there has been a plethora of publications devoted to the inverse Radon transform. Therefore we shall limit our mathematical discussion to a straightforward derivation of the inverse transform, with some comments made about algorithms appropriate to optical reconstruction methods. Readers interested in an in-depth mathematical development should consult some of the other literature, notably Rowland (1979), Deans (1983), and Barrett (1984).

The inverse Radon transform is most easily derived by applying the central-slice theorem to the polar form of the inverse 2-D Fourier transform:

$$\mathrm{FT}_2^{-1}[F(\boldsymbol{\rho})] \equiv f(\mathbf{r}) = \int_{-\pi}^{\pi} d\theta_p \int_0^\infty d\rho\,\rho\, F(\boldsymbol{\rho})\, e^{+2\pi i \boldsymbol{\rho}\cdot\mathbf{r}} \tag{14}$$

Invoking the central-slice theorem [Eq. (7)], we set $\boldsymbol{\rho} = \hat{\mathbf{n}}\nu$, $\rho = \nu$, $\theta_p = \phi$, and $F(\boldsymbol{\rho}) = F(\hat{\mathbf{n}}\nu) = \Lambda(\nu, \phi)$ in Eq. (14), yielding

$$f(\mathbf{r}) = \int_0^\pi d\phi \int_{-\infty}^\infty d\nu\,|\nu|\Lambda(\nu, \phi)\, e^{+2\pi i \nu \hat{\mathbf{n}}\cdot\mathbf{r}}$$
$$= \int_0^\pi d\phi [\mathrm{FT}_1[|\nu|\Lambda(\nu, \phi)]]|_{\rho = \mathbf{r}\cdot\hat{\mathbf{n}}} \tag{15}$$

This is one form of the inverse Radon transform. In words, it reconstructs a 2-D function $f(\mathbf{r})$ from a complete set of projections $\lambda(p, \phi)$ by the following steps:

1. 1-D Fourier transform $\lambda(p, \phi)$, yielding $\Lambda(\nu, \phi)$;
2. multiply by $|\nu|$;
3. inverse 1-D Fourier transform the product $[|\nu|\Lambda(\nu, \phi)]$;
4. smear this 1-D function perpendicular to the line defined by $p = \mathbf{r} \cdot \hat{\mathbf{n}}$;

and

5. sum over all angles ϕ.

Step 4 generates a 2-D function from the 1-D projections and is referred to as backprojection since it is the complementary operation to projection. Step 2 is a filtering operation in Fourier space to correct for the sampling nonuniformity of the transformation from Cartesian to Radon space mentioned previously.

It is instructive to rearrange the steps to obtain another recipe for the inverse transform. Backprojection and summation (Steps 4 and 5) may be performed first to generate a 2-D unfiltered summation image (sometimes called a layergram). The point spread function (PSF) of the layergram has been shown to be $p(\mathbf{r}) = |\mathbf{r}|^{-1}$ (Peters, 1974), which implies a transfer function $\mathrm{FT}_2[|\mathbf{r}|^{-1}] = |\boldsymbol{\rho}|^{-1}$. This distortion can be corrected by filtering in 2-D with transfer function $|\boldsymbol{\rho}|$, an operation commonly known as rho filtering (often, albeit imprecisely, the 1-D filter $|\nu|$ in Step 2 is also referred to as a rho filter). In reality, of course, the noise dominant at high spatial frequencies requires either filter to be rolled off, or apodized. Since our rationale for signal processing in Radon space was to avoid unnecessary 2-D operations, we shall not consider implementations of the alternative recipe. Interested readers should consult Barrett and Swindell (1977, 1981) or Barrett (1984).

We can also express the inverse Radon transform in operator notation (Barrett, 1984), expanding the operator R_2^{-1} into the sequences

$$R_2^{-1} = B_2 \, \mathrm{FT}_1^{-1} |\nu| \, \mathrm{FT}_1$$
$$= \mathrm{FT}_2^{-1} |\boldsymbol{\rho}| \, \mathrm{FT}_2 B_2 \qquad (16)$$

where B_2 is the operator notation for backprojection.

The inverse Radon transform algorithm [Eq. (15)] can be recast into a more concise form by invoking the filter theorem of Fourier transforms to create a convolution of functions instead of a product of their Fourier transforms. That is,

$$\mathrm{FT}_1^{-1}[|\nu|\Lambda(\nu, \phi)] = h(p) * \lambda(p, \phi) \qquad (17)$$

where $h(p) = \mathrm{FT}_1^{-1}[|\nu|]$ is the filter function in the coordinate-space representation. Lighthill (1962) showed that $h(p) = \mathrm{FT}_1^{-1}[|\nu|] = -1/2\pi^2 p^2$, where the singularity at the origin requires that it be interpreted as a generalized function that has a Dirac delta function at the origin. A realizable interpretation is (Gmitro *et al.*, 1980)

$$h(p) = \lim_{\varepsilon \to 0} \left[\begin{matrix} -1/p^2, & |p| \geq \varepsilon \\ 1/\varepsilon^2, & |p| < \varepsilon \end{matrix} \right] \tag{18}$$

Note that $h(p)$ is bipolar. We can now represent the inverse Radon transform in one equation, with the important proviso that the true nature of the filter function be recognized:

$$f(\mathbf{r}) = -\frac{1}{2\pi^2} \int_0^\pi d\phi \left[\lambda(p, \phi) * \frac{1}{p^2} \right]_{p = \mathbf{r} \cdot \hat{\mathbf{n}}} \tag{19}$$

The operations required to implement this algorithm for the inverse Radon transform are the source of its common name, filtered backprojection. Integration of the convolution product by parts yields other possible expressions for filtered backprojection (Barrett, 1984):

$$f(\mathbf{r}) = \frac{1}{2\pi^2} P \left[\int_0^\pi d\phi \left[\lambda'(p, \phi) * \frac{1}{p} \right] \right]_{p = \mathbf{r} \cdot \hat{\mathbf{n}}} \tag{20}$$

$$= \frac{1}{2\pi^2} \int_0^\pi d\phi [\lambda''(p, \phi) * \ln|p|]_{p = \mathbf{r} \cdot \hat{\mathbf{n}}} \tag{21}$$

$$= \frac{1}{2\pi^2} \int_0^\pi d\phi \left[\frac{\partial^2}{\partial p^2} [\lambda(p, \phi) * \ln|p|] \right]_{p = \mathbf{r} \cdot \hat{\mathbf{n}}} \tag{22}$$

where $P[\int dx]$ denotes the Cauchy principal value of the integral, and the primes [e.g., $\lambda'(p, \phi)$] represent derivatives of the function with respect to p. Each representation of the inverse Radon transform [Eqs. (19–22)] requires a bipolar filter function, a fact having important consequences for optical implementation. Which representation is optimum depends strongly on the limitations of the signal and available hardware. For instance, the dynamic range of the 1-D filter function $\ln|p|$ in Eqs. (21) and (22) is much less than that of $-p^{-2}$ or $P[p^{-1}]$, thus reducing the dynamic range required of the 1-D convolver at the cost of increased noise inherent in taking the second derivative of the projection.

An alternative development of the reconstruction problem was made independently by Cormack. Though not as straightforward in application as filtered backprojection it can potentially be implemented by optical methods (Ein-Gal, 1974; Hansen and Goodman, 1978). Cormack's development is based on the periodicity in angle of every physically realizable object [i.e., $f(r, \theta) = f(r, \theta + 2\pi)$]. As a result $f(r, \theta)$ can be expanded in a discrete Fourier series of angular basis functions that are called circular harmonics:

$$f(r, \theta) = \sum_{n=-\infty}^{\infty} f_n(r) \, e^{in\theta} \tag{23}$$

where

$$f_n(r) = \frac{1}{2\pi} \int_{-\infty}^{\infty} d\theta \, f(r, \theta) \, e^{-in\theta} \tag{24}$$

Cormack expanded the projections $\lambda(p, \phi)$ in the same manner and derived the space-variant transformation between these two representations. The transformation can be made space-invariant via a Mellin transform (Casasent and Psaltis, 1977) and can then be processed by optical methods (Hofer, 1979; Hansen, 1981a, b). However, the Cormack reconstruction algorithm is not directly applicable to our task, so we shall not consider it further.

C. APPLICATION TO OPTICAL SIGNAL PROCESSING

To summarize the mathematical development, we have demonstrated that the classic 2-D signal-processing operations of Fourier transformation and convolution (filtering) can be performed via the equivalent 1-D operations on the Radon projections, producing central slices of the 2-D Fourier transform or projections of the 2-D convolution. Of course, there are optical methods available for performing these 2-D operations as well. Coherent computation of the 2-D Fourier transform has always been the basis of optical signal processing, but limitations of speckle noise and performance of available spatial light modulators have generally restricted application to static film transparencies in liquid gates. By placing the input in the front focal plane of the transform lens, we produce the correct magnitude and phase of the 2-D Fourier transform in the back focal plane (limited by lens aberrations). However, the phase of the transform is coded in the relative phases of the coherent wave front at the various locations in the Fourier plane. Preserving this phase information requires a precise and stable optical configuration, and square-law detection necessitates heterodyne techniques to decode it. Optical convolution/correlation can be performed by spatial filtering in the Fourier plane or by a joint transform arrangement (Weaver and Goodman, 1966; Rau, 1966). Problems still abound, however: Stability and positioning requirements are stricter yet, generation of a true complex (magnitude and phase) spatial filter is non-trivial, and deriving the phase of a complex convolution remains difficult. Incoherent optics avoids the speckle noise problems, and architectures are available for performing Fourier transformation and convolution (Rogers, 1977; Monahan *et al.*, 1977); but representation of negative quantities requires a bias or two signal channels.

On the other hand, the corresponding 1-D operations of Fourier transformation and convolution can be performed easily and rapidly by devices based on electronics, acoustic interactions, or charge transfer. By constructing optical systems to perform the dimensional transduction to and from Radon space, we can use these technologies to perform the corresponding 2-D operation. By so doing we may be able to loosen the constraints on signal input format and system stability, at the cost of some processing parallelism. The resulting hybrid systems can emphasize the strengths and minimize the weaknesses of each technology. If the optical dimensional transducers and the 1-D processors are fast enough, we may still be able to perform the complete 2-D processing operation at a usefully rapid rate (e.g., 30 frames/s).

1. *Optical Radon Transformer*

The forward Radon transform [Eq. (2)] is generated by integrating the input function $f(\mathbf{r})$ along the set of lines perpendicular to the azimuth ϕ. This can be done optically in several ways, depending on the format of the input data and the type of signal processor to be used. Radon projections can be generated as temporal data by scanning the input function with a line of light (usually from a laser) and integrating the resultant intensity on a detector. This method is suitable for transmissive or reflective input data. At one instant the detector signal is proportional to the line integral of input transmittance or reflectance. Sweeping the line of light perpendicular to itself generates a temporal signal proportional to one line-integral projection. The azimuth of the scan can be optically rotated (e.g., by a dove prism) to derive the complete set of projection data sequentially. For obvious reasons this optical Radon transformer is called a flying-line scanner and is shown schematically in Fig. 4 (Easton *et al.*, 1984). Since the light transmitted or reflected by the 2-D input is integrated on the detector, speckle noise is irrelevant, and a laser can be usefully employed as a light source. Indeed, the coherence of the laser becomes an advantage because it allows the use of a fast acoustooptic beam deflector or a slower and cheaper hologon holographic deflector (Rallison and Lowe, 1982). The technology of optical scanners and image rotators permits a system to be built capable of performing Radon transforms at video rates with video resolution (30 frames/s, 500×500 points). This would require scanning 500 azimuth angles with 500 resolvable data points per scan every 30 ms. Acoustooptic Bragg-cell scanners capable of resolving more than 1000 points per

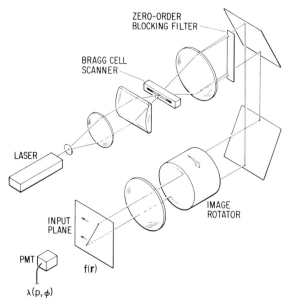

Fig. 4. Flying-line scanner in transmissive mode. Anamorphic optics image a line of laser light on the input plane. The light transmitted by the input function $f(\mathbf{r})$ is integrated by a detector, yielding an output proportional to the line integral of intensity transmittance. The Bragg cell sweeps the line across the transparency to generate one projection. The azimuth is rotated by the prism, and the cycle repeats. The output is a sequence of temporal projection signals. The flying-line scanner can be used for reflective signals as well.

10-μs scan have been reported (Gottlieb *et al.*, 1983). To preserve the phase of the projection, the temporal center of the flying-line scan must intersect the image rotation axis each time (i.e., the optical rotation axis of the prism must not wobble). Scanning a full projection set in 30 ms requires an image rotation rate of $180°/30\ \text{ms} = 900\ \text{rpm}$, implying a prism rotation rate of 450 rpm. Such systems have been constructed and demonstrated (Gmitro and Gindi, 1985). Indeed, much higher rotation rates have been reported while preserving holographic image quality (Stetson and Elkins, 1977). Radon transformers based on the flying-line scanner are most useful for 2-D signals on transparencies (e.g., movies) or for real reflective scenes.

Projection data can also be generated by collapsing an image of the 2-D signal onto a linear array or imaging detector with anamorphic optics (Fig. 5). The anamorphic optical element can be a cylindrical lens (Gindi and Gmitro, 1984) or a coherent optical fiber bundle (Farhat *et al.*, 1983). Alternatively, if an N-element 1-D linear array detector can be obtained with an aspect ratio of $N:1$ (i.e., a square 1-D array with each detector element 1 unit in width and N units long), anamorphic imaging is

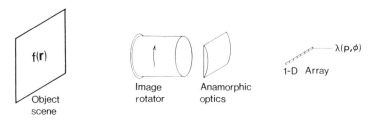

Fig. 5. System for deriving projections by anamorphic imaging. An object scene that is self-luminous (e.g., CRT image) or naturally illuminated is anamorphically imaged onto a 1-D detector.

unnecessary. An array detector samples the projection, making this arrangement especially useful if the data are to be processed digitally. An image rotator is still required, and hence the projections are again generated sequentially. This type of system is adaptable to naturally illuminated scenes or to self-luminous signals as from a CRT.

2. 1-D Signal Processor Technologies

As was demonstrated in Eqs. (19–22), the inverse Radon transformation requires convolution of the projection data with a bipolar 1-D filter function. Therefore we shall now shift gears somewhat to investigate the types and capabilities of available 1-D signal processors. These will be lumped into four categories: electronic devices (both digital and analog, charge-transfer devices (mainly CCDs), acoustoelectric devices (primarily those based on surface acoustic waves, or SAWs), and acoustooptics (AO). In the first case, the Radon transform allows direct application to 2-D problems of the very technologies that optical methods are supposedly competing against on the signal-processing battlefield.

a. Electronic Systems. Electronic systems (analog and digital) for processing temporal signals are no doubt familiar to the reader. They can be as simple as an *RC* filter or as complex as a digital supercomputer. The accuracy, precision, stability, and flexibility of electronics are products of many decades of theoretical and engineering effort with the result that electronic systems are generally preferred for signal-processing applications. This is the target at which proponents of optical signal processing must aim, but it is moving ahead all the time. New materials such as GaAs and new fabrication technologies such as x-ray lithography promise further improvements in packing density, speed, and cost of electronic devices. Even the traditional advantage of parallelism offered by optical processing is fading as new algorithms and chip architectures are adding parallel capability to the electronic world.

Electronic signal processing is generally divided into analog and digital domains, each having its own advantages and disadvantages. Analog processing represents signal amplitudes by proportional voltages that can be added, subtracted, and divided. Some nonlinear operations (e.g., thresholding) are easily performed as well. Analog processing with active and passive components can be fast, with bandwidths reported to ≈ 2 GHz for silicon devices and up to 20 GHz for GaAs (Bierman, 1985). More complicated operations (e.g., multiplication and root finding) are possible with special analog modules, but operation is much slower and subject to severe limitations in linearity, stability, and precision. For some applications the restrictions can be eased by using the analog voltage signal to modulate a radio-frequency (rf) carrier. There are rf devices available that are capable of several useful operations including multiplication, phase shifting, and phase detection. Though still limited in linearity and stability these devices can be profitably used for analog signal processing.

The advantages of digital systems are well known—probably too well known to the optical processing community. But they have their limitations too, lack of speed and large power consumption being two of the most important. Sampling limits system bandwidth and subjects the sampled signal to aliasing. A/D and D/A conversions may have to trade speed for precision and dynamic range. Clock rates are limited to ≈ 500 MHz for silicon-based logic. However, improvements are being made continuously. For instance the increased mobility of gallium arsenide charge carriers allows clock rates up to several gigahertz with lower power consumption (Bierman, 1985). Generally the limited disadvantages of digital processing have been more than offset by its inherent noise immunity and linearity. An unlimited variety of signal-processing operations are amenable to solution by digital means, and new special-purpose hardware promises to increase speeds dramatically. The very high-speed integrated circuit (VHSIC) program of the Department of Defense is stimulating the design and production of new devices such as the Westinghouse complex arithmetic vector processor, which can perform a 1024-point 16-bit complex Fourier transform in 130 μs, compute one point of a 256-element 16-bit correlation in 6 μs, and multiply a 64×64 16-bit matrix by a 64-element vector in 35 μs (Marr, 1982). Digital parallel operation is becoming more economical as design costs drop and fabrication yields increase, but cost is still a significant limitation for such devices and is likely to remain so.

b. Charge-Transfer Devices.   Charge-transfer devices can store and manipulate packets of electronic charge using two structurally different circuit technologies. The older bucket-brigade device is a series of MOS transistors and capacitors, in which the charge is moved between capacitors by alternate switching of the transistors. These have been largely superseded by charge-coupled devices (CCDs), in which minority charge carriers are stored under closely spaced electrodes. Charges are moved to detectors at the edges of the array by sequential pulsing of the electrodes. The most familiar use of CCD devices has been as 1-D and 2-D optical detector arrays, in which the amount of charge in a detector cell is proportional to the photon flux. However, it is also possible to use them as signal processors in which the sampled data values are denoted by the varying amounts of charge. By moving, summing, and detecting the charge packets in various ways, a variety of processing operations can be performed. The resulting devices are an interesting hybrid of analog and digital qualities since the amplitude of each discrete sample is a continuous variable. CCDs can obviously be used as delay lines with applications to signal-time and bandwidth compression. Tapped delay lines and fixed-transversal filters can be constructed by spacing nondestructive charge detectors along the charge pathway and summing the tapped signals (Buss *et al.*, 1973; Beynon and Lamb, 1980). With variable weights, the filter is programmable. Multiplying adjacent tapped signals from two CCD delay lines and summing the products allows computation of a discrete convolution. The useful dynamic range of these CCD devices is limited by the quantum noise floor and the saturation level, with typical specifications of 60–70 dB (30 dB for the convolver). The bandwidth of the CCD devices is determined by the analog electronics and the sampling clock rate, ranging from a few hertz to 5 MHz.

Combining the CCD devices described above makes possible a wide variety of 1-D signal-processing operations. The utility of fixed and programmable CCD transversal filters and of the CCD convolver for signal processing is obvious. With two or three filters having linear FM (or chirp) impulse responses, the chirp z-transform algorithm can be implemented (Rabiner *et al.*, 1969). This algorithm will be discussed in some detail later. CCD spectrum analyzers using the chirp z-transform algorithm that are capable of computing a 512-point z-transform at a 5 MHz sampling rate have been demonstrated.

c. Acoustoelectric Devices. Piezoelectric materials distort when placed in an electric field and also generate an electric field when mechanically stressed. By applying a modulated rf electric field to a piezoelectric medium, one can generate a corresponding acoustic distortion that can be processed and detected. This acoustic wave propagates in the medium at a characteristic velocity $v_s \simeq 10^{-5}c$, where c is the velocity of light. Thus the acoustic wavelengths are much shorter than the electromagnetic wavelengths, allowing signal processing devices that are many wavelengths long to be constructed in small packages. Components based on acoustic waves in bulk materials, such as the quartz oscillator and delay line, have been used for many years. More recently, however, much attention haas been paid to using acoustic waves on the surface of a medium (surface acoustic waves, or SAWs) due to their accessibility. Once a wave has been generated on the surface of a medium, it can be sampled at any point in its journey along the surface. A diagram of a simple SAW device is shown in Fig. 6. A pair of conductive transducers is deposited on the surface of the piezoelectric crystalline medium. The input signal (often on a carrier) is applied to the input transducer, which consists of a set of interleaved fingers connected to buss bars. The field distorts the medium piezoelectrically, and the acoustic wave travels along the surface of the crystal to a similar transducer where it generates an electric rf signal.

If we think of the SAW devices in Fig. 6 as a delay line, the sampling of the acoustic wave by the output transducer is a tapping and summing operation performed in parallel for many points in the acoustic wave. Hence the SAW device is another example of a transversal filter. Variation of the spacing and overlap of the transducer fingers produces different impulse responses, allowing a wide variety of operations to be performed. The utility of SAW filters is such that several design procedures have been developed

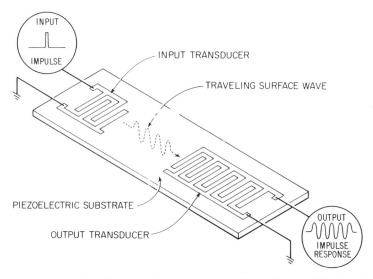

Fig. 6. Schematic of a simple surface acoustic-wave filter. The interdigital conductive transducers are deposited onto a piezoelectric substrate. Applying an impulsive electric signal across one transducer generates an acoustic wave on the surface of the substrate. The receiving transducer reconverts the acoustic wave into an electric signal which is the impulse response of the filter. By design of the overlap and separation of the interdigital fingers, a wide variety of impulse responses can be created.

(Matthews, 1977; Gerard, 1978), and the filters themselves are manufactured by standard photolithographic techniques (Smith, 1978). SAW bandpass filters are available for center (carrier) frequencies from 10 MHz to 2 GHz and bandwidths from $\leq$100 kHz up to 50% of center frequency (Morgan, 1985). The noise-limited dynamic range is typically 70 dB, comparable to that available from CCDs. Indeed, it is interesting that CCDs and SAW devices are so complementary, offering similar signal processing capability over a wide range of input frequencies (Roberts, 1977).

Linear FM (or chirp) SAW filters are easily made and have found wide application to radar systems (Klauder et al., 1960; Gerard et al., 1973). More recently they have been employed in spectrum analyzers and Fourier transformers (Jack and Paige, 1978; Jack et al., 1980). The transducers are designed such that the impulse response of the filter is a signal whose frequency increases or decreases linearly with time. SAW interdigital chirp filters are limited to bandwidths of about 500 MHz, dispersion times of 50 µs and effective time–bandwidth products of about 1000 (Morgan, 1985). Frequency dispersion can also be achieved by spacing acoustic reflectors on the substrate. These so-called reflective array compressors (RACs) have been reported with bandwidths to 180 MHz, dispersion times to 90 µs, and time–bandwidth products of 16,200 (Gerard et al., 1977).

Other useful SAW signal processors can be made by using the nonlinear response of the substrate to severe distortions. If strong acoustic signals are applied to each end of a substrate, the two waves interact nonlinearly to generate higher harmonics. The second harmonic of the carrier frequency contains information about the product of the two signal amplitudes. Integration of the second harmonic frequency over the substrate by an area electrode produces a temporal signal proportional to the convolution of the input signals. Since second harmonic generation is inefficient, the convolution signal is weak, typically 80 dB below the input signal levels. Even so, noise-limited dynamic ranges of 60 dB and spurious-signal-limited dynamic ranges of 30 dB have been reported (Ash, 1978). Acoustic convolvers are available commercially with time–bandwidth products approaching 2000 (Morgan, 1985).

d. Acoustooptics. Acoustooptic processors are reviewed in detail elsewhere in this volume (Part III), so we shall discuss their capabilities only briefly. As mentioned, an rf electromagnetic wave can be transformed into an acoustic wave in a medium by the piezoelectric effect. The variation in material density modulates the refractive index, producing a phase grating that can diffract light. Devices based on the interaction of sound and light have long been used in signal processing as efficient 1-D spatial light modulators and beam deflectors (Korpel, 1981). Developments in materials and architectures in the last 15 years or so have led to new applications for bulk AO devices in signal processing including time-integrating and space-integrating correlators/convolvers (Berg *et al.*, 1979; Rhodes, 1981a; Abramovitz *et al.*, 1983), Fourier transformers (Lee *et al.*, 1982; Pancott and Reeve, 1985), and generation of 1-D time-frequency representations (e.g., the Woodward ambiguity function, Athale *et al.*, 1983; Casasent, 1983). The interaction of light and surface acoustic waves has also been applied to various signal processing operations (Das and Ayub, 1982; Casseday *et al.*, 1983). Indeed, AO devices and SAW devices are inherently compatible for the obvious reason that the processing mechanisms are so similar. Limits on carrier frequency, bandwidth, and dispersion time are comparable for both types. AO materials support carrier frequencies in the range of ($1 \text{ MHz} \leq \nu_0 \leq 1 \text{ GHz}$) with bandwidths of up to 500 MHz, interaction times of up to 80 μs, and time–bandwidth products greater than 10,000 (Berg *et al.*, 1979).

3. *Optical Implementation of the Inverse Radon Transform*

Having discussed the technologies available for 1-D signal processing, we are now ready to describe methods for reconstructing the 2-D processed signal from the 1-D projections. Two mathematical algorithms for reconstruction have already been discussed: filtered backprojection and circular harmonic expansion. As stated, the latter is more complicated to implement and not as appropriate for signal processing applications and so will not be considered further here. Interested readers should consult the work of Hansen and Goodman (1978), Hofer (1979), Hofer and Kupka (1979), and Hansen (1981a, b).

In our mathematical development of filtered backprojection we stated that 1-D filtering can be performed before backprojection or 2-D filtering afterwards. Optical reconstruction systems have been built that filter in 2-D (Peters, 1974), but again we are more concerned with application of 1-D technologies to the problem. Several hybrid optical systems have been proposed or built to implement 1-D filtered backprojection, and we shall give a brief overview of those systems here. Readers desiring more detail should consult the original papers or the review articles by Barrett and Swindell (1977) and Gmitro *et al.* (1980). To lessen problems associated with coherent noise these systems used incoherent illumination. However, it is essential to recall that the filtered projection is bipolar, requiring that any reconstruction scheme preserve sign information. Because of this constraint, systems based on incoherent optics must place the projection signal on a bias or employ two signal channels. Neither of these alternatives is desirable; biased signals reduce the contrast of the reconstruction, and dual-channel systems are subject to differential signal errors.

After 1-D filtering, the algorithms of Eqs. (19–22) require two more steps: backprojection and summation. Backprojection (i.e., generation of a 2-D function from a 1-D projection by smearing perpendicular to the projection azimuth) has been demonstrated by anamorphic optics. The projection is written on the face of a 1-D display device (e.g., a CRT or LED array) located one focal length from a cylindrical lens and is imaged onto an integrating 2-D detector or display device. As this operation is performed for each projection, the reconstructed image is built up at the output plane. Any integrating 2-D detector can be used for summation of the backprojections (e.g., photographic film, video camera, or human eye if the system is fast enough).

The hybrid optical–electronic reconstruction schemes have differed greatly in detail and degree of success. The system of Duinker *et al.* (1978) was mostly based on analog electronics, with only filtering performed optically. The projections were displayed in sequence on a CRT and imaged onto two area-weighted optical masks representing the positive and negative parts of the filter function. The images of the projections were swept across the filter masks by electronic deflection and the integrated transmitted signals electronically subtracted to obtain the bipolar temporal filtered signals. Backprojection and summation were performed electronically. Edholm *et al.* (1978) stored the Radon projections on film in sinogram format $\lambda(p, \phi)$. A filtered, biased sinogram was generated by sandwiching a positive image of $\lambda(p, \phi)$ and a negative image of $\lambda(p, \phi) * h_-(p)$, where $h_-(p)$ represents the negative part of the filter function in Eq. (18). Backprojection was performed for each line of the sinogram by a cylindrical lens, with summation on a suitably rotated piece of photographic film. Despite the dynamic range limitation inherent in the use of a bias this system produced some good reconstructions.

Probably the most successful incoherent optical reconstruction systems synthesized the required filter function by optical transfer function (OTF) synthesis. This method is based on the fact that the OTF is the autocorrelation of the pupil function (Lohmann, 1977; Rhodes, 1977; Rhodes and Lohmann, 1978; Stoner, 1978). Two pupil functions are calculated for which the difference of the autocorrelations is the Fourier transform of the required filter point spread function (PSF). An infinite number of pairs of pupil functions are theoretically possible, with the optimum choice determined by system requirements such as light throughput or noise considerations. Since the required positive part of the filter PSF is a delta function [Eq. (18)], a clear pupil in the positive channel is appropriate. Two negative-channel pupils successfully demonstrated are the so-called Ronchi pupil (Barrett *et al.*, 1979a) and a logarithmic phase plate (Barrett *et al.*, 1979b). The envelope of the PSF of either pupil falls off as $1/p$ as required. Optical reconstruction systems based on OTF synthesis include the drum processor (Gordon, 1977; Gmitro et al., 1980), the loop processor (Greivenkamp et al., 1981), and a hybrid digital–optical system (Gmitro et al., 1980). An example of image reconstruction with the loop processor is shown in Fig. 7.

A reconstruction system that is most applicable to tomographic signal processing tasks was proposed recently by Gmitro and Gindi (1985). It is capable of performing a 500×500 point reconstruction of projection data at video rates. The system, depicted in Fig. 8, implements the algorithm of Eq. (19). Filtering is performed by a space-integrating acoustooptic convolver, as shown in Fig. 9, though a SAW convolver could be used as suggested in Section I.C.2.c. The projection data are stored in a fast digital memory and read out line-by-line to a fast D/A converter. The analog signal modulates an rf carrier and is then impressed on a Bragg cell. The diffracted light is Fourier transformed by a lens and filtered by a spatial binary transmission mask. The diffracted light is retransformed, collected by the detector, and demodulated. The filtered projection is displayed on a CRT and backprojected by a cylindrical lens. Azimuth selection for the backprojection is accomplished by an image-rotating prism, and the 2-D image is collected by a video camera and displayed on a conventional CRT. The image data are read out rapidly enough for operation at video rates (30 reconstructed frames/s). The design goal is to process projections at video rates with a dynamic range of 12 bits, implying an SNR of about 4000. Preliminary results are presented in Fig. 10.

II. Applications

A. OPERATIONS ON TWO-DIMENSIONAL SIGNALS

As was evident from our mathematical development, the application of the Radon transform to signal processing primarily exploits the central-slice and filter theorems, which allow operations based on Fourier transforms and/or convolutions to be performed on the 1-D projections. Useful operations of this type include the Fourier transform and its relative, the Hartley transform, 2-D filtering, some pattern-recognition algorithms, bandwidth compression, and spectrum estimation. Some of these operations require the flexibility of digital operation but are included to indicate the scope of application of Radon methods. Since application of projection operations to signal processing is a field that has yet to be fully plowed, much of our treatment will deal with the feasibility rather than actual results.

1. Fourier Transformation

Since it is a signal-processing staple and also because of its close relationship to the Radon transform via the central-slice theorem, it seems natural

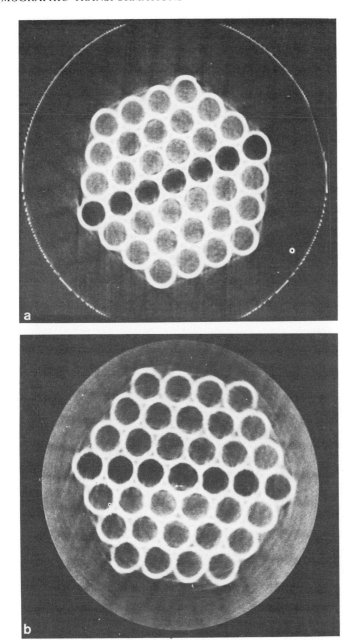

Fig. 7. Reconstruction obtained with the optical loop processor (Greivenkamp *et al.*, 1981). The object is an array of tubes filled with liquids of two different x-ray attenuation coefficients. (a) Reconstruction with a digital system and (b) the optical reconstruction.

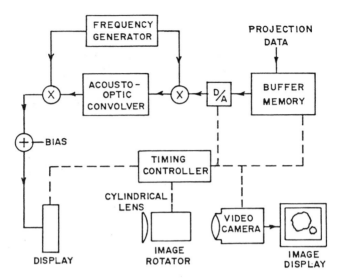

Fig. 8. The system of Gmitro and Gindi (1985) for video-rate filtered backprojection. The projections are read in from a fast digital buffer memory and modulate an rf carrier. The projections are filtered in the acoustooptic convolver, demodulated, biased up, and displayed on a CRT. A cylindrical lens and image rotator perform the backprojection.

to commence our discussion of applications with 2-D Fourier transformation. After having been generated by one of the systems described in Section I.C.1, each projection is Fourier transformed, and the result is displayed in the polar format required by the central-slice theorem. To perform the 1-D Fourier transform, we introduce the chirp transform algorithm, which is derived by decomposing the Fourier kernel:

$$e^{-2\pi i\nu t} = e^{-i\pi(\nu/\beta)^2} \cdot e^{-i\pi(\beta t)^2} \cdot e^{+i\pi(\nu/\beta - \beta t)^2} \tag{25}$$

The three complex exponentials are quadratic phase terms or linear FM signals (i.e., the instantaneous frequency of each varies linearly with time). Such signals are commonly called chirps by the radar community. The factor β, with dimensions of temporal frequency, has been introduced to rationalize the units of the exponent. A 1-D temporal Fourier transform can now be written as

$$
\begin{aligned}
F(\nu) &= \int_{-\infty}^{\infty} dt\, f(t)\, e^{-2\pi i\nu t} \\
&= e^{-i\pi(\nu/\beta)^2} \int_{-\infty}^{\infty} dt \{ [f(t)\, e^{-i\pi(\beta t)^2}] \cdot e^{+i\pi(\nu/\beta - \beta t)^2} \} \\
&= e^{-i\pi(\beta t)^2} \cdot [[f(t)\, e^{-i\pi(\beta t)^2}] * e^{+i\pi(\beta t)^2}]|_{(\nu = \beta^2 t)}
\end{aligned}
\tag{26}
$$

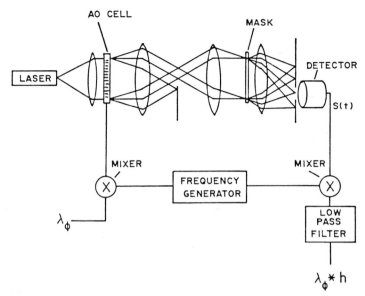

Fig. 9. Diagram of the acoustooptic convolver used by Gmitro and Gindi (1985). The projection signal modulates an rf carrier and is impressed on the Bragg cell. After the −1st diffraction order is eliminated; the signal is imaged onto a binary transmission mask that encodes the filter function. The transmitted light is collected, detected, and demodulated to obtain the filtered signal.

Thus by employing three temporal chirp signals (one with positive exponential term, or upchirp, and two with negative terms, or downchirps), we can implement the Fourier transform of $f(t)$ in three steps:

1. multiplication of $f(t)$ by a downchirp;
2. convolution of the product in a filter with an upchirp impulse response; and
3. multiplication by a downchirp.

The resulting temporal signal is a scaled version of the Fourier transform in which the frequency is related to the output temporal coordinate by $\nu = \beta^2 t$. The pre- and postmultiplication chirp signals can be generated by applying impulsive inputs to filters with upchirp responses. Note that this analysis has assumed that the chirp signals are complex and of infinite length. If only the power spectrum is required the postmultiplication in Step 3 can be eliminated. Because of the order of operations, this algorithm is usually referred to as the M–C–M chirp transform (for multiply–convolve–multiply). The duality of multiplication and convolution in coordinate and Fourier space imply that the operations can be exchanged to produce a

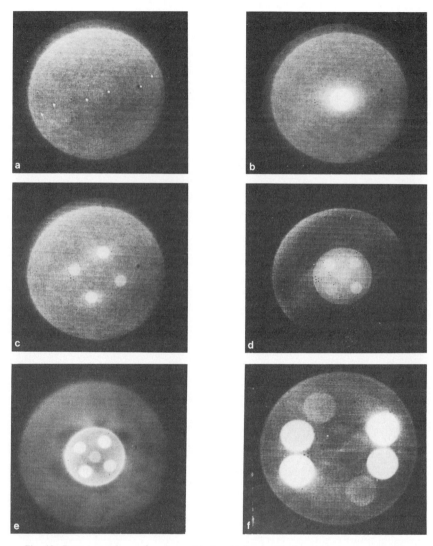

Fig. 10. Reconstructions of various objects, obtained with the video tomography system of Gmitro and Gindi shown in Fig. 8. Images (a)–(d) are all-optical reconstructions (i.e., filtering via the AO convolver and optical backprojection); images (e) and (f) are digitally filtered before optical backprojection. The objects are (a) six discrete points, (b) a single circular disk, (c) four disks with two intensities, (d) five circular disks of varying brightness within one larger disk. Image (e) is a digitally filtered version of image (d), and the object reconstructed in image (f) by digital means consists of eight circles: two each of relative intensities 1, 0.5, 0.1, and 0.01. Examination of images (d)–(f) demonstrates that the contrast resolution of the digital system is of the order of 10 and is somewhat better than that of the all-optical reconstructions.

second arrangement for chirp transforms, the C–M–C transform (Jack *et al.*, 1980). It has the disadvantage of requiring three filters even if only the power spectrum is required. For sampled data Fourier transformation is equivalent to evaluation of the *z*-transform on the unit circle. The comparable implementation using sampled chirps is therefore called the chirp *z*-transform (Rabiner *et al.*, 1969).

It is instructive to reconsider coherent optical Fourier transformation in light of the chirp transform algorithm. Propagation of light in the Fresnel region can be described as convolution of the wave front with a quadratic-phase impulse response, and the action of a spherical lens on a wave front is multiplication by a quadratic phase, so the common 2-*f* single-lens coherent Fourier transformer is a version of the C–M–C chirp algorithm. An optical version of M–C–M is also possible (Whitehouse, 1977).

The chirp Fourier or *z*-transform can be implemented for real 1-D data (as would be obtained from a flying-line scanner) using the technologies described previously, but the analysis differs somewhat from that given in Eqs. (25) and (26). A basic temporal signal filter has a real, finite-length impulse response, often modulating a carrier. For example, the impulse response of a SAW chirp filter is of the form

$$h_{\pm}(t) = A(t) \cos\left[\omega_0 t \pm \frac{\alpha t^2}{2} \right] \tag{27}$$

where $A(t)$ is the apodizing function of the filter, ω_0 the initial carrier frequency, and α the chirp rate, or rate of change of the instantaneous frequency. For SAW filters the carrier frequency ω_0 is in the rf region (≈ 15–300 MHz). The frequency of $h_+(t)$ rises with time, so this function is again called an upchirp. Using these realizable filters, one can still implement the chirp Fourier transform, but the phase of the transform is now determined relative to the phase of the carrier (Jack and Paige, 1978). The recipe for the chirp transform becomes

1. premultiplication by a downchirp;
2. convolution (filtering) with an upchirp;
3. postmultiplication by two upchirps separately, with phase difference of $\pi/2$; and
4. low-pass filtering of both signals from Step 3.

The complex transform is thus generated as two parts simultaneously. The signal derived from the in-phase chirp of Step 3 is the real part of the complex Fourier transform or cosine transform. The quadrature signal yields the sine transform or imaginary part of the Fourier transform. Note that the sign of the slope of the postmultiplication chirp differs for the realizable algorithm relative to that for complex chirps. This is due to double-sideband multiplication of the carrier-borne signals, which yields signals at the sum and difference frequencies of the carriers. Selecting the difference frequency sideband with the low-pass filter makes the operation equivalent to post-multiplication by a chirp of the opposite sign. The output temporal signal maps linearly to frequency with constant of proportionality α. Since the real chirp signals are apodized by $A(t)$, their time–bandwidth product (TBW) is finite, thus limiting the frequency resolution of the transformer. The maximum system TBW is one-fourth the TBW of the convolution chirp (Ash, 1978). It should be noted that the SAW chirp transform algorithm can also be implemented for complex input data by premultiplying the imaginary part of the input signal by a chirp in quadrature to the real-part premultiplication chirp (Jack and Paige, 1978). Using surface acoustic wave reflective array compressive filters, Gerard et al. (1977) demonstrated a system capable of transforming signals 60 μs long with 60 MHz bandwidth. SAW chirp Fourier transformers are faster and require less power and bulk than all-digital systems but are less accurate.

This chirp Fourier transform algorithm can be implemented with AO devices as well. Hotz (1984) and Pancott and Reeve (1985) have demonstrated M–C–M transforms using space-integrating architectures incorporating two Bragg cells. The 1-D input is multiplied by an electronically generated chirp signal in an rf mixer, and the product is applied to one Bragg cell. The +1st diffraction order is selected and imaged on the second Bragg cell, which is driven by the same electronic chirp signal. The −1st diffraction order emerging from the second cell is selected, integrated on a detector, and demodulated. Hotz reports a system bandwidth of 25 MHz for a signal duration of 5 μs, limited by the capabilities of the AO cells and by problems with generating the proper postmultiplication chirp slope. Such a system has mechanical stability requirements similar to those of other coherent optical systems but is readily applicable to signal processing in Radon space.

a. Two-Dimensional Power Spectra.   Ticknor et al. (1985) demonstrated production of 2-D power spectra via the Radon transform and the SAW chirp Fourier transform. Their system is diagrammed in Fig. 11. The Radon projection of a 2-D transparency $f(\mathbf{r})$ is generated by a Bragg-cell-driven flying-line scanner. One projection is derived in 10 μs. Premultiplication by the SAW chirp is performed in an rf mixer. This product signal is applied to the convolution chirp filter whose output is the Fourier transform on an rf carrier. Since the phase of the Fourier transform is not required, the output of the convolution filter is detected incoherently with a diode, producing a unipolar signal proportional to the squared-modulus of the Fourier transform. The SAW filters used had time dispersions of 10 MHz

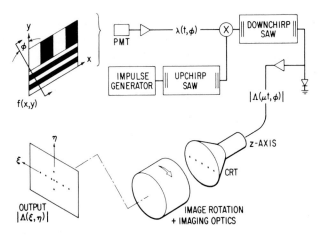

Fig. 11. System for generating the Fourier power spectrum of 2-D transparencies (Ticknor *et al.*, 1985). The input transparency is illuminated by the flying-line scanner, and the integrated transmitted light is detected by a photomultiplier. This projection signal is premultiplied by the SAW-generated chirp. After convolution with a chirp of opposite sign, the envelope signal is detected by a diode and applied to the z-axis of a CRT. The 1-D transform signal is rotated to the proper orientation and imaged onto the output plane.

and bandwidths of 20 μs. Power spectra were generated by the system within 28 μs after commencement of the flying-line scan. The spectra were 20 μs long with 50 resolvable frequencies. By the central-slice theorem the detected signal must be displayed in a polar format to generate one line through the 2-D power spectrum. However, as the 2-D spectrum is built up, the polar raster oversamples the low spatial frequencies, producing a displayed time-averaged intensity that is too bright in the center. Mathematically this problem is due to the sampling nonuniformity of the Radon transform and is corrected by rho filtering (i.e., the central slices of the power spectrum are multiplied by $|\nu|$ in an rf mixer before detection). After one transform slice has been displayed, the prism is rotated and a new projection generated. The power spectrum of that projection is displayed at the new azimuth on the CRT. Integration of the result can be done on film, or by eye if the system is fast enough. System speeds up to 5 frames/s have been demonstrated, limited by the rotation rate of the stepper motor driving the image rotator in the flying-line scanner. Results for a 2-D function are shown in Fig. 12.

b. Two-Dimensional Complex Fourier Transforms. The same group (Easton *et al.*, 1985b) added a postmultiplication chirp to their system to generate the complex Fourier transform, as diagrammed in Fig. 13. The

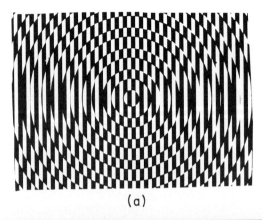

(a)

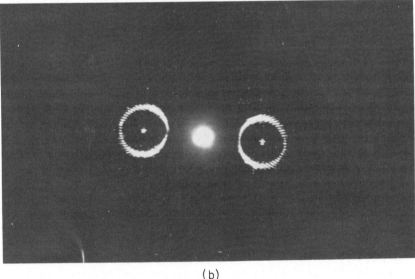

(b)

Fig. 12. (a) Input signal and (b) 2-D power spectrum obtained by the system of Fig. 11. The object is the grid-coded magnitude of the signum of a J_0 Bessel function. The Fourier power spectrum consists of ring-delta functions located at the $\pm$1st orders of the grid carrier frequency.

time delay of the postmultiplication chirp is derived from a digital delay generator (1-ns resolution). To obtain more precise time delay the phase of the postmultiplication chirp can be varied with a continuously adjustable rf phase shifter. The postmultiplication itself occurs in an rf phase comparator that generates voltages proportional to the in-phase and quadrature products of two input signals. The in-phase term is the cosine transform,

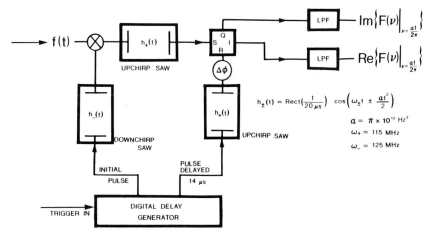

Fig. 13. SAW complex chirp Fourier transformer. The temporal input function $f(t)$ is mixed with the premultiplication downchirp, and the product is applied to a filter with upchirp impulse response. The filtered signal is demodulated by a precisely timed and phase-shifted upchirp signal in an rf phase comparator. After low-pass filtering the portion of the filtered signal that is in phase relative to the postmultiplication chirp is proportional to the real part of the Fourier transform (cosine transform). Similarly, the filtered signal in quadrature to the postmultiplication chirp is the imaginary part of the Fourier transform (sine transform) (Easton *et al.*, 1985b).

and the quadrature term is the sine transform. Performance of the complex SAW chirp transformer is shown in Fig. 14.

Rho filtering of the complex transform before display is somewhat more difficult than for the power spectrum. The frequency of the demodulated signal is too low for multiplication in rf mixers and too high for analog multipliers. An integrated-circuit balanced modulator was used instead. The two bipolar complex Fourier transform signals were then biased up before application to the z-axis of the CRT. Results are shown in Fig. 15.

Since the phase of the transform is derived from the time differences of the projection signal relative to the chirps, the coherence of the scanner beam is immaterial. This method is therefore applicable to reflective scenes as well as to transparencies. An example of complex Fourier transformation of a reflective scene is shown in Fig. 16.

Another 2-D processing situation in which Radon space Fourier transformation may prove very useful is with spatial light modulators whose image quality is relatively poor. Recently there has been much interest in applying an inexpensive liquid-crystal television receiver to optical processing operations (Liu *et al.*, 1985; McEwan *et al.*, 1985). The poor phase uniformity of the LCTV limits its utility for coherent operations though various means have been suggested for improvement. Again, this is not a problem when

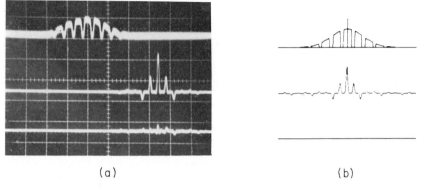

(a)   (b)

Fig. 14. Performance of the 1-D chirp Fourier transformer. The input object is a grating (75% clear, 25% opaque) in a circular aperture. In (a), the top trace is the output of the flying-line scanner [i.e., $f(t)$ in Fig. 13], where the line of light is oriented parallel to the grating lines. The Gaussian-like character of the signal envelope is due to the circular aperture. The second trace is the real part of the Fourier transform of $f(t)$ [i.e., Re$\{F(\nu)\}$ in Fig. 13], and the third trace is the imaginary part of the Fourier transform [Im$\{F(\nu)\}$ in Fig. 13]. The grating is centered in the aperture, giving a symmetric object with no imaginary part of the transform. The time scale is 5 μs/division. A computer simulation of the same case is shown in (b) (Easton *et al.*, 1985b).

used as input for a flying-line scanner (Easton *et al.*, 1985a). Some results in that application are shown in Fig. 17.

Farhat *et al.* (1983) also demonstrated 2-D complex Fourier transforms via Radon space operations but used a 2-channel incoherent optical correlator to generate the 1-D transforms. A 2-D complex signal was displayed on a CRT in two colors (e.g., real part in red, imaginary part in green). The image was rotated by a dove prism, spectrally filtered to separate channels, and collapsed to 1-D by two coherent optical fiber bundles. The real and imaginary 1-D signals were correlated incoherently with a fixed cosine and sine reference mask, respectively. The 1-D correlator outputs represented the real and imaginary parts of the 1-D Fourier transform, which were then detected and displayed in the polar raster. The system is fast but also suffers

Fig. 15. Complex 2-D Fourier transforms obtained by the Radon transform. The object $f(\mathbf{r}) = f[x, y]$ is a circular aperture of diameter 1 mm, as shown in (a). The projections are generated optically by the flying-line scanner of Fig. 4, and the 1-D complex Fourier transform of each projection is produced by the SAW system of Fig. 13. Each 1-D transform is written on the face of a vector CRT at the proper azimuth defined by the central-slice theorem, Eq. (7). In the transforms, light areas represent positive Fourier amplitude and dark areas negative amplitude. In (a) the circular aperture $f(\mathbf{r})$ is centered at the origin, giving a symmetric transform: the Airy disk. As the aperture is shifted off-center in (b) and (c), fringes are produced in the transforms by the linear phase term. Note the fringes are symmetric in the cosine transform (left) and antisymmetric in the sine transform (right).

$$\text{Re}\{F(\,\boldsymbol{\rho}\,)\} \qquad\qquad \text{Im}\{F(\,\boldsymbol{\rho}\,)\}$$

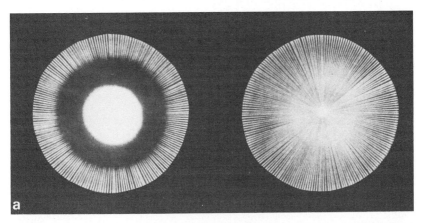

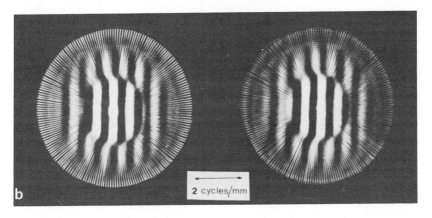

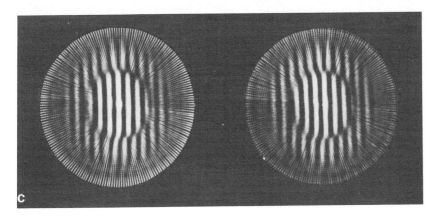

f(r)

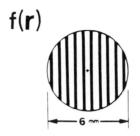

Re{F(ρ)}   Im{F(ρ)}

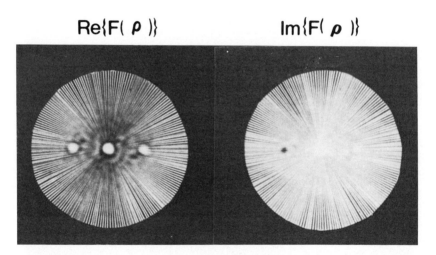

Fig. 16. Complex transforms of a reflective object generated by the Radon–Fourier transformer. The object is a Ronchi ruling in a 6 mm aperture centered on the optic axis. Since the reflectance of the object is much less than its transmittance, and since the modulation in reflectance is much less as well, the SNR is much worse for the reflective case. The object was located off-center to give a nonvanishing imaginary part of the transform. The real part of the Fourier transform (left), biased up to demonstrate the bipolar character; also note that the pattern is symmetric about the center. Imaginary part of the transform (right), which is antisymmetric.

from the familiar limitations on bandwidth and dynamic range common to other geometrical-optics incoherent correlators (Rogers, 1977).

c. Hartley Transforms. A 2-D operation that is receiving some attention in the signal processing community is the Hartley transform (Bracewell, 1983; Bracewell *et al.*, 1985). For a 2-D function $f(\mathbf{r})$, the Hartley transform is defined as

$$H(\boldsymbol{\rho}) = \int\int_{\infty} d^2 r f(\mathbf{r}) \, \text{cas}(2\pi \mathbf{r} \cdot \boldsymbol{\rho}) \tag{28}$$

(a)

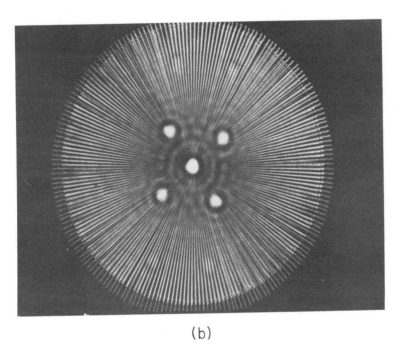

(b)

Fig. 17. Fourier transforms of patterns generated by the low-cost liquid-crystal television. (a) Object, a checkerboard pattern. (b) Cosine transform produced by the Radon–Fourier transformer.

where $cas(x) \equiv \cos(x) + \sin(x)$. The kernel of the Hartley transform is again a function of the scalar product of conjugate variables and is in fact the difference of the real and imaginary parts of the Fourier kernel. Being purely real, the Hartley transform may be preferred over the Fourier transform for digital computation since the storage requirements could be halved. Being a linear combination of the real and imaginary parts of the 2-D Fourier transform and hence of the 1-D Fourier transform of the Radon projections, the Hartley transform is easily implemented in Radon space. By subtraction of the real and imaginary outputs of the SAW chirp transformer with a simple difference amplifier, the 1-D central slices of the Hartley transform are generated. They are displayed in the same fashion as the Fourier transform.

2. Filtering and Correlations

The filter theorem demonstrates that a projection of a 2-D convolution (correlation) is the convolution (correlation) of the corresponding projections of the 2-D functions. Since devices or systems exist to perform 1-D convolutions (SAW devices, CCD convolvers, and AO convolution systems), it is feasible to perform the 2-D operations in Radon space (Gmitro *et al.*, 1983). With a fast 1-D SAW convolver such an operation can be performed at video rates. A system capable of video-rate 2-D convolution or filtering is depicted in Fig. 18. The projections of the filter function may

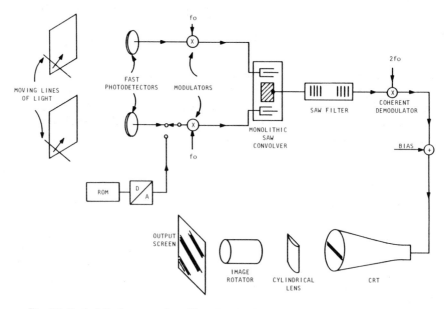

Fig. 18. Optical Radon convolver–filter. By the filter theorem, the convolution of two functions can be performed in 1-D on their projections. With this system a 2-D signal can be convolved with another 2-D signal or a stored filter function. After the projections are generated with a flying-line scanner, a SAW convolver is used to perform the 1-D filtering. The required rho filtering is also performed by a suitably designed SAW filter. The bipolar signal is biased up, applied to the *z*-axis of a CRT, backprojected by the cylindrical lens and image rotator, and imaged on the output detector.

be generated as needed from a 2-D image or stored in digital memory and read out through a fast D/A converter. A simulation of 2-D high-pass filtering is shown in Fig. 19 where the projections were generated optically, the 1-D convolutions and rho filtering performed in a digital computer, and the backprojection again performed optically.

If the projections of the filter function are stored in an addressable digital memory, as suggested above, we have the capability to alter the impulse response of the 2-D filter by updating its digitally stored 1-D projections. This could be useful if filtering a noisy signal that varies over time and would enable the application of 1-D adaptive filtering methods to 2-D situations. For example, consider a signal corrupted by noise. An adaptive filter acts on noise in a reference channel (correlated in some unknown way with the noise in the signal channel) to maximize the output SNR. This is accomplished by adjusting the filter's impulse response to minimize an appropriate error signal. The filter parameters are derived from correlations between the signals in the input and reference channels—operations that can be legitimately performed on the Radon projections of 2-D signals. In 1-D the technique has been successfully applied to a number of problems [e.g., telephone echo cancellation (Gritton and Lin, 1984), electrocardiography, and antenna sidelobe interference (Widrow *et al.*, 1975)]. To the knowledge of the authors there is only one demonstrated example of 2-D adaptive filtering: Tao and Weinhaus (1985) applied adaptive noise cancellation techniques to removal of periodic signal-dependent noise in digital imagery. By filtering the Radon projections with 1-D updatable stored functions in a 1-D convolver, one can implement these adaptive algorithms while avoiding the limitations of available 2-D hardware.

3. Pattern Recognition

Some very useful pattern recognition operations can be profitably performed in Radon space. We have already demonstrated generation of the 2-D Fourier power spectrum. Gindi and Gmitro (1984) have used optical methods to extract integrated features of the power spectrum rapidly from the Radon projections. They have also demonstrated the feasibility of evaluating a set of invariant moments, deriving the Hough transform and finding the convex hull of a 2-D input by operations on the Radon projections. Since the first three operations are probably of most interest, we shall briefly discuss each.

a. Fourier Spectrum Features. Optical computation of features in the Fourier power spectrum has been feasible for some years and has been applied to some industrial uses (Casasent, 1981). The wedge–ring detector

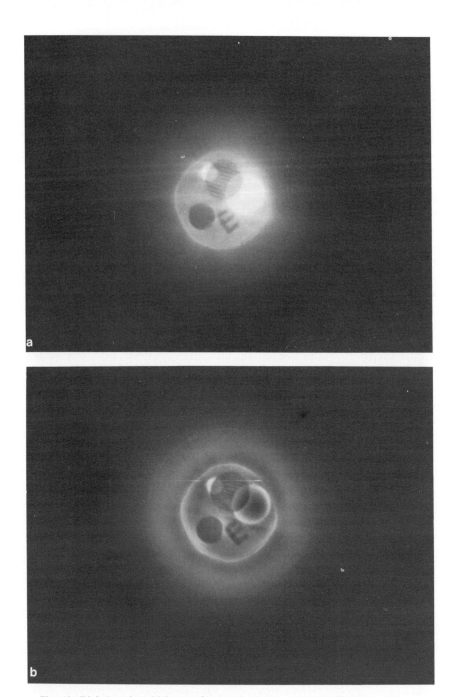

Fig. 19. Digital–optical high-pass filtering in Radon space. Projections are generated optically, stored in digital memory, and high-pass and rho-filtered digitally. The backprojection and summation are performed optically. (a) Object. (b) Resulting edge enhancement.

was developed for use in a coherent processor to compute the energy in the power spectrum in discrete segments of magnitude and orientation of spatial frequency. By manipulation of the 1-D power spectra in various ways the same kind of Fourier feature extraction can be performed. Integration of the power spectra of adjacent projections produces information equivalent to that from the wedge segments. Sampling the 1-D spectra and integrating over projections generates information from discrete spatial frequency intervals, corresponding to the annular segments of the wedge-ring detector. Results from a computer simulation by Gindi and Gmitro (1984) are shown in Fig. 20.

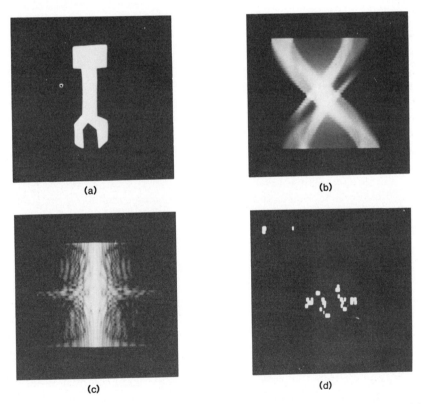

(a)

(b)

(c)

(d)

Fig. 20. Feature extraction in Radon space. (a) Simulated object and (b) its sinogram. (c) Log of the power spectrum of the sinogram slices (i.e., Fourier spatial frequency along a radial line is displayed horizontally and azimuth angle vertically). (d) Digitally derived Hough transform, obtained by high-pass filtering each projection of the sinogram and then thresholding. Bright spots in the feature space represent the presence of straight lines in coordinate space. Clustering near the center corresponds to the vertical lines in the object (Gindi and Gmitro, 1984).

b. Image Moments.   Hu (1962) described a system of linear combinations of image moments that are invariant to translation, rotation, and scale change. Later, Maitra (1979) modified the system to include invariance to relative image contrast. Six combinations of ten image moments m_{pq} are required, where

$$m_{pq} = \int_{-\infty}^{\infty} \int_{-\infty}^{\infty} dx\, dy\, x^p y^q f(x, y) \tag{29}$$

The ten necessary image moments are m_{00}, m_{11}, m_{10}, m_{01}, m_{20}, m_{02}, m_{12}, m_{21}, m_{30}, and m_{03}. Gindi and Gmitro (1984) demonstrated that the ten moments can be computed from four projections spaced $\pi/4$ radians apart. The ten image moments and the linear combinations can be rapidly computed by digital means from optically generated projections. (See also Chapter 2.1 by Casasent.)

c. Hough Transform.   The Hough transform was developed as a technique to speed detection of straight-line segments in digital imagery. Edges of the object are mapped by the Hough transform to a parameter space wherein peaks indicate the presence of straight lines in the object. Deans (1981) described the close similarity between the Hough and Radon transforms; for binary pictures, in fact, they are identical. Eichmann and Dong (1983) have proposed a coherent system to generate the Hough transform, and Gindi and Gmitro (1984) demonstrated that 1-D filtering of Radon projections can be used to edge-enhance a 2-D image and derive the Hough transform simultaneously. Their digital simulations of the computation of the Hough transform are shown in Fig. 20.

4. *Image Coding and Bandwidth Compression*

The potential of x-ray tomography in medical applications led to investigation of the collected data required to obtain good image quality (Rowland, 1979). In turn this has led to application of the tomographic transformation to reduce image storage and transmission requirements while maintaining image quality (Mersereau and Oppenheim, 1974). Since only 1-D compression operations are required after the projections are collected, rapid coding is possible. To date the work has been aimed at digital compression of the 1-D projections. Smith and Barrett (1983) truncated and quantized the Fourier components of each projection of a scene to reduce the data from 8 bits/pixel to 1.1 bits/pixel while retaining good image quality. As they point out, the approach works very well with rectilinear scenes since significant Fourier components predominate in a limited number of projections. Fraser *et al.* (1985) investigated the effect of gross reduction of the number of projections used as well as quantization effects of various spatial frequency ranges. Using 256×256 8-bit images, they obtained good image quality with as few as 0.86 bits/pixel.

5. *Spectrum Estimation*

In temporal signal processing, the estimation of frequencies of a signal buried in uncorrelated noise is a classic problem (Robinson, 1982). Averaging and modeling techniques have been developed appropriate for distinguishing various types of signals (Kay and Marple, 1981). Most are based on Fourier transform and/or correlation operations and are hence adaptable to operations in Radon space for 2-D signals. Traditional methods incorporating averaging operations, such as the periodogram and the Blackman–Tukey spectrum estimate, are most useful for detecting the presence of sinusoidal signals. To compute the periodogram, windowed segments of the 1-D input are sampled and padded with zeros. The size of the data window determines the frequency resolution of the periodogram. The power spectra of the segments are computed and averaged. Since the noise is uncorrelated, the signal spectrum should dominate in the periodogram. This approach has become popular since the invention of the FFT algorithm, and 2-D periodograms are used in a similar manner for spatial signals (Dudgeon and Mersereau, 1984). For 2-D signals optical processing techniques can be used to estimate the spectrum. Indeed, one of the success stories of optical processing, Labeyrie stellar speckle interferometry, generates a form of 2-D periodogram in which the signal segmentation is over time rather than over space. Computation of the traditional periodogram is easily adaptable to Radon space implementation. The projections of a noisy signal are computed and segmented. The individual segments are padded with zeros and Fourier transformed. The power spectra of the segments of the projection are averaged to derive an estimate of the power spectrum of that one projection. The same procedure is carried out for each projection to generate the 2-D power spectrum estimate.

The Blackman–Tukey algorithm derives a spectral estimate via the Wiener–Khintchine theorem (i.e., the power spectrum of a stochastic signal is the Fourier transform of its autocorrelation). For a sampled 1-D signal the autocorrelation is computed for a number of allowed lags (shifts) and Fourier transformed. For a 2-D signal the calculation of the 2-D autocorrelation makes this approach computationally expensive. However, once the projections have been derived, this approach can be performed in 1-D rapidly and cheaply. By the filter theorem the projection of the autocorrelation is the autocorrelation of the projections. The 1-D autocorrelation of each projection can be rapidly computed, Fourier transformed, and displayed in sinogram or polar format to give an estimate of the 2-D power spectrum.

6. Linear, Space-Variant Operations

In recent years a considerable amount of effort has been directed at developing optical methods of implementing space-variant operations to broaden the applicability of optical processing. For a review of this work see Goodman (1981). It is natural, therefore, for us to investigate the application of the Radon transform to such operations. We shall see that Radon-space implementation of general space-variant operations, though theoretically possible, usually offers little if any advantage over direct processing. For some special cases, however, the Radon approach can be very useful.

A general linear, space-variant operation on a 2-D function $f(\mathbf{r})$ can be expressed as a superposition integral:

$$g(\mathbf{r}) = \int\int_{\infty} d^2r'\, f(\mathbf{r}')h(\mathbf{r}; \mathbf{r}') \tag{30}$$

where the kernel $h(\mathbf{r}; \mathbf{r}')$ can be regarded as a space-variant impulse response. Since the superposition kernel is a function of both the input and output coordinates and is therefore 4-D, we cannot derive unique 1-D projections of $h(\mathbf{r}; \mathbf{r}')$ in the matter described by Eq. (2). We could derive a generalized projection $\lambda_h(p, \phi; p', \phi')$ of $h(\mathbf{r}; \mathbf{r}')$ by integration over the input and output variables and examine the relationship between λ_f and λ_h that yields λ_g. We have already seen some cases (e.g., the Fourier and Hartley transforms) in which the close kinship of the space-variant integral kernel and the Radon kernel allow the operations to be directly performed in this manner. But for the general space-variant operation, we shall instead consider an alternative treatment made by Bamler and Hofer-Alfeis (1982). They proved that 2-D space-variant operations can be considered to be a special case of 4-D space-invariant convolution, that is,

$$g(\mathbf{r}) = g'(\mathbf{r}; \mathbf{r}' = 0) = [f'(\mathbf{r}; \mathbf{r}') * * * * h(\mathbf{r}; \mathbf{r}')]|_{\mathbf{r}'=0} \tag{31}$$

where $f'(\mathbf{r}; \mathbf{r}') \equiv f(\mathbf{r})\, \delta(\mathbf{r}+\mathbf{r}')$, and the operator $* * * *$ denotes 4-D convolution. Deriving $f'(\mathbf{r}; \mathbf{r}')$ involves sampling a 4-D smeared version of $f(\mathbf{r})$ and so is somewhat akin to backprojection. Bamler and Hofer-Alfeis proposed a means of implementing the 4-D convolution optically by sequential 2-D convolutions for the case of a bandlimited space-variant impulse response. By extension of the filter theorem [Eq. (13)] to 4-D the convolution can theoretically be performed by 1-D convolutions in Radon space once the projections of the 4-D functions have been derived. The 4-D generalization of the projection operation [Eq. (2)] is obtained in analogous fashion to the 3-D case (Section I.B.1), that is, the 1-D projection of a 4-D function is generated by integration over the 3-D volume normal to the 4-D unit vector defining the azimuth of the projection. Three angles (α, β, γ) are required to specify this unit normal. For clarity we respecify the arguments $(\mathbf{r}; \mathbf{r}')$ of the 4-D functions by the notation $(\mathbf{r}_4)$, where the subscript denotes the dimensionality of the space. Similarly, we define the 4-D volume element $d^4 r = d^2 r \, d^2 r'$. The 1-D projection of the 4-D input function $f'(\mathbf{r}_4)$ is therefore

$$\lambda_{f'}(p, \alpha, \beta, \gamma) = \int\int\int\int_\infty d^4 r f'(\mathbf{r}_4) \, \delta[p - \mathbf{r}_4 \cdot \hat{\mathbf{n}}_4] \qquad (32)$$

Note that the definition of $f'(\mathbf{r}_4) = f(\mathbf{r}) \, \delta(\mathbf{r} + \mathbf{r}')$ allows some simplification of this expression by evaluating the integral over $d^2 r'$. However, the projection of the kernel $h(\mathbf{r}_4)$ cannot be so simplified, in general. Extending the filter theorem [Eq. (13)] to 4-D, we have

$$g'(\mathbf{r}_4) = R_4^{-1}[\lambda_{g'}(p, \alpha, \beta, \gamma)] = R_4^{-1}[\lambda_{f'}(p, \alpha, \beta, \gamma) * \lambda_h(p, \alpha, \beta, \gamma)] \qquad (33)$$

where R_4^{-1} is the 4-D inverse Radon transform. The desired output $g(\mathbf{r})$ of the 2-D space-variant operation is obtained by evaluation of $g'(\mathbf{r}_4) = g'(\mathbf{r}; \mathbf{r}')$ at the 2-D plane defined by $\mathbf{r}' = 0$. Since each 1-D convolution influences every point in the 4-D convolution (and hence every point in the 2-D output plane) via backprojection, there are no computational shortcuts—only nonessential 4-D output. In Radon terms, mapping the 2-D input function to 4-D space and performing a 4-D space-invariant convolution avoids the necessity of operating on one projection of the 2-D input $f(\mathbf{r})$ with multiple generalized projections of the 4-D kernel $h(\mathbf{r}; \mathbf{r}')$ to obtain one projection of the 2-D output $g(\mathbf{r})$. However, the forward and inverse Radon transforms of 4-D functions are very intensive computational processes that would require special-purpose hardware if they are to be performed rapidly and economically. To see the scope of the problem, consider that the forward transform requires the calculation of a volume integral for each point in each projection. For a 500×500 input $f(\mathbf{r})$, the general space-variant kernel $h(\mathbf{r}; \mathbf{r}')$ has $500^4 = 6.25 \times 10^{10}$ data points. Calculation of each of 500^4 projections requires 500 volume integrals over 500^3 points. The difficulties of performing the 4-D backprojection are similarly prodigious. As will be discussed, Barrett (1981) proposed a hybrid 3-D Radon-space signal processor that could be adapted to these 4-D applications, but the addition of one more dimension significantly complicates the data storage and manipulation requirements. Hence performing the general space-variant operation in Radon space via the 4-D convolution algorithm has no obvious advantage over direct digital processing at this time.

7. Bilinear and Nonlinear Operations

For 1-D signals a number of processing algorithms have been developed that operate on the signal in a multilinear or nonlinear manner for such purposes as voice pattern recognition and echo deconvolution. Examples include coordinate–frequency representations [e.g., sliding-window spectrum, Woodward ambiguity function, and Wigner distribution function (WDF)], triple correlation (Lohmann and Wirnitzer, 1984), and the cepstrum (Childers et al., 1977). The success of these algorithms for certain 1-D signal-processing tasks has stimulated research into 2-D analogs, but these are usually computationally intensive and hence not often implemented digitally. In some cases optical processing has been profitably applied, notably for coherent optical computation of the Wigner distribution function of 2-D data (Bamler and Glünder, 1983). Those operations based on Fourier transforms (e.g., WDF) or on nonlinear point processing (e.g., cepstrum) may be implemented in Radon space. With a fast optical Radon transformer and 1-D analog or fast digital processing, the 2-D operation can be performed profitably. An example of such an operation is coordinate–frequency representation of 2-D functions.

A simultaneous representation of the coordinate and frequency distribution of the energy in a nonstationary signal has proven useful in a number of applications [e.g., radar signal processing (Woodward, 1953) and speech processing (Oppenheim, 1970)]. Such a representation is intended to give a picture of the local frequency spectrum of the signal (i.e., the frequency content of the signal arising from a particular region of coordinate space). Obviously such a picture requires twice as many dimensions in the representation space as in the signal space. Several such representations have been proposed. The most direct path to a local spectrum is the complex spectrogram (CS), or sliding-window spectrum, in which a constant window function is shifted over the signal to specify the region to be Fourier analyzed; that is, for a 1-D signal $f(t)$ the complex spectrogram S_{fg} is defined

$$S_{fg}(t; \nu) = \int_{-\infty}^{\infty} dt' \, f(t')g^*(t'-t) \, e^{-2\pi i \nu t'} \tag{34}$$

This representation is easily computed by coherent optics, but the output is affected as much by the window $g(t)$ as by the input $f(t)$. This potential problem can be alleviated by using a self-windowed representation such as the Wigner distribution function (WDF), which is commonly defined as

$$W_f(t; \nu) = \int_{-\infty}^{\infty} dt' \, f\left(t + \frac{t'}{2}\right) f^*\left(t - \frac{t'}{2}\right) e^{-2\pi i \nu t'}$$

$$= \mathrm{FT}_{t' \to \nu}\left[f\left(t + \frac{t'}{2}\right) f^*\left(t - \frac{t'}{2}\right) \right] \tag{35}$$

where FT_1 is the 1-D Fourier operator transforming coordinate t' to
$t' \to \nu$
frequency ν. This representation was introduced by Wigner (1932) and introduced into optics by Bastiaans (1978). Another closely related function is the Woodward ambiguity function (AF), which is defined as

$$
A_f(\nu; t') = \int_{-\infty}^{\infty} dt\, f\left(t + \frac{t'}{2}\right) f^*\left(t - \frac{t'}{2}\right) e^{-2\pi i \nu t}
$$

$$
= \underset{t \to \nu}{FT_1}\left[f\left(t + \frac{t'}{2}\right) f^*\left(t - \frac{t'}{2}\right) \right] \tag{36}
$$

It is related to the WDF through a double Fourier transform. Several optical methods for computing these representations for 1-D functions have been introduced (Bartelt *et al.*, 1980; Brenner and Lohmann, 1982; Eichmann and Dong, 1982; Athale *et al.*, 1983).

Generation of such representations for 2-D functions presents another problem since the resultant is a function of four variables. Generally, 2-D slices of the 4-D representation are produced. Real input functions are assumed, eliminating the need for conjugating the shifted function. In addition the computation of the bilinear product function is expensive if done digitally, increasing the motivation for optical processing. Of the representations listed, the WDF is most readily computed optically since the Fourier transform of the product function is over the shifted coordinate variable. Optically the product function is generated by passing coherent light twice through a transparency of the signal, either by reflecting an image of the transparency onto itself, by overlaying copies (Bamler and Glünder, 1983), or by imaging onto a copy (Conner and Li, 1985). The bilinear product function is then Fourier transformed to generate one slice $W_f(\mathbf{r}_0; \boldsymbol{\rho})$. Shifting the position of the input functions generates 2-D slices for different values of $\mathbf{r}_0$.

Computation of the WDF can also be performed in Radon space by taking projections of the optically derived bilinear product and Fourier transforming in 1-D. Easton *et al.* (1984) demonstrated generation of 1-D central slices of the squared modulus of the 4-D WDF and later used the 1-D SAW complex Fourier transformer to produce bipolar 2-D slices of the 4-D WDF of a 2-D real function. An example is shown in Fig. 21.

B. OPERATIONS ON THREE-DIMENSIONAL SIGNALS

Earlier we stated that we would emphasize processing of 2-D signals by a tomographic transform. However, it may be even more profitable to use the Radon transform to reduce 3-D problems to 1-D operations since digital

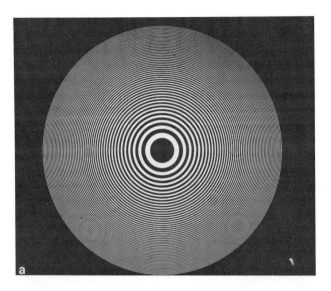

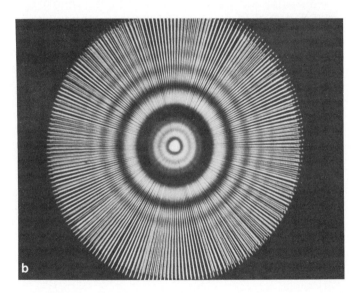

Fig. 21. Two-dimensional slices of the 4-D Wigner distribution function. The object is a transparent Fresnel zone plate; the slices produced represent the 2-D spatial frequency plane of the WDF at a point $r_0 = [x_0, y_0]$. (a) When the zone plate is centered in coordinate space (i.e., $r_0 = 0$), the bilinear product function is identical to the input, and the WDF is the Fourier transform of the zone plate (b). Shifting r_0 off center generates (c) a product function with fringes that results in (d) a symmetric delta-function pair in the WDF.

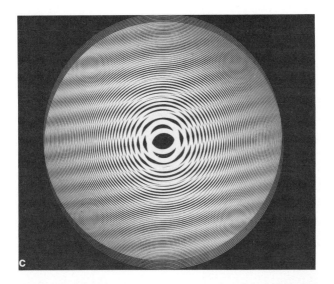

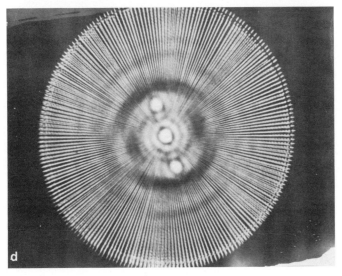

Fig. 21 (*continued*).

data manipulation is even more time-consuming in that case. Two kinds of 3-D problems will be discussed: 3-D purely spatial data and 2-D spatial data with a third dimension (e.g., time or spectrum). We shall briefly describe the required operations and suggest potential applications.

1. *Three-Dimensional Spatial and Two-Dimensional*
    Spatial + One-Dimensional Temporal Signals

In Section I.B.1 we described the decomposition of a 3-D function into a set of 1-D projections by integration over parallel planes. The projection operation is identical to Eq. (2) except that the delta function reduces the volume integral to a set of planar integrals. Given a 3-D function $f(x, y, z)$, we wish to integrate the function over a set of planes normal to the 3-D unit vector $\hat{\mathbf{n}}$. Two angles are required to define the normal to a plane, commonly the azimuth ϕ and the colatitude θ. The displacement of the parallel plane from the origin is again defined as p, so that $\hat{\mathbf{n}} = \mathbf{p}/p$. The 3-D projection operation can then be expressed as

$$\lambda(p, \phi, \theta) = \int \int \int_{\infty} d^3 r f(\mathbf{r}) \, \delta(p - \mathbf{r} \cdot \hat{\mathbf{n}}) \qquad (37)$$

The 3-D version of the central-slice theorem states that the 1-D Fourier transform of a projection of a 3-D function yields one line through the origin of the 3-D Fourier transform.

The 3-D backprojection operation is again very similar to the 2-D case, but now the 1-D function is smeared over the original projection plane normal to $\hat{\mathbf{n}}$. Repeating this for all directions $\hat{\mathbf{n}}$ generates a 3-D summation image $b(\mathbf{r})$. In the filtering step, however, there is a significant qualitative difference between the 2-D and the 3-D cases. Recall that in 2-D the Fourier space filter for the 1-D projection is $H(\nu) = |\nu|$, and the coordinate space counterpart is $h(p) = -1/2\pi^2 p^2$, which falls off slowly with p. The corresponding filter for the inverse 3-D Radon transform is $H(\sigma) = 2\pi\sigma^2$, where σ is the magnitude of the 3-D spatial frequency vector $[\xi, \eta, \zeta]$ (Barrett, 1981). The coordinate space filter is easily found since multiplication by $-(2\pi^2\sigma^2)$ in the frequency domain corresponds to taking the Laplacian in the space domain (Gaskill, 1978). The expression for the inverse 3-D Radon transform is therefore

$$f(\mathbf{r}) = -\frac{1}{2\pi} \nabla^2 [b(\mathbf{r})] \qquad (38)$$

where $b(\mathbf{r})$ is the 3-D summation image. Filtering for the 3-D inverse transform is therefore a local operation, in contrast with the 2-D case.

Barrett (1981) proposed a hybrid 3-D Radon-space signal processor composed of an optical system to derive the projections, digital storage, 1-D signal processing, and optical backprojection. The input function was assumed to be a collection of 2-D image frames (i.e., a movie film) in which each frame is assumed to be a slice through the 3-D object. All of the 3-D versions of the operations described in Section II.A could be performed by this system, including 3-D Fourier transformation and convolution. Such a system should be capable of performing 3-D complex Fourier transforms on 500^3 data points in less than 4 h. A digital system common at the time (PDP 11/34 + array processor) would have required two days.

Such a system can also be applied to 2-D spatial + 1-D temporal signals (e.g., movies) for joint spatial–temporal filtering. A possible application would be to stellar speckle interferometry, allowing the averaging filter impulse response to vary temporally. Such operations are feasible by digital means but are expensive and time-consuming.

2. *Two-Dimensional Spatial + One-Dimensional Spectral Data*

Optical detection and display systems are best suited to 2-D data formats. In white-light images a third dimension of information has been encoded in the spectrum of each image point. The Radon transform provides a mechanism by which we can use 2-D detectors, signal processors, and display devices to manipulate the spectral data while retaining the ability to regenerate the image. For example, if we have a white-light 2-D image, we can derive the set of 1-D projections of that image as described in Section I.C.1. The 1-D projections can be spectrally dispersed in the orthogonal dimension, allowing 2-D filtering to be performed on the joint spatial–spectral projection. The 2-D filtered signal can be inversely dispersed, to rederive spectrally filtered 1-D projections, and a 2-D filtered image then reconstructed by the inverse Radon transform. Such a system could be used for spectral matched filtered imaging (Lohmann and Maul, 1981; Yu, 1984) or imaging spectroscopy.

III. Summary and Conclusions

We have discussed the reduction of 2-D signal processing operations to 1-D operations by the Radon transform for the purpose of gaining flexibility, precision, and mechanical advantages over direct optical signal processing. This technique is most readily applicable to operations based on Fourier transforms and convolution. Several optical systems were discussed that are capable of performing the forward and inverse dimensional transformations, and a number of applications were considered, some already demonstrated and some postulated. The authors believe that many of the fruits of this technique have yet to be harvested, and we encourage workers in signal processing to investigate the utility of projection operations in their own applications.

Acknowledgments

The authors have benefitted greatly from discussions with many coworkers and colleagues, including Adolf Lohmann, Stanley Deans, John Walkup, H. Harold Szu, Arthur Gmitro, Gene Gindi, Anthony Ticknor, Warren Smith, and Kyle Myers.

References

Abramovitz, I. J., Berg, N. J., and Casseday, M. W. (1983). *In* "Acousto-Optic Signal Processing" (N. J. Berg and J. N. Lee, eds.), pp. 289–323. Dekker, New York.

Ash, E. A. (1978). *In* "Acoustic Surface Waves" (A. A. Oliner, ed.), pp. 97–186. Springer-Verlag, Berlin and New York.

Athale, R. A., Lee, J. N., Robinson, E. L., and Szu, H. H. (1983). *Opt. Lett.* **8**, 166–168.

Bamler, R., and Glünder, H. (1983). *Opt. Acta* **30**, 1789–1803.

Bamler, R., and Hofer-Alfeis, J. (1982). *Opt. Commun.* **43**, 97–102.

Barrett, H. H. (1981). *SPIE Semin. Proc.* **373**, 179–190.

Barrett, H. H. (1984). *In* "Progress in Optics" (E. Wolf, ed.), Vol. XXI, pp. 219–286. Elsevier, Amsterdam.

Barrett, H. H., and Swindell, W. (1977). *Proc. IEEE* **65**, 89–107.

Barrett, H. H., and Swindell, W. (1981). "Radiological Imaging," Vol. II. Academic Press, New York.

Barrett, H. H., Greivenkamp, J., Gordon, S. K., Gmitro, A. F., Chiu, M. Y., and Swindell, W. (1979a). *Opt. Commun.* **28**, 287–290.

Barrett, H. H., Chiu, M. Y., Gordon, S. K., Parks, R. E., and Swindell, W. (1979b). *Appl. Opt.* **18**, 2760–2766.

Bartelt, H. O., and Lohmann, A. W. (1981). *SPIE Semin. Proc.* **373**, 3–10.

Bartelt, H. O., Brenner, K.-H., and Lohmann, A. W. (1980). *Opt. Commun.* **32**, 32–38.

Bastiaans, M. J. (1978). *Opt. Commun.* **25**, 26–30.

Berg, N. J., Lee, J. N., and Casseday, M. W. (1979). *Opt. Eng.* **18**, 420–428.

Beynon, J. D. E., and Lamb, D. R. (1980). "Charge-coupled Devices and the Applications." McGraw-Hill, London.

Bierman, H. (1985). *Electronics* **58**(48), 139.

Bracewell, R. N. (1983). *J. Opt. Soc. Am.* **73**, 1832–1835.

Bracewell, R. N., Bartelt, H., Lohmann, A. W., and Streibl, N. (1985). *Appl. Opt.* **24**, 1401–1402.

Brenner, K.-H., and Lohmann, A. W. (1982). *Opt. Commun.* **42**, 310–314.

Buss, D. D., Collins, D. R., Bailey, W. H., and Reeves, C. R. (1973). *IEEE J. Solid-State Circuits* **SC-8**, 138–146.

Casasent, D. P. (1978). *In* "Optical Data Processing" (D. Casasent, ed.), pp. 241–282. Springer-Verlag, Berlin and New York.

Casasent, D. P. (1981). *In* "Optical Information Processing" (S. H. Lee, ed.), pp. 181–233. Springer-Verlag, Berlin and New York.

Casasent, D. (1983). *In* "Acousto-Optic Signal Processing" (N. J. Berg and J. N. Lee, eds.), pp. 325–367. Dekker, New York.

Casasent, D., and Psaltis, D. (1977). *Proc. IEEE* **65**, 77–83.

Casseday, M. W., Berg, N. J., and Abramovitz, I. J. (1983). *In* "Acousto-Optic Signal Processing" (N. J. Berg and J. N. Lee, eds.), pp. 165–203. Dekker, New York.

Childers, D. G., Skinner, D. P., and Kemerait, R. C. (1977). *Proc. IEEE* **65**, 1428–1443.

Connor, M., and Li, Y. (1985). *Appl. Opt.* **24**, 3825–3829.

Cormack, A. M. (1963). *J. Appl. Phys.* **34**, 2722–2727.

Cormack, A. M. (1964). *J. Appl. Phys.* **35**, 2908–2913.

Das, P., and Ayub, F. M. M. (1982). *In* "Applications of Optical Fourier Transforms" (H. Stark, ed.), pp. 289–331. Academic Press, New York.

Deans, S. R. (1981). *IEEE Trans. Pattern Anal. Mach. Intell.* **PAMI-3**, 185–188.

Deans, S. R. (1983). "The Radon Transform and Some of its Applications." Wiley, New York.

Dudgeon, D. E., and Mersereau, R. M. (1984). "Multidimensional Digital Signal Processing." Prentice-Hall, Englewood Cliffs, New Jersey.

Duinker, S., Geluk, R. J., and Mulder, H. (1978). *Oldelft Sci. Eng. Q.* **1**, 41–66.

Easton, R. L., Jr., Ticknor, A. J., and Barrett, H. H. (1984). *Opt. Eng.* **23**, 738-744.

Easton, R. L., Jr., Ticknor, A. J., and Barrett, H. H. (1985a). *J. Opt. Soc. Am. A* **2**, P108.

Easton, R. L., Jr., Ticknor, A. J., and Barrett, H. H. (1985b). *Appl. Opt.* **24**, 3817-3824.

Edholm, P., Hellstrom, L. G., and Jacobson, B. (1978). *Phys. Med. Biol.* **23**, 90-99.

Eichmann, G., and Dong, B. Z. (1982). *Appl. Opt.* **21**, 3152-3156.

Eichmann, G., and Dong, B. Z. (1983). *Appl. Opt.* **22**, 830-834.

Ein-Gal, M. (1974). Ph.D. Thesis, Stanford Univ., Stanford, California.

Farhat, N. H., Yi Ho, C., and Chang, L. S. (1983). *SPIE Semin. Proc.* **388**, 140-150.

Fraser, D., Hunt, B. R., and Su, J. C. (1985). *Opt. Eng.* **24**, 298-306.

Gaskill, J. D. (1978). "Linear Systems, Fourier Transforms, and Optics." Wiley (Interscience), New York.

Gerard, H. M. (1978). *In* "Acoustic Surface Waves" (A. A. Oliner, ed.), pp. 61-96. Springer-Verlag, Berlin and New York.

Gerard, H. M., Smith, W. R., Jones, W. R., and Harrington, J. B. (1973). *IEEE Trans. Microwave Theory Tech.* **MTT-21**, 176-186.

Gerard, H. M., Yao, P. S., and Otto, O. W. (1977). *Proc. IEEE Ultrason. Symp.* pp. 947-951.

Gindi, G. R., and Gmitro, A. F. (1984). *Opt. Eng.* **23**, 499-506.

Gmitro, A. F., and Gindi, G. R. (1985). *Appl. Opt.* **24**, 4041-4045.

Gmitro, A. F., Greivenkamp, J. E., Swindell, W., Barrett, H. H., Chiu, M. Y., and Gordon, S. K. (1980). *Opt. Eng.* **19**, 260-272.

Gmitro, A. F., Gindi, G. R., Barrett, H. H., and Easton, R. L., Jr. (1983). *SPIE Semin. Proc.* **388**, 132-139.

Goodman, J. W. (1981). *In* "Optical Information Processing" (S. H. Lee, ed.), pp. 235-260. Springer-Verlag, Berlin and New York.

Gordon, S. K. (1977). Ph.D. Thesis, Univ. of Arizona, Tucson.

Gottlieb, M., Ireland, C. L. M., and Ley, J. M. (1983). "Electro-Optic and Acousto-Optic Scanning and Deflection." Dekker, New York.

Greivenkamp, J. E., Swindell, W., Gmitro, A. F., and Barrett, H. H. (1981). *Appl. Opt.* **20**, 264-273.

Gritton, C. W. K., and Lin, D. W. (1984). *IEEE ASSP Mag.* **1**(2), 30-38.

Hansen, E. W. (1981a). *J. Opt. Soc. Am.* **71**, 304-308.

Hansen, E. W. (1981b). *Appl. Opt.* **20**, 2266-2274.

Hansen, E. W., and Goodman, J. W. (1978). *Opt. Commun.* **24**, 268-272.

Helgason, S. (1980). "The Radon Transform." Birkhaeuser, Boston.

Hofer, J. (1979). *Opt. Commun.* **29**, 22-26.

Hofer, J., and Kupka, W. (1979). *SPIE Semin. Proc.* **211**, 62-65.

Hotz, D. F. (1984). *Appl. Opt.* **23**, 1613-1619.

Hu, M. K. (1962). *IRE Trans. Inf. Theory* **IT-8**, 113-121.

Jack, M. A., and Paige, E. G. S. (1978). *Wave Electron.* **3**, 229-247.

Jack, M. A., Grant, P. M., and Collins, J. H. (1980). *Proc. IEEE* **68**, 450-468.

John, F. (1955). "Plane Waves and Spherical Means Applied to Partial Differential Equations." Wiley (Interscience), New York.

Kay, S. M., and Marple, S. L., Jr. (1981). *Proc. IEEE* **69**, 1380-1419.

Klauder, J. R., Price, A. C., Darlington, S., and Albersheim, W. J. (1960). *Bell Syst. Tech. J.* **34**, 745-808.

Korpel, A. (1981). *Proc. IEEE* **69**, 48-53.

Lee, J. N., Lin, S.-C., and Tventen, A. B. (1982). *SPIE Semin. Proc.* **341**, 86-93.

Lighthill, M. J. (1962). "Fourier Analysis and Generalized Functions." Cambridge Univ. Press, London and New York.

Liu, H.-K., Davis, J. A., and Lilly, R. A. (1985). *Opt. Lett.* **10**, 635-637.

Lohmann, A. (1977). *Appl. Opt.* **16**, 261-263.

Lohmann, A., and Maul, M. (1981). *Angew. Opt., Annu. Rep., Phys. Inst. Univ. Erlangen-Nuernberg* pp. 28–29.
Lohmann, A. W., and Wirnitzer, B. (1984). *Proc. IEEE* **72**, 889–901.
McEwan, J. A., Fisher, A. D., Rolsma, P. B., and Lee, J. N. (1985). *J. Opt. Soc. Am. A* **2**, P8.
Maitra, S. (1979). *Proc. IEEE* **67**, 697–699.
Marr, J. D. (1982). *SPIE Semin. Proc.* **341**, 245–251.
Matthews, H. (1977). "Surface Wave Filters." Wiley, New York.
Mersereau, R. M., and Oppenheim, A. V. (1974). *Proc. IEEE* **62**, 1319–1338.
Monahan, M. A., Bromley, K., and Bocker, R. P. (1977). *Proc. IEEE* **65**, 121–129.
Morgan, D. P. (1985). "Surface Wave Devices for Signal Processing." Elsevier, Amsterdam.
Oppenheim, A. V. (1970). *IEEE Spectrum* **7**(8), 57–62.
Pancott B., and Reeve, C. D. (1985). *J. Opt. Soc. Am. A* **2**, P38.
Peters, T. M. (1974). *IEEE Trans. Biomed. Eng.* **BME-21**, 214–219.
Rabiner, L. R., Schafer, R. W., and Rader, C. M. (1969). *IEEE Trans. Audio Electroacoust.* **AU-17**, 86–92.
Radon, J. (1917). *Ber. Saech. Akad. Wiss. Leipzig, Math.-Phys. Kl.* **67**, 262–267. Transl. in Deans (1983).
Rallison, R., and Lowe, R. (1982). *SPIE Semin. Proc.* **353**, 47–51.
Rau, J. (1966). *J. Opt. Soc. Am.* **56**, 1490–1497.
Rhodes, W. T. (1977). *Appl. Opt.* **16**, 265–267.
Rhodes, W. T. (1981a), *Proc. IEEE* **69**, 64–79.
Rhodes, W. T. (1981b). *SPIE Semin. Proc.* **373**, 11–20.
Rhodes, W. T., and Lohmann, A. (1978). *Appl. Opt.* **17**, 1141–1151.
Roberts, J. B. G. (1977). *Proc. Advis. Group Aerosp. Res. Dev. NATO* **230**, 1.2-1–1.2-16.
Robinson, E. (1982). *Proc. IEEE* **70**, 885–907.
Rogers, G. L. (1977). "Noncoherent Optical Processing." Wiley (Interscience), New York.
Rowland, S. W. (1979). *In* "Image Reconstruction from Projections" (G. T. Herman, ed.), pp. 9–79. Springer-Verlag, Berlin and New York.
Smith, H. I. (1978). *In* "Acoustic Surface Waves" (A. A. Oliner, ed.), pp. 305–324. Springer-Verlag, Berlin and New York.
Smith, W. E., and Barrett, H. H. (1983). *Opt. Lett.* **8**, 395–397.
Stetson, K. A., and Elkins, J. N. (1977). Tech. Rep. AFAOL-TR-77-51. United Technol. Res. Cent., East Hartford, Connecticut.
Stoner, W. (1978). *Appl. Opt.* **17**, 2454–2467.
Tao, K. M., and Weinhaus, F. M. (1985). *Proc. Int. Conf. Acoust., Speech, Signal Process,* pp. 18.9.1–18.9.4.
Thomas, C. E. (1966). *Appl. Opt.* **5**, 1782–1790.
Ticknor, A. J., Easton, R. L., Jr., and Barrett, H. H. (1985). *Opt. Eng.* **24**, 82–85.
Weaver, C. S., and Goodman, J. W. (1966). *Appl. Opt.* **5**, 1248–1249.
Whitehouse, H. J. (1977). *SPIE Semin. Proc.* **118**, 118–123.
Widrow, B., Glover, J. R., Jr., McCool, J. M., Kaunitz, J., Williams, C. S., Hearn, R. H., Zeidler, J. R., Dong, E., Jr., and Goodlin, R. C. (1975). *Proc. IEEE* **63**, 1692–1716.
Wigner, E. (1932). *Phys. Rev.* **40**, 749.
Woodward, P. M. (1953). "Probability and Information Theory with Applications to Radar." Pergamon, New York.
Yu, F. T. S. (1984). *Opt. Eng.* **23**, 690–694.

VI

Optical Numerical Processing

6.1

Optical Linear Algebra Processors

DAVID CASASENT AND
B. V. K. VIJAYA KUMAR
DEPARTMENT OF ELECTRICAL AND COMPUTER ENGINEERING
CARNEGIE-MELLON UNIVERSITY
PITTSBURGH, PENNSYLVANIA 15213

I. Introduction

Optical processors have been, for a long time, special-purpose devices relying heavily on a few basic operations such as Fourier transform, imaging, and correlation. But recently there has been a tremendous effort to find optical architectures capable of accomplishing general-purpose operations. It is a well-known fact that linear systems can be conveniently represented in terms of matrices and vectors. Thus optical systems capable of operating on vectors and matrices have received a great deal of attention and are referred to as optical linear algebra processors (OLAPs).

OLAPs represent one of the most attractive and viable uses of optical computing that has emerged in recent years. The majority of work on this topic is summarized in a recent journal special issue [1] and in various Society of Photo-Instrumentation Engineers (SPIE) conference proceedings [2]. Several different linear algebra operations can be categorized as OLAP,

389

including matrix–vector multiplications, matrix–matrix multiplications, vector outer products, vector inner products, and eigenvalue–eigenvector calculations. We shall focus on matrix–vector operations that do not involve 2-dimensional (2-D) spatial light modulators (SLMs) because such devices do not yet have the necessary system maturity. Optical numerical processors that concern the realization of logical operations [3] and numerical processors that consider implementation of basic operations (such as addition, subtraction, and multiplication) are not considered. We also do not consider processors that involve the use of more than two data planes because such systems have light-efficiency problems at present. With appropriate device developments such advanced architectures offer improved realization of the basic concepts and techniques addressed in this chapter.

Our present concern is to document and critically review the wealth of OLAP architectures, number representations, algorithms, and applications. In Section II we advance a generic OLAP architecture and assess components available and unique features of this basic architecture. Our emphasis is on presently realizable systems, initial laboratory results, and an assessment of the issues to be addressed and decisions on such architectures. Section III advances several other major architectures published, with critical remarks on each. In Section IV we consider an iterative algorithm for the solution of systems of linear algebraic equations. Section V presents two optical matrix decomposition methods. Error sources, their modeling, and their use are then briefly summarized in Section VI. Number representation issues associated with bipolar and complex-valued data representation, high-accuracy (including floating point) performance, and the base or radix to be used are then summarized in Section VII, in which we also detail the digital multiplication by analog convolution (DMAC) algorithm. Section VIII contains detailed case studies on a space-integrating frequency-multiplexed architecture and a hybrid space-integrating and time-integrating multichannel architecture, with attention to initial laboratory performance results, the electronic support system required, and the flexibility of such processors. Applications are then briefly noted by reference in Section IX, and our summary is then advanced in Section X.

II. Generic OLAP Architecture and Its Component Evaluation

A generic OLAP system is shown in Fig. 1. At plane P_1 one can place a 1-D or 2-D array of point modulators (a 1-D array is the more realistic choice). Candidates for P_1 devices include 1-D laser diode (LD) and light-emitting diode (LED) arrays as well as multichannel acoustooptic (AO) cells with short apertures. We refer to this latter device as a multichannel AO point modulator. We consider M processor channels at P_1. Generally

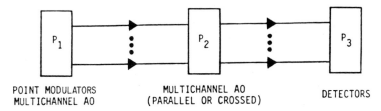

Fig. 1. Conceptual generic two-plane optical linear algebra processor architecture.

the interconnections between P_1 and P_2 are not random but involve imaging (generally a one-to-many connection between each channel of P_1 and the 2-D data we consider at P_2). At P_2 a multichannel AO cell with N channels is assumed. This achieves the best real-time throughput (high per channel input data rate) with a realistic presently available spatial light modulator (SLM), a multichannel AO cell. Between P_2 and P_3 we consider and allow random and global interconnections. At present, simple global interconnections appear in most systems. As detailed elsewhere [4, 5], we also allow frequency multiplexing at P_2 (this is preferred to P_1 frequency multiplexing) to allow more processing capacity. The angular (space multiplexing combined with an integrating lens) and frequency-multiplexing features of optical systems, together with their global interconnection features (realizable by spatial integrating and frequency multiplexing and the use of lenses and detectors) are unique aspects of OLAP architectures that are exploited and addressed in the systems we consider.

We now briefly address several of the unique aspects of optical systems and their appropriateness for linear algebra operations. OLAP architectures presently offer high accuracy (floating point [6]) without the need for interferometric positioning tolerances (as required in other optical systems) and can be fabricated with available components. These reasons make OLAP systems attractive and realistic. Optical systems allow parallel multiplication and addition, as do currently advanced and suggested digital architectures. Thus the parallelism of optics is no longer unique. However, optical systems allow one-to-many connections or broadcasting (by collimation). This property is unique and is also useful in optical interconnections for integrated circuit use at the chip and board level [7]. Optical systems also allow many-to-one connections (using lenses and detectors) which provide the summing operation. A variety of global operations (using lenses) as well as local operations (through the traveling-wave nature of AO cells) are possible because of the parallelism of light. Random and space-variant interconnections are also possible but have not yet been used in OLAPs.

The way in which a spatially or temporally modulated light beam accomplishes multiplication and the control of its direction by angular and frequency multiplexing are unique and not present in other parallel and multiprocessor technologies. We now review the important concepts and differences that distinguish OLAPs from other parallel architectures. If N modulated regions of the light leaving P_1 in Fig. 1 are angle modulated (by a lens) to pass through the same region of P_2, each local P_1 data segment is multiplied by the same P_2 data, and each of the N products leaves P_2 at a different angle and can thus be spatially separated by another lens. If one modulated region of an incident light beam passes through a region of a material at P_2 with N signals present in it (each on a different frequency), these N signals multiply the one input signal, and the N products leave P_2 at N different angles. Such angle and frequency control of the direction of light in 1-D and 2-D are features used in many OLAPs. These concepts are illustrated in more detail in Section VIII using Fig. 9.

III. Basic OLAP Architectures

We now consider the basic OLAP architectures proposed and include critical remarks on each. Figure 2 shows the basic time-integrating (TI) AO OLAP architecture [8]. The data b_n from P_1 are expanded to multiply all elements of the vector data $\mathbf{a}_n$ in the AO cell at P_2, which is then imaged to a linear output detector array at P_3 where $b_n\mathbf{a}_n$ is formed. At each T_B (bit time: the time at which each input point modulator is pulsed on or the time at which a new operation occurs in the processor), a new b_n value enters P_1, the vector in the AO cell at time n is a shifted version of the vector in the AO cell at time $n-1$, and the $b_n\mathbf{a}_n$ product is added to prior such products on the TI detectors at P_3. After N such T_B times (for N element vectors), the output in plane P_3 is the convolution of the sequence b_n with the sequence a_n. This convolution operation and the associated use of this processor is most attractive in the digital multiplication by analog convolution (DMAC) high-accuracy OLAP algorithm (detailed in Section

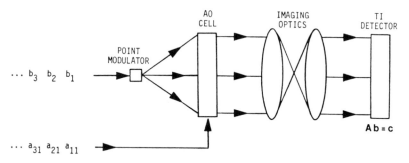

Fig. 2. Basic time-integrating acoustooptic optical linear algebra processor architecture. (From Casasent [8].)

VII) and in forming the matrix-vector product **Ba** when **B** is a Toeplitz matrix. When **B** is Toeplitz (i.e., all elements on diagonals parallel to the main diagonal are all the same), the matrix-vector product can be obtained as the convolution of the vector with the first row of the matrix. This TI architecture is especially attractive when **a** is of large dimensionality. This TI architecture has significant data-flow problems since the output data (for an N element vector) is not valid until NT_B time units (i.e., the input and output data rates of the processor differ significantly), and then all N outputs at P_3 must be read out and processed (i.e., dead time can result). If P_3 is read out in parallel each NT_B time units, then output delay and buffering circuitry is necessary.

In Fig. 3 a multichannel TI AO OLAP architecture with a linear charge-coupled device (CCD) detector array is shown [9]. At each T_B, the P_1 and P_2 data are multiplied point-by-point and added to the prior output P_3 data, and the contents of P_3 are shifted by one position. If the diagonals (or the skewed columns) of the matrix **A** are fed to the P_1 point modulators, and the vector **b** is fed to the AO cell at P_2, the P_3 outputs in time are the vector result of the associated matrix-vector product. The zero-padding needed can be avoided by omitting the CCD shift register (SR) output (however, a parallel 1-D output or dead time is then required [10]). In Fig. 3 the detector dynamic range required can be large and cannot be reduced unless a parallel detector output is employed and associated partial sums are obtained and appropriately processed. The major limitations of the TI architecture of Fig. 3 are that the CCD SR rate limits T_B (and hence the

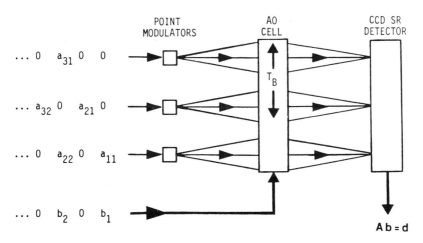

Fig. 3. Time-integrating acoustooptic optical linear algebra processor architecture with multiple point modulator inputs and a CCD time-integrating detector. (From Casasent [8].)

speed of the system) and that to utilize fully the potential of the system we require $N \simeq \text{TBWP}_A \simeq 1000$ point modulators at P_1 (where TBWP_A is the time bandwidth product of the AO cell). Thus the full utilization of this architecture can cause a prohibitive fabrication problem and can result in data-feeding problems.

The prior architectures computed point-by-point vector products and scalar–vector products. The architecturre of Fig. 4 uses two crossed linear parallel addressed modulators and a 2-D TI detector to produce the vector outer product (VOP) of two vectors [11]. One VOP is produced each T_B (new P_1 and P_2 data vector inputs are required each T_B to achieve this rate). If N VOPs are accumulated at P_3 with the $\mathbf{a}_n$ and $\mathbf{b}_n$ vector inputs being the columns and rows of matrices $\mathbf{A}$ and $\mathbf{B}$, then the matrix–matrix product $\mathbf{AB}$ results at P_3. This architecture is also suitable for the digital multiplication by analog convolution (DMAC) algorithm. The use of VOPs is generally most appropriate for matrix–matrix rather than matrix–vector operations. A major practical problem with this system is that the output is not valid until NT_B; and when it is valid, a 2-D array of N^2 detectors must be read out in parallel. If this is not achieved, dead-time and data-flow problems can result, or excessive postdetection electronics may be required.

The basic space-integrating (SI) vector inner product (VIP) AO OLAP architecture [8] is shown in Fig. 5. In this architecture the data $\mathbf{a}_n$ from the point modulators in P_1 are again imaged through an AO cell at P_2 with contents $\mathbf{b}_n$, and the point-by-point products of the elements of $\mathbf{a}_n$ and $\mathbf{b}_n$ are formed. The output lens now forms the sum on a single output detector where the VIP $\mathbf{a}^T\mathbf{b}$ results. At each T_B, new $\mathbf{a}_n$ data can be entered, and as before $\mathbf{b}_{n+1}$ is a shifted version of $\mathbf{b}_n$. With $\mathbf{a}_n$ fixed, the output is the convolution of the sequence a_n with the sequence b_n, and the system is thus

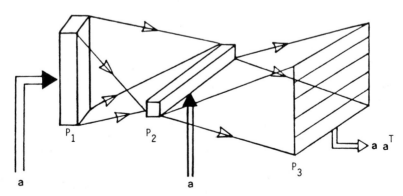

Fig. 4. Vector outer product time-integrating acoustooptic optical linear algebra processor architecture. (Adapted from Carlotto and Casasent [30].)

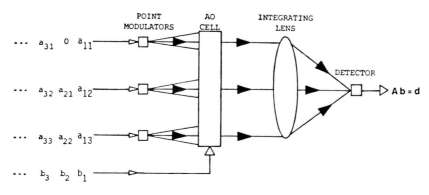

Fig. 5. Space-integrating vector inner product acoustooptic optical linear algebra processor architecture. (From Casasent [8].)

suited for the DMAC algorithm or multiplication by Toeplitz matrices. If $\mathbf{a}_n$ are rows of a matrix presented at each T_B, the system performs the matrix–vector multiplication $\mathbf{Ab}$. The advantages of the system are the simple single detector output and the higher-level basic operation of a VIP performed at each T_B (data flow is greatly simplified with a VIP processor [12]). The disadvantage is again that $N = \text{TBWP} \simeq 1000$ point modulators are necessary at P_1 to utilize the potential of the system fully.

Figure 6 shows the basic SI frequency-multiplexed AO OLAP architecture [4]. This system is similar to Fig. 5 except that M frequency-multiplexed signals (vectors) are fed to the AO cell at P_2. The P_1 point modulator data $\mathbf{a}_n$ multiplies that M signals $\mathbf{b}_m$ in the AO cells at P_2, and M VIPs $\mathbf{a}_n^T\mathbf{b}_m$ are formed in parallel each T_B on the M output detectors at P_3. If the $\mathbf{b}_m$ vectors are the rows of a matrix $\mathbf{B}$, the output (each T_B) is the matrix–vector

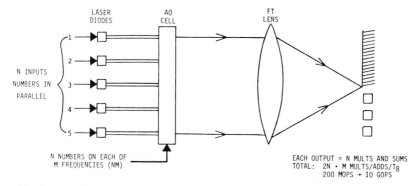

Fig. 6. Space-integrating frequency-multiplexed vector inner product acoustooptic optical linear algebra processor architecture. (From Casasent *et al.* [4].)

TABLE I

Data Encoding for Fig. 6 to Achieve All Basic Linear Algebra Equations[12]

Operation	Notation	AO cell	Point modulators	Applications
Matrix-vector multiplication	**Ab**	$\mathbf{b} = b[t]$	$\mathbf{A} = a[t, x]$	Banded matrix multiplication Solve banded matrix problems Solve triangular matrix problems (feedback to AO cell or point modulators)
Matrix-vector multiplication	**Ab**	$\mathbf{b} = b(t)$	$\mathbf{A} = a(t)$ (one row)	Solve Toeplitz matrix problem (feedback to AO cell)
Matrix-vector multiplication	**Ab**	$\mathbf{A} = a(t)$ (one column)	$\mathbf{b} = b(t)$ (serially)	Solve Toeplitz matrix problem (feedback to point modulators)
Matrix-vector multiplication	**Ab**	$\mathbf{A} = a[f, t]$	$\mathbf{b} = b[x]$	Solve systems of LAEs (feedback to point modulators)
Matrix-matrix multiplication	**BA**	$\mathbf{A} = a[t, f]$	$\mathbf{B} = b[t, x]$	Triple matrix product **CBA** LU matrix decomposition Direct LAEs solution by LU or QR Least-squares solution by LU or QR (feedback to AO)
Matrix-matrix multiplication	**AB**	$\mathbf{A} = a[f, t]$	$\mathbf{B} = b[x, t]$	Triple matrix product **ABC** (feedback to AO) QR Matrix decomposition without vector outer-product processor (feedback to point modulators and AO cell)

product **Ba** formed as M VIPs. This architecture is attractive since with $MN \simeq 1000$ we can use $M = N \simeq 33$ and thus require only $N = 33$ input P_1 point modulators (rather than 1000 point modulators as in the system of Fig. 5) and $M = 33$ detectors (rather than 1000 detectors as required in Figs. 2 or 3) to achieve the full system potential of this processor. The major practical problem in the system of Fig. 6 is the rf frequency-multiplexing electronics required at the input to P_2 and obtaining adequate bandwidth for the AO cell at P_2. These issues are surmountable and are detailed elsewhere [5].

The data flow necessary for the architecture of Fig. 6 to realize iterative and all direct algorithms and triangular system solutions has been detailed elsewhere [12]. From this detailed study, the ease with which a VIP processor allows data flow has been verified. In the realization of QR decomposition, a hybrid VIP/VOP processor has been found to be the best realization. In Table I we summarize the operations performed (the first two columns), the AO plane P_2 and point modulator plane P_1 inputs (the third and the fourth columns) with attention to the use of the space (x), time (t), and frequency (f) multiplexing variables possible in the data-encoding scheme used in this processor, as well as the applications (the last column) for which each of these cases is appropriate.

IV. Iterative Algorithm for Solving Linear Algebraic Equations

It is often of interest to find the solution to the linear algebraic equation (LAE) $\mathbf{Ax} = \mathbf{b}$. In this section we shall consider four linear iterative algorithms to solve this LAE. These solutions emerge by splitting the matrix $\mathbf{A}$:

$$\mathbf{A} = \mathbf{D} - \mathbf{L} - \mathbf{U} \tag{1}$$

where $\mathbf{D}$ is a diagonal matrix, $\mathbf{L}$ a lower triangular matrix, and $\mathbf{U}$ an upper triangular matrix. The four iterative algorithms are as follows.

Richardson algorithm:

$$\mathbf{x}(j+1) = \mathbf{x}(j) - \omega \mathbf{Ax}(j) + \omega \mathbf{b} \tag{2}$$

Jacobi algorithm:

$$x(j+1) = [\mathbf{D}^{-1}(\mathbf{L}+\mathbf{U})]\mathbf{x}(j) + \mathbf{D}^{-1}\mathbf{b} \tag{3}$$

Gauss–Seidel algorithm:

$$\mathbf{x}(j+1) = [(\mathbf{D}-\mathbf{L})^{-1}\mathbf{U}]\mathbf{x}(j) + (\mathbf{D}-\mathbf{L})^{-1}\mathbf{b} \tag{4}$$

Successive overrelaxation algorithm:

$$\mathbf{x}(j+1) = \{(\mathbf{D}-\omega\mathbf{L})^{-1}[(1-\omega)\mathbf{D} + \omega\mathbf{U}]\}\mathbf{x}(j) + \omega(\mathbf{D}-\omega\mathbf{L})^{-1}\mathbf{b} \tag{5}$$

In these equations ω can be selected to control the convergence behavior.

Selection among the four iterative algorithms depends on several factors including the application at hand, the number of required iterations, and the ease of implementation.

To see how these iterative algorithms can be implemented using the matrix–vector multipliers, we consider the algorithm in Eq. (2) to solve $\mathbf{Ax} = \mathbf{b}$. We use $\mathbf{x}(0)$ as the initial guess for the solution vector $\mathbf{x}$. This initial estimate is multiplied by the matrix $\mathbf{A}$ to yield the matrix–vector product $\mathbf{Ax}(0)$. The vector $\mathbf{b}$ is then subtracted from this matrix–vector product, and the resultant vector is multiplied by the scalar ω. Finally, the initial vector $\mathbf{x}(0)$ is added back to this vector to produce starting vector $\mathbf{x}(1)$ for the next iteration. The new $\mathbf{x}$ vector computed is fed back to the system to start the iterative process once more. These iterations continue until the solution vector stabilizes. When $\mathbf{x}(j+1)$ equals $\mathbf{x}(j)$, we see from Eq. (2) that $\mathbf{A}\,\mathbf{x}(j)$ is equal to $\mathbf{b}$, thus satisfying the original LAE. The basic element of the iterative processor to solve LAEs is thus a matrix–vector multiplier.

The matrix–vector multiplication architecture of Fig. 6 is considered the basic element in this system. For this system the $\mathbf{x}(j)$ components are fed in parallel to the point modulators, and the matrix $\mathbf{A}$ elements are fed to the AO cell using frequency multiplexing. After the matrix data are completely loaded into the AO cell, the elements of $\mathbf{x}(j)$ are input to the point modulators, producing immediately the matrix–vector product $\mathbf{Ax}(j)$ in parallel. The data flow in this system is such that it is kept fully active. The associated architecture and data flow for this algorithm are shown in Fig. 7. This architecture uses the encoding noted in the second line of Table I.

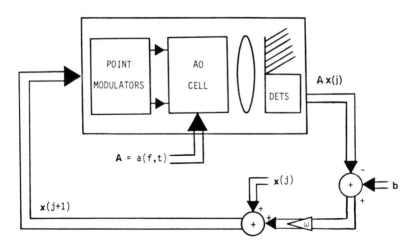

Fig. 7. Simplified schematic of an optical processor to solve linear algebraic equations with general matrices using indirect algorithms. (From Casasent *et al.* [4].)

After NT_B time units the system of Fig. 7 yields the solution based on N iterations of the Richardson algorithm in Eq. (2). If the problem is such that acceptable convergence is not attained in this time interval, the matrix components in the AO cell are completely recycled. The length of the AO cell need be only NT_B, and only N point modulators are needed. Experimental demonstrations of this algorithm as well as guidelines for the parameter selection are discussed in detail elsewhere [12–14].

V. Optical Matrix Decomposition Techniques

In the previous section we outlined an iterative algorithm for the solution of a linear algebraic equation. The main problem with that approach is that the number of iterations required is not known a priori, and thus the time required for solution varies from problem to problem. A method to overcome this difficulty is to use direct algorithms. By this, we refer to methods that decompose the full matrix $\mathbf{A}$ into simpler matrices such as lower triangular, upper triangular, and unitary matrices and solve the LAE by simple operations such as back substitution. Although several decomposition methods exist we shall outline the important LU matrix decomposition method and present appropriate optical architectures for it.

In LU decomposition the matrix $\mathbf{A}$ is decomposed as the product of $\mathbf{L}$, a lower triangular matrix, and $\mathbf{U}$, an upper triangular matrix. We assume that the diagonal elements of $\mathbf{L}$ are all equal to 1. Then the original problem can be written as two simpler problems: Solve $\mathbf{Ly} = \mathbf{b}$ for $\mathbf{y}$, and solve $\mathbf{Ux} = \mathbf{y}$ for $\mathbf{x}$. Once $\mathbf{L}$ and $\mathbf{U}$ are obtained, $\mathbf{x}$ can be easily obtained by back substitution. We now concentrate on the more difficult task of matrix decomposition.

All matrix decomposition solutions to $\mathbf{Ax} = \mathbf{b}$ involve multiplying both $\mathbf{A}$ and $\mathbf{b}$ by a series of matrices $\mathbf{P}_m$. Let the matrix obtained after multiplication by $\mathbf{P}_m$ be denoted by $\mathbf{A}_m$. The matrices $\mathbf{P}_m$ are constructed such that each matrix–matrix multiplication $\mathbf{P}_m \mathbf{A}_m$ affects only columns (or rows) m through N of $\mathbf{A}_{m-1}$. In LU decomposition $\mathbf{P}_m$ is chosen to force all elements below the diagonal in the mth column of $\mathbf{A}_m$ to zero. Each successive cycle of this system thus requires a matrix–matrix multiplication and the construction of the $\mathbf{P}_m$ matrix for the next cycle. On each cycle of the processing we obtain one row of the upper triangular matrix $\mathbf{U}$ and one column of the inverse of the lower triangular matrix $\mathbf{L}$. The construction of the matrix $\mathbf{P}_m$ is easy because it requires that we calculate the ratio of the (k, m) and (m, m) entries of the matrix $\mathbf{A}_{m-1}$. Further details of this procedure are available elsewhere [15].

The data flow for the use of a systolic processor for LU decomposition is shown in Fig. 8. The matrix $\mathbf{A}_m$ (augmented by the vector $\mathbf{b}_m$) is fed to

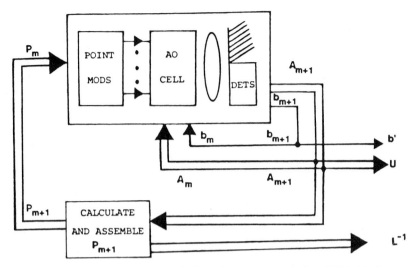

Fig. 8. Simplified schematic of an optical systolic processor to perform LU matrix decomposition of a general matrix. (From Casasent and Ghosh [15].)

the AO cell, multiplied by $\mathbf{P}_m$ to obtain the new augmented matrix $\mathbf{A}_{m+1}$. After each matrix–matrix multiplication, one row of the upper triangular matrix $\mathbf{U}$ is produced and removed to make the size of the subsequent matrix–matrix multiplication smaller by one. The new elements to be calculated in $\mathbf{P}_{m+1}$ require only the elements in one column of the matrix $\mathbf{A}_{m+1}$. These operations can be carried out in special-purpose analog hardware in $1\,T_B$ time unit. After N matrix–matrix multiplications, the full LU decomposition is achieved, and the upper triangulr matrix $\mathbf{U}$ and the lower triangular matrix $\mathbf{L}$ are produced.

Another important matrix decomposition method is the QR decomposition. In this, the matrix $\mathbf{A}$ is expressed as the product of an orthogonal matrix $\mathbf{Q}$ and an upper triangular matrix $\mathbf{R}$. Since the inverse of an orthogonal matrix is simply its transpose, the solution of the equation $\mathbf{Ax} = \mathbf{b}$ can be obtained via the following two simple steps: Solve $\mathbf{Qy} = \mathbf{b}$ for the vector $\mathbf{y}$, and solve $\mathbf{Rx} = \mathbf{y}$ for the vector $\mathbf{x}$. The first solution is obtained by multiplying vector $\mathbf{b}$ by the matrix $\mathbf{Q}^T$ and the second solution is obtained by back substitution. An optical architecture for this decomposition is presented in detail elsewhere [16].

VI. Error Sources and Modeling

In OLAPs (whether analog- or digital-encoded high-accuracy systems), various error and noise sources are present and must be considered, and their effects must be analyzed. Conventional linear algebra error source analyses are not appropriate for optical systems, and new definitions of errors and models for each of these error sources are thus required [17]. A brief review of this issue is now provided. The P_1, P_2, and P_3 devices have spatial response variations. Frequency response variations in P_2 are transformed as spatial response errors in plane P_3 and are included as detector spatial response differences. All of these spatial errors are correctable. They are modeled as additive, zero-mean, Gaussian random numbers (uncorrelated but fixed in time) that are added to each new input at each T_B. The P_3 detectors include time-varying noise that we model as additive, zero-mean, Gaussian random variables with a new independent noise random variable added to the P_3 output at each T_B. The acoustic attenuation of the AO cell at P_2 is modeled as a fixed (spatial) error. However, it is a function of frequency (and thus cannot be compensated at each frequency), and its value can be large (if the aperture time of the AO cell at P_2 is large). If the acoustic attenuation is small, the error effects can be separated into additive spatial errors and additive time-varying errors. For a more complete understanding (including crosstalk and temporal coupling error sources), simulation is required as no closed-form solution is possible.

Such analyses are essential to obtain quantitative data. They also allow the dominant error sources to be identified (and thus the level to which each of these error sources must be corrected in an optical processor laboratory system can be quantified) and determination of how multiple errors combine (we have found that acoustic attenuation errors dominate iterative algorithms and detector noise dominates direct algorithms [14]). The final item of concern is the performance measure to be used in evaluation of a given algorithm. This is application dependent. Two specific examples that are quite illustrative concern the solution of LAEs arising in a control application and in the adaptive phased array radar weight solution. For the first case we consider the percentage error in the norm of $\mathbf{x}$, or we could consider the maximum difference from the ideal. In the second case we could consider the signal-to-noise ratio (SNR) in the adaptive phased array radar application or an analogous adaptive noise cancellation application. These measures of performance noted are more appropriate for each specific case. A major reward of such an error source analysis is an assessment of the best algorithm and data flow to be used on a given processor for a given application.

VII. Number Representation

The number representation to be used has generally not been given adequate attention in the various proposed optical systems and architectures. Handling complex and bipolar-valued data are issues of concern in OLAPs, since in such systems light intensity (positive valued) is used. The methods thus far suggested for bipolar data representation in OLAPs include biased data [18–20], two's complement [21, 22], space or time multiplexing [4, 20], frequency multiplexing [23], sign magnitude [24], and negative base [25] representations. General remarks on these methods are now advanced. Biased data reduces the dynamic range of the components and detectors, and two's-complement representation requires twice as many bits (unless the newer two's-complement techniques [22] are used). Time multiplexing reduces speed by a factor of two, and space multiplexing increases input hardware by a factor of two. Sign magnitude and related methods are not necessarily useful when multiple data channels are present and must be added in parallel. This is generally necessary for high throughput, global connections, and reduced detector postprocessing. Frequency multiplexing is attractive since the TBWP of the AO cell is generally not fully utilized. Negative base is presently the most generally attractive and usable technique for most OLAP architectures.

Complex-valued data must be handled in many cases. The methods suggested for this have included space or time multiplexing [4, 20] or frequency multiplexing [23] of three-tuple data [18] or space-, time-, and frequency-multiplexing of real and imaginary part data [23]. In both the three-tuple and real–imaginary point representation, two positive nonzero numbers are present, and which of the three or four positions these numbers occupy denotes the complex number associated with this positive-valued number representation. Generally, the three-tuple number representation is preferable since it requires the allotment of one less data slot.

The decisions on the number representation for high-accuracy is much simpler. Residue representation has large dynamic range requirements when parallel systems with multiple data channels and global summations are employed. The DMAC algorithm [26–28] in which the bits of two encoded numbers are convolved to achieve a multiplication is the most favored technique and the one that is most suitable for optical realization (especially with AO devices). To see how the DMAC algorithm works, consider the multiplication of two numbers a and b, each having an $N+1$ bit binary representation:

$$a = a_0 + a_1 2 + a_2 2^2 + \cdots + a_N 2^N$$
$$b = b_0 + b_1 2 + b_2 2^2 + \cdots + b_N 2^N \tag{6}$$

The multiplication of these two numbers can be accomplished by convolving their binary representations as shown here:

$$ab = \left(\sum_{m=0}^{N} a_m 2^m \right) \cdot \left(\sum_{n=0}^{N} b_n 2^n \right) = \sum_{p=0}^{2N} \left(\sum_{n=0}^{N} a_{p-n} b_n \right) 2^p \tag{7}$$

This algorithm and its extensions to multilevel DMAC with a general radix R are preferable [24] since these representations can achieve increased performance and reduced fabrication requirements. The radix R to be chosen depends upon the number of channels, the number of bits, and the detector A/D dynamic range used and desired [24].

Many high-accuracy OLAP architectures have been suggested [1]. In one [29], the relative differences between the velocities of propagation in two AO cells appears to limit the accuracy achievable. Space does not permit evaluation of each of these high-accuracy AO architectures. This requires attention to data flow, dynamic range requirements, ease of fabrication, light budget, and bipolar and complex data handling issues noted earlier. To achieve floating-point operations, the presently preferable technique appears to be to use the conventional mantissa-exponential representation, with a shift of the mantissa dependent upon the exponential value, and to handle the mantissa operations optically, and to employ dedicated digital hardware for the exponential data processing required.

VIII. Two System Case Studies

We now briefly consider two OLAP architectures to allow fabrication, number representation, and data-flow issues to be most clearly seen. The architecture of Fig. 9 is considered first. It uses space multiplexing at P_1 to represent bipolar data (with the positive- and negative-valued $\mathbf{a}(+)$ and $\mathbf{a}(-)$ input vector data $\mathbf{a}$ fed to the separate linear point modulator input arrays). P_1 is imaged onto P_2 where an AO cell fed with three frequency-multiplexed signals $\mathbf{b}^n$ is placed. The data leaving P_2 is $\mathbf{a}(+)$ times $\mathbf{b}^n$ (these signals and waves leave P_2 at three different horizontal angles) and $\mathbf{a}(-)$ times $\mathbf{b}^n$ at the same three horizontal angles but at a different vertical angle. Six VIP products are thus formed in parallel on separate output detectors at P_3. With the three frequency signals $\mathbf{b}^n$ used to represent complex-valued data, the system achieves the VIP of a bipolar vector $\mathbf{a}$ (this vector can be complex if a third P_1 linear point modulator input array is employed) and

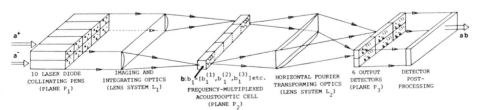

Fig. 9. Laboratory space-integrating frequency-multiplexed vector inner product acoustooptic optical linear algebra processor system. (From Casasent and Jackson [23].)

a complex-valued vector **b**. This system presented is quite versatile. It can operate on analog data. For bipolar data it can operate using biased data at each P_1 channel and employ multiple biased vectors at P_3. This results in six VIPs performed at each T_B and thus a significant increase in system throughput. Finally, if the P_1 data are fixed while the P_2 data move through the AO cell, then the six outputs at P_3 are six convolutions. If the data fed to the system are encoded (in radix $R = 2$ or higher), the same system thus also implements the DMAC and multilevel DMAC algorithms. This system has been fabricated [23] using laser diodes with individual collimating optics at P_1. It has successfully demonstrated all basic operations and is presently under test for larger problem demonstrations. The digital electronic support system for this or any OLAP or digital system of such a magnitude is of concern. One approach to this is detailed elsewhere [23].

The final architecture to be addressed (Fig. 10) is a hybrid time- and space-integrating OLAP system [24]. A linear array of M point modulators at P_1 are imaged vertically onto all N channels of a multichannel AO cell at P_2, and a vertical integration of the light leaving P_2 onto a linear detector array at P_3 is performed. Consider one of the M processor channels of this system. Time-sequential data s_1 enter one of the P_1 point modulators for NT_B. During this time the same signal s_2 is present horizontally in the associated vertical region of P_2. When the P_3 output detector is a CCD shift register type, the P_3 output in time is the convolution of the two signals s_1 and s_2 (i.e., a high-accuracy product is achieved by the DMAC algorithm). Each of the N channels of the system achieves this on different data, and the results are summed. Thus the P_3 output is a VIP of the M-element vectors. The encoded elements of one vector are fed time-sequentially to the M channels of P_1, and each encoded element of the other vector is fed

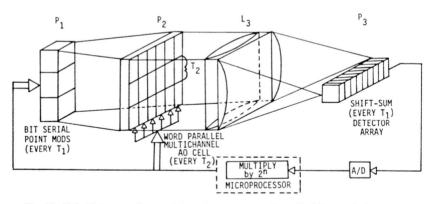

Fig. 10. Hybrid time- and space-integrating acoustooptic optical linear algebra processor architecture. (From Casasent and Taylor [24].)

in parallel time-sequentially to the N channels of P_2. The system is attractive because of its single-output data line, its parallel channels, global connections, vertical space integration, and time integration on the detector. For matrix processing, M of the diagonals of the matrix are fed to the P_1 inputs and then another M diagonals are fed to P_1 and hence partitioning is easily achieved. This architecture also easily achieves the matrix–matrix multiplications required in the matrix decomposition algorithms using only one channel of the system. The details of this new matrix decomposition algorithm for the specific case of LU decomposition are available elsewhere [24].

IX. Applications

Attention to applications and specific problems is essential to see and show the best way to orchestrate the variety of linear algebra operations required, to select the best algorithms and arrangement of data, and to determine the preferable number representation to be employed. Computation of the adaptive weights in adaptive phased array radar (APAR) is one application being given attention. Initial results [30] on this problem have been published. The solution of partial differential equations (PDEs) is another major application. Simulation studies of the system of Fig. 10 for finite element problems and structural mechanics have recently been advanced with attention to error sources in the DMAC algorithm [31]. Much attention has been given to nonlinear matrix problems since these represent very formidable linear algebra applications. The first application considered for parallel algorithms was the algebraic Ricatti equation solution. These results have been detailed elsewhere [32]. The technique proposed involves the use of a two-loop iterative algorithm. Convergence issues of the algorithm have been addressed [32], and initial simulation and experimental laboratory verification [17] have been obtained. The second nonlinear matrix operation addressed has been Kalman filtering. When measurements are linear and the noise statistics are known, a simple architecture and algorithm results [33]. For a more demanding extended Kalman filter case, a two-processor system has been suggested [34]; however, recent work involving a factorized algorithm [6] appears to be far more attractive and represents a case in which attention to the marriage of an algorithm and a processor architecture produced optimal solutions.

X. Summary and Discussion

OLAPs represent attractive, general-purpose systems. A wealth of architectures and number representations are possible for these systems. With these, OLAPs with significant performance (including high-accuracy and floating-point computations) can be fabricated. The parallel algorithms for these architectures differ considerably for others and have included all major basic linear algebra functions, including linear algebraic equation solutions with different matrix structures by both iterative and direct methods, the solution of nonlinear matrix equations, and a wealth of applications. We did not deal with the number of multiplications performed by the optical processor for each A/D conversion. This number must be large (>1) for the OLAPs to become attractive. These issues have started receiving attention only lately, and we expect to see much more interesting work in this area. The future for this technology appears to be quite bright and attractive. It requires digital VLSI support and laboratory system fabrication efforts and tests to achieve further realization and transition of technology.

Acknowledgments

We acknowledge the research support of the Carnegie–Mellon Universtiy work included here by NASA Langley Research Center (Grant NAG 1-575), National Science Foundation (Grant ECS-8500830), the Air Force Office of Scientific Research (Grant AFOSR-84-0239), and the partial support by the Innovative Science and Technology Office of the Strategic Defense Initiative Organization.

References

1. *Proc. IEEE* **72**, July (1984).
2. *SPIE Real Time Signal Process. Proc.*
3. A. A. Sawchuck and T. C. Strand, *Proc. IEEE* **72**, 758–779 (1984).
4. D. Casasent, J. Jackson, and C. P. Neuman, *Appl. Opt.* **22**, 115–124 (1983).
5. D. Casasent and J. Jackson, *SPIE Semin. Proc.* **465**, 104–112 (1984).
6. J. Fisher, D. Casasent, and C. P. Neuman, *SPIE Semin. Proc.* **564**, Aug. (1985).
7. J. W. Goodman, F. J. Leonberger, S. Y. Kung, and R. A. Athale, *Proc. IEEE* **72**, 909–930 (1984).
8. D. Casasent, *Appl. Opt.* **21**, 1859–1865 (1982).
9. H. J. Caulfield, W. T. Rhodes, M. J. Foster, and S. Horvitz, *Opt. Commun.* **40**, 86–90 (1981).
10. P. Tamura, private communication.
11. R. A. Athale and J. N. Lee, *Proc. IEEE* **72**, 931–941 (1984).
12. D. Casasent, *Proc. IEEE* **72**, 831–849 (1984).
13. J. W. Goodman and M. S. Song, *Appl. Opt.* **21**, 502–506 (1982).
14. D. Casasent, A. Ghosh, and C. P. Neuman, *Appl. Opt.* **24**, 3883–3892 (1985).
15. D. Casasent and A. Ghosh, *Opt. Commun.* **46**, 270–273 (1983).
16. D. Casasent and A. Ghosh, *Appl. Opt.* **22**, 3572–3578 (1983).
17. D. Casasent and A. Ghosh, *Opt. Lett.* **10**, 252–254 (1985).
18. D. Casasent and C. Perlee, *Appl. Opt.* **25**, 1033–1035 (1986).
19. J. W. Goodman, *BMD Tech. Rep.* No. L-723-1 (1979).
20. M. Carlotto and D. Casasent, *Appl. Opt.* **21**, 147–152 (1982).
21. R. Bocker, S. Clayton, and K. Bromley, *Appl. Opt.* **23**, 2019–2011 (1983).
22. B. K. Taylor and D. Casasent, *Appl. Opt.* **24**, 956–961 (1986).
23. D. Casasent and J. Jackson, *Appl. Opt.* **24**, 2258–2263 (1986).

24. D. Casasent and B. K. Taylor, *Appl. Opt.* **24**, 1476–1480 (1985).
25. C. Perlee and D. Casasent, *Appl. Opt.* **25**, 168–169 (1986).
26. E. Swartzlander, *IEEE Trans. Comput.* **C-22**, 317–321 (1973).
27. H. J. Whitehouse and J. M. Speiser, *in* "Aspects of Signal Processing—Part II" (G. Tacconi, ed.), NATO Advanced Study Institute, pp. 669–702. Reidel, Boston, Massachusetts, 1976.
28. D. Psaltis, D. Casasent, D. Neft, and M. Carlotto, *SPIE Semin. Proc.* **232**, 151–156 (1980).
29. P. S. Guilfoyle, *Opt. Eng.* **23**, 20–25 (1984).
30. M. Carlotto and D. Casasent, *Opt. Eng.* **21**, 814–821 (1982).
31. D. Casasent and B. K. Taylor, *SPIE Semin. Proc.* **564**, Aug. (1985).
32. D. Casasent, A. Ghosh, and C. P. Neuman, *J. Large-Scale Syst.* **9**, 35–49 (1985).
33. J. Jackson and D. Casasent, *Appl. Opt.* **23**, 376–378 (1984).
34. D. Casasent, C. P. Neuman, and J. Lycas, *Appl. Opt.* **23**, 1960–1966 (1984).

6.2

Algorithms and Software

H. J. CAULFIELD

CENTER FOR APPLIED OPTICS
THE UNIVERSITY OF ALABAMA IN HUNTSVILLE
HUNTSVILLE, ALABAMA 35899

I. Perspectives

A. Why This Chapter Was Hard to Write

With few exceptions, optical computers are aimed at special purposes, and though the number of special purposes may be large, there is a special optical architecture for each purpose. Architecture and algorithm blur into archirithms and algotectures. My task is, therefore, to describe algorithms suitable for optical implementation. Unfortunately, "suitability" may be less in the algorithm than in the current state of the art in architecture.

B.   OPTICAL VERSUS ELECTRONIC COMPUTERS

Rather than rehearse the relative advantages of optics and electronics, we concentrate here only on their differences as these affect software. Those differences go far to explain why this chapter differs so drastically from any similar chapter in a book on ordinary (electronic) computers.

The most striking difference is in maturity. By the mid-1940s modern electronic computer theory was reasonably well developed, and large working systems were at hand. In the mid-1980s optical computer theory is just beginning, and the working hardware is very primitive. The relative immaturity of optical computing will be most noticeable to those readers whose background is in electronic computing.

A yet, optical computers are far less flexible than electronic computers. Decisions and branching are very difficult. Most nonlinear operations are best done in electronics. A major overhead in time and power occurs for every conversion from optics to electronics or electronics to optics, which causes optical computer algorithmicists to look for ways to avoid or minimize such conversions. As a result we often use algorithms in optics that we would not use in electronics.

While both electronics and optics can offer parallelism, optics can, in principle, offer truly massive parallelism, say 10^{12} channels, which is achievable in electronics only with equally massive inconvenience. Optical computer algorithmicists are always in search of ways to use this parallelism effectively.

One of the most limiting aspects of optical computers, as of this writing, is the lack of a convenient way to do floating-point calculations. This makes questions of accuracy and "conditioning" of constant concern. These were an equal concern for electronic computers until floating-point arithmetic become popular. This gives "optikers" a useful clue: look into the early electronic algorithms for ways to deal with this problem.

Optics, as yet, has not higher-level language. It will have—but not until it develops some standard architectures, some standard routines, and much more flexibility. This chapter is a progress report in a field of active research. No text of lasting significance is possible at this stage.

C.   LEVELS OF OPERATIONS

Only two operations are natural to optics: multiplication and addition. Multiplication is usually electronically controlled optical attenuation, but it could, in principle, be gain as well. Addition is of two types: Multiple beams striking the same detector at the same time from different directions produce a sum by space integration; a single beam can carry multiple pulses in sequence to a single detector to produce a sum by time integration. All operations other than multiplication and addition are nontrivial. How do we achieve high accuracy? How do we handle negative or even complex numbers?

Finally, not all operations of interest are inherently numerical. We might consider sorting, inference, logic, and so on. These may be especially suitable for optics because great accuracy is not always necessary.

D. Algorithm Sources

At least half of the greatest mathematicians of this century have invented algorithms for electronic computers. Almost without exception the optical computer architects come from optics not from mathematics. Under these circumstances the prudent course for optical computer architects is to select a promising electronic computer algorithm, adapt it for optical computers, and check the usefulness of the resulting algorithm.

Rather than discuss this approach generally, we shall illustrate it with specific examples.

E. Properties of Algorithms for Optics

1. *Parallelism and Linearity*

Whereas both electronics and optics offer parallelism, optics may offer more easily used channels. Linear operations are inherently parallel.

Suppose that we want to form a Fourier transform of a function $f(x, y)$. If we can weight $f(x, y)$ at any point with a function $\exp[-i(xu + yv)]$ in parallel and then perform their sum, we obtain the desired Fourier transform $F(u, v)$. Since, to a first approximation, coherent imaging does this, Fourier optics has become a major part of optical computing.

In general, if

$$F(\cdot) = L[f(\cdot)]$$

and

$$f = \sum_i f_i \tag{1}$$

We can also write

$$F(\cdot) = \sum_i L[f_i(\cdot)] \tag{2}$$

Here $L(\cdot)$ is any linear operator on the variables generated by $f(\cdot)$ and $F(\cdot)$ the Fourier transform operator.

It may be true that parallel nonlinear operations are valuable as well. A commonly postulated optical computer component is an array of thresholding gates. For each gate the output signal S_o is related to the input signal S_i by

$$S_o = \begin{cases} 1, & \text{if } S_i \geq T \\ 0, & \text{otherwise} \end{cases} \tag{3}$$

2. Space Invariance

Because space is the common domain of optical operators, and parallel operations are to be preferred, it is a clear convenience if all of the operations are identical (making array manufacture relatively easy) and an overwhelming advantage if one operator can operate simultaneously on all of the parallel data streams. In Fourier filtering both the lenses and the filter have this property.

3. Pipelining

A nested set of operations

$$(O_N \cdots O_3(O_2(O_1(\cdot)))) \cdots)$$

can be calculated in a pipeline of N operators. Again, it is desirable that all of the operators be identical. It is also desirable to keep the operations in the optical domain. For short chains this can be directly implemented. For long chains periodic amplication may be necessary.

Pipelines correspond to such readily available optical components as acoustooptic delay lines, surface acoustic waves, and charge-coupled devices (CCDs).

4. Interconnections

Optical computer algorithmicists look for highly interconnected calculation channels. Feedforward and feedback are favored features. In the joint transform pattern recognition, two parallel Fourier transforms are performed in such a way that perfect spatial alignment occurs. A nonlinear real-time recording of their mutual interference is addressed with a coherent optical beam. The resulting wavefront is then Fourier transformed to obtain the cross-correlation. Thus two parallel channels become one. Less developed but also clearly important is lateral interconnect.

5. *Accuracy Requirements*

Analog optical processor arrays with 10^6 parallel channels, each working to at least 1% absolute accuracy, are dreamed of and can certainly be made. Doing much better than that will clearly be expensive and unreliable. Thus the accuracy required of a single channel must be strictly limited. The 1% figure seems desirable but is clearly somewhat arbitrary.

What is important is that 1% is between 8 (1/64) and 9 (1/128) bits. Therefore we must choose channel operations in which 8- to 9-bit accuracy is acceptable. If we need greater accuracy, we must use multiple channels (in space, time, or both). The ways in which this can be done are not the subject of this chapter. Suffice it to note that using these multiple channels is often very costly in speed, size, power consumption, cost, and so on. It is a cost worth avoiding when possible.

6. *Limited Primitives*

Algorithms that use only operations that are easy (natural?) to optics are to be preferred because we are not required to get in and out of the optical domain and pay the very unpleasant power, speed, size, and cost penalties that this always entails.

The only two linear primitives available are addition and multiplication. Furthermore, except in coherent optics, we restrict ourselves to addition and multiplication of nonnegative quantities. Signed (real) numbers are represented using multiple nonnegative channels.

Relatively easy nonlinear primitives are thresholding for single signals and the classical binary logic functions.

Of course we can have what we call derived primitives, which are subroutines involving the true primitives. We shall see later that division and square rooting, for example, can be derived primitives. So can multivalued logic [2].

7. *Electronic Difficulty*

As the newer of the two technologies, optics will be used only when it offers a clear and lasting superiority over electronics. This drives optical computer algorithmicists to look only at problems for which optics appears to offer the hope of such advantages. Electronics is a rapidly moving target, so applying this criterion is a difficult and often (since extrapolations of both technologies are required) controversial art. We offer the reader only one counsel in this regard: Projecting the superiority of one technology over the other for a particular task even five years from now is at best difficult and likely impossible. Both are in rapid flux.

8. *Imbedding*

As we develop more optical computing systems, we must come to view them as paradigms. An algorithm is attractive if it can be made isomorphic with an algorithm already successfully used in optical computing.

F. A Note on Complexity

A straightforward multiplication of two $N \times N$ matrices requires precisely N^3 multiples and N^3 additions. The computational complexity is said to be precisely N^3. More complex operations can allow computation in a number of steps of order roughly $N^{2.5}$, $O(N^{2.5})$. Other, unfortunately common, problems scale exponentially [e.g., $O(2^N)$]. We shall not discuss complexity theory here but rather its implications for optical computing.

First, given an algorithm, the complexity is fixed and represents a price that must be paid. The way we pay the price may be somewhat under our control. Fully parallel calculation of N channels can be said to have $O(1)$ temporal complexity, but the hardware complexity must scale as the algorithm demands. Alternatively, we can use a fixed and limited spatial complexity and pay the rest of the price in temporal complexity. This requires some form of problem partitioning and stitching. A rather general approach to the partitioning problem for optical computers is given elsewhere [2].

Second, complexity-decreasing algorithms usually drive us to noniterative uses on optical nonprimitives. This recalls the tradeoffs discussed earlier with regard to direct versus iterative algorithms. For large N, $N^3/N^{2.5} = N^{0.5}$ can be very large, and the complexity savings is worth the price.

Third, for the notorious exponentially complex problems (e.g., the large and interesting set of problems called NP complete) direct solution is precluded for any reasonably large N. By precluded we mean that one nanosecond operations would not allow solution before the universe either dies the heat death or recollapses: The approach in this case is always heuristic, that is, the calculation proceeds in steps, with each step being chosen according to some rule of thumb. This appears to offer a possible niche for optics in that calculation of the heuristic decision function may be computationally difficult, but it need not necessarily be done to high accuracy.

G. Prior Work: What Sort of Review?

It would be highly presumptious to label best algorithms for any application, particularly in view of all the previous caveats. What then can be accomplished in this chapter beyond the systematic list of considerations just offered? Our library contains perhaps 50 texts on numerical methods, but our library is relatively small. All of the algorithms discussed there are applicable (with wildly differing degrees of difficulty) to optical computing. Many algorithms have been specifically suggested for optical computers, some, but by no means all, of which were the subject of a recent fine review [3]. An update of that review is likely to prove repetitive, much longer, and equally incomplete. Our approach is to be deliberately incomplete and to offer instead some examples that illustrate interesting directions. Of course, "interesting" is, itself, somewhat subjective. Furthermore "exhaustive" sounds, and is, exhausting to readers.

II. Linear Analog Processor Algorithms

A. FOURIER ANALYSIS

Because Fourier analysis is natural to coherent optics, the early trend in optical analog processors was Fourier analysis and variants thereon. This work is covered in Chapter 5.1 by Saleh and Freeman.

B. ALGEBRA

Let us consider the special case of linear equations.

$$\mathbf{A}\mathbf{x} = \mathbf{b} \tag{4}$$

where $\mathbf{A}$ is an $n \times n$ matrix, $\mathbf{x}$ the n component vector of unknowns, and $\mathbf{b}$ the given vector of n components.

In other words, this is n equations with n unknowns. The matrix is

$$\mathbf{A} = \begin{bmatrix} a_{11} & a_{12} & \cdots & a_{12} \\ a_{21} & a_{22} & \cdots & a_{22} \\ \vdots & \vdots & & \vdots \\ a_{n1} & a_{n2} & \cdots & a_{nn} \end{bmatrix} \tag{5}$$

As we choose $\mathbf{x}$ and $\mathbf{b}$ to be column vectors their transposes $\mathbf{x}^T$ and $\mathbf{b}^T$ are row vectors. We have

$$\mathbf{x}^T = (x_1, x_2, \ldots, x_n) \tag{6}$$

and

$$\mathbf{b}^T = (b_1, b_2, \ldots, b_n) \tag{7}$$

Formally,

$$\mathbf{x} = \mathbf{A}^{-1}\mathbf{b} \tag{8}$$

where $\mathbf{A}^{-1}$ is the inverse matrix whose defining property is

$$\mathbf{A}^{-1}\mathbf{A} = \mathbf{A}\mathbf{A}^{-1} = \mathbf{E} \tag{9}$$

where

$$\mathbf{E} = \begin{bmatrix} 1 & 0 & \cdots & 0 \\ 0 & 1 & \cdots & 0 \\ \vdots & \vdots & & \vdots \\ 0 & 0 & \cdots & 1 \end{bmatrix} \tag{10}$$

In practice, finding $\mathbf{A}^{-1}$ requires n times more calculations than direct calculation of $\mathbf{x}$, so Eq. (8) is seldom used.

A solution of $\mathbf{Ax} = \mathbf{b}$ exists provided that the determinant of $\mathbf{A}$ is not zero. Suppose, however, that within the accuracy of our number representation we cannot tell whether or not that determinant is zero. Such a matrix is called ill-conditioned. When $\mathbf{A}$ is ill-conditioned, small errors in the components of $\mathbf{A}$ and $\mathbf{b}$ may (but need not) produce larger errors in $\mathbf{x}$ components.

Let us try to make these observations semiquantitative. We want to solve

$$\mathbf{Ax} = \mathbf{b} \tag{11}$$

but we pose the problem inaccurately by writing $\mathbf{b} + \delta\mathbf{b}$ instead of $\mathbf{b}$. The resulting exact equation is

$$\mathbf{A}(\mathbf{x} + \delta\mathbf{x}) = \mathbf{b} + \delta\mathbf{b} \tag{12}$$

from which, using $\mathbf{Ax} = \mathbf{b}$,

$$\delta\mathbf{x} = \mathbf{A}^{-1}\delta\mathbf{b} \tag{13}$$

Applying any norm $\|\cdot\|$ and using the triangle inequality,

$$\|\delta\mathbf{x}\| \leq \|\mathbf{A}^{-1}\| \|\delta\mathbf{b}\| \tag{14}$$

and

$$\|\mathbf{b}\| \leq \|\mathbf{A}\| \|\mathbf{x}\| \tag{15}$$

Dividing, we get

$$\frac{\|\delta\mathbf{x}\|}{\|\mathbf{x}\|} \leq \frac{\|\mathbf{A}\| \|\mathbf{A}^{-1}\| \|\delta\mathbf{b}\|}{\|\mathbf{b}\|} \tag{16}$$

We call

$$\chi(\mathbf{A}) = \|\mathbf{A}\| \|\mathbf{A}^{-1}\| \tag{17}$$

the condition number of $\mathbf{A}$. With somewhat more difficulty we can show (for a posing error in $\mathbf{A}$, that is, for an inability to represent $\mathbf{A}$ exactly) that

$$\frac{\|\delta\mathbf{x}\|}{\|\mathbf{x} + \delta\mathbf{x}\|} \leq \frac{\chi(\mathbf{A})\|\delta\mathbf{A}\|}{\|\mathbf{A}\|} \tag{18}$$

Thus $\chi(\mathbf{A})$ is a multiplier of $\|\delta\mathbf{b}\|/\|\mathbf{b}\|$ or $\|\delta\mathbf{A}\|/\|\mathbf{A}\|$ which gives $\|\delta\mathbf{x}\|/\|\mathbf{x}\|$. Unfortunately,

$$\chi(\mathbf{A}) > 1 \tag{19}$$

for all matrices. For an ill-conditioned matrix,

$$\chi(\mathbf{A}) \gg 1 \tag{20}$$

Some common vector norms are

$$\|\mathbf{x}\|_2 = [x_1^2 + x_2^2 + \cdots + x_n^2]^{1/2} \tag{21}$$

$$\|\mathbf{x}\|_1 = \sum_{i=}^{n} |x_i| \tag{21a}$$

$$\|x\|_\infty = \max\{|x_1|, |x_2|, \ldots, |x_n|\} \tag{21b}$$

Most writers use $\|\mathbf{x}\|_2$.

The corresponding matrix norm is

$$\|\mathbf{A}\| = \max\|\mathbf{Ax}\| \tag{22}$$

for $\|\mathbf{x}\| = 1$. It follows that

$$\|\mathbf{A}\| = |\lambda|_{\max} \tag{23}$$

is the dominant eigenvalue of $\mathbf{A}$. Of course, for a singular matrix $|\lambda|_{\min} = 0$, and no meaningful $\mathbf{x}$ can be calculated. Also,

$$\chi(\mathbf{A}) = \frac{|\lambda|_{\max}}{|\lambda|_{\min}} \tag{24}$$

We need not accept $\chi(\mathbf{A})$ as given, however. Consider the two equations $100x_1 + 200x_2 = 160$ and $x_1 + 4x_2 = 2$. We have

$$A = \begin{bmatrix} 100 & 200 \\ 1 & 4 \end{bmatrix}$$

and

$$\chi(\mathbf{A}) \sim 200$$

This is fully equivalent to the equations $x_1 + 2x_2 = 1.6$ and $x_1 + 4x_2 = 2$, for which

$$\mathbf{A} = \begin{bmatrix} 1 & 2 \\ 1 & 4 \end{bmatrix}$$

and $\chi(\mathbf{A}) = 4$. A simple normalization has changed an ill-conditioned matrix into a well-conditioned one. In general, we can change

$$\mathbf{Ax} = \mathbf{b} \tag{25}$$

into $\mathbf{SA'x} = \mathbf{A'x} = \mathbf{Sb} = \mathbf{b'}$, where $\mathbf{S}$ is diagonal. Thus, in the 2×2 case,

$$\mathbf{S} = \begin{bmatrix} S_1 & 0 \\ 0 & S_2 \end{bmatrix}$$

and

$$\mathbf{SA} = \begin{bmatrix} S_1 \cdot 100 & S_1 \cdot 200 \\ S_2 \cdot 1 & S_2 \cdot 4 \end{bmatrix}$$

so we used

$$\mathbf{S} = \begin{bmatrix} 0.01 & 0 \\ 0 & 1 \end{bmatrix}$$

A good general rule is to equilibrate the rows, that is,

$$S_i[(a_{i1})^2 + (a_{i2})^2 + \cdots + (a_{in})^2]^{1/2} = 1$$

Thus, in our case,

$$S_1[(100)^2 + (200)^2]^{1/2} = 1 \quad \text{and} \quad S_2[(100)^2 + (4)^2]^{1/2} = 1$$

Unfortunately, this leads to complex eigenvalues. There appears to be no general rule that always works.

Besides ill-posing (poor conditioning), two other major error sources occur: roundoff and error accumulation. Roundoff comes from inequate dynamic range. Chains of calculations can easily allow errors to add. Both problems can be severe.

In an excellent analog processor a $1:100$ repeatability might be achieved. We can, in principle, expect to solve equations with $\chi(\mathbf{A}) < 100$. But to get $\mathbf{x}$ to 10% accuracy we need a problem with $\chi(\mathbf{A}) < 10$. This is fairly restrictive, especially if no equilibrium is done. Even for an $\mathbf{A}$ with a promising $\chi(\mathbf{A})$, the dynamic range can still be a problem if it approaches 100. Thus a purely analog $\mathbf{Ax} = \mathbf{b}$ solver will have a fairly limited set of amenable problems.

C. ITERATIVE VERSUS DIRECT ALGORITHMS

The simple problem of linear equations with N unknowns is a good paradigm for discussing iterative versus direct algorithms. We represent the problem as seeking a solution vector $\mathbf{x}$ satisfying

$$\mathbf{Ax} = \mathbf{b} \tag{26}$$

where $\mathbf{A}$ is a given N by N matrix and $\mathbf{b}$ a given N-component vector.

There are certainly hundreds of algorithms for solving this problem, all of which could be implemented optically. Which should we choose? Certainly all of the criteria discussed in Section II apply. Another important criterion is solution accuracy. Given the limited accuracy of an optical computer (which can, of course, greatly exceed the channel accuracy), we should choose only those algorithms that give adequately accurate results adequately often. Note two things: First, better than adequate is acceptable, but not if other costs are too high, and second, adequacy is highly situation dependent. Other criteria of importance are speed, size, cost, and power consumption. Tradeoffs are necessary.

A famous direct algorithm is Gaussian elimination with pivoting. All linear algebra books teach this method. It gives the answer in a fully predictable number of operations. However, the basic operations involve such optical nonprimitives as division, search for the largest number, and rearrangement of the rows in the matrix. It gives relatively good accuracy (a concept we shall refine later).

Iterative $\mathbf{Ax} = \mathbf{b}$ solvers are somewhat less familiar but also abundant. The one shown here is chosen for only one reason: It is easy to explain. Let us rewrite $\mathbf{A}$ in the form

$$\mathbf{A} = \mathbf{L} + \mathbf{D} + \mathbf{U} \tag{27}$$

where

$$\mathbf{D} = \begin{bmatrix} a_{11} & & & \\ & a_{22} & & 0 \\ & & \ddots & \\ 0 & & & a_{nn} \end{bmatrix}, \tag{28}$$

$\mathbf{L}$ is a matrix nonzero and equal to $\mathbf{A}$ only below the diagonal, and $\mathbf{U}$ is nonzero and equal to $\mathbf{A}$ only above the diagonal. If $A_{kk} \neq 0$ for $k = 1, 2, \ldots, N$; then

$$\mathbf{D}^{-1} = \begin{bmatrix} a_{11}^{-1} & & & \\ & a_{22}^{-1} & & 0 \\ & & \ddots & \\ 0 & & & a_{nn}^{-1} \end{bmatrix} \tag{29}$$

Obviously,

$$\mathbf{D}^{-1}(\mathbf{L} + \mathbf{U})\mathbf{x} + \mathbf{x} = \mathbf{D}^{-1}\mathbf{b} \tag{30}$$

or

$$\mathbf{x} = \mathbf{A}'\mathbf{x} + \mathbf{b}' \tag{31}$$

where

$$\mathbf{A}' = \mathbf{D}^{-1}(\mathbf{L} + \mathbf{U}) \tag{32}$$

and

$$\mathbf{b}' = \mathbf{D}^{-1}\mathbf{b} \tag{33}$$

It is easy to precalculate $\mathbf{A}'$ and $\mathbf{b}'$. We can then guess a vector $\mathbf{x}_0$ and calculate

$$\mathbf{x}_1 = \mathbf{A}'\mathbf{x}_0 + \mathbf{b}'$$
$$\mathbf{x}_2 = \mathbf{a}'\mathbf{x}_1 + \mathbf{b}' \tag{34}$$
$$\vdots$$

Under some convergence conditions on $\mathbf{A}$, we have

$$\lim_{n \to \infty} \mathbf{x}_n \to \mathbf{x} \tag{35}$$

The speed of convergence varies with $\mathbf{x}_0$, $\mathbf{A}$, and $\mathbf{b}$. Therefore we must either go to the predetermined large n or test $\mathbf{x}_n$ for satisfactory convergence. The disadvantages (unpredictability, perhaps lower accuracy, convergence testing, etc.) may be overwhelmed in some cases by some clear advantages for optics. The only operations are multiplication and addition, both optical primitives. It is well suited for continuous feedback. In other words, it is well matched to optics.

Which type of algorithm is better for optics? The answer is clear but unsatisfying: It depends on the details of the particular problem.

D. RELAXATION METHOD

One difficulty with algorithms borrowed from digital computing is that time (iteration number, etc.) in digital computing is definitely discretized. This need not be the case in optics. Caulfield and Cheng [4] described a method borrowed more from control theory than from digital computing. A parallel $\mathbf{A}\mathbf{x} = \mathbf{y}$ solver is assumed to exist. We then compared y_i at any time with the target b_i and drive x_i in a direction to compensate for the observed discrepancies. When this does converge (which it will if all the eigenvalues of $\mathbf{A}$ are positive), it converges to the desired answer continuously in time with a rate of roughly $\exp(-\lambda_{\text{MIN}}t)$, where λ_{MIN} is the minimum eigenvalue of $\mathbf{A}$. Thus the temporal complexity is $O(1)$ independent of N. Of course the spatial complexity is $O(N^2)$, the matrix size.

III. Nonlinear Mathematics

A. FUNDAMENTAL NATURE OF POLYNOMIALS

The most general form of nonlinear function is the polynomial. Some functions are polynomial, but all can be expressed (approximated) as polynomials by Taylor series, Pade rational functions, Chebyshev approximation, and so on. Thus, if we can evaluate polynomials, we can evaluate any function.

B. POLYNOMIAL EVALUATION

Two types of methods are available for polynomial evaluation: matrix–matrix multiplication and most other deterministic operations. We can either work with the coefficients as given or we can preprocess the coefficients prior to evaluation. Thus matrix–matrix multiplication has $O(N^3)$ complexity without preprocessing but an approach $O(N^{2.5})$ complexity with preprocessing. An Nth-order polynomial evaluation must involve at least N multiples and at least N additions without preprocessing. That is, it is $O(N)$. The unique optimum algorithm for evaluating the Nth-order polynomial P_n is Horner's rule:

$$P_N(x) = a_N x^N + a_{N-1} x^{N-1} + \cdots + a_0$$
$$= (\cdots ((a_N x + a_{N-1})x + a_{N-2})x \cdots a_0 \tag{36}$$

Here, of course, a_k is the coefficient of x^k in P_n, that is, it is a pipeline of operations of the form

$$C_N = a_N \tag{37a}$$

$$C_{N-1} = a_N x + a_{N-1} \tag{37b}$$

$$C_{N-2} = C_{N-1} x + a_{N-2} \tag{38}$$

$$\vdots$$

$$C_0 = C_1 x + a_0$$
$$= P_N(x)$$

Performing the

$$C_k = C_{k+1} x + a_k$$

operation and pipelining the results is a straightforward optical operation (although straightforward does not mean without experimental difficulty). All a and x can be real or complex, analog or digital. Extension to functions of multiple variables is also straightforward [5]. Since this chapter is about algorithms not hardware, we omit the hardware description here.

C. Accuracy

Because all a and x cannot be represented with perfect accuracy, $P_N(x)$ does not give perfect accuracy. But how are those accuracies or inaccuracies related? This is the conditioning problem explored earlier for linear algebra. As might be expected, conditioning for nonlinear problem is much more complex. There appears to be no general theory of conditioning in polynomial evaluation schemes. The Horner form is known to be stable in the sense that a small relative error in any coefficient produces only a small relative error in $P_N(x)$. Other polynomial forms (e.g., Chebyshev or root product) are even better conditioned, but they are not so amenable to optical evaluation.

For root finding, the conditioning can be quite complex and disasterous. Root-finding methods for optics are, as yet, quite primitive.

D. Analog Evaluation

By definition, nonlinear functions such as $P(x)$ can change very rapidly with S. Thus the range of x values over which a purely analog evaluation might be accurate could be quite small. Of course, a Taylor or similar expression helps. We might, on the other hand, be concerned not with accuracy at all $P_N(x)$ values but only with accuracy near $P_N(x) = 0$. An analog scan of x from 0 to a and of $y = 1/x$ from 0 to $1/a$ might help find approximate roots of $P_N(x)$.

E. Algorithms

We have noted earlier that all functions can be represented accurately as polynomials or, better, rational functions (ratios or polynomials). This allows one or two polynomial evaluators with a few stored coefficients per function to serve as a general function evaluator or look-up table.

A second application is as nonlinear operator. Perhaps the two most useful operators are

$$D(x) = \frac{1}{x} \tag{39}$$

and

$$R(x) = \sqrt{x} \tag{40}$$

Having dealt with division earlier [6]. We turn now to the square-root operation for illustration.

These and other operators can be evaluated as follows. Write the operation as an equation, for instance,

$$f(x) = a - \frac{1}{x} \tag{41a}$$

or

$$f(x) = a - x^2 \tag{41b}$$

or

$$f(x) = a - \frac{1}{x^2} \tag{41c}$$

or (2) use Newton's method to improve on initial guess x_0, that is,

$$x_{n+1} = \frac{x_n - f(x_n)}{f'(x_n)} \tag{42}$$

where f' indicates the derivative. Let us illustrate with

$$f(x) = \frac{a-1}{x^2} \tag{43}$$

It is easy to find

$$f'(x) = \frac{2}{x^3} \tag{44}$$

Thus

$$f(x_n) = a - \frac{1}{x_n^2} \tag{45}$$

and

$$f'(x_n) = \frac{2}{x_n^3} \tag{46}$$

Thus

$$x_{n+1} = x_n - \frac{a - 1/x_n^2}{2/x_n^3}$$

$$= x_n - \frac{ax_n^3 - x_n}{2} \tag{47}$$

Starting with a good guess x_0, we have

$$x_1 = x_0 - \frac{ax_0^3 - x_0}{2} = f_1(x_0) \tag{48}$$

and

$$x_2 = x_1 - \frac{ax_1^3 - x_1}{2}$$

$$= \left(\frac{X_0}{4}\right) - \left(\frac{aX_0^3}{4}\right) + \left(\frac{aX_0^3}{16}\right)(1 - 3ax_0^2 + 3a^2x_0^4 - a^3X_0^6) \qquad (49)$$

We can progress in this way through enough iterations to give good first-pass accuracy.

IV. Hybrid Processors

Having noted accuracy problems with analog processors, we now seek ways to use digital processors to improve their accuracy. Presumed in this is the assumption that the net hybrid processor offers some advantage over its purely digital equivalent. Generally, this means that the analog task must be of greater computational complexity than the digital task. The digital processor, however, provides accuracy bootstrapping. We illustrate the process with the $\mathbf{Ax = b}$ problem. We have also applied it to $\mathbf{A}^{-1}$ and to $\mathbf{Ae} = \lambda\mathbf{e}$.

Suppose we "solve" $\mathbf{Ax = b}$ by analog optics to obtain a solution $\mathbf{x}_0$.

We now accept $\mathbf{X}_0$ to final accuracy (e.g., 16 bits) and store in scratchpad memory.

Using a digital computer we calculate

$$\mathbf{r = b - Ax_0} \qquad (50)$$

to that same accuracy. Next we solve

$$\mathbf{A \, \Delta x}^0 = \mathbf{r} \qquad (51)$$

using analog optics. Note that this is the same problem we started with except that $\mathbf{b}$ has been replaced by $\mathbf{r}$.

If we could calculate $\mathbf{\Delta x}_0$ accurately enough, we would find that

$$\mathbf{x}_1 = \mathbf{x}_0 + \mathbf{\Delta x}^0 \qquad (52)$$

is the exact solution. Thus,

$$\mathbf{Ax}_1 = \mathbf{Ax}_0 + \mathbf{A \, \Delta x}_0 \, d$$
$$= \mathbf{Ax}_0 + (\mathbf{b - Ax}_0)$$
$$= \mathbf{b} \qquad (53)$$

Unfortunately, we have not calculated $\mathbf{\Delta x}_0$ exactly, so $\mathbf{x}_1$ is not the exact solution. However, it may be closer than $\mathbf{x}_0$. In this case we can restart the iteration.

It is easy to show that if each iteration leads to an improvement, convergence is assured. Roughly speaking, the situation guranteeing convergence is

$$\chi(A) \cdot E(c) \leqq \frac{1}{2} \tag{54}$$

here $E(c)$ is the accuracy of the anlog computer. For a 5% accurate computer [$E(c) = 0.02$]; we require $\chi(a) \leqq 25$. In practice, convergence usually occurs for $\chi(A)$ up to a few thousand. Our recent work (unpublished) allows convergence independent of χ, even for singular A.

V. Digital Processors

Digital optics must either be limited in scope to fixed-point multiplication and addition or by hybrid optical–digital. The former greatly restricts the number of applications. The latter puts a great burden of proof on the system designer to show that the hybrid system is distinctly superior to pure digital electronics.

VI. General-Purpose Optical Computers

So far we have assumed that the optical processor was a special-purpose design. Workers in the Soviet Union and at AT & T Bell Laboratories are designing general-purpose optical computers. Workers around the world are designing readily reprogrammable cellular array processors. Even here, however, we cannot freely borrow all electronic algorithms. The reason is that we lack a read–write memory worthy in speed, format, and capacity of such a task. We do, however, have a suitable rad-only memory: the page-oriented holographic memory. Thus programming for general-purpose optical computers and for optical cellular array processors must seek to make a virtue of this necessity. Since we can almost instantaneously access any of, say, 10^5 fixed "programs" to be read into an optical processor in parallel, can we define a simple approach for using this ability? This is a new area, so no results worth mentioning are available.

VII. Fault Tolerance

Unlike most electronic computers, optical computers provide little if any hardware fault tolerance. Surely this will change. For the moment, however, fault tolerance in optics is largely in the domain of a software burden.

The simplest task in fault tolerance is error detection. For instance, in matrix–vector or matrix–matrix multiplication, a simple checksum method should suffice. Rather than

$$\begin{bmatrix} a_{11} & a_{12} \\ a_{21} & a_{22} \end{bmatrix} \begin{bmatrix} x_1 \\ x_2 \end{bmatrix} = \begin{bmatrix} y_1 \\ y_2 \end{bmatrix} \tag{55}$$

$$\begin{bmatrix} a_{11} & a_{12} \\ a_{21} & a_{22} \\ S_1 & S_2 \end{bmatrix} \begin{bmatrix} x_1 \\ x_2 \\ 0 \end{bmatrix} = \begin{bmatrix} y_1 \\ y_2 \\ C \end{bmatrix} \tag{56}$$

where

$$S_1 = \frac{(a_{11} + a_{21})}{2} \tag{57}$$

$$S_2 = \frac{(a_{12} + a_{22})}{2} \tag{58}$$

and

$$C = \frac{(y_1 + y_2)}{2} \tag{59}$$

it is easier to check C to determine if an error has occurred.

The next task is fault location. Caulfield and Putnam [7] have shown that this is very simple since the postulated optical components are very simple and arranged in distinctly accessible channels.

As no no redundant optical computer has yet been designed, the traditional task of fault masking has not yet been undertaken.

VIII. Partitioning

Optical processors tend to have fixed dimensions, whereas real problems do not. Matching the problem to the processor may mean simple padding with zeros for problems smaller than the processor. For linear algebra problems larger than the processor, Caulfield et al. have developed a very general approach, which is described elswhere (2).

IX. Conclusion

Algorithms and software for optical processors must trail the processors themselves, for if the processors at the time of this writing are quite primitive, the algorithms and software are even more so. This is an area of great interest simply because we cannot, in general, directly transfer results from the electronic computer domain. The greatest challenges lie in the future.

References

1. *Opt. Eng.* Spec. Issue, Jan. (1986).
2. H. J. Caulfield, C. M. Verber, and R. L. Sterner, *Opt. Commun.* **51**, 213 (1984).
3. D. Casasent, *Proc. IEEE* **72**, 831 (1984).
4. H. J. Caulfield and W. K. Cheng, *Opt. Commun.* **43**, 251 (1982).
5. H. J. Caulfield, C. M. Verber, R. P. Kenan, J. E. Ludman, and P. D. Stilwell, Jr., *Appl. Opt.* **23**, 817 (1984).
6. H. J. Caulfield, *Appl. Opt.* **23**, 373 (1984).
7. H. J. Caulfield and R. S. Putman, *Opt. Eng.* **24**, 65 (1984).

VII

Devices and Components with Applications

7.1

Fiber-Optic Delay-Line Signal Processors

K. P. JACKSON* AND H. J. SHAW

EDWARD L. GINZTON LABORATORIES
STANFORD, CALIFORNIA 94305

I. Introduction

The advantages of optical fiber for use in communications (Li, 1985) and sensing (Giallorenzi *et al.*, 1982) are well known. Becasue of the low-loss [<0.2 dB/km (Nagel, 1984)] and large modulation bandwidth [>100 GHz km (Marcuse, 1981)], optical fibers are capable of transmitting wideband signals over large distances with little attenuation or distortion. The optical phase of the signal guided by the fiber is particularly sensitive to environmental fluctuations (temperature and pressure changes, etc.) that perturb the index of refraction of the fiber. As a result, fibers can be used in interferometers to detect extremely small changes in the surrounding environment.

Over the last few years, however, another application has been emerging in which optical fibers are used to process very wideband signals. The approach has been to make use of the low-loss and large modulation

*Present address: IBM T. J. Watson Research Center, Yorktown Heights, New York 10598.

bandwidth of the fiber and construct delay-line processors capable of performing a variety of important signal processing operations. The operations include coded sequence generation, convolution, correlation, matrix–vector multiplication, frequency filtering, and many other operations based on delay-line concepts.

Due to the excellent propagation characteristics of optical fiber, these processing operations can be performed at far higher data rates than are possible with present digital or analog techniques such as charge-coupled or surface-acoustic wave devices. These mature technologies are very effective at data rates of about one gigabit per second (Gb/s) and below. However in very high data-rate applications (>1 Gb/s), new technologies capable of performing wideband signal processing operations are required. Optical fiber delay-line processors are potential candidates for these high data-rate applications.

The type of signal processing considered in this chapter is delay-line signal processing. The signals are not optical but radio-frequency (rf) signals whose frequency and bandwidth can extend to very high values. The rf signals are modulated onto optical carriers. When the modulated carriers propagate through fiber-optic delay-line structures, the rf modulation function is transformed or processed.

Fiber-optic signal processing makes use of two basic structures: the recirculating delay line and the tapped delay line. The fiber recirculating delay line in its most basic form is a loop of fiber that is closed upon itself. Light introduced into one end can lead to waves that travel repeatedly around the loop giving output signals at the other end of the loop on each transit. The most basic fiber tapped delay line is a section of fiber having the property that as light propagates through it signals are output at points distributed periodically along its length, which we refer to as taps. An alternative to the basic fiber tapped delay line is a structure having multiple fibers of different lengths, which are connected at their ends so that signals introduced into one end of the structure are divided among the fibers and differentially delayed by amounts corresponding to the differences in fiber lengths.

Tapped and recirculating delay lines can be implemented by many different technologies. For example, they can be constructed by connecting lengths of coaxial cable. More sophisticated approaches make use of planar semiconductor processing techniques to fabricate charge-coupled devices (CCDs) using both silicon (Buss et al., 1976) and, more recently, gallium arsenide (GaAs) (McKnight et al., 1984). CCDs have been fabricated that are capable of providing delays of up to 1s and operating at frequencies of about 10 MHz for silicon devices and up to several hundred megahertz for GaAs.

Other well-developed technologies make use of bulk- or surface-acoustic waves. Acoustooptic Bragg cells using bulk acoustic-wave propagation in crystalline materials have been demonstrated in a variety of signal processing applications with bandwidths of several hundred megahertz (Rhodes and Guilfoyle, 1984). The use of surface acoustic waves propagating along planar substrates is perhaps the most widely known delay-line processing technology. The technology uses planar processing techniques to construct compact devices operating at signal bandwidths of several hundred megahertz (Claiborne et al., 1976).

More recently, new technologies are being developed that operate at higher bandwidths. These include magnetostatic wave (MSW) devices that make use of slow, dispersive spin waves in low-loss ferromagnetic materials (Adam and Daniel, 1981). Another approach uses superconducting striplines operating at temperatures of around 4 K (Withers et al., 1985; Reible, 1985). Both approaches use planar processing techniques and can produce delay-line devices operating at bandwidths of up to 20 GHz.

Optical fiber as a delay-line medium was suggested by Wilner and van den Heuvel (1976) who noted that the low-loss and large modulation bandwidth makes it particularly attractive for broadband signal processing applications. Initially, multiple differential-length fiber systems were developed and demonstrated. Ohlhaber and Wilner (1977) reported on the use of three multimode fibers of different lengths to generate and correlate a 4-bit, 88 Mb/s optical pulse sequence. Chang et al. (1977) described an experiment that examined the response of a similar type of fiber system as a function of the input modulation frequency. The delay-line structure consisted of a bundle of 15 multimode fibers, each of different length so that the relative delays were separated by 5.2 ns. The fiber bundle was simultaneously illuminated with a light-emitting diode, and the outputs from each fiber were collected on a single detector. The frequency response of the structure exhibited a fundamental passband at 193 MHz.

A number of other experiments demonstrating specific time- and frequency-domain functions have since been reported (Marom and Ramer, 1978; Chang et al., 1979; Pappert et al., 1985). The early development of fiber-optic delay-line signal processing focused on the fabrication of multimode fiber devices. In recent years, however, the emergence of single-mode fiber and single-mode fiber components has allowed single-mode fiber structures to be investigated as well (Wang et al., 1984; Moslehi et al., 1984; Jackson et al., 1985). Single-mode fiber technology can be used to construct both recirculating delay lines and tapped delay lines. Delay lines with taps distributed along a single fiber in addition to multiple, differential-length fiber systems have been investigated. For many applications multimode fiber structures are sufficient. However, for very high data-rate applications, in excess of several gigabits per second, multimode fiber implementations are inadequate due to the dispersive characteristics of the fiber. Single-mode fiber, on the other hand, because of the very low dispersion, can transmit signals having bandwidths of up to 100 GHz over a 1-km length of fiber. Therefore in very wide bandwidth applications in which the propagation characteristics of the delay-line medium are critical, single-mode fiber must be used.

In this chapter the fundamental concepts of fiber-optic delay-line processing are reviewed. Basic delay-line structures are presented, and the use of these structures in various time- and frequency-domain applications is described. Experimental devices are presented to illustrate various implementations of the basic structures in fiber form. We focus on single-mode fiber structures because they have the potential for much greater processing capacity than comparable multimode fiber devices. The concepts, however, apply to multimode fiber implementations as well.

Most fiber delay-line processors are operated incoherently. That is to say, the coherence time of the optical source is much shorter than the smallest differential delay in the device. It is also of interest to consider coherent operation. In this instance, the coherence time of the source is considerably longer than the largest differential delay in the device. In Section IV, coherent fiber processing is discussed. The operation of two prototype coherent systems is described, and the main features of coherent and incoherent processing are compared. In the last section, some potential applications of high-speed fiber-optic delay-line processors are discussed.

II. Optical Fiber Characteristics

In this section we summarize those properties of optical fiber that are most important in establishing its utility for use in the delay-line signal processing devices described in subsequent sections. This utility primarily depends on three basic characteristics; loss, dispersion, and linearity. The propagation loss, along with the group velocity, determines the maximum delay that can be achieved before the signal is attenuated below some acceptable level. Dispersion sets a limit on the signal bandwidth for a given delay. The linearity, or dynamic range, is the range of signal strengths over which the input is linearly related to the output. The dynamic range is a measure of the accuracy of the delay-line processor. The dynamic range of a fiber delay line is a function of whether the system is coherent or incoherent. Consequently the discussion of this characteristic is deferred to Section IV where coherent fiber processing is described.

A. Loss

Attenuation in an optical fiber arises from a number of wavelength-dependent loss mechanisms. They include scattering (Pinnow *et al.*, 1973) and absorption from impurities and the glass constituents (Midwinter, 1979) as well as externally induced losses such as those due to bending (Keck, 1983). In silica fibers (the most commonly used) there are spectral regions where each loss mechanism is minimal. However, the combined effect of these mechanisms restricts the useful operation of an optical fiber to the wavelength range from 0.6–1.6 μm.

Among the loss mechanisms, Rayleigh scattering is dominant at wavelengths below 1.55 μm. It is a process whereby the electromagnetic wave is scattered off small (on the order of a few tenths of a micron) inherent inhomogeneities in the medium. Rayleigh scattering is strongly wavelength dependent. The attenuation per unit length varies inversely as the fourth power of wavelength. Therefore it is advantageous to operate at long wavelengths. Infrared absorption losses from the glass constituents, however, increase with wavelength and limit the useful operation to wavelengths below 1.6 μm. As a result the lowest overall loss (approximately 0.2 dB/km) in silica fiber occurs at a wavelength of about 1.5 μm, where the Rayleigh scattering losses are comparable to the infrared absorption losses.

An attractive feature of optical-fiber delay lines is that the loss is independent of the modulation frequency. Since the signals to be processed are impressed onto a very high-frequency optical carrier, the fractional optical bandwidths can be very small, usually much less than 0.1% even for very large rf modulation bandwidths. Consequently, although the loss varies over the optical spectrum, it is virtually constant within the frequency interval of the modulation signal.

The loss of a typical single-mode fiber is plotted in Fig. 1 as a function of the signal frequency for a 1-μs delay. Other delay-line technologies are included for comparison. On the basis of this comparison it is seen that fiber delay lines offer extremely low propagation loss at very high signal frequencies.

B. DISPERSION (BANDWIDTH LIMITATIONS)

As an optical pulse propagates along a fiber, it becomes distorted because the group velocity is a nonlinear function of frequency. The dominant dispersive mechanisms in a fiber depend on the construction of the waveguide and the spectral characteristics of the optical source.

In multimode fibers the modulation bandwidth is usually limited by modal dispersion. Multimode fibers guide a number of transverse modes that in general, do not propagate at the same velocity. As a result the transmission of very broadband signals is limited. Step-index multimode fibers have transmission bandwidths of a few to a few tens of megahertz for a 1-km length. Graded-index fibers have extended capabilities with bandwidths of up to a few gigahertz.

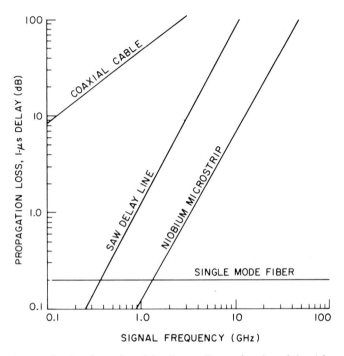

Fig. 1. Propagation loss for various delay-line media as a function of signal frequency for a delay of 1 μs. A loss of 1 dB/km was assumed for the single-mode fiber case. The propagation losses for nonfiber delay-line media have been calculated using typical values.

For extremely broadband processing it is desirable to use single-mode fiber. Since modal dispersion is virtually absent, very short pulses can be transmitted over large distances with little distortion. The modulation bandwidth of a single-mode fiber is most often limited by material dispersion (the variation of the refractive index with frequency) and a basic waveguide dispersion of the propagating mode. For silica fibers there exists a wavelength (roughly 1.3 μm) at which the first-order dispersion passes through zero. Consequently, at wavelengths in the vicinity of 1.3 μm the modulation bandwidth can be very large, limited by higher-order dispersion effects. The modulation bandwidth of a single-mode fiber operating at this wavelength has been estimated (Marcuse, 1981) to be

$$B = \frac{1}{2\sqrt{3}} \left(\left| \frac{d^3\beta}{d\omega^3} \right| \frac{L}{\sqrt{2}} \right)^{-1/3} \tag{1}$$

where $\beta = 2\pi n_e/\lambda$ is the propagation constant of the fundamental fiber mode having an effective index of refraction n_e, and L is the fiber length.

This expression describes the maximum theoretical transmission bandwidth of a single-mode fiber. It assumes that the spectral width of the unmodulated source is much smaller than the modulation frequency. As an example, a typical single-mode fiber operating near 1.3 μm has a value of $d^3\beta/d\omega^3 = 0.07\ ps^3/km$. The modulation bandwidth of the fiber is therefore over 780 GHz for a 1-km length.

In practice, however, these large modulation bandwidths are never realized because polarization dispersion is larger than either the material or waveguide dispersion (Marcuse, 1981). Polarization dispersion results from noncircular fiber cores and residual stress that cause the two polarization modes of the fiber to propagate at different velocities. Nevertheless, if proper care is exercised in fabrication, winding, and handling of the fiber, bandwidths of more than 100 GHz over one-kilometer lengths are achievable. It should be noted that polarization dispersion can be eliminated by using polarization-maintaining fiber.

These large modulation bandwidths suggest that single-mode fiber delay lines have the potential for providing enormous processing capacity. One measure of the processing capacity is the TB-product, where T is the maximum signal delay time through the device, and B is the signal bandwidth. The time–bandwidth product TB is a measure of the maximum number of time samples in a signal segment that can be processed by the device. A TB-product of about 1000 is a respectable value for many applications. Figure 2 is a plot of the maximum achievable TB-product of a single-mode fiber delay line as a function of the signal bandwidth. At high signal bandwidths the maximum achievable TB-product is limited by the dispersion given by Eq. (1). At low signal bandwidths the TB-product is limited by the propagation loss of the fiber. In Fig. 2 a loss of 0.5 dB/km has been assumed so that a 100-km length (which corresponds to about 500 μs of delay) has almost 50 dB of loss. As indicated in the figure, the maximum achievable TB-product of a single-mode fiber delay line exceeds 5×10^5 over a frequency range from 1 to 1000 GHz.

C. OTHER CONSIDERATIONS

Single-mode fibers have several other characteristics that make them attractive for delay-line applications. For example, the flexibility of optical fibers allows the construction of relatively small, compact devices. Moreover, the flexibility of optical fiber does not lead to any significant bending losses if the fiber is not bent to less than a critical radius, which is a threshold radius below which the loss increases rapidly for decreasing bend radii. It depends on the wavelength and waveguide properties and can be as small as a few millimeters for commercial fiber.

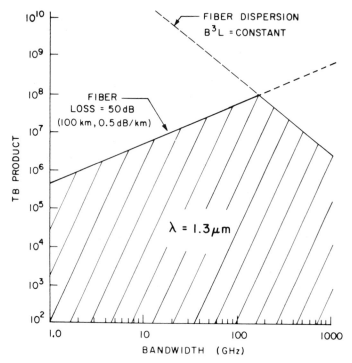

Fig. 2. Maximum achievable *TB*-product for a single-mode fiber delay line operating at the minimum dispersion wavelength ($\lambda \simeq 1.3$ μm).

Another important advantage of optical fiber is that the velocity of light in the medium is high. That means tapping or delay intervals can be made with great precision. Measurement of the fiber length to an accuracy of ±1 mm guarantees timing intervals to better than ±5 ps. Such a feature is particularly important when constructing delay-line devices operating at frequencies near 100 GHz, at which the time delay between taps is on the order of 10 ps.

Other attractive features of optical fibers for delay-line applications are their immunity to electromagnetic interference (EMI), relative compactness, and absence of crosstalk. These features are important in hostile electromagnetic environments where bulky conductive delay lines suffer from strong interference.

III. Fiber-Optic Delay-Line Processors

Fiber-optic delay-line signal processors are conceptually similar to conventional delay-line transversal filters such as the well-known surface acoustic wave (SAW) types. Surface acoustic waves with frequencies up to the lower end of the gigahertz range, propagating on the polished surfaces of solid substrates, have propagation delays in the microsecond range for path lengths in the centimeter range. The propagation surface is typically piezoelectric, and taps in the form of electrodes with submillimeter or micron widths are deposited on the substrate surface along the delay path. The rf voltages are produced at these tap electrodes by the passing acoustic waves, and the outputs from all taps are summed electrically.

All fiber-optic tapped delay lines have the same generic components, namely, a propagation medium for the transient storage (delay) of analog signals and means distributed along the propagation medium for sampling the analog signals. However, there are significant differences in details between fiber-optic and conventional systems. Fiber-optic systems have more circuit flexibility, allowing a wider range of circuit topologies than is the case, for example, for SAW devices. This stems from the mechanical flexibility of the fiber itself, which allows more or less arbitrary interconnections of components. It also stems from the high propagation velocity of the optical waves, about five orders of magnitude greater than for acoustic waves, meaning that components such as taps are relatively widely spaced along fiber delay lines.

Another significant difference between fiber-optic and conventional systems is that the latter are operated with coherent acoustic waves whereas fiber systems are most often operated with incoherent light. The reasons for incoherent operation, and the consequences of it, are discussed later. We shall see that this may or may not limit the processing speed, depending on the application. Alternatively, fiber-optic signal processors operated with coherent light are being explored, and an initial result is described in Section IV. This case corresponds most closely to surface acoustic-wave devices wherein the acoustic carrier waves are coherent. In the fiber-optic case it will allow general signal processing at the highest ultimate data rates.

A. BASIC DELAY-LINE TYPES

As mentioned previously, fiber-optic delay-line signal processing makes use of two basic structures: the recirculating delay line and the tapped delay line. Both structures can be used to perform a variety of time- and frequency-domain signal processing operations. These basic structures are described, and the use of them to perform simple signal processing operations is discussed. Experimental prototypes are also included to illustrate the fiber implementations. It should be repeated that most of the concepts apply to both multimode and single-mode fiber systems. However, because of the potential for ultrawide bandwidth operation, only single-mode fiber prototypes are presented.

We shall see later that tapped delay lines and recirculating delay lines can be used cooperatively to perform complementary functions and that recirculating delay-line and tapped delay-line mechanisms can be combined in a single-fiber circuit.

1. Tapped Delay Lines

The basic tapped delay line (Fig. 3) consists of a fiber with taps distributed along its length. Signals to be processed are launched into one end of the fiber and successively sampled at regular or irregular intervals. The tapped signals are weighted, which usually involves varying the relative intensity of the samples and then summing optically before detection or electronically after detection.

When an optical pulse that is short compared with the tapping interval is launched into one end of the delay line, the output consists of a series of pulses that correspond to the distribution of taps along the delay line. Figure 4 schematically illustrates the operation of a delay line with four equally spaced taps. The output (labeled impulse response) consists of a series of equally spaced pulses whose amplitudes correspond to the tap weights. In this instance the tapped delay line performs as an optical code generator. Since the time between taps can be made as short as a few picoseconds, tapped fiber delay lines are capable of generating pulse sequences of tens of gigabits per second.

An example of coded sequence generation using a fiber tapped delay line is illustrated in Fig. 5. The four different 8-bit, 2-Gb/s, on–off sequences were generated with a device that accomplishes tapping by abruptly bending or kinking the optical fiber. The device, called a macrobend tapped delay line, is formed by winding single-mode fiber around a mandrel that has a

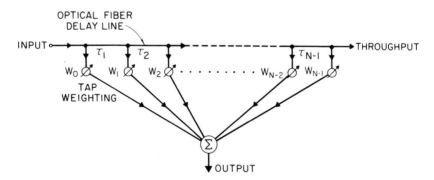

Fig. 3. Fiber-optic tapped delay line with tap intervals τ_n and weighting elements W_n $(n = 0, 1, \ldots, N - 1)$; τ_0 is the initial reference delay, which is zero in this example.

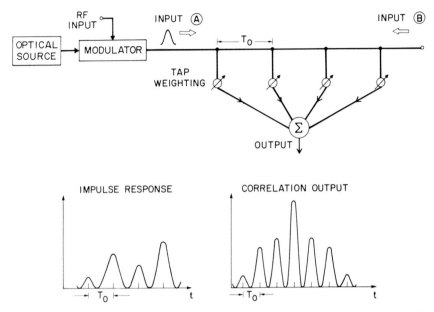

Fig. 4. Coded sequence generation (input A) and correlation (matched filtering) (input B) with a 4-tap fiber delay line.

small diameter tapping pin located at one point along the circumference (Jackson *et al.*, 1983) (Fig. 6). The tapping pin kinks the fiber and causes a portion of the propagating signal to be tangentially radiated. The portion of the mandrel containing the tapping pin is immersed in a bath of index-matching fluid that serves to extract radiated light that is otherwise guided by the fiber cladding. The optical imaging system, consisting of two lenses and a transmission mask, provides the tap-weighting and summing operations. The first lens forms an image of the horizontal array of taps which is then spatially filtered by the transmission mask. The second lens simultaneously sums the transmitted tapped outputs by focusing them onto a single detector. In the results shown in Fig. 5, the tap weights were simple on–off weightings (i.e., the image of the tap was blocked or passed by the transmission mask). The circumference of the mandrel was approximately 10 cm, corresponding to a pulse separation of 500 ps (a 2-Gb/s data rate). The variations in pulse amplitudes were due to tension variations during fabrication of the macrobend device.

When operated with incoherent light (i.e., the coherence time of the source is much less than the smallest differential delay in the device), the tapped outputs do not interfere coherently and their intensities add. In this instance the system is linear in the intensities of the optical waves, and the

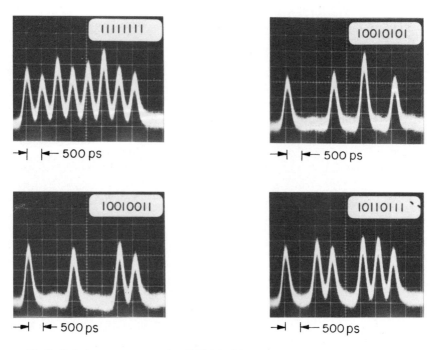

Fig. 5. Coded sequence generation (2 Gb/s) with a programmable 8-tap macrobend delay-line device.

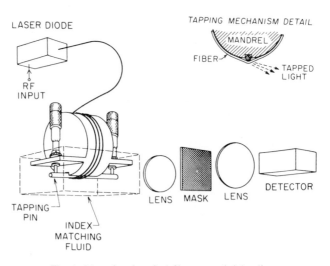

Fig. 6. Macrobend optical fiber tapped delay line.

output signal is given by the convolution of the input signal, represented by the modulation envelope and the impulse response of the device. In matched-filtering operations the tap weights represent samples of a particular modulation signal reversed in time. When the input corresponds to this modulation signal, the output contains a strong correlation peak (correlation output, Fig. 4). As a result the fiber tapped delay line performs as a matched receiver that recognizes a specific code while rejecting others.

These kinds of operations have been demonstrated experimentally with a device having taps consisting of polished, evanescent, single-mode fiber couplers fabricated on a single substrate. A close-up view of the couplers is illustrated in Fig. 7. This V-groove device, as it is referred to, is fabricated by bonding adjacent turns of a single-mode fiber delay-line coil into grooves of a preferentially etched silicon wafer that has been mounted on a curved quartz substrate (Newton *et al.*, 1983a). The substrate is then ground and polished until the fiber cladding is removed to within a few microns of the

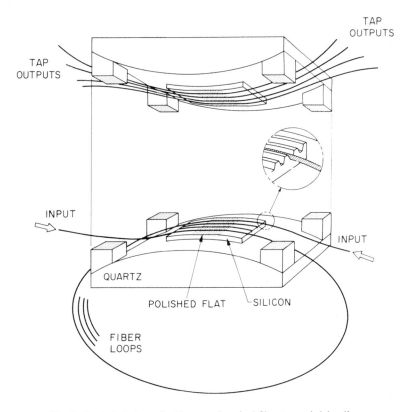

Fig. 7. Exploded view of a V-grooved optical-fiber tapped delay line.

core. A similarly constructed array of individual output fibers is mated with the first array. The result is an array of evanescently coupled taps. The relative offset of the two arrays at each tap can be adjusted by lateral translation of the entire output array, thus changing the coupling at every tap by the same amount. As the signal propagates along the delay-line coil, it is tapped each time it encounters the polished region. The tapped portions of the signal are collected by the individual output fibers, weighted, and then summed by focusing onto a single detector.

The upper trace in the photograph of Fig. 8 is the response of a four-tap V-groove device to a single input pulse from a laser diode (LD) pulser. The tapped outputs emerge at output A where they are weighted and optically

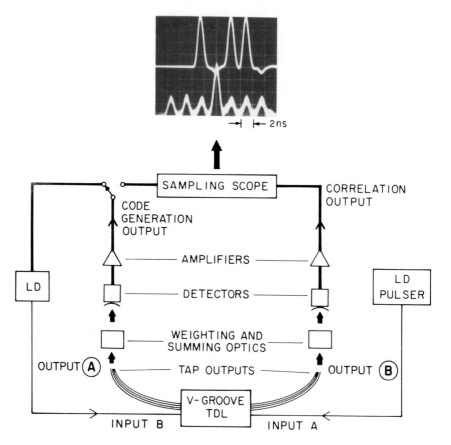

Fig. 8. Experimental arrangement for demonstrating coded sequence generation and correlation with a V-groove tapped delay line. Photograph shows the generation (upper trace) and autocorrelation (lower trace) of the coded sequence 1011.

summed by combining them on a single detector. This generated signal is then coupled into the opposite (left-hand) end of the delay line by modulating a laser diode (LD) whose output is coupled to the left-hand end (input B) of the delay line. This sequence is then sampled, weighted, and again combined onto a single detector (output B). In this instance, since the weightings at output B are equal to the weightings at output A, the output is the autocorrelation of the generated sequence 1011.

Fiber-optic tapped delay lines can also perform as rf frequency filters that respond differently to different modulation frequencies. The frequency response, or transfer function, of a fiber delay line can be tailored by adjusting the tap weights. The transfer function of a tapped delay line is given by the Fourier transform of its response to a modulation impulse (impulse response). For example, the frequency response of a device having N uniformly spaced taps with equal amplitudes consists of a series of $\sin(x)/x$-like functions centered at dc, $1/T_0$, $2/T_0$, ..., with T_0 equal to the tapping interval. The width of the passbands is inversely proportional to the number of taps. Figure 9 is a series of photographs that illustrate this dependence. The experiments were performed using the same device that generated the results of Fig. 8. The 2.5-ns tapping interval gives rise to passbands centered every 400 MHz.

Note that the measured frequency response of this and other fiber tapped delay lines is presently limited by electronic components (e.g., laser, detector, and network analyzer) external to the fiber circuits themselves. Consequently, with the introduction of faster detectors and modulators the useful frequency range of a fiber tapped delay line will be extended well beyond the frequencies indicated in Fig. 8.

2. Recirculating Delay Lines

The other structure basic to fiber-optic delay-line signal processing is the recirculating delay line, which consists of a loop of fiber that has been closed upon itself with a directional coupler (Fig. 10). Signals launched into the input end of the structure circulate repeatedly, producing outputs on each transit.

One important application of a recirculating delay line is as a buffer-memory device. Optical pulses can be read into the device, temporarily stored, and then recovered at a later time. If a short optical pulse is input, the output consists of a decaying series of pulses separated by the loop delay that corresponds to the loop length (Fig. 11a).

The effective storage time of a passive recirculating loop with a fixed coupler is relatively limited since a portion of the signal energy is coupled out on each circulation. However, the storage time can be increased by

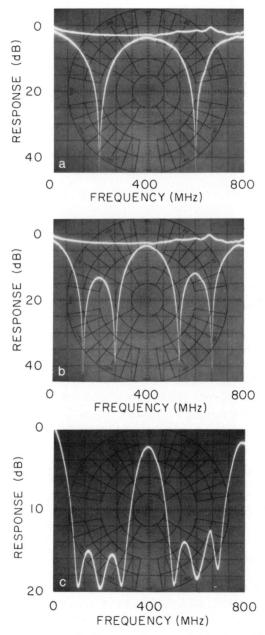

Fig. 9. Frequency response of a V-groove fiber tapped delay line with (a) two taps, (b) three taps, and (c) four taps. Upper trace in (a) and in (b) is the frequency response of the measurement system.

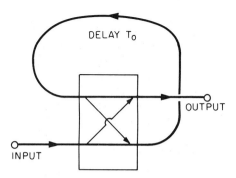

Fig. 10. Fiber-optic recirculating delay line.

using a dynamic coupling element that switches at the appropriate instant to read the signal into the loop and then switches at a later instant to extract the signal. In this approach the maximum storage time is limited to the number of circulations that can be made before the loop propagation loss attenuates the signal below some acceptable level.

Another approach is to introduce gain in the loop to compensate for both the loop and coupling loss. This approach has been successfully demonstrated using a second optical source that acts as a pump for a Raman gain process in the fiber loop (Desurvire *et al.*, 1985). Figure 11 describes the experiment demonstrating the amplification process. A short optical pulse (at a wavelength $\lambda = 1.12~\mu m$) is launched into one end of the fiber loop. With no pump signal present, the effective storage time of the loop is limited to a few circulations (Fig. 11a). When the pump is included, and the wavelength of the pump is chosen so that the maximum of the Raman gain coincides with the signal wavelength, the pulse is amplified and circulates for relatively long intervals without loss (Fig. 11b).

In the results shown in Fig. 11 a recirculating delay line with a loop length of 810 m, corresponding to a transit time of about 4 μs, was used. The optical pump source at 1.06 μm greatly increased the number of circulations of the signal pulse. The lower photograph shows a pulse that has been stored for almost 200 μs, which corresponds to 50 circulations. In other words the last pulse has traveled the equivalent of 47 km without loss. Storage times of up to 10 times this amount were observed and have been reported by Desurvire *et al.* (1986a). The maximum number of circulations that can be achieved with the Raman process is ultimately limited by the buildup of spontaneous Stokes noise in the loop (Desurvire *et al.*, 1986b).

The temporary storage characteristics of recirculating delay lines can be useful for data-rate transformations (Newton *et al.*, 1982). A recirculating delay line can be used to change an incoming sequence of pulses to an

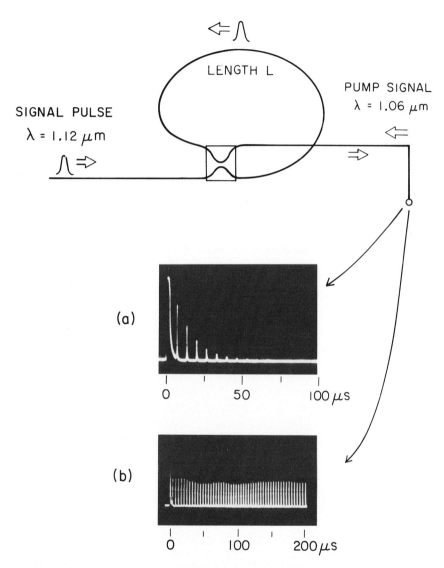

Fig. 11. Experimental optical pulse storage in a recirculating delay line using Raman amplification: (a) output of loop without pump signal and (b) output of loop with pump signal. The fiber loop length was 810 m corresponding to a 4-μs delay.

outgoing sequence of pulses with a different data rate. In the slow-in fast-out mode of Fig. 12a, an incoming pulse sequence with data rate $1/T_0$ is coupled into a recirculating delay line with loop delay $T_0 - \tau$. The pulses are separated by the time interval τ as they circulate in the loop. Once the entire pulse stream has been fed into the loop, it can be recovered at the higher bit rate of $1/\tau$.

In the fast-in slow out mode of Fig. 12b, a high-speed pulse sequence is fed into a loop that also has transit time $T_0 - \tau$. Individual pulses can then be read out one by one at a regular interval T_0 until the entire sequence is recovered at the slower data rate $1/T_0$.

In practice, both of these transformer modes require amplification to compensate propagation and coupling loss, as well as switchable, gated coupling to inject or extract selectively the individual pulses or groups of pulses. Whereas the slow in–fast out mode requires a relatively slow gate with a switching time on the order of T_0, the fast in–slow out mode requires a fast gate with a switching time less than τ to extract individual pulses from a circulating high-speed pulse train.

Recirculating delay lines can also be used in frequency-domain applications. Incoherently operated recirculating structures have been demonstrated both as notch filters and bandpass filters (Bowers *et al.*, 1980) with measured frequency responses extending out to almost 18 GHz (Newton and Cross, 1983). The frequency response is given by the Fourier transform

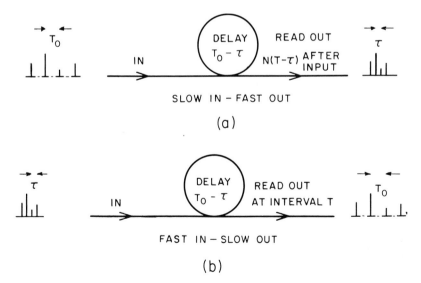

Fig. 12. Data-rate transformations using a recirculating delay line. (a) Slow in–fast out. (b) Fast in–slow out.

of its impulse response. As before, the modulation frequency characteristics of the structures can be tailored by adjustment of the loop delays and coupling coefficients.

B. INCOHERENT OPERATION

The phase of optical waves on fibers is very sensitive to environmental factors such as temperature variations and vibration. This is one basis for the large interest in optical fibers for sensor applications. For signal processing applications these effects must be suppressed, and the simplest approach to this is to discard optical phase and operate the system with incoherent light. All of the prototypes described above were operated incoherently.

Incoherent operation can be most easily implemented by using an optical source whose spectrum contains a broad range of frequency components. In this instance the frequency components of the carrier beat against each other, and if the detector integration time is sufficiently long, the tapped portions of the carrier are temporally averaged, resulting in the addition of optical intensities. The necessary condition for obtaining temporal averaging is given by

$$\tau_c \ll T_{int} \ll T_0 \tag{2}$$

where T_0 is the time delay between tapped signals and T_{in} the integration time of the detector and where τ_c, the coherence time of the carrier, is inversely related to the spectral linewidth of the source.

Semiconductor laser diodes can exhibit both a broad output spectrum and the ability to be directly modulated at speeds up to several gigahertz. Consequently, they have been the sources of choice in most optical-fiber delay-line implementations.

Figure 13 is a generalized block diagram of an incoherent fiber-optic delay-line processing system. It consists primarily of an optical source, a fiber delay-line structure, and one or more photodetectors. An input rf

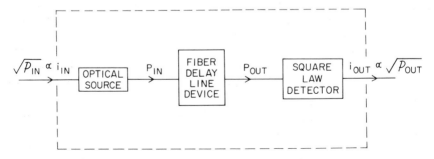

Fig. 13. Block diagram of an incoherent fiber-optic delay-line processing system.

signal with power P_{in} modulates the intensity of an optical source by way of an input voltage or input current that is proportional to the square root of the input electrical power. The modulation can be accomplished using an external modulator that controls the amount of transmitted light from a cw optical source. Or more commonly, the source is a semiconductor laser diode whose optical intensity can be directly modulated by varying the bias current. When the laser is operated above threshold, the optical power coupled to the fiber delay line is linearly related to the input current.

The optical power emerging from the output of the fiber delay line is linearly proportional to the input optical power, provided the input power is sufficiently low so that nonlinear effects are insignificant (described in Section IV) and that coherent interference is negligible. The optical output of the fiber delay line is detected with a square-law device whose output photocurrent is linearly related to the optical intensity. The photocurrent is proportional to the square root of the electrical output power P_{out}.

The overall system from electrical input port to electrical output port is linear and time-invariant. Thus the electrical output signal is given by the convolution of the electrical input signal with the impulse response of the system as measured between electrical input and output ports. Given these properties, the response of a fiber delay-line processor can be analyzed using classical transform techniques.

In the case of incoherent operation the phase of the optical carrier is discarded, and only its intensity is retained. An unfortunate consequence of this type of operation is that all signals in the device can represent only positive numbers since intensity cannot be negative. There are several possible approaches to dealing with this situation.

On the other hand there are applications areas in which positivity is appropriate, and positive systems constitute a class of systems that have been studied at some length. Positive-systems theory has been applied to incoherent fiber delay-line devices (Moslehi *et al.*, 1984). These analyses are helpful in that general conclusions about the behavior of these systems can be ascertained without knowing the details of their topology and device parameters. For example, the transfer function of any incoherent delay-line filter is maximum at the origin. Also, information about the locations of the poles and zeros of the transfer function of a fiber filter can be obtained. For instance, it can be shown that there cannot be an odd number of zeros to the right of the pole with the largest magnitude (which is real and positive) (Moslehi *et al.*, 1984).

A second approach to dealing with the inherent positivity of incoherent systems is to expand these systems, with some modest cost in terms of complexity and ultimate speed, so that all real numbers or even complex numbers can be handled. For time-domain applications, encoding algorithms exist that allow bipolar or, in general, complex signal weightings (Goodman *et al.*, 1979). For frequency-domain as well as time-domain applications, bipolar (or, in general, complex) tap weightings can be implemented by collecting the tapped outputs with either of two separate detectors that are electrically inverted with respect to each other (Rausch *et al.*, 1982) (Newton *et al.*, 1983b). By collecting the tapped outputs with a second detector and electrically subtracting the signal from that of the other, one can generate an electronic signal that contains both positive and negative values. This approach can be extended to complex-valued systems by using multiple detectors and appropriately adding the electrical outputs.

Figure 14 illustrates the implementation of this approach for a bipolar system. The results were obtained with two macrobend delay-line devices in which the first device generated a bipolar code (upper traces) and the second device acted as a matched-filter for the generated code. The tapped outputs from each macrobend device were separated individually by collecting them in short pieces of multimode optical fiber. The outputs of the multimode fibers were then directed either toward a positive or negative photodetector. Since the impulse response of the second macrobend device was a time-reversed version of the impulse response of the first device, the output from the second (lower traces) was the autocorrelation of the sequence generated by the first.

A third approach to providing bipolar or complex number capability, plus other features, involves operating the fiber-optic systems with coherent light. This topic is discussed in Section IV.

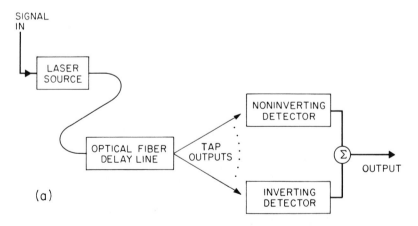

Fig. 14. (a) Bipolar signal processing configuration with an optical fiber tapped delay line. (b)–(d) 1-Gb/s Barker code generation (upper traces) and compression (lower traces) using two macrobend fiber tapped delay lines.

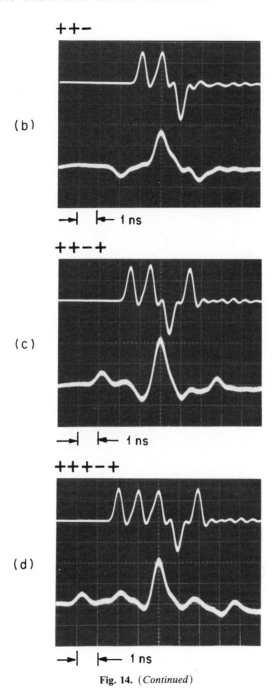

Fig. 14. (*Continued*)

C. Hybrid Tapped Delay Lines

We have seen that an N-tap delay line provides means for distributing an input signal into N different paths, each being capable of providing an arbitrary time delay, and means for summing the N signals from the separate paths. It is basic to fiber-optic delay-line signal processing that fibers are used to provide the time delays, but it is possible to do the signal distribution and/or summing operations electronically. We shall refer to such systems as hybrid systems.

To see how hybrid systems arise, consider again the prototype tapped delay-line devices just described, in which the several tapped optical outputs are summed at the surface of a single detector. This has the advantage of simplicity; however, as the number of taps increases and/or the photo-sensitive area decreases (for high data rates), it becomes increasingly difficult to image all of the tapped outputs onto a single detector efficiently. Consequently, in many applications, such as those involving large numbers of taps and/or high data rates, more than one detector must be used and their outputs summed electrically. In the limit such a hybrid system would have a separate detector for every tap (Fig. 15).

Such hybrid systems are attractive due to their processing flexibility since additional weighting operations can be carried out on the electrical outputs of each detector. However, this flexibility is obtained at the expense of increased electronic interconnect complexity, and therefore hybrid systems are limited to data processing rates that are well below the capabilities of the fiber optics. A prototype system employing electronic signal distribution rather than electronic summing is described in Section IV.

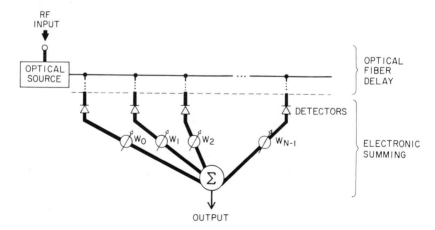

Fig. 15. Hybrid, fiber tapped delay line with one detector per tap. Weighting and summing operations are performed electronically.

As a result, it is of particular interest to investigate all-fiber systems which perform the summing operation optically by combining the tapped outputs into a single fiber. These systems may use up to several detectors at the output, but the great majority of signal processing operations are carried out in the fiber circuits, and the electronics perform only a minimal number of operations. In the next section, some all-fiber topologies are presented and their features discussed. All-fiber prototypes are also included to illustrate their operation.

D. ALL-FIBER APPROACHES

In this section we consider systems that maximize the number of operations performed in the fiber portions and minimize the number of operations in the electronic portions, an approach that should ultimately lead to the highest possible data rate. Basically these are all-fiber circuits interconnecting a single high-speed source with a high-speed detector. Since the basic recirculating delay lines described earlier are already in this form, our concern here is essentially with tapped delay lines, although we shall see in some cases that the tapped delay-line system can contain internal substructure having recirculating delay-line behavior.

In the tapped delay lines to be described the functions of signal branching, delay, weighting, and summing are all done optically in all-fiber circuitry. These systems can be subdivided into ladder and lattice forms. As indicated in Figs. 16 and 17, tapping is accomplished using directional couplers. The exact form of these components need not be specified except that certain features such as low loss and high directivity must be available. Tap weightings (not shown in the figures) are carried out by attenuating (or amplifying) the signal. Attenuation can be accomplished by sharply bending the fiber so that a portion of the propagating signal is radiated from the fiber core. The summing operation is provided by directional couplers that combine the delayed signals into a single output fiber.

The ladder structures in Fig. 16 have certain tradeoffs among them, and the use of one form or the other depends on the application. For example, the forward-flow structure of Fig. 16a can have arbitrarily small tapping intervals since the time between taps is determined by the difference in propagation delays along adjacent fiber lines. This feature can be especially important in high data-rate applications in which the physical size of the tap (or directional coupler) limits the smallest possible tapping interval in the backward-flow case of Fig. 16b. Here a 100-Gb/s data rate corresponds to a tapping interval of about 10 ps or a tap separation of 2 mm.

Another important all-fiber delay-line structure is the lattice (Moslehi *et al.*, 1984). The basic tapped and recirculating delay lines form the foundation for the development of these complex fiber networks. Fiber-optic lattices

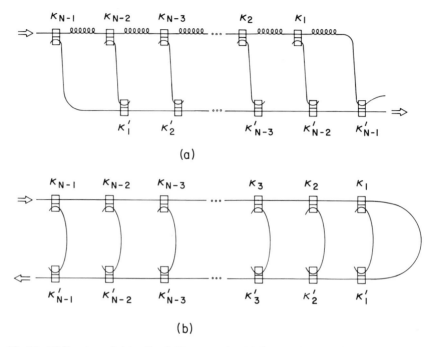

Fig. 16. All-fiber tapped delay-line ladder networks: (a) forward-flow and (b) backward-flow.

provide a systematic approach for synthesizing complicated processing systems. Fiber lattices are composed of simple nonrecursive and recursive sections (Figs. 17a and b) that embody certain aspects of the tapped and recirculating delay lines. For example, the nonrecursive section is a simple two-tap delay line with differential delay $T_2 - T_1$. The recursive section contains a recirculating path and thus is a variation of the basic recirculating delay line.

Referring to the basic all-fiber delay lines of Figs. 16 and 17, we see that the lattice circuits of Fig. 17 feature an economy of components by eliminating one of the directional couplers associated with each tap. They also eliminate the power loss at the otherwise unused port of the remaining directional coupler by employing it to feed into the fiber delay-line bus previously serviced by the eliminated coupler. This has several interesting functional effects in addition to those noted previously. For one, it increases the number of separated signal paths between source and detector from the original N paths (for N-tap ladder-type delay lines) to 2^{N-1} so that the system becomes a 2^{N-1} tap delay line. This can lead to a great economy of directional couplers when N is large. The tradeoff is that the system is still

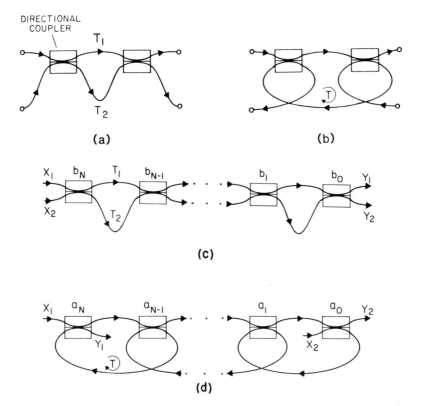

Fig. 17. Fiber-optic lattices: (a) and (b) elementary nonrecursive and recursive sections, respectively; (c) and (d) Nth-order feed-forward and Nth-order feed-backward structures, respectively.

only an $(N-1)$-parameter system ($N-1$ directional coupler ratios); so, unlike in the networks of Fig. 16, we cannot arbitrarily adjust all tap weights unless we incorporate optical attenuators or amplifiers in the different paths. This is seen in the matrix–vector multiplier described below, which is constrained to Toeplitz matrix operations.

The elementary nonrecursive and recursive lattice sections act as building blocks from which complicated feed-forward and feed-backward fiber lattices are formed. The two lattice forms shown in Figs. 17c and d are constructed by interconnecting N-nonrecursive and N-recursive sections in tandem. Mixed arrays of cascaded nonrecursive and recursive sections are also easily formed.

Fiber lattices are capable of performing a variety of signal processing operations in both the time- and the frequency-domain. One important time-domain operation is that of matrix–vector multiplication. A feed-backward fiber lattice (Fig. 17d) can be used to perform high-speed multiplications between a matrix whose elements are represented by the coupling coefficients of the fiber couplers and an input vector whose components are represented by a series of optical pulses. The clock rate of the processor is set by the basic loop delay of an individual recursive section. The operation of the multiplier involves $2N - 1$ couplers, which corresponds to the $2N - 1$ main- and off-diagonals of an $N \times N$ matrix.

The detailed operation of a 2×2 matrix multiplier of this kind is illustrated in Fig. 18. The coupling coefficients, which represent the elements of the matrix, are assumed to be sufficiently weak that the energy of the signals is not significantly depleted and that recirculations after the first circulation are negligible. The components of the input vector, which are represented by the intensities of the pulses in a sequence, are serially fed into the structure. The time separation of the pulses corresponds to the round-trip propagation delay between adjacent couplers. As the pulses propagate through the structure, a portion of their energy is coupled to the backward flowing line. This process represents multiplication between elements of the vector and of the matrix. Since the device uses a short coherence length

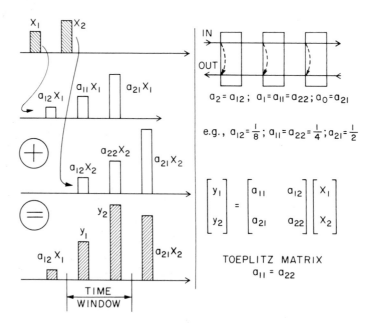

Fig. 18. Systolic Toeplitz matrix–vector multiplier for 2×2 matrices. $[a_i]$ are the coupling ratios of the three couplers. The output is the sum of the contributions made by each of the vector components.

laser source, the pulse intensities add, and the output response is equal to the sum of the responses to the two components of the input vector. As illustrated in Fig. 19, the matrix–vector product appears in a time slot, with a width of two unit time delays, following the first pulse. In the general case of an N-dimensional matrix–vector multiplication, the N components of the output vector follow the $(N-1)$th output pulse.

Figures 19a and b show experimental matrix–vector operations obtained with a single-mode fiber structure having a basic loop delay of 10 ns, which corresponds to a clock rate of 100 MHz. The elements of the matrix were

(a)
$$\begin{bmatrix} 2 \\ 1 \end{bmatrix} = \begin{bmatrix} 1 & 1 \\ 0 & 1 \end{bmatrix}\begin{bmatrix} 1 \\ 1 \end{bmatrix}$$

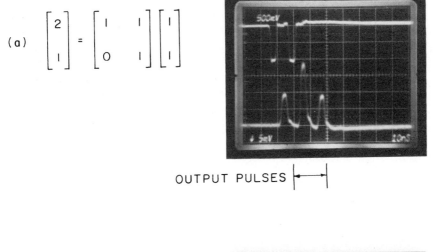

OUTPUT PULSES

(b)
$$\begin{bmatrix} 1.5 \\ 1.5 \end{bmatrix} = \begin{bmatrix} 1 & 1 \\ 1 & 1 \end{bmatrix}\begin{bmatrix} 1 \\ 0.5 \end{bmatrix}$$

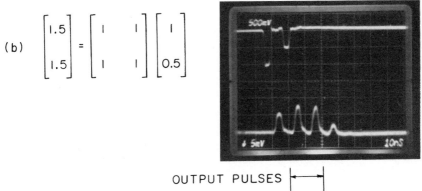

OUTPUT PULSES

Fig. 19. Experimental matrix–vector products (arbitrary vertical scales). The electronic input pulses are shown in the upper traces. The undershoots that follow the pulses result from the high-pass characteristics of the electronic circuitry.

introduced into the device by manually adjusting the couplers to yield an impulse response with the first three pulse heights proportional to a_{12}, $a_{11}(= a_{22})$, and a_{21}, respectively.

The arrangement presently uses couplers that are adjusted manually. consequently, only matrices in which all the elements along each diagonal are equal (Toeplitz matrices) can be performed. Fortunately, this restriction is not very serious since many important signal processing functions such as convolution, correlation, and Fourier transformation can be represented by Toeplitz matrix operations. With the introduction of fast switchable couplers, however, general matrix operations will become possible.

Fiber lattices are also important in frequency-domain applications in which complicated filter responses can be synthesized. Classical Z-transform procedures for synthesizing electronic lattice filters to provide prescribed frequency response characteristics can be applied directly to fiber-optic arrays of lattice sections. The response of an individual recursive or nonrecursive section can be represented by a matrix whose elements relate the input and output terminals of the section. These response matrices can in turn be multiplicatively cascaded in prescribed ways to analyze the overall response of the fiber lattice containing any number of elementary sections (Moslehi et al., 1984). The technique of manipulating the locations of poles and zeros in the complex Z-plane aids in the synthesis process.

This analytical approach has been used to derive the frequency response of the feed-backward structure shown in Fig. 20. The structure contains three basic loops and is therefore a third-order lattice. The structure performs as an all-pole filter with each loop contributing a single pole in the Z-plane (Figs. 20a and b). By adjusting the power-coupling coefficients of the couplers, one can position the poles at various locations within the unit circle. For one particular set of adjustments (Fig. 20a) all of the poles reside on the positive real axis. The frequency response for this case contains only one peak per basic period. For another setting (Fig. 20b) the poles are distributed within the unit circle with one pole on the positive real axis. In this case the corresponding frequency response (upper curve) exhibits two additional peaks within one basic period.

Similar kinds of analyses can also be carried out on feed-forward structures as well as structures that combine both feed-forward and feed-backward sections. Feed-forward structures contain zeros in the complex Z-plane. By combining feed-forward (all-zero) with all-pole type feed-backward filters, one can obtain independent adjustment of the poles and zeros in the Z-plane (Moslehi et al., 1984). Structures of this kind offer great flexibility in filter design.

Fiber-optic lattices are attractive for high-speed signal processing applications for a number of reasons. For example, their modular construction

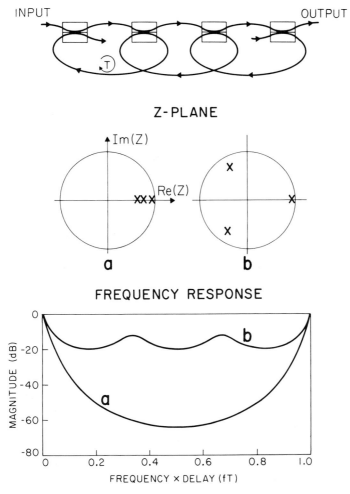

Fig. 20. Theoretical Z-plane pole diagrams and corresponding frequency responses for a third-order all-pole fiber-optic lattice filter for two different settings of coupling coefficients. T is the propagation delay of a single loop.

simplifies the design and fabrication of complicated filtering systems. Also, the analysis of these complicated systems is relatively simple since the overall response is obtained by cascading the responses of the elementary sections. Finally, since fiber lattices are all-fiber systems with single inputs and outputs, they can be easily interfaced to high-speed, small-area photodetectors. It is anticipated that the frequency capabilities will eventually be extended to many tens of gigahertz.

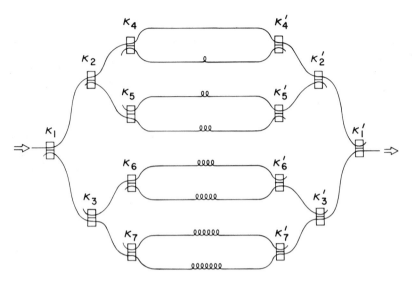

Fig. 21. All-fiber double binary-tree structure with eight delay paths.

We conclude this section with the mention of one further all-fiber topology. The structure, referred to as a double binary tree (Fig. 21), is analogous to the early, multiple, parallel, fiber systems developed with multimode technology. The double binary tree is similar to the single-mode ladder forms described earlier in that a system with N independently controlled signal paths is constructed with $2N - 2$ couplers. However, the double binary tree has one significant advantage over the ladder forms. In systems having uniform impulse responses, the coupling ratios in the double binary tree structure are equal, whereas in the ladder forms the coupling ratios must be contoured. This can be of practical importance when fabricating systems of this kind with large numbers of components.

IV. Coherent Fiber-Optic Delay-Line Signal Processing

In coherent fiber delay-line signal processing systems the coherence time of the optical source is much longer than the largest differential delay in the system. As a result the delayed signals are coherent with one another, and their electric fields add at the output of the delay line. In general, coherent processing systems use both the phase and amplitude of the optical waves to carry information. Therefore coherent systems are capable of performing complex-valued signal processing operations.

To recover the processed signals a second optical signal, derived from the primary carrier, is mixed with the delay-line output for heterodyne or homodyne detection. In coherent fiber communications systems the additional optical signal is a separate source, so the signal-to-noise ratio (SNR) at the output of the system can be significantly larger than that of a comparable incoherent system (Yamamoto and Kimura, 1981). This feature is one reason for the interest in coherent fiber signal processing systems since a greater SNR implies greater dynamic range and therefore greater processing accuracy. Fortunately, since the input and output of a fiber processing system are in close proximity (unlike coherent fiber communications systems in which the output may be located some distance away from the input), there are greater opportunities for stabilizing the optical sources with one another.

Coherent signal processing systems, however, are sensitive to environmental fluctuations, and precautions must be taken to stabilize them. In the following, some simple experimental systems are described that illustrate the basic operation of coherent systems and address some of the stability concerns.

A. Experimental Prototypes

One of the first examples of a coherent fiber-optic signal processing system was proposed and demonstrated by Davies and James (1984) (Fig. 22). In their system, a signal to be processed is first modulated onto an electrical subcarrier, which in turn is applied simultaneously to a number of phase modulators distributed along a single-mode fiber delay line. The phase modulators encode weighted samples of the input electrical signal into the phase of a cw optical carrier propagating in the fiber. The tapped-in signals are successively added in the phase of the carrier at each point along the fiber. In this way, the output of the delay line consists of a phase-modulated carrier with the modulation corresponding to the sum of the

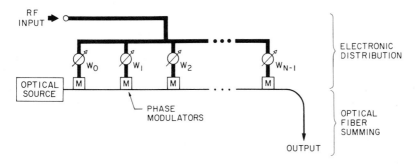

Fig. 22. Coherent fiber-optic tapped delay line. Taps are implemented with phase modulators that tap in the rf signal by modulating the phase of a cw optical carrier.

delayed input samples. The processed signal is recovered from the phase of the carrier using a second optical signal with heterodyne detection.

Unfortunately, as was the case with the incoherent hybrid systems, this coherent, phase-modulated system is ultimately limited at high data rates by the electronic operations involving the distribution of the input signal to the phase modulators. As a result, even though the processing capabilities are increased by taking advantage of the optical phase, the highest processing speed is ultimately limited by electronic operations.

To minimize electronic limitations, it is of interest to consider coherent operation of the all-fiber systems described earlier. As before, the outputs of these fiber systems are interfaced to a single high-speed photodetector. In this way the electronics are simplified and optimized for speed. The fiber networks retain their original form, and only the temporal characteristics of the source are changed.

In the all-fiber system shown in Fig. 23, signals to be processed are impressed onto a cw optical carrier by modulating its amplitude or phase or both. The modulated carrier propagates through the fiber delay line where it is separated, delayed, and then recombined. Since a long coherence length source is used, the delayed signals coherently interfere and the output of the delay line is a function of their relative phases. The relative phases are determined by the phase delays in the optical paths, which can be

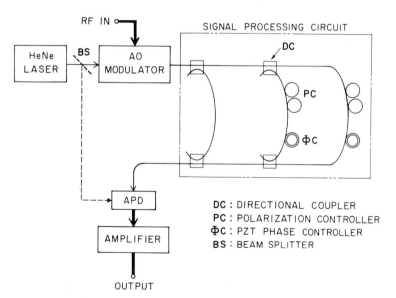

Fig. 23. Schematic of an experimental coherent backward-flow, all-fiber, tapped delay line with three signal paths.

changed, for example, by phase modulators (ΦC) consisting of electroded piezoelectric cylinders having several turns of fiber wound around them. When the applied voltage is varied, the cylinder expands or contracts, stretching the fiber and thus changing the optical path length. This method can be employed to obtain phase shifts of several radians.

A relatively simple set of experiments was carried out with the prototype coherent system shown in Fig. 23 to demonstrate the basic operation. A single-frequency HeNe laser ($\lambda = 0.63$ μm) was modulated with an acoustooptic cell that impressed the input electrical signal onto the phase and amplitude of the optical carrier. The modulated signal was then coupled into a single-mode fiber network having three delay paths. The relative amplitudes of the signals in the delay paths could be varied by adjustment of the directional couplers, and their relative phases could be varied by changing the voltage applied to piezoelectric phase controllers. The signal emerging from the output of the delay line was combined with an optical reference signal that was derived from the primary source for heterodyne detection. In this instance, since the frequency of the output signal is shifted from that of the reference, the generated photocurrent contains an IF beat signal whose frequency corresponds to the difference in frequencies between the two optical signals. The phase and amplitude of the IF correspond to the phase and amplitude of the optical wave propagating in the delay line. The output of the photodetector is subsequently filtered to isolate the desired beat signal.

A system operated in this fashion is linear in the electric field of the optical waves. Given this, the response to an arbitrary input signal is given by the convolution of the input with the impulse response. The response of the system to a modulation impulse is shown in Fig. 24. The acoustooptic cell was modulated with a tone burst having a carrier frequency corresponding to the center frequency of the acoustooptic cell. The relative amplitudes and phases of the output pulses describe the effective weightings of each delay path in the system. In this particular result the weightings were adjusted to have equal amplitudes, and the phase controllers were adjusted so that the longest delay path was 180° out of phase with respect to the shorter two paths.

Figure 25 shows the response of the 3-tap system to a series of input pulses whose time separations correspond to the relative delays of the optical paths: (a) shows the response of the system to a series of three input pulses of equal amplitude and phase, and (b) shows the response to three equal amplitude pulses with the relative phase of the last pulse shifted by 180° with respect to the first two. In both cases the outputs correspond to the convolution of the input signal with the signal encoded in the tap weights. In Fig. 25a the waveform corresponds to the characteristic triangle

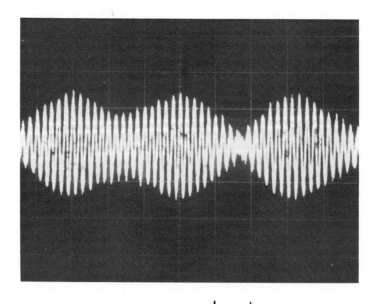

→| |← 5 ns

Fig. 24. Impulse response of 3-tap coherent all-fiber delay line. The relative phases of the delay paths were adjusted so that the last path was 180° out of phase with the first two.

response expected for this input sequence. The waveform in Fig. 25b corresponds to the autocorrelation of the 3-bit Barker sequence ++−.

The time-domain operation of this simple system is intended to demonstrate the basic principles of coherent fiber delay-line signal processing. The experiments performed thus far suggest that coherent systems have features that may be advantageous in a variety of signal processing applications. However, to exploit these superior features certain precautions must be taken to stabilize the systems. As a result one would need to determine on a case-by-case basis whether the advantages of a coherent processing system outweigh the additional complexity. Coherent systems, however, have other features, not addressed in the preliminary experiments, that are beneficial. Some of these features are described in the next section in which the main aspects of coherent and incoherent delay-line processing are analyzed and compared.

B. COMPARATIVE FEATURES OF COHERENT AND INCOHERENT DELAY LINES

A coherent fiber delay-line system differs from an incoherent system because the optical phase is retained. In a fiber the optical phase is sensitive

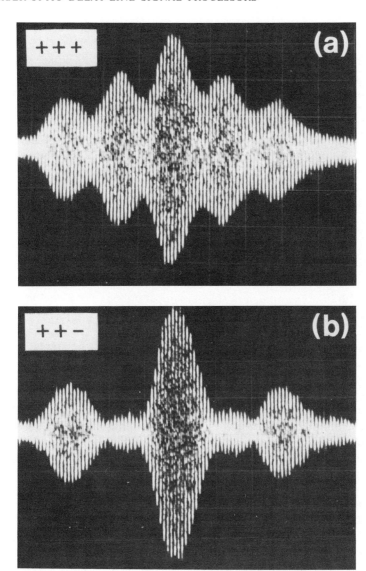

Fig. 25. Response of 3-tap coherent all-fiber delay line, with different weightings, to various input sequences. (a) Input: three equal amplitude pulses with equal relative phases. System weights: equal amplitudes and phases. (b) Input: three equal amplitude pulses with the last pulse 180° out of phase with the first two. System weights: equal amplitudes with the last two delay paths 180° out of phase with the first one.

to source frequency fluctuations as well as environmental fluctuations that perturb the optical path length. Therefore coherent delay-line systems must use sources with very narrow linewidths, and the fiber delay paths must be shielded from changes in the surrounding environment.

The coherent 3-tap experimental system described above used a single-frequency HeNe laser with a frequency drift of about 1 MHz over a 5-min interval. The fiber network was enclosed in a sealed insulating container that isolated the fiber delays from acoustic vibrations and reduced temperature variations to about 0.01°C over a 1-h interval. Temperature fluctuations were the dominant effect, causing the relative phase between the first and last delay path in the system to change by almost 10 radians. However, actively stabilizing the temperature in the container reduced the phase fluctuations by almost two orders of magnitude.

Incoherent delay-line systems, on the other hand, are not susceptible to optical phase fluctuations since the optical phase is discarded. Incoherent systems are affected only by gross perturbations that change the relative delay by an amount that is large compared with the inverse of the processing bandwidth. For example, a change in temperature of 140°C would cause a 0.1% variation in delay.

Coherent and incoherent systems have other important differences that may affect their processing capabilities. For example, coherent systems make use of an additional optical source in the detection process. Consequently, the output SNR can be larger than that of a comparable incoherent system (Okoshi et al., 1981). This feature is reflected in Fig. 26 where the theoretical sensitivities of coherent and incoherent systems are compared as a function of the processing bandwidth (or data rate). The model used in these calculations is a fiber-optic circuit of zero insertion loss connecting a 1.3-μm optical source with a PIN diode receiver. The minimum detectable power is calculated by setting the SNR at the output of the receiver to unity. In this calculation, various noise sources were assumed including shot noise from the optical signal itself, detector dark current, and circuit noise arising from nonideal electrical components in the receiver circuitry (Muoi, 1984). (Phase-induced intensity noise, which will be discussed below, has been neglected.) Unfortunately, at bandwidths beyond 10 GHz the detector-receiver characteristics are not well established. Consequently, the plots have been extrapolated to provide an approximate comparison. However, one can say that, in general, coherent systems are within range of the quantum limit, whereas incoherent systems are some 30 dB or so away from it.

Another quantity of importance is the dynamic range, which is the range of optical power levels over which the input signal is linearly proportional to the output signal. From the same basic model that was used in the

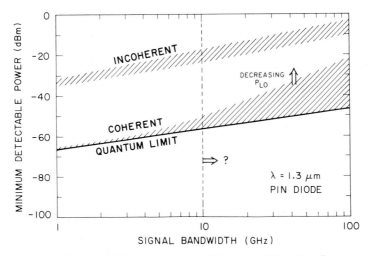

Fig. 26. Theoretical sensitivities for coherent and incoherent fiber delay-line processors as a function of the signal bandwidth. The shaded regions represent system performance using different receiver designs. For coherent systems, the predicted sensitivity approaches the quantum limit for sufficiently high local oscillator powers.

previous plot, the maximum theoretical dynamic range for coherent and incoherent processing systems was estimated (Fig. 27). The minimum optical power level used in the calculation is obtained from the previous graph.

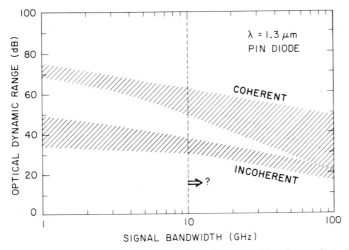

Fig. 27. Theoretical optical dynamic range for coherent and incoherent fiber delay-line processors as a function of the signal bandwidth. Dissapative loss in components and fiber has been neglected.

The maximum optical power level is based on the appearance of optical nonlinearities in the fiber that are different for coherent and incoherent systems.

At high optical powers incoherent systems are primarily limited by stimulated Brillouin and stimulated Raman scattering. Both scattering processes cause energy in the forward-propagating wave to be transferred to a secondary wave (forward- or backward-propagating) at a lower frequency (longer wavelength). Brillouin scattering is the dominant effect when the spectral linewidth of the optical source is relatively narrow. However, in broadband signal processing operations (in excess of several gigahertz) the spectral width of the modulated optical carrier becomes relatively wide. In these instances the fiber delay-line system is dominated by stimulated Raman scattering. The critical input power above which stimulated Raman scattering becomes important is given roughly by (Stolen, 1979)

$$P_{crit} \simeq 18 \frac{A}{\gamma_0 L} \tag{3}$$

where A is the cross-sectional area of the fiber core, L the fiber length, and γ_0 the Raman gain coefficient. Assuming $\gamma_0 = 5 \times 10^{-10}$ cm/W (Johnston et al., 1968) and a 200-m (1-μs delay) length of single-mode fiber having an 8-μm diameter core, the critical power level is $P_{crit} = 0.9$ W.

In a coherent delay-line system the maximum input optical power level is set by self-phase modulation. As the optical signal propagates along the fiber, the electric field of the wave interacts with the medium and causes a local variation in the index of refraction. At sufficiently high optical powers, the index variation can be significant. When the index changes, the optical phase changes, and as a result the relative phases of the delayed signals are a function of the optical intensity. It can be shown (Stolen, 1979) that the phase shift Φ due to the nonlinear intensity dependent index of refraction is given by

$$\Phi(t) = \frac{2\pi L}{\lambda} \delta n \tag{4}$$

where $\delta n = \frac{1}{2} n_2 E^2$ and $E^2 = 10^7 (8\pi P(t)/n c_0 A)$. L is the fiber length, λ the wavelength of the light, n the index of refraction of the fiber, n_2 the coefficient for self-focusing in esu, E the peak field amplitude in cgs, $P(t)$ the optical power in units of watts and A the cross-sectional area of the fiber. As an example, if the maximum allowed phase shift between two optical paths is 0.1 radians, and $\lambda = 1.3$ μm, then the maximum allowed power in one of the delay paths is given by

$$P_{SPM} \simeq \frac{A[cm^2]}{n_2 L[cm]} \times 7.4 \times 10^{-4} \text{ W} \tag{5}$$

For a fiber with core diameter of 8 μm, $n_2 = 1.14 \times 10^{-13}$ (Stolen and Lin, 1978), and a differential fiber length of 200 m, the maximum input power is 160 mW. This power limitation is about one-fifth the power limitation imposed by stimulated Raman scattering.

In Fig. 27 the effects of both stimulated Raman and stimulated Brillouin scattering have been included as well as the effects of saturation of the photodetector. As shown in the figure, dynamic ranges of around 30–70 dB appear possible for coherent systems and somewhat less for incoherent systems.

One other important feature of coherent systems is that phase-induced intensity noise, arising from the conversion of source phase fluctuations to intensity fluctuations by the optical circuit, is minimized. In an all-fiber incoherent circuit the phase-induced intensity noise power varies with the ratio of $\tau_c/T \sim B\tau_c$ where τ_c is the coherence time of the source and T the smallest differential delay in the system, inversely related to the bandwidth B. For a given coherence time, as the smallest differential delay decreases (B increases), the phase-induced intensity noise power increases. In a coherent system, on the other hand, the noise power varies as T/τ_c or $1/B\tau_c$; so for a given coherence length, the noise power tends to decrease as the bandwidth increases.

Although coherent fiber processing systems require substantial stabilization procedures, we point out that stabilization is a viable process for these systems. Unlike fiber communication or sensor systems, which are distributed in space, the entire system is contained within a limited space such that it can be placed within the stabilized interior of a single container. Because of the miniaturization that is made possible by the small volume requirements of optical fiber, the controlled enclosure can be small, even for very complex optical circuits. Fortunately these characteristics are reinforced at higher data rates because of smaller differential path delays. This will become more and more effective as the state of the art moves toward full exploitation of the extreme speed capabilities of fiber signal processing.

Finally, it should be emphasized that by operating at longer wavelengths, coherent systems are less sensitive to environmental perturbations and thus are easier to stabilize. Operating at a wavelength of 1.55 μm, for example, would reduce the stability requirements by almost a factor of three from the HeNe wavelength of 0.63 μm.

V. Applications

High-speed fiber-optic delay-line signal processors have great potential for use in multi-gigabit per second applications. For example, one area that may benefit from the broadband capabilities of fiber delay lines is in the real-time processing of radar signals. The idea is to use fiber-optic delay lines to process radar returns in-band, without down-converting to a lower frequency which ultimately limits the capabilities of the radar system. Over the last few years some simple preliminary systems using multimode (Chang *et al.*, 1979; Pappert *et al.*, 1985) and single-mode (Wang *et al.*, 1984) fibers have been demonstrated with encouraging results.

Another area of application is in the use of high-speed fiber devices to increase the data throughput of a large optical or electronic sensing system gathering huge amounts of relatively low bandwidth data. One possible scenario is illustrated in Fig. 28. In a large sonar or radar system the data-throughput requirement can overwhelm the capabilities of the electronics used to process the data in real time. In a radar system, for example, the transmitter sends a coded signal, and the receiver output is cross-correlated with that code. These operations are necessary to increase both the SNR and the resolving power of the radar system.

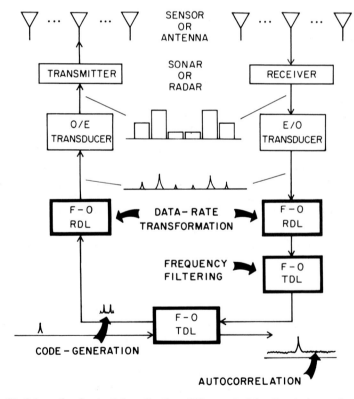

Fig. 28. Schematic of potential application of fiber-optic delay-line devices to large data-throughput processing.

Fiber-optic delay-line devices might be employed to enhance the system in the following way. A fiber-optic tapped delay line generates a high data-rate code that is radiated by the radar antenna. The returns from individual receiving antennas are fed into a fiber-optic recirculating delay line where they are temporarily stored and read out at a higher data rate. The high-speed data could then be filtered using another fiber tapped delay line and finally fed into the tapped delay-line code generator where cross-correlation operations are performed. Since the correlation operations can be performed at considerably higher data rates than those of the return signals, the throughput can be increased by multiplexing a number of returns onto the single input channel of the fiber correlator. In this way the high-speed capabilities of the fiber systems are used to increase the data throughput of a large data-volume electronic system.

Finally, fiber-optic delay-line devices may be of great practical use in the preprocessing of signals in optical communications networks (Hui, 1985). The compatibility of fiber devices with these optical systems allows high-speed operations to be performed in the optical domain, thus relaxing the processing requirements of the electronics.

VI. Summary and Future Directions

This article has reviewed some of the fundamental concepts of fiber-optic delay-line signal processing. Basic delay-line structures have been described, and experimental devices have been presented demonstrating the operation of these devices. The experimental results presented emphasized single-mode fiber structures, although the basic concepts apply to multimode fiber implementations as well. For extreme broadband processing applications, however, only single-mode devices meet the performance requirements.

Over the last few years much of the research effort has been directed towards the development of multimode fiber devices, with single-mode implementations beginning to emerge in more recent years. Fiber-optic delay-line signal processors have great potential for use in very high-speed applications due to the superior propagation characteristics of the optical fibers themselves. Optical fibers have extremely low loss that is independent of the modulation frequency and, in the case of single-mode fibers, have an enormous modulation bandwidth. These two features suggest that fiber delay lines have the potential to operate at signal bandwidths far greater than those that are possible with other more conventional delay-line technologies.

Figure 29 shows plots of TB- and TB^2-products for various signal processing technologies. As can be seen from the plot, fiber-optic devices (single-mode fiber devices in particular) have the potential for TB-products

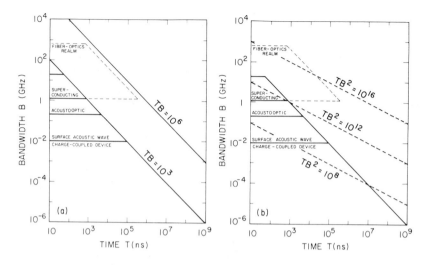

Fig. 29. Potential capability of single-mode fiber delay-line devices relative to other technologies: (a) *TB*-product and (b) *TB²*-product.

of around 10^4, and perhaps 10^5 or higher. These large *TB*-products result mainly from the large modulation bandwidth of the fiber (Section II.B).

The effect of the large fiber bandwidth is felt even more strongly in the TB^2-product, which is a measure of the number of arithmetic operations such as multiplications that can be performed per second by the device. A product of about 10^6 is large by today's standards, applicable to large electronic digital computers. From the plot in Fig. 29 it appears that fiber-optic systems have the possibility of exceeding this by a substantial margin.

It should be pointed out that these comparisons are tentative. For some of the technologies being compared, real devices exist whose performance ranges have been proven in practice. For fiber optics, on the other hand, no fieldable devices yet exist. Therefore the comparisons make some assumptions on the part of fiber optics to provide some estimates of the future capabilities of fiber-optic devices.

The high velocity of light in optical fibers requires much longer propagation paths to achieve given signal delays than is the case for some other technologies, a fact that works against compactness for fiber devices. However, the very small fiber diameters result in small values for total fiber volume and will allow the required fiber lengths to be coiled into such small spaces that when devices are compared on the basis of data throughput, fiber devices can be expected to emerge as miniature devices.

Additional research is needed in a number of areas. Reduction of the losses in tapping components is important. Although directional coupler development has succeeded in reducing excess losses into the 1% range, any further progress in this area would be important for systems employing very large numbers of taps. Also, for compensating for reductions in signal levels due to signal branching and component losses, further development of in-line optical amplifiers, such as the Raman type (Section III.B.2) and laser amplifiers using doped single crystal or glass fibers, are felt to be very promising. The capabilities of both coherent and incoherent fiber processors would be greatly increased with the introduction of fast switchable taps, and work is beginning in this area with encouraging results (Heffner *et al.*, 1986; Sorin, 1986). Further study of coherent systems is needed to establish performance limits. Fiber-optic signal processing is in its early stages, and new modes of operation, not now known, can be expected.

References

Adam, J. D., and Daniel, M. R. (1981). *IEEE Trans. Mag.* **MAG-17**, 2951.
Bowers, J. E., Newton, S. A., Sorin, W. V., and Shaw, H. J. (1980). *Electron. Lett.* **18**, 110.
Buss, D. D., Broderson, R. W., and Hewes, C. R. (1976). *Proc. IEEE* **64**, 801.
Chang, C. T., Cassaboom, J. A., and Taylor, H. F. (1977). *Electron. Lett.* **13**, 678.
Chang, C. T., Altman, D. E., Wehner, D. R., and Albares, D. J. (1979). *IEEE Trans. Circuits Syst.* **CAS-26**, 1132.
Claiborne, L. T., Kino, G. S., and Stern, E., eds. (1976). *Proc. IEEE* **64**.
Davies, D. E. N., and James, G. W. (1984). *Electron. Lett.* **20**, 95.
Desurvire, E., Digonnet, M., and Shaw, H. J. (1985). *Opt. Lett.* **10**, 83.
Desurvire, E., Digonnet, M., and Shaw, H. J. (1986a). *IEEE J. Lightwave Tech.* **LT-4**, 426.
Desurvire, E., Tur, M., and Shaw, H. J. (1986b). *IEEE J. Lightwave Tech.* **LT-4**, 560.
Giallorenzi, T. G., Bucaro, J. A., Dandridge, A., Sigel, G. H., Jr., Cole, J. H., Rashleigh, S. C., and Priest, R. G. (1982). *IEEE J. Quantum Electron.* **QE-18**, 626.
Goodman, J. W., Dias, A. R., Woody, L. M., and Erickson, J. (1979). *SPIE Semin. Proc.* **190**, 485.
Heffner, B. L., Kino, G. S., Khuri-Yakub, B. T., and Risk, W. P. (1986). *Opt. Lett.* **11**, 476.
Hui, J. Y. (1985). *IEEE Trans. Selected Areas Commun.* **SAC-3**, 916.
Jackson, K. P., Newton, S. A., and Shaw, H. J. (1983). *Appl. Phys. Lett.* **42**, 556.
Jackson, K. P., Newton, S. A., Moslehi, B., Tur, M., Cutler, C. C., Goodman, J. W., and Shaw, H. J. (1985). *IEEE Trans. Microwave Theory Tech.* **MIT-33**, 193.
Johnston, W. D., Jr., Kaminow, I. P., and Bergman, J. G., Jr. (1968). *Appl. Phys. Lett.* **13**, 190.
Keck, D. B. (1983). *IEEE Spectrum* **20**, 30.
Li, T. (1985). *Phys. Today* **38**, 24.
McKnight, A. J., Mun, J., and Vance, I. A. W. (1984). *Electron. Lett.* **20**, 84.
Marcuse, D. (1981). *IEEE J. Quantum Electron.* **QE-17**, 869.
Marom, E., and Ramer, O. G. (1978). *Electron. Lett.* **14**, 48.
Midwinter, J. E. (1979). "Optical Fibers for Transmission." Wiley, New York.
Moslehi, B., Goodman, J. W., Tur, M., and Shaw, H. J. (1984). *Proc. IEEE* **72**, 909.
Muoi, T. V. (1984). *IEEE J. Lightwave Tech.* **LT-2**, 243.
Nagel, S. R. (1984). *J. Lightwave Tech.* **LT-2**, 792.
Newton, S. A., and Cross, P. S. (1983). *Electron. Lett.* **19**, 480.
Newton, S. A., Bowers, J. E., and Shaw, H. J. (1982). *SPIE Semin. Proc.* **326**, 108.
Newton, S. A., Bowers, J. E., Kotler, G., and Shaw, H. J. (1983a). *Opt. Lett.* **8**, 60.
Newton, S. A., Jackson, K. P., and Shaw, H. J. (1983b). *Appl. Phys. Lett.* **43**, 149.

Ohlhaber, R. L., and Wilner, K. (1977). *Electro-Opt. Syst. Des.* **9**, 33.

Okoshi, T., Emura, K., Kikuchi, K., and Kersten, R. Th. (1981). *J. Opt. Commun.* **2**, 89.

Pappert, S. A., Mclandrich, M. N., and Chang, C. T. (1985). *J. Lightwave Tech.* **LT-3**, 273.

Pinnow, D. A., Rich, T. C., Ostermayer, F. W., Jr., and DiDomenico, M., Jr. (1973). *Appl. Phys. Lett.* **22**, 527.

Rausch, E. O., Efurd, R. B., and Corbin, M. A. (1982). *IEE Int. Conf. Radar.*

Reible, S. A. (1985). *IEEE Trans. Magn.* **MAG-21**, 193.

Rhodes, W. T., and Guilfoyle, P. S. (1984). *Proc. IEEE* **72**, 820.

Sorin, W. V. (1986). Rep. G.L. No. 3977. Edward L. Ginzton Lab., Stanford Univ., Stanford, California.

Stolen, R. H. (1979). *In* "Optical Fiber Telecommunications" (S. E. Miller and A. G. Chynoweth, eds.), pp. 125–150. Academic Press, New York.

Stolen, R. H., and Lin, C. (1978). *Phys. Rev. A* **17**, 1448.

Wang, C. C., Moeller, R. P., Burns, W. K., and Kaminow, I. P. (1984). *Electron. Lett.* **20**, 486.

Wilner, K., and van den Heuvel, A. P. (1976). *Proc. IEEE* **64**, 805.

Withers, R. S., Anderson, A. C., Green, J. B., and Reible, S. A. (1985). *IEEE Trans. Magn.* **MAG-21**, 186.

Yamamoto, Y., and Kimura, T. (1981). *IEEE J. Quantum Electron.* **QW-17**, 919.

7.2

Spatial Light Modulators: Applications and Functional Capabilities

CARDINAL WARDE

DEPARTMENT OF ELECTRICAL ENGINEERING AND
COMPUTER SCIENCE
MASSACHUSETTS INSTITUTE OF TECHNOLOGY
CAMBRIDGE, MASSACHUSETTS 02139

ARTHUR D. FISHER

OPTICAL SCIENCES DIVISION
NAVAL RESEARCH LABORATORY
WASHINGTON, D.C. 20375

I. Introduction

The fundamental building blocks of optical information processing systems are a variety of active optical devices called spatial light modulators (SLMs). These devices spatially modify the phase, polarization, amplitude, and/or intensity of a one- or two-dimensional readout light distribution as a function of space and time. The control or write signal is a time-varying electrical signal for an electrically addressed SLM (E-SLM), and the intensity distribution of another time-varying write-light beam for an optically addressed SLM (O-SLM).

This chapter discusses SLMs from a functional and applications perspective. Throughout the chapter, optical information processing is broadly defined to include such fields as optical signal processing, image processing, and computing. A brief introduction to SLM technology that includes a framework for classifying SLMs according to their functional capabilities is provided in Section II, and a brief overview of past, current, and contemplated applications of SLMs is presented in Section III.

A generic information processing architecture is then abstracted in Section IV to highlight the various functional roles assumed by SLMs in applications. This theme is elaborated on in Section V by explicitly delineating the fundamental operations performed by SLMs in applications. Section VI considers the performance limitations of SLMs by examining the materials and design constraints that determine how well SLMs carry out these basic functions.

A variety of specific devices are mentioned in examples throughout the chapter. The reader is referred to Section VII for descriptions of these and other major classes of available SLMs; the descriptions are brief, as it is not our purpose to provide a comprehensive overview of SLM technology. Finally, a few summarizing remarks are provided in Section VIII.

II. Basic SLM Structures

The most general SLM structure consists essentially of a charge-generation element and a light-modulation element, as illustrated in Fig. 1a. Optically addressed SLMs tend to employ either photoconductors or photocathodes as the charge-generation element, while E-SLMs generally employ electron beams, a matrix of electrodes, or an array of active devices such as charge-coupled devices (CCDs) or transistors. Examples of light-modulating elements include liquid crystals, electrooptic crystals, magnetooptic materials, and membranes.

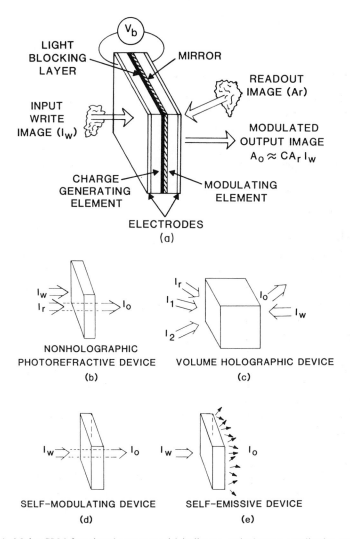

Fig. 1. Major SLM functional structures (A indicates optical wave amplitudes and I the intensities or currents). These fall into three functional classes: (a, b, c) signal multiplying and amplifying, (d) self-modulating, and (e) self-emissive.

In the generic sandwich structure shown in Fig. 1a, the bias voltage V_b is shunted to the light-modulating element by charges generated within the illuminated regions of the photosensor. The resulting electric fields cause the light-modulating material to modify the polarization, phase, and/or amplitude of the readout light. The mirror and light-blocking layers at the center of the sandwich permit the written information to be read out by reflection and prevent leak through of the readout light to the photosensor.

Optically addressed SLMs also take on a variety of modified structures (as illustrated in Figs. 1b–e) in which a single material serves both as the charge-generation transducer and the light-modulating element. Devices employing these structures generally use a material whose refractive index, optical transparency, mechanical dimensions or radiative properties are modified by the incident light. Such devices are often not cascadable and generally cannot match the flexibility of an SLM in which the constituent elements are distinct, as in Fig. 1a.

Functionally it is useful to divide SLMs into three basic classes: signal multiplication and amplification devices, self-modulation devices, and self-emissive devices. Some materials (e.g., photorefractive crystals) can be operated as devices that belong in more than one class, because their operating mechanisms permit a variety of write–read configurations.

A. SIGNAL-MULTIPLYING SLMs

Signal multiplication devices are three-port devices that can have any of the structures illustrated in Figs. 1a–c. In a typical amplitude-modulation application, for example, the amplitude at each point in the readout image is multiplied by the effective transmittance or reflectance of the modulating element, which is determined by the write image intensity or the electrical write signal at a corresponding point on the device. Thus the amplitude of the processed output image is essentially the product of the write image intensity, voltage or current, and the readout image amplitude.

Examples of signal-multiplying O-SLMs, which are described in Section VII, include the photoactivated LCLV (Bleha et al., 1978; Efron et al., 1983), the photo-MSLM (Warde et al., 1981), the photoemitter membrane light modulator (PEMLM) (Somers, 1972; Fisher et al., 1986a), the Pockels Readout Optical Light Modulator (PROM) (Horwitz and Corbett, 1978), the Photo DKDP light valve (Donjon et al., 1973), and the photorefractive incoherent-to-coherent (PICOC) device (Marrakchi et al., 1985).

Similarly, examples of signal-multiplying E-SLMs include the electron-beam-addressed DKDP light valve (Groh and Marie, 1970; Marie and Donjon, 1973; Casasent, 1978a), the CCD-addressed liquid crystal light valve (CCD-LCLV) (Efron et al., 1983), the electron-beam-addressed Micro-channel Spatial Light Modulator (e-beam MSLM) (Schwartz et al., 1985), and the Litton Iron Garnet H-triggered Modulator (LIGHTMOD) (Ross et al., 1983).

The volume-holographic modulator of Fig. 1c, which can be operated as a signal multiplication and amplification device, is an *n*-port device in which multiple write and readout beams can interact interferometrically with the medium simultaneously. These devices generally employ photore-fractive or other nonlinear materials. Because information is written onto these devices by interferometric means, they are constrained by a require-ment for coherent write-light.

B. SELF-MODULATING SLMs

Self-modulating devices are generally two-port O-SLMs, as illustrated in Fig. 1d. The optical properties of the modulating material are modified by the input light, which is itself modified as it is transmitted through or reflected from the device to become the output beam. In most cases the output light intensity of a self-modulating O-SLM bears a simple (often nonlinear) relationship to the input light intensity. Examples of self-modu-lating O-SLMs include the semiconductor etalon and other bistable optical devices (Gibbs, 1985; Smith *et al.*, 1985) and passive self-pumped phase-conjugate mirrors based on photorefractive crystals (Feinberg, 1982; Cronin-Golomb *et al.*, 1982).

C. SELF-EMISSIVE SLMs

Self-emissive modulators generate a coherent or incoherent spatial light distribution under the control of input electrical or optical information (see Fig. 1e). Examples include CRTs and other emissive displays, image intensifiers, platelet lasers (Seko and Nishikata, 1977), and proposed integrated circuits with interconnected arrays of, for example, photodiodes and surface-emitting injection lasers (Uchiyama and Iga, 1985; Liau *et al.*, 1984; Goodman *et al.*, 1984).

III. SLM Applications

This applications overview provides insight into (1) the important signal processing applications that rely on or could benefit from the use of SLMs, (2) the basic operations that are performed by SLMs in these applications, and (3) the specifications that these applications impose on SLM design (e.g., in functional capabilities and minimal performance requirements).

Considering the rich variety of SLMs referred to in Sections II and VII, one may be surprised that very few SLMs have progressed to the point of routine use, mass production, and/or commercialization. The attainment of high-performance, versatile SLMs has proven to be more difficult than initially anticipated. In many cases the device shortcomings can be traced to device fabrication and materials limitations. There is reason for optimism, however, as recent advances in materials and fabrication techniques are beginning to produce a new generation of 2-dimensional (2-D) SLMs.

A number of these are making the transition from the laboratory into commercial production (Fisher and Lee, 1986). Furthermore, with some of the currently available SLMs, researchers are beginning to prototype simple cases of a number of sophisticated applications. Consequently, some very exciting optical information processing concepts that offer the potential of significantly exceeding the projected capabilities of conventional electronic processors are being proposed.

A. INITIAL MOTIVATING APPLICATIONS

Historically, the quest for projection and flat screen devices for television and computer display applications provided much of the initial motivation for the development of light-control devices. Other related early applications included proposals to use the high information densities of 2-D data fields for memory applications and for page composers or formatters for printing purposes. Also, many of the addressing schemes employed in today's E-SLMs, such as scanning electron beams, electrode matrices, arrays of thin-film transistors in amorphous silicon, and direct silicon addressing, were first pioneered in the development of display devices. Unfortunately, most display devices tend to be self-emissive and nonflat; only a few offer the important signal-multiplication function. An exception is the commercially available, low-cost (<$100), nematic liquid-crystal television displays which offer reasonable optical quality and up to 240×240 resolution elements (Blechman, 1986). These are currently being converted by researchers to electrically addressed signal-multiplying SLMs for applications in optical information processing (Liu et al., 1985; McEwan et al., 1985b). Display device research is still a very active field which continues to hold promise of impacting future SLM development.

The next major impetus for SLM development followed from the discovery of holography and the recognition of the Fourier transformation properties of free-space propagation and simple lenses. The invention of the laser made both of these areas practical and was a tremendous stimulus for the field (Pollock et al., 1963; Tippett et al., 1965; Goodman, 1968). Initially proposed applications of holography included (a) robust optical memory that exploited the distributed nature of holographic recordings and (b) nondestructive testing using the ability of double-exposure and time-exposure holography to visualize tiny deformations and vibrations. The applications of Fourier principles progressed from spatial-filtering systems for image enhancement and deblurring (O'Neill, 1956; Tsujiuchi, 1962) to the matched-filter correlator (Fig. 2) for pattern recognition (Vander Lugt, 1964) and to a major success in the processing of synthetic aperture radar (SAR) signals (Cutrona et al., 1966; Goodman, 1968). These applications

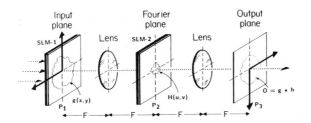

Fig. 2. Real-time two-lens optical correlator. The Fourier transform $G(u, v)$ of the input $g(x, y)$ illuminates the filter $H(u, v)$ in the plane P_2. The output $g * h$ is the convolution operation between g and h. With the complex conjugate filter $H^*(u, v)$, the output is the correlation, $g \star h$.

were pioneered with photographic film, but to be truly practical they require real-time SLMs for electrical-to-optical input signal conversion, programmable spatial filtering, and real-time holographic recording.

Although the classical two-lens coherent optical processor in Fig. 2 is simple and extremely powerful, interest in this correlator waned for many years owing to difficulties associated with the sensitivity of the Fourier transform operation to scale and orientation variations in the input image and with the critical alignment required of the filter.

Fourier transform techniques and 1-D acoustooptic Bragg modulators have also been employed with much success to process temporal electrical signals (Berg and Lee, 1983; also see Section VII of this chapter and Part III of this volume). For example, Fig. 2 becomes a schematic of a space-integrating correlator when the lenses are 1-D cylindrical lenses and SLM-1 and SLM-2 are 1-D acoustooptic modulators. With acoustic signals $g(t)$ and $h(t)$ propagating with velocity v in opposite directions in the two SLMs, an output signal proportional to

$$c(t) = \int g(x - vt) h(x + vt) \, dx$$

can be obtained with an on-axis detector in the output plane (Berg and Lee, 1983). A variety of acoustic processors have been configured to perform real-time operations such as spectrum analysis, convolution, correlation, adaptive filtering, laser beam steering and scanning, heterodyne detection, triple-product processing, numeric matrix–vector calculations, and generation of time-frequency representations (e.g., ambiguity functions and Wigner distributions).

B. MORE RECENT APPLICATIONS

From these roots, the number of potential SLM applications has expanded rapidly because of recent advances in SLM technology and a resurgence of interest in optical information processing. For example, the acoustooptic processors described represent one of the few technologies that are currently making the transition to routine use. They are becoming superior to conventional electronic approaches by offering a higher information throughput and through the use of some of the speed and parallelism capabilities of optics. They often also have practical size, weight, and power consumption advantages. Real-time holographic nondestructive testing is another area that is progressing to the point of regular use because of recent SLM technologies such as the thermoplastic and photorefractive/volume-holographic devices that now offer sufficient resolution to record off-axis holograms. Additionally, prototype systems under development may help SLM-based matched-filter correlators (Bell, 1986) and SAR processors to make the transition to routine use in the near future.

Other recent directions in optical information processing that are beginning to exploit the capabilities of SLMs include:

1. pattern recognition techniques based on enhanced matched filters (Casasent and Psaltis, 1977; Casasent, 1985), phase-only filters (Psaltis *et al.*, 1984; Horner and Gianino, 1984; Horner and Leger, 1985; Flannery *et al.*, 1986) and noncorrelation approaches (Leger and Lee, 1982; Gu and Lee, 1984a, b);

2. white-light and color image processing (Yu, 1983);

3. tomographic transformations (see Chapter 5.2 by Barrett and Easton);

4. solutions of partial differential and integral equations (Lee, 1985);

5. high-resolution adaptive wave-front estimation, compensation, and conjugation; and

6. analog and digital optical numeric processing.

The last two application areas have engendered widespread interest, and will be further elaborated below.

High-resolution adaptive optical systems for real-time wave-front estimation, correction, and/or conjugation have been a more recent motivation for SLM development (Jacobs *et al.*, 1978; Ludman, 1985; Fisher and Warde, 1979, 1983). These systems facilitate communications, imaging, and high-power laser transmission through aberrating media (e.g., the earth's atmosphere) and the correction of distortions in large optical systems. Older, conventional adaptive optical approaches employed spatial arrays of individual phase sensors hard-wired to discrete modulator elements. The new SLM-based approaches are all-optical configurations, extendable to millions of wave-front resolution elements with no significant increase in system complexity.

As a specific example, Fig. 3a shows a microchannel spatial light modulator (MSLM) device in a specific configuration called an interference phase

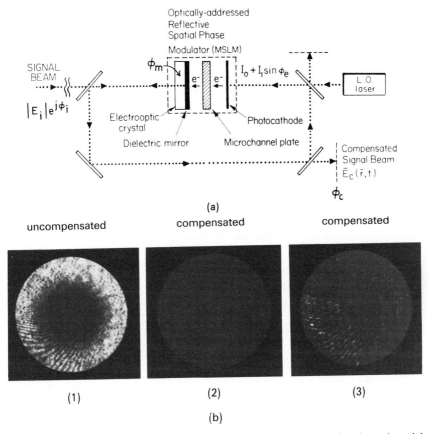

(a)

(b)

Fig. 3. (a) Interference phase loop (Fisher and Warde, 1983) using microchannel spatial light modulator (MSLM) for high-resolution wave-front estimation, compensation, and/or conjugation; (b) self-compensation results for the convex wave front produced by the MSLM crystal: (1) interferogram before compensation, (2) interferogram after compensation ($\frac{1}{8}$-s exposure), and (3) interferogram after compensation (1.5-s exposure).

loop (Fisher and Warde, 1979, 1983; Fisher, 1985a). The phase of the input aberrated wave front $\phi_i(x, y, t)$ is multiplied by a correcting phase $-\phi_m(x, y, t)$ as it reflects from the MSLM. The residual error in the corrected wavefront $\phi_c = \phi_i - \phi_m$ is fed back through a homodyne interferometer to produce an intensity that drives the MSLM. A conjugate wave can be generated by reading ϕ_m from the MSLM with an auxiliary planar wave front. This system can continuously estimate, compensate, and conjugate wave-front phase with no phase-quadrant ambiguity over multiple-π radians of dynamic range, even in the presence of wave-front amplitude variations. Figure 3b is an interferogram of the crystal in a MSLM which is operating in an interference phase loop. The results show compensation of the convex wave front produced by the crystal (Fisher and Warde, 1979).

Real-time holography and multiwave mixing in photorefractive and other nonlinear materials also show strong promise for high-resolution wave-front compensation and conjugation and are beginning to find practical application in areas such as laser-resonator beam cleanup and phase locking of independent lasers.

There has also been considerable interest in optical numeric processing, generally in the form of linear algebraic processors for solving problems that can be decomposed into matrix–vector and/or matrix–matrix products. Figure 4 illustrates a basic analog configuration for multiplying an $n \times n$ matrix by an n-element vector. In Fig. 4, n^2 simultaneous parallel multiplications are performed by the 2-D SLM, and n^2 parallel additions are performed by focusing the individual products onto the appropriate detector elements (Goodman *et al.*, 1978; Tamura and Wyant, 1976). A related "flash" matrix–matrix multiplier achieves n^3 parallelism by employing a clever spatial frequency multiplexing scheme (Tamura and Wyant, 1976).

A large variety of significantly different analog matrix–vector and matrix–matrix multiplication architectures have been proposed, many of which exploit the better analog numeric performance available from Bragg acoustooptic and other 1-D modulators and/or CCD detector arrays. Examples include systolic architectures (Caulfield *et al.*, 1982), engagement architectures (Speiser and Whitehouse, 1982; Guilfoyle, 1982), outer-product concepts (Athale and Collins, 1982), the PRIMO outer-product processor

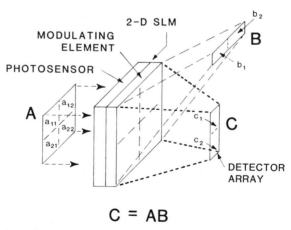

$$C = AB$$

Fig. 4. Matrix–vector multiplier geometry. The matrix **A** is first recorded in the 2D SLM. The optics stretch vector **B** vertically and compress the modulator output horizontally to form the sum vector **C**. The SLM serves as a parallel analog multiplier.

(Owechko *et al.*, 1986), and the RUBIC engagement processor (Bocker, 1984).

A variety of digital–optical matrix-processing architectures have also been proposed for achieving higher numeric accuracy. These architectures employ such techniques as residue arithmetic, binary multiplication by analog convolution, and/or two's-complement arithmetic. In addition, iterative-feedback matrix processors using SLMs have been proposed for such applications as matrix inversion, solution of systems of linear equations, eigenvalue and eigenvector determination, adaptive beam-forming, least-squares solution, Kalman filtering, and singular value decomposition (Psaltis *et al.*, 1979; Kumar and Casasent, 1981; Caulfield *et al.*, 1981, 1984). The digital–optical approaches to high-accuracy numeric computing often produce a mixed binary output which requires further electronic postprocessing. This reduces processing throughput and can greatly diminish any competitive advantages the optical approaches may hold over competing electronic architectures.

C. Current Trends

There is now a growing trend toward more fully exploiting the innate parallel processing and unique 3-D geometric capability of optics to provide reconfigurable interconnections between 2-D processing planes in VLSI circuits and in optical information processing systems. Many of the new directions complement rather than compete with electronic systems by addressing problem domains that are taxing the capabilities of conventional electronic processors. Examples of the problems being addressed include pattern recognition and classification, multisensor processing, large numeric models, image understanding, robotic vision and manipulation, speech understanding, high-level symbolic processing, and a variety of problems in artificial intelligence. Real-time SLMs are expected to play key roles in all these applications.

With regard to the development of algorithms and architectures, electronic approaches to parallel processing have thus far provided little guidance on how to utilize effectively the 3-D interconnection and parallel processing capabilities of optics. Consequently, optical researchers are being called upon to make contributions at the forefront of the science of parallel processing (Jenkins and Giles, 1986; Huang, 1985). Nevertheless, the limited but steadily increasing body of knowledge concerning intrinsically parallel computational models and algorithms is already beginning to impact the design of efficient parallel optical architectures. For example, there have been promising recent proposals for highly parallel optical computing architectures that employ SLMs to implement cellular automata (Sawchuk and Jenkins, 1984; Jenkins and Sawchuk, 1985; Yatagai, 1986), generalized parallel state machines (Huang, 1985), associative and neural-network processing (references follow below), parallel symbolic logical inference (Warde and Kottas, 1986; Eichmann and Caulfield, 1985; Schmidt and Cathey, 1986; Casasent and Lee, 1986), and parallel low-level vision processing (e.g., stereopsis) (Ichioka and Ono, 1985). A few of these new SLM applications are outlined below.

There is currently much interest in the development of novel electronic processors that are augmented by parallel optical interconnections between systems, boards, processors, integrated circuits (ICs), and even individual devices on an integrated circuit (see Figs. 5a and b) (Hutcheson, 1986; Horvitz and Neff, 1986; Goodman et al., 1984). Spatial light modulators, and in particular those technologies that can be directly fabricated in semiconductors, can play a central role in many of these configurations. In this interconnection context, the matrix–vector multiplier of Fig. 4 can implement a cross-bar switch when the matrix is loaded with one binary element per row (Horvitz and Neff, 1986).

The general parallel iterative processor geometry outlined in Fig. 6 can be configured to implement parallel finite-state machines, cellular automata, and a variety of other advanced parallel computing concepts (Sawchuk and Jenkins, 1984; Sawchuk and Strand, 1984; Jenkins and Sawchuk, 1985; Huang, 1985). Spatial light modulators are employed here to implement processor, memory, and interconnect functions.

Symbolic logic problems are another area in which there is considerable interest. These problems involve, in an abstract sense, a set of data objects

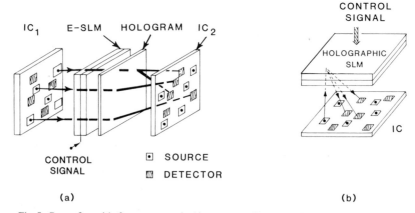

Fig. 5. Reconfigurable free-space optical interconnection system between integrated circuits (ICs) in two configurations (a and b). The ICs incorporate detectors, sources, and/or modulators.

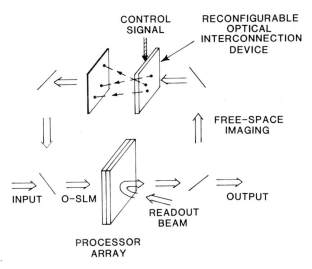

Fig. 6. General parallel, iterative optical processor.

and a set of relationships describing the data objects. The data objects and relationships constitute a knowledge base that is generally arranged as a set of facts and rules. Conclusions are inferred in response to queries by applying logical inference to the knowledge base. The solutions to such problems involve operations such as searching, pattern matching, and logic.

Because the parallel processing capability of optics permits these operations to be performed at high speed, and furthermore, since high accuracy and large dynamic range are not required, 2-D optical processors appear to be well suited for these problems. Such optical inference engines should be more efficient than their electronic counterparts because the parallel searching operation eliminates the need for backtracking through the knowledge base. Through the use of electrically addressed SLMs as interfacing elements, these optical systems become compatible with electronic computers and have been proposed as auxiliary processors to electronic mainframes (Warde and Kottas, 1986).

The mapped-template inference machine, proposed by Warde and Kottas (1986) (Fig. 7) is an example of a hybrid symbolic logic processor. It uses mapping templates to store the facts, which are the relationships between the data objects. Conclusions are inferred to the queries by applying the mapping templates to the data objects in the order prescribed by the rules. As illustrated in Fig. 7a, the input data set is treated as a horizontal row D_i and is stretched vertically so that it forms a 2-D mask. This expanded form of D_i is first overlaid with the mapping template using imaging optics,

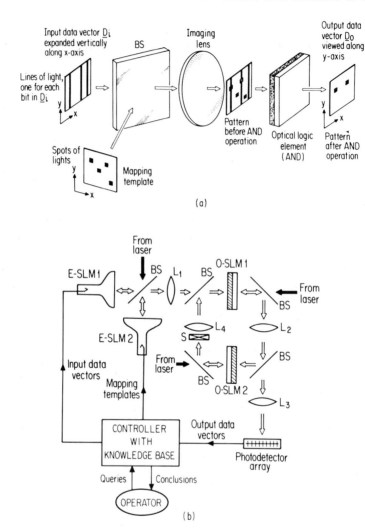

Fig. 7. (a) Basic structure of the mapped-template optical inference machine and (b) hardware implementation of the mapped-template inference machine.

and then a 2-D logical AND is performed. The resulting output viewed along horizontal rows corresponds to the output vector $\mathbf{D}_i$. A hardware implementation of the mapped-template inference engine is illustrated in Fig. 7b. The input data vectors are written onto E-SLM$_1$ and stretched therein; the mapping templates are written onto E-SLM$_2$; O-SLM$_1$ performs the logical AND; and O-SLM$_2$ performs latching and feedback for iterative processing.

Associative processing by optical means is currently a particularly active and rapidly growing area of optical information processing. An associative memory has the basic capability of storing a number of associated information patterns (u, v), so that subsequent presentation of one pattern u recalls its paired pattern v.

Associative processing is inherently parallel. For example, a content-addressable digital memory should ideally compare the current input pattern simultaneously with all possible matching patterns. As another example, a simple associative neural network capable of storing pairs of n-element vectors $(\mathbf{u}, \mathbf{v})$ generally requires n^2 parallel multiplications and additions to perform recall (Kohonen, 1984; Hopfield, 1982). This innate parallelism suggests implementations using the parallel processing and interconnection capabilities of optics. For example, the n^2 parallelism of neural-net recall can be expressed in the form $\mathbf{v} = \mathbf{Mu}$ and has been implemented by the matrix–vector multiplier configuration of Fig. 4 (Psaltis and Farhat, 1985; Fisher and Giles, 1985). Furthermore, most associative-processing applications do not tax the limited analog dynamic range capabilities of optical hardware because they use only a few analog levels or binary information.

The attractiveness of optical implementations of associative processing has been recognized for some time. There were early proposals for optical holographic associative memories (Collier and Pennington, 1966; Lohmann and Werligh, 1967; Gabor, 1969), optical "perceptron" neural networks (Babcock *et al.*, 1963; Hawkins and Munsey, 1963), and other optical associative schemes (Willshaw *et al.*, 1969). The current rapid growth in optical associative processing is coupled to a rebirth in the field of associative/neural network or "connectionist" processing in general (Rumelhart and McClelland, 1986; Kohonen, 1984; Sanderson and Zeevi, 1983; Hopfield, 1982; Grossberg, 1982; Hinton and Anderson, 1981). A number of matrix-algebraic and neural-net optical associative architectures have recently been demonstrated, including Hopfield-type iterative-recall configurations (Psaltis and Farhat, 1985), Widrow–Hoff-type adaptive-learning systems (Fisher and Giles, 1985), "attentive" implementations (Athale *et al.*, 1986), and Boltzmann machines (Ticknor *et al.*, 1985). Other new optical associative directions include real-time and nonlinear holographic concepts (Mada, 1985; Kim and Guest, 1986; Jannson *et al.*, 1986; Yariv *et al.*, 1986; Soffer *et al.*, 1986), nonlinear holographic resonators (Soffer *et al.*, 1986; Anderson, 1986; Yariv and Kwong, 1986; Cohen, 1986), window-addressable memory (Condon *et al.*, 1985), and symbol substitution (Brenner *et al.*, 1986).

An optical adaptive-learning associative processor that also illustrates a variety of the processing capabilities of 2-D SLMs, is shown in Fig. 8 (Fisher *et al.*, 1986b). It performs real-time learning of pairs of n-element associated

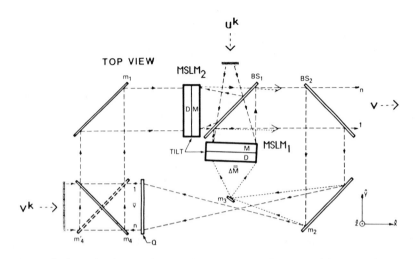

Fig. 8. Optical adaptive-learning associative processor (Fisher, 1986). D is the detector side and M the modulator side of the microchannel spatial light modulators (MSLMs). The MSLMs perform multiplication, addition, subtraction, accumulation, and storage in this architecture.

vectors $(\mathbf{u}^k, \mathbf{v}^k)$, in the form of 1-D arrays of light intensities, by implementing the dynamic-learning equation

$$\frac{d\mathbf{M}}{dt} = g'(\mathbf{v}^k - \mathbf{M}\mathbf{u}^k)\mathbf{u}^{kT}$$

Here g' is a gain factor, k designates a particular associated vector pair, and T is the matrix transpose operator. The operation of the architecture in Fig. 8 has been described elsewhere (Fisher *et al.*, 1986b). Briefly, the current state of the memory matrix $\mathbf{M}$ is stored as an electronic charge distribution in the microchannel spatial light modulator $MSLM_1$. Associations are retrieved by the matrix–vector equation of recall

$$\mathbf{v} = \mathbf{M}\mathbf{u}^k$$

with a geometry similar to Fig. 4. The difference equation form,

$$\mathbf{M}_{n+1} = \mathbf{M}_n + g\mathbf{v}^k\mathbf{u}^{kT} - g\mathbf{v}\mathbf{u}^{kT}$$

where $g = g'\Delta t$, is implemented by utilizing the capability of $MSLM_1$ to add or subtract charge to or from its stored image.

D. SUMMARIZING REMARKS ON APPLICATIONS

A variety of important, traditional applications in optical information processing are beginning to benefit from the development of optical processors that employ real-time SLMs. There is hope that the associative, symbolic inference, and other new, highly parallel optical-computing concepts discussed above will be able to solve some of the new and more demanding problems that are defying the capabilities of conventional electronic processors.

An appreciation of these applications helps to delineate the various basic processing operations provided by SLMs and to establish the performance and functional requirements that must guide future device research. For further details concerning these applications, the reader is referred to the other chapters of this book as well as a number of recent books, special journal issues, and conference proceedings on optical computing and related areas (see, e.g., Goodman, 1982; Caulfield *et al.*, 1984; Neff, 1984; Psaltis, 1984; Caulfield, 1985; Dove, 1985; Horvitz and Neff, 1986).

The sections that follow elaborate upon these themes by (1) abstracting a generic optical information processing architecture that highlights the various roles assumed by SLMs, (2) explicitly delineating the fundamental functions required by applications and offered by specific SLM device technologies, and (3) addressing application performance requirements and SLM performance limitations.

IV. Architectural Considerations of Optical Processors

A. OPTICAL PROCESSOR ARCHITECTURES

As illustrated in Fig. 9 and in the foregoing section, most optical information processing systems are an architectural arrangement of optical elements that generally include input and output transducers, processor and memory elements, and interconnection devices (Tanguay, 1985).

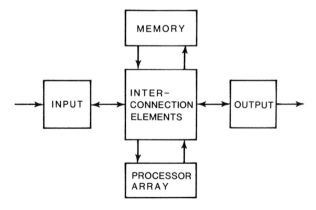

Fig. 9. Generic optical processing architecture showing major roles assumed by SLMs.

Depending on the characteristics of the signals to be processed, the input data-formatting SLM may perform incoherent-to-coherent optical conversion, electrical-to-optical image conversion, raster or vector signal formatting, preprocessing such as thresholding or A/D conversion, or simply buffering. All three functional classes of SLMs are possible input transducers, depending on the signal and the application.

The processor array is typically one or more SLMs implementing optically connected processing elements that execute transformations and computations that are central to the operation of interest. Some examples of SLM classes employed here include:

1. signal multiplying 2-D SLMs functioning as reprogrammable spatial filters in a classical two-lens correlator,

2. self-modulating real-time nonlinear switching or bistable devices functioning as logic elements in a digital-optical processor,

3. two-dimensional arrays of self-emissive electronic circuits with optical input and output (e.g., logic gates, analog multipliers, adders, and threshold devices), and

4. one-dimensional acoustooptic cells functioning as dynamical masks in a space or time integrating correlator.

The required memory devices may be classified as either location addressed or content/associative addressed. In a location-addressed memory, specification of the memory location yields the data stored at the location. This is in contrast to a content-addressed or associative memory in which information is accessed by specifying an associated data pattern. In some cases, the data to be retrieved are not even localized, being spread and intermingled among a number of storage elements. Associative memories can also have additional capabilities such as the ability to recall perfectly a complete block of stored data from only a partial or distorted specification of the associated input. Memories with fast access times and large capacity ($\sim 10^{12}$ bits) are desirable for optical information processing systems. Volume holographic SLMs and other high-resolution SLMs are candidate memory devices.

Reconfigurable interconnection devices are the central element of a wide variety of optical information processing systems. They implement the parallel control and information structures that underlie the algorithms being executed. More specifically, the interconnections provide global communication among the processing elements, sequencing and feedback, and parallel communication between the processor, memory, and input and output devices. Although fixed interconnections based on static holograms, classical optical components, and fiber optics may find limited applications in the near term, the future of several proposed advanced optical information processing architectures may well be determined by the availability, cost, and performance of dynamically reconfigurable optical interconnection devices. Photorefractive crystals, high resolution E-SLMs and O-SLMs, and systems consisting of combinations of such devices look particularly promising for implementing the reconfigurable interconnection operation.

The output device generally performs one of the following functions: optical-to-electronic conversion, optical-to-optical conversion, format conversion (e.g., parallel to serial), buffering, optical or electronic thresholding, and further signal processing. The technologies that currently serve as output devices include semiconductor detector arrays, optical fiber bundles, vidicon cameras, and SLMs.

Clearly there is a role for real-time SLMs in each of the subsystems of Fig. 9 that constitute an optical processor. Since it is unlikely that a single device can simultaneously meet the demands of these various roles, a variety of specialized devices appears to be the most practical approach. Collectively these SLMs should offer high spatial resolution, high framing speed, both linear and nonlinear input/output characteristics, short-term memory (min), and a variety of internal 2-D processing operations such as contrast reversal, edge enhancement, Boolean logic, and thresholding. In addition, the optically addressed devices should offer high optical sensitivity and cascadability.

V. Fundamental Operations Performed by SLMs

A. APPLICATION-DRIVEN FUNCTIONS

1. *Transducer Functions*

One of the primary functions of E-SLMs is input transducer and/or data formatter for an optical processor. For example, such devices are often used with nonoptical sources such as multisensor arrays or the results of digital manipulations in a hybrid electrooptical processor. The formatting role depends on the specific addressing mechanism, with sequential-electronic to 1-D or 2-D parallel-optical conversion being common. Optically addressed SLMs can also function as input transducers and are often used for incoherent-to-coherent light conversion, input image amplification, wavelength conversion, or input image preprocessing such as contrast reversal. Thus all three classes of SLMs find applications as input transducers.

2. *Amplification*

The generic O-SLM, illustrated in Fig. 1a, is a 3-port device that can also be loosely interpreted as a 2-D "optical transistor." Signal amplification is achieved by operating the device in its multiplication mode with an intense, spatially uniform readout beam. The output beam then becomes an amplified version of the weak write-beam, and the desirable feature of decoupling the optical system producing the weak write-beam from the amplified output beam is usually also obtained. Furthermore, when the uniform readout beam has different properties from the write-beam, conversion operations such as incoherent-to-coherent light conversion and image wavelength conversion are performed.

Sophisticated applications often employ several optically addressed light modulators in cascade and/or in optical feedback configurations (Fisher and Warde, 1983; Fisher and Giles, 1985). Thus it is desirable that the output of one device be sufficiently intense and of the appropriate wavelength to act as the input to one or more successive devices in the optical train. Cascadable SLMs should therefore exhibit optical gain so as to obviate the need for signal regeneration between stages.

Included among the many cascadable SLMs are the MSLM, the PEMLM, the LCLV, photo-DKDP light valve, and some of the etalon bistable optical devices. Devices such as the PROM and the PRIZ are not cascadable because, as outlined in Section VII, they are typically written on with blue light and read out with red light.

3. *Arithmetic Operations*

Signal multiplication is intrinsic to most SLMs, as was discussed in Section II, and has been exploited for operations such as numeric vector-matrix multiplication, programmable matched filtering, wave-front conjugation, programmable template matching, optical mask generation from electronic computer data, and computer or optically controlled reconfigurable optical interconnections.

Besides this basic multiplication function, virtually all O-SLMs can also perform addition between simultaneously applied incoherent input images. SLMs exhibiting storage can also perform numeric intensity addition on successively stored input image intensities. Some SLMs can also directly perform image subtraction. For example, in the MSLM and PEMLM devices (discussed in Section VII) it is possible to add or remove electrons to or from a stored-charge image distribution on the modulating element. This permits algebraic subtraction between the stored image and a new image written with opposite charge polarity. A few other SLMs, such as the Phototitus, can also be operated in an analogous subtraction mode. With the inclusion of additional optics, the arithmetic operations of parallel subtraction (Marom, 1986) and division (Efron *et al.*, 1985b) of image fields can also be implemented with most SLMs.

4. *Memory*

Short-term storage is another desirable basic function of SLMs, with the output image becoming the product of a previously stored write image and the current readout image. SLMs with storage can perform memory or information latching functions, and in particular, O-SLMs with storage can be a reusable substitute for photographic film. Storage can be especially important in the electronically addressed devices to avoid continuous updating of a 2-D data array and thereby relieving the information bandwidth demands on the driving electronic processor.

In O-SLMs, storage capabilities are often accompanied by the ability to detect very low light level input imagery by integration over an extended period. Modulators mentioned in Section VII that can store images for about an hour, and in some instances much longer, include the Photo-DKDP and e-beam DKDP light valves, PROM, PRIZ, MSLM, PEMLM, PICOC, LIGHTMOD, and bistable devices, as well as modulators employing smectic and ferroelectric liquid crystals, PLZT, thermoplastic, VO_2, and photo-refractive materials.

5. *Linear and Nonlinear Transfer Characteristics*

Optical information processing applications use SLMs to perform both linear and nonlinear operations (e.g., thresholding) on each point in the input write image. In practice most modulators are intrinsically nonlinear. For example, the output intensity is proportional to $\sin^2(\text{input-intensity}^2)$ in some configurations of mechanical modulators (cantilevered beam, PEMLM, or deformable mirror devices mentioned in Section VII). Similarly, exponential dependence of the readout intensity on the write-light intensity is characteristic of electroabsorption devices (Kingston *et al.*, 1984), although thin electroabsorption devices can offer amplitude modulation approximately proportional to input intensity.

Modulators that are read out either between crossed polarizers or interferometrically produce output beam intensities that are related to the write-beam intensity by sinusoidal functions. However, modulation approximately linearly proportional to the input intensity can be obtained by operation in the regions midway between the turning points of the sinusoidal modulation characteristic. A linear intensity input/output transfer function is required of an SLM for most of the previously mentioned arithmetic operations.

In the PEMLM and MSLM, for example, approximately linear modulation is achieved by using a static uniform stored-charge distribution to bias the modulator to one of the 50% modulation points of the sine-squared characteristic. In these devices, contrast-reversed modulation is also possible by operating about an adjacent 50% bias modulation point, where the sinusoid has a slope of the opposite sign. These SLMs can also perform contrast reversal by alternate means: for instance, by switching between their electron accumulation and depletion modes. In addition, the contrast of a previously stored image can be reversed by adjusting the readout optics: for example, by reorienting the crossed polarizers used to read out the MSLM or by changing the diffraction stop in a phase-contrast system used to read out the PEMLM.

6. *Thresholding*

The ideal nonlinear binary thresholding characteristic shown in Fig. 10a is a desirable SLM transfer function that finds application in a wide variety of optical information processing algorithms. SLMs exhibiting this characteristic may be thought of as 2-D arrays of nonlinear optical switches. As can be seen from Fig. 10a, in binary or hard-clip thresholding (solid curve), there is little or no change in the output intensity until the input write-beam intensity exceeds a specific threshold level. However, in the analog thresholding case (dashed curve), the output intensity varies linearly as a function of the input intensity after the input intensity has exceeded the threshold.

Hard-clip image thresholding allows dicisions (e.g., yes/no) to be made in an optical processor and can be used to regenerate binary optical signals in cascaded systems. Furthermore, Boolean logic operations can be performed between multiple input beams. For example, setting the input threshold at $\frac{1}{2}$ of the logical 1 input intensity level produces the OR operation between two input beams, and setting the input threshold at $\frac{3}{2}$ of the logical 1 input level produces an AND operation on the two input beams. With contrast reversal, the NOT, NAND, and NOR operations become available. Hard-clip thresholding is implicit in the transfer function of most bistable optical devices. The bistable characteristic, which is shown in Fig. 10b, also exhibits hysteresis.

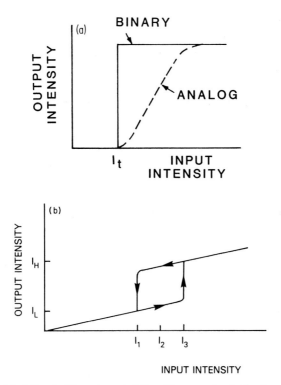

Fig. 10. (a) Ideal thresholding characteristics: binary or hard-clip thresholding (solid curve); analog thresholding (dashed curve). (b) Typical nonlinear transfer function of most bistable optical devices.

Hard-clipping can also be exploited to realize analog-to-digital converters for optical image fields or to form the nucleus of an optical halftone processor that can implement a wide variety of nonlinear intensity functions (Dashiell and Goodman, 1975; Armand *et al.*, 1982). Particularly useful nonlinear functions that can accrue from such halftone processing include contrast enhancement, level slicing, A/D conversion, quantization, pseudocolor encoding, logarithmic transforms for converting multiplicative signals and/or noise into additive signals, and square-root for obtaining output amplitude modulation directly proportional to the write-beam amplitude.

Certain materials, such as liquid crystals, YIG, PLZT, and VO_2, have a nonlinear relation between their controlling input and the resulting modulation, which can be directly employed for thresholding and other nonlinear operations. Alternatively, nonlinear operations can be implemented by employing particular aspects of the overall device physics, as in the MSLM and PEMLM, the platelet laser, and most of the bistable optical devices. The MSLM and PEMLM devices, for example, have a very useful intrinsic hard-clipping mode in which all three critical parameters (i.e., input threshold level, below-threshold output level, and above-threshold output level) are fully adjustable (McEwan *et al.*, 1985a). This mode permits inversion by setting the above-threshold output to be less intense than the below-threshold output.

7. *Optical Limiting*

The relatively flat regions below and above the hard-clip threshold in Fig. 10a or below and above the hysteresis region of Fig. 10b can provide an optical limiting function that can be used, for example, to supress intensity fluctuations in a noisy beam.

B. DEVICE-SPECIFIC ADVANCED PROCESSING FUNCTIONS

Some SLMs have intrinsic abilities to perform more advanced processing functions directly. While these functions are of immense utility to applications, most of them were not developed to meet the needs of specific applications but were discovered and developed in the course of basic device research.

1. *Edge Detection*

The programmable hard-clipping mode of the MSLM and PEMLM devices can be used to implement edge detection between regions of the input image having intensities above and below the threshold level (Warde and Thackara, 1983; McEwan *et al.*, 1985a). Essentially, both output levels are set to produce the same output intensity (e.g., dark) but separated by one full cycle of the device's sinusoidal modulation characteristic. Due to finite device resolution, a line of the intermediate half-cycle intensity level (e.g., bright) is produced along portions of the input image that are divided by the threshold. Other devices such as the PRIZ (Petrov, 1981; Owechko and Tanguay, 1982) and photorefractive configurations (Feinberg, 1980) also offer intrinsic spatial differentiation or edge detection capabilities.

2. *Intensity-to-Spatial Frequency Conversion*

This is a very powerful signal processing transformation which is an intrinsic operation of only a small number of SLMs. In a specific device called the variable grating mode (VGM) liquid-crystal modulator, the readout beam is scattered by gratings whose local periodicity varies with the local intensity of the input write-beam (Tanguay *et al.*, 1983). With such an intensity-to-spatial frequency converter, a wide range of nonlinear functions of the input intensity can be implemented by spatially filtering the readout beam.

3. Synchronous Detection

The MSLM and PEMLM devices can be operated as a 2-D pixel array of lock-in amplifiers or synchronous detectors (McEwan et al., 1985a). This function is implemented by oscillating the device between its charge deposition and removal modes at a rapid rate. Portions of the write image that are flashing on in synchronism with, for example, the charge-deposition cycles result in net charge accumulation over many cycles. This integrated charge eventually reaches a high modulation level. However, portions of the write image that are continuously illuminated or oscillating at a slightly different frequency result in no net charge accumulation. Applications of this lock-in amplifier array include discrimination from the ambient background of a structured light pattern projected into a scene for robot vision, removal of the dc bias from a heterodyne interferometric image, and target designation.

4. Demonstrations of Advanced Processing Operations

Actual experimental demonstrations of some of these more advanced processing functions are illustrated in Fig. 11. These demonstrations were implemented with MSLMs (McEwan et al., 1985a; Warde and Thackara, 1983). The MSLM used for parts 1–4 was provided by Hamamatsu Photonics. Parts 1b–1f of Fig. 11 show real-time hard-clip thresholding of the 6-level gray scale in part 1a, at five different adjustable-threshold levels. Part 2a is an image of two people, and 2b shows the corresponding MSLM output in its normal nonthreshold mode. Reverse-contrast hard-clip thresholding of this image at two different threshold levels is illustrated in parts 2c and 2e. Parts 2d and 2f demonstrate real-time edge detection, with the below- and above-threshold output levels separated by one full modulation cycle. (The object on the left of 2e and 2f is the darker leg of the left person.)

Part 3 depicts algebraic addition and subtraction by charge deposition and charge removal, respectively. The intermediate results of the following series of matrix additions and subtractions are shown.

$$\begin{pmatrix} 0 & 0 & 0 \\ 0 & 0 & 0 \\ 0 & 0 & 0 \end{pmatrix} + \begin{pmatrix} 1 & 0 & 0 \\ 1 & 0 & 0 \\ 1 & 0 & 0 \end{pmatrix} - \begin{pmatrix} 0 & 0 & 1 \\ 0 & 0 & 1 \\ 0 & 0 & 1 \end{pmatrix} + \begin{pmatrix} 1 & 1 & 1 \\ 0 & 0 & 0 \\ 0 & 0 & 0 \end{pmatrix} - \begin{pmatrix} 0 & 0 & 0 \\ 0 & 0 & 0 \\ 1 & 1 & 1 \end{pmatrix} = \begin{pmatrix} +2 & +1 & 0 \\ +1 & 0 & -1 \\ 0 & -1 & -2 \end{pmatrix}$$

The lock-in amplifier or synchronous detection function is demonstrated in part 4, where 4a–4c show the output response elicited by three LEDs

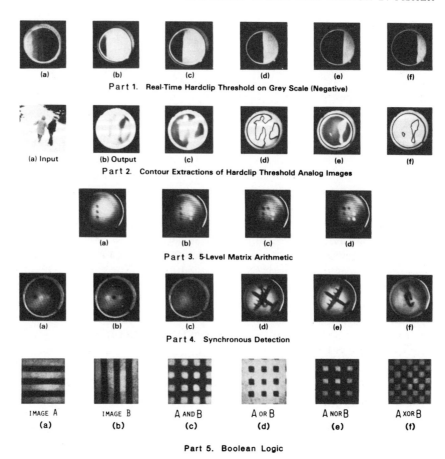

(a)   (b)   (c)   (d)   (e)   (f)

Part 1.   Real-Time Hardclip Threshold on Grey Scale (Negative)

(a) Input   (b) Output   (c)   (d)   (e)   (f)

Part 2.   Contour Extractions of Hardclip Threshold Analog Images

(a)   (b)   (c)   (d)

Part 3.   5-Level Matrix Arithmetic

(a)   (b)   (c)   (d)   (e)   (f)

Part 4.   Synchronous Detection

IMAGE A   IMAGE B   A AND B   A OR B   A NOR B   A XOR B
(a)   (b)   (c)   (d)   (e)   (f)

Part 5.   Boolean Logic

Fig. 11. Experimental demonstrations of five advanced intrinsic processing operations of the MSLM.

simultaneously pulsing at 19, 20, and 21 Hz as the MSLM is successively locked to each frequency. The normal, noncycling response of the MSLM to the simultaneous presentation of a C-clamp image oscillating at 18 Hz superimposed with an airplane image at 20 Hz is shown in part 4d. In parts 4e and 4f, the cycling MSLM is synchronized to detect only one image despite the simultaneous presence of the other image oscillating at nearby frequency. This synchronous detection mode can easily operate with kilohertz cycling rates, and discrimination bandwidths as small as 0.1 Hz have been demonstrated.

Parts 5c, 5d, and 5e show the Boolean AND, OR, NOR, and XOR logic operations performed between the striped input patterns of parts 5a and 5b.

VI. Performance Limitations of Electrooptic SLMs

The parameters by which optically addressed SLMs are characterized and compared include spatial resolution and device space–bandwidth product (number of pixels), framing speed, storage time, write-light exposure (including its spectral dependence), readout phase dynamic range, contrast ratio, spatial uniformity, readout wavelength range, cascadability, power supply holding currents and/or voltage levels, optical and electrical input power dissipation, readout light loss, readout optical power handling capacity, thermal stability, ruggedness, and difficulty and cost of manufacture. For electrically addressed devices, electrical input signal current, voltage, and power levels, rather than input exposure, are the appropriate input signal characteristics.

For the sake of brevity, we have chosen a charge-integrating 2-D longitudinal-electrooptic SLM with the generic structure of Fig. 1a as an example to illustrate the factors that limit the performance of SLMs. The analysis, therefore, applies to devices such as the MSLM and the photo-DKDP and e-beam DKDP light valves. Corresponding arguments and reasoning can be applied to other types of modulators.

Materials parameters that influence the characteristics of such electrooptic devices include electrooptic coefficients, refractive index and optical dispersion, optical absorption, spectral transmittance, photoconductivity and photorefractivity, optical activity, bulk and surface resistivity, pyroelectric and piezoelectric effects, dielectric constants, crystal symmetry, thermal conductivity, bulk photovoltaic effects, vapor pressure, dielectric strength, hardness, tensile strength, crystal thickness, and temperature coefficients. In the sections that follow, we examine how some of these materials characteristics impact the more important device operating characteristics.

A. WRITE-LIGHT EXPOSURE

The full-modulation exposure is a measure of the input sensitivity of an optically addressed device. In a longitudinally addressed electrooptic SLM that is read out in reflection (see Fig. 1a), the full-modulation exposure can be specified by the half-wave exposure $\mathscr{E}_{\pi R}$, which is the write-light power density (J/cm^2) that is required to change the phase retardation Γ of the readout light by π radians. For an amplitude modulator, $\Gamma = \Delta\phi_x - \Delta\phi_y$, where $\Delta\phi_x$ is the electrically induced phase change for light polarized along the x axis of the crystal. For phase-only modulators, the definition applies to an absolute phase shift of π radians.

For such a device, the factors that influence the half-wave exposure are the quantum efficiency η of the photosensor at the write wavelength λ_w, the internal electronic gain G, if any, and the half-wave surface charge density $\sigma_{\pi R}$ required for π radians of phase retardation. In general, $\sigma_{\pi R}$ depends on the dielectric constants ε_i, the crystal thickness l_x, the effective electrooptic coefficient tensor element r_{ij}, and the refractive index n of the crystal at the readout wavelength λ_r. For a high-resistivity crystal that integrates the driving charge distribution at its surface and is read out in reflection between crossed polarizers, the low-frequency half-wave exposure $\mathscr{E}_{\pi R}$ for amplitude modulation is given by

$$\mathscr{E}_{\pi R} = I_w t_\pi = \frac{hc\sigma_{\pi R}}{\eta e G \lambda_w} \tag{1}$$

where h is Planck's constant, c the speed of light, e the charge of an electron, I_w the write-light intensity and t_π the time taken to accumulate the reflection half-wave surface charge density $\sigma_{\pi R}$.

$$\sigma_{\pi R} = \frac{\varepsilon_\parallel \varepsilon_0 \lambda_r}{4n^3 r_{ij} l_x} \tag{2}$$

Here $\varepsilon_\parallel$ is the dielectric constant of the crystal parallel to the applied electric field and ε_0 is the permittivity of free space. As an example, for a 55°-cut LiNbO$_3$ MSLM (Warde and Thackara, 1982) in which $(n^3 r_{ij})_{\text{eff}} = 1.3 \times 10^{-10}$ m/V at $\lambda_r = 633$ nm, $\varepsilon_\parallel = 36$, $l_x = 100$ μm, $G = 10^3$, and $\eta = 0.1$ at $\lambda_w = 633$ nm, the calculated value of $\sigma_{\pi R}$ is 0.4 μC/cm^2 and $\mathscr{E}_{\pi R}$ is 8 nJ/cm^2.

Half-wave exposures ranging from 2 to 30 nJ/cm^2 have been reported for MSLMs employing one microchannel plate (Warde et al., 1978; Hara et al., 1986). Typical half-wave exposure values for other electrooptic devices, such as the photo-DKDP light valve and the PROM, are in the μJ/cm^2 range. In comparison, Kodak 649F film has a sensitivity of approximately 50 μJ/cm^2. The spectral dependence of the half-wave exposure is determined primarily by the spectral responsivity of the photosensor and the spectral transmission of the input window.

Devices such as the MSLM and PEMLM derive their very large gain through the use of microchannel plates (MCPs) and consequently can offer very high exposure sensitivity. However, at very high gains the useful dynamic range diminishes, because in this quantum-limited regime only a few input photons are used to achieve the full-modulation exposure. In practice it is often desirable to decrease the MCP gain so that the number of photons required to drive a pixel to the required modulation depth are also sufficient to obtain the desired signal-to-noise ratio.

B. Framing Speed

The factors that generally influence the framing speed of a light modulator are:

1. the combined charge delivery capability of the photosensor and gain elements,

2. the charge-to-light modulation sensitivity of the light-modulating element, and

3. joule heating in the device components.

For electrooptic crystals, the charge-to-light modulation sensitivity is dictated by the electrooptic coefficients, the dielectric constants, and the thickness of the crystal, and can be expressed in terms of the half-wave surface charge density. In most cases, the framing speed of longitudinal electrooptic light modulators is limited by the capacity of the charge delivery system. Examples include MCP current saturation in the MSLM, joule heating in the silicon DKDP light valve (Armitage *et al.*, 1985), and maximum electron gun beam current in the e-beam DKDP light valve. Typical half-wave framing speeds of, for example, the MSLM vary from a few to about 200 Hz at present.

Consider the case where the framing speed is limited by joule heating in the device components. For example, in a device consisting of a photoconductor layer addressing a high-resistivity electrooptic crystal, the crystal is essentially lossless and most of the heat is dissipated in the photoconductor. In this case, the average power dissipated per unit surface area of the crystal is given by

$$P = \frac{\bar{E}_{\pi R}}{t_{\pi}} \tag{3}$$

where $\bar{E}_{\pi R}$ (J/cm^2), the capacitively stored half-wave energy per unit area, is given by

$$\bar{E}_{\pi R} = \frac{\sigma_{\pi R}^2}{2\bar{C}} = \frac{\varepsilon_{\parallel}\varepsilon_0 \lambda_r^2}{32 l_x n^6 r_{ij}^2} \tag{4}$$

and $\bar{C}$ is the capacitance per unit area of the crystal. Since the electrical power dissipation goes as $\varepsilon_{\parallel} n^{-6} r_{ij}^{-2}$, for high-speed operation it is advantageous to choose an electrooptic material with large refractive index, large electrooptic coefficient, and small dielectric constant. This electrical power dissipation figure of merit shows that DKDP operated at $-51°$C is approximately 5 times more efficient than 55°-cut LiNbO$_3$ and about 20 times more efficient than Bi$_{12}$SiO$_{20}$ as far as joule heating is concerned. Considering again the numerical example of the 55°-cut LiNbO$_3$ MSLM from the previous section, we find that $\bar{E}_{\pi R} = 240\ \mu$J/cm^2, and for $t_{\pi} = 1$ ms, $P = 240$ mW/cm^2.

C. SPATIAL RESOLUTION

The spatial resolution of an SLM may be expressed in terms of a spatial charge-to-light modulation transfer function (MTF). With spatially varying sinusoidal input charge patterns of frequency f on the crystal surface, the MTF of the device is defined by

$$\text{MTF}(f) = \frac{1}{m} \frac{I_{max} - I_{min}}{I_{max} + I_{min}} \tag{5}$$

where I_{max} and I_{min} are the intensities at the peaks and valleys of the spatially modulated readout light pattern as a function of spatial frequency f, and m is the modulation index of the sinusoidal input intensity.

Typically, in a longitudinal electrooptic SLM the spatial resolution is limited by the fringing of the electric fields in the crystal and therefore by the thickness of the crystal. For surface-charge-addressed crystals with the sandwich structure of Fig. 1a, it has been shown (Roach, 1974) that the crystal-limited spatial MTF exhibits a low-pass-filter type of characteristic, with a charge-to-voltage sensitivity roll-over point f^* (cycles per unit length) that is given by

$$f^* = \frac{\varepsilon_\parallel / l_x + \varepsilon_d / l_d}{2\pi[(\varepsilon_\perp \varepsilon_\parallel)^{1/2} + \varepsilon_d]} \tag{6}$$

where ε_d and l_d are the dielectric constant and thickness of the photosensor, and $\varepsilon_\parallel$ and $\varepsilon_\perp$ are the dielectric constants of the crystal parallel and perpendicular to the applied electric field. In devices such as the MSLM, $\varepsilon_d \ll \varepsilon_\parallel$ and $\varepsilon_\perp$, and Eq. (6) simplifies to

$$f^* = \frac{1}{2\pi l_x} \left(\frac{\varepsilon_\parallel}{\varepsilon_\perp} \right)^{1/2} \tag{7}$$

If we take $m = 1$, and assume that (1) the driving charge distribution consists only of charges of the same sign and (2) the average value of the induced exciting sinusoidal voltage distribution is $V_A = V_\pi/2$, then it can be shown from the results of Roach (1974) that the roll-over point ($\sim 71\%$ modulation) on the charge-to-light MTF curve is at approximately $1.6f^*$ and that the 50% point is at about $2.8f^*$. The resolution of an SLM is usually quoted at either of these two points. The resolution of surface-charged-addressed devices such as the MSLM and the DKDP light valves tends to fall in the range 5–15 cycles/mm at 50% contrast because of the thicknesses of the crystals used. The PROM and PRIZ devices store charge in the bulk, and consequently they tend to have a much more complicated MTF characteristic (Owechko and Tanguay, 1984). In materials that lack cylindrical symmetry, $\varepsilon_\perp$ is a function of direction, which causes f^*, and hence the spatial resolution, to be direction dependent (Liu and Warde, 1986). This phenomenon can lead to image distortion at high spatial frequencies.

D.   SWITCHING ENERGY PER PIXEL

For high-throughput applications it is essential simultaneously to maximize the number of pixels per unit area N and minimize the energy required to switch each pixel. In optically addressed devices there is generally also an electrical contribution to the switching energy. Thus, in longitudinal electrooptic O-SLMs, the total switching energy per pixel is given by

$$E_{p\pi} = \frac{\mathscr{E}_{\pi R} + \bar{E}_{\pi R}}{N} \tag{8}$$

If we take $N = (2 \times 2.8f^*)^2$, then for our example of the 55°-cut LiNbO$_3$ MSLM, with $l_x = 100$ μm, $\varepsilon_\parallel = 36$, $\varepsilon_\perp = 44$ (maximum), and $G = 10^3$, we find with the help of Eqs. (1), (4), and (7) that $N = 63$ pixels/mm^2 and that the electrical and optical switching energy components are 38 nJ/pixel and 1.3 pJ/pixel, respectively.

E.   CONTRAST RATIO AND USEFUL DYNAMIC RANGE

The contrast ratio of an amplitude or intensity modulator can be defined as the ratio $\langle I_{max}\rangle/\langle I_{min}\rangle$ where I_{max} and I_{min} are the maximum and minimum readout light intensities, under uniform write excitation and the angle brackets denote spatial averaging. For a spatially uniform SLM the contrast ratio is limited by the physical characteristics of the materials involved in the light modulation mechanism (e.g., dielectric breakdown strength in electrooptic SLMs). In practice, however, the contrast ratio of longitudinal electrooptic SLMs is determined by factors such as inhomogeneities in the crystal lattice, surface blemishes that tend to scatter and depolarize the readout light, and the quality of the polarizers used. Contrast ratios of 1000:1 are achievable with the LiNbO$_3$ MSLM, whereas liquid-crystal light modulators typically have contrast ratios less than 100:1 (Efron et al., 1983).

In a typical SLM both the contrast ratio and the MTF vary from region to region because of static fixed-pattern noise and spatial variations in the response of the device to the same input excitation. Consequently, it is expedient to define the "useful dynamic range" R of the device (the number of resolvable gray-scale levels) as

$$R = \frac{\langle I_{max}\rangle - \langle I_{min}\rangle}{\Delta I} \tag{9}$$

where ΔI is the spatial rms fluctuation in the readout light when the device is excited with a uniform write source that biases the device about the center of the most sensitive region of its transfer characteristic. Although the contrast ratio at a single point on a currently available 2-D SLM may be greater than 10^3 levels, the "useful dynamic range" of most of these devices rarely exceeds 20 levels (i.e., 5% uniformity).

Similar definitions hold for phase-only modulators. However, fixed-pattern noise in phase-only SLMs is easily removed by the use of static optical components such as phase plates and holographic optical elements. In longitudinal electrooptic devices, for example, the maximum phase modulation range achievable is often limited by the dielectric breakdown strength of the electrooptic crystal. Several waves of modulation have been demonstrated with an MSLM employing thin LiNbO$_3$ wafers with a breakdown strength of about 50 kV/mm (Warde *et al.*, 1978). Similarly, some deformable membrane devices are capable of displacements that are several visible wavelengths in amplitude (Fisher *et al.*, 1986a).

F. STORAGE TIME

Surface and bulk dark resistivities, photoconductivity, and dielectric constants of the modulating materials are the primary parameters that control the storage time in electrooptic and photorefractive SLMs. For surface-charge-addressed electrooptic light modulators, the bulk discharge time constant is given by $\tau = \rho \varepsilon \varepsilon_0$. Here ρ and ε are the resistivity and dielectric constant, respectively, of the electrooptic material. In many instances surface conductivity, which causes lateral diffusion of charge, is the dominant mechanism tending to degrade resolution. Photoconductivity accelerates both the transverse diffusion and the longitudinal discharging processes.

G. READOUT POWER LIMITATIONS

The readout optical power handling capability of SLMs is generally limited by the absorption and photorefractive effects in the crystal. Deuterated potassium dihydrogen phosphate (DKDP) is among the electrooptic crystals best suited for high power laser readout. Power densities of several MW/cm^2 have been successfully transmitted through this material. On the other hand, LiNbO$_3$ is readily damaged at high optical power densities due to large photorefractive and photovoltaic effects. Similarly, photorefractive materials such as BaTiO$_3$, Bi$_{12}$SiO$_{20}$ and Sr$_{1-x}$Ba$_x$Nb$_2$O$_6$ are damaged at densities of several kW/cm^2. Spectral absorption characteristics also play a critical role in determining the readout power handling capability of the SLM. For most applications in optical information processing, the goal is to use the minimum readout optical power necessary to maintain a sufficiently high signal-to-noise ratio. Thus the ability of the modulator to tolerate high power readout is not always essential.

VII. Specific SLM Structures

A few of the most common devices, representing the major classes of SLMs, are briefly discussed in this section. A more detailed perspective of previous, current, and proposed SLM devices can be found in a variety of SLM review articles and special journal issues, such as Flannery (1973), Meitzler and Kurtz (1973), Casasent (1977), Knight (1981), Tanguay (1983), Efron (1984), Tanguay and Warde (1985), Tanguay (1985), Fisher (1985b), Fisher and Lee (1987), and Warde and Efron (1986).

A variety of optical phenomena in materials have been exploited to realize real-time spatial light modulation. These include the electrooptic effect in organic and inorganic materials; the Faraday effect in magnetic materials; the acoustooptic effect in elastooptic materials; the Franz–Keldysh and other electroabsorption effects in insulators and semiconductors; the photochromic effect in alkali halides; the piezoelectric effect in ceramics; electrostatic deformation of membranes, elastomers, gels, and cantilevers; and phase transitions and thermal expansion of materials.

The SLMs in the following discussions are divided into two primary classes (O-SLMs and E-SLMs). The devices are then further classified into signal-multiplying, self-modulating, and self-emissive functional categories.

A. OPTICALLY ADDRESSED SLMs

1. Signal-Multiplying Devices

a. Microchannel Plate Devices. The optically addressed microchannel spatial light modulator (photo-MSLM) (Warde *et al.*, 1978, 1981; Warde and Thackara, 1982, 1983; Hara *et al.*, 1985, 1986) and the photoemitter membrane light modulator (PEMLM) (Somers, 1972; Fisher *et al.*, 1986a) fall into the structural class illustrated in Fig. 1a. Their specific structure is shown in Fig. 12. A unique feature of these devices is their large electron gain, which is provided by a microchannel plate (MCP) (Wisa, 1979) located between the photocathode and the modulating element. In operation, an incident write image is converted by the photocathode into an electron image. This electron image is amplified by the MCP and deposited onto the surface of the light-modulating material, which is an electrooptic crystal in the MSLM and a reflective, flexible membrane covering the MCP in the PEMLM. In the MSLM the electric field set up by the charge distribution on the surface of the crystal modulates the readout light via the longitudinal electrooptic effect. Whereas in the PEMLM the accumulated charge distribution causes electrostatic forces that deform the reflective membrane. A grid between the MCP and the modulating material facilitates the active removal of electrons by secondary emission from the surface of the modulating

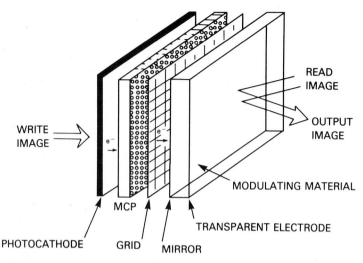

Fig. 12. Generic structure of MSLM and PEMLM incorporating photoemission and micro-channel plate electron amplification.

material. These devices can offer long-term (months) storage of images as a net positive or negative charge distribution on the modulating material.

The MSLM and the PEMLM are among the most versatile of the electrooptic SLMs. They offer high exposure sensitivity ($\sim$2–30 nJ/cm^2), long storage time (days), and high framing speed ($\sim$200 Hz and 1 kHz for the MSLM and the PEMLM, respectively) and can internally perform several real-time sophisticated optical parallel processing operations on stored or time-varying images. These include image addition and subtraction, contrast enhancement, contrast reversal, edge enhancement, and binary-level optical logic operations such as AND, OR, NOR, NAND, XOR, and NXOR. Several of these operations are illustrated in Fig. 11. The write-light wavelength range may vary from the soft x-ray to the near infrared. The readout light wavelength range of the MSLM and PEMLM is also broad. In the MSLM it is limited by the spectral transmittance of electrooptic crystals.

b. Liquid-Crystal Devices. The optically addressed liquid-crystal light valves (LCLVs) (Bleha *et al.*, 1978; Efron *et al.*, 1983; Aubourg *et al.*, 1982) have the generic structure of Fig. 1a. They employ a liquid-crystal layer as the light-modulating element and such photoconductors as cadmium sulfide, silicon, or bismuth silicon oxide as the charge-generation transducer. In the twisted nematic liquid-crystal device, for example, the liquid-crystal molecules are oriented with a 45° twist in going from one electrode to the other. An alternating electric field from an ac bias voltage supply is impressed across the liquid-crystal layer by optically induced impedance changes in the photoconductor layer. This field tends to tip the axes of the molecules along the field lines, which alters the material birefringence and thereby the polarization state of the readout light. This light-induced change in polarization rotation of the readout light can be converted to amplitude modulation by reading out the device between crossed polarizers.

In the typical nematic liquid devices, the photoconductor is 5–10 μm thick, and the liquid crystal layer is 2–15 μm thick. These devices offer a spatial resolution of about 20 cycles/mm at 50% MTF, an exposure sensitivity of about 1–5 $\mu J/cm^2$ and rms operating voltages of about 5–10 V. Image storage time is very short (ms), and the framing speeds are approximately 40 Hz, being limited by the natural reorientation time of the liquid-crystal molecules when the write-light is turned off. Ferroelectric liquid-crystal devices (Clark *et al.*, 1983; Armitage *et al.*, 1986) offer increased framing speeds over nematic devices, because the polar nature of the ferroelectric molecules permit the molecules to be actively reoriented by an applied electric field.

c. Photo-DKDP Light Valve. The photo-DKDP light valve is a sandwich of the form in Fig. 1a, consisting of a thin photoconductor (amorphous selenium), a dielectric mirror layer, and a thin deuterated potassium dihydrogen phosphate (DKDP) crystal operated near its Curie temperature ($-51°C$) (Donjon *et al.*, 1973; Marie, 1976; Casasent, 1978b; Armitage *et al.*, 1985).

When blue write-light is incident on the photoconductor, charge carriers (holes or electrons, depending on the polarity of the applied field) migrate to the photoconductor–crystal interface and establish a spatially varying electric field across the DKDP crystal. The electric field in the DKDP alters the birefringence of the crystal, and thus readout light making a double pass through the crystal is polarization modulated. The device is read out between crossed polarizers, and erasure is accomplished by flooding the photoconductor with light while short-circuiting the electrodes. A sensitivity of 10 $\mu J/cm^2$ at $\lambda = 420$ nm, a contrast ratio of 70:1, and a limiting resolution of 75 cycles/mm have been reported (Marie, 1976).

d. Photorefractive Signal-Multiplying Devices. Photorefractive devices employ a single material that simultaneously exhibits the photoconductive and electrooptic effects. Signal-multiplying devices employing photorefractive materials fall into two structural classes: a nonholographic structure as illustrated in Fig. 1b and a volume-holographic structure with the configuration shown in Fig. 1c. The Pockels readout optical modulator (PROM) (Horwitz and Corbett, 1978; Owechko and Tanguay, 1982) and the PRIZ (*preobrasovatel izobrazheniy,* meaning "image transducer" in

Russian) (Petrov, 1981) employ $Bi_{12}SiO_{20}$ (BSO) or $Bi_{12}GeO_{20}$ (BGO) crystals and are examples of devices with the nonholographic structure. Devices with the holographic structure include the photorefractive in-coherent-to-coherent (PICOC) modulator (Kamshilin and Petrov, 1980; Marrakchi et al., 1985) and the multiwave mixing devices (Huignard et al., 1985; Pepper, 1982).

The PROM uses a thin ($\sim$500 μm) wafer of photorefractive BSO with a pair of transparent electrodes that are separated from the crystal by blocking layers of paralene that are about 5 μm thick. Blue or near-ultraviolet light incident on the device generates an image-wise distribution of hole–electron pairs within the bulk of the crystal. The mobile electrons drift through the bulk to the electrodes under the influence of an applied electric field. The space-charge field set up by the immobile hole pattern and the transparent electrodes modulates the refractive index of the crystal and thereby the phase (or amplitude, when polarizers are employed) of the readout light. To avoid destructive readout, red readout light is employed. Erasure of the stored image is accomplished by flooding the crystal with light containing blue or near-ultraviolet components. Current devices exhibit a spatial reso-lution of about 5–10 cycles/mm at 50% MTF, framing rates of 10–30 Hz, $1/e$ exposures in the neighborhood of 10 μJ/cm^2, contrast ratios of 1000:1, and operating bias voltages in the neighborhood of 4 kV. The storage time depends on the ambient illumination. Storage times of about one hour in the dark have been reported for $Bi_{12}SiO_{20}$.

Unlike the nonholographic devices, volume-holographic modulators (Glass, 1978; Burke et al., 1982; Huignard et al., 1985; Pepper, 1982) are generally written on with light having an energy less than the material bandgap. Volume-holographic devices often consist simply of a rectangular block of the photorefractive material, as depicted in Fig. 1c. Sometimes electrodes are added. Nonuniform write-light incident on the material ionizes impurity ions and/or lattice defects, creating spatially varying inter-nal charge distributions. This charge is subsequently transported by drift and/or diffusion from the brighter to the darker regions of the material. The resulting space-charge electric fields modulate the refractive index of the material via the electrooptic effect. Best performance is generally obtained by operating these materials in the regime where the spatial structure in the input image is comparable to the drift and diffusion lengths in the materials. Consequently, holographic recording techniques are used, and spatial resolutions on the order of 2000 cycles/mm can be achieved (Huignard et al., 1980). Materials exhibiting this effect include $Bi_{12}SiO_{20}$, $BaTiO_3$, $Sr_xBa_{1-x}Nb_2O_6$, $LiNbO_3$:Fe, $KNbO_3$:Fe, and $GaAs$:Fe.

By employing 2-, 3-, or 4-wave mixing, these volume-holographic devices can perform multiplication, amplification, and incoherent-to-coherent image conversion (Huignard et al., 1985; Pepper, 1982; Huignard and

Marrakchi, 1981; Marrakchi *et al.*, 1985). However, readout is often destructive. Because the writing process is interferometric, applications of these devices are usually constrained by the need for (1) a source of polarized coherent light, (2) a mechanically stable platform suitable for holographic recording, and (3) auxiliary light beams with specific geometric, polarization, and/or intensity characteristics (Pepper, 1982; Huignard *et al.*, 1985; Marrakchi *et al.*, 1985; Tanguay, 1985).

e. Thermoplastic Modulator. The thermoplastic modulator (Colburn and Chang, 1978) is a two-element device consisting of a photoconductor and a thermoplastic layer in the basic sandwich configuration of Fig. 1a. This device is often used to record holograms. The interference pattern set up by the write-beams on the photoconductor produces a spatially varying charge pattern at the interface with the thermoplastic material. When the thermoplastic is heated above its softening point, the electrostatic forces arising from the interface charge deform the thermoplastic, thereby recording the information. The hologram is erased by flooding the photoconductor with light and reheating the thermoplastic layer above the softening point. This modulator has a cycle time on the order of tenths of a second, a bandpass spatial frequency response whose peak varies with the thickness of the thermoplastic layer, and an exposure sensitivity of about $10 \ \mu J/cm^2$ for 10% diffraction efficiency.

f. Semiconductor O-SLMs. An important new class of optically addressed hybrid SLM structures is beginning to emerge that is compatible with planar semiconductor microcircuits. For example, some versions of the deformable membrane device (DMD) (Pape, 1985a; Pape and Hornbeck, 1983; Hornbeck, 1983) employ an array of silicon phototransistors that address a deformable membrane mirror, or arrays of tiny SiO_2 diving-boardlike, cantilever-beam mirror structures (Brooks, 1985). Monolithic planar structures combining Si phototransistors with PLZT electrooptic modulators are also under development (Lee *et al.*, 1986). This Si-PLZT device has a transverse electrooptic geometry in which the propagation direction of the readout light is orthogonal to the driving electric field in each pixel. In yet another semiconductor SLM structure (Kingston *et al.*, 1984), photogenerated charges in a GaAs charge-coupled device array set up electric fields that modify the optical absorption characteristics of the GaAs substrate via electroabsorption.

2. Self-Modulating Devices

a. Bistable Optical Devices. Optical bistability is observed in a light-modulating material when an optical feedback mechanism exists in conjunction with an optically induced change in one of the optical properties of the material. Most bistable optical devices employ the self-modulating structure of Fig. 1d in which a single material performs the functions of charge generation and light modulation. A commonly used configuration is an etalon, such as a Fabry–Perot cavity or multilayer interference filter containing a nonlinear material whose optical absorption, refractive index, and/or physical length is a function of the incident optical intensity. Nonlinear materials that have been used in Fabry–Perot cavities include Na vapor, CS_2, nitrobenzene, CdHgTe, CdS, CuCl, ZnS, ZnSe, InAs, InSb, GaAs, and multiple quantum well (MQW) structures consisting of very thin (0.5–100 nm) layers of GaAs and $Al_{1-x}Ga_xAs$. Recent attention has focused on the latter three materials and on interference filters with layers of ZnS or ZnSe, all of which offer fairly large nonlinearities at room temperature.

In a bistable etalon device, part of the incident intensity is transmitted or reflected to form an output beam. The optical intensity in the etalon changes the refractive index or absorption of the nonlinear material which alters the effective cavity length and in turn modifies the cavity intensity. The net transmission or reflection follows a nonlinear transfer function of the general bistable form shown in Fig. 10b, which is characterized by hysteresis with two possible stable outputs for input intensities near I_2.

Bistability has also been realized in other feedback configurations, such as (1) the self-electrooptic effect device (SEED) which places an MQW structure inside a p-i-n photodiode (Miller *et al.*, 1984), (2) hybrid structures in which the output intensity from an etalon is incident on a detector that in turn drives an electrooptic modulator within the cavity (Smith and Turner, 1977), (3) laser diode amplifiers in which the external intensity tunes the cavity resonance (Dagenais and Sharfin, 1986), (4) a conventional SLM with its output beam fed back to its input (Fisher and Warde, 1979; Collins, 1980; Garmire *et al.*, 1978), and (5) reflection at an interface with a nonlinear material.

Unlike many SLMs which have a passive storage mode requiring no holding power, the bistable devices require the continuous application of illumination to store information. Other disadvantages of semiconductor bistable devices are their high optical switching powers and/or electrical power consumption, their low contrast ratios, and the difficulties associated with fabricating large 2-D arrays of devices on a single wafer. To date, simultaneous parallel operation of up to 25 elements has been demonstrated. Sustained operation of most of the bistable devices has generally required 1–10 mW of optical power per pixel (for switching times in the nanosecond to picosecond range), which implies that sustained operation of a large array at these speeds may demand impractically large optical intensities. For example, a 10^6 element array constructed in 1 cm^2, would require 1–10 kW/cm^2 of optical intensity, with 1 kW/cm^2 or more being dissipated as heat (Gibbs, 1985). These power requirements can be reduced by operating in a low duty-cycle mode, with occasional transient high-speed decisions being made. A major strength of these devices is their high switching speeds, with some of the bistable etalons offering nanosecond to picosecond switching times, as opposed to the millisecond operation for most SLMs.

b. Passive Phase-Conjugate Mirrors. These are self-modulating devices that consist of a single block of volume-holographic material and produce a phase-conjugate beam when a single input beam is incident on the material (Feinberg, 1982; Cronin-Golomb *et al.*, 1982). It is believed that the mechanism responsible for the phase-conjugating property involves: (1) the generation of weak noisy diffraction gratings from the interference between the primary beam and scattered light, and (2) subsequent scattering of the primary beam off these gratings to produce several diffracted beams, one of which is internally retroreflected from a corner of the crystal, scatters off the amplified grating, and exits the crystal counterpropagating and phase conjugated with respect to the input beam. Applications of passive phase-conjugate mirrors include image subtraction, optical associative memories, phase locking of lasers, and adaptive compensation of aberrations in laser cavities.

3. *Optically Addressed Self-Emissive SLMs*

These devices are generally used as input transducers for wavelength conversion and as gain stages in optical processors. They include devices such as image intensifier tubes, photoconductor-accessed LED arrays (Tippett *et al.*, 1965), and photoconductor-accessed electroluminescent devices (Shaefer and Strong, 1975; Bray, 1963). Currently there is interest in platelet lasers (Seko and Nishikata, 1977) for image processing and in photodiode-activated LED's or surface-emitting injection lasers (Liau *et al.*, 1984; Uchiyama and Iga, 1985; Goodman *et al.*, 1984) for applications in optical interconnections for VLSI.

B. ELECTRICALLY ADDRESSED SLMs

Electrically addressed SLMs tend to be either the signal-multiplying or the self-emissive type, with the generic configuration shown in Figs. 1a or 1e, respectively. Many of the signal-multiplying E-SLMs are related to a corresponding O-SLM, sharing the same modulator material and hence the same materials-dictated performance limitations. Examples include the electrically addressed DMD (Pape, 1985a), the electron-beam addressed MSLM (e-beam MSLM) (Schwartz, *et al.*, 1985), the electron-beam addressed DKDP light valve (Groh and Marie, 1970; Casasent, 1978a), and the CCD-addressed liquid-crystal light valves (CCD-LCLV) (Efron *et al.*, 1983).

Overall, a wider variety of modulating materials and principles have been employed in E-SLMS than in O-SLMs. Examples include the magnetooptic effect in the LIGHTMOD (Ross *et al.*, 1983) devices, the electrocapillary effect device (Lea, 1984), the anisotropic particle-in-liquid suspension optical tunnel array (OTA) device, and self-emissive devices such as cathode ray tubes, LEDs, and arrays of surface-emitting injection lasers (Uchiyama and Iga, 1985; Liau *et al.*, 1984).

One-dimensional SLMs have tended to be electronically, rather than optically, addressed, and a wide variety of signal-multiplying E-SLMs have been produced in 1-D formats. These include magnetooptic, acoustooptic, micromechanical (Brooks, 1985), electroabsorption (Kingston *et al.*, 1984), Canon liquid-film (Minoura *et al.*, 1984), integrated-optical electrooptic (Verber *et al.*, 1981), and total internal refection (TIR) (Johnson *et al.*, 1983) devices.

1. *Magnetooptic SLMs*

The most common magnetooptic device, called the LIGHTMOD/SIGHTMOD, uses the Faraday magnetooptic effect in an epitaxial garnet film (Ross *et al.*, 1983). The film is thulium iron garnet that is heavily doped with bismuth to increase the Faraday rotation. The film is divided into an array of square mesas, and the magnetization direction of each mesa-pixel can be individually flipped through the combined magnetic field from an x–y matrix of conductors. The two magnetization orientations produce opposite rotations of the polarization of a transmitted beam. Therefore an amplitude-modulated image is obtained by reading out The device between polarizers. The Faraday rotation and absorption of the garnet film vary with film thickness and wavelength of illumination. When the LIGHTMOD is operated with white light, the transmission of the device thus becomes color dependent.

2. *Acoustooptic SLMs*

The acoustooptic Bragg cell modulators (Berg and Lee, 1983) deserve special mention because they are the most well developed and widely used 1-D modulator technology. These are generally operated in a 1-D mode and employ a single transducer to launch a surface or bulk acoustic wave in an elastooptic material. The resulting compressions and rarefactions lead to spatial variations in the refractive index that scatter the readout optical beam as it passes through the material. The transducer is generally operated in the neighborhood of a central carrier frequency ν_0 where the electrical input signal energy is coupled most efficiently into the modulator material.

Some of the most frequently used materials include, $LiNbO_3$ quartz, TeO_2, and GaP. Desirable materials properties include large acoustooptic figures of merit, good optical quality and high transparency, birefringence, low acoustic attenuation, low nonlinear acoustic coefficient, high thermal conductivity, and high optical damage threshold (Chang, 1985).

The input electrical signal is usually mixed with the carrier and applied to the transducer. Either bulk material or surface acoustic wave geometries can be used. Time–bandwidth products on the order of 1000–10,000 are achievable. Bragg cells have also been configured as 2-D E-SLMs by employing a linear array of transducers to launch parallel acoustic beams across the optical aperture (Vander Lugt *et al.*, 1983; Pape, 1985b). The inability to store information is a major shortcoming of Bragg cells.

3. *Self-Emissive E-SLMs*

Spatial light modulators in this class are used primarily as transducers for electrical-to-optical conversion. As such, they generally find applications in the input plane of optical processors. Most self-emissive devices generate incoherent light, although active research continues on coherently combining arrays of semiconductor lasers on the same chip. Examples of electrically addressed self-emissive devices include cathode ray tubes, arrays of LEDs, electroluminescent and gas-plasma panels, arrays of hard-wire addressed or electron-beam pumped semiconductor lasers, and surface-emitting 2-D planar arrays of injection lasers (Uchiyama and Iga, 1985; Liau *et al.*, 1984).

VIII. Concluding Remarks

We have identified a variety of important applications in optical information processing that rely critically upon SLMs. These applications dictate the various basic processing operations required of SLMs and establish performance requirements that provide direction for future device research. Included in the applications are areas such as pattern recognition, real-time signal processing, numerical array processing (e.g., matrix–matrix operations), medical imaging, and imaging and communications through randomly fluctuating media. There is also promising research in progress that will expand the applications of SLMs into advanced processing areas, such as image understanding, speech understanding, high-level symbolic processing, and a variety difficult problems within the domain of artificial intelligence. Although several sophisticated optical information processing architectures have been proposed for these applications, only a few have thus far been demonstrated at the feasibility level in the laboratory.

A small number of 2-D SLMs are beginning to emerge from the laboratory into commercial manufacture. The performance level of current SLMs is on the order of 100×100 resolution elements, 10-Hz framing rate, 1-s storage time, less than 100 $\mu J/cm^2$ exposure for full contrast modulation, five levels of useful dynamic range (20% spatial uniformity), and a few visible wavelengths of flatness. We note, however, that even these modest perform-ance levels are seldom simultaneously achievable in a single device.

To satisfy the requirements of the more important signal processing applications, current SLM research is moving in the direction of devices with better than 1000×1000 resolution elements in an active area less than $20\ cm^2$, kilohertz framing rates, high sensitivity (O-SLMs), 1 hour of storage time, 100 levels of useful dynamic range, and $\frac{1}{5}$ wavelength flatness. These values are actually a compromise between truly ideal performance and reasonable device expectations for the near future. The associated practical issues that should guide present and future SLM development include ease of use, reproducibility and reliability of operation, minimal and unsophisti-cated support electronics, simple low-loss optical readout system, small device footprint, and nonintimidating cost ($<\$5000$). In practice the per-formance levels required are application specific, and all of these features are seldom required simultaneously.

Research on the development of new materials and on new techniques for employing existing materials is sorely needed. The electrooptic SLM technology, for example, would benefit significantly from an electrooptic material with large electrooptic coefficients that couple only to longitudinal fields, small dielectric constants, large refractive index, high crystallographic symmetry, high dielectric strength, high surface and bulk resistivities, good optical quality, good mechanical strength and hardness, small temperature coefficients, and insolubility in the common solvents. Because no material has been found that exhibits all of the above characteristics, it is customary to trade performance in one device characteristic for another (e.g., sensitivity and framing speed for spatial resolution).

Although available devices fall short of attaining the overall features and performance levels eventually required by many important applications, some do perform well enough for use in feasibility demonstrations of some of the recently proposed sophisticated concepts. This has been particularly true when the requirements of the application match the specific strengths of a given device technology, and it suggests that there may be merit in designing current optical architectures to employ the strengths of particular existing devices while de-emphasizing the device weaknesses. The future of SLM development is expected to be marked by increased interplay between applications and devices.

References

Anderson, D. Z. (1986). *Opt. Lett.* **11**, 56.
Armand, A., Strand, T. C., Sawchuk, A. A., and Soffer, B. H. (1982). *Opt. Lett.* **7**, 451.

Armitage, D., Anderson, W. W., and Karr, T. J. (1985). *IEEE J. Quantum Electron.* **QE-21**, 1241.

Armitage, D., Thackara, J. I., Clark, N. A., and Handschy, M. A. (1986). *Dig. Conf. Lasers Electroopt.* (*CLEO*) p. 366.

Athale, R. A., and Collins, W. C. (1982). *Appl. Opt.* **21**, 2089.

Athale, R. A., Friedlander, C. B., and Kushner, B. H. (1986). *SPIE Semin. Proc.* **625**, 179.

Aubourg, P., Huignard, J. P., Hareng, M., and Mullen, R. A. (1982). *Appl. Opt.* **21**, 3706.

Babcock, T. R., Friend, R. C., and Hegges, P. (1963). *In* "Optical Processing of Information" (C. K. Pollock, C. J. Koester, and J. T. Tippet, eds.), p. 145. Spartan Books, Baltimore, Maryland.

Bell, T. E. (1986). *IEEE Spectrum.* **23**, 34.

Berg, N. J., and Lee, J. N. eds. (1983). "Acoustooptic Signal Processing: Theory and Implementation." Dekker, New York.

Blechman, F. (1986). *Radio Electron.* **57**, July, p. 39; Aug. p. 47.

Bleha, W. P., Lipton, L. T., Wiener-Avnear, E., Grinberg, J., Reif, P. G., Casasent, D., Brown, H. B., and Markevitch, B. V. (1978). *Opt. Eng.* **17**, 371.

Bocker, R. P. (1984). *Opt. Eng.* **23**, 26.

Bray, T. E. (1963). *In* "Optical Processing of Information" (D. K. Pollock, C. J. Koester, and J. T. Tippett, eds.), p. 216. Spartan Books, Baltimore, Maryland.

Brenner, K. H., Huang, A., and Streibl, N. (1986). *Appl. Opt.* **25**, 3054.

Brooks, R. E. (1985). *Opt. Eng.* **24**, 101.

Burke, W. J., Staebler, D. L., Phillips, W., and Alphonse, G. A. (1982). *Opt. Eng.* **17**, 308.

Casasent, D. (1977). *Proc. IEEE* **65**, 143.

Casasent, D. (1978a). *Opt. Eng.* **17**, 344.

Casasent, D. (1978b). *Opt. Eng.* **17**, 365.

Casasent, D. (1985). *Opt. Eng.* **24**, 27.

Casasent, D., and Lee, A. J. (1986). *SPIE Semin. Proc.* **625**, 234.

Casasent, D., and Psaltis, A. (1977). *Proc. IEEE* **65**, 770.

Caulfield, H. J., gen. chm. (1985). *Tech. Dig. OSA '85 Top. Meet. Opt. Comput. Lake Tahoe, Nev.*

Caulfield, H. J., Dvore, D., Goodman, J. W., and Rhodes, W. (1981). *Appl. Opt.* **20**, 2263.

Caulfield, H. J., Rhodes, W. T., Foster, M. J., and Horvitz, S. (1982). *Opt. Commun.* **40**, 86.

Caulfield, H. J., Horvitz, S., Tricoles, G. P., and Von Winkle, W. A., guest eds. (1984). *Proc. IEEE* **72**, 755.

Chang, I. C. (1985). *Opt. Eng.* **24**, 132.

Clark, N. A., Handschy, M. A., and Lagerwall, S. T. (1983). *Mol. Cryst. Liq. Cryst.* **94**, 213.

Cohen, M. S. (1986). *SPIE Semin. Proc.* **625**, 214.

Colburn, W. S., and Chang, B. J. (1978). *Opt. Eng.* **17**, 334.

Collier, R. J., and Pennington, K. S. (1966). *Appl. Phys. Lett.* **8**, 44.

Collins, S. A., guest ed. (1980). *Opt. Eng.* **19**, 441.

Condon, D. J., Reichenbach, M. C., Taresevich, A., and Rhodes, W. T. (1985). *Dig. Postdeadline Pap., OSA '85 Top. Meet. Opt. Comput., Lake Tahoe, Nev.* p. PD2.

Cronin-Golomb, M., Fisher, B., White, J. O., and Yariv, A. (1982). *Appl. Phys. Lett.* **41**, 689.

Cutrona, L. J., Leith, E. N., Porcello, L. J., and Vivian, W. E. (1966). *Proc. IEEE* **54**, 1026.

Dagenais, M., and Sharfin, W. F. (1986). *Opt. Eng.* **25**, 219.

Dashiell, S. R., and Goodman, J. W. (1975). *Appl. Opt.* **14**, 1813.

Donjon, J., Dumont, F., Grenot, M., Hazan, J. P., Marie, G., and Pergrale, J. (1973). *IEEE Trans. Electron Devices* **Ed-20**, 1037.

Dove, B. L., ed. (1985). *Digital Opt. Circuit Technol. AGARD Conf. Proc.* No. 362. NTIS, Springfield, Virginia.

Efron, U., ed. (1984). *SPIE Semin. Proc.* **465**.

Efron, U., Braatz, P. O., Little, M. J., and Schwartz, R. N. (1983). *Opt. Eng.* **22**, 682.

Efron, U., Grinberg, J., Braatz, P. O., Little, M. J., Reif, P. G., and Schwartz, R. N. (1985a). *J. Appl. Phys.* **57**, 1356.

Efron, U., Marom, E., and Soffer, B. H. (1985b). *Tech. Dig. OSA '85 Top. Meet. Opt. Comput. Lake Tahoe, Nev.* p. TuF2.

Eichmann, G., and Caulfield, H. J. (1985). *Appl. Opt.* **24**, 2051.

Feinberg, J. (1980). *Opt. Lett.* **5**, 330.

Feinberg, J. (1982). *Opt. Lett.* **7**, 486.

Fisher, A. D. (1985a). *SPIE Semin. Proc.* **551**, 102.

Fisher, A. D. (1985b). *Tech. Dig. OSA '85 Top. Meet. Opt. Comput., Lake Tahoe, Nev.* p. TuC1.

Fisher, A. D., and Giles, C. L. (1985). *Proc. IEEE 1985 COMPCON Spring Meet.* CH135-2/85, p. 342.

Fisher, A. D., and Lee, J. N. (1986). *SPIE Semin. Proc.* **634**, 352.

Fisher, A. D., and Warde, C. (1979). *Opt. Lett.* **4**, 131.

Fisher, A. D., and Warde, C. (1983). *Opt. Lett.* **8**, 353.

Fisher, A. D., Ling, L. C., Lee, J. N., and Fukuda, R. C. (1986a). *Opt. Eng.* **25**, 261.

Fisher, A. D., Fukuda, R. C., and Lee, J. N. (1986b). *SPIE Semin. Proc.* **625**, 196.

Flannery, D. L., Biernacki, A., Loomis, J., and Cartwright, S. (1986). *Appl. Opt.* **25**, 466.

Flannery, J. B. (1973). *IEEE Trans. Electron. Devices* **ED-20**, 41.

Gabor, D. (1969). *IBM J. Res. Dev.* **13**, 156.

Garmire, E., Marburger, J. H., and Allen, S. D. (1978). *Appl. Phys. Lett.* **32**, 320.

Gibbs, H. M. (1985). "Optical Bistability: Controlling Light with Light." Academic Press, New York.

Gibbs, H. M., Jewell, J. L., Lee, Y. H., Macleod, A., Olbright, G., Ovadia, S.,Peyghambarian, N., Rushford, M. C., Warren, M., Weingerber, D. A., and Venkatesan, T. (1985). *Digital Opt. Circuit Technol., AGARD Conf. Proc.* No. 362, p. 8.1. NTIS, Springfield, Virginia.

Glass, A. M. (1978). *Opt. Eng.* **17**, 470.

Goodman, J. W. (1968). "Introduction to Fourier Optics." McGraw-Hill, New York.

Goodman, J. W. (1982). *J. Electr. Electron. Eng. Aust.* **2**, 139.

Goodman, J. W., Dias, A., and Woody, L. M. (1978). *Opt. Lett.* **2**, 1.

Goodman, J. W., Leonberger, F. J., Kung, S. Y., and Athale, R. A. (1984). *Proc. IEEE* **72**, 850.

Groh, G., and Marie, G. (1970). *Opt. Commun.* **2**, 133.

Grossberg, S. (1982). "Studies of Mind and Brain." Reidel, Boston, Massachusetts.

Gu, Z. H., and Lee, S. H. (1984a). *Appl. Opt.* **23**, 822.

Gu, Z. H., and Lee, S. H. (1984b). *Opt. Eng.* **23**, 723.

Guilfoyle, P. S. (1982). *SPIE Semin. Proc.* **352**, 2.

Hara, T., Sugiyama, M., and Suzuki, Y. (1985). *Adv. Electron. Electron Phys.* **64B**, 637.

Hara, T., Ooi, Y., Kato, T., and Suzuki, Y. (1986). *SPIE Semin. Proc.* **613**, 153.

Hawkins, J. K., and Munsey, C. J. (1963). *In* "Optical Processing of Information" (D. K. Pollock, C. J. Koester, and J. T. Tippett, eds.), p. 233. Spartan Books, Baltimore, Maryland.

Hinton, G. E., and Anderson, J. A. (1981). "Parallel Models of Associative Memory." Erlbaum, Hillsdale, New Jersey.

Hopfield, J. J. (1982). *Proc. Natl. Acad. Sci. U.S.A.* **79**, 2554.

Hornbeck, L. J. (1983). *IEEE Trans. Electron Devices* **ED-30**, 539.

Horner, J. L., and Gianino, P. D. (1984). *Appl. Opt.* **23**, 812.

Horner J. L., and Leger, J. R. (1985). *Appl. Opt.* **24**, 609.

Horvitz, S., and Neff, J. A., guest eds. (1986). *SPIE Semin. Proc.* **625**.

Horwitz, B. A., and Corbett, F. J. (1978). *Opt. Eng.* **17**, 353.

Huang, A. (1985). *Tech. Dig. OSA '85 Top. Meet. Opt. Comput., Lake Tahoe, Nev.* p. WA2-1.

Huignard, J. P., Herriau, J. P., Rivet, G., and Günter, P. (1980). *Opt. Lett.* **5**, 102.

Huignard, J. P., and Marrakchi, A. (1981). *Opt. Commun.* **38**, 249.

Huignard, J. P., Rajbenbach, H., Refregier, P., and Solymor, L. (1985). *Opt. Eng.* **24**, 586.

Hutcheson, L. D., guest ed. (1986). *Opt. Eng.* **25**, 1075.

Ichioka, Y., and Ono, S. (1985). *Proc. Image Sci. '85, Helsinki* p. 241.

Jacobs, S. F., Sargent, M., III, and Scully, M. O., eds. (1978). "Adaptive Optics and Short Wavelength Sources." Addison-Wesley, Reading, Massachusetts.

Jannson, T., Stoll, H. M., and Karaguleff, C. (1986). *SPIE Semin. Proc.* **698**, 157.

Jenkins, B. K., and Giles, C. L. (1986). *SPIE Semin. Proc.* **625**, 22.

Jenkins, B. K., and Sawchuk, A. A. (1985). *Dig. IEEE Conf. Comput. Archit. Pattern Anal. Image Database Manage. (CAPAIDM)* p. 61.

Johnson, R. V., Hecht, D. L., Sprague, R. A., Flares, L. N., Steinmetz, D. L., and Turner, W. D. (1983). *Opt. Eng.* **22**, 665.

Kamshilin, A. A., and Petrov, M. P. (1980). *Sov. Tech. Phys. Lett. (Engl. Transl.)* **6**, 144.

Kim, M. S., and Guest, C. C. (1986). *SPIE Semin. Proc.* **625**, 174.

Kingston, R. H., Burke, B. E., Nichols, K. B., and Leonberger, F. J. (1984). *SPIE Semin. Proc.* **465**, 9.

Knight, G. R. (1981). *In* "Optical Information Processing" (S. Lee, ed.), p. 111. Springer-Verlag, Berlin and New York.

Kohonen, T. (1984). "Self-Organization and Associative Memory." Springer-Verlag, Berlin and New York.

Kumar, B. V. K., and Casasent, D. (1981). *Appl. Opt.* **20**, 3703.

Lea, M. (1984). *SPIE Semin. Proc.* **465**, 12.

Lee, S. H. (1985). *Opt. Eng.* **24**, 41.

Lee, S. H., Esener, S. C., Title, M. A., and Drabik, T. J. (1986). *Opt. Eng.* **25**, 250.

Leger, J., and Lee, S. H. (1982). *J. Opt. Soc. Am.* **72**, 556.

Liau, Z. L., Walpole, J. N., and Tsang, D. Z. (1984). *Tech. Dig. Top. Meet. Integr. Guided-Wave Opt., 7th OSA, Washington, D.C.* p. TuC5.

Liu, H.-K., Davis, J. A., and Lilly, R. A. (1985). *Opt. Lett.* **10**, 635.

Liu, L.-Y., and Warde, C. (1986). *IEEE Trans. Electron Devices* **ED-33**, 1593.

Lohmann, A. W., and Werlich, H. W. (1967). *Phys. Lett. A* **25**, 570.

Ludman, J. E., ed. (1985). *SPIE Semin. Proc.* **551**.

McEwan, J. A., Fisher, A. D., and Lee, J. N. (1985a). *Dig. Conf. Lasers Electroopt. (CLEO)* p. PD-1.

McEwan, J. A., Fisher, A. D., Rolsma, P. B., and Lee, J. N. (1985b). *J. Opt. Soc. Am. A* **2**, 8.

Mada, M. (1985). *Appl. Opt.* **24**, 2063.

Marie, G. (1976). *Ferroelectrics* **10**, 9.

Marie, G., and Donjon, J. (1973). *Proc. IEEE* **61**, 942.

Marom, E. (1986). *Opt. Eng.* **25**, 274.

Marrakchi, A., Tanguay, A. R., Yu, J., and Psaltis, D. (1985). *Opt. Eng.* **24**, 124.

Meitzler, A. H., and Kurtz, S. K., guest eds. (1973). *Proc. IEEE* **61**.

Miller, D. A. B., Chelma, D. S., Damen, T. C., Gossard, A. C., Wiegmann, W., Wood, T. H., and Burrus, C. A. (1984) *Appl. Phys. Lett.* **45**, 13.

Minoura, K., Usui, M., Matsouka, K., Baba, T., Suzuki, M., and Asai, A. (1984). *Dig. Conf. ICO ICO-13, 13th* p. 154.

Neff, J. A., guest ed. (1984). *SPIE Semin. Proc.* **456**.

O'Neill, E. L. (1956). *IEEE Trans. Inf. Theory* **IT-2**, 56.

Owechko, Y., and Tanguay, A. R. (1982). *Opt. Lett.* **7**, 587.

Owechko, Y., and Tanguay, A. R. (1984). *J. Opt. Soc. Am. A* **1**, 644.

Owechko, Y., Marom, E., Grinberg, J., and Soffer, B. H. (1986). *SPIE Semin. Proc.* **625**, 72.

Pape, D. R. (1985a). *Opt. Eng.* **24**, 107.

Pape, D. R. (1985b). *Tech. Dig. OSA '85 Top. Meet. Opt. Comput., Lake Tahoe, Nev.* p. TuC6.

Pape, D. R., and Hornbeck, L. J. (1983). *Opt. Eng.* **22**, 675.

Pepper, D. M., guest ed. (1982). *Opt. Eng.* **21**, 156.

Petrov, M. P. (1981). *In* "Current Trends in Optics" (F. T. Arecchi and F. R. Aussenegg, eds.), p. 161. Taylor & Francis, London.

Pollock, D. K., Koester, C. J., and Tippett, J. T., eds. (1963). "Optical Processing of Information." Spartan Books, Baltimore, Maryland.

Psaltis, D., guest ed. (1984). *Opt. Eng.* **23**, 1.

Psaltis, D., and Farhat, N. (1985). *Opt. Lett.* **10**, 98.

Psaltis, D., Casasent, D., and Carlotto, M. (1979). *Opt. Lett.* **4**, 348.

Psaltis, D., Paek, E., and Venkatesh, S. (1984). *Opt. Eng.* **23**, 698.

Roach, W. R. (1974). *IEEE Trans. Electron Devices* **ED-21**, 453.

Ross, W. E., Psaltis, D., and Anderson, R. H. (1983). *Opt. Eng.* **22**, 485.

Rumelhart, D. E., and McClelland, J. L., eds. (1986). "Parallel Distributed Processing: Explorations in the Microstructure of Cognition," Vols. 1 and 2. MIT Press, Cambridge, Massachusetts.

Sanderson, A. C., and Zeevi, Y. Y., eds. (1983). *IEEE Trans. Syst. Man Cybern.* **SMC-13**.

Sawchuk, A. A., and Jenkins, B. K. (1984). *Tech. Dig. OSA '85 Top. Meet. Opt. Comput.* p. TuA2.

Sawchuk, A. A., and Strand, T. C. (1984). *Proc. IEEE* **72**, 758.

Schmidt, R. A., and Cathey, W. I. (1986). *SPIE Semin. Proc.* **625**, 226.

Schwartz, A., Wang, X.-Y., and Warde, C. (1985). *Opt. Eng.* **24**, 119.

Seko, A., and Nishikata, M. (1977). *Appl. Opt.* **16**, 1272.

Shaefer, D. H., and Strong, J. P. (1975). *NASA Rep. S-943-75-14.* Goddard SFC, Greenbelt, Maryland.

Sheridon, N. K. (1972). *IEEE Trans. Electron Devices* **ED-19**, 1003.

Smith, P. W., and Turner, E. H. (1977). *Appl. Phys. Lett.* **30**, 280.

Smith, S. D., Janossy, I., MacKenzie, H. A., Mathew, J. G. H., Reid, J. J. E., Taghizadeh, M. R., Tooley, F. A. P., and Walker, A. C. (1985). *Opt. Eng.* **24**, 569.

Soffer, B. H., Dunning, G. J., Owechko, Y., and Marom, E. (1986). *Opt. Lett.* **11**, 118.

Somers, L. E. (1972). *Adv. Electron. Electron Phys.* **33A**, 493.

Speiser, J. M., and Whitehouse, H. J. (1982). *SPIE Semin. Proc.* **298**, 2.

Tamura, P. N., and Wyant, J. C. (1976). *SPIE Semin. Proc.* **83**, 97.

Tanguay, A. R., guest ed. (1983). *Opt. Eng.* **22**, 663.

Tanguay, A. R. (1985). *Opt. Eng.* **24**, 2.

Tanguay, A. R., and Warde, C., guest eds. (1985). *Opt. Eng.* **24**, 91.

Tanguay, A. R., Wu, C. S., Chaval, P., Strand, T. C., Sawchuck, A. A., and Soffer, B. H. (1983). *Opt. Eng.* **22**, 687.

Ticknor, A. J., Barrett, H. H., and Easton, R. L. (1985). *Dig. Postdeadline Pap. OSA '85 Top. Meet. Opt. Comput.*, Lake Tahoe, Nev. p. PD3.

Tippett, J. T., Berkowitz, D. A., Clapp, L. C., Koester, C. J., and Vanderburgh, A., Jr., eds. (1965). "Optical and Electrooptical Information Processing." MIT Press, Cambridge, Massachusetts.

Tsujiuchi, J. (1962). *Prog. Opt.* **2**, 133.

Uchiyama, S., and Iga, K. (1985). *Dig. Conf. Lasers Electroopt. (CLEO)* p. 44.

Vander Lugt, A. B. (1964). *Trans. IEEE Inf. Theory* **IT-10**, 139.

Vander Lugt, A., Moore, G. S., and Mathe, S. S. (1983). *Appl. Opt.* **22**, 3906.

Verber, C. M. (1984). *Proc. IEEE* **72**, 942.

Verber, C. M., Kenan, R. P., and Busch, J. R. (1981). *Appl. Opt.* **20**, 1626.

Warde, C., and Efron, U., guest eds. (1986). *Opt. Eng.* **25**, 197.

Warde, C., and Kottas, J. (1986). *Appl. Opt.* **25**, 940.

Warde, C., and Thackara, J. I. (1982). *Opt. Lett.* **7**, 344.

Warde, C., and Thackara, J. I. (1983). *Opt. Eng.* **22**, 695.

Warde, C., Fisher, A. D., Cocco, D. M., and Burmawi, M. Y. (1978). *Opt. Lett* **3**, 196.

Warde, C., Weiss, A. M., Fisher, A. D., and Thackara, J. I. (1981). *Appl. Opt.* **20**, 2066.

Willshaw, D. J., Buneman, O. P., and Longuet-Higgins, H. C. (1969). *Nature (London)* **222**, 960.

Wisa, J. L. (1979). *Nucl. Instrum. Methods* **162**, 587.

Yariv, A., and Kwong, S.-K. (1986). *Opt. Lett.* **11**, 186.

Yariv, A., Kwong, S.-K., and Kyuma, K. (1986). *Appl. Phys. Lett.* **48**, 1114.

Yatagai, T. (1986). *SPIE Semin. Proc.* **625**, 54.

Yu, F. T. S. (1983). "Optical Information Processing." Wiley, New York.

7.3

Optical Feedback Processing

J. N. CEDERQUIST

ENVIRONMENTAL RESEARCH INSTITUTE OF MICHIGAN

ANN ARBOR, MICHIGAN 48107

I. Introduction

In other chapters of this book, a number of devices are described that sometimes or always use optical feedback. Examples are acoustooptic and fiber-optic processors and optical logic and memory devices. Most of the applications discussed in earlier chapters can benefit from the use of optical feedback. Examples here are pattern recognition, temporal and nonlinear processing, iterative transformation algorithms, and all-optical numerical computing. Optical feedback is therefore an important technique in the field of optical signal processing. It is the goal of this chapter to provide a comprehensive discussion of optical feedback.

Section II provides important prerequisites to the study of optical feedback: a general discussion of feedback and related concepts, a summary of the use of feedback in electronic systems, and a review of the history of optical feedback research. Section III describes the operation of the broad range of optical feedback devices. For clarity, the equally broad range of applications is discussed separately in Section IV. The chapter is summarized in Section V; advantages gained by the use of optical feedback in optical signal processing are described, and speculations as to future developments in optical feedback are given.

II. Background

A. FEEDBACK CONCEPTS

A block diagram of a simple feedback system is shown in Fig. 1. Blocks A though D represent subsystems. The feedback loop consists of a forward path (A to B to C) and a feedback path (C to D to A). Block A combines the input signal with the feedback signal from D. Block B performs the forward path processing operation. Block C provides the output signal and also redirects part of the output into the feedback path. Block D performs the feedback path processing operation.

This description is general in that the subsystems may consist of optical, electronic, or other components; the signals may be in any convenient physical form and may represent any physical quantities in n-dimensional space; and the combination, processing, and redirection operations are arbitrary in nature. However, it is important to note that reference to one physical quantity—time—is always necessary in the description of feedback systems. The various subsystems operate sequentially on a given signal, and the output signal from a feedback system is therefore always a function of time. The cycle time, defined as the time taken for a signal to make one

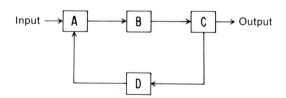

Fig. 1. Block diagram of a simple feedback system. Blocks A through D represent subsystems. (From Cederquist and Lee, 1979.)

cycle around the feedback loop, is an important parameter in characterizing feedback systems.

The above usage of the term feedback is consistent with that of electrical engineering and, in particular, control theory. In other fields, other terms are used to express related concepts. In applied mathematics, iterative methods are defined as those that use a repeated cycle of operations to generate successive approximations to the solution of a problem. If the algorithm is properly chosen, the approximation improves with every cycle; and there is, in principle, no limit to the number of cycles desired. Applications of iterative methods include the determination of square roots and the solution of partial differential equations. A feedback system (such as that of Fig. 1) can perform iterative processing if blocks A and D perform the appropriate operations and if, once given, the input signal is not changed. The output signal as a function of time is then the series of approximations to the desired result.

In computer science, the term iteration is used to describe the process of repeating a cycle of operations (with minor modifications) a specified number of times. Usually the input to each cycle is different, and the output of every cycle is equally important in later computations. In this case the output of one cycle is not input to the next cycle, and systems with feedback are not necessary to perform the desired processing. Note that under this definition, iteration must terminate after a finite number of cycles and does not involve approximate results.

A related term in computer science is recursion. It is used to describe a process in which each operation cycle first reduces the complexity of the problem and then hands over the simplified problem to the next cycle. Usually no cycle can be completed until the next cycle completes. Infinite regress is avoided by allowing a cycle to complete immediately if the problem has been reduced to a sufficiently elementary form. For example, recursive methods can be used to compute integer powers of real numbers and to make fractal drawings. Some recursive methods can be expressed in an iterative form (in the computer science sense). In this case the output from one cycle is input to the next cycle, and only the output of the final cycle is important. A feedback system can perform recursive processing if the processing subsystems perform the appropriate functions, if the input is not changed, and most importantly, if some means is available to use or store the output signal after the appropriate number of cycles.

Finally, the term adaptive is used in fields as widely separated as psychology and information science. It can be used to describe systems whose properties change with and depend upon the history of the input signals they have received. Animal learning and memory are possible because the brain is an adaptive system. Control and prediction algorithms function by altering some of their parameters dependent upon recently received input signals or upon an error signal equal to the difference between the current input and a feedback signal. Feedback systems can perform adaptive processing on a time-varying input signal if the feedback signal (or signals in systems with multiple feedback loops) is used to control some parameters in the processing subsystems.

B. ELECTRONIC FEEDBACK

An analog electronic circuit is said to use feedback if a portion of its time-varying output signal, possibly in modified form, is combined with the input signal and returned to the circuit. Analog electronic feedback is often used to produce temporal frequency response characteristics that are difficult or impossible to obtain otherwise. It is also used in control systems. In more complicated circuits, signals from various points in the circuit can be fed back to other points, but usually only a single output signal is of interest. The emphasis in analog electronic feedback, then, is on the processing of a one-dimensional (1-D) (time-varying) signal.

Digital electronic components can be used to replace some or all of the analog components in the circuits just discussed. The circuit function and its application to 1-D signals can remain the same. More importantly, the development of digital electronics and digital computers has made it possible to process data with algorithms that use feedback (e.g., iterative approximation). The output data now range in dimensionality from zero (a single scalar) to, commonly, one or two (signals and images) to, often, three or more. The domain of the data can be temporal, spatial, frequency, or some other parameter. The range of processing operations achievable with this type of digital electronic feedback is therefore very wide.

Signal amplification or gain is very important in electronic feedback. In analog systems having the form of Fig. 1, a high gain in the forward path gives a system frequency response that is approximately the inverse of the frequency response of the feedback path. Thus the useful operation of inverse filtering is obtained. Amplification is also routinely used throughout analog feedback circuits to achieve desired signal levels. In digital computing systems, multiplication (usually with high precision) is used for proper operation of the feedback algorithms. In both cases, components that achieve gain or multiplication are readily available.

C. HISTORY OF OPTICAL FEEDBACK RESEARCH

The first steps in the development of optical feedback techniques were taken in the 1950s. It was difficult at that time to make good photographic prints from negatives having a wide density range. Detail contrast was lost in regions at the density extremes. A solution to this problem was a device that used a cathode ray tube (CRT) as a light source to scan the negative (Craig, 1954, 1955). The light passed by the negative was detected and electronically fed back to control the intensity of the CRT. The CRT brightness was increased in regions of high average density and decreased in regions of low density. The dynamic range of the print exposure was thus reduced while detail contrast was maintained. This device and others for contrast control were also studied by Lohmann (1959) and by Spitzberg and Sunder-Plassmann (1963).

The invention of the laser greatly facilitated the development of coherent optical processing. Lasers depend upon feedback, and in the 1960s, experiments were performed in which transmissive objects were placed inside laser cavities (Pole et al., 1966, 1967; Wieder and Pole, 1967). Consider an object that is encoded as the spatially varying modulation depth of a phase grating. If the phase grating is illuminated by a laser beam, the first diffraction order can be used to form an image of the object. However, most of the power is in the undiffracted beam and not used for displaying the image. In the experiments, the phase grating was placed inside a laser cavity in which one of the cavity mirrors was in a Fourier plane with respect to the grating plane. The undiffracted and diffracted light are then spatially separated at the mirror plane. The undiffracted light was reflected by the mirror, but the diffracted light bypassed the small mirror and was externally inverse Fourier transformed to form an image of the object. With this configuration, the undiffracted light is not lost but is fed back to the laser gain medium. The same laser can therefore project an image of greater intensity.

Despite the good results obtained, little notice was taken of this very early work. Interest in feedback began again with the work of Jablonowski and Lee (1975). Their work along with that of many others will be discussed in Sections III and IV. By the end of the 1970s, several research groups in the United States, Germany, and the Soviet Union were extensively engaged in optical feedback processing research. Even at that date, however, the use of feedback was still a curiosity in the broad field of optical processing research. It is very gratifying to those who were involved in the early feedback research to see, since 1980, the use of feedback techniques become much more widespread, to the point that new optical processor designs more often than not incorporate optical feedback.

In the following sections our goal is to include all significant work but not to give an exhaustive review of all work. Complete reviews of optical feedback to about 1980 were given by Cederquist and Lee (1979), Akins et al. (1980), and Collins and Wasmundt (1980). Devices and applications that with hindsight are judged as not likely to contribute to the further development of optical feedback processing are omitted. It is hoped that by concentrating on the main concepts and their variations, the reader will be most effectively equipped to understand and to perform further research in optical feedback processing.

III. Devices for Optical Feedback

We now describe devices using feedback for optical processing, beginning with all-optical devices, both analog and digital. Then hybrid optical-electronic devices, again both analog and digital, are described. Devices that are properly the subject of other chapters of this book [e.g., fiber-optic processors (Chapter 7.1)] are given only a brief treatment. Systems in which a significant portion of the processing is performed by digital electronics, even though optical processing is also used, are not included; the basic structure of these systems is that of an electronic digital computer that controls both optical and electronic processors. Such systems are very general, and their study lies outside of the field of optical feedback processing.

Some of the more important features that can be used to describe optical processors in general are the degree of space variance, the extent of non-linearity, and the presence of memory capability. For optical feedback devices, some additional factors are the presence of gain in the feedback loop, the possibilities for the phase of the feedback signal (positive, negative, or complex feedback), the cycle time of the loop, and the number of dimensions that are useful in describing the input and output signals. In the following descriptions, these terms will be used to aid the comparison of the capabilities of the many different optical feedback devices.

A. ANALOG OPTICAL FEEDBACK DEVICES

Historically, most all-optical analog processors without feedback have used a few lenses and optical filters with spatially varying transmittance to perform the desired processing operation. The addition of some mirrors and/or beamsplitters to these processors makes it possible to feed back the output signal to the input. Devices with single and multiple feedback loops, devices with gain, and fiber-optic feedback devices are discussed in this section.

1. *Single Feedback Loop Devices*

Analog optical devices with a single feedback loop are described below in order of increasing complexity of the optical system. It is important to note that complexity does not necessarily increase performance.

a. Two-Plane-Mirror Feedback Device. The simplest possible device consists of two plane, partially reflecting mirrors (a Fabry–Perot interferometer) as shown in Fig. 2 (Lee *et al.*, 1976). The input light a_i enters the device through mirror M_1 (corresponding to block A of Fig. 1), passes through the region between the mirrors (block B), and is partially transmitted by mirror M_2 (block C) to become the output a_o. Mirror M_2 also reflects part of the light into the feedback path where it again passes through the region between the mirrors (block D) before being partially reflected by mirror M_1 and combined with the input. The data are input via the amplitude transmittance $t_i(x, y) \exp[i\,\delta(x, y)]$ of photographic film or real-time recording media placed between the mirrors.

If the input light is noncoherent, then the intensities of the input and feedback light are summed at mirror M_1, giving positive feedback. If the input light is coherent, then the input and feedback light adds in amplitude. The phase between the two light fields depends on the round-trip path length. If one of the mirrors is mounted on a precision translator, then this path length can be adjusted to give positive, negative, and even complex feedback. To maintain a desired phase, the components must be kept stable to within a fraction of a wavelength of the light being used. The simplicity of the two-mirror feedback device is an advantage in maintaining the needed stability. A disadvantage is that the forward and feedback paths (and therefore their processing operations) are identical, which limits the range of possible device operations. Because diffraction in propagating the distance d between the mirrors is not compensated by any lens, the space-bandwidth product of the spatial information that can be processed is also limited. Variations on the device shown in Fig. 2 include a device with one

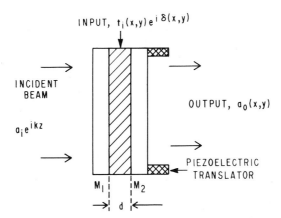

Fig. 2. Two-plane-mirror feedback device. The input light is a_i, the input data to be processed is $t_i(x, y) \exp[i\,\delta(x, y)]$. (From Lee *et al.*, 1976.)

mirror slightly tilted (Indebetouw, 1980) and a three-mirror device (Bartholomew and Lee, 1980).

b. Two-Lens, Two-Mirror Feedback Device. A device using two plane, partially reflecting mirrors and two lenses with focal lengths f and designed to operate with coherent light is shown in Fig. 3 (Jablonowski and Lee, 1975). The input light distribution $a_i(x, y)$ passes through mirror M_1 (block A of Fig. 1) and is Fourier transformed by the first lens. After spatial filtering (block B) by function $F(u, v)$ (where u and v are the spatial frequency coordinates), the light is inverse transformed by the second lens and partly transmitted by mirror M_2 (block C) to become the output light distribution $a_o(x, y)$. However, most of the light is reflected into the feedback path where it is Fourier transformed, spatially filtered by $G(u, v)$ (block D), inverse transformed, and, finally, combined with the input by mirror M_1. The two Fourier transforms in the midplane of the device can be spatially separated, as shown in Fig. 3, by tilting the mirrors at equal and opposite angles θ with respect to the optical axis. The ability to perform, in the feedback path, a different processing operation from that in the forward path gives the device a processing capability in two (spatial) dimensions that is similar to that which traditional analog electronic feedback devices have in one (temporal) dimension. The coherent transfer function $H(u, v)$ is

$$H(u, v) = \frac{F(u, v)}{1 - t_h F(u, v) G(u, v) \exp(i\phi)} \qquad (1)$$

where t_h is the round-trip amplitude transmittance and ϕ the feedback phase. By appropriate choices of real-valued $F(u, v)$, $G(u, v)$, and ϕ, complex-valued $H(u, v)$ are produced, which would be difficult to obtain without feedback.

Because this device images the input plane to the output plane, it can also have a much greater space–bandwidth product than the two-mirror device discussed in the previous section. However, because of the additional lenses and greater round-trip path length, maintaining a spatially constant phase between the input and feedback light is more difficult. The device of

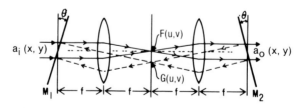

Fig. 3. Two-lens, two-mirror feedback device. The feedback light path is shown dashed. (From Jablonowski and Lee, 1975.)

Fig. 3 has also been used without tilting the mirrors, in which case identical processing operations are performed in both the forward and the feedback paths (Tamura and Wyant, 1976).

c. Two-Spherical-Mirror Feedback Device. A device using two spherical, partially reflecting mirrors is shown in Fig. 4 (Cederquist and Lee, 1980, 1981). The two mirrors have identical radii of curvature R and are confocally separated by a distance R. In Fig. 4a, lenses L_1 and L_2 telecentrically image the input $a_i(x, y)$ to the upper part of the midplane P of the device. In Fig. 4b, the upper part of mirror M_2 produces a Fourier transform of the input in the midplane P (centered slightly above the horizontal center line because the zero spatial frequency of the input propagates at a small angle θ with respect to the horizontal) where it is spatially filtered by $F(u, v)$. The light continues to the lower part of mirror M_1 which produces an inverse Fourier transform in the lower part of the midplane P. This light distribution is, in turn, Fourier transformed by the lower part of mirror M_2, spatially filtered by $G(u, v)$ (centered slightly

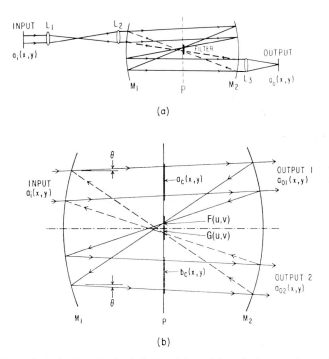

Fig. 4. Two-spherical-mirror feedback device: (a) provisions for input and one of the two outputs; (b) possible filter locations and the two possible outputs. (From Cederquist and Lee, 1980, 1981.)

below the center line), inverse Fourier transformed by the upper part of mirror M_1, and combined with the input in the upper part of the midplane P. As shown in Fig. 4a, the light transmitted by the lower part of mirror M_2 can be imaged to a detector.

The two-spherical-mirror device can perform all of the processing operations possible with the two-lens device of the previous section but is simpler because it uses the spherical mirrors as both Fourier transforming and reflecting elements. An advantage is that the spherical-mirror device is less sensitive to mirror alignment than are devices incorporating plane mirrors. Since the device has two internal image planes, image domain filters $a_c(x, y)$ and $b_c(x, y)$ can be used to add space-variance to the range of achievable processing operations. The device also has two possible outputs $a_{o1}(x, y)$ and $a_{o2}(x, y)$. They differ in that the second has been filtered by $F(u, v)$ and multiplied by $b_c(x, y)$ relative to the first. The choice of which output to use depends upon the application under consideration.

The aberrations of the spherical-mirror device have been more extensively analyzed than those of the two-lens device. The effect of aberrations is to reduce the space–bandwidth product that can be processed and to reduce computation accuracy. An improved design uses the back surface of the spherical mirrors as the reflecting surface and uses the front (theoretically perfectly transmitting) spherical surface to control aberrations (Johnston and Lee, 1983). Such a device has been built and shown to have improved performance, with a space–bandwidth product of 500 by 500 (Fainman and Lee, 1985).

d. Two-Lens, Four-Mirror Feedback Device.   A device using two lenses and four plane mirrors to produce optical feedback is shown in Fig. 5 (Händler and Röder, 1977, 1979). The input $a_i(x, y)$ is Fourier transformed by lens 1 to the front focal plane P_1 of lens 2 (located between the prism and the beamsplitter). The input is then inverse transformed by lens 2 to location B in the image plane P_2 (indicated by solid lines). Lens 3 Fourier transforms the light in plane P_2 to the Fourier plane P_1. The light reflected by the beamsplitter is again inverse transformed by lens 2, but because of the tilt angle of the beamsplitter, to location D in plane P_2 (indicated by dotted lines). When this light reaches the beamsplitter, it is now traveling in a direction such that the reflected light combines with the input and follows the path indicated by the solid lines.

A similarity to the two-spherical-mirror device is that this device also has two possible outputs. The diaphragm determines which output is inverse Fourier transformed to the output plane. If the output is first taken after two circuits around the two lenses and four mirrors (as depicted in Fig. 5), then the feedback path is of zero length and no processing is performed in

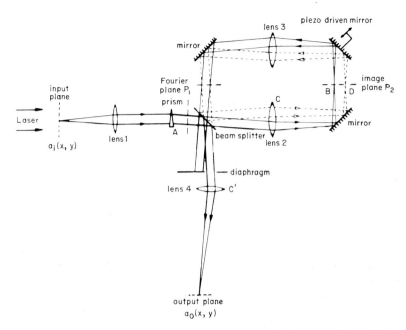

Fig. 5. Two-lens, four-mirror feedback device. (From Händler and Röder, 1977.)

the feedback loop. Another similarity is that two images (but only one Fourier transform) are available for filtering. Redefinition of the image and Fourier domains permits filtering of two Fourier transforms and one image. However, the greater number of optical components makes it more difficult to maintain the total path length stability required when the system is used with coherent light.

e. Four-Lens, Four-Mirror Feedback Device. A device using four mirrors and four lenses is shown in Fig. 6 (Nezhevenko and Spektor, 1975, 1976; Kotljar *et al.*, 1978). The input is imaged into the device by lens L_1 and travels around the loop, alternately being transformed into the Fourier and

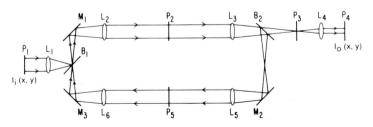

Fig. 6. Four-lens, four-mirror feedback device. Light travels clockwise. (From Nezhevenko and Spektor, 1975.)

image domains. This device has four possible outputs depending on which mirror is partially transmitting. For the output used in Fig. 6, the forward path is from beamsplitter B_1, through lenses L_2 and L_3, to beamsplitter B_2, and the feedback path is from B_2, through L_5 and L_6, to combination with the input at B_1. Because the forward and feedback paths are separate, this device has the greatest space–bandwidth product (for given focal lengths and aperture dimenions) of any analog feedback device. It also has the most components and may be the most difficult to maintain in stable alignment.

2. Multiple Feedback Devices

All of the devices described so far have a single feedback loop. Multiple feedback loops are also possible, as shown in Fig. 7 (Cederquist and Lee, 1981; Cederquist, 1981). Here a second, smaller, two-spherical-mirror device is placed inside of a larger one. They are positioned so that the upper image of the larger device coincides with the lower image of the smaller device. Other placements of the smaller device are also possible. The use of multiple feedback loops increases the complexity of the transfer function and therefore the range of processing operations, but it also reduces the space-bandwidth product that can be processed and increases alignment sensitivity.

3. Devices with Gain

All of the above devices are passive, and in propagation around the feedback loop, light is lost both in less-than-perfect reflection and transmission at the various optical elements and in filtering to perform the desired

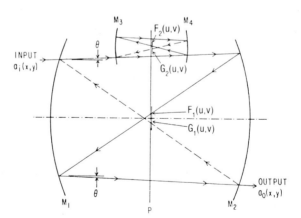

Fig. 7. Device with multiple feedback loops. Other locations for smaller loop and use of other outputs are possible. (From Cederquist and Lee, 1981.)

processing operations. Experimentally, great care is usually taken to minimize these losses. For example, in the device of Fig. 4, the spherical mirrors have an amplitude reflectance of 98.5%, and the processing filter substrates are antireflection coated for a transmittance of 98%. Even so, it is difficult to achieve a round-trip transmittance greater than 90%, not including losses in the processing filters (Cederquist and Lee, 1981). This 10% loss severely limits the number of round-trips that can contribute to the output light and in turn limits the processing capabilities of the feedback device.

The solution to this problem is to use a gain device in the feedback loop to amplify the light. Two device types have been experimentally demonstrated in all-optical systems; dye amplification (Hänsch *et al.*, 1971; Akins and Lee, 1979, 1984; Schneeberger *et al.*, 1981) and photorefractive amplification (Pellat-Finet and de Bougrenet de la Tocnaye, 1985; Anderson, 1986; Soffer *et al.*, 1986; Fainman *et al.*, 1986). Amplifier stability has also been studied theoretically (Hagler, 1971; Hagler and Bell, 1986). Unlike lasers, gain sufficient for oscillation to occur is usually not desirable in optical processors. Both device types operate by transferring energy from a relatively high-power pump beam to the lower-power signal beam. They are both suitable for use in the coherent operation of the feedback devices described in Sections III.A.1 and III.A.2. With dye devices, amplitude gain factors of 1.3–5 have been achieved, which are more than enough to overcome the loop losses discussed in the previous paragraph. With the same device, ratios of amplified signal to amplifier noise of 500 to 1 and a space–bandwidth product of 500 by 500 have been obtained (Akins and Lee, 1984). Photorefractive devices have achieved a gain of about 30 for images with 100 to 1 dynamic range and a space–bandwidth product of 500 by 500 (Fainman *et al.*, 1986). This large gain is useful if the forward or feedback processing operations have low transmittance (e.g., high-pass filtering). If the technology can be developed for the routine inclusion of gain in feedback devices, then there is great potential for the improvement of device performance. Hybrid optical–electronic methods for implementing gain in a feedback device are discussed in Sections III.C and III.D.

4. Fiber-Optic Feedback Devices

A device consisting of optical fibers interconnected at selected points by coupling between the fibers can perform signal processing. The signal paths can be arranged so that some of the optical signals are fed back to other parts of the device (Tur *et al.*, 1982). These devices are discussed extensively in Chapter 7.1. They use noncoherent light and perform linear operations on the light intensity. In their present form, rather than operating on 1- or 2-D spatial arrays of data, they use high-speed point sources and point detectors to achieve a high processing rate on a single or, at most, a few temporal signals.

B.   DIGITAL OPTICAL FEEDBACK DEVICES

To justify the use of the term digital, an all-optical digital device must operate on light amplitudes, intensities, or polarizations that take on only a finite number of discrete values. Nearly all such devices in fact use only two values, most often of intensity. This bistable operation requires feedback and nonlinearity. These devices are of great interest because the fabrication techniques, device sizes, and device specifications closely approach those of digital electronic computers. Although these devices can be fabricated as 2-D arrays and used for signal processing, the feedback is in each device and is used to achieve bistable operation. Therefore these devices are not discussed further here. A number of interesting digital optical-electronic devices do use feedback (of 2-D arrays) for processing and are discussed in Section III.D.

C.   ANALOG OPTICAL–ELECTRONIC FEEDBACK DEVICES

The all-optical analog feedback devices described in Section III.A consisted of mirrors and lenses and are closely related to each other. In contrast, the analog hybrid optical–electronic devices discussed in this section make use of a wide range of electronic technology and are very different from each other.

1.   *Television-Based Feedback Devices*

Television technology with its inherent ability to handle 2-D signals can be used as a component in a hybrid feedback device (Häusler and Lohmann, 1977; Lohmann, 1977; Sato *et al.*, 1978; Görlitz *et al.*, 1978). For example, in Fig. 8a, the input intensity $I_i(x, y)$ is imaged onto a vidicon and the resulting signal subjected to analog electronic processing. The resulting signal can be displayed on CRT monitor T_1 as the output $I_o(x, y)$ and also sent into the feedback path where it can be processed further, both electronically and optically, before being combined with the input and imaged once again onto the vidicon.

The characteristics of this device contrast with those of all-optical devices. Because noncoherent light is used, the input and feedback images can only add in intensity. This limits the device primarily to positive feedback, although operation on a bias and the use of contrast reversal on monitor T_2 permits negative feedback to be simulated. The cycle time of the feedback is relatively long, on the order of milliseconds (33 ms for American standard television). Depending on the application, the long cycle time may be an

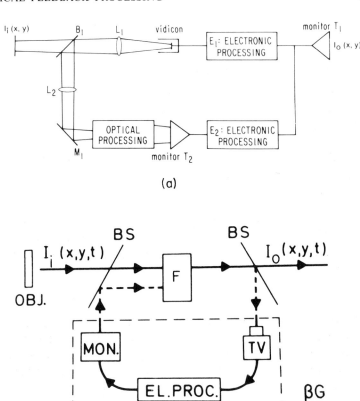

(a)

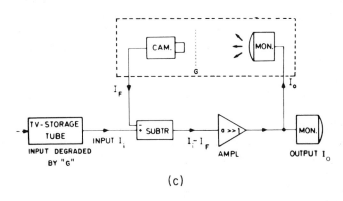

(b)

(c)

Fig. 8. Several configurations for television-based feedback devices (a, b, and c). Still other arrangements are possible. (From Häusler and Lohmann, 1977; Goetz *et al.*, 1979.)

advantage because it allows the time behavior of the device to be more easily studied. Signal amplification and nonlinear operations are easily performed in the electronic processing stages.

Figures 8b and 8c show two of the many other possible television-based feedback devices (Häusler and Lohmann, 1977; Goetz *et al.*, 1979). In Fig. 8c, the combination of the input and feedback images is performed electronically. Here subtraction is indicated, which amounts to negative feedback. Experimentally the main disadvantage in the use of television-based feedback devices has been distortion, primarily in the image displayed on the monitors (Häusler and Streibl, 1982). This has limited the space–bandwidth product of the images that can be processed.

2. Light-Emitting-Diode-Based Feedback Devices

The optical matrix–vector multiplier has been important in the development of optical numerical processing (see Chapters 6.1 and 6.2). This device uses a linear array of light–emitting diodes (LEDs) to input the data. The light is spread in one dimension and passes through a mask with spatially varying transmittance. The resulting 2-D light distribution is then focused in one dimension (orthogonal to the spreading dimension) onto a linear detector array. The processing operation is that of multiplication of a matrix (represented by the mask) by a vector (represented by the LED intensities). If the output data are combined electronically with the input data and used as input to the LED array, then the LED-based feedback device shown in Fig. 9 results (Psaltis *et al.*, 1979; Goodman and Song, 1982).

Apart from the fact that the input and output data are only 1-D, this device has many similar characteristics to the television-based device. The feedback can be positive or negative, gain is easily obtained, and nonlinearity can be obtained by including electronic processing. The cycle time depends upon the electronics, which usually is built specially for the particular device. Laser diodes can also be used as the sources, and a variety of

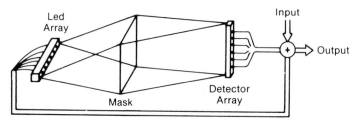

Fig. 9. Light-emitting-diode-based feedback device. Part of the output is fed back to the LED array. An acoustooptic cell and point source of light may be used in place of the LED array. (From Goodman and Song, 1982.)

detector arrays can be used. Currently, the 1-D space–bandwidth product is limited to about 100.

3. Acoustooptic-Transducer-Based Feedback Devices

Acoustooptic (AO) transducers play an important role in optical signal processing (see Chapter 3.3). They can also be used in feedback configurations. For example, the LED array of Fig. 9 can be replaced by a single LED illuminating an AO cell (Casasent, 1982). Most AO processors use AO cells rather than masks for data storage, and these processors can also use feedback (Vander Lugt, 1982). A device of this type with two forward paths and one feedback path is shown in Fig. 10 (Psaltis and Hong, 1984; Hong and Psaltis, 1985). The input is given to AO cell AOD1 and is divided by the beamsplitter BS into two parts. One part is correlated at AOD3 with

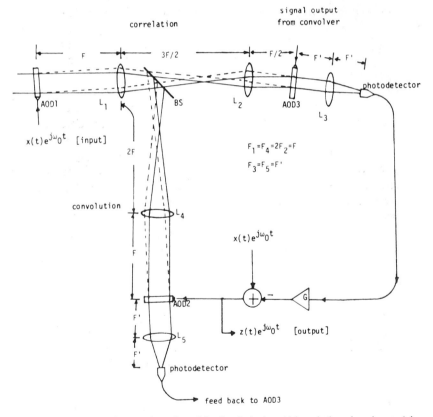

Fig. 10. Acoustooptic-transducer-based feedback device. Although there is only one (electronic) feedback path, the forward path has two branches. (From Psaltis and Hong, 1984.)

the feedback signal while the other is convolved at AOD2 with the difference between the input and the correlation signal (an error signal). Note that unlike most other feedback devices, the feedback signal is not added but is convolved with the input signal. Apart from this difference, AO-based feedback devices have the same characteristics as LED-based devices except that here the 1-D space–bandwidth product can be 1000 or more.

4. Two-Dimensional Spatial-Light-Modulator-Based Feedback Devices

Two-dimensional spatial light modulators (SLMs) are also important in optical processing (see Chapter 7.2). Some of the more important types are those based on microchannel plates, electrooptic crystals, and liquid-crystal compounds. Each of these has also been used as a component in a feedback device (Fisher and Warde, 1983; Nezhevenko and Gofman, 1984; Marom et al., 1985). Since SLMs transfer their 2-D input signal to the output side of the device by electronic effects, the resulting feedback devices are optical-electronic hybrids.

In optical processors without feedback, SLMs are most often used to convert noncoherent or electronic signals to 2-D coherent signals. In a feedback device, if the feedback signal is given to the input side of the SLM, and the input signal is used to read out the SLM, then point-by-point multiplication of the 2-D input by the 2-D feedback signal is achieved. This is a very useful operation that cannot be achieved simply by combining two images optically. The SLM can also be used for gain, to produce a desired nonlinear operation, and for integration of a 2-D signal. This last effect come about either because the SLM has memory (e.g., some electrooptic crystals) or simply because the SLM response time is relatively slow (e.g., liquid crystals). The feedback-loop cycle time can be no shorter than about 30 ms when using most SLMs.

An example of a feedback device using a liquid crystal SLM is shown in Fig. 11 (Rhodes, 1983). The application is in adaptive filtering in which it is desired to produce an estimate $\hat{x}(t)$ of an input signal $x(t)$. The error signal $e(t) = x(t) - \hat{x}(t)$ is fed back to the point electrooptic modulator. This application is discussed further in Section IV.B. The SLM is used to provide temporal integration of the product of the input $x(t)$ and the error signal $e(t)$ and also for gain. Note that AO cells are also used in the device.

D. DIGITAL OPTICAL–ELECTRONIC FEEDBACK DEVICES

Most, if not all, of the analog hybrid feedback devices just discussed potentially can also operate in a digital mode. In those that are described here, feedback is used both to create digital operation through bistability and to interconnect the digital processing units.

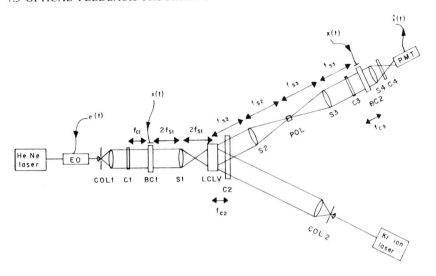

Fig. 11. Two-dimensional spatial-light-modulator-based feedback device. Symbols are S, spherical lens; C, cylindrical lens; COL, collimination optics; POL, polarizer; EO, electrootopic modulator; BC, Bragg (AO) cell; LCLV, liquid-crystal light valve; PMT, photomultiplier tube; and f, focal length. (From Rhodes, 1983.)

1. Television-Based Digital Feedback Devices

The television-based feedback devices of Fig. 8 can also be operated in a bistable mode by using feedback to increase a small nonlinearity. If the input/output characteristic of the vidicon, electronic processing, and monitor in combination is slightly nonlinear and the feedback is positive, then input light above a threshold level causes a high-intensity signal to circulate in the feedback loop. Similarly, input light below the threshold gives a low-intensity signal. Since these signals continue to circulate even if the input is withdrawn, the device has memory. As for the analog television-based device, distortion due to the monitor limits performance. For the digital device, a lenslet array can be used to eliminate distortion effects, but experimentally demonstrated 2-D space–bandwidth products have been no more than 8 by 8.

2. Liquid-Crystal-Based Digital Feedback Devices

Liquid-crystal devices and feedback concepts have been combined in several ways to produce optical processing devices. A single pixel of one of the simplest is shown in Fig. 12 (Athale and Lee, 1981). The input light I_{in} is absorbed by the cadmium sulfide photoconductor, alters the voltage across the liquid crystal, and permits the reference light I_R to pass through

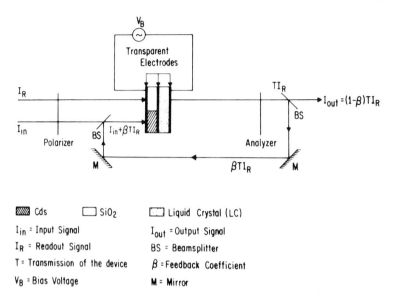

Fig. 12. Simple liquid-crystal-based digital feedback device. (From Athale and Lee, 1981.)

the analyzer. Part of the output light I_{out} is reflected by a beamsplitter, fed back, and added (positive feedback) to the input light. As for the television-based device, feedback increases the inherent nonlinearity of the liquid-crystal response, and a bistable device is produced. If the input light is removed, the output remains unchanged, so the device also has memory. It also has gain in the sense that all input signals above threshold are converted to output signals of a constant level. It should be noted that experimental work has been limited to pixel arrays not larger than 8 by 8. Strictly speaking, this device does not perform any data processing, but it can be a part of a system using several liquid-crystal devices and several feedback paths that is capable of optical digital data processing (Athale *et al.*, 1980). Similar devices have been built by Vlad (1982, 1985) and studied by Kompanets *et al.* (1981a, b).

A device that uses two Hughes liquid-crystal light valves (LCLVs) (see Chapter 7.2), and feedback to produce an optical flip-flop is shown in Fig. 13 (Fatehi *et al.*, 1984). Application of a light pulse in the set beam causes the read beam to be reflected from LCLV1. The polarization is manipulated so that in the absence of the reset beam, light is also reflected from LCLV2, and therefore the read beam propagates to the input side of LCLV1. There it functions in a manner similar to the feedback beam in Fig. 12, and the device maintains itself in a high-intensity state. Application of a light pulse in the reset beam rotates the polarization of the beam reflected from LCLV2.

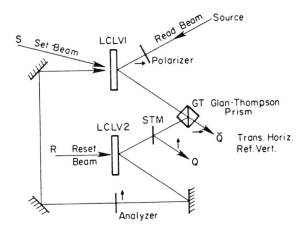

Fig. 13. Optical flip-flop using two liquid-crystal light valves. STM is a semitransparent mirror. Other implementations are possible. (From Fatehi *et al.*, 1984.)

This beam is then blocked by the analyzer and therefore does not propagate to the input side of LCLV1, and the device switches to a low-intensity state. Devices of this type have been theoretically studied by Collins *et al.* (1979) and Gerlach *et al.* (1980). Extensions of the configuration of Fig. 13 can function as shift registers and accumulators (Fatehi *et al.*, 1980). The Hughes LCLV has sufficient resolution for digital devices to be built which process 500 by 500 pixels in parallel. Experimental results, however, have not shown more than an 8 by 8 array.

In the two devices just discussed feedback was used to increase nonlinearities and to produce bistable operation. A different use of feedback is shown in Fig. 14 (Jenkins *et al.*, 1984a). Here the LCLV is built and operated such that, if the input is the sum of two 2-D spatial signals, the output is the logical NOR operation point-by-point between the two inputs. The LCLV is thus an array of NOR logic gates. The feedback path returns the LCLV output to its input but also contains a hologram that allows the light from a given logic gate to be redirected by diffraction to the inputs of other logic gates. The hologram allows the NOR gates to be interconnected to perform a desired digital processing operation. It is important to note that the LCLV supplies the nonlinearity and gain and that feedback is used to permit sequential processing of the 2-D data. Processing architectures of this type have been studied by Jenkins *et al.* (1984b). Applications and experimental results are discussed in Section IV.F.

Materials other than liquid crystals can also be used in digital feedback devices. Devices using electroluminescence have been built (Porada, 1983), and devices using nonlinear media proposed (Yakimovich, 1983, 1984).

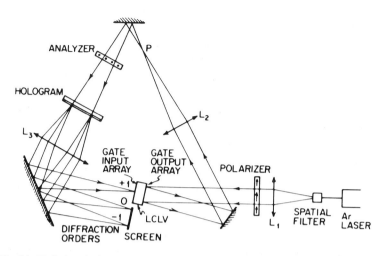

Fig. 14. Digital optical processor using feedback. Lens L_2 images the LCLV output to the hologram. The hologram is an array of subholograms. Lens L_3 Fourier transforms the hologram output to the LCLV input. (From Jenkins *et al.*, 1984a.)

Since liquid crystals have undesirably slow response times, further research into other materials could be rewarded by improved device performance.

IV. Applications of Optical Feedback

Devices using optical feedback have been applied to many processing problems. This section surveys the wide range of applications including analog computing, signal and image processing, analog-to-digital operations and digital processing, and some unusual applications in associative memory and in the study of chaotic and cooperative systems. Although the feedback device used in the experimental work will be specified for each application, many of the other devices described in Section III could also be used. What is important is that optical feedback is necessary or advantageous for performing the processing required by the application, not that a particular feedback device was used in an experiment.

A. ANALOG COMPUTING

Analog computing applications of optical feedback devices include spatial frequency filtering, differential and integral equation solution, linear algebra problem solution, adaptive phase compensation, nonlinear operations, and division.

1. *Spatial Frequency Filtering*

Optical processors are often used to perform spatial frequency domain filtering or, equivalently, spatial domain convolution. This operation is needed in many problems to which analog computing can be applied and also in image processing. Optical feedback devices have greater capability and flexibility in performing spatial frequency filtering than other optical processors. The spatial frequency transfer function H of a device with a single feedback loop is given by Eq. (1). The three quantities F, G and ϕ can be independently varied to produce the desired H. In addition, the denominator term gives division and inversion capabilities to the feedback device. There has been much experimental work demonstrating the spatial frequency filtering capabilities of optical feedback devices (Jablonowski and Lee, 1975; Tamura and Wyant, 1976; Goetz *et al.*, 1979; Indebetouw, 1980). For example, the two-lens, four-mirror device shown in Fig. 5 was used with filters F and G whose phases were linear in the absolute value of one of the spatial frequency variables. The resultant bandpass filtering operation is shown in Fig. 15 which gives the measured coherent transfer function as a function of spatial frequency (Händler and Röder, 1979). The location of the bandpass varied with the feedback phase and could be rapidly changed by moving a mirror mounted on a piezoelectric translator.

2. *Differential and Integral Equation Solution*

Spatial filtering can be applied to the solution of partial differential equations (Jablonowski and Lee, 1975; Cederquist and Lee, 1980; Ferrano and Häusler, 1980b; Cederquist and Lee, 1981; Akins and Lee, 1982; Lee, 1985). For example, it can be shown that the solutions of the Poisson, wave, and diffusion equations in two dimensions can be expressed as the convolution of a function determined by the form of the differential equation with a function that expresses the initial or boundary conditions. Figure 16 shows (a) the forward and feedback path spatial filters for the solution of the wave equation and (b) plots of optical solutions obtained for two sets of boundary conditions using the two-spherical-mirror device of Fig. 4 (Cederquist and Lee, 1980). With the addition of image plane filters (and therefore the production of a space-variant optical system), this device has also been used to solve Fredholm and Volterra integral equations of the second kind (Cederquist, 1981).

The method can be extended to higher-order partial differential equations and to equations in three dimensions. A prism of very small wedge angle can be placed in one of the Fourier transform planes of the two-spherical-mirror device of Fig. 4. The effect of the linear phase shift is to translate the processed image a small distance each time it makes one round trip

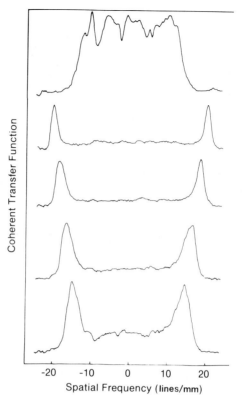

Fig. 15. Application to spatial frequency filtering: coherent transfer function of the device in Fig. 5 versus spatial frequency for various values of the feedback phase. The location of the bandpass can be rapidly varied by submicron motion of a piezoelectric translator. (From Händler and Röder, 1979.)

through the loop. The output of the optical processor is a series of non-overlapping images, each having made a different number of round trips through the loop. When the proper filters are also used, the output is the solution of a partial differential equation in three dimensions with the third dimension varying discretely from one output image to the next. Figure 17 shows a photograph of one such optical solution (Cederquist and Lee, 1981).

3. Linear Algebra Problem Solution

A number of optical processors perform linear algebra operations such as matrix–vector multiplication (see Chapters 6.1 and 6.2). Since some of the more important problems in linear algebra can be solved by iterative algorithms, it is natural to use optical feedback. For example, consider the

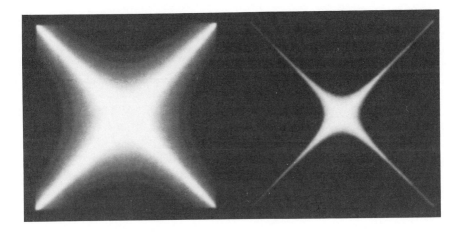

(a)

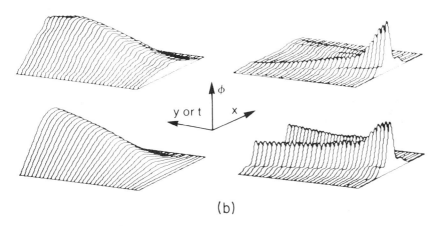

(b)

Fig. 16. Application to differential and integral equation solution using the device of Fig. 4. (a) Spatial filters for the solution of the wave equation. (b) Optical solutions (above) compared with numerical solutions (below), for boundary conditions of the first time derivative of wave amplitude equal to a triangle function (left) and wave amplitude shown on x-axis at $t = 0$ (right). Rms errors of optical solution are 8 and 15%, respectively. (From Cederquist and Lee, 1980.)

Fig. 17. Application to solution of differential equation in three dimensions using a modified version of the device in Fig. 4. Shown is the optical solution of $\partial\phi/\partial t + \phi = \partial^2\phi/\partial x\,\partial y$ for $t = n\,\Delta t$ where, from left to right, $n = 0$ to 5. For this equation each image is the previous one differentiated in x and y. (From Cederquist and Lee, 1981.)

problem of solving a set of simultaneous linear equations, $\mathbf{Ax} = \mathbf{b}$, for the unknown vector $\mathbf{x}$ given the matrix $\mathbf{A}$ and the vector $\mathbf{b}$. A possible iterative algorithm is

$$\mathbf{x}_{i+1} = (\mathbf{I} - \mathbf{A})\mathbf{x}_i + \mathbf{b} \tag{2}$$

If it converges, then the $\mathbf{x}$ obtained is a solution to $\mathbf{Ax} = \mathbf{b}$. The light-emitting diode based device of Fig. 9 has been used to compute this algorithm (Psaltis *et al.*, 1979; Casasent *et al.*, 1979). Additional work, all based on the above iterative equation, has shown theoretically improved convergence and accuracy (Goodman and Song, 1982), a method for eigenvector determination (Caulfield *et al.*, 1981), Kalman filtering (Casasent *et al.*, 1983), singular value decomposition (Kumar, 1983), applications to systolic processing (Caulfield and Gruninger, 1983), and extension to nonlinear equations (Lewak *et al.*, 1984). It is unfortunate that none of these theoretical developments has yet been tested experimentally.

4. *Adaptive Phase Compensation*

A common type of adaptive system measures the difference between a signal and an estimate of that signal and uses this error signal to improve future estimates of the signal. An unusual and interesting feedback device (a 2-D spatial light modulator-based device discussed in Section III.C.4) that estimates the phase of an aberrated wave front and adaptively compensates the wave front is shown in Fig. 18 (Fisher and Warde, 1983). The incoming wave front or signal beam passes through the input beamsplitter and is reflected from an optically controlled 2-D phase shifter (a microchannel SLM). After further reflections, it passes through the output beamsplitter as the phase-compensated wave front. However, part of this wave front is mixed with a local oscillator to become an error signal that controls further phase shifting and maintains phase compensation. The microchannel SLM has a low-pass temporal response that effectively integrates the error signal. The device is insensitive to amplitude variations of the incoming wave front,

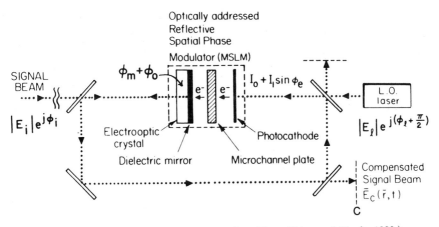

Fig. 18. Application to adaptive compensation. (From Fisher and Warde, 1983.)

can estimate phase over many multiples of 2π radians, and, if self-interference is used instead of a local oscillator, does not require monochromatic light (Fisher and Warde, 1979; Fisher, 1985).

5. *Multiplication, Division, and Other Operations*

Other analog computing applications have also been experimentally demonstrated. For example, if a filter with intensity transmittance $I_i(x, y)$ is placed in plane P_5 of the four-lens, four-mirror device shown in Fig. 6, then output light that has made n round trips through the feedback loop has an intensity $[I_i(x, y)]^n$. Experimental results are shown in Fig. 19

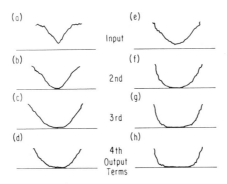

Fig. 19. Application to nonlinear image transformation of the device in Fig. 6. Two different inputs are shown: (a) $I_i = |x|$ and (e) $I_i = x^2$. The 2nd–4th output terms (corresponding to I_i raised to the 2nd–4th powers) are shown in (b)–(d) and (f)–(h). (From Nezhevenko and Spektor, 1975.)

(Nezhevenko and Spektor, 1975). If a prism with a small wedge angle is placed in plane P_2, light that has made different numbers of round trips can be separated in a Fourier plane, filtered, and recombined in an image plane, so that arbitrary power series in $I_i(x, y)$ can be generated (Kotljar et al., 1978):

$$I_o(x, y) = \sum_{n=1}^{N} c_n [I_i(x, y)]^n \tag{3}$$

Experimental results showing point-by-point division of two 2-D functions have been obtained using a device based on a liquid-crystal SLM (Marom et al., 1985). This type of device had previously been considered only theoretically (Crosta, 1978a, b; Grinberg and Marom, 1978). For completeness, the general theoretical discussion of the application of analog feedback devices to optimization problems (Nezhevenko and Gofman, 1984) and experimental use of a feedback device with gain to generate spheroidal wave functions (Pellat-Finet and de Bougrenet de la Tocnaye, 1985) should also be mentioned.

B. SIGNAL PROCESSING

In this section, applications in the processing of 1-D signals are considered. Research has focused on adaptive filtering and, in particular, on adaptive linear prediction. Adaptive linear prediction has many applications including equalization and redundancy removal in communication systems, antenna array processing, inteference rejection, and noise suppression.

Adaptive optical signal processors using feedback were theoretically analyzed by Vander Lugt (1982) and Cohen (1985). The first experimental results were obtained using the feedback system shown in Fig. 11 (Rhodes, 1983). The goal is to produce an estimate $\hat{x}(t)$ of a signal $x(t)$ where t is time. The estimate is a linear combination of past values of the signal,

$$\hat{x}(t) = \sum_{n=1}^{N} w_n x(t - nT) \tag{4}$$

where T is the time between samples, and the weights w_n are adaptively changed depending on the error signal $e(t) = x(t) - \hat{x}(t)$. In this implementation, the correlation cancellation loop method is used in which w_n is set equal to the correlation of $e(t)$ with $x(t - nT)$. It can be shown that, in equilibrium, the mean-squared error is minimized.

To perform these computations optically, the input signal $x(t)$ is biased, placed on a carrier, and sent to Bragg cells BC1 and BC2 (see Fig. 11). The current error signal is sent to a point electrooptic modulator EO. The HeNe laser beam passing through the modulator is spread in one dimension and multiplies the signal $x(t)$ in Bragg cell BC1. Because the signal $x(t)$ is propagating across the Bragg cell, the product $e(t)x(t-nT)$ for all values of n is produced simultaneously. This light is imaged onto the liquid-crystal SLM (LCLV) and effectively integrated by the relatively slow response time of the LCLV. Thus all of the desired correlations giving the w_n are computed in parallel. A Kr ion laser is used to read out the LCLV, and this light is imaged to Bragg cell BC2 where the product of the w_n and $x(t-nT)$ is performed. Spatial integration of this light gives the signal estimate $\hat{x}(t)$ by Eq. (4). Analog electronics are used to produce the error signal $e(t)$, which is fed back to the modulator (EO).

Experimental results are shown in Fig. 20 (Rhodes, 1983). For an input signal $x(t)$, which is a 3.6-MHz sine wave, the error signal as a function of time for a relative feedback gain of 10 is shown in (a). The weights adapt and reach equilibrium in about 500 μs. The spectrum of the input signal is shown in (b). The central peak is at dc, and the other two large peaks are at ± 3.6 MHz. The spectrum of the error signal is shown in (c) for a gain of 10. The 3.6-MHz components are decreased by about 20 dB. The upper trace in (d) shows an input signal that is a series of impulses. The lower trace is the estimate $\hat{x}(t)$ when a gain of 10 is used. Part (e) shows the spectrum of the corresponding error signal with a decrease of about 10 dB in the main frequency components.

Since many optical devices have been built that process temporal signals, a wide variety of systems using feedback could be constructed to perform 1-D signal processing. As another example, the system of Fig. 10 (Psaltis and Hong, 1984) performs adaptive Wiener filtering for minimum mean-squared error signal estimation in the presence of additive noise. It is surprising that the use of optical feedback has been confined to adaptive filtering. It seems that many other avenues of research remain unexplored.

C. IMAGE PROCESSING

We now examine applications in the processing of 2-D signals (images). The applications include image restoration, image enhancement, computation of iterative algorithms for signal recovery, and generation of scaled and rotated images for pattern recognition.

1. Image Restoration

Optical feedback devices have been used for inverse filtering and generalized inversion in image restoration. When an image has been degraded by a known spatial frequency transfer function $K(u, v)$ where u and v are spatial frequency coordinates, the use of an approximate inverse filter is a possible method to restore the image. In a feedback device, if the forward

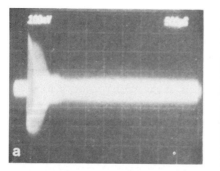
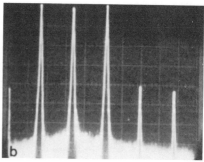
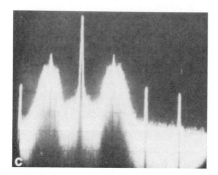
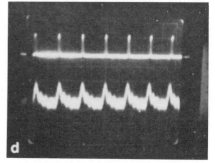
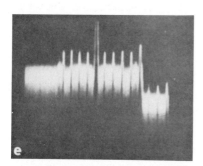

Fig. 20. Application of the device in Fig. 11 to adaptive signal processing. (a) Error signal versus time for relative feedback gain of 10; (b) spectrum of input signal; (c) spectrum of error signal; (d) input signal (upper trace) and estimate $\hat{x}(t)$ (lower trace); and (e) spectrum of error signal with 10 dB decrease in main frequency components. (From Rhodes, 1983.)

path filter $F(u, v)$ is set equal to unity, the phase ϕ taken as zero, and the feedback filter $G(u, v)$ set equal to $1 - K(u, v)$, then by Eq. (1) the transfer function of the device becomes $1/[1 - t_h + t_h K(u, v)]$ which, for $1 - t_h \cong 0$, is approximately $1/K(u, v)$, the desired inverse filter. If $1 - K(u, v)$ is easier to implement than $1/K(u, v)$, then it is an advantage to use a feedback device. Several devices have been used for inverse filtering (Jablonowski and Lee, 1975; Tamura and Wyant, 1976; Goetz et al., 1979; Ferrano and Häusler, 1980b). Experimental results using the two-lens, two-mirror device of Fig. 3 are shown in Fig. 21 (Jablonowski and Lee, 1975).

In a feedback system with gain in the forward path, the forward path filter F can be made much larger than unity. Then, again using Eq. (1), the transfer function of the device becomes $1/G(u, v)$. More generally, if the feedback path applies an operator G to the image, then the effect of the feedback device is to apply the inverse operator G^{-1}. This method can restore images degraded by nonlinear and space-variant effects. Experimental results have been obtained using the television-based feedback device of Fig. 8 (Goetz et al., 1979). A similar device when expanded to include more feedback loops can also perform the Jacobi method for inverting the effect of an image degradation (Maitre, 1981; Ferrano and Maitre, 1981). Other work in this area includes removal of ghost images (Sato et al., 1978), suppression of multiplicative noise (Händler and Röder, 1977), and removal of nonuniform bias (Görlitz et al., 1978).

2. Image Enhancement

Optical feedback devices have been used for image enhancement. If one of the elements internal to a feedback device has a transmittance proportional to the intensity of an image, then the output intensity becomes a nonlinear function of the image intensity. (A similar effect was described in Section IV.A.5.) If coherent light is used in the feedback device, then the phase of the feedback can be used to control this function and, for example, to increase or decrease the image contrast (Jablonowski and Lee, 1975; Tamura and Wyant, 1976; Lee et al., 1976). Feedback devices can also be used for edge enhancement (Sato et al., 1978; Vlad, 1982, 1985).

3. Signal Recovery

There exist a number of algorithms that proceed by iteratively Fourier transforming the data from an image domain to a spectral domain and back again, with various relatively simple operations performed in each domain. These algorithms are used for extrapolation, interpolation, superresolution, and phase retrieval in radio astronomy, tomography, and optical and acoustic imaging. Theoretical work was suggested that optical feedback devices can be used to compute these algorithms (De Santis et al., 1976;

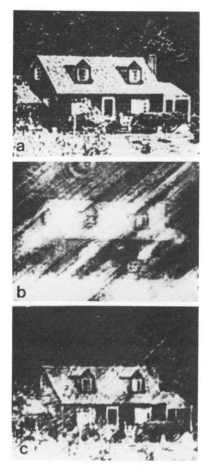

Fig. 21. Application to linear image restoration of the device in Fig. 3. The original image (a) is degraded (b) and restored (c). (From Jablonowski and Lee, 1975.)

Cesini *et al.*, 1978; Marks, 1980). For example, optical implementation of the Gerchberg algorithm for image extrapolation has been investigated (Marks and Smith, 1981). Preliminary experimental results have been obtained with the two-mirror, two-lens feedback device of Fig. 3 (Marks and Smith, 1980; Sato *et al.*, 1981). Only simple images were used, and much developmental work remains to be done.

4. *Pattern Recognition*

Pattern recognition is an important application of optical processing. Most pattern recognition devices, optical or electronic, must have special provisions for handling rotated or scaled versions of a pattern. The ability of feedback devices to provide a third dimension to optical processing can be used to advantage here. For example, the insertion of a Dove prism image rotator and a slightly demagnifying lens combination into the four-lens, four-mirror device of Fig. 6 produces output images that are rotated and scaled versions of the input (Kotljar *et al.*, 1978). Some samples are shown in Fig. 22 (Nezhevenko and Spektor, 1976). In an all-optical feedback device, the scaled and rotated versions are produced very rapidly (in 100 ns or less) and remain present at the output until the input is removed. Television-based feedback devices have been used to detect periodic structures and differences between successive images (Maitre and Ferrano, 1981; Fleuret *et al.*, 1983).

D. ASSOCIATIVE MEMORY

An associative memory is characterized by the ability to store and recall information based on memory content rather than by memory location.

(a)

(b)

Fig. 22. Application to pattern recognition using the device of Fig. 6. Generation of (a) scaled and (b) rotated versions of two input test images. (From Nezhevenko and Spektor, 1976.)

Since it is often desirable to interrogate the memory with the information that has just been recalled, either to improve the accuracy of the recalled information or to recall additional members of a chain of associations, feedback methods are frequently used in associative memory devices. Optical associative memories have been proposed and experimentally demonstrated (Mager et al., 1973; Wess and Röder, 1977, 1978). Recent experimental work includes the use of the light emitting diode-based feedback device of Fig. 9 (Psaltis and Farhat, 1985; Farhat et al., 1985) and all-optical devices using some of the gain methods described in Section III.A.3 (Anderson, 1986; Soffer et al., 1986; Yariv and Kwong, 1986). A proposed system uses feedback and a microchannel SLM to create an adaptive associative memory (Fisher and Giles, 1985). Chapter 2.3 gives a detailed discussion of this application of optical processing.

E. ANALOG TO DIGITAL CONVERSION

Analog-to-digital (A/D) operations are necessary in some optical processors. Since feedback can be used to produce bistable and multistable devices, optical feedback devices can be used to perform A/D conversion. For example, if a phase object is present between the two plane mirrors of the device of Fig. 2, the output image is bright only in those regions that lead to a positive feedback phase (Lee et al., 1976). This operation is level selection. If the mirror separation is varied, and the input light also appropriately varied, the time-integrated output image can be a thresholded version of the phase object or one of the bit planes of a digitized version of the object. Other experimental results in this area include the use of the two-spherical-mirror system of Fig. 4 for level selection, use of a three-plane-mirror device for color coding of phase levels (Bartholomew and Lee, 1980), and use of a television-based device for 1- and 2-bit A/D conversion (Ferrano and Häusler, 1980b).

F. DIGITAL COMPUTING

The digital optical–electronic feedback devices described in Section III.D have been used to perform some of the basic operations of digital computing. The operations demonstrated so far are latching and memory, flip-flops of various types, logic operations, and clock signal generation.

Several devices have demonstrated latching and memory (Athale and Lee, 1981; Ferrano and Häusler, 1980a). Although these devices had only about 8 by 8 memory cells, other devices could be built with at least 500 by 500 independent memory locations (Fatehi et al., 1984).

Flips-flops (Sengupta et al., 1978) and some of the basic logic operations (Collins et al., 1980; Ferrano and Häusler, 1980a) have also been experimentally demonstrated. Figure 13 (Fatehi *et al.*, 1984) shows one possible flip-flop device. One of the most powerful digital computing devices so far constructed using optical feedback is that of Fig. 14. As described in Section III.D, it uses the liquid-crystal light valve to perform the NOR operation and a hologram in the feedback path to achieve the desired interconnections between logic gates. In one experiment, 16 logic gates were interconnected to create a synchronous master–slave flip-flop and a driving clock. The outputs of some of the NOR gates are shown in Fig. 23 (Jenkins *et al.*, 1984a). In this figure, the clock signal is shown as the output of gate 12, and the output of the flip-flop is gate 15.

Unfortunately none of this research has progressed to the point at which all of the operations required by any ditigal computing application can be performed. Operations for which devices have been proposed, but not yet experimentally demonstrated, are shift registers (Fatehi *et al.*, 1980) and adders (Yakimovich, 1983, 1984). Other devices for sequential logic operations on 2-D data have also been proposed (Athale *et al.*, 1980).

G. STUDY OF CHAOS AND COOPERATION

A final and unusual application of optical feedback devices is in the study of certain nonlinear systems. Of interest are chaotic systems whose temporal behavior is extremely sensitive to arbitrarily small changes in initial conditions and cooperative systems where spatial order can evolve and be maintained over much greater distances than would be expected

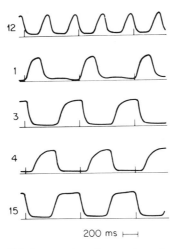

200 ms

Fig. 23. Application to digital computing. Outputs (as a function of time) of some the NOR gates in the device of Fig. 14. (From Jenkins *et al.*, 1984a.)

simply from the extent of the spatial interaction between elements. Simple systems of these types can be studied theoretically, and more complex ones can be simulated on a digital computer. However, as the number of spatial elements increases, it may be advantageous to use optical feedback processors. Also, since continuous-valued systems behave differently from discrete-valued ones (a quantized system cannot be arbitrary sensitive), true analog proccessing using optics may be desirable.

The television-based feedback devices of Fig. 8 have been used in such studies (Häusler *et al.*, 1986a, b, c). A chaotic system was created by including a nonmonotonic point nonlinearity in the feedback loop. Figure 24a shows the input (or initial conditions) and the results after various numbers of round trips through the feedback loop (Häusler and Streibl, 1983). A cooperative system was made by combining a bipolar point spread function in the feedback loop with a nonmonotonic nonlinearity. The result, shown in Fig. 24b, is that order is established over a much greater distance than the width of the point spread function (Häusler and Striebl, 1984). It was discovered that simply by varying the strength (not the form) of the nonlinearity, the spatial structure could be changed from the dot pattern of Fig. 24b to that of the line pattern of Fig. 24c. Related work has demonstrated the generation of spatial and temporal oscillations (Häusler and Simon, 1978) and studied the stability of feedback devices and their sensitivity to noise (Häusler and Streibl, 1983).

V. Conclusion

A. Summary

Optical feedback has been implemented in optical processors in diverse ways ranging from all-optical devices, both analog and digital, to hybrid optical–electronic devices, again both analog and digital, using television, light-emitting diode, acoustooptic, and 2-D spatial light modulator components. The characteristics of the devices are similarly varied as to the presence (or absence) of gain, the phase of the feedback signal, the cycle time of the feedback loop, and the dimensionality of the processing. The applications of optical feedback processors include special-purpose analog computing, signal and image processing, and, potentially, general-purpose digital computing.

B. Advantages of Optical Feedback

The use of feedback can give several important advantages to an optical processor. First, the two spatial dimensions of optics plus the temporal dimension in which the feedback occurs make the system three-dimensional.

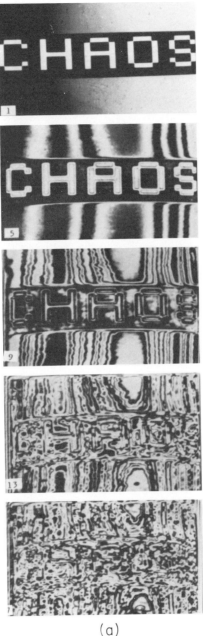

(a)

Fig. 24. Application to study of chaos and cooperation using the device of Fig. 8. (a) Chaos created by nonmonotonic point nonlinearity in the feedback loop; insets give the number of round trips through the loop. (b) and (c) Cooperative behavior over a long range generated by a short-range bipolar point spread function and a nonlinearity of varying strength (see insets). (From Häusler and Streibl, 1983, 1984.)

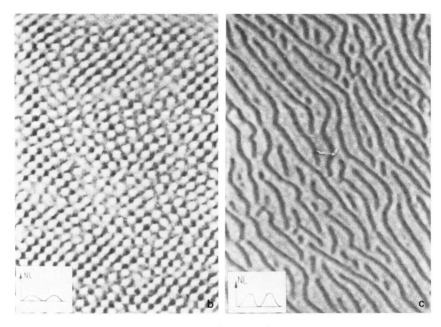

Fig. 24. (*Continued*).

Second, it increases the computational abilities of the processor by allowing the use of iterative and recursive algorithms. Third, feedback gives the system an inversion capability [see Eq. (1)]. Fourth, if the feedback can alter some of the system parameters, then the processing is adaptive, a powerful principle in system design. Fifth, feedback can create and enhance nonlinearities and produce bistability and multistability. Nonlinear processing is often advantageous, and bistability is required for digital processing.

C. FUTURE DEVELOPMENTS

In the 1980s, the importance of the advantages of optical feedback has become more generally recognized. The use of optical feedback is no longer a curiosity and is, more often than not, a vital part of new optical processor designs. It is to be expected that future research will widen the range of feedback devices and applications and will deepen our understanding of the potential of optical feedback.

The nature of future research in optical feedback will depend greatly on developments in optical processing devices and applications. Optical feedback processors, like all optical processors, must allow data input and output. In addition, many feedback devices are hybrids and require means for efficient data conversion from optical to electronic form and vice versa.

The success of optical feedback (and of optical processing in general) is contingent upon the development of high-performance optoelectronic devices and, in particular, optical and/or electronically addressed 2-D spatial light modulators.

As appropriate for an engineering, rather than a scientific, discipline, the achievements of optical processing research must be measured by the useful applications of the technology. However, in spite of the considerable research and development effort already expended, optical processing has become the method of choice in very few commercial, defense, or research applications. There are, importantly, some notable exceptions (such as image formation from synthetic aperture radar data and spectral analysis of wideband temporal signals), but optical processors have not found the widespread use that electronic processors (whether they be calculators, supercomputers, or even analog devices) have. It is extremely important that researchers in optical processing identify viable applications for which optical approaches offer distinctive advantages and aim to achieve the specific performance requirements. The use of feedback techniques with their potential for more processing power and complexity should assist this enterprise.

References

Akins, R. P., and Lee, S. H. (1979). *Appl. Phys. Lett.* **35**, 660–663.
Akins, R. P., and Lee, S. H. (1982). *Appl. Opt.* **21**, 4515–4520.
Akins, R. P., and Lee, S. H. (1984). *J. Opt. Soc. Am. A* **1**, 533–536.
Akins, R. P., Athale, R. A., and Lee, S. H. (1980). *Opt. Eng.* **19**, 347–358.
Anderson, D. Z. (1986). *Opt. Lett.* **11**, 56–58.
Athale, R. A., and Lee, S. H. (1981). *Appl. Opt.* **20**, 1424–1432.
Athale, R. A., Barr, H. S., Lee, S. H., and Bartholomew, B. J. (1980). *SPIE Semin. Proc.* **241**, 149–154.
Bartholomew, B. J., and Lee, S. H. (1980). *Appl. Opt.* **19**, 201–206.
Casasent, D. (1982). *Appl. Opt.* **21**, 1859–1865.
Casasent, D., Psaltis, D., Kumar, B. V., and Carlotto, M. (1979). *SPIE Semin. Proc.* **209**, 47–52.
Casasent, D., Jackson, J., and Neuman, C. (1983). *Appl. Opt.* **22**, 115–124.
Caulfield, H. J., and Gruninger, J. (1983). *Opt. Lett.* **8**, 398–400.
Caulfield, H. J., Dvore, D., Goodman, J. W., and Rhodes, W. (1981). *Appl. Opt.* **20**, 2263–2265.
Cederquist, J. N. (1981). *J. Opt. Soc. Am.* **71**, 651–655.
Cederquist, J. N., and Lee, S. H. (1979). *Appl. Phys.* **18**, 311–319.
Cederquist, J. N., and Lee, S. H. (1980). *J. Opt. Soc. Am.* **70**, 944–953.
Cederquist, J. N., and Lee, S. H. (1981). *J. Opt. Soc. Am.* **71**, 643–650.
Cesini, G., Guattari, G., Lucarini, G., and Palma, C. (1978). *Opt. Acta* **25**, 501–508.
Cohen, J. D. (1985). *Appl. Opt.* **24**, 4247–4259.
Collins, S. A., and Wasmundt, K. C. (1980). *Opt. Eng.* **19**, 478–487.
Collins, S. A., Gerlach, U. H., and Zakman, Z. M. (1979). *SPIE Semin. Proc.* **185**, 36–41.
Collins, S. A., Fatehi, M. T., and Wasmundt, K. C. (1980). *SPIE Semin. Proc.* **232**, 168–173.
Craig, D. R. (1954). *Photogr. Eng.* **5**, 219–226.

Craig, D. R. (1955). *Photogramm. Eng.* **21**, 556-563.

Crosta, G. (1978a). *Opt. Quantum Electron.* **10**, 9-15.

Crosta, G. (1978b). *Opt. Quantum Electron.* **10**, 361-363.

De Santis, P., Gori, F., Guattari, G., and Palma, C. (1976). *Opt. Acta* **23**, 505-518.

Fainman, Y., and Lee, S. H. (1985). *Opt. Eng.* **24**, 535-540.

Fainman, Y., Klancnik, E., and Lee, S. H. (1986). *Opt. Eng.* **25**, 228-234.

Farhat, N. H., Psaltis, D., Prata, A., and Paek, E. (1985). *Appl. Opt.* **24**, 1469-1475.

Fatehi, M. T., Wasmundt, K. C., Yen, C. Y., and Collins, S. A. (1980). *SPIE Semin. Proc.* **241**, 139-148.

Fatehi, M. T., Wasmundt, K. C., and Collins, S. A. (1984). *Appl. Opt.* **23**, 2163-2171.

Ferrano, G., and Häusler, G. (1980a). *Opt. Commun.* **32**, 375-379.

Ferrano, G., and Häusler, G. (1980b). *Opt. Eng.* **19**, 442-451.

Ferrano, G., and Maitre, H. (1981). *Opt. Commun.* **38**, 336-339.

Fisher, A. D. (1985). *SPIE Semin. Proc.* **551**, 102-112.

Fisher, A. D., and Giles, C. L. (1985). *Proc. IEEE Compcon, Spring Meet.*, pp. 342-344.

Fisher, A. D., and Warde, C. (1979). *Opt. Lett.* **4**, 131-133.

Fisher, A. D., and Warde, D. (1983). *Opt. Lett.* **8**, 353-355.

Fleuret, J. P., Clainchard, A., and Maitre, H. (1983). *SPIE Semin. Proc.* **397**, 104-107.

Gerlach, U. H., Sengupta, U. K., and Collins, S. A. (1980). *Opt. Eng.* **19**, 452-455.

Görlitz, D., Lanzl, F., and Mischke, T. (1978). *Proc. ICO* **11**, 239-242.

Goetz, J., Häusler, G., and Sesselmann, R. (1979). *Appl. Opt.* **18**, 2754-2759.

Goodman, J. W., and Song, M. S. (1982). *Appl. Opt.* **21**, 502-506.

Grinberg, J., and Marom, E. (1978). *Proc. ICO* **11**, 245-248.

Händler, E., and Röder, U. (1977). *Opt. Commun.* **23**, 352-356.

Händler, E., and Röder, U. (1979). *Appl. Opt.* **18**, 2787-2791.

Hänsch, T. W., Varsanyi, F., and Schawlow, A. L. (1971). *Appl. Phys. Lett.* **18**, 108-110.

Häusler, G., and Lohmann, A. (1977). *Opt. Commun.* **21**, 365-368.

Häusler, G., and Simon, M. (1978). *Opt. Acta* **25**, 327-336.

Häuser, G., and Streibl, N. (1982). *Opt. Commun.* **42**, 381-385.

Häusler, G., and Streibl, N. (1983). *Opt. Acta* **30**, 171-187.

Häusler, G., and Streibl, N. (1984). *In* "Optical Bistability 2" (C. M. Bowden, H. M. Gibbs, and S. L. McCall, eds.), pp. 151-157. Plenum, New York.

Häusler, G., Seckmeyer, G., and Weiss, T. (1986a). *Appl. Opt.* **25**, 4656-4663.

Häusler, G., Seckmeyer, G., and Weiss, T. (1986b). *Appl. Opt.* **25**, 4664-4667.

Häusler, G., Seckmeyer, G., and Weiss, T. (1986c). *Appl. Opt.* **25**, 4668-4672.

Hagler, M. O. (1971). *Appl. Opt.* **10**, 2783-2784.

Hagler, M. O., and Bell, S. V. (1986). *J. Opt. Soc. Am. A* **3**, 308-318.

Hong, J., and Psaltis, D. (1985). *SPIE Semin. Proc.* **551**, 81-88.

Indebetouw, G. (1980). *SPIE Semin. Proc.* **232**, 224-229.

Jablonowski, D. P., and Lee, S. H. (1975). *Appl. Phys.* **8**, 51-58.

Jenkins, B. K., Sawchuk, A. A., Strand, T. C., Forchheimer, R., and Soffer, B. H. (1984a). *Appl. Opt.* **23**, 3455-3464.

Jenkins, B. K., Chavel, P., Forchheimer, R., Sawchuk, A. A., and Strand, T. C. (1984b). *Appl. Opt.* **23**, 3465-3474.

Johnston, S., and Lee, S. H. (1983). *Appl. Opt.* **22**, 1431-1438.

Kompanets, I. N., Parfenov, A. V., and Popov, Y. M. (1981a). *Opt. Commun.* **36**, 415-416.

Kompanets, I. N., Parfenov, A. V., and Popov, Y. M. (1981b). *Opt. Commun.* **36**, 417-418.

Kotljar, P. E., Nezhevenko, E. S., Spektor, B. I., and Feldbush, V. I. (1978). *In* "Optical Information Processing" (E. S. Barrekette, G. W. Stroke, Y. E. Nesterikhin, and W. E. Kock, eds.), Vol. 2, pp. 155-170. Plenum, New York.

Kumar, B. V. (1983). *Appl. Opt.* **22**, 962-963.

Lee, S. H. (1985). *Opt. Eng.* **24**, 41-47.

Lee, S. H., Bartholomew, B. J., and Cederquist, J. N. (1976) *SPIE Semin. Proc.* **83**, 78-84.

Lewak, G., Lee, S. H., and Cathey, W. T. (1984). *Appl. Opt.* **23**, 3144-3148.

Lohmann, A. (1959). *Opt. Acta* **6**, 319-338.

Lohmann, A. (1977). *Opt. Commun.* **22**, 165-168.

Mager, H. J., Wess, O., and Waidelich, W. (1973). *Opt. Commun.* **9**, 156-160.

Maitre, H. (1981). *Comput. Graphics Image Process.* **16**, 95-115.

Maitre, H., and Ferrano, G. (1981). *Opt. Acta* **28**, 553-557.

Marks, R. J. (1980). *Appl. Opt.* **19**, 1670-1672.

Marks, R. J., and Smith, D. K. (1980). *SPIE Semin. Proc.* **231**, 106-111.

Marks, R. J., and Smith, D. K. (1981). *SPIE Semin. Proc.* **373**, 161-178.

Marom, E., Soffer, B. H., and Efron, U. (1985). *Opt. Lett.* **10**, 43-45.

Nezhevenko, E. S., and Gofman, M. A. (1984). *Optik* **67**, 199-210.

Nezhevenko, E. S., and Spektor, B. I. (1975). *Avtometriya* No. 3, 98-103.

Nezhevenko, E. S., and Spektor, B. I. (1976). *Avtometriya* No. 6, 14-18.

Pellat-Finet, P., and de Bougrenet de la Tocnaye, J.-L. (1985). *Opt. Commun.* **55**, 305-310.

Pole, R. V., Wieder, H., and Myers, R. A. (1966). *Appl. Phys. Lett.* **8**, 229-231.

Pole, R. V., Wieder, H., and Barrekette, E. S. (1967). *Appl. Opt.* **6**, 1571-1575.

Porada, Z. (1983). *Thin Solid Films* **109**, 213-216.

Psaltis, D., and Farhat, N. H. (1985). *Opt. Lett.* **10**, 98-100.

Psaltis, D., and Hong, J. (1984). *Appl. Opt.* **23**, 3475-3481.

Psaltis, D., Casasent, D., and Carlotto, M. (1979). *Opt. Lett.* **4**, 348-350.

Rhodes, J. F. (1983). *Appl. Opt.* **22**, 282-287.

Sato, T., Sasaki, K., and Yamamoto, R. (1978). *Appl. Opt.* **17**, 717-720.

Sato, T., Sasaki, K., Nakamura, Y., Linzer, M., and Norton, S. J. (1981). *Appl. Opt.* **20**, 3073-3076.

Schneeberger, B., Laeri, F., Tschudi, T., and Heiniger, F. (1981). *Opt. Commun.* **36**, 107-110.

Sengupta, U. K., Gerlach, U. H., and Collins, S. A. (1978). *Opt. Lett.* **3**, 199-201.

Soffer, B. H., Dunning, G. J., Owechko, Y., and Marom, E. (1986). *Opt. Lett.* **11**, 118-120.

Spitzberg, W., and Sunder-Plassmann, F.-A. (1963). *Optik* **20**, 440-449.

Tamura, P. N., and Wyant, J. C. (1976). *SPIE Semin. Proc.* **74**, 57-61.

Tur, M., Goodman, J. W., Moslehi, B., Bowers, J. E., and Shaw, H. J. (1982). *Opt. Lett.* **7**, 463-465.

Vander Lugt, A. (1982). *Appl. Opt.* **21**, 4005-4011.

Vlad, V. I. (1982). *Opt. Commun.* **41**, 411-416.

Vlad, V. I. (1985). *Opt. Acta* **32**, 1235-1250.

Wess, O., and Röder, U. (1977). *Biol. Cybern.* **27**, 89-98.

Wess, O., and Röder, U. (1978). *In* "Progress in Cybernetics and Systems Research" (R. Trappl, G. J. Klir, and L. Ricciardi, eds.), Vol. III, pp. 580-590. Wiley, Chichester, England.

Wieder, H., and Pole, R. V. (1967). *Appl. Opt.* **6**, 1761-1765.

Yakimovich, A. P. (1983). *Sov. J. Quantum Electron.* (*Engl. Transl.*) **13**, 1296-1297.

Yakimovich, A. P. (1984). *Sov. J. Quantum Electron.* (*Engl. Transl.*) **14**, 464-467.

Yariv, A., and Kwong, S.-K. (1986). *Opt. Lett.* **11**, 186-188.

Index